Ghosts
wont
EASY
Answers —

CHARACTER ANALYSIS

BY WILHELM REICH

The Bioelectrical Investigation of Sexuality and Anxiety

The Bion Experiments

The Cancer Biopathy

Character Analysis

Children of the Future

Early Writings, Volume One

Ether, God and Devil / Cosmic Superimposition

The Function of the Orgasm

Genitality

The Invasion of Compulsory Sex-Morality

Listen, Little Man!

The Mass Psychology of Fascism

The Murder of Christ

Passion of Youth

People in Trouble

Reich Speaks of Freud

Selected Writings

The Sexual Revolution

WILHELM REICH

Character Analysis

Third, enlarged edition

Newly translated by
VINCENT R. CARFAGNO

*Edited by Mary Higgins
and Chester M. Raphael, M.D.*

The Noonday Press

Farrar, Straus and Giroux

NEW YORK

Love, work and knowledge are the wellsprings of our life. They should also govern it.

WILHELM REICH

CONTENTS

PART ONE: TECHNIQUE

PART TWO: THEORY OF CHARACTER FORMATION

PART THREE: FROM PSYCHOANALYSIS TO ORGONE BIOPHYSICS

EDITOR'S NOTE

This new translation of the third, enlarged edition of *Character Analysis* has been prepared from the original German language book and manuscripts with the exception of the preface to the third edition and the chapter on "The Schizophrenic Split" which were written in English by the author.

It was discovered that, except for a few minor changes, the note preceding "The Masochistic Character" that was previously signed by a translator was, in fact, written by Reich himself. It is, therefore, presented in its original form in this translation.

It should also be noted that the chapter entitled "The Emotional Plague," written in 1943 and slightly revised by Reich before its inclusion in *Character Analysis,* has been placed at the end of the book so that its terminology will be comprehensible within the context of this work and, also, to enable the reader to follow without interruption Reich's development from character analysis to orgone biophysics.

Mary Higgins, Trustee

The Wilhelm Reich Infant Trust Fund
New York, 1972

PREFACE TO THE THIRD EDITION

The second edition of this book (1945) was soon sold out, and the great demand for it could not be satisfied for more than two years. Our press was busy with publications devoted to the newer field of orgone biophysics (*The Discovery of the Orgone,* Vol. II: *The Cancer Biopathy,* 1948, etc.). Furthermore, I hesitated to issue a new edition of *Character Analysis.* This book still uses psychoanalytic terminology and a *psychological* description of the neuroses. In the fifteen years since the publication of the first edition, I had to redesign and rewrite our picture of emotional disease. During this time, many important developments took place: "character" became a term signifying typical *biophysical* behavior. The "emotions," more and more, came to mean manifestations of a tangible *bio-energy,* of the organismic orgone energy. Slowly, we learned to handle it practically by what is now called "medical orgone therapy." In the preface to the second edition, I pointed out that "character analysis" is still valid in the realm of depth psychology, where it originated and where it still belongs. We no longer practice character analysis as described in this book. However, we still use the character-analytic method in certain situations; we still proceed from character attitudes to the depths of human experience. But in orgone therapy, we proceed *bio-energetically* and no longer psychologically.

Why then publish a third edition of this book, in its original form? The main reason is that one cannot easily find one's way toward an understanding of orgonomy and medical orgone therapy without being well acquainted with their development from the study of human emotional pathology of twenty or twenty-five years ago.

Character analysis is still valid and helpful in psychiatry, but it is far from being sufficient to cope with the *bio-energetic core* of emotional functions. It is indispensable for the medical orgone therapist who, without having studied psychoanalysis, comes directly to the orgone biophysics of the 40's. The psychiatrist who has not studied the bio-energetic functions of the emotions is apt to overlook the organism as such and to remain stuck in the psychology of words and associations. He will not find his way to the *bio-energetic* background and origin of every type of emotion. The orgone therapist, on the other hand, trained to see a patient first of all as a biological organism, may easily forget that, besides muscular armoring, bodily sensations, orgonotic streamings, anorgonotic attacks, diaphragmatic or pelvic blocks, etc., there is a vast field of functioning such as marital distrust, specifically distorted ideas about genital functions in puberty, certain social insecurities and anxieties, unconscious intentions, rational social fears, etc. Although the "psychic realm" of the emotions is much narrower than their "bio-energetic realm"; although certain diseases, such as vascular hypertension, cannot be attacked by psychological means; although language and thought association cannot possibly penetrate more deeply than to the phase of speech development, that is, about the second year of life, the psychological aspect of emotional disease remains important and indispensable; however, it is no longer the foremost aspect of orgonomic biopsychiatry.

The third edition of *Character Analysis* has been considerably enlarged. I have added "The Emotional Plague," previously published as an article in the *International Journal of Sex-Economy and Orgone Research,* 1945. Also, a paper on "The Expressive Language of the Living," not previously published. It deals with the realm of *biophysical* emotional expressions, the main realm of medical orgone therapy. Finally, an extensive case history of a paranoid schizophrenia will introduce the student of human nature to the new field of *biopathology* which was opened up only a few years ago by the discovery of the organismic orgone energy (= bio-energy). This case history will convince the reader that the organismic orgone energy is the *physical reality* which corresponds to the classical, merely psychological, concept of "psychic energy."

The old term "vegetotherapy" has been replaced by "orgone therapy." Otherwise, the book remains unchanged in its main structure. It represents the essential first step, taken from 1928 to 1934, from psychoanalysis toward the bio-energetic study of the emotions (orgone biophysics) and deserves to be preserved as such.

The discovery of the atmospheric (cosmic) orgone energy has forced major revisions in our basic physical as well as psychological concepts. These are not dealt with in this book. It will take many years of painstaking work to elucidate the main trends which have developed since the discovery of the orgone. Such things as a "psychic idea," for example, appear today in an entirely different light, as a result of disclosures made by orgonomic experiments. But this should not distract the psychotherapist and orgone therapist from his everyday task with emotionally sick people. At present, it is mainly the natural scientist and the natural philosopher who are being challenged by the disclosure of a universal primordial energy: orgone energy.

W. R.

December 1948

PREFACE TO THE SECOND EDITION

In the twelve years since the first publication of *Character Analysis,* the character-analytic technique has developed into vegetotherapy. In spite of this, no changes have been undertaken in the present edition. There is a good reason for this.

The character-analytic technique was clinically worked out and tested between 1925 and 1933. At that time, sex-economy was still in its infancy. The individual and social importance of the function of the orgasm had been recognized only a few years earlier. Naturally, this recognition had considerable influence on the theory and technique of psychoanalytic therapy. Today, as twelve years ago, character analysis definitely belongs within the framework of Freudian psychoanalysis. It was in this framework and only in this framework that this book was written and can still claim validity today. It was intended for students as well as practitioners of psychoanalysis. I do not want to change its original purpose and intention. Hence, I have not added anything, nor have I made any revisions.

Yet, as time went on, the analytic conception of the human character structure, particularly the pathologically and therapeutically so important *"character armor,"* continued to develop. Character armor represents the point of departure of present-day *orgone biophysics* and of the therapeutic techniques corresponding to it, *vegetotherapy* and *orgone therapy,* the basic features of which are set forth in Vol. I of my book *The Discovery of the Orgone,* 1942, and in various essays dealings specifically with orgone physics. It is interesting and important for every psychiatrist to comprehend how the original psychiatric problem of the encrustation of the human character opened the road to biologic energy and biopathies. Orgone biophysics did not refute the character-analytic contentions set forth in this book. Quite the contrary, it provided them with a solid natural scientific foundation.

The appendix to the present edition of *Character Analysis* contains the last paper I delivered to the International Psychoanalytic Association at the 13th Congress in Lucerne, 1934. This paper represents the transition from Freud's depth psychology to biology and then to orgone biophysics. The problems of the orgone are not dealt with in this book. However, the reader who is familiar with my later writings will have no difficulty in discovering those passages in which orgone biophysics picks up the thread of the problems of character structure. Through the insertion of footnotes, I have attempted to point out those passages in which we find the transition from depth psychology to orgone biophysics.

The burden of drawing the line of demarcation which led to the exclusion of sex-economy and the theory of the orgasm from official psychoanalysis lies with those members of the International Psychoanalytic Association who were responsible for my expulsion. Later, they began to feel pricks of conscience and tried to make it appear as if I had been the one who had detached my theories from psychoanalysis. However, this much must be made quite clear here: sex-economy never sought to detach itself from Freud's basic scientific findings. It was false social considerations, which have become meaningless as a result of the social revolutions of the past ten years, that caused the psychoanalytic movement to detach itself from sex-economy. Sex-economy is not a rival of psychoanalysis any more than Newton's law of gravitation is a rival of Kepler's law of harmony. Sex-economy represents the continuation of Freudian psychoanalysis and provides it with a natural scientific foundation in the sphere of biophysics and social sexology. Today, it is sex-economy which can claim the success of having led to the discovery of the biologic energy, *orgone,* which, governed by definite physical laws, lies at the basis of the human sexual functions first described by Freud. The *"biopathies"* which orgone biophysics was able to detect in the *organic* sphere are the correlate of Freud's "psychoneuroses" in the psychological sphere.

Summing up, I should like to say that "character analysis" is still valid within the theoretical frame of reference of depth psychology and the *psycho*therapeutic techniques which pertain to it. It is also still valid as an indispensable auxiliary technique in vegetotherapy and orgone therapy. But as time goes on, we continue to move forward: the sex-economist and vegetotherapist is essentially a *biotherapist,* and no longer merely a psychotherapist.

W. R.

New York
November 1944

PREFACE TO THE FIRST EDITION

The psychoanalytic investigations of the human character which I am setting forth in this book tie in with the problems of the Vienna Psychoanalytic Clinic which, nine years ago, I attempted to outline in the introduction to my book *Der triebhafte Charakter*, without, however, offering even a tentative solution. Those familiar with psychoanalytic research will not be surprised that well-nigh a decade has had to elapse between the formulation of the problem and its partial solution. When I suddenly undertook to treat several impulsive psychopaths at the clinic, I was immediately faced with a number of therapeutic problems. To be sure, the insights into the impulsive type's fragmentary ego-structure were more or less adequate to cope with these problems. Yet, it was possible even then to surmise that a genetic-dynamic theory of the character, a rigid differentiation between the actual content and the form of the resistances with which the "personality" attempts to thwart the exposure of what is repressed, and a well-founded examination of the genetic differentiation of character types would be of importance for the theory and therapy of the instinct-inhibited character neuroses which, at that time, I contrasted to the impulsive character neuroses.

The explanations of therapeutic technique and the dynamic-economic conception of the character as a totality are, in the main, the fruits of my vast experiences and countless discussions in the Seminar for Psychoanalytic Therapy at the Vienna Psychoanalytic Clinic. I was the head of this seminar for a period of six years, during which I enjoyed the active cooperation of a number of enthusiastic young colleagues. Even now, however, I must caution the reader to expect neither a complete elucidation of the problems under consideration nor their complete solution. Today, as nine years ago, we are still a long way from a comprehensive, systematic psychoanalytic characterology. Yet, in all modesty, I feel that the present volume is no mean contribution toward this end.

The chapters on technique were written in the winter of 1928–29, and their validity could be verified over a period of four years. There were no essential changes to be made. The chapters on theory, up to Chapter III (Part II), are enlarged, in part revised, reprints of papers of mine which, over the past years, have appeared in the *Internationalen Zeitschrift für Psychoanalyse*.

For a number of reasons, one of them being lack of time, I was not able to comply with the wishes of my colleagues, who wanted me to write a book dealing with all phases of analytic technique. In this regard, I had to confine myself to a description and substantiation of the principles of technique which follow from character analysis. Besides, the analytic technique cannot be learned from books—practical application is vastly too complicated for that. One becomes intimate with it only through a thorough study of cases in seminars and in monitored sessions.

However, we shall have to deal more thoroughly with a serious criticism (an obvious one which is to be expected from a certain quarter), for on first impression it gives one pause for thought and makes one question the necessity of the effort and expenditure involved in such a publication as this one. It runs as follows: doesn't this publication as such constitute an extravagant and one-sided overvaluation of individual psychotherapy and characterology? In a city the size of Berlin, there are millions of neurotic people, people whose psychic structure and capacity for work and pleasure have been severely impaired; every hour of every day fresh thousands of neuroses are produced by family education and social conditions. In view of the present lack of interest in such matters, is there any point in printing detailed material on individual analytic technique, relations between various psychic structures, character dynamics, and similar matters? And this question is all the more pointed in view of the fact that I have no immediately applicable advice for a mass therapy of neuroses, for short, certain, and quickly effective treatments. For a long time I myself was not able to shake off the strong impression of such an objection. Finally, I had to tell myself that this was a shortsighted standpoint—in the long run, even worse than the present-day obsession with questions of individual psychotherapy. From a social point of view, the position of individual psychotherapy is a hopeless one. It might even be regarded as a typical dialectical ruse that it was precisely this insight, i.e., that neuroses are socially produced on a mass scale, which led to an even more thorough, even more intensive concern with the problems of individual therapy. I have endeavored to demonstrate that neuroses are the results of a home atmosphere that is patriarchal and sexually suppressive; that, moreover, the only *prophylaxis* worthy of serious consideration is one for the practical implementation of which the present social system lacks every prerequisite; that it is only a thorough turnover of social institutions and ideologies, a turnover that will be dependent upon the outcome of the political struggles of our century, which will create the preconditions for an extensive prophylaxis of neuroses. Hence, it is clear that a prophylaxis of neuroses is out of the question unless it is prepared theoretically; in short, that the study of the dynamic and economic conditions of human structures is its most important prerequisite. What does this have to do with the technique of individual therapy? To make a study of human structures in a way that would have relevance for the prophylaxis of neuroses, it is first necessary to perfect our analytic technique. It will be shown in the course of the present work to what extent the existing technical knowledge cannot fulfill such a purpose. Hence, the chief concern of psychotherapy, insofar as it wants to prepare itself for the future tasks of the prevention of neuroses, must be to derive a theory of technique and therapy based on the dynamic and economic processes of the psychic mechanism. First of all, we need therapists who know why they were able to effect a change in a structure or can explain why they failed. When we undertake to combat an epidemic in any other branch of medicine, we use the best available methods to investigate and to understand typical individual cases of this epidemic in order then to be able to offer advice on social hygiene. Thus, we are concerned with the technique of individual analysis not because we have such a high regard for individual therapy, but because, without a good technique, we cannot gain the insights which we need for the more comprehensive goal of research on the human structure.

There is a further consideration, and it constitutes the general background of the following clinical investigations. Let us briefly sketch it at this point. Unlike other branches of medical science, we do not deal with bacteria or tumors but with human reactions and psychic illnesses. An offspring of medical science, psychoanalysis has developed far beyond it. If, according to a famous saying, man is the author of his own history, depending upon certain economic conditions and presuppositions; if the materialistic[1] conception of history does indeed proceed from the basic premise of sociology, the natural and psychic organization of man, then it is clear that, at a certain point, our research assumes decisive sociological importance. We study psychic structures, their economy and dynamics. The most important productive power, the productive power called working power, is dependent upon man's psychic structure. Neither the so-called "subjective factor" of history nor the productive power, working power, can be comprehended without a natural scientific psychology. This requires a detachment from those psychoanalytic concepts which explain culture and the history of human society on the basis of drives, instead of understanding that social conditions must first have impinged upon and changed human needs before these transformed drives and needs could begin to have an effect as historical factors. The most famous of today's characterologists endeavor to comprehend the world on the basis of "values" and "character," instead of vice versa: to deduce character and valuations from the social process.

In the broader scope of the question concerning the sociological function of character formation, we have to focus our attention on a fact which, while it is known well enough, is hardly understood in its details, namely that certain average human structures are native to certain social organizations. Or, to put it another way, every social organization produces those character structures which it needs to exist. In class society, the existing ruling class secures its position, with the help of education and the institution of the family, by making its ideologies the ruling ideologies of all members of the society. However, it is not solely a matter of implanting the ideologies in all members of the so-

[1] Footnote, 1945: today we would say "functional" conception.

ciety. It is not a matter of indoctrinating attitudes and opinions but of a far-reaching process in every new generation of a given society, the purpose of which is to effect a change in and mold psychic structures (and this in all layers of the population) in conformity with the social order. Hence, natural scientific psychology and characterology have a clearly defined task: they have to put their finger on the ways and mechanisms by means of which man's social entity is transformed into psychic structure and, thereby, into ideology. Thus, the social production of ideologies has to be differentiated from the reproduction of these ideologies in the people of a given society. While the investigation of the former is the task of sociology and economics, the ascertaining of the latter is the task of psychoanalysis. It has to study how not only the immediate material existence (nourishment, shelter, clothing, work process, i.e., the way of life and the way in which needs are gratified) but also the so-called social superstructure (morality, laws, and institutions) affect the instinctual apparatus. It has to determine, as completely as possible, the myriad intermediate links in the transforming of the "material basis" into the "ideologic superstructure." It cannot be immaterial to sociology whether psychology fulfills this task adequately and to what extent it fulfills it, for man is, first and foremost, the *object* of his needs and of the social organization which regulates the gratification of his needs in this or that way. In his position as the object of his needs, however, man is also and at the same time the *subject* of history and of the social process of which he "himself is the author," not, to be sure, exactly as he would like to be, but under definite economic and cultural presuppositions, which determine the content and outcome of human action.

Since society became divided into those who possess the means of production and those who possess the commodity, working power, every social order has been established by the former, at least independent of the wills and minds of the latter, indeed usually against their wills. However, in that this social order begins to mold the psychic structures of all members of the society, it *reproduces* itself in the people. And insofar as this takes place through the utilization and transformation of the instinctual apparatus, which is governed by the libidinal needs, it also affectively *anchors* itself in it. Ever since the beginning of the private ownership of the means of production, the first and most important organ for the reproduction of the social order has been the patriarchal family, which lays in its children the character groundwork for the later influencing by the authoritarian order. While, on the one hand, the family represents the primary reproduction organ of character structures, the insight into the role of sexual education in the educational system as a whole teaches us that, first and foremost, they are *libidinal* interests and energies which are employed in the anchoring of the authoritarian social order. Hence, the character structures of the people of a given epoch or of a given social system are not only a mirror of this system. More significantly, they represent its anchoring. In the course of an investigation of the change in sexual morality during the transition from matriarchy to patriarchy,[2] it was possible to demonstrate that this anchoring by means of adapting the structures of people's characters to the new social order constitutes the conservative nature of so-called "tradition."

It is in this anchoring of the social order in the character structure that we find the explanation of the toleration on the part of the suppressed layers of the population toward the rulership of an upper social class that has the means of power at its disposal, a toleration that sometimes goes so far as to affirm authoritarian suppression at the expense of its own interests. This is far more obvious in the sphere of sexual suppression than it is in the sphere of the material and cultural gratification of needs. And yet, precisely in the formation of the libidinal structure, it can be demonstrated that, coeval with the anchoring of a social order, which completely or partially obstructs the gratification of one's needs, the psychic preconditions begin to develop which undermine this anchoring in the character structure. As time goes on, an ever widening divergency springs up between forced renunciation and the increased strain on one's needs. This divergency takes place along with the development of the social process, and it has a disintegrating effect upon "tradition"; it constitutes the psychological core of the formation of mental attitudes that undermine this anchoring.

[2] Cf. *Der Einbruch der Sexualmoral*, now published in English as *The Invasion of Compulsory Sex-Morality*. Ed.

It would be wrong to equate the conservative element of the character structure of the men and women of our society with the arbiter which we call the "superego." While it is certainly true that a person's moralistic arbiters derive from the definite prohibitions of the society, of which the parents function as the chief representatives in life, it is equally true that the first changes in the ego and the instincts, changes that occur during the earliest frustrations and identifications, long before the superego is formed, are dictated by the economic structure of the society and represent the initial reproductions and anchorings of the social system, in the same way as they begin to develop the first contradictions. (If a child develops an anal character, he will be sure to develop a corresponding stubbornness at the same time.) The superego receives its special importance for this anchoring in that it groups itself in the core around the child's incestuous genital demands; it is here that the best energies are bound and that the formation of the character is determined.

The dependence of the character formation upon the historical-economic situation in which it takes place is most clearly shown in the changes exhibited by the members of primitive societies as soon as they fall under the influence of an alien economy or culture, or begin to develop a new social order on their own accord. It follows quite clearly from Malinowski's studies that the character distinctions change relatively rapidly in the same region when the social structure is changed. For example, he found the natives of the Amphlett Islands (South Sea) to be distrustful, shy, and hostile, as opposed to the neighboring Trobrianders, whom he found to be simple, frank, and open. The former were already living under a patriarchal social system with strict familial and sexual mores, whereas the latter were still to a large extent enjoying the freedom of matriarchy. These findings confirm the conception, formulated at the Vienna Psychoanalytic Clinic and developed elsewhere,[3] that the social and economic structure of a society impinges upon the character formation of its members in an indirect, very complicated, circuitous way. The society's socioeconomic structure dictates definite modes of famil-

---

[3] *The Invasion of Compulsory Sex-Morality,* and "Dialektischer Materialismus und Psychoanalyse," published in *Unter dem Banner des Marxismus,* 1929.

ial life, but these modes not only presuppose definite forms of sexuality; they also produce them inasmuch as they influence the instinctual life of the child and adolescent, from which changed attitudes and modes of reaction result. At this point we can extend our earlier statement about the reproduction and anchoring of the social system, and say: *the character structure is the congealed sociological process of a given epoch.* A society's ideologies can become a material force only on condition that they actually change the character structures of the people. Hence, research on character structure is not of clinical interest only. It can reveal essential material if we turn to the question of why ideologies undergo revolutionary changes at a much slower pace than the socioeconomic basis, i.e., why man usually lags far behind that which he produces and which should and could actually change him. In addition to the hindrance to participation in cultural enjoyment due to class, we have the fact that character structures are acquired in early childhood and remain intact, without undergoing many changes. On the other hand, the socioeconomic situation that formed their basis at one time changes rapidly with the development of the forces of production, later makes different demands and requires other kinds of adaptations. To be sure, it also creates new attitudes and modes of reaction that superimpose on and penetrate the old, earlier-acquired characteristics, without, however, eliminating them. These two sets of characteristics, which correspond to different, historically differentiated sociological situations, now become involved in a contradiction with one another. Let me cite an example by way of illustration. A woman reared in the family of 1900 develops a mode of reaction corresponding to the socioeconomic situation of 1900; by 1925, however, as a result of the process of economic distintegration brought about by capitalism, familial conditions have changed to such a degree that she becomes involved in a critical contradiction, despite a partial surface adaptation of her personality. For instance, her character requires a strict monogamous sexual life; in the meantime, however, monogamy has become socially and ideologically disintegrated. Intellectually, the woman can no longer require monogamy of herself or her husband; in terms of her structure, however, she is not equal to the new conditions and the demands of her intellect.

Similar questions arise when one follows the difficulties involved in the transformation of privately owned farms into the collective cultivation of the soil in the Soviet Union. The Soviet economy has had to wrestle not only with economic difficulties but also with the character structure which the Russian peasant acquired under the tsars and private enterprise. The role played in these difficulties by the dissolution of the family through the collectives and, above all, through the revolutionary change in sexuality can be roughly understood from the literature on this subject. The old structures not only lag behind; they struggle against the new in many different ways. If the old ideology or orientation which corresponds to an earlier sociological situation were not anchored in the structure of the instincts or, more properly speaking, in the structure of the character, as a chronic and automatic mode of reaction and, in addition, with the help of libidinal energy, it would be able to adapt to the economic revolutions more easily and much more rapidly. No detailed proof is needed to show that an exact knowledge of the mechanisms that mediate between economic situation, instinctual life, character formation, and ideology would make possible a number of practical measures, above all in the field of education, but perhaps even in the manner of mass influencing.

All these things still have to be worked out. But the science of psychoanalysis cannot demand to be practically and theoretically recognized on a social scale if it *itself* does not get control of those fields which belong to it and in which it can prove that it does not want to remain outside the great historical events of our century. For the time being, research in the field of characterology must persist in its clinical investigations. Perhaps the material set forth in Part II will reveal of itself where the transitions lie to the more comprehensive sociological questions. Elsewhere an attempt has already been made to pursue these questions briefly. They led to an unexpected field, which we will not enter into in *this* work.

W. R.

Berlin
January 1933

PART ONE
Technique

CHAPTER I

SOME PROBLEMS OF PSYCHOANALYTIC TECHNIQUE

In the practice of his profession, the analyst is daily confronted with problems, for whose solution neither theoretical knowledge nor practical experience alone is adequate. It can be said that all questions of technique cluster around the one essential question, namely whether and how a clearly defined technique of analytic treatment can be deduced from the psychoanalytic theory of psychic illness. It is the question of the possibilities and limits of the application of theory to practice. However, in view of the fact that analytic practice itself does not yield the theory of psychic processes until practical tasks have been set, we have, to proceed correctly, to seek out the avenues which lead from purely empirical practice, pass through theory, and terminate in a theoretically well-grounded practice. Vast experience in the Vienna Seminar for Psychoanalytic Therapy and in monitored analytic sessions has shown that we have hardly progressed beyond the preliminary work toward the solution of the problem sketched above. It is true that we have the basic material, the so-called ABC of analytic technique, in Freud's various essays and his scattered remarks on the subject; and the very informative works on technique by Ferenczi and other writers have increased our understanding of many individual problems of technique. Generally speaking, however, there are just as many techniques as there are analysts, notwithstanding Freud's commonly shared, partially positive and partially negative suggestions, which are few compared with the welter of questions centered on practice.

These generally valid principles of technique which have become a matter of course among analysts are deduced from the general basic theoretical concepts of the neurotic process. All neuroses can be traced back to the conflict between repressed instinctual demands—among which the sexual demands of early childhood are never missing—and the ego forces which ward them off. The result of the failure to resolve this conflict is the neurotic symptom or the neurotic character trait. In terms of technique, therefore, the resolution of the conflict necessitates the "elimination of the repression"; in other words, the making conscious of the unconscious conflict. But the psychic agency known as the preconscious has erected psychic "counter-cathexes" against the breakthrough of repressed, unconscious impulses, "counter-cathexes" which act as a strict censor of one's own thoughts and desires by preventing them from becoming conscious; so it is necessary in analytic treatment to dispense with the usual ordering of one's thoughts required in everyday thinking and to allow one's train of ideas to flow freely and without critical selection. In the course of analytic work, traces of one's unconscious repressed demands and childhood experiences stand out ever more clearly amid the emerging material and, with the help of the analyst, these traces have to be translated into the language of the conscious. The so-called basic rule of psychoanalysis, which requires that the censor be abolished and one's thoughts be allowed to "associate freely," is the strictest, most indispensable measure of analytic technique. It finds a powerful support in the force of the unconscious impulses and desires pressing toward action and consciousness; however, it is opposed by another force, which is also unconscious, namely the "counter-cathexis" of the ego. This force makes it difficult and sometimes impossible for the patient to follow this basic rule. This same force also feeds the neurosis through the moralistic agencies. In the analytic treatment, these forces show up as "resistances" to the elimination of the repression. This theoretical insight dictates a further rule of practice, namely that the making conscious of the unconscious must not proceed directly but by the breaking down of the resistances. This means the patient has to realize that he is resisting, then by what means, and finally against what.

The work of making the unconscious conscious is called "interpretation"; it consists either in the unveiling of veiled expressions of the unconscious or in the reestablishment of relations which were torn asunder by the repressions. The patient's unconscious and repressed desires and fears are constantly seeking release or, more precisely, contact with real persons and situations. The most important driving force of this behavior is the patient's ungratified libido. Hence, it is to be expected that he will relate his unconscious demands and fears to the analyst and the analytic situation. This results in the "transference," i.e., the establishment of relationships to the analyst which are prompted by hate, love, or fear. But these attitudes which are expressed toward the analyst in the analytic situation are merely repetitions of older, usually childish attitudes toward people of the patient's childhood who had a special importance for him at one time. The patient has no awareness of their meaning. These transferences must be principally handled as such, i.e., they must be "resolved" by discovering how they are related to the patient's childhood. Since every neurosis, without exception, can be traced back to conflicts of childhood prior to the fourth year of life, conflicts which could not be handled at that time but become resuscitated in the transference, the analysis of the transference, i.e., that part of it which deals with the breaking down of the resistances, constitutes the most important piece of analytic work. Since, moreover, in the transference the patient either tries to supplant the explanatory work of the analysis, e.g., by gratifying the old love demands and hate impulses which have remained unsatisfied, or refuses to take cognizance of these attitudes, the transference usually develops into a resistance, i.e., it impedes the progress of the treatment. The negative transferences, i.e., the attitudes expressive of hate which are projected upon the analyst, are easily recognized as resistances from the beginning, whereas the transference of positive attitudes of love becomes a resistance only through a sudden change into a negative transference as a consequence of disappointment or fear.

Only as long as analytic therapy and technique were not discussed at any great length, or were insufficiently and unsystematically discussed, could the view prevail that a technique practiced by everyone in the same way had developed from the common basis sketched above. This view was true of many individual questions; but in the comprehension of the concept of "analytic passivity," for instance, the most varied interpretations exist. The most extreme and surely the least correct is the view that one need merely be silent; everything else will follow of itself. Confused views prevailed and still prevail on the function of the analyst in the analytic treatment. It is generally known, to be sure, that he has to break down the resistances and to "manage" the transference, but how and when this is to take place, how diverse his approach has to be in the handling of this task in various cases and situations, was never systematically discussed. Hence, even in the simplest questions dealing with everyday analytic situations, the views are of necessity vastly divergent. When, for instance, a certain resistance situation is described, one analyst thinks that this, another that that, and a third that the other should be done. And when, then, the analyst who described the situation returns to his case with the various suggestions of his colleagues, countless other possibilities arise, and the confusion is often much greater than it was in the first place. And yet it is to be assumed that, under given circumstances and conditions, *a* definite analytic situation admits of only *one single,* optimal possibility of solution, that there is only one application of technique that can really be correct in any given case. This applies not only to a particular situation; it applies to analytic technique as a whole. Hence, the task is to establish the criteria of this correct technique and, above all, how one arrives at it.

It took a long time to realize what is important: *to allow the technique of a given situation to grow out of the specific analytic situation itself by an exact analysis of its details.* This method of developing the analytic technique was strictly adhered to at the Vienna seminar, and it proved successful in many cases—in all cases where a theoretical comprehension of the analytic situation was possible. Suggestions which, in the final analysis, were a matter of taste, were avoided. A given difficulty was discussed—for example, a resistance situation—until the measure necessary to deal with it emerged of itself from the discussion, in a clear and definite form. Then one had the feeling that it could be correct only in this way and in no other way. Thus, a method had been found which made it possible to apply analytic material to the analytic technique, if not in every case, then at least in many cases and—above all—fundamentally. Our technique is not a principle that rests upon firmly fixed practices but a method built upon certain basic theoretical principles; as for the rest, it can be determined in the individual case and in the individual situation only. One might say that the making conscious of all manifestations of the unconscious through interpretations is a basic principle. But does this imply that this unconscious material has to be immediately interpreted as soon as it begins to show itself with some degree of clarity? That all transference manifestations are to be traced back to their infantile source is another basic principle. But does this tell us at what point and how this is to take place? The analyst is faced with negative and positive transferences at one and the same time; fundamentally, both have to be "resolved." But isn't one justified in asking what is to be resolved first and in what sequence, and which conditions are decisive for determining this? In this connection, is it sufficient to say that there are indications of ambivalent transference?

Against the attempt to deduce from the particular situation as a whole the sequence, emphasis, and depth of the interpretations necessary in each individual case, it would be easy to contend: interpret everything as it appears. To this contention, we reply: when countless experiences and the subsequent theoretical assessment of these experiences teach us that the interpretation of the entire material in this way and in the sequence in which it appears does not, in a very large number of cases, achieve the purpose of interpretation, namely therapeutic influencing, then it becomes necessary to search for the conditions that determine the therapeutic effectiveness of an interpretation. These are different in every case, and even if, from the point of view of technique, some basic general principles applicable to interpretation are yielded, they do not signify that much as compared with the supreme principle, namely that the analyst must endeavor to wrest the special technique of the case and the individual situation from each individual case and from each individual situation, without, while so doing, losing the general continuity in the development of the analytic process. Suggestions and views such as that this or that has "to be analyzed," or it is simply "a matter of analyzing correctly," are matters of taste; they are not principles of technique. What is precisely meant by "analyze" usually remains a dark secret. Nor can the analyst seek consolation by trusting to the duration of the treatment. Time alone will not do it. Having faith in the duration of the treatment is meaningful only when the analysis is developing, i.e., when the analyst understands the resistances and can pursue the analysis accordingly. Then, naturally, time is not and cannot be a factor. But it is absurd to expect that a success can be achieved merely by waiting.

We shall have to show how important the correct comprehension and handling of the *first* transference resistance is for the natural development of the treatment. It is not immaterial which detail and which layer of the transference neurosis is approached for the first time in the work of analysis, whether the analyst selects this or that piece from the wealth of material offered by the patient, whether the analyst interprets the unconscious material that has become manifest or the resistance pertaining to it, etc. If the analyst interprets the material in the sequence in which it is offered, he proceeds upon the preconceived notion that "material" is always capable of being used analytically, i.e., that all material is therapeutically effective. In this connection, however, it is its dynamic value that is most important. The prime objective of my efforts to secure a theory of technique and therapy is to establish general as well as particular points of view for the *legitimate application* of material to the technical handling of the case; to secure a theory, in other words, which will enable the analyst to know, in each interpretation, precisely why and toward what end he is interpreting—and not merely to interpret. If the analyst interprets the material in the sequence in which it appears in *each* case, whether or not the patient is deceiving, using the material as a camouflage, concealing an attitude of hate, laughing up his sleeve, is emotionally blocked, etc., he (the analyst) will be sure to run into hopeless situations. Proceeding in such a way, the analyst is caught in a scheme which is imposed on all cases, without regard to the *individual* requirements of the case with respect to the timing and depth of the necessary interpretations. Only by strict adherence to the rule of deducing the technique from every situation can the analyst begin to meet the demand that he be able to state, in each and every case, exactly why he succeeded or failed to effect a cure. If the analyst cannot, at least in the average case, satisfy this demand, no proof is necessary to show that our therapy does not deserve the name of a scientific causal therapy. However, in explaining the reasons for the failure of a particular case, the analyst must avoid statements such as that the patient "did not want to get well," or he or she was not accessible; for this is precisely what we want to know: *why* didn't the patient want to get well, *why* wasn't he or she accessible.

No attempt shall be made to establish a "system" of technique. It is not a matter of outlining a scheme valid for all cases but of establishing a groundwork, based on our theory of neurosis, for the comprehension of our therapeutic tasks; in short, to trace a broad frame of reference allowing sufficient latitude for the application of the general groundwork to individual cases.

I have nothing to add to Freud's principles on the interpretation of the unconscious and his general formula that the analytic work depends on the elimination of the resistances and the handling of the transference. However, the following explication must be regarded as a consistent application of the basic principles of psychoanalysis, in the course of which new areas of analytic work are opened. If our patients adhered to the basic rules at least roughly, there would be no reason to write a book on character analysis. Unfortunately, only a very small fraction of our patients are capable of analysis from the outset; most patients adhere to the basic rule only after the resistances have been successfully loosened. Hence, we shall concern ourselves merely with the initial phases of the treatment up to the point at which the course of the analysis can be confidently left to the patient. The first problem is "to teach the patient to be analyzed." The second is the termination of analysis, the problem of resolving the transference and of teaching the patient to deal with reality. The middle part, the body of the analysis, as it were, will be of interest to us only insofar as it follows from the initial phase of the treatment and leads to its termination.

Before we begin, however, a brief theoretical consideration of the libido-economic basis of analytic therapy is called for.

CHAPTER II

THE ECONOMIC VIEWPOINT IN THE THEORY OF ANALYTIC THERAPY

When Freud moved away from the position of cathartic therapy, gave up hypnosis as a device of analysis, and assumed the standpoint that what the patient was able to tell the analyst while asleep could also be communicated while awake, he tried for a time to make the patient aware of the unconscious meaning of the symptoms by direct interpretation of the traces of repressed elements. It wasn't long before he discovered that this method was dependent upon the readiness on the part of the patient to accept what the analyst pointed out. He divined that the patient put up a "resistance," which was usually unconscious, to the analyst's statements. Thus, he adapted his technique to the new knowledge, i.e., he dispensed with direct interpretation and attempted, from then on, to enable the unconscious to become conscious by eliminating the resistances directed against the repressed elements.

This fundamental change in the theoretic conception and technique of analytic therapy was a turning point in its history, which marked the beginning of the newer, still valid technique. This was never understood by those students who turned away from Freud; even Rank returned to the old method of direct symptom interpretation. In the present work, we have merely applied the new technique of dealing with resistances to the analysis of the character, entirely in keeping with the development of analytic therapy from symptom analysis to the analysis of the personality as a whole.

Whereas, in the period of cathartic therapy, the idea existed that it was necessary "to liberate the strangulated affect from repression" to bring about the disappearance of the symptom, it was later stated, in the period of resistance analysis (this was perhaps a carry-over from the direct interpretation of the symptom's meaning) that the symptom would *of necessity* disappear when the repressed idea upon which it rested had been made conscious. Then, when it turned out that this thesis was untenable, when it was repeatedly observed that symptoms, despite the consciousness of their formerly repressed contents, often continued to exist, Freud, in a discussion at a meeting of the Vienna Psychoanalytic Society, changed the first formula to read that the symptom *might* disappear when its unconscious content had become conscious but that it *did not have to* disappear.

Now one was confronted by a new and difficult problem. If becoming conscious, by itself, was not enough to effect a cure, what other factors were necessary to cause the symptom to disappear; what further conditions decided whether becoming conscious would lead to a cure or not? Hence, the making conscious of the repressed contents remained *the* indispensable precondition of cure; it did not, however, specifically account for it. Once this question had been posed, it was immediately joined by another, namely whether those opponents of psychoanalysis were right, after all, who had always exhorted that analysis had to be followed by "synthesis." However, closer examination showed quite clearly that this exhortation was but a hollow phrase. At the Budapest Congress, Freud himself completely refuted it by pointing out that analysis and synthesis went hand in hand, since every drive which is set free from one relationship immediately forms another relationship. Was this perhaps a key to the solution of the problem? Which drives and which new relationships were we dealing with? Doesn't it make any difference what kind of libido structure the patient has when he leaves the analysis? As an analyst, one has ceased to search for a godhead in psychotherapy and must content oneself with the finding of a solution more in keeping with the pretensions of the average man. Surely, all psychotherapy suffers from the fact that the primitive-biological and the sociological bases of all the so-called higher aspirations have been neglected. The way out was again indicated by Freud's inexhaustible libido theory, which in many cases had been more than neglected in recent years of analytic research. But there were still too many questions all at once. For the sake of brevity, we shall arrange them according to metapsychological points of view.

Topographically, the problem could not be solved. Such an attempt would only have proved inadequate: the mere translation of an unconscious idea into consciousness is not enough to effect a cure. A solution from the *dynamic* point of view was promising but likewise inadequate, notwithstanding the fact that Ferenczi and Rank had made successful efforts in this connection.[1] It is true that the abreaction of the affect related to an unconscious idea almost always alleviates the patient's condition, but usually for a short time only. It must be borne in mind that, apart from certain forms of hysteria, it is difficult to achieve abreaction in the concentrated form necessary to produce the desired result. Thus, only the *economic* point of view remained. It is quite clear that the patient suffers from an inadequate, disturbed libido economy; the normal biological functions of his or her sexuality are in part pathologically distorted, in part completely negated—both contrary to the average healthy person. And surely the normal or abnormal functioning of the libido economy is dependent upon the libido's organization. Hence, one must be able to make a functional distinction between those libido organizations which enable the libido economy to function normally and those which disrupt it. Our later differentiation between two prototypes, the "genital" character and the "neurotic" character, is an attempt to solve this problem.

Whereas, however, the topographical and the dynamic points of view were, from the outset, easy to handle in everyday practice (consciousness or unconsciousness of an idea, intensity of the affective breakthrough of a repressed element, etc.), it was not immediately clear how the economic point of view could be applied in practice. We are dealing here of course with the quantitative factor of psychic life, with the amount of libido which is dammed up or discharged. But how were we to tackle this quantitatively determined difficulty, in view of the fact that in psychoanalysis we deal directly with qualities only? To begin with, we had to understand why we were continually coming up against the quantitative factor in our theory of neurosis and why

[1] Cf. *Development of Psychoanalysis.*

the qualitative factor of psychic life was not, in itself, sufficient to explain psychic phenomena. While experience and deliberation on the problem of analytic therapy always pointed to the problem of quantities, an empirical solution turned up unexpectedly.

We learn from analytic practice that some cases, notwithstanding protracted and copious analysis, remain refractory; whereas other cases, despite incomplete examination of the unconscious, can achieve lasting practical recovery. In comparing these two groups,[2] it turned out that, after the analysis, the former cases, namely those which remained refractory or readily relapsed, had not succeeded in establishing a regulated sexual life or had continued to live in abstinence; whereas the latter, enabled to do so by a partial analysis, quickly took up a lasting and satisfactory sexual life. In an investigation of the prognosis of average cases, it was further shown that, under otherwise equal conditions, the chances of cure were that much more favorable the more completely genital primacy had been achieved in childhood and adolescence. Or, to put it another way, the cure was impeded to the extent to which the libido had been withheld from the genital zone in early childhood. The cases that proved to be more or less inaccessible were those in which genital primacy had not been established at all in childhood, the cases in which the activity of genitality had been restricted to anal, oral, and urethral eroticism.[3] However, in view of the fact that genitality proved to have such prognostic importance, it seemed obvious to investigate in these cases the evidence of genitality, their potency. It turned out that there were no female patients whose vaginal potency was not disturbed and hardly any male patients whose ejaculative or erective potency was not impaired. However, the patients whose potency was intact in the usual sense, the small number of erectively potent neurotics, were enough to erode the value of genitality for the understanding of the economics of cure.

Eventually, one had to reach the conclusion that it doesn't

[2] Cf. Reich: "Über Genitalität" and "Die therapeutische Bedeutung der Genitallibido," *Internationalen Zeitschrift für Psychoanalyse*, Vol. X (1924) and XI (1925).

[3] In the meantime, we have discovered possibilities of considerably improving even such cases.

make any difference whether erective potency exists; this fact tells us nothing about the *economy* of the libido. What is important, evidently, is *whether the capacity to achieve adequate sexual gratification* is intact. This is quite clearly not the case in female patients suffering from vaginal anesthesia; here it is clear from which source the symptoms derive their energy, and what sustains the libido stasis, which is of course the specific energy source of the neurosis. The *economic* concept of *orgastic* impotence, i.e., the incapacity to achieve a resolution of sexual tension satisfactory to the libidinal demands, was first derived from the more thorough investigation of male patients having erective potency. The far-reaching importance of genitality or, more precisely, of orgastic impotence for the etiology of the neurosis was set forth in my book *The Function of the Orgasm*. It wasn't until its implications for the theory of the *actual neurosis* were shown that the genital function became theoretically important—for investigations of the character also. Suddenly it was clear where the problem of quantity was to be sought: it could be nothing other than the organic groundwork, *the "somatic core of the neurosis,"* the actual neurosis which results from dammed-up libido. And, therefore, the economic problem of the neurosis as well as its cure lay, to a large extent, in the somatic sphere, i.e., was accessible only by way of the somatic content of the libido concept.[4]

Now one was also in a better position to decide what other factors, apart from the making conscious of the unconscious, were necessary to cause the symptom to disappear. It is only the *meaning* (ideational content) of the symptom that becomes conscious. In terms of dynamics, the process of becoming conscious brings about a certain alleviation through the emotional discharge which goes hand in hand with it, and through the elimination of a part of preconscious counter-cathexis. But these processes in themselves do not effect very much of a change at the *source* of the energy of the symptom or neurotic character trait. The libido stasis remains, notwithstanding the consciousness of the symptom's meaning. The pressure of the high-strung libido can be partially relieved through intensive analytic work, but the over-

[4] Cf. Reich: "Die Rolle der Genitalität in der Neurosentherapie," *Zeitschrift für Aerztliche Psychotherapie,* Vol. I (1925).

whelming majority of our patients require *genital* sexual gratification (because the pregenital cannot produce an orgasm) for a permanent resolution of sexual tension. It is only after this step, which is made possible by the analysis, that an economic readjustment also takes place. At that time, I tried to formulate this conception in the following way: by removing sexual repressions, the analysis creates the possibility of a *spontaneous organotherapy of neuroses.* Hence, *the ultimate therapeutic agent is an organic process in the metabolic sexual economy,* a process which is related to the sexual gratification achieved in the genital orgasm and, with the elimination of the actual neurosis, the somatic core, also erodes the groundwork of the psychoneurotic superstructure. At the outset, when the neurosis begins to develop, an external inhibition (tangible fear), which then becomes internalized, produces the libido stasis, which in turn imparts its pathological energy to the experiences of the Oedipal stage and, perpetuated as a consequence of sexual repression, keeps the psychoneurosis constantly supplied with energy in a kind of cyclic motion. Therapy works in reverse order in that it first breaks down the psychoneurosis by making conscious the unconscious inhibitions and fixations, thus opening the way to the elimination of the libido stasis. Once this stasis has been eliminated, again in a kind of cycle, the repression and the psychoneurosis have also become unnecessary, indeed impossible.

Roughly speaking, this is the concept which, in the book mentioned above, I developed with respect to the role of the somatic core of the neurosis. From this concept, a larger framework and a clearly defined therapeutic goal ensue for the technique of analysis: the establishment of genital primacy not only in theory but also in practice; *that is to say, the patient must, through analysis, arrive at a regulated and gratifying genital life*—if he is to be cured and permanently so. No matter how short of this goal we may fall in some cases, it is, on the basis of our insights into the dynamics of the libido stasis, the actual goal of our efforts. It is not without danger to lay less stress upon the therapeutic demand for effective sexual gratification as a goal than upon the demand for sublimation, if only because the ability to sublimate is still an ill-understood endowment, whereas the capacity for sexual gratification, even if significantly restricted by social factors, is on the average attainable through analysis. It is easily understood that the shifting of the stress of the goal of the treatment from sublimation to direct sexual gratification broadens considerably the sector of our therapeutic possibilities. Yet it is precisely in this shifting that we encounter difficulties of a social nature, difficulties that we cannot underestimate.

However, that this goal is not achieved by means of instruction, "synthesis," or suggestion but solely through the thorough analysis of the sexual inhibitions rooted in the *character* will have to be demonstrated in the following discussions dealing with technique. But first let us make a few comments on Nunberg's conception of the task.

In his book *Allgemeine Neurosenlehre,* Nunberg attempts to interpret the theory of psychoanalytic therapy; we extract the most important of his views. He is of the opinion that the "first therapeutic task is . . . to help the instincts to achieve discharge and to provide them with access to consciousness." Nunberg further sees an important task "in the establishment of peace between the two poles of the personality, the ego and the id, in the sense that the instincts will no longer lead an isolated existence shut off from the organization of the ego and that the ego will regain its synthesizing power." This, even if incomplete, is essentially correct. But Nunberg is also the exponent of the old view, proved erroneous by practical experience, that, in the act of remembering, psychic energy is discharged, that it is, so to speak, "detonated" in the act of becoming conscious. Thus, in the explanation of cure from the point of view of dynamics, he draws the line at the becoming conscious of what is repressed, without asking whether the minimal quantities of affect which are discharged in this process are also sufficient to release the dammed-up libido in its entirety and to balance the energy economy. If, to counter this objection, Nunberg contended that in the course of the many acts of becoming conscious the entire quantity of the dammed-up energy is indeed disposed of, he could be confronted with a wealth of clinical experiences which clearly indicate the following: only a small fraction of the affect attached to a repressed idea is unlocked in the act of becoming conscious; the far greater and more important part is soon after shifted to another segment of unconscious activity if the affect is attached to the idea itself; or a resolution of the affect does not take place at all if, for instance, it is absorbed into and made a part of the character. In such a case, the becoming conscious of unconscious material remains without therapeutic effect. In short, the dynamics of the cure can by no means be deduced solely from the act of becoming conscious.

This leads to another inevitable criticism of Nunberg's formulations. He writes that the repetition compulsion operates independent of the transference and that it is based on the attractive force of repressed infantile ideas. This would be correct if the repetition compulsion were a primary, irreducible psychic datum. Clinical experience shows, however, that the great attractive force exercised by the unconscious and infantile ideas derives from the energy of the unsatisfied sexual needs, and that it retains its compulsive repetitive character only as long as the possibility of mature sexual gratification is blocked. In short, the neurotic repetition compulsion is contingent on the libido's economic situation. Seen from this perspective as well as from the point of view to be encountered later in the formulations on the neurotic and genital characters, the peace between ego and id which Nunberg is justified in postulating can be secured only on a given sex-economic basis: first, through the supplanting of pregenital strivings by genital strivings; second, through effective gratification of the genital demands, which, in turn, would solve the problem of the permanent elimination of stasis.

Nunberg's theoretical assumption leads to an attitude toward technique which we cannot look upon as the proper analytic attitude. Nunberg claims that the resistances should not be attacked directly; as he sees it, the positive transference should be exploited by the analyst for the purpose of insinuating himself into the patient's ego, from which vantage point he should set about their destruction. It is Nunberg's contention that a relationship similar to the one existing between a hypnotized person and the hypnotist would result from this. "Since, inside the ego, the analyst is surrounded by libido, he neutralizes to some extent the severity of the superego itself." In this way, he argues, the analyst becomes capable of bringing about the reconciliation of the two cloven parts of the neurotic personality.

In opposition to this, it is necessary to point out:

a) It is precisely this "insinuation" into the ego that is therapeutically dangerous in many cases, for in the beginning, as will be thoroughly elaborated later, there is no durable and genuine positive transference. In the initial stages of the analysis, we are always dealing with narcissistic attitudes, e.g., an infantile need for protection. In view of the fact that the reaction of disappointment is stronger than the positive object-relationship, this narcissistic dependence can readily change into hate. Such an "insinuating into" for the purpose of evading the resistances and "destroying" them from "within" constitutes a danger inasmuch as the resistances could become disguised in this way. What is more important, the old condition (if not the severest reactions of disappointment) will be reestablished as soon as the weak object-relationship falls apart or is usurped by other transferences. It is precisely through such procedures that we bring about the most severe, most devious, and least controllable manifestations of negative transference. Termination of the analysis by the patient or even suicide is very often the result of such procedures. It is necessary to point out that incidents of suicide are especially likely when the establishment of an artificially positive, hypnoidal attitude has succeeded all too well, whereas an open and clear working through of the aggressive and narcissistic reactions, also borne by positive attitudes of course, prevents a suicide as well as an abrupt termination of the analysis. This may sound paradoxical, but it mirrors the workings of the psychic apparatus.

b) In the process of insinuating oneself into the positive transference (instead of allowing it to become crystallized out of its infantile fixations), the danger arises of accepting superficial interpretations which can delude the analyst as well as the patient about the true situation until, very often, it becomes too late to correct. Unfortunately, a hypnotic relationship ensues of its own accord all too often; it should be unmasked and eliminated as a resistance.

c) When anxiety subsides at the beginning of treatment, this merely attests to the fact that the patient has channeled a portion of his libido into the transference—the negative transference also —not that he has resolved anxiety. To make analytic work possible, the analyst may, by some form of reassurance, have to relieve anxieties that are too acute. Apart from this, however, it must be made clear to the patient that he can be cured only by mobilizing the greatest possible quantity of aggression and anxiety.

My own experiences have made me very familiar with Nunberg's description of the typical course of an analytic treatment. I can only add that I do my utmost to obviate such an imbroglio; indeed, it is precisely for this reason that I give so much attention to the technique of dealing with resistances at the beginning of the treatment. The following is the most frequent result of an analysis in which the negative transference has not been worked out at the beginning of the treatment and the durability of the patient's positive transference has been falsely appraised:

For a time, an undisturbed harmony exists between the patient and the analyst; indeed, the patient completely relies on the analyst, also on his interpretations, and, if it were possible, would rely on him in his recollections also. But the moment soon arrives at which this accord is disturbed. As we already mentioned, the deeper the analysis proceeds, the stronger the resistances become, and this is all the more the case as the original pathogenic situation is approached. Added to these difficulties, moreover, is the frustration that occurs inevitably at some point of the transference, for the patient's personal demands upon the analyst cannot be satisfied. Most patients react to this frustration by slacking off in the analytic work, by enactment, i.e., they behave as they once did in analogous situations. This could be interpreted to mean that they are expressing a certain activity; . . . on the contrary, they are evading it. At bottom, they behave passively toward it. In short, the repetition compulsion, which of course helps to bring about the fixations, also governs, in the transference situation, the psychic utterances of what is repressed. Now the patient relegates a piece of active work to the analyst: the divination of what he wants but cannot express. As a rule, it is a matter of wanting to be loved. The actual omnipotence of the means of expression (which can also be mute) and the supposed omnipotence of the analyst are put to a crucial test. To some extent, the analyst is capable of unmasking these resistances; for the rest, he is hard put to know what the patient is trying to communicate. The conflict, which is no longer an internal one but one between the patient and the analyst, is thus brought to a head. *The analysis threatens to go to pieces, i.e., the patient is faced with the choice of losing the analyst and his love or of again performing active work.* [My italics, W.R.] If the transference is a durable one, i.e., if the patient is again in control of a modicum of the object-libido which has already been loosened from the fixations, he is alarmed at the possibility of losing the analyst. A peculiar thing often occurs in such cases. Just when the analyst has given up hope of a favorable outcome of the analysis, has lost interest in the case, a wealth of material suddenly appears betokening a rapid conclusion of the analysis. (Nunberg: *Allgemeine Neurosenlehre,* p. 305)

A determined, consistent, systematic resistance analysis does not succeed in all cases. Where it does succeed, such hopelessness is not part of the analysis. Where it does not succeed, such a situation occurs quite frequently. Uncertain of the outcome, we are forced, precisely because of it, to pay the greatest attention to the technique of resistance analysis.

CHAPTER III

ON THE TECHNIQUE OF
INTERPRETATION AND OF
RESISTANCE ANALYSIS[1]

(The Natural Development of the Transference Neurosis)

1. SOME TYPICAL ERRORS IN THE TECHNIQUE OF INTERPRETATION AND THEIR CONSEQUENCES

In analytic work, we have to differentiate two parts: the *recovery* of the patient and his *immunization* insofar as this is possible in the course of treatment. The first task too falls into two parts: the preparatory work of the *introductory period* and the actual *healing process*. True, this is merely an artificial differentiation, for even the very first resistance interpretation has a lot to do with the actual cure. But we do not allow ourselves to be deterred by this. Even the preparations for a journey (to which Freud compared analysis) have a lot to do with the journey itself —its success could depend upon them. In analysis, at any rate, everything depends upon the way in which the treatment is initiated. A case which is incorrectly or confusedly begun can be salvaged only with difficulty—often not at all. Most cases offer the greatest difficulties in the introductory period, whether they are "going well" or not. It is precisely those cases in which the introductory period proceeds with apparent smoothness that later offer the greatest difficulties, for the untrammeled course in the beginning complicates the timely recognition and elimination of the difficulties. Errors committed during the introductory period of the treatment become that much more difficult to eliminate, the longer the treatment has progressed without their correction.

[1] First presented in the Seminar for Psychoanalytic Therapy, Vienna, June 1926, published in the *Internationalen Zeitschrift für Psychoanalyse*, 1927–28.

What is the nature of these special and typical difficulties of the introductory period?

Let us sketch, for the time being merely to gain a better orientation, the goal toward which the analysis must advance from the introductory period. Its aim is to reach the energy source of the symptoms and of the neurotic character in order to set the healing process in motion. Obstructing this effort are the patient's resistances, the most tenacious of which are those which derive from the transference conflicts. They have to be made conscious, interpreted, and relinquished by the patient, i.e., their psychic value has to be annulled. Thus, the patient penetrates ever deeper into the affect-laden remembrances of early childhood. For us, the widely discussed question of what is more essential, affective reanimation (enactment) or remembering, is of no importance. Clinical experience confirms Freud's dictate that the patient who likes to reenact what he has experienced not only must understand what he enacts but also must remember affectively if he is to get at the core of his conflicts.[2] But I do not want to anticipate our program. I mention this merely to avoid creating the impression that the analysis of the resistances and transference constitutes the entire analytic effort. It must be borne in mind that in this section we are dealing solely with the principles of resistance technique.

What is the course taken by many of our cases in lieu of affective remembering?

There are the cases which fail to achieve a cure because, as a result of the many heterogeneous transferences, the analyst is no longer able to keep track of the welter of unearthed material. We call this a "chaotic situation" and find that it is caused by certain errors in the technique of interpretation. Let us but think of the many cases in which the negative transference is overlooked because it is hidden behind manifest positive attitudes. And last but not least let us consider those cases which, notwithstanding far-reaching recall work, do not lead to a successful cure because

---

[2] Footnote, 1945: This technical problem of psychoanalysis has been completely solved in the meantime. In orgone therapy, the pathogenic remembrances emerge *spontaneously* and *effortlessly* when the somatic emotions break through the muscular armor.

their affect-paralysis is not accorded sufficient attention or is not, at the very beginning, subjected to analysis.

In contrast to these cases, which appear to be going well but actually end chaotically, there are those which are "not going well," i.e., do not come up with any associations and oppose our efforts with passive resistance.

If, now, I sketch some of my own gross failures, we shall soon recognize that they can be traced back to typical errors. And the similarity of most of these failures is indicative of typical errors that we make in the introductory period, errors that can no longer be ascribed to the gross sins which beginners are known to commit. We must not be disheartened by this, for, as Ferenczi once said, every new experience costs us a case. What is important is to recognize errors and to translate them into experience. It is no different in any other branch of medicine; but let us leave extenuation and the concealment of failures to our colleagues.

In analysis, a patient who suffered from an inferiority complex and self-consciousness enacted his impotence by adopting an apathetic attitude ("What's the use?"). Instead of divining the nature of this resistance, clarifying it, and making conscious the deprecatory tendency concealed behind it, I told him again and again that he did not want to cooperate and had no desire to get well. I was not entirely unjustified in this, but the analysis was not successful because I failed to probe further into his "not wanting," because I did not make an effort to understand the reasons for his "not being able to." Instead, I allowed myself to be trapped into futile reproaches by my own inability. Every patient has the tendency to remain sick, and I know that many analysts, when they themselves are not clear about a particular case, simply accuse the patient of not wanting to get well, without giving any further explanation. Such accusations should disappear from analytic practice altogether and be replaced by self-control. For this too we must realize: a stagnation in an analysis which remains unclear is the fault of the analyst.

Another patient, in the course of three years of analysis, had recalled the primal scene together with all material pertaining to it, but not *once* had there been any loosening of his affect-paralysis, not once had he accused the analyst of those feelings which—however emotionless—he harbored toward his father. He was not cured. I had not known how to elicit his repressed hate. This example will make some people jubilant: finally it is admitted that the unearthing of the primal scene is of no use therapeutically. Such people are deceived. There is no real cure without analysis of the earliest experiences. What is important is that the act of remembering be accompanied by the affects pertaining to the remembered material.

In still another case, it happened that in a dream during the second week of treatment the incest fantasy appeared quite clearly and the patient himself recognized its true meaning. For a whole year I heard nothing more about it; consequently, there was no real success. However, I had learned that at times material that is emerging too rapidly has to be suppressed until the ego is strong enough to assimilate it.

A case of erythrophobia failed because I pursued the material which the patient offered in every direction, interpreting it indiscriminately, without first having clearly eliminated the resistances. They eventually appeared, of course, but much too strongly and chaotically; I had used up my ammunition; my explanations were without effect; it was no longer possible to restore order. I assure you that at the time, with three or four years' analytic practice behind me, I was no longer such a novice that, contrary to Freud's teaching, I would have given an interpretation before the unconscious had clearly and unequivocally revealed itself and the patient himself was close to the solution. Evidently, however, this alone was not enough, for the chaotic situation was similar to those which are encountered in seminars and monitored analyses.

A case of classical hysteria marked by twilight states would have recovered beautifully (subsequent experiences with similar cases permit me to say this) if, at the right time, I had understood and correctly handled the patient's reactions to the analysis of the positive transference, i.e., her reactive hate. Instead, I allowed myself to be lured into a chaos by her recollections, a chaos from which I was not able to find my way out. And the patient continued to have her twilight states.

A number of bad experiences as a consequence of incorrect

handling of the transference when reactions of disappointment set in taught me to respect the danger to the analysis of the original negative transference or the negative transference resulting from the frustration of the love transference. And it was not until a patient told me, some months after the termination of an unsuccessful analysis, that he had never trusted me that I learned to appreciate the danger of the negative transference that remains latent. That patient had recalled beautifully for a year and a half in a good positive transference. This experience prompted me successfully to seek a means of drawing the negative transference out of its concealment in order to avoid such a thing ever happening again, and so as to fulfill my therapeutic duties in a wiser way.

Most of our meetings at the Vienna seminar were also concerned with the negative transference, especially the latent transference. In short, we see that this was not the blind spot of one analyst. Failure to recognize the negative transference appears to be a general occurrence. Undoubtedly, this can be traced back to our narcissism, which makes us highly receptive to compliments but quite blind to all negative tendencies in the patient unless they are crudely expressed. Psychoanalytic literature is conspicuous for its references to the transference in its positive sense. To my knowledge, apart from Landauer's article on "Passive Technique," the problem of negative transference has been largely neglected.

The failure to recognize negative transference is only one of the many mistakes which confuse the course of the analysis. We have all had experiences of what we have termed the "chaotic situation"; hence, my description of it need not be anything more than the roughest sketch.

The remembrances and actions are quite numerous, but they follow one another in great confusion; the analyst learns a great deal; the patient produces abundant material from all layers of his unconscious, from all periods of his life; everything is there in large chunks, as it were. Yet nothing has been worked through in accordance with the therapeutic goal; notwithstanding the wealth of material, the patient has not gained any conviction of its importance. The analyst has done a good deal of interpreting, but the interpretations have not deepened the analysis one way or another. It is clear that everything the patient has offered serves a secret, unrecognized resistance. Such a chaotic analysis is dangerous inasmuch as, for a long time, the analyst believes that it is going very well, simply because the patient is "coming up with material." Usually too late, the analyst realizes that the patient has been going around in circles and has turned up the same material again and again, only in a different light. In this way, the patient is able, for years on end, to use up his analytic hour without the slightest change taking place in his nature.

Here is a characteristic case which I took over from a colleague. A patient with a number of perversions had been under analysis for eight months, during which time he had rattled on incessantly and had yielded material from the deepest layers of his unconscious. This material had been continuously interpreted. The more it was interpreted, the more copiously flowed the stream of his associations. Finally, the analysis had to be broken off for external reasons, and the patient came to me. At that time I was already familiar with the dangers of concealed resistances. It struck me that the patient uninterruptedly produced unconscious material, that he knew, for instance, how to give an exact description of the most intricate mechanisms of the simple and double Oedipus complex. I asked the patient whether he really believed what he was saying and what he had heard. "Are you kidding!" he exclaimed. "I really have to contain myself not to burst out laughing at all this." To my question why he had not told this to the first analyst, he answered that he had not considered it necessary. There was no longer anything to be done, notwithstanding a vigorous analysis of his levity. He already knew too much. My colleague's interpretations had all fizzled out, and my own interpretations merely ricocheted from his levity. I gave him up after four months, but it is possible that a longer and more consistent interpretation of his narcissistic defense would have achieved some result. At any rate, I had gained a new understanding. At that time, however, I had not yet had the full experience gained from working on this type of behavior continuously for a period of time.

If we look for the causes of such chaotic situations, we soon see that the technique of interpretation falls short on the following points:

1. *Premature interpretation* of the meaning of the symptoms

and other manifestations of the deep unconscious, particularly of symbols. Compelled by the resistances which have remained concealed, the patient gets control of the analysis, and only too late the analyst notices that the patient is going around in circles, completely untouched.

2. Interpretation of the material in the sequence in which it yields itself, without due consideration to the structure of the neurosis and the stratification of the material. The error consists in the fact that interpretations are made simply because the material has come to light clearly *(unsystematic interpretation of meaning)*.

3. The analysis is embroiled not only because interpretations are pursued in every direction but also because this is done before the cardinal resistance has been worked through. The error here is that the interpretation of meaning precedes the interpretation of resistance. The situation becomes even more confused in that the resistances soon become entangled in the relationship to the analyst; hence, *unsystematic interpretation of resistances* also complicates the transference situation.

4. The interpretation of the transference resistances is not only unsystematic but also *inconsistent,* i.e., not enough attention is given to the fact that the patient has the tendency to conceal his resistances anew, or, more specifically, to mask them by sterile accomplishments or acute reaction formations. The latent transference resistances are usually overlooked, or the analyst shies away from developing and following them up consistently when they are hidden, whatever their form.

Presumably, an incorrect comprehension of the Freudian rule, namely that the course of the analysis should be left to the patient, lies at the root of these errors. This Freudian rule can only be taken to mean that the patient's work should not be disturbed when it is following a course in keeping with his conscious will to get well and our intention to cure him. Clearly, however, we must intervene when the patient's fear of struggling with his conflicts and his desire to remain sick disrupt this course.

2. SYSTEMATIC INTERPRETATION AND RESISTANCE ANALYSIS

I have now subjected our efforts to sufficient criticism, and I fear that I may have overtaxed the reader's patience. I fear this all the more since, when he now asks us to describe the correct technique, that is not so easily done. Yet I am convinced that the reader has gained sufficient insight into the difficulties of the subject so that a rough outline will suffice. He can then draw conclusions from the errors outlined and will be able to apply them to general aspects of the problem.

Before I begin, I must express my concern about the danger of being caught in a snare in the discussion of this very peculiar subject. We are dealing with living and fluid psychic events; that they take on a rigid character as soon as we put them into words and try to communicate them in sentences cannot be helped. What follows may easily create the impression of being a rigid system, but in fact it is hardly more than a rough sketch of a field which we are in the process of surveying and must still study in detail. Only some things which stand out conspicuously are marked in; other things which are just as important must be passed over *for the time being*. The differentiating detail work is also missing. Hence, we must be prepared at all times to correct the sketch when some aspect of it turns out to be incorrect, less important, or not universally valid. It is important that we understand one another and not speak at cross purposes, each of us talking a different language. Whatever appears to be schematic in the following exposition is intended merely to serve as a means of orientation. There is no getting out of a thicket if one fails to establish one's bearings by means of various landmarks, e.g., conspicuous formations of the terrain, or if one does not use a compass. Our investigation of the psychic processes during treatment will be "held together" by similar "landmarks," which will be created *ad hoc* solely for the purpose of orientation. The same holds true for the schema which automatically emerges as soon as one particular phenomenon is isolated and viewed as a separate unit; it is merely a scientific makeshift. It must also be borne in mind that we do not impose the system, the rule, or the principle on the case. We approach the case free of preconceived notions and establish our bearings on the basis of *its* material, *its* behavior, on what the patient conceals or represents as its opposite. Only then do we turn to the question: how do I best make use of what I know about *this* case for the technique of *this* case? Should it turn out, after vast experience, that we are able to differentiate various types of resistances—a possibility Freud spoke of favorably at the Budapest Congress—this would make it easier for us. But even then, in each individual case, we would have to wait to see whether the patient reveals this or that kind of typical resistance or, perhaps, shows no similarity with other cases. The latent negative transference is only *one* of such typical resistances. Hence, we should not look solely for this resistance and immediately apply a different means of orientation in the event we don't find it. The means must be derived solely from the individual patient's material.

We have already agreed that interpretations involving deeper probing have to be avoided as long as the first front of the cardinal resistances has not become manifest and been eliminated, regardless of how abundant, clear, and obviously interpretable the material may be. The more material a patient recollects without having produced corresponding resistances, the more circumspect one must become. Faced with the choice of interpreting unconscious contents or taking up evident resistances, the analyst will choose the latter. Our principle is: *No interpretation of meaning when a resistance interpretation is still to come.* The reason for this is simple enough. If the analyst offers an interpretation *before* the dissolution of the germane resistances, the patient will accept the interpretation for reasons related to the transference, in which case he will wholly depreciate its importance at the first sign of a negative bearing, or the resistance will follow afterwards. In either case, the interpretation has forfeited its therapeutic force; it has fizzled out. Such an error is very difficult, if at all possible, to correct. The path which the interpretation must take into the deep unconscious has been blocked off.

It is important not to disturb the patient in the unfolding of his "analytic personality" during the first weeks of treatment. Neither should the resistances be interpreted before they have been fully developed and in essence understood by the analyst. Naturally, the moment at which a resistance is interpreted will depend largely upon the analyst's experience. Small signs will suffice for the experienced analyst, while the beginner will need gross actions to understand the same case. Not infrequently, it depends solely upon experience whether and by which indications *latent resistances* are recognized. When the analyst has grasped the meaning of such resistances, he will make them conscious by consistent interpretation, i.e., he will first make it clear to the patient that he has resistances, then what mechanism they are making use of, and finally what they are directed against.

If the first transference resistance has not been preceded by sufficient recall work, a major difficulty is encountered in dissolving it, a difficulty, however, which diminishes as the analyst gains practice and experience. This obstacle consists in the fact that, to dissolve the resistance, the analyst must know the unconscious material pertaining to and contained in it, yet he has no way of reaching this material because it is shut off by the resistance. Like the dream, every resistance has a historical meaning (an origin) and a contemporary relevance. The impasse can be penetrated by first divining the *contemporary* meaning and purpose of the resistance from the *contemporary* situation (the unfolding of which the analyst has observed) and from the form and mechanisms of the resistance, and then working through it with corresponding interpretations in such a way that the germane infantile material is brought to the surface. It is only with the help of the latter that the resistance can be wholly dissolved. There are of course no rules for the ferreting out of the resistances and the divining of their contemporary meaning. To a large extent, this is a matter of intuition—and here we have the beginning of the nonteachable art of analysis. The less blatant, the more concealed the resistances are (i.e., the more the patient deceives), the more certain the analyst will have to be of his intuitions in order to gain control. In other words, the analyst himself must be analyzed and, over and above this, he must have special gifts.

What is a "latent resistance"? They are attitudes on the part of the patient which are not expressed directly and immediately, i.e., in the form of doubt, distrust, tardiness, silence, obstinacy, apathy, etc., but indirectly in the analytic performance. Exceptional docility or complete absence of manifest resistances is indicative of concealed and, for that reason, much more dangerous passive resistance. I am in the habit of tackling latent resistances as soon as I perceive them; and I do not hesitate to interrupt the flow of communications when I have learned all that is necessary to understand them. For I have learned from experience that the therapeutic effect of analytic communications is lost as long as there are unresolved resistances.

The one-sided and therefore incorrect assessment of analytic material and the not infrequent incorrect application of the Freudian thesis, namely that the analyst must proceed from the specific surface, easily lead to catastrophic misunderstandings and technical difficulties. To begin with: what is meant by "analytic material"? This is usually taken to mean the patient's communications, dreams, associations, slips. Theoretically, to be sure, it is known that the patient's behavior is of analytic importance; but unequivocal experiences in the seminar show that the patient's behavior (manner, look, language, countenance, dress, handshake, etc.) not only is vastly underestimated in terms of its analytic importance but is usually completely overlooked. At the Innsbruck Congress, Ferenczi and I, independent of one another, stressed the therapeutic importance of these formal elements. As time went on, they became for me the most important fulcrum and point of departure for the analysis of the character. The overestimation of the content of the material usually goes hand in hand with an underestimation, if not total neglect, of the patient's bearing, the manner in which the patient makes his communications, recounts his dreams, etc. and when the patient's bearing is neglected or not given importance equal to content, a therapeutically catastrophic comprehension of the "psychic surface" is unintentionally arrived at. When a patient is very polite, at the same time producing a great deal of material, e.g., on his relationship to his sister, we have two contents of the "psychic surface" existing side by side: his love for his sister and his bearing —the politeness. Both are grounded in the unconscious. In view of all this, it is no longer a simple matter of stating that the analyst must proceed from the surface. We learn from analytic experience that, beneath this politeness and nicety, a more or less unconscious, if not downright distrustful or derogatory attitude is *always* concealed. More correctly, the patient's stereotype politeness is in itself indicative of negative criticism, distrustfulness, or derogation. From this point of view, should the incestuous love for the sister be interpreted without any further consideration, if a dream or association pertaining to it arises? There are special reasons why one part of the psychic surface, and not another, is dealt with first in analysis. It would be a mistake to wait until the patient himself begins to speak about his politeness and the reasons for it. Since in analysis this character trait immediately becomes a resistance, the same holds true for it as for every other resistance: the patient will never bring it up of his own accord. The analyst must unmask the resistance for what it is.

At this point we can expect an important objection. It will be contended that my assumption, i.e., that the politeness immediately becomes a resistance, does not tally with the facts of the situation, for if it did, the patient would not produce any material. Yes, but this is precisely the point: it is not solely the content of the material which is important; at the beginning of the analysis, the formal aspect of the material is also of special importance. To return to our example of politeness: owing to his repressions, the neurotic has every reason to set an especially high value on politeness and social convention and to make use of them as a means of protection. It may be much more agreeable to treat a polite patient than it is to treat an impolite, highly outspoken patient who might, for example, tell the analyst straight off that he is too young or too old, hasn't a beautifully furnished apartment or has an ugly wife, is not very bright or looks too Jewish, acts like a neurotic, should be undergoing analysis himself, and similar flattering things. This is not necessarily a transference phenomenon: that the analyst should be a "blank piece of paper" is an ideal. It can never be wholly realized. The "true nature" of the analyst is a fact which at first has nothing to do with transference. And patients are exceptionally sensitive to our weaknesses; indeed, in scenting these weaknesses, some patients directly revenge themselves for the stress they have to endure because of the imposition of the basic rule. Only a few patients (usually they are sadistic characters) derive sadistic pleasure from the frankness demanded of them. In therapeutic terms, their behavior is valuable, even if it becomes a resistance for a time. But the majority of patients are still much too diffident and apprehensive, too burdened with guilt feelings, to bring this frankness into play spontaneously. Unlike many of my colleagues, I must subscribe to the contention that every case, without exception, begins the analysis with a more or less pronounced attitude of distrust and skepticism, *which usually remains concealed.* To persuade himself of this, the analyst must not of course rely upon the patient's need to confess or, for that matter, his need for punishment;

rather, he must use all his wits to elicit from the patient the quite obvious reasons for being distrustful and exercising negative criticism (the novelty of the situation, the lack of familiarity with the analyst, the public's contempt for psychoanalysis, etc.) which are inherent in the analytic situation. Thus, it is only through his own frankness that the analyst gains the patient's confidence. One technical question remains, namely at what point should the analyst deal with those attitudes of distrust and negative criticism, which cannot yet be called neurotic, determined as they are by the contemporary situation. What is important here is that deeper interpretations of the unconscious be avoided as long as the wall of conventional politeness exists between patient and analyst.

We cannot continue our discussion of the technique of interpretation without going into the development and treatment of the transference neurosis.

In an analysis that is proceeding correctly, it is not long before the first substantial transference resistance arises. To begin with, we must understand why the first significant resistance against the continuation of the analysis is automatically, and in keeping with the legitimacy of the case's structure, tied in with the relationship to the analyst. What is the motive of "transference compulsion" (Ferenczi) ? As a result of the basic rule, adherence to which we insist on, we have hit upon the taboo that is so disagreeable to the ego. Sooner or later, the patient's defense against his repressions becomes stronger. At first, the resistance is directed solely against what is repressed, but the patient knows nothing about it, neither that he bears something forbidden in himself nor that he is fending it off. As Freud demonstrated, the resistances themselves are unconscious. But the resistance is an emotional stirring corresponding to an increased expenditure of energy, and for that reason cannot remain buried. Like everything else that is irrationally motivated, this emotional stirring also strives to achieve a rational foundation, i.e., to become anchored in a real relationship. Now what could be closer to hand than to project, and to project upon that person who brought about the whole conflict through his insistence on the disagreeable basic rule? As a result of the displacement of the defense (from the unconscious to the analyst), the particular content of the unconscious also creeps into the resistance; that is, the content is also projected upon the analyst. He becomes a miserable creature like the father or a lovable creature like the mother. It is clear that this defense can lead only to a negative attitude at first. As the disturber of the neurotic balance, the analyst necessarily becomes the enemy, whether it is a matter of projected love or projected hate, for in both cases defense and rejection are also always present.

If hate impulses are projected first, the transference resistance is clearly negative. If, on the other hand, the impulses that are projected first are of a loving nature, then the real transference resistance is preceded for a time by a manifest but not conscious positive transference. However, its fate is always the same, i.e., it becomes a reactive negative transference, on the one hand because of the inevitable disappointment ("disappointment reaction") and on the other hand because it is warded off as soon as it endeavors to become conscious under the pressure of sensuous strivings; and every defense encompasses negative attitudes.

The problem of technique pertaining to the latent negative transference is so important that it will be necessary to make a separate investigation of the forms in which this transference becomes manifest and how it is to be treated. At this time, I want merely to list a few typical cases in which we are most likely to encounter a latent negative transference. They are:

1. The obsequious, obtrusively friendly, implicitly trustful, in short, the *"good" patients;* those who are always in a positive transference and never show a disappointment reaction. (Usually passive-feminine characters or female hysterics having nymphomanic tendencies.)

2. Those who are always *rigidly conventional and correct.* They are usually compulsive characters who have converted their hatred into "being polite at all costs."

3. *Patients whose affects are paralyzed.* Like those who are rigidly correct, these patients are characterized by an exaggerated but blocked aggressiveness. They, too, for the most part, are compulsive characters; however, female hysterics also show a surface affect-paralysis.

4. *Patients who complain about the artificiality of their feelings and emotionality*—patients, in short, who suffer from de-

personalization. Among these we also have those patients who consciously and at the same time compulsively "play act," i.e., who know at the back of their minds that they are deceiving the analyst. In such patients, who usually belong to the group of narcissistic neuroses of the hypochondriac type, we always discover a *"secret chuckle"* at everything and everybody, a chuckle which becomes a torture to the patient himself. It entails the greatest difficulties in analysis.

Since the form and stratification of the first transference resistance are determined by the individual's infantile experience of love, it is possible to analyze the infantile conflicts in a systematic way, free of unnecessary complications, only if we make strict allowances for this stratification in our interpretations of the transference. It is not, of course, that the contents of the transferences are dependent upon our interpretations; but there can be no doubt that the sequence in which they become acute is decided by the technique of interpretation. It is important not only that a transference neurosis develop but also that in its development it follow the same pattern as its prototype, the primal neurosis, and that it exhibit the same stratification as the other in its dynamics. Freud taught us that the original neurosis becomes accessible only through the transference neurosis. Thus, it is clear that our task will be that much easier, the more completely and systematically the original neurosis has coiled around the spools of the transference. Naturally, this coiling takes place in reverse sequence. Hence, one can see that a faulty analysis of the transference—e.g., the interpretation of an attitude stemming from a deeper layer of the unconscious, regardless of how distinct the attitude is and how accurate the interpretation may be —will blur the blueprint of the original neurosis and entangle the transference neurosis. We learn from experience that the transference neurosis will develop of its own accord, in keeping with the structure of the original neurosis. But we must avoid premature and unsystematic interpretations and interpretations that penetrate too deeply.

Let us take the following schematic example to illustrate our point. A patient first loves his mother, then hates his father, and eventually withdraws his love from his mother out of fear and converts his hatred of his father into a passive-feminine love of

him. If the resistance is correctly analyzed, it will be the passive-feminine attitude, i.e., the last result of his libidinal development, that manifests itself first in the transference. Next, a systematic resistance analysis will bring out the hatred of the father
concealed behind this passive-feminine attitude, and only after
this hatred has been worked through will a new cathexis of the
mother follow, at first through the transference of the love for
the mother to the analyst. From here, then, it can be transferred
to a woman in real life.

Let us now consider a less favorable but no less possible development. The patient, for example, might exhibit a manifest
positive transference and produce in this connection not only
dreams reflecting his passive-feminine attitude but also dreams
embodying his tie to his mother. Let us further assume that both
sets of dreams are clear and capable of interpretation. If the analyst recognizes the true stratification of the positive transference;
if it is clear to him that the reactive love for the father represents
the top layer of this transference, the hatred of him the second
layer, and the transferred love for the mother the deepest layer,
then he will certainly leave the last untouched, no matter how
importunate. If, however, he should choose to work first on the
love for the mother which is projected upon him as part of the
transference, then the latent hatred of the father transferred to
the analyst in a reactive form would constitute a powerful and
impenetrable resistance block between his interpretations pertaining to the incestuous love and the experience of the patient.
The interpretation that would have had to pass through the topographically higher layers of distrust, disbelief, and rejection will
be superficially accepted but will be therapeutically ineffective
and have but one result: it will cause the patient, internally
frightened and made cautious by this interpretation, to conceal
the hatred of his father even more thoroughly and, because of intensified guilt feelings, to become an even "nicer" person. In one
form or another, we would have a chaotic situation on our
hands.

What is important, therefore, is to single out from the welter
of material flowing from many psychic layers that element which
assumes a central position in the existing or preceding transference resistance and is not laden with other attitudes. As theoreti-

cal as this may sound, it is a principle which has to be applied in every average case.

Now we have to ask what happens to the remainder of the material which is of less contemporary importance. Usually it is enough just to ignore it. Thus it will automatically recede into the background. It often happens, however, that the patient will obtrude an attitude or a definite sphere of experience in order to conceal material of greater immediate importance. It follows from everything we have said that such a resistance has to be eliminated. In elucidating the situation, the analyst "steers the material," i.e., *unceasingly points to that which is being buried* and disregards that which is being pushed forward. A typical example of this is the patient's behavior in a latent negative transference. He tries to conceal his secret criticism and discredit the analyst and the analysis by means of hypocritical praise. Analyzing this resistance, the analyst easily arrives at the patient's motive, his fear of expressing criticism.

Only seldom is the analyst forced to check rapidly flowing material—for instance, when unconscious perverse fantasies or incestuous desires become conscious prematurely and cumulatively—before the ego has become strong enough to handle them. When this happens, if disregarding the material is not enough, the analyst will have to ward it off.

Thus, the central content of the transference resistance remains always in contact with the patient's remembrances, and the affects aroused in the transference are automatically passed on to them. And in this way the analytically dangerous situation of remembering without affects is avoided. It is indicative of the chaotic situation, on the other hand, that a concealed resistance remains unresolved for months on end and binds all affects, while the remembrances flit about in wild succession, e.g., one day the castration anxiety, another day the oral fantasy, and still another day the incest fantasy.

By correctly selecting the material that is to be interpreted, we achieve a *continuity in the analysis.* In this way, we are not only conversant with the existing situation at all times; we are also able to keep a close watch on the legitimacy with which the transference develops. Our work is made easier and the groundwork of the cure is thoroughly prepared by the fact that the resistances, which of course are nothing other than individual pieces of the neurosis, appear *one after the other*, yet tied together by a historically determined structure.

3. CONSISTENCY IN RESISTANCE ANALYSIS

Thus far, we have merely described the technique of interpreting the meaning of unconscious material and the technique of interpreting resistances, and we have agreed that interpretation must be systematic and must be carried out in keeping with the individual structure of the neurosis. In listing the errors made in interpretation, we differentiated between disorganized and inconsistent interpretations. There was good reason for this, for we know cases which, notwithstanding systematic interpretation, become disorganized; and we perceive the cause of this in the *lack of consistency in the further working through of the already interpreted resistances.*

If we have happily passed the barrier of the first transference resistance, the work of recalling usually moves forward rapidly and penetrates into the period of childhood. But it isn't long before the patient runs into fresh layers of forbidden material, which he endeavors to ward off with a second front of transference resistances. The game of resistance analysis begins anew, but this time it has a somewhat different character. Before, we were dealing with a virgin difficulty, whereas the new resistance has an analytic past which was not without influence on its formation. In keeping with the new material, it has, to be sure, a structure and meaning different from the first resistance. It might be assumed that the patient has learned from the first resistance analysis and will himself help to eliminate the difficulty this time. However, it doesn't work out that way in practice. In the large majority of cases, it turns out that, in addition to the new resistance, the patient reactivates the old one. Indeed, the patient may relapse into the old resistance without showing the new one. This stratification complicates the whole situation. There is no set pattern as to which resistance will gain the upper hand, the reactivated old one or the new one. But this is not significant with respect to the tactics of analysis. What is important is that the patient restores a large portion of his counter-cathexis to the old resistance position which had apparently been disposed of. If the analyst takes up the new resistance first or exclusively, he will be neglecting an intermediate layer, namely the reactivated old resistance. He will then run the risk of wasting his costly interpretations. Disappointments and failures can be averted if *the old difficulty is reverted to* every time, regardless of how conspicuous or inconspicuous it makes itself, and is used as the point of departure for the work of dissolution. In this way, the analyst slowly advances to the new resistance and avoids the danger of conquering a new piece of land while the enemy reestablishes itself in a previously conquered area.

Using the cardinal resistance as a kind of citadel, as it were, the analyst must *undermine the neurosis from all sides,* instead of taking up individual peripheral resistances, i.e., attacking many different points which have only an indirect relation to one another. By consistently broaching the resistances and the analytic material from the first transference resistance, the analyst is able to survey the situation as a whole, both past and present. The required continuity of the analysis does not have to be fought for and a thorough working through of the neurosis is guaranteed. Assuming that we are dealing with typical case histories and that the resistance analysis has been correctly carried out, we are able to foresee the sequence in which recognized tendencies will appear as acute transference resistances.

There is no point in trying to persuade us that the major problems of psychotherapy are to be coped with by "bombarding" the patient with interpretations of his unconscious material or, for that matter, by treating all patients according to one scheme, e.g., from *one* assumed primal source of the neurosis. The analyst who tries such a thing shows that he has not comprehended the real problems of psychotherapy and does not know what the "cutting of the Gordian knot" really means, namely a destroying of the conditions of analytic cure. An analysis carried out in such a way can hardly be salvaged. Interpretation is comparable to a valuable drug, which must be used sparingly if its effectiveness is not to be lost. This, too, we have learned from experience: the complicated way of disentangling the knot is the shortest—yes, the shortest—way to *true* success.

On the other side of the fence, we have those analysts who, incorrectly apprehending the concept of analytic passivity, are experts in the art of waiting. They would be able to furnish us with much valuable material on the casuistry of the chaotic situation. In the resistance period, the difficult task of steering the course of the analysis devolves upon the analyst. The patient holds the reins only in phases which are free of resistance. Freud could not have had anything else in mind. And the danger, both for the patient and for the development of analytic therapy, of making a rigid principle of analytic passivity or of "letting matters ride" is no less than that of "bombardment" or interpretation according to a theoretical scheme.

There are forms of resistance in which this kind of passivity is in the nature of a classic mistake. For instance, a patient might fight shy of a resistance or, more specifically, the discussion of the material pertaining to it. He will make allusions to a remote subject until he has also produced resistances there, then switch to a third subject, etc. This "zigzag technique" can go on ad infinitum, whether the analyst looks on "passively" or follows him offering one interpretation after the other. Since, as is evident, the patient is constantly on the run and his efforts to satisfy the analyst with substitute accomplishments are to no avail, it is the analyst's obligation *to lead him back to the first resistance position again and again* until he summons up the courage to get control of it analytically.[3] The other material is of course not lost.

Or the patient reverts to an infantile phase and divulges otherwise valuable secrets merely for the sake of holding on to a particular position. Naturally, such divulgences have no therapeutic value—the reverse is more likely the case. The analyst can listen all he wants if he prefers not to interrupt, but then he will have to be consistent in the working through of that position which the patient refused to face. The same holds true when the patient takes refuge in the contemporary situation. Ideal and optimal is a rectilinear development and analysis of the transference neu-

---

[3] Footnote, 1945: Compulsive talking is a form of resistance offered by many patients. To begin with, this compulsion is a purely *biological manifestation* of a contraction of the deep musculature of the neck and throat. Speaking without any regard to content is a necessity, e.g., "the chatterbox." In orgone therapy, we enjoin such patients to be *silent,* and eventually the anxiety which nourishes this compulsive symptom comes to the surface. The curing of a compulsion to speak is brought about by the loosening of the muscular armor of the throat.

rosis along the same lines as the primal neurosis. The patient develops his resistances systematically and performs, intermittently, affective recall work which is free of resistance.

The controversial question of which is better, an "active" or a "passive" attitude has no real meaning when phrased this way. It can be said generally that *resistances cannot be taken up soon enough in the analysis, and that, apart from the resistances, the interpretation of the unconscious cannot be held back enough.* Usually, the procedure is the reverse of this: the analyst is in the habit, on the one hand, of showing much too much courage in the interpretation of meaning and, on the other hand, of cringing as soon as a resistance turns up.

CHAPTER IV

ON THE TECHNIQUE OF CHARACTER ANALYSIS[1]

1. INTRODUCTION

Our therapeutic method is contingent upon the following basic theoretical concepts. The *topographical* point of view determines the principle of technique to the effect that the unconscious has to be made conscious. The *dynamic* point of view dictates that this making conscious of the unconscious must not proceed directly, but by way of resistance analysis. The *economic* point of view and the knowledge of *structure* dictate that, in resistance analysis, each individual case entails a definite plan which must be deduced from the case itself.

As long as the making conscious of the unconscious, i.e., the *topographical* process, was regarded as the sole task of analytic technique, the formula was justified that the patient's unconscious manifestations had to be translated into the language of the conscious *in the sequence in which they appeared.* In this process, the *dynamics* of the analysis were left largely to chance, that is, whether the act of becoming conscious actually released the germane affect and whether the interpretation had anything more than an intellectual influence on the patient. The very inclusion of the dynamic factor, i.e., the demand that the patient had not only to remember but also to experience what he remembered, complicated the simple formula that "the unconscious had to be made conscious." Since the dynamic effect of analysis depends not on the material which the patient produces but on the resistances which he brings into play against this material and on the emotional intensity with which they are mas-

[1] First presented at the Tenth International Psychoanalytic Congress, Innsbruck, September 1927.

tered, the task of analysis undergoes no insignificant shift. Whereas it is sufficient, from the topographical point of view, to make the patient conscious of the clearest and most easily interpretable elements of the unconscious in the sequence in which they appear, in other words, *to adhere to the pattern of the contents of the material,* it is necessary, when the dynamic factor is taken into consideration, to relinquish this plan as a means of orientation in the analysis. Instead, another must be adopted, which embraces both the content of the material and the affect, namely *the pattern of successive resistances.* In pursuing this plan, however, a difficulty arises in most cases, a difficulty which we have not considered in the foregoing presentation.

2. CHARACTER ARMORING AND CHARACTER RESISTANCE

a) *The inability to follow the basic rule*

Our patients are seldom capable of analysis at the outset. Only a very small number of patients are prepared to follow the basic rule and to open themselves completely to the analyst. First of all, it is not easy for the patient to have immediate trust in the analyst, if only because he is a stranger. Added to this, however, is the fact that years of illness, the unrelenting influence of a neurotic milieu, bad experiences with mental specialists—in short, the entire secondary fragmentation of the ego—have created a situation that is adverse to the analysis. The elimination of this difficulty becomes a precondition of the analysis, and it could be accomplished easily if it were not complicated by the characteristic, indeed character of the patient, which is itself a part of the neurosis and has developed on a neurotic basis. It is known as the "narcissistic barrier." Fundamentally, there are two ways of getting at these difficulties, especially at the difficulty entailed by the resistance to the basic rule. The first way, and the one usually pursued, I believe, is to prepare the patient for analysis through instruction, reassurance, challenge, exhortation, persuasion, and more of the same. In this case, by establishing a kind of positive transference, the analyst seeks to convince the patient of the necessity of being open and honest in the analysis. This roughly corresponds to the technique suggested by Nunberg. Vast experience has taught us, however, that this pedagogic or active approach is highly uncertain, is dependent upon uncontrollable contingencies, and lacks the secure basis of analytic clarity. The analyst is constantly at the mercy of the oscillations of the transference and treads on uncertain terrain in his efforts to make the patient capable of analysis.

The second method is more complicated, and not yet feasible for all patients. It is a far more secure approach. Here the attempt is made *to replace the instructional measures by analytic interpretations*. There is no question that this is not always possible, yet it remains the ideal goal toward which analysis strives. Instead of inducing the patient to enter into the analysis by persuasion, suggestion, transference maneuvers, etc., the analyst takes a more passive attitude and attempts to get an insight into the *contemporary* meaning of the patient's behavior, *why* he or she doubts, arrives late, speaks in a ranting or confused manner, communicates only every third idea or so, criticizes the analysis, or produces deep material, often in uncommon amounts. In other words, the analyst can do one of two things: (1) attempt to persuade a narcissistic patient who speaks in grandiloquent technical terminology that his behavior is detrimental to the analysis and that he would do better to rid himself of analytic terminology and to come out of his shell; or (2) dispense with any kind of persuasion and wait until he understands why the patient behaves as he does. It may turn out, for instance, that the patient's ostentatious behavior is an attempt to cover up a feeling of inferiority toward the analyst. In this case, the analyst will endeavor to influence him through a consistent interpretation of the meaning of his actions. In contrast to the first, this second approach is entirely in keeping with the principles of analysis.

From this endeavor to use purely analytic interpretations wherever possible in place of all the instructional or otherwise active measures which become necessary as a result of the patient's characteristics, a method of analyzing the *character* emerged in an unsought and unexpected way.

Certain clinical considerations make it necessary for us to designate as *"character resistances"* a special group of the resistances that we encounter in the treatment of our patients. *These derive their special character not from their content but from the spe-*

cific mannerisms of the person analyzed. The compulsive character develops resistances whose form is specifically different from
that of the hysterical character, the form of whose resistances, in
turn, is different from that of the genital narcissistic, impulsive,
or neurasthenic character. *The form of the ego's reactions,* which
differs from character to character even where the contents of
the experiences are the same, *can be traced back to infantile experiences in the same way as the content of the symptoms and
fantasies.*

b) Where do the character resistances come from?

Some time ago, Glover made an effort to discriminate between character neuroses and symptom neuroses. Alexander also
operated on the basis of this distinction. I adhered to it in earlier
works, but it turned out, on closer comparison of the cases, that
this distinction makes sense only insofar as there are neuroses
with circumscribed symptoms ("symptom neuroses") and neuroses
without them ("character neuroses"). In the former, understandably, the symptoms are more conspicuous; in the latter, the
neurotic character traits stand out. But are there symptoms
which do not have a neurotic reaction basis, which, in other
words, are not rooted in a neurotic character? The only difference between character neuroses and symptom neuroses is that,
in the case of the latter, the neurotic character also produces
symptoms, has become, so to speak, concentrated in them. That
the neurotic character is at one time exacerbated in circumscribed symptoms and at another time finds other ways of discharging the libido stasis requires more detailed investigation
(cf. Part II). But if it is acknowledged that the symptom neurosis is always rooted in a neurotic character, then it is clear that,
in *every* analysis, we are dealing with resistances that are manifestations of a neurotic character. The individual analysis will
differ only with respect to the importance ascribed to the analysis of the character in each case. However, a retrospective glance
at analytic experiences cautions us against underestimating this
importance in any one case.

From the point of view of character analysis, the differentiation between neuroses which are chronic, i.e., have existed since childhood, and those which are acute, i.e., appeared later, has no importance whatever; it is of no great moment whether the symptoms appear in childhood or later. What matters is that the neurotic character, i.e., the reaction basis for the symptom neurosis, is formed, at least in its principal features, by the time the Oedipal stage comes to a close. We have ample clinical experience to show that the boundary which the patient draws between health and the outbreak of sickness always vanishes in the analysis.

Since the symptom formation does not hold up as a descriptive characteristic, we have to look for others. Two which readily come to mind are *illness insight* and *rationalizations*.

A lack of insight into the illness is not, of course, absolutely reliable but it is certainly an essential indication of character neurosis. The neurotic symptom is sensed as something alien, and it engenders a feeling of being ill. On the other hand, the neurotic character trait, e.g., the exaggerated sense of order of the compulsive character or the anxious shyness of the hysterical character, is organically incorporated into the personality. One might complain of being shy, but one does not feel sick for that reason. Not until the characterological shyness becomes a pathological blushing or until the compulsive-neurotic sense of order becomes a compulsive ceremony, not until, in other words, the neurotic character exacerbates symptomatically, does one feel that one is sick.

Naturally, there are symptoms for which no insight, or insufficient insight, exists. They are regarded by patients as bad habits or something which has to be accepted (e.g., chronic constipation, mild ejaculatio praecox). Then there are some character traits which are sometimes felt to be pathological, e.g., irrational, violent fits of anger, gross negligence, a penchant for lying, drinking, splurging, and other such. Generally, however, an insight into the sickness is indicative of a neurotic symptom, whereas lack of insight points to a neurotic character trait.

In practical terms, the second important difference consists in the fact that symptoms never exhibit such complete and credible *rationalizations* as neurotic character traits. Neither hysterical vomiting nor abasia; neither compulsive counting nor compulsive thinking can be rationalized. There is no question about the senselessness of a symptom, whereas the neurotic character trait has a sufficiently rational motivation so as not to appear pathological or senseless.

Furthermore, there is a justification for neurotic character traits which is immediately rejected as absurd when it is applied to symptoms. We often hear it said: "That's simply the way I am." The implication here is that the person concerned was born that way; he simply cannot behave differently—that's his character. However, this does not tally with the facts, for the analysis of its development shows that the character had to become what it is, and not something else, for very specific reasons. Fundamentally, therefore, it is capable of analysis and of being changed, just like the symptom.

Occasionally, symptoms have become so ingrained in the personality that they are like character traits. An example is compulsive counting that is wholly absorbed within the framework of one's need to be orderly, or compulsive methodicalness that is fulfilled in the rigid subdivisions of each day. The latter is especially true of the compulsion to work. Such modes of behavior are held to be indicative more of eccentricity or excessiveness than of pathology. Hence, we see that the concept of illness is highly flexible, that there are many shades, ranging from the symptom as an isolated foreign body through the neurotic character trait and the "wicked habit" to rationally sound behavior. However, in view of the fact that these shades are not very much help to us, the differentiation between symptom and neurotic character trait recommends itself, even insofar as rationalizations are concerned, notwithstanding the artificiality of all divisions.

With this reservation, another differentiation occurs to us with respect to the structure of the symptom and of the character trait. In the process of analysis, it is shown that, in terms of its meaning and origin, the symptom has a very simple structure compared with that of the character trait. True enough, the symptom too is indeterminate; but the more deeply we penetrate into its reasons, the more we move away from the actual compass of the symptom and the more clearly we perceive its basis in the character. Hence, theoretically, the reaction basis in the character can be worked out from any symptom. The symptom is directly determined by a limited number of unconscious attitudes; hysterical vomiting, for example, is based on a repressed fellatio desire or an oral desire for a child. Each of them is expressed in the character, the former in a kind of childishness, the latter in a maternal attitude. But the hysterical character, which determines the hysterical symptom, is based on a multiplicity of —to a large extent antagonistic—strivings, and is usually expressed in a specific *attitude* or *mode of existence*. It is not nearly so easy to analyze the attitude as it is to analyze the symptom; fundamentally, however, the former, like the latter, can be traced back to and understood on the basis of drives and experiences. Whereas the symptom corresponds solely to one definite experience or one circumscribed desire, the character, i.e., the person's specific mode of existence, represents an expression of the person's entire past. So a symptom can emerge quite suddenly, while the development of each individual character trait requires many years. We must also bear in mind that the symptom could not have suddenly emerged unless a neurotic reaction basis already existed in the character.

In the analysis, the neurotic character traits as a whole prove to be a compact *defense mechanism* against our therapeutic efforts, and when we trace the origin of this character "armor" analytically, we see that it also has a definite economic function. Such armor serves on the one hand as a defense against external stimuli; on the other hand it proves to be a means of gaining mastery over the libido, which is continuously pushing forward from the id, because libidinal and sadistic energy is used up in the neurotic reaction formations, compensations, etc. Anxiety is continually being bound in the processes which are at the bottom of the formation and preservation of this armor in the same way that, according to Freud's description, anxiety is bound in the compulsive symptoms. We shall have more to say about the economy of the character formation.

Since, in its economic function as defensive armor, the neurotic character trait has established a certain, albeit *neurotic balance*, analysis constitutes a danger to this balance. It is from this narcissistic defense mechanism of the ego that the resistances originate which give the analysis of the individual case its special features. If, however, a person's mode of behavior represents the result of a total development which is capable of analysis and resolution, then it must also be possible to deduce the technique of character analysis from that behavior.

c) On the technique of analyzing the character resistance

In addition to the dreams, associations, slips, and other communications of the patients, the *way in which* they recount their dreams, commit slips, produce associations, and make their communications, in short their bearing, deserves special attention.[2] Adherence to the basic rule is something rare, and many months of character-analytic work are required to instill in the patient a halfway sufficient measure of candidness. The way the patient speaks, looks at and greets the analyst, lies on the couch, the inflection of the voice, the degree of conventional politeness which is maintained, etc., are valuable cues in assessing the secret resistances with which the patient counters the basic rule. And once they have been understood, they can be eliminated through interpretation. It is not only *what* the patient says but *how* he says it that has to be interpreted. Analysts are often heard to complain that the analysis is not progressing, that the patient is not producing any "material." By material, what is usually meant is merely the content of the associations and communications. But the nature of the patient's silence or sterile repetitions is also material which has to be used fully. There is scarcely a situation in which the patient does not produce *any* material, and we have to lay the blame upon ourselves if we can't make use of the patient's bearing as material.

There is of course nothing new in the statement that behavior and the form of the communications are of analytic importance. What we are concerned with here, however, is the fact that they give us access to the analysis of the character in a very definite and relatively complete way. Bad experiences in the analysis of some neurotic characters have taught us that, *at the outset* of such cases, the form of the communications is of greater importance than the content. We want merely to allude to the con-

[2] Footnote, 1945: The *form* of expression is *far more important* than the ideational *content.* Today we use only the form of expression to arrive at the *decisively* important experiences of childhood. It is the form of expression and not the ideational content that leads us to the biological reactions which lie at the basis of the psychic manifestations.

cealed resistances produced by the emotionally paralyzed, by the "good" men and women, the excessively polite and correct patients; by those patients, moreover, who always give evidence of a deceptive positive transference or, for that matter, by those who raise a passionate and monotonous cry for love; those who conceive of analysis as a kind of game; the eternally "armored" who laugh in their sleeve at anything and everything. The list could be extended indefinitely. Hence, one has no illusions about the painstaking work which the innumerable individual problems of technique will entail.

To allow what is essential in character analysis to stand out more clearly in contrast to symptom analysis, and to give a better idea of our thesis in general, let us consider two pairs of cases. The first pair consists of two men being treated for ejaculatio praecox: one is a passive-feminine character, the other a phallic-aggressive character. Two women suffering from an eating disturbance constitute the second pair: one is a compulsive character, the other a hysteric.

Let us further assume that the ejaculatio praecox of the two male patients has the same unconscious meaning: fear of the (paternal) phallus assumed to be in the woman's vagina. On the basis of the castration anxiety which lies at the root of the symptom, both patients produce a negative father transference in the analysis. They hate the analyst (father) because they perceive in him the enemy who limits their pleasure, and each of them has the unconscious desire to dispose of him. While the phallic-sadistic character will ward off the danger of castration by means of vituperations, disparagements, and threats, the passive-feminine character will become more and more confiding, more and more passively devoted, and more and more accommodating. In both of them the character has become a resistance: the former wards off the danger aggressively; the latter gets out of its way by compromising his standards, by deceptiveness and devotion.

Naturally, the character resistance of the passive-feminine type is more dangerous, for he works with devious means. He produces material in abundance, recalls infantile experiences, appears to adapt himself beautifully—but at bottom he glosses over a secret obstinacy and hate. As long as he keeps this up, he will not have the courage to show his true nature. If the analyst does not pay any attention to his manner and merely enters into *what* the patient produces, then, according to experience, no analytic effort or elucidation will change his condition. It may even be that the patient will recall his hatred of his father, but he will not *experience* it unless the meaning of his deceptive behavior is consistently pointed out to him in the transference, *before* a deep interpretation of the father-hatred is begun.

In the case of the second pair, let us assume that an acute positive transference has developed. In both women, the main content of this positive transference is the same as that of the symptom, namely an oral fellatio fantasy. However, the transference resistance ensuing from this positive transference will be wholly different in form. The woman suffering from hysteria, for example, will be *apprehensively* silent and behave timidly; the woman having a compulsive neurosis will be *obstinately* silent or behave in a cold, haughty way toward the analyst. The transference resistance employs various means in warding off the positive transference: in the one instance, aggression; in the other, anxiety. We would say that in both cases the id conveyed the same wish, which the ego warded off differently. And the form of this defense will always remain the same in both patients; the woman suffering from hysteria will always defend herself in a way expressive of anxiety, while the woman suffering from a compulsive neurosis will always defend herself aggressively, no matter what unconscious content is on the verge of breaking through. In other words, *the character resistance always remains the same in the same patient and disappears only when the neurosis has been uprooted.*

The character armor is the molded expression of *narcissistic* defense chronically embedded in the psychic structure. In addition to the known resistances which are mobilized against each new piece of unconscious material, there is a constant resistance factor which has its roots in the unconscious and pertains not to content but to *form*. Because of its origin in the character, we call this constant resistance factor "character resistance."

On the basis of the foregoing statements, let us summarize the most important features of character resistance.

Character resistance is expressed not in terms of content but formally, in the way one typically behaves, in the manner in which one speaks, walks, and gestures; and in one's characteristic habits (how one smiles or sneers, whether one speaks coherently or incoherently, *how* one is polite and *how* one is aggressive).

It is not what the patient says and does that is indicative of character resistance, but *how* he speaks and acts; not what he reveals in dreams, but *how* he censors, distorts, condenses, etc.

The character resistance remains the same in the same patient, regardless of content. Different characters produce the same material in a different way. The positive father transference of a woman suffering from hysteria is expressed and warded off differently than that of a woman suffering from a compulsive neurosis. Anxiety is the defense mechanism in the former; aggression in the latter.

The character resistance which is manifested in terms of form is just as capable of being resolved, with respect to its content, and of being traced back to infantile experiences and instinctual interests as the neurotic symptom is.[3]

In given situations, the patient's character becomes a resistance. In everyday life, in other words, the character plays a role similar to the one it plays as a resistance in the treatment: that of a psychic defense apparatus. Hence, we speak of the "character armoring" of the ego against the outer world and the id.

If we trace the formation of the character into early childhood, we find that, in its time, the character armor ensued for the same reasons and for the same purposes the character resistance serves in the contemporary analytic situation. The resistive projection of the character in the analysis mirrors its infantile genesis. And those situations which seem to appear by chance but actually are brought about by the character resistance in the analysis are exact duplicates of those childhood situations which caused the formation of the character. Thus, in the character resistance, the function of defense is combined with the projection of infantile relationships to the outer world.

Economically, the character in everyday life and the character resistance in the analysis serve as a means of avoiding what is unpleasant *(Unlust),* of establishing and preserving a psychic

[3] In light of this clinical experience, the element of form has been incorporated into the sphere of psychoanalysis, which, until now, has focused predominantly on content.

(even if neurotic) balance, and finally of consuming repressed quantities of instinctual energy and/or quantities which have eluded repression. The binding of free-floating anxiety or—what amounts to the same thing—the absorbing of dammed-up psychic energy, is one of the cardinal functions of the character. Just as the historical, i.e., the infantile, element is embodied and continues to live and operate in the neurotic symptom, so too it lives and operates and is embodied in the character. This explains why the consistent loosening of the character resistance provides a sure and direct approach to the central infantile conflict.

How do these facts bear upon the analytic technique of character analysis? Is there an essential difference between character analysis and the usual resistance analysis?

There are differences and they relate to:

a) the sequence in which the material is to be interpreted

b) the technique of resistance interpretation itself

With respect to (a): In speaking of "selection of material," we shall have to be prepared to encounter an important objection. It will be said that any selection is in contradiction to the basic principle of psychoanalysis, namely that the analyst must follow the patient, must allow himself to be led by him. Every time the analyst makes a selection, he runs the risk of falling prey to his own inclinations. First of all, we have to point out that, in the kind of selection we are speaking of here, it is not a matter of neglecting analytic material. The whole point here is *to insure* that the material is interpreted in a *legitimate sequence,* in keeping with the structure of the neurosis. All material is in turn interpreted; it is only that one detail is momentarily more important than another. We also have to realize that the analyst always selects anyhow, for in the very act of singling out individual details of a dream instead of interpreting them successively, he has made a selection. And as far as that goes, the analyst has also made a biased selection when he considers only the content and not the form of the communications. Hence, the very fact that the patient produces material of the most diverse kinds in the analytic situation forces the analyst to make selections in interpreting this material. It is merely a question of selecting *correctly,* i.e., in keeping with the analytic situation.

With patients who, because of a particular character development, repeatedly disregard the fundamental rule, as well as with all cases in which the character is obstructing the analysis, it will be necessary to single out the germane *character resistance from the welter of material and to work it through analytically by interpreting its meaning*. Naturally, this does not mean that the rest of the material is neglected or disregarded. On the contrary, everything is valuable and welcome which gives us an insight into the meaning and origin of the recalcitrant character trait. The analyst merely puts off the analysis, and, above all, the interpretation of the material which does not have an immediate bearing upon the transference resistance, until the character resistance has been understood and broken through, at least in its basic features. In Chapter III, I tried to point out the dangers of giving deep interpretations before the character resistances have been resolved.

With respect to (*b*) : Now we turn our attention to some special problems of the technique of character analysis. First, we must anticipate a likely misunderstanding. We stated that character analysis begins with the singling out and consistent analysis of the character resistance. This does not mean that the patient is enjoined not to be aggressive, not to be deceptive, not to speak in an incoherent manner, to follow the basic rule, etc. Such demands would not only be contrary to analytic procedure, they would be fruitless. It cannot be sufficiently stressed that what we are describing here has nothing whatever to do with the so-called education of the patient and similar matters. In character analysis, we ask ourselves why the patient is deceptive, speaks in an incoherent manner, is emotionally blocked, etc.; we endeavor to arouse his interest in the peculiarities of his character in order to elucidate, with his help, their meaning and origin through analysis. In other words, we merely single out from the orbit of the personality the character trait from which the cardinal resistance proceeds, and, if possible, we show the patient the surface relation between the character and the symptoms. But for the rest, we leave it up to him whether or not he wants to make use of his knowledge to change his character. Fundamentally, our procedure in this is no different from the one followed in the analysis of a symptom; the one exception is that, in character analysis, we have to *isolate* the character trait and put it before the patient *again and again* until he has succeeded in breaking clear of it and in viewing it as he would a vexatious compulsive symptom. In breaking clear of and objectifying the neurotic character trait, the patient begins to experience it as something alien to himself, and ultimately gains an insight into its nature.

In this process, it becomes apparent, surprisingly, that the personality changes—at least temporarily. And as the character analysis progresses, that impetus or disposition which gave rise to the character resistance in the transference automatically comes to the surface in an unconcealed form. Applying this to our example of the passive-feminine character, we can say that the more thoroughly the patient objectifies his inclinations to passive devotion, the more aggressive he will become. For, of course, his feminine, deceptive behavior was, in the main, an energetic reaction against repressed aggressive impulses. Hand in hand with the aggressiveness, however, the infantile castration anxiety also reappears which, at one time, caused the aggression to be transformed into a passive-feminine attitude. Thus, through the analysis of the character resistance, we arrive at the center of the neurosis, the Oedipus complex.

Let there be no illusions, however: the isolation and objectification as well as the analytic working through of such a character resistance usually take many months, demand great effort and, most of all, steadfast patience. Once the breakthrough has been achieved, the analytic work usually proceeds by leaps and bounds, borne by *affective* analytic experiences. If, on the other hand, such character resistances are left untended; if the analyst merely follows the patient, continually interpreting the content of his material, such resistances will, as time goes on, form a ballast that will be almost impossible to remove. When this happens, the analyst begins to feel in his bones that all his interpretations of content were wasted, that the patient continues to doubt everything, to accept it merely *pro forma,* or to laugh in his sleeve at everything. In later stages of the analysis, after the essential interpretations of the Oedipus complex have already been given, the analyst will find himself embroiled in a hopeless situation, if he has neglected to clear away these resistances right from the beginning.

I have already tried to refute the objection that resistances cannot be taken up until their *infantile* determinants are known.

In the beginning of the treatment, it is merely necessary for the analyst to discern the *contemporary* meaning of the character resistance, for which purpose the infantile material is not always required. This material we need for the *dissolution* of the resistance. If, at the beginning, the analyst contents himself with putting the resistance before the patient and interpreting its contemporary meaning, it is not long before the infantile material emerges and, with its help, the resistance can then be eliminated.

When stress is laid upon a previously neglected fact, the impression is unwittingly created that other facts are being deprived of their importance. If in this work we lay such strong emphasis on the analysis of the *mode* of reaction, this does not mean that we neglect the content. We merely add something which had not been properly appreciated before this. Our experience teaches us that the analysis of the character resistance must be given absolute precedence; but this does not mean that the analysis is confined solely to character resistance until a certain date, when the analyst then takes up the interpretation of content. To a large extent, the two phases, resistance analysis and analysis of the early infantile experiences, overlap one another. It is merely that the analysis of the character is given priority at the beginning of the treatment ("preparing the analysis through analysis") , while the main accent in the later stages falls upon the interpretation of content and infantile experiences. This, however, is not a rigid rule; its application will depend upon the behavior pattern of the individual patient. The interpretation of infantile material will be taken up early with one patient, later with another. There is one rule, however, which must be strictly adhered to, namely that deep analytic interpretations have to be avoided, even in the case of fairly clear material, until the patient is prepared to assimilate them. This is of course nothing new. Yet, in view of the many different ways in which analysts work, it is obviously important to know what is meant by "prepared for analytic interpretation." In deciding this, we shall doubtless have to differentiate those contents which pertain directly to the character resistance and those which pertain to other spheres of experience. Normally, in the beginning of analysis, the analysand is prepared to take cognizance of the former but not of the latter. On the whole, the main idea behind character analysis is to gain the greatest possible security both in the preparatory work of the analysis and in the interpretation of infantile material. At this point, we are confronted with the important task of investigating and systematically describing the various forms of character transference resistances. The technique of dealing with them will emerge of itself from their structure.

d) The technique of dealing with individual situations as derived from the structure of the character resistance (technique of interpreting ego defense)

We now turn to the problem of the character-analytic technique of dealing with individual situations, and how this technique is derived from the structure of the character resistance. To illustrate this, we shall take a patient who develops resistances right at the outset, the structure of which, however, is far from immediately clear. In the following case, the character resistance had a very complicated structure; there were many determining factors, intermingled with one another. An attempt will be made to set forth the reasons which induced me to begin my interpretation precisely with one particular element of the resistance. Here, too, it will become apparent that a consistent and logical interpretation of the ego defense and of the mechanism of the "armor" leads into the very heart of the central infantile conflicts.

A CASE OF MANIFEST FEELINGS OF INFERIORITY

A thirty-year-old man turned to analysis because he "didn't really enjoy life." He could not really say whether or not he felt sick. Actually, he didn't think that he was really in need of treatment. Yet he felt that he should do whatever he could. He had heard of psychoanalysis—perhaps it could help him gain insight into himself. He was not aware of having any symptoms. It turned out that his potency was very weak; he seldom engaged in sexual intercourse, approached women only with great reluctance, did not derive any gratification from coitus, and, moreover, suffered from ejaculatio praecox. He had very little insight into his impotence. He had—so he said—reconciled himself to its meagerness. There were so many men who had no need of it.

His demeanor and behavior betrayed at a glance that he was a severely inhibited and oppressed man. He didn't look into one's eyes while speaking, spoke softly, in a muffled way, with many hesitations and embarrassed clearings of the throat. In all this, however, one detected that he was making a strenuous effort to suppress his shyness and to appear bold. Nonetheless, his nature bore all the earmarks of severe feelings of inferiority.

Familiarized with the basic rule, the patient began to speak softly and hesitatingly. The first communications included the recollection of two "horrible" experiences. While driving a car, he had once run over a woman, who had died from the effects of the accident. Another time he had gotten into a situation where he had to perform a tracheotomy on a person who was suffocating (the patient had been a medical orderly in the war). He could think of these two experiences only with horror. During the first sessions, he spoke about his home in an unvaried, somewhat monotonous, soft, and muffled way. As the second youngest of several brothers and sisters, he had a second-rate position in the household. The oldest brother, some twenty years his senior, was the darling of the parents. He had traveled a great deal and he knew his way around "in the world." At home he vaunted his experiences, and when he returned from a trip, "the entire household revolved around him." Though the envy and hatred of his brother were clearly evident from the content of the communication, the patient vehemently denied having any such feelings when I made a cautious inquiry in this direction. He had, he said, never felt any such thing against his brother.

Then he talked about his mother, who had been very good to him and who had died when he was seven years old. While speaking about her, he began to cry softly, was ashamed of his tears, and didn't say anything for a long time. It seemed clear that the mother had been the only person who had given him a bit of attention and love, that her demise had been a severe shock to him, and he could not hold back his tears in remembering her. After the death of his mother, he had spent five years in the house of his brother. It was not from what he said but from the way he said it that his enormous animosity toward the domineering, cold, and unfriendly nature of his brother became evident.

Then, in short, not very pregnant sentences, he related that he had a friend now who very much loved and admired him. Following this communication, there was a prolonged silence. A few days later he reported a dream: *he saw himself in a strange city with his friend, except that the face of his friend was different.* Since, for the purpose of the analysis, the patient had left the town in which he had been living, it was reasonable to assume that the man in the dream represented the analyst. The fact that the patient identified him with his friend could be interpreted as an indication of an incipient positive transference; but the situation as a whole militated against conceiving of this as a positive transference, and even against its interpretation. The patient himself recognized the analyst in the friend but had nothing to add to this. Since he was either silent or monotonously expressing doubts about *his* ability to carry out the analysis, I told him that he had something against me but lacked the courage to articulate it. He vehemently denied this, whereupon I told him that he had also never dared to express his hostile emotions toward his older brother, indeed had not even dared to think of them consciously. I also pointed out that he had obviously established some kind of a connection between me and his older brother. This was true, but I committed the error of interpreting his resistance too deeply. The interpretation did not achieve its purpose, so I waited a few days, observing his demeanor the while, to see what relevance the resistance had for the contemporary situation. This much was clear to me: in addition to the transference of the hatred of the brother, there was a strong defense against a feminine attitude (the dream about the friend). Naturally, I couldn't risk an interpretation in this direction. So I continued to point out that, for one reason or another, he was fighting shy of me and the analysis. I told him that his whole manner was indicative of a block against the analysis. He agreed with this and went on to say that this had always been his way in life —rigid, inaccessible, defensive. While I constantly and consistently, in every session and at every opportunity, called his attention to his recalcitrance, I was struck by the monotonous tone in which he expressed his complaints. Every session began with the same remarks: "What's this all leading to, I don't feel a thing, the analysis has no influence on me, will I be able to go through with it, I can't, nothing comes to mind, the analysis has no influence on me," and so on. I couldn't understand what he was trying to express. And yet it was clear that here lay the key to the understanding of his resistance.[4]

This offers us a good opportunity to study the difference between the character-analytic and the active-suggestive preparation of the patient for analysis. I could have urged the patient in a nice way and endeavored to exercise a kind of comforting influence to get him to produce additional communications. It is even possible that, by so doing, I might have brought about an artificial positive transference; but experiences with other cases had taught me that one does not get very far with this approach. Since his entire demeanor left no room for doubt that he opposed the analysis in general and me in particular, there was no reason why I should not continue in this interpretation and wait for further reactions. One time, when we returned to the dream, he said the best proof that he did not reject me was the fact that he identified me with his friend. I took this opportunity to suggest that perhaps he had expected me to have the same liking and admiration for him that his friend had, that he had been disappointed, and now very much resented my reserve. He had to admit that he had harbored such thoughts but had not had the courage to tell me. Subsequently he told me that he had always merely demanded love and especially recognition and that he had always behaved very *defensively,* especially toward manly-looking men. He felt that he was not on a par with them, and in his relationship with his friend he played the feminine role. Again he offered me material toward the interpretation of his feminine transference, but his demeanor as a whole cautioned me against making such a disclosure. The situation was difficult, for the elements of his resistance which I already understood, the transference of the hatred he felt for his brother and the narcissistic-feminine attitude toward his superiors, had been sharply

[4] Footnote, 1945: While this explanation is psychologically correct, it is not the whole story. We understand now that such complaints are the direct expression of vegetative, i.e., muscular, armor. The patient complains of an affect-paralysis because his plasmatic currents and sensations are blocked. In short, this defect is essentially of a purely *biophysical* nature. In orgone therapy, the motility block is loosened by means of biophysical methods and not by means of psychological methods.

rejected. Hence, I had to be very careful if I did not want to risk the abrupt termination of the analysis at that time. Moreover, in each session, he complained almost without letup and always in the same way that the analysis was not having any effect on him, etc. Even after some four weeks of analysis, I still did not understand this attitude, though it appeared to me as an essential and momentarily acute character resistance.

I fell ill at this time and had to interrupt the analysis for two weeks. The patient sent me a bottle of cognac as a tonic. He seemed pleased when I resumed the analysis, but continued to complain in the same way, and told me that he was tortured by thoughts of death. He couldn't get it out of his mind that something had happened to someone in his family, and while I was sick he couldn't stop thinking that I might die. One day, when he was especially tortured by this thought, he made up his mind to send me the cognac. It was a very tempting opportunity to interpret his repressed death wishes. There was more than ample material for such an interpretation, yet I was held back by the consideration and the definite feeling that it would have been sterile, merely ricocheting from the wall of his complaints: "Nothing gets through to me"; the "analysis has no affect on me." In the meantime, of course, the concealed ambiguity of the complaint that "nothing gets through to me" had become clear. This was an expression of his deeply repressed passive-feminine transference desire for anal intercourse. But would it have been sensible and justified to interpret his homosexual desire, however clearly manifested, while his ego continued to protest against the analysis? First, the meaning of his complaint about the fruitlessness of the analysis had to become clear. I might have shown him that his complaint was unfounded. He always had new dreams to report, the thoughts of death became more pronounced, and many other things were taking place in him. I knew from experience that telling him this would not have eased the situation, despite the fact that I clearly felt the armor which stood between the analysis and the material offered by the id. Moreover, in all probability, I had to assume that the existing resistance would not allow any interpretation to pass through to the id. Thus, I continued to dwell on his behavior—interpreting it to him as an expression of his strong defense—and told him we both had to wait until the meaning of this behavior became clear to us. He had already grasped that the thoughts of death which he had had on the occasion of my illness did not necessarily have to be an expression of his loving concern for me.

In the course of the following weeks, the impressions of his behavior and his complaints multiplied. It became more and more clear that these complaints were intimately related to the defense of his feminine transference, but the situation was still not ripe for exact interpretation. I lacked a tight formulation of the meaning of his behavior as a whole. Let us summarize the fundamental aspects of the solution which followed later:

a) He wanted recognition and love from me as well as from all other men who appeared masculine to him. The fact that he wanted love and had been disappointed by me had already been interpreted repeatedly, without success.

b) His attitude toward me, the transference of his unconscious attitude toward his brother, was clearly full of hate and envy; to avoid the danger of having the interpretation fizzle out, it was best not to analyze this attitude at this point.

c) He warded off his feminine transference; the defense could not be interpreted without touching upon the forbidden femininity.

d) He felt inferior to me because of his femininity—and his continuous complaints could only be an expression of his inferiority complex.

I now interpreted his feelings of inferiority toward me. At first, this had no success. After several days of consistently dwelling upon his nature, however, he finally produced some communications on his inordinate envy, not of me but of other men he also felt inferior to. And now I was suddenly struck by the idea that his continual complaints that "the analysis has no effect on me" could have no other meaning than, "It's worthless." It follows, therefore, that the analyst is inferior, impotent, and could not achieve anything with him. Thus *the complaints were to be understood partially as a triumph over and partially as a reproach against the analyst.* Now I told him how I viewed his continual complaints; even I was amazed at the success. He accepted my interpretation as quite plausible. He immediately came up with a large number of examples which revealed that he always acted this way when someone wanted to influence him. He said that he could not endure another person's superiority and always endeavored to disparage those toward whom he felt inferior. He went on to say that he had always done the exact opposite of what a superior had demanded of him. He brought forward a wealth of recollections about his insolent and deprecatory attitude toward teachers.

Here, then, lay his pent-up aggressiveness, the most extreme expression of which, until this point, had been the death wish. But our joy was short-lived. The resistance returned in the same form—the same complaints, the same depression, the same silence. But now I knew that my disclosure had very much impressed him and, as a consequence, his feminine attitude had become *more pronounced.* The immediate result of this, naturally, was a renewed warding off of the effeminacy. In the analysis of this resistance, I again proceeded from his feelings of inferiority toward me, but I enlarged upon the interpretation by pointing out that he not only felt inferior but also, indeed precisely for this reason, felt himself cast in a feminine role toward me, a fact which was too much of an insult to his manly pride.

Notwithstanding the fact that he had, before this, produced a great deal of material about his feminine behavior toward manly men and had also showed complete understanding of it, he no longer wanted to know anything about it. This was a new problem. Why did he refuse to admit something he himself had described earlier? I continued to interpret the meaning of his acute behavior, namely that he felt so inferior toward me, that he refused to accept what I explained to him, though this refusal constituted reversal of his earlier position. He admitted that this was true, and went on to give a detailed account of his relationship to his friend. It turned out that he had indeed played the feminine role; there had often been intercouse between the thighs. I could now show him that his defensive behavior was nothing other than the expression of a struggle against the surrender to analysis which, for his unconscious, was obviously related to the idea of surrendering to the analyst in a feminine way. This too, however, was an insult to his pride and was the reason for his tenacious opposition to the influence of the analysis. He reacted to this with a confirmatory dream: he is lying on a sofa with the analyst and is kissed by him. However, this clear dream released a new wave of resistance, again in the old form of complaints (the analysis was not having any affect on him, couldn't have any influence on him, what was it leading to anyhow, he was completely cold, etc.). I interpreted his complaints as a deprecation of the analysis and a defense against surrendering to it. At the same time, I began to explain to him the economic meaning of his block. I told him that, even on the basis of what he had related about his childhood and adolescence, it was clear he had immured himself against all the disappointments which he had experienced in the outside world and against the rough, cold treatment on the part of father, brother, and teachers. This had been his only salvation, even if a salvation which entailed many restrictions upon his enjoyment of life.

He immediately accepted this explanation as plausible and followed it up with remembrances of his behavior toward teachers. He had always found them so cold and alien (a clear projection of his own feelings), and even if he were outwardly agitated when they beat or scolded him, he remained inwardly indifferent. In this connection, he told me that he had often wished I were more strict. At first, the meaning of this desire did not appear to fit into the situation; much later it became clear that at the bottom of his obstinacy lay the intent to put me and my prototypes, the teachers, in the wrong.

For several days the analysis proceeded free of resistances; now he went on to relate that there had been a time in his early childhood when he had been very wild and aggressive. At the same time, curiously, he produced dreams which revealed a strong feminine attitude toward me. I could only surmise that the recollection of his aggressiveness had simultaneously mobilized the guilt feeling which was expressed in these dreams of a passive-feminine nature. I avoided an analysis of the dreams not only because they were not directly related to the existing transference situation but also because he did not appear prepared to grasp the connection between his aggression and dreams expressing a guilt feeling. I assume that some analysts will regard this as an arbitrary selection of material. Against this, however, I have to defend the clinically tested position that the optimum in therapy will be achieved when a direct connection has been established between the contemporary transference situation and the infantile material. So I merely voiced the supposition that his recollection of the wild conduct of his childhood indicated he had once been wholly different, the exact opposite of what he was today, and the analysis would have to uncover the time and the circumstances that led to the transformation of his character. Presumably, his present effeminacy was a moving out of the way of aggressive masculinity. The patient did not react to this disclosure at all; instead, he sank back into the old resistance: he couldn't manage it, he didn't feel anything, the analysis had no effect on him, etc.

I again interpreted his feelings of inferiority and his repeated attempt to show up the powerlessness of the analysis or, more to the point, of the analyst; but I also endeavored now to work out the transference of the attitude he held toward his brother. He himself had said that the brother had always played the dominant role. He entered into this only with great hesitation, evidently because it concerned the central conflict situation of his childhood. He repeated that the mother had paid a great deal of attention to the brother, without, however, going into his subjective attitude toward this preference. As was brought out by a cautious inquiry in this direction, he was completely closed to an insight into his envy of his brother. This envy, it had to be assumed, was so intimately associated with an intensive hate and repressed out of fear that not even the feeling of envy was permitted to enter consciousness. An especially strong resistance resulted from my attempt to draw out his envy of his brother; it lasted many days and was marked by stereotyped complaints about his powerlessness. Since the resistance did not give way, it had to be assumed that we were dealing with a very immediate defense against the person of the analyst. I again urged him to speak openly and without fear about the analysis and particularly about the analyst and to tell what impression the analyst had made on him on first encounter.[5] After a long hesitation, he told me in a faltering voice that the analyst had appeared crudely masculine and brutal to him, as a man who would be absolutely

[5] Since then, I am in the habit of urging the patient to give me a description of my person. This always proves to be a fruitful measure for the removal of blocked transference situations.

ruthless toward women in sexual matters. How did this fit in with his attitude toward men who appeared potent?

We were at the end of the fourth month of analysis. Now, for the first time, that repressed relationship to the brother broke through which was intimately related to the most disruptive element of the existing transference, envy of potency. Revealing strong affects, he suddenly remembered that he had always condemned his brother in the most rigorous manner because he (the brother) chased after all the girls, seduced them, and, moreover, made a show of it. My appearance had immediately reminded him of his brother. Given greater confidence by his last communication, I again explained the transference situation and showed him that he identified me with his potent brother and, precisely for this reason, could not open himself to me; that is, he condemned me and resented my alleged superiority, as he had once condemned and resented his brother's alleged superiority. I told him, furthermore, that it was clearly evident now that the basis of his inferiority was a feeling of impotence.

After this explanation, *the central element of the character resistance emerged spontaneously.* In a correctly and consistently carried out analysis, this will happen every time, *without the analyst having to push matters or give anticipatory conceptions.* In a flash he remembered that he had repeatedly compared his own small penis with his brother's big penis, and had envied his brother because of it.

As was to be expected, a powerful resistance again ensued; again he complained, "I can't do anything," etc. Now I was able to go a step further in my interpretations and show him that these complaints were a verbalization of his feeling of impotence. His reaction to this was completely unexpected. After my interpretation of his distrust, he declared for the first time that he had never believed any man, that he believed nothing at all, probably not even the analysis. Naturally, this was a big step forward. But the meaning of this communication, its connection to the preceding situation, was not immediately clear. He spoke for two hours on the many disappointments which he had experienced in his life, and was of the opinion that his distrust could be rationally traced back to these disappointments. The old resistance reappeared. Since I was not sure what lay behind it this time, I decided to wait. For several days the situation remained unchanged —the old complaints, the familiar behavior. I continued to interpret the elements of the resistance which had already been worked through and were very familiar to me, when suddenly a new element emerged. He said that *he was afraid of the analysis because it might deprive him of his ideals.* Now the situation was clear again. He had transferred to me the castration anxiety which he felt toward his brother. He was afraid of me. Naturally, I made no mention of the castration anxiety, but again proceeded from his inferiority complex and his impotence and asked him whether he did not feel himself superior to all people on the basis of his high ideals, whether he did not regard himself as better than all the others. This he readily admitted; indeed, he went even further. He asserted that he really was superior to all the others, who chased after women and were like animals in their sexuality. With less certitude he added that, unfortunately, this feeling was frequently disturbed by his impotence. Evidently, he had not yet entirely come to terms with his sexual debility. Now I was able to elucidate the neurotic manner in which he was attempting to deal with his feeling of impotence and to show him that he was seeking to regain a feeling of potency in the sphere of ideals. I showed him the compensation and again drew his attention to the resistances to the analysis which stemmed from his secret feeling of superiority. It was not only that he secretly thought of himself as better and more intelligent; it was precisely for this reason that he had to resist the analysis. For if it turned out to be a success, then he would have needed someone's help and the analysis would have vanquished his neurosis, the secret value of which we had just uncovered. From the point of view of the neurosis, this constituted a defeat and, in terms of his unconscious, this also meant becoming a woman. In this way, moving forward from his ego and its defense mechanisms, I prepared the ground for the interpretation of the castration complex and the feminine fixation.

Thus, using the patient's demeanor as its point of departure, character analysis had succeeded in penetrating directly to the center of the neurosis, his castration anxiety, the envy of his brother stemming from the mother's preference of the brother, and the concomitant disappointment in her. The outlines of the

Oedipus complex were already coming into view. Here, however, what is important is not that these unconscious elements emerged —this often happens spontaneously. What is important is the legitimate sequence in which they emerged and the intimate contact they had with the ego defense and the transference. Last but not least, it is important that this happened without pushing but through pure analytic interpretation of the patient's bearing and with accompanying affects. This constitutes what is specific to consistent character analysis. It means a thorough working through of the conflicts assimilated *by the ego.*

Let us compare this with what might have resulted if we had not consistently focused on our patient's ego defense. Right at the beginning, the possibility existed of interpreting both his passive homosexual relationship to his brother and the death wish. We have no doubt that dreams and subsequent associations would have yielded additional material for interpretation. However, unless his ego defense had been systematically and thoroughly worked through beforehand, no interpretation would have evoked an affective response; instead, we would have obtained an intellectual knowledge of his passive desire on the one hand and a narcissistic, highly affective defense against these desires on the other hand. The affects pertaining to the passivity and murder impulses would have remained in the function of defense. The result would have been a chaotic situation, the typical bleak picture of an analysis rich in interpretation and poor in success. Several months of patient and persistent work on the ego resistance, with particular reference to its form (complaints, inflection, etc.), lifted the ego to the level necessary to assimilate what was repressed, loosened the affects, and brought about a shifting in their direction to the repressed ideas.

Thus, it cannot be said that there were *two* techniques which could have been applied in this case; there was only one, if the intent was to change the case *dynamically.* I hope that this case has made sufficiently clear the predominant difference in the conception of the application of theory to technique. The most important criterion of effective analysis is the use of *few* (but accurate and consistent) interpretations, instead of many unsystematic interpretations which fail to take the dynamic and economic moment into account. If the analyst does not allow himself to be tempted by the material but correctly assesses its dynamic position and economic role, the result is that, though he will receive the material later, it will be that much more thorough and affect-laden. The second criterion is the maintaining of a continuous connection between the contemporary situation and the infantile situation. The initial disconnectedness and confusion of the analytic material is transformed into an orderly sequence, that is, the succession of the resistances and contents is now determined by the special dynamics and structural relations of the particular neurosis. When the work of interpretation is not performed systematically, the analyst must always make a fresh start, search about, divine more than deduce. When the work of interpretation proceeds along character-analytic lines, on the other hand, the analytic process develops naturally. In the former case, the analysis runs smoothly in the beginning only to become more and more entangled in difficulties; in the latter case, the most serious difficulties present themselves in the first weeks and months of the treatment, only to give way to smoother work, even in the deepest material. Hence, the fate of each analysis depends upon the introduction of the treatment, i.e., upon the correct or incorrect unraveling of the resistances. Thus, the third criterion is the unraveling of the case, not arbitrarily from any position which happens to be conspicuous and intelligible, but from those positions where the strongest ego resistance is concealed, followed by the systematic expansion of the initial incursion into the unconscious and the working through of the important infantile fixations, which are affect-laden at any given time. An unconscious position which manifests itself in dreams or in an association, at a certain point in the treatment and notwithstanding the fact that it is of central importance for the neurosis, can play a completely subordinate role, i.e., have no contemporary importance with respect to the technique of the case. In our patient, the feminine relationship to the brother was the central pathogen; yet in the first months the fear of losing the compensation for impotence provided by the fantasized ego ideals constituted the problem with respect to technique. The error which is usually made is that the analyst attacks the central element in the neurotic formation (which usually manifests itself in some way right at the outset), instead of first attacking those positions which have a specific contemporary importance. Systematically worked through in succession, these positions *must* eventually lead to the central pathogenic element. In short, it is important, indeed decisive for the success of many cases, *how*, *when*, and from which side the analyst penetrates to the core of the neurosis.

It is not difficult to fit what we are describing here as character analysis into Freud's theory of resistance formation and resistance resolution. We know that every resistance consists of an id impulse which is warded off and an ego impulse which wards off. Both impulses are unconscious. In principle, it would seem to be a matter of choice whether the striving of the id or the striving of the ego is interpreted first. For example: if a homosexual resistance in the form of silence is encountered right at the outset of an analysis, the striving of the id can be taken up by telling the patient that he is presently engaged in tender intentions toward the person of the analyst. His positive transference has been interpreted and, if he does not take flight, it will be a long time before he becomes reconciled to this hideous idea. Hence, the analyst must give precedence to that aspect of the resistance which lies closer to the conscious ego, namely *the ego defense*, by merely telling the patient, to begin with, that he is silent because he rejects the analysis *"for one reason or another,"* presumably because it has become dangerous to him in some way. In short, the resistance is attacked without entering into the striving of the id. In the former case, that aspect of the resistance which pertains to the id (in the above instance, the love tendency) has been attacked through interpretation; in the latter case, that part of the resistance pertaining to the ego, i.e., the rejection, is attacked through interpretation.

By using this procedure, we simultaneously penetrate the negative transference, in which every defense finally ends, and also the character, the armor of the ego. The surface layer of *every* resistance, i.e., the layer closest to consciousness, must of necessity be a negative attitude toward the analyst, whether the id striving is based on hate or love. The ego projects onto the analyst its defense against the striving of the id. Thus, the analyst becomes an enemy and is dangerous because, by his imposition of the irksome basic rule, he has provoked id strivings and has disturbed the neurotic balance. In its defense, the ego makes use of very old forms of defensive attitudes. In a pinch it calls upon hate impulses from the id for help in its defense, even when it is warding off a love striving.

Thus, if we adhere to the rule of tackling that part of the resistance which pertains to the ego, we also resolve a part of negative transference in the process, a quantity of affect-laden hate, and thereby avoid the danger of overlooking the destructive tendencies which are very often brilliantly concealed; at the same time the positive transference is strengthened. The patient also comprehends the ego interpretation more easily because it is more related to his conscious feelings; in this way, he is also more prepared for the id interpretations which follow later.

No matter what kind of id strivings we are dealing with, the ego defense always has the same form, namely one that corresponds to the patient's character; and the same id striving is warded off in various ways in various patients. Thus, we leave the character untouched when we interpret only the striving of the id; on the other hand, we include the neurotic character in the analysis when we tackle the resistances fundamentally from the defense, i.e., from the ego side. In the former case, we tell the analysand immediately *what* he is warding off; in the latter case, we first make it clear to him *that* he is warding off "something," then *how* he is going about it, what means he is employing to do it (character analysis), and only much later, when the analysis of the resistance has progressed sufficiently, he is told or finds out for himself what the defense is directed against. In this very roundabout way to the interpretation of the id strivings, all the germane attitudes of the ego are taken apart analytically, thus precluding the grave danger that the patient will learn something too soon, or that he will remain unemotional and unconcerned.

Analyses in which the attitudes are accorded so much analytic attention proceed in a more orderly and more effective manner, without the least detriment to the theoretical research work. It is only that the important events of childhood are learned later than usual. However, this is amply compensated for by the emotional freshness with which the infantile material springs forth *after* the character resistances have been worked through analytically.

Yet, we must not fail to mention certain unpleasant aspects of consistent character analysis. Character analysis subjects the patient to far more psychic strain; the patient suffers much more than when the character is left out of consideration. This has, to be sure, the advantage of a weeding out: those who don't hold out would not have been cured anyhow, and it is better to have a case fail after four or six months than to have it fail after two years. But experience shows that if the character resistance does not break down, a satisfactory success cannot be counted on. This is especially true of cases having concealed character resistances. The overcoming of the character resistance does not mean that the patient has changed his character; this is possible only after the analysis of its infantile sources. He must merely have objectified it and have gained an analytic interest in it. Once this has been accomplished, a favorable continuation of the analysis is very probable.

e) The breaking down of the narcissistic defense apparatus

As we already mentioned, the essential difference between the analysis of a symptom and that of a neurotic character trait consists in the fact that, from the very outset, the former is isolated and objectified, whereas the latter must be continually singled out in the analysis so that the patient gains the same attitude toward it as toward a symptom. It is only seldom that this happens easily. There are patients who show very little inclination to take an objective view of their character. This is understandable, for it is a question of the breaking down of the narcissistic defense mechanism, and the working through of the libido anxiety which is bound in it.

A twenty-five-year-old man sought analytic help because of a few minor symptoms and a disturbance in his work. He exhibited a free, self-confident bearing, yet one sometimes had the vague impression that his behavior required great strain and that he did not establish a genuine relationship with the person with whom he happened to be speaking. There was something cold in his manner of speaking; his voice was soft and subtly ironic. Once in a while he smiled, but it was hard to know whether it was a smile indicative of embarrassment, superiority, or irony.

The analysis commenced with violent emotions and a vast amount of enactment. He cried when he spoke of his mother's demise and swore when he described the usual upbringing of children. He divulged only very general information about his past: his parents had had a very unhappy marriage; his mother had been very strict with him; and it wasn't until he had reached maturity that he established a rather superficial relationship with his brothers and sisters. All his communications sharpened the original impression that neither his crying nor his swearing nor any of his other emotions was sincere and natural. He himself stated that it really wasn't so bad as all that, and indeed he was forever smiling at everything he said. After several sessions, he took to provoking the analyst. When I had concluded the session, for example, he would continue to lie on the couch ostentatiously for a while; or he would strike up a conversation afterwards. Once he asked me what I would do if he seized me by the throat. Two sessions later he tried to frighten me by a sudden movement of his hand toward my head. I shrank back instinctively and told him that the analysis required of him only that he say everything, not that he do everything. Another time, he stroked my arm on taking leave. The deeper but inexplicable meaning of this behavior was an incipient homosexual transference which was expressing itself sadistically. When I translated these actions superficially as provocations, he smiled to himself and immured himself even more. The actions as well as the communications ceased; only the stereotyped smile remained. He began to immerse himself in silence. When I called his attention to the resistive character of his behavior, he merely smiled again and repeated, after a period of silence, the word "resistance" several times, in a clearly ironic tone of voice. In this way, his smiling and his tendency to treat everything ironically became the fulcrum of the analytic task.

The situation was difficult enough. Apart from the scanty information about his childhood, I knew nothing about him. So I had to concentrate on his mode of behavior in the analysis. For the time being, I withdrew into a passive position and waited to see what would come, but there was no change in his behavior.

About two weeks elapsed in this way. Then it struck me that, in point of time, the intensification of his smiling coincided with my warding off his aggression. So, to begin with, I tried to make him understand the contemporary reason for his smiling. I told him that there was no doubt his smiling meant many different things, but at the moment it was his reaction to my cowardice as testified by my instinctive drawing back. He said that this was very likely true, but he would continue to smile nonetheless. He spoke little and on matters of subsidiary importance, treated the analysis ironically, and stated that he couldn't believe anything I told him. Gradually, it became more and more clear that his smiling served as a defense against the analysis. I repeatedly pointed this out to him throughout several sessions, but several weeks elapsed before he had a dream, the content of which was that a pillar made of brick was cut down into individual bricks by a machine. What relation this dream had to the analytic situation was all the more difficult to fathom inasmuch as he did not produce any associations at first. Finally, he stated that the dream was altogether quite clear; obviously, it dealt with the castration complex —and he smiled. I told him that his irony was merely an attempt to disavow the sign that the unconscious had given him through the dream. This evoked a screen memory, which was of the greatest importance for the future development of the analysis. He remembered that once, when he was about five, he had "played horsy" in the courtyard of his parents' home. He had crawled about on all fours, letting his penis hang out of his pants; his mother had caught him in the act and asked him what he was doing—he had merely smiled. For the time being, there was nothing else to be gotten out of him. Yet, some clarity had been gained; his smiling was a part of the mother transference. When I now told him that, obviously, he was acting here as he had acted toward his mother and that his smiling must have a definite meaning, he merely smiled. All this was of course very nice, he said, but its meaning eluded him. For several days we had the same smiling and silence on his part and, on my part, consistent interpretation of his behavior as a defense against the analysis and of his smiling as the conquering of a secret fear of this interpretation. Yet he warded off this interpretation of his behavior with his typical smile. This, too, was consistently interpreted as a block against my influence, and I pointed out to him that he evidently was always smiling in life. He admitted that this was the only possibility of holding one's own in the world. In admitting this, however, he had unwittingly concurred with my interpretation. One day he came into the analysis wearing his usual smile and said, "You'll be happy today, Doctor. I was struck by something funny. In my mother tongue, bricks mean the testicles of a horse. That's pretty good, isn't it? You see, it is the castration complex." I told him that this might or might not be the case, but as long as he persisted in his defensive attitude, it was out of the question to think of analyzing his dream. He would be sure to nullify every association and every interpretation with his smiling. We have to append here that his smile was hardly more than a suggestion of a smile; it expressed, rather, a sense of mockery. I told him that he had no need to be afraid to laugh heartily and loudly at the analysis. From then on, he came out much more clearly with his irony. But the verbal association, so ironically communicated, was a very valuable cue toward an understanding of the situation. It seemed very probable that, as is often the case, the analysis had been conceived of as a castration threat and had been warded off in the beginning with aggression and later with smiling. I returned to the aggression he had expressed at the beginning of the analysis and supplemented my earlier interpretation by pointing out that he had used his provocation to test to what extent he could trust me, to see how far he could go. In short, his lack of trust was very likely rooted in a childhood fear. This explanation made an evident impression on him. He was momentarily shaken, but quickly recovered and began once again to deride the analysis and the analyst. Well aware, from the few indications derived from the reactions to his dream, that my interpretations were hitting home and were undermining his ego defense, I refused to be diverted. Unfortunately, he was not too happy about this, and he stuck to his smiling just as tenaciously as I stuck to my explanatory work. Many sessions elapsed without any apparent progress. I intensified my interpretations not only by becoming more insistent but also by more closely relating his smiling to the supposed infantile fear. I pointed out that he was afraid of the analysis because it would arouse his childhood conflicts. He had, I said, at one time come to terms with these conflicts, even if not in a very satisfactory way, and now he recoiled from the possibility of having again to go through all that he thought he had mastered with the help of his smile. But he was deceiving himself, for his excitement in telling of his mother's death had certainly been genuine. I also ventured the opinion that his relationship to his mother had not been unambiguous; surely he had not only feared her and derided her but also loved her. Somewhat more seriously than usual, he related details of his mother's loveless attitude toward him. Once, when he had been naughty, she had even injured his hand with a knife. To this, however, he added, "Right, according to analytic theory, this is again the castration complex?" But something serious seemed to be preparing itself inside of him. On the basis of the analytic situation, I continued to interpret the contemporary and latent meaning of his smile. During this time, additional dreams were reported. Their manifest content was rather typical of symbolic castration fantasies. Finally, he produced a dream in which horses appeared, and another dream in which the fire department was mobilized and out of a truck rose a high tower from which a powerful column of water was discharged into the flames of a burning house. At this time, occasional bed-wettings were also reported. He himself recognized, albeit still with a smile, the connection between the "horse dream" and his playing "horsy." He recalled, indeed, that the long genital of horses had always been of special interest to him, and added spontaneously that he had no doubt imitated such a horse in the childish game. Micturition had also afforded him great pleasure. He did not remember whether he had wet his bed as a child.

Another time when we were discussing the infantile meaning of his smile, he put a different interpretation on the smile of the childhood incident in which he had been playing "horsy." It was quite possible, he said, that it had been intended not as a sneer but as an attempt to disarm his mother, out of fear that she would scold him. In this way, he came closer and closer to what, on the basis of his behavior in the analysis, I had been interpreting to him for months. Thus, the function and meaning of the smile had changed in the course of his development: *at first it had been an attempt to propitiate, later it had become a compen-*

sation for inner fear, and finally it served a feeling of superiority.
The patient himself hit upon this explanation when, in the course
of several sessions, he reconstructed the way he had found to
keep at bay the misery of his childhood. Hence, the meaning
was: "Nothing can harm me; I am immune to everything." It
was in the latter sense that the smile had become a resistance in
the analysis, a defense against the resuscitation of the old conflicts. Infantile fear seemed to be the essential motive for this defense. A dream which the patient had at about the end of the
fifth month of analysis revealed the deepest layer of his fear, the
fear of being deserted by his mother. The dream went as follows:
"Accompanied by an unknown person, I am riding in a car through
a completely deserted and dreary looking town. The houses
are dilapidated, the windows smashed. No one is to be seen.
It is as if death had ravaged this place. We come to a gate, and
I want to turn back. I tell my companion we should have another look around. A man and a woman in mourning are kneel-
ing on the sidewalk. I walk toward them with the intent of asking
them something. As I touch their shoulders, they are startled,
and I wake up in fear." The most important association was
that the town was similar to the one he had lived in until he was
four. Symbolically, the death of the mother and the feeling of infantile desertion were clearly intimated. The companion was the
analyst. For the first time the patient took a dream completely
seriously and without smiling. The character resistance had been
broken through and the connection had been established to the
infantile material. From this point on, apart from the usual in-
terruptions caused by relapses into the old character resistance,
the analysis proceeded without any particular difficulty. But a
deep depression ensued, which disappeared only with time.

Naturally, the difficulties were far greater than may be evident
from this brief summary. The resistance phase from beginning to
end lasted almost six months and was marked by continuing
mockery of the analysis. If it had not been for the necessary patience and confidence in the effectiveness of consistent interpretation of the character resistance, one might easily have "thrown in
the sponge."

Let us now endeavor to decide whether the subsequent analytic insight into the mechanism of this case would justify the use

of a different technical procedure. It is true that the manner of
the patient's behavior could have been given less prominence in
the analysis; instead, the scanty dreams could have been subjected to more exact analysis. It is also true that he might have
produced interpretable associations. Let us pass over the fact
that, until he entered analysis, this patient always forgot his
dreams or didn't dream at all. And it wasn't until his behavior
was consistently interpreted that he produced dreams of a definite content and of a specific relevance to the analytic situation. I
am prepared for the objection that the patient would have produced the corresponding dreams spontaneously. To enter into
such a discussion is to get into an argument about things that
cannot be proven. There are ample experiences which show that
a situation such as the one presented by this patient is not easily
resolved solely through passive waiting; and if it is, then it happens only by chance, i.e., the analyst does not have the analysis
under control.

Let us assume that we had interpreted his associations relating
to the castration complex, that is, tried to make him conscious of
the repressed content, the fear of cutting or of being cut. Eventually this approach, too, *might have* achieved success. But the
very fact that we cannot say with certainty that that would have
been the case, the fact that we admit the element of chance,
compels us to reject as unanalytic this kind of technique which
violates the essence of psychoanalytic work. Such a technique
would mean a reversion to that stage of analysis where one did
not bother about the resistances because one did not recognize
them, and therefore interpreted the meaning of the unconscious directly. It is evident from the case history itself that this technique
would also have meant a neglect of the ego defenses.

It might also be objected that, while the technical handling of
the case was absolutely correct, my polemics were uncalled for.
What I am saying is quite obvious and not at all new—that's the
way all analysts work. I do not deny that the general principles
are not new, that character analysis is merely the special application of the principle of resistance analysis. But many years of experience in the seminar have clearly and unequivocally shown
that while the principles of resistance technique are generally
known and acknowledged, in practice one proceeds almost ex-

clusively according to the old technique of direct interpretation of the unconscious. This discrepancy between theoretical knowledge and actual practice was the cause of all the mistaken objections to the systematic attempts on the part of the Vienna seminar to develop the consistent application of theory to therapy. Those who said that all this was commonplace and that there was nothing new in it were basing their statements on their theoretical knowledge; those who contended that this was all wrong and not "Freudian analysis" were thinking of their own practice, which, as we have said, deviated considerably from theory.

A colleague once asked me what I would have done in the following case. For four weeks he had been treating a young man who immured himself in complete silence but who was otherwise very friendly and, before and after the analytic session, feigned a very genial disposition. The analyst had already tried everything possible, threatened to terminate the analysis, and finally, when even a dream interpretation failed to achieve any results, had set a definite termination date. The scanty dream material had contained nothing but sadistic murders; the analyst had told the patient that his dreams showed quite clearly that he conceived of himself as a murderer in fantasy. But this had not served any purpose. The analyst was not satisfied with my statement that it does not do to make a deep interpretation to a patient who has an acute resistance, even though the material appears quite manifestly in a dream. He was of the opinion that there was no alternative but to do that. To my suggestion that, to begin with, the patient's silence should have been interpreted as a resistance, he said that this was not possible: there was "no material" available for such an interpretation. Wasn't there, quite apart from the content of the dreams, sufficient "material" in the patient's behavior itself, the contradiction between his silence during the analytic session and his friendliness outside of it? Wasn't at least one thing clear from the situation, namely that through his silence the patient—to put it in very general terms—expressed a negative attitude or a defense; expressed, to judge from his dreams, sadistic impulses which he sought to counter and conceal through his obtrusively friendly behavior? Why is it that an analyst will venture to infer unconscious processes from a patient's slip—e.g., the forgetting of an object in the analyst's consultation room—but is afraid to make inferences, from the patient's behavior, which will have bearing on the meaning of the analytic situation? Does a patient's behavior offer less conclusive material than a slip? Somehow I couldn't get this across to my colleague. He stuck to his view that the resistance could not be tackled because there was "no material." There can be no doubt that the interpretation of the sanguinary wish was a mistake; the result of such an interpretation can only be that the patient's ego becomes even more frightened and even more inaccessible to analysis. The difficulties offered by the cases presented in the seminar were of a similar nature. There was always an underestimation of or disregard for the patient's behavior as interpretable material; the repeated attempt to eliminate the resistance from the position of the id, instead of through the analysis of the ego defense; and finally the oft-repeated idea, which served as an excuse, that the patient simply did not want to get well or was "much too narcissistic."

The technique of breaking down the narcissistic defense in other types is not fundamentally different from that described above. If, for example, a patient never becomes emotionally involved and remains indifferent, regardless of what material he produces, one is dealing with a dangerous emotional block, the analysis of which must take precedence over everything else if one does not want to run the risk of having all the material and interpretations lost. If this is the case, the patient may acquire a good knowledge of psychoanalytic theory, but he will not be cured. If, confronted with such a block, the analyst elects not to give up the analysis because of the "strong narcissism," he can make an agreement with the patient. The patient will be given the option to terminate the analysis at any time; in turn, he will allow the analyst to dwell upon his emotional lameness until it is eliminated. Eventually—it usually takes many months (in one case it took a year and a half)—the patient begins to buckle under the continual stressing of his emotional lameness and its causes. In the meantime, the analyst will gradually have obtained sufficient clues to undermine the defense against anxiety, which is what an emotional block is. Finally, the patient rebels against the threat of the analysis, rebels against the threat to his protective psychic armor, of being put at the mercy of his drives, particularly his aggressive drives. By rebelling against this "non-sense," however, his aggressiveness is aroused and it is not long before the first emotional outbreak ensues (i.e., a negative transference) in the form of a paroxysm of hate. If the analyst succeeds in getting this far, the contest has been won. When the aggressive impulses have been brought into the open, the emotional block has been penetrated and the patient is capable of analysis. From this point on, the analysis runs its usual course. The difficulty consists in drawing out the aggressiveness.

The same holds true when, because of the peculiarity of their character, narcissistic patients vent their resistance verbally. For example, they speak in a grandiloquent manner, use technical terminology, always rigidly chosen or else confused. This manner of speaking constitutes an impenetrable wall; until it is subjected to analysis, no real progress can be made. Here, too, the consistent interpretation of the patient's behavior provokes a narcissistic rebellion: the patient does not like to hear that he speaks in such a stilted, grandiloquent manner, or uses technical terminology to conceal his inferiority complex from himself and from the analyst, or that he speaks confusedly because he wants to appear especially clever—the truth of the matter being that he cannot formulate his thoughts simply. In this way the hard terrain of the neurotic character has been loosened in an essential area and an approach has been paved to the infantile foundation of the character and the neurosis. Needless to say, it is not enough to make passing allusions to the nature of the resistance. The more tenacious it proves to be, the more consistently it must be interpreted. If the negative attitudes toward the analyst which are provoked by this consistent interpretation are simultaneously analyzed, then there is little danger that the patient will terminate the treatment.

The immediate result of the analytic loosening of the character armor and the disruption of the narcissistic protective apparatus is twofold: (1) *the loosening of the affects from their reactive anchorings and concealments;* (2) *the establishment of an entry into the central area of the infantile conflict, the Oedipus complex and the castration anxiety.* There is an advantage in this procedure which should not be underestimated: it is not only the content of infantile experiences that is reached. More important, they are brought directly to analysis in the specific context in which they have been assimilated, i.e., *in the form in which they have been molded by the ego.* It is seen again and again in analysis that the dynamic value of the same element of repressed material varies depending on the degree to which the ego defenses have been loosened. In many cases the affect-cathexis of the childhood experiences has been absorbed into the character as a defensive mechanisms, so that, by simply interpreting the content, one reaches the remembrances but not the affects. In such cases, to interpret the infantile material *before* the affects assimilated into the character have been loosened is a grave mistake. It is, for example, to this neglect that the long, bleak, and more or less fruitless analyses of compulsive characters are to be traced.[6] If, on the other hand, the affects pertaining to the defensive formation of the character are liberated first, then a new cathexis of the infantile instinctual expressions takes place automatically. The character-analytic interpretation of resistances all but excludes remembering without affects because of the disturbance of the neurotic balance, which always occurs at the outset in character analysis.

In still other cases, the character erects itself as a hard protective wall against the experiencing of infantile anxiety and thus maintains itself, notwithstanding the great forfeiture of *joie de vivre* which this entails. If a patient having such a character enters analytic treatment because of some symptom or other, this protective wall continues to serve in the analysis as a character resistance; and it soon becomes apparent that nothing can be

---

[6] Let the following case serve as an example of how decisive it is to take into consideration or neglect a patient's mode of behavior. A compulsive character who had twelve years of analysis behind him without any commensurate improvement and was well informed on his infantile motivations, e.g., on the central father-conflict, spoke in a strange monotone in the analysis, in a somewhat singsong cadence and kept wringing his hands. I asked whether this behavior had ever been analyzed. It had not. At first, I had no insight into the case. One day it struck me that he spoke as if he were praying. I informed him of my observation, whereupon he told me that as a child he had been forced by his father to attend prayer meetings, which he had done very reluctantly. He had prayed, but under protest. In the same way he had recited to the analyst for twelve years, "Fine, I'll do as you say, but under protest." The uncovering of this apparently insignificant detail in his behavior threw open the analysis and led to the most deeply buried affects.

accomplished until the character armor, which conceals and consumes the infantile anxiety, has been destroyed. This, for example, is the case in moral insanity and in manic, narcissistic-sadistic characters. Here, the analyst is often faced with the difficult question whether the existing symptom justifies a thoroughgoing character analysis. For let there be no doubt about it: when the analysis of the character destroys the character compensation, especially in cases where that defense is a relatively good one, a temporary condition is created which approximates a breakdown of the ego. In some extreme cases, it is true, such a breakdown is necessary before the new reality-oriented ego structure can develop. (However, we must admit that the breakdown would have come of itself sooner or later—the formation of a symptom was the first sign of this.) Yet one is reluctant, unless an urgent indication exists, to adopt a measure which involves such grave responsibility.

Nor can it be ignored in this connection that, in every case in which it is used, character analysis provokes violent emotions; indeed, often creates dangerous situations. Hence, the analyst must have technical mastery of the analysis at all times. Some analysts will perhaps reject the character-analytic procedure for this reason. If such is so, however, the analytic treatment of quite a number of patients can be counted upon to fail. There are neuroses which simply cannot be reached through mild means. The methods employed in character analysis, the consistent stressing of the character resistance and the persistent interpretation of its forms, means, and motives, are as powerful as they are disagreeable to the patient. This has nothing to do with preparing the patient for analysis; it is a strict analytic principle. However, it is good policy to make the patient aware, at the very outset, of all the foreseeable unpleasantness and difficulties of the treatment.

f) On the optimal conditions for the analytic reduction to the infantile situation from the contemporary situation

Since the consistent interpretation of a patient's behavior spontaneously provides access to the infantile sources of the neurosis, a new question arises: are there criteria for determining when the contemporary mode of behavior should be reduced to its infantile prototype? Indeed, one of the main tasks of analysis consists precisely in this reduction. In these general terms, however, the formula is not applicable in everyday practice. Should this reduction take place immediately, as soon as the first signs of the germane infantile material become apparent, or are there factors which indicate that it would be better to wait until a certain specific time? To begin with, it must be borne in mind that the purpose of reduction, namely the dissolution of the resistance and the elimination of amnesia, is not immediately encompassed in many cases. This much we know from definite experiences. Either the patient does not get beyond an intellectual understanding or the attempt at reduction is foiled by doubt. This is explained by the fact that, just as in the case of making an unconscious idea conscious, the topographical process of conversion actually culminates only when combined with the *dynamic-affective* process of becoming conscious. Two things are necessary to achieve this: (1) the main resistance must at least be loosened; (2) the cathexis of the idea which is to become conscious or (as in the case of reduction) which is to be exposed to a definite connection must have attained a minimum degree of intensity. As we know, however, the libido-charged affects of the repressed ideas are usually split off, i.e., bound in the character or in the acute transference conflicts and transference resistances. If the contemporary resistance is now reduced to its infantile source, before it has been fully developed (that is, as soon as a trace of its infantile foundation has been spotted), then the intensity of its cathexis has not been fully taken advantage of. The content of the resistance has been analytically utilized in the interpretation, but the corresponding affect has not been included. If, in other words, both the topographical and the dynamic points of view are taken into consideration in making one's interpretations, then we have the following stricture imposed upon us: the resistance must not be nipped in the bud. On the contrary, it must be allowed to reach full maturity in the heat of the transference situation. In the case of torpid character encrustations which have become chronic, the difficulties cannot be gotten at in any other way. To Freud's rule that the patient has to be led from acting out to remembering, from the contemporary to the infantile, must be added that, *before* this takes place, what has been chronically stultified has to attain a new living reality in the contemporary transference situation. This is the same process involved in the healing of chronic inflammations—i.e., they are first made acute by means of irritation—and this is always necessary in the case of character resistances. In advanced stages of the analysis, when the analyst is sure of the patient's cooperation, "irritation therapy," as Ferenczi called it, is no longer as necessary. One gets the impression that when an analyst reduces a wholly immature transference situation he does so out of fear of the stresses which are part and parcel of strong transference resistances. So, despite one's better theoretical knowledge, the resistance is often regarded as something highly unwelcome, as merely disruptive. This is also the reason for the tendency to circumvent the resistance, instead of allowing it to develop and then attacking it. It seems to be forgotten that the neurosis itself is contained in the resistance, that, in dissolving a resistance, we also dissolve a part of the neurosis.

Allowing the resistance to develop is necessary for another reason. In view of the complicated structure of each resistance, all its determinants and meaningful contents are comprehended only with time; and the more thoroughly a resistance situation has been comprehended, the more successful its interpretation will be, quite apart from the previously mentioned dynamic factor. The double nature of the resistance, its contemporary and its historical motives, requires that the forms of the ego defense which it contains must be brought to complete consciousness first. Only after the contemporary meaning of the resistance has become clear should its infantile origin be interpreted in light of the material which has been produced. This also holds true for patients who have already revealed the infantile material necessary to the understanding of the *subsequent* resistance. In other cases, probably the majority, it is necessary to allow the resistance to develop, if only to be able to obtain the infantile material in sufficient measure.

Thus, the resistance technique has two aspects: (1) *comprehending the resistance from the contemporary situation through interpretation of its contemporary meaning;* (2) *dissolving the resistance by linking the ensuing infantile material with the contemporary material.* In this way, escape into the contemporary as well as the infantile situation is easily avoided, inasmuch as both are given equal consideration in interpretation.

Thus, the resistance, once a therapeutic obstruction, becomes the most powerful vehicle of analysis.

g) *Character analysis in the case of abundantly flowing material*

In cases in which the patient's character impedes the recall work from the very beginning, character analysis as described above is unquestionably indicated as the solely legitimate analytic method of introducing the treatment. But what about those patients whose characters admit of ample recall work in the beginning? We are faced with two questions. Is character analysis as we have described it here also necessary in these cases? If so, how should the analysis be introduced? The first question would have to be answered in the negative if there were any patients who did not exhibit character armor. However, since there are no such patients, since the narcissistic protective mechanism sooner or later becomes a character resistance, varying only in intensity and depth, no *fundamental* difference exists. There is merely a circumstantial difference: in patients whose character impedes the recall work, the mechanism of narcissistic protection and defense lies wholly on the surface and immediately appears as a resistance, whereas in the other patients the protective and defensive mechanism lies deeper in the personality, so that it is not at all obvious at first. But it is precisely these patients who are dangerous. With the former, one knows in advance where one stands. With the latter, one goes on believing for quite some time that the analysis is progressing very well because the patient seems to accept everything very readily; indeed, even shows signs of improvement, and produces prompt reactions to the interpretations. It is with such patients that one experiences the greatest disappointments. The analysis has been carried out, but there is no sign of final success. One has used up all one's interpretations, is confident that the primal scene and the infantile conflicts have been made completely conscious; yet the analysis is stuck in bleak, monotonous repetitions of the old material—the cure refusing to take effect. It is still worse when a transference success deludes the analyst into thinking that the patient is cured, only to find that he suffers a complete relapse soon after discharge.

The countless bad experiences with such cases lead me to believe—a self-evident belief, really—that something has been neglected, not with regard to content, for the thoroughness of these analyses leaves little to be desired in this area. What I have in mind is an unknown and unrecognized, a concealed resistance which causes all therapeutic efforts to fail. Closer examination shows that these concealed resistances are to be sought precisely in the patient's docility, in his manifestly weak defense against the analysis. And these analyses, on closer comparison with other cases which succeed, are shown to have followed a steady, even course, never disrupted by violent affective outbursts, and, above all—something which did not become clear until the very end—to have been conducted almost exclusively in a "positive" transference. Seldom or never had there been violent negative impulses against the analyst. Although the hate impulses had been analyzed, they just had not appeared in the transference or had been remembered without affects. The narcissistic affect-lame and the passive-feminine characters are the prototypes of these cases. The former are characterized by a tepid and steady "positive" transference; the latter by an effusive "positive" transference.

So it had to be admitted that in these so-called going cases—referred to as "going" because they produce infantile material, i.e., again on the basis of a one-sided overestimation of the contents of the material—the character had operated as a resistance in a concealed form throughout the entire analysis. Very often these cases were held to be incurable, or at least difficult to master, an appraisal for which, formerly, I too thought I saw sufficient evidence in my own experiences. However, since I gained a knowledge of their concealed resistances, I can consider them among my most rewarding cases.

In terms of character analysis, the introductory phase of such cases differs from other cases in that the flow of the communications is not disturbed and the analysis of the character resistance is not taken up until the flood of material and the behavior itself have become clearly recognizable resistances. The following typical case of a passive-feminine character is intended to illustrate this and, moreover, to demonstrate how, here too, the entry into the deeply repressed infantile conflicts ensues of itself. Furthermore, by pursuing the analysis into advanced stages, we want to demonstrate the legitimate unwinding of the neurosis on the spool of the transference resistances.

3. A CASE OF PASSIVE-FEMININE CHARACTER

a) *Anamnesis*

A twenty-four-year-old bank employee turned to analysis because of the anxiety states which had seized him a year before while he was visiting a hygiene exhibition. And prior to that occasion, he had suffered from acute hypochondriac fears, e.g., that he had a *hereditary taint,* would become *mentally ill* and *perish in a mental institution.* He was able to offer a number of rational reasons to account for these fears: his father had contracted syphilis and gonorrhea ten years before his marriage. His paternal grandfather was also supposed to have had syphilis. One of his father's brothers was very nervous and suffered from insomnia. On his mother's side the hereditary taint was even worse: his maternal grandfather had committed suicide, as had one of his maternal uncles. One of the sisters of his maternal grandmother was "mentally abnormal" (apparently melancholic-depressive). The patient's mother was a nervous, anxiety-ridden woman.

This double "hereditary taint" (syphilis on his father's side; suicide and psychosis on his mother's side) made the case that much more interesting: psychoanalysis does not deny a hereditary etiology of the neurosis but merely accords it the importance of one of many etiologies and, for this reason, finds itself in opposition to orthodox psychiatry. We shall see that the patient's idea about his heredity also had an irrational basis. Notwithstanding his severe handicaps, he was cured. His subsequent freedom from relapses was followed up over a period of five years.

This report covers only the first seven months of treatment, which were taken up with the unfolding, objectification, and analysis of the character resistances. The last seven months are considered only very briefly; from the point of view of resistance and character analysis, this part had little of interest to offer. For us it is chiefly important to describe the introductory phase of the treatment, the course pursued by the analysis of the resistances, and the way in which it found access to the early infantile material. In deference to the difficulties of describing an analysis and also to make it easier to comprehend, we shall report the analysis without any of the accessories and repetitions. We shall concentrate solely on the resistances and how they were worked through. We shall, as it were, reveal only the scaffolding of the analysis and attempt to lay bare its most important stages and to relate them to one another. In reality, the analysis was not so simple as it may appear here in print. As the months passed, however, one manifestation was added to another and a definite outline began to take shape regarding certain events; it is this outline which we shall attempt to describe here.

The patient's *attacks of anxiety* were accompanied by *palpitations* and a paralysis of all *volition*. Even in the intervals between these attacks he was never wholly free of a feeling of *uneasiness*. Frequently, the attacks of anxiety occurred quite suddenly, but they were also easily provoked when, for example, he read about mental illnesses or suicide in the newspaper. In the course of the previous year his work capacity had shown marked signs of deteriorating, and he feared that he might lose his job because of his *reduced performance*.

He had severe *sexual* disturbances. Shortly before his visit to the *hygiene exhibition*, he had attempted to have intercourse with a prostitute but had failed. This had not bothered him very much, or so he said. Nor were his conscious sexual needs very strong. Apparently, abstinence created no problem for him. Several years earlier, a sexual act had worked out, but he had had a premature and pleasureless ejaculation.

Asked whether he had ever suffered states of anxiety before this time, the patient reported that even as a *child* he had been *very timorous* and, especially during puberty, had been *afraid of world catastrophes*. He had been very much afraid in 1910 when there was talk of the end of the world through a collision with a comet, and he had been astonished that his parents spoke about it so calmly. This "fear of catastrophes" subsided gradually, but it was later replaced by the idea of having a hereditary taint. He had suffered from vivid states of anxiety ever since he was a child. In recent years, however, they had become less frequent.

Apart from the *hypochondriac idea of having a hereditary taint,* the *states of anxiety,* and the *sexual debility,* there were no other neurotic symptoms. At the beginning of the treatment, the patient had an insight into his states of anxiety, for he suffered the most from these. The hereditary idea was too well rationalized, and his libido debility (impotence) did not trouble him enough to make him sense them as an illness. In terms of the symptoms, we had here the *hypochondriac form of anxiety-hysteria* having the customary, in this case especially well developed, *actual neurotic core (stasis neurosis).*

The diagnosis, *hysterical character with hypochondriac anxiety-hysteria,* was based on the analytic findings with respect to his fixations. Phenomenologically, he came under the type of the *passive-feminine character:* his demeanor was always excessively friendly and humble; he was forever excusing himself for the most trifling matters. Both when he arrived and when he departed, he bowed deeply several times. In addition, he was *awkward, shy,* and *ceremonious.* If he were asked, for example, whether he had any objection to rescheduling his hour, he would not simply answer "no." He would assure me that he was at my service, that everything was quite agreeable with him, etc. If he had a request to make, he stroked the arm of the analyst while making it. Once, when it was intimated that perhaps he distrusted the analyst, he returned on the same day very much upset. He could not, he said, endure the thought that his analyst regarded him as distrustful, and he repeatedly begged forgiveness in the event he had said something that might have caused me to make such an assumption.

b) *The development and analysis of the character resistance*

The analysis, marked by resistances which stemmed from his character, developed as follows:

Acquainted with the basic rule, he began, fluently and seldom at a loss for words, to tell about his family background and the hereditary taint. Gradually, he came to talk about his relationship to his parents. He maintained that he loved both of them the same; indeed, he said that he had a very high regard for his father. He depicted him as an energetic, level-headed person. *His father had repeatedly warned him against masturbation and extramarital intercourse.* The father had told him about his own bad experiences in this area, about his syphilis and gonorrhea, about his relationships with women which had ended badly. All this had been done with the best of intentions, i.e., in the hope of sparing the son similar experiences. The father had never beaten him as a means of enforcing his will. He had always used a more subtle approach: "I'm not forcing you; I'm merely advising you . . ." Needless to say, this was said with great energy. The patient described his relationship to his father as being extremely good; he was devoted to him; he had no better friend in the whole world.

He did not dwell upon this subject very long. The sessions were taken up almost exclusively with descriptions of his relationship to the mother. She had always been affectionate and extremely attentive to his welfare. He, too, behaved affectionately toward her. On the other hand, he let himself be waited on hand and foot. She laid out his clothes for him, served him breakfast in bed, sat beside his bed until he fell asleep (still at the time of the analysis), combed his hair; in a word, he led the life of a pampered child.

He progressed rapidly in the discussion of his relationship to his mother and *within six weeks was on the verge of becoming conscious of the desire for coitus.* With this exception, he had become fully conscious of his affectionate relationship to his mother—to some extent he had been aware of this even before the analysis: he was fond of throwing her on his bed; to which she submitted with *"glowing eyes* and *flushed cheeks."* When she came in her nightgown to wish him goodnight, he would embrace her impetuously. Though he always endeavored to stress the sexual excitement of the mother—in an effort, no doubt, to betray his own intentions as little as possible—he mentioned several times, parenthetically as it were, that he himself had felt clear sexual excitation.

My extremely cautious attempt to make him aware of the real meaning of these practices met with prompt and violent resistance. He could assure me, he said, that he would have responded in the same way to other women. I had not made this attempt with the intent of interpreting the incest fantasy but merely to ascertain whether I had been right in assuming that his rigid advance in the direction of the historically important incestuous love was a clever evasion of other material having greater *con-*

temporary importance. The material which he produced on the relationship to his mother was not in the least ambiguous; it really appeared as if he were on the verge of grasping the true situation. In principle, therefore, there was no reason why an interpretation could not be given. Yet the striking disparity between the content of his communications and the content of his dreams and his excessively friendly demeanor cautioned me against such an interpretation.

Thus, my attention had to become more and more focused on his behavior and dream material. He did not produce any associations to his dreams. During the session itself, he was enthusiastic about the analysis and the analyst; outside of the session, he was deeply worried about his future and had sullen thoughts about his hereditary taint.

The dream material had a twofold nature: in part, it was concerned with his incestuous fantasies. What he did not express during the day, he betrayed in the manifest content of his dreams. Thus, in his dream he followed his mother with a paper knife, or he crawled through *a hole* in front of which *his mother was standing.* On the other hand, it *frequently* dealt with a *dark story of murder,* with the *hereditary idea,* a *crime* which someone had committed, jeering *remarks* made by somebody, or an expression of distrust.

In the first four to six weeks, I had the following analytic material at my disposal: his communications about his relationship to his mother; his contemporary states of anxiety and the hereditary idea; his excessively friendly, submissive behavior; his dreams, those which clearly followed up his incest fantasies and those which dealt with murder and distrust; certain indications of a positive mother transference.

Faced with the choice of interpreting his completely clear incest material or of stressing the indications of his distrust, I chose the latter. For, in fact, we were dealing here with a *latent resistance* which, over a period of weeks, remained concealed. And it was precisely for this reason that the patient offered too much material and was not sufficiently inhibited. As was shown later, this was also the first major *transference resistance,* the special *nature* of which was determined by the patient's character. *He gave a deceptive impression:* (1) through his divulgence of therapeutically worthless material relating to his experiences; (2) through his excessively friendly demeanor; (3) through the frequency and clarity of his dreams; (4) through the sham trust which he showed in the analyst. *His attitude toward the analyst was "complaisant,"* in the same way as he had been devoted to his father throughout his life, and, in fact, for the same reason, i.e., *because he was afraid of him.* If this had been my first case of this kind, it would have been impossible for me to know that such behavior is a strong, dangerous resistance; nor would I have been able to resolve it, for I could not have divined its meaning and its structure. However, previous experiences with similar cases had taught me that such patients are not capable of producing any manifest resistance for months, indeed years on end, and that they do not react at all therapeutically to the interpretations which the clear material induces the analyst to give. Hence, it cannot be said that, in such cases, one has to wait until the transference resistance sets in; the truth of the matter is that it is already completely developed from the very beginning. The resistance is concealed in a form peculiar to the patient's character.

Let us consider also whether the heterosexual incest material which was offered actually represents material that had broken through from the depth of the unconscious. The answer must be in the negative. If the contemporary function of the material currently offered is considered, it can often be ascertained that deeply repressed impulses, without any change whatever in the fact of repression, are temporarily drawn upon by the ego to ward off *other* contents. This very peculiar fact is not easily comprehensible in terms of depth psychology. It is a decided error of judgment to interpret such material. Such interpretations not only do not bear fruit, they thwart the maturation of this repressed content for future use. In theory, we can say that psychic contents can appear in the conscious system under one of two highly diverse conditions: borne by *native,* specifically libidinal affects which pertain to them, or by *foreign,* nonrelated interests. In the first instance, the internal pressure of dammed-up excitation forces the content into consciousness; in the second instance, the content is brought to the surface for purposes of defense. An illustration of this is freely flowing expressions of love as compared with those whose purpose is to cover up repressed hate, i.e., reactive testimonies of love.

The resistance had to be tackled, a task which was of course much more difficult in this case than if the resistance had been manifest. Though the meaning of the resistance could not be derived from the patient's communications, it was certainly possible to derive it from his demeanor and from the seemingly insignificant details of some of his dreams. From these it could be seen that, fearing to rebel against his father, he had masked his obstinacy and distrust with reactive love and by means of his obedience had spared himself anxiety.

The first interpretation of the resistance was made as early as the fifth day of the analysis, in connection with the following dream: *"My handwriting is sent to a graphologist for an expert evaluation. Answer: this man belongs in an insane asylum. Deep despair on the part of my mother. I want to make an end of my life. I wake up."*

He thought of Professor Freud in connection with the graphologist; the professor had told him, the patient added, that sicknesses such as the one from which he suffered could with "absolute certainty" be cured by analysis. I called his attention to the contradiction: since, in the dream, he thought of an insane asylum and was afraid, he was undoubtedly of the opinion that the analysis could not help him. He refused to admit this, insisting that he had full confidence in the efficacy of the analysis.

Until the end of the second month, he had many dreams, though few were capable of interpretation, and continued to talk about his mother. I allowed him to go on speaking, without interrupting or inciting him, and was careful not to miss any indication of distrust. After the first resistance interpretation, however, he masked his secret distrust even better, until finally he had the following dream:

"A crime, possibly a murder, has been committed. I have become involuntarily implicated in this crime. Fear of being detected and punished. One of my co-workers, by whose courage and determined nature I am impressed, is present. I am aware of his superiority."

I singled out only his fear of detection and related it to the analytic situation by telling him point-blank that his entire demeanor indicated that he was concealing something.

On the very next night, he had a longer dream confirming what I had said:

"*I have learned that there is a plan to commit a crime in our apartment. It is night and I am on the dark staircase. I know that my father is in the apartment. I want to go to his aid, but I am afraid of falling into the hands of the enemy. It occurs to me to notify the police. I have a roll of paper in my possession which contains all the details of the criminal plot. A disguise is necessary, otherwise the leader of the gang, who has planted many spies, will frustrate my undertaking. Putting on a large cape and a false beard, I leave the house stooped over like an old man. The chief of the adversaries stops me. He orders one of his subordinates to search me. The roll of paper is noticed by this man. I feel that all will be lost if he reads its contents. I try to appear as innocent as possible and tell him that they are notes having no meaning whatever. He says that he has to have a look anyhow. There is a moment of agonizing suspense; then, in desperation, I look for a weapon. I find a revolver in my pocket and pull the trigger. The man has disappeared, and I suddenly feel very strong. The chief of the adversaries has changed into a woman. I am overcome by a desire for this woman; I seize her, lift her up, and carry her into the house. I am filled with a pleasurable sensation and I wake up.*"

The entire incest motif appears at the end of the dream, but we have also, at the beginning, unmistakable allusions to his dissimulation in the analysis. I stressed only this element, again bearing in mind that a patient who is so self-sacrificing would first have to give up his deceptive attitude in the analysis before deeper interpretations could be given. But this time I went one step further in the interpretation of the resistance. I told him that not only was he distrustful of the analysis but he feigned to be the exact opposite. The patient became terribly excited at this and produced three different hysterical actions over a period of six sessions.

1. He reared up, his arms and legs thrashing in all directions, as he screamed, "Leave me alone, do you hear, don't come near me, I'll kill you, I'll pulverize you." This action often modulated imperceptibly into a different one:

2. He seized himself by the throat, produced a whining sound, and cried in a rattling voice, "Oh, leave me alone, please leave me alone, I won't do anything again."

3. He did not behave like one who has been violently attacked but like a girl who has been raped: "Leave me alone, leave me alone." This was spoken without sounds of strangulation and, whereas he had curled up in the earlier action, he now spread his legs wide apart.

During these six days, the flow of his communications faltered; he was definitely in a state of manifest resistance. He spoke continuously of his hereditary taint; between times he occasionally lapsed into that peculiar condition in which, as we described, he reenacted the above scenes. The strange thing was that, as soon as the action ceased, he went on speaking calmly as if nothing had happened. He merely remarked, "But this is a strange thing that is going on in me here, Doctor."

I now explained to him, without going into any details, that he was obviously enacting something for me which he must have experienced or at least fantasized sometime in his life. He was visibly delighted with this first explanation, and he enacted far more frequently from then on. It had to be admitted that my interpretation of the resistance had roused an important unconscious element, which now expressed itself in the form of these actions. But he was a long way from an analytic clarification of the actions; he was still making use of them as part of his resistance. He thought that he was being especially pleasing to me with his frequent reenactments. I learned later that, during his evening attacks of anxiety, he behaved as described in 2 and 3 above. Though the meaning of the actions was clear to me and I could have communicated it to him in connection with the murder dream, I persisted in the analysis of his character resistance, toward the understanding of which his reenactments had already contributed a great deal.

I was able to form the following picture of the *stratification of the contents of the character transference resistance.*

The *first action* represented the transference of the murderous impulses which he harbored toward the father (the deepest layer).

The *second action* portrayed the fear of the father because of the murderous impulses (intermediate layer).

The *third action* represented the concealed, crudely sexual content of his feminine attitude, the identification with the (raped) female, and at the same time the passive-feminine warding off of the murderous impulses.

Thus, *he surrendered himself to prevent the father from executing the punishment* (castration).

But even the actions which corresponded to the topmost layer could not be interpreted yet. The patient might have accepted every interpretation *pro forma* ("to be pleasing"), but none would have had therapeutic effect. For, between the unconscious material which he offered and the possibility of a deep understanding, there was the inhibiting factor of the *transferred feminine warding off of a similarly transferred fear of me,* and this fear, in turn, was related to a *hate impulse* and a distrust which were transferred from the father. In short, hate, fear, and distrust were concealed behind his submissive, confiding attitude, a wall against which every symptom interpretation would have been dashed to pieces.

So I continued to restrict myself to the interpretation of the intentions of his unconscious deceptions. I told him that he was now reenacting so frequently in an effort to win me over to his side; I added that this acting out was in fact very important. But we could not begin to understand it until he had grasped the meaning of his contemporary behavior. His opposition to the interpretation of the resistance weakened, but he still did not agree.

During the following night, he dreamed, for the first time *openly,* of his distrust of the analysis:

"Dissatisfied with the failure of the analysis thus far, I turn to Professor Freud. As a remedy for my illness, he gives me a long rod, which has the form of an ear-pick. I have a feeling of gratification."

In the analysis of this dream fragment, he admitted for the first time that he had been mildly distrustful of Freud's words, and then had been disagreeably surprised that he had been recommended to so young an analyst. I was struck by two things: first, this communication about his distrust was made to oblige me; second, he was suppressing something. I called his attention to both of these points. Sometime later I learned that he had cheated me in the matter of remuneration.

While his character resistance, his deceptive obedience and

submissiveness, was being consistently worked on, more and more material continued to flow automatically from all periods of his life, material about his childhood relationship to his mother and his relationship to young men, his childhood anxiety, the pleasure he had had in being sick as a child, etc. This was interpreted only insofar as it related to his character resistance.

He began to have more and more dreams relating to his distrust and to his suppressed sarcastic attitude. Among others, he had this dream several weeks later:

"To a remark by my father that he does not have any dreams, I reply that this is definitely not the case, that he evidently forgets his dreams, which, to a large extent, are prohibited fancies. He laughs derisively. I point out in excitement that this is the theory of no less a person than Professor Freud, but I feel ill at ease in saying this."

I explained that he had his father laugh derisively because he himself was afraid to, and I substantiated my claim by referring to the uneasiness which he experienced in the dream. This I interpreted as the sign of a bad conscience.

He accepted this interpretation, and during the next ten days the question of remuneration was discussed. It turned out that, during the preliminary talk before the beginning of the analysis, he had consciously lied to me, inasmuch as, without having been asked, he quoted a smaller sum than he actually had at his disposal. He had done this, he said, "to protect himself," that is, because he doubted my honesty. As is my custom, I had quoted him my usual fee and my minimum fee, and I had accepted him as a patient at the latter rate. However, he could afford to pay more, not only because he had a larger savings and a better income than he had said he had, but also because his father was covering half of the cost of the analysis.

c) *Linking the analysis of the contemporary material to the infantile*

In the discussion of the "money matter," which was always taken up in connection with his character resistance (i.e., his concealed fear and concealed distrust), he once committed a slip of the tongue. He said, "I wanted my savings in the bank to get *bigger!"* instead of saying that he wanted his savings to increase. Thus, he betrayed the relationship of money to the phallus and the relationship of *the fear of losing money to the fear for the phallus.* I did not point any of this out to him, nor did I analyze his slip of the tongue, for I did not want to interpret the castration anxiety as such too soon. I merely made a few remarks to the effect that his thrift must be related to his fear of catastrophes, that he evidently felt more secure when he had more money. He showed a good and genuine understanding of this explanation and produced confirmatory associations from his childhood: he had begun to save pennies at a very early age, and he could never forget the fact that his father had once taken his savings and spent it, without asking his permission. *For the first time he spontaneously expressed disapproval of the father;* on a conscious level, this disapproval related to the money, but unconsciously of course it was related to the castration danger. In this connection I also explained that, while his father had evidently acted in good faith, he had been unwise to suppress his son's sexuality to such an extent. The patient admitted that he himself had often puzzled about these things in secret but had never had the courage to oppose his father, who, as the patient assumed, had only the patient's best interest in mind. I still could not tell him that a deep guilt feeling and fear of the father were the driving forces of his obedience.

From now on, the analysis of the transference resistance went hand in hand with the analysis of the concealed rebellious attitude toward the father. Every element of the transference situation was related to the father and understood by the patient, while producing a wealth of *new material on his true attitude toward his father.* To be sure, everything which he brought forward was still strictly censored, still inaccessible to deep interpretation, but the analysis of his childhood had been duly begun. He no longer divulged the material for the purpose of escaping other things; now, because of the analysis of the character resistance, he was deeply shaken and the conviction had begun to grow in him that his relationship to his father was not what he had thought it was and that it had had a detrimental influence on his development.

Every time he came close to the murder fantasy, his fear grew stronger. He dreamed less frequently and had shorter dreams, but they were more compact and had a closer connection to the analytic situation. To a large extent, the material which had been previously *pushed forward* now faded into the background. What came forth from other psychic layers had a close connection to the father complex: his fantasy of being a woman and his incest desire. In the course of the next six weeks, undisguised castration dreams appeared for the first time, notwithstanding the fact that I had given no interpretations or suggestions along these lines.

1. *"I am lying in my bed, suddenly I am roused and notice that my former high-school principal, Mr. L, is sitting on me. I overpower him and get him under me, but he frees one of his hands and threatens my phallus."*

2. *My older brother climbs through a window in our hallway and gets into our apartment. He commands that someone bring him a sword because he wants to kill me. I beat him to it and I slay him."*

Thus, we see how the central father conflict emerges more and more clearly, *without* any special effort on my part, but solely as a result of correct resistance analysis.

Repeated stagnations occurred in this phase, and there were loud exclamations of distrust concerning the analysis. Now the resistance was tied up with the question of remuneration: he doubted my honesty. Doubt and distrust always cropped up when he came close to his antipathy toward the father, the castration complex, and the murder fantasy. True, the resistances sometimes masked themselves behind feminine devotedness, but it was no longer difficult to draw them out of their concealment.

After a five-week vacation, we resumed the analysis. Because his parents were away on a trip and he was afraid to stay alone, the patient, who had not taken a vacation, had lived with a friend during this time. There had been no letup in his anxiety states; on the contrary, they had become very severe after my departure. In this connection he told me that as a child he had always been afraid when his mother went away, that he had always wanted to have her with him and was angry with his father when he took her to the theater or to a concert.

Thus, it was fairly clear that, alongside the negative father transference, he had realized a strong, affectionate mother transference. Comparing the situation during the vacation with the situation in the months before my departure, the patient said he had felt quite well and secure with me. This shows that the mother transference had been present from the very beginning, alongside the reactive passive-feminine attitude. He himself deduced that he felt as sheltered with me as he felt with his mother. I did not go into this communication any further, for the affectionate mother transference was not causing any trouble then. It was still premature for an analysis of the mother relationship and, as a result of the interruption, his reactive-feminine father transference was again as strong as ever. He spoke in a meek and submissive manner, as he had done at the beginning of the analysis, and his communications were again focused upon his relationship to his mother.

On the third and fourth day after we had resumed the analysis, he had two dreams which contained *the incest desire,* his *infantile attitude toward his mother, and his womb fantasy.* In connection with these dreams, the patient remembered scenes which he had experienced with his mother in the bathroom. She had washed him until he was twelve years old, and he could never understand why his school friends teased him about this. Then he remembered his childhood fear of criminals who might force their way into the apartment and murder him. Thus, the analysis had already brought to the surface the infantile anxiety-hysteria, without any interpretations or suggestions along these lines. A deeper analysis of the dreams was avoided, because the remainder of his behavior was again marked by deceptive tendencies.

The dreams of the following night were even more distinct:

1. *"I am hiking through the Arnbrechtthal (the site of our summer vacations when I was five and six) with the intent of refreshing my childhood impressions. Suddenly, I come to a large place, to leave which one has to go through a castle. The doorkeeper, who is a woman, opens the gate for me and explains that I cannot visit the castle at this time. I reply that this is not my intention; I merely want to go through the castle to get into open country. The owner of the castle appears, an elderly lady who seeks to find favor with me flirtatiously. I want to withdraw, but suddenly notice that I have forgotten my key (which opens my*

*suitcase and also appears to be of great importance to me
otherwise) in the private coffer of the lady of the castle. Unpleasant feeling, which soon passes, however, for the coffer is
opened and the key is given back to me."*

2. *"I am called by my mother, who lives on the floor above
mine. I seize a newspaper, form it into a penis, and go to my
mother.*

3. *"I am in a large hall in the company of my cousin and her
mother. My cousin, who causes a tingle of delight in me, is clad
solely in a shift. I, too. I embrace her. It strikes me that I am
suddenly considerably smaller than she, for my penis is only
halfway up her thighs. I have an involuntary ejaculation and feel
terribly ashamed because I fear that this will cause stains on my
shift which might be easily noticed."*

He himself recognizes his mother in the cousin. With respect
to his nudity, he remembered that he never undressed in his attempts at sexual intercourse. He had a vague fear of doing so.

Thus, the incest fantasy (parts 2 and 3) and the castration
anxiety (part 1) were revealed quite clearly. Why did he censor
so little? In view of his barefaced diversions, I did not give any
interpretations, nor did I make any effort to get the patient to
produce further communications or associations. On the other
hand, I did not interrupt the patient's associations. I wanted this
subject to develop further and, most important of all, *I did not
want anything to happen until the next transference resistance
had emerged and had been eliminated.*

It wasn't long in making its appearance, and it was touched
off by a remark, which I had made involuntarily and against my
better judgment, relating to the second dream. I called his attention to the fact that once before he had had a dream about a
paper penis. It was a needless observation. Notwithstanding the
unambiguous manifest content of the dream, he reacted to it defensively in his usual way. He saw my point, he said, "but . . ."
On the night following this incident, he had a violent attack of
anxiety and had two dreams: the first related to his "money resistance" (transferred castration anxiety); the second revealed
the primal scene for the first time, which, when all was said and
done, motivated the money resistance.

1. *"I am standing in front of an amusement stand in the midst*

of a large crowd at the Prater. Suddenly, I notice that a man standing behind me is trying to purloin my wallet from my back pocket. I reach for my wallet and prevent the theft at the last moment.

2. *"I am riding in the rear car of a train in a part of the country south of Wörther See. At a curve I suddenly notice that another train is coming toward me on the single-line stretch of railroad. There seems to be no way of averting the catastrophe; to save myself, I jump from the platform."*

This dream made it quite clear that I had been right in not interpreting his incest dreams. A latent but strong resistance was in front of it. We also see that the resistance dream was intimately related to his infantile anxiety (fear of castration, fear of the primal scene). Between the ages of three and six, he had spent his summer vactions at Wörther See.

No associations came to mind with reference to the dream. Relating the man in the first dream to myself, I once again focused the discussion upon his entire attitude, his suppressed fear of me and his concealed distrust in the matter of remuneration, without, for the time being, touching upon the connection with the fear of catastrophes. In the second dream, I singled out only the "unavoidable catastrophe." We of course already knew, I told him, that for him money meant protection against catastrophes, and he feared I could deprive him of this protection.

He did not admit this immediately (indeed, he appeared to be shocked at the idea that he might conceive of me as a thief), but he did not reject it either. During the next three days, he produced dreams in which he assured me of his devotion and trust. I also appeared as his mother. There was also a new element: *his mother as a man;* she appeared in the dream as a Japanese. We didn't understand this element until many months later, when the meaning of his childhood fantasies about the Russo-Japanese War became clear. The Russian represented the father; the Japanese, because of his slight stature represented the mother. His mother, moreover, had worn Japanese pajamas at that time: *the mother in pants.* He made repeated slips, referring, e.g., to "mother's penis." Even his "school friend" who appeared in some dreams represented his cousin, who resembled his mother.

However, the clear incest dreams were resistance dreams, the intent of which was to conceal his fear of woman (having a penis).

From this point on—for about six weeks—the analysis followed a strange zigzag course: dreams and communications relating to his money resistance alternating with dreams which revealed his longing for the mother, the mother as a man, the dangerous father, and the most diverse variations of the castration anxiety. In my interpretations, I always proceeded from his money resistance (= castration anxiety) and, using this as a base, continued to deepen the analysis of the infantile situation. This was quite easy since *the infantile material was always intimately connected with the transference situation.* Of course all the childhood fears and desires which now emerged did not appear in the transference, which was brought to a head more and more every day. (At this time, the salient feature of the transference was the castration anxiety.) Only the core of the infantile situation had appeared in the transference resistance. Since I had a secure feeling that the analysis was proceeding correctly, I had no misgivings about reserving the deep content interpretations for the proper time. Instead, I consistently worked on his fear of me by always relating it to his fear of his father.

It was my intention, by working through and eliminating as thoroughly as possible the transferred father resistance, to penetrate to his childhood incest fantasies. In this way I would receive them relatively free of resistance and be able to interpret them. Thus, I hoped to prevent the wasting of my main interpretations. For the time being, therefore, I made no effort to interpret the incest material which flowed ever more clearly and compactly from the unconscious.

At the beginning of this phase, the topographical stratification of the resistance and of the material was as follows:

1. The castration anxiety, in the form of his money resistance, occupied the top layer.

2. He continually sought to ward this off by means of his feminine behavior toward me; but this was no longer so easy for him as it had been in the beginning.

3. The feminine behavior concealed a sadistic-aggressive attitude toward me (toward his father) and was accompanied by

4. a deep affectionate attachment to the mother, which was also transferred to me.

5. Connected with this ambivalent behavior, which was concentrated in the transference resistance, were the incest desires, the fear of masturbation, his longing for the womb, and the great fear stemming from the primal scene, all of which appeared in his dreams but were not interpreted. Only his intent to deceive and its motives, the fear of an antipathy toward the father, were interpreted.

This situation, which of course had been latently present from the very beginning but had not become concentrated in all points until now (above all, in the transference of the castration anxiety), developed in the following way.

In the fifth month of the analysis he had his first incestuous masturbation anxiety dream:

"I am in a room. A young woman with a round face is sitting at a piano. I see only the upper part of her body, for the piano conceals the rest of her body. I hear the voice of my analyst beside me: 'You see, this is the cause of your neurosis.' I feel myself being drawn closer to the woman, am suddenly overwhelmed by fear and scream loudly."

On the previous day, in reference to a dream, I had told him, "You see, this is one of the causes of your neurosis," by which I meant his childish behavior, his demand to be loved and cared for. As if the patient had known the true cause of his neurosis, he connected this "statement of the preceding day" with his repressed *masturbation anxiety*. The masturbation idea was again associated with the incest idea. He woke up in a state of fear. There was a good reason for the fact that the lower part of the woman's body was concealed. (Representation of the aversion to the female genital.)

However, since his resistance was still at its height and nothing occurred to him with respect to the dream, I did not pursue the subject.

The patient subsequently had a dream in which a "naked family," father, mother, and child, were clasped by an enormous snake.

Another dream ran as follows:

1. *"I am lying in bed; my analyst is sitting beside me. He says to me: 'Now I will show you the cause of your neurosis.' I cry out in fear (not only fear, perhaps with a trace of voluptuousness) and almost lose consciousness. He repeats that he will analyze me in our bathroom. I am pleasantly taken with this idea. It is dark as we open the door to the bathroom."*

2. *"I am walking with my mother through a woods. I notice that we are being pursued by a robber. I notice a revolver in my mother's dress and I take it into my possession to shoot down the robber when he gets closer. Walking at a rapid pace, we reach an inn. The robber is hard on our heels as we climb up the steps. I fire a shot at him. However, the bullet is transformed into a banknote. We are safe for the time being, but I am not sure whether the robber, who is sitting in the lobby, still has evil intentions. To put him in a good humor, I give him another banknote."*

That I made the right move in not going into these clear dreams was confirmed by the fact that the patient, who already had sufficient analytic knowledge, made no reference whatever to the figure of the robber. Nor was he able to come up with any associations. Either he said nothing or he spoke excitedly about the "large sums of money" which he had to pay and about his doubts as to whether the analysis would help him, etc.

There could be no doubt, of course, that this resistance was also directed against the discussion of the incest material, but an interpretation to this effect would not have served any purpose. I had to wait for a suitable opportunity to interpret his money anxiety as phallus anxiety.

In the first part of the robber dream it is said that I am going to analyze him in the bathroom. It came out later that he felt safest in the bathroom when he masturbated. In the second part of the dream, I (the father) appeared as a robber (= castrator). Thus, *his contemporary resistance* (distrust due to money) *was intimately related to the old masturbation anxiety* (castration anxiety).

With respect to the second part of the dream, I told him that he was afraid I might hurt him, that I might endanger his life. Unconsciously, however, it was his father he was afraid of. After some opposition, he accepted this interpretation and, in this connection, he himself began to discuss his exaggerated friendliness. He required very little help in this. He recognized the meaning of his obsequious attitude toward his boss as an expression of a vague fear of being blamed for something. Nor were other people to notice that he sneered at them in secret. The more he succeeded in objectifying and unmasking his character, the more free and more open he became, both in and outside the analysis. Already he ventured to offer criticism and began to be ashamed of his former mode of behavior. *For the first time he began to sense the neurotic character trait as something alien.* This, however, also marked the first success of the character analysis: *the character had been analyzed.*

The money resistance continued. *Without the least bit of help from me,* the deepest layer of material, the *fear for his penis,* began to appear in his dreams more and more clearly in connection with *the primal scene.*

This fact has to be especially emphasized: when the analysis of the character resistance is carried out in a systematic and consistent manner, it is not necessary to make a special effort to obtain the infantile material pertaining to it. It emerges of its own accord, always more clearly and always more closely connected with the contemporary resistance, provided, naturally, that this process has not been disturbed by premature interpretations of the childhood material. The less effort that is made to penetrate to the childhood sphere and the more accurately the contemporary resistance material is worked through, the more rapidly the infantile material is reached.

This was again proven when he dreamed, after the interpretation, that he was afraid of being hurt. He dreamed that he was walking past a chicken farm and saw how a chicken was killed. A woman also lay stretched out on the ground, and another woman stuck a large fork into her a number of times. Then he embraced one of his female co-workers; his *phallus was halfway up her thighs* and he had an involuntary ejaculation.

Since his money resistance had grown somewhat weaker, an attempt was made to analyze this dream. With respect to the chicken farm, he was now able to remember that as a child he had often witnessed animals in the act of copulation during his summer vacations in the country. We had no way of knowing at this time what meaning the detail "summer in the country" had. He identified the first woman as his mother, but had no way of explaining her position in the dream.

However, he was able to tell us more about the involuntary ejaculation. He was convinced that he appeared as a child in the dream. He remembered that he liked to and was in the habit of pressing himself against women until he ejaculated involuntarily.

It appeared to me to be a good sign that this intelligent patient did not offer an interpretation, despite the fact that everything lay before him in a rather transparent state. If, *prior* to the analysis of his resistances, I had interpreted symbols or essential contents of the unconscious, he would have immediately accepted these interpretations for reasons of resistance, and we would have leaped from one chaotic situation into another.

Through my interpretation of his fear of being injured, the analysis of his character had been brought into full swing. For days on end there was no trace of his money resistance; he discussed his infantile behavior at great length, and produced one example after another of his "cowardly" and "furtive" way of doing things, which now he wholeheartedly condemned. I made an effort to persuade him that his father's influence had been chiefly responsible for this. Here, however, I encountered the most passionate opposition. *He still lacked the courage to speak critically of his father.*

Sometime after this, he again dreamed about that subject behind which I surmised the primal scene:

"I am standing along the shore of the ocean. A number of large polar bears are romping about in the water. Suddenly they become restless. I see the back of a gigantic fish emerging. The fish pursues one of the polar bears, upon which he inflicts injuries by terrible bites. Finally, the fish turns away from the mortally wounded bear. However, the fish itself has been severely wounded; a stream of blood shoots out of its gills as it struggles to breathe."

I call his attention to the fact that his dreams always have a cruel character. He responded to this and went on for several sessions to tell about the sexual fantasies he had while masturbating and the cruel acts he had indulged in until the age of puberty. I had him write them down after they had been analyzed.

Almost all of them were determined by the "sadistic conception of the sexual act."

" (Three to five years old). At the *summer resort* I accidentally witness how pigs are slaughtered. I hear the squealing of the animals and see the blood spurting from their bodies, which have a white gleam in the darkness. I feel a deep sensation of pleasure.

" (Four to six years old). The idea of slaughtering animals, especially horses, evokes a sensation of deep pleasure in me.

" (Five to eleven years old). I very much like to play with tin soldiers. I stage battles which always end up in hand-to-hand fighting. In this, I press the bodies of the soldiers against one another. The soldiers which I favor overpower the enemy.

" (Six to twelve years old). I press two ants together in such a way that they fasten upon one another with their nippers. Thus locked into one another, these two insects are forced to fight to the death. I also engineer battles between two different colonies of ants by sprinkling sugar in the area between their hills. This lures the insects from their hostile camps and causes them to engage in regular battles. It also affords me pleasure to imprison a wasp and a fly in a water glass. After a while, the wasp pounces upon the fly and bites off its wings, legs, and head, in that order.

" (Twelve to fourteen years old). I keep a terrarium and like to observe how the males and the females engage in the sexual act. I like to observe the same thing in the chicken yard; it also gives me pleasure to see the stronger cocks drive away the weaker ones.

" (Eight to sixteen years old). I like to scuffle with the housemaid. In later years, I usually lifted the girls up, carried them to a bed, and threw them down on it.

" (Five to twelve years old). I like to play with trains. I run my little trains throughout the apartment, whereby tunnels improvised out of boxes, stools, etc., are gone through. In this, I also attempt to imitate the sound of the locomotive as it builds up steam and picks up speed.

"(Fifteen years old; masturbation fantasies). I am always an onlooker. The woman defends herself against the man, who, in many instances, is considerably smaller than she is. After a struggle of some duration, the woman is overpowered. Brutally, the man clutches at her breasts, thighs, or hips. *Neither the male nor female genital nor the sexual act itself is ever part of the fantasy.* At the moment that the woman ceases to offer resistance, I have an orgasm."

The two major aspects of the situation at this time were: (1) he was ashamed of his cowardice; (2) he remembered his past sadism. The analysis of the fantasies and acts which are summarized above lasted until the end of the treatment. He became much freer in the analysis, bolder and more aggressive; but his behavior was still characterized by fear. His states of anxiety were not as frequent, but they always reappeared with the money resistance.

Here again we can be assured that the chief object in producing the genital-incest material was to conceal the infantile sadism, even though, at the same time, it represented an attempt to move toward a genital-object cathexis. But his genital strivings were imbued with sadism and, economically, it was important to extract them from their entanglement with the sadistic impulses.

At the beginning of the sixth month of the analysis, the first opportunity presented itself to interpret his *fear for the penis*. It was in connection with the following dream:

1. *"I am lying on a sofa in an open field (at the summer resort!). One of the girls whom I know comes toward me and lies on top of me. I get her under me and attempt to have intercourse. I get an erection, but I notice that my phallus is too short to complete the sexual act. I am very sad about this.*

2. *"I am reading a drama. The characters: three Japanese— father, mother, and a four-year-old child. I sense that this play will have a tragic ending. I am deeply moved by the role of the child."*

For the first time, an attempt to have intercourse appeared as a manifest part of a dream. The second part, which alludes to the primal scene (four years old), was not analyzed. In continuously discussing his cowardice and timidity, he himself began to speak about his penis. I took this opportunity to point out that his fear of being injured and cheated, etc., referred in actual fact to his genital. Why and of whom he was afraid were not yet discussed. Nor was any effort made to interpret the real meaning of the fear. The explanation seemed plausible to him, but now he fell into the clutches of a resistance which lasted for six weeks and *was based on a passive-feminine homosexual defense against the castration anxiety.*

It was the following which told me that he was in a fresh state of resistance: he did not rebel openly, expressed no doubt, but again became excessively polite, docile, and obedient. His dreams, which had become shorter, clearer, and less frequent during the analysis of the previous resistance, were again as they had been at the beginning—long and confused. His states of anxiety were again very prevalent and intense. But he did not voice any doubts about the analysis. The hereditary idea also cropped up again, and in this connection his doubts about the analysis were expressed in a veiled manner. As he had done at the beginning of the analysis, he again enacted a raped woman. The passive-homosexual attitude was also dominant in his dreams. He no longer had any dreams involving coitus or an involuntary ejaculation. Hence, we see that, notwithstanding the advanced stage of the analysis of his character, the old character resistance immediately assumed its full force when a new layer of his unconscious—this time the most crucial layer for his character, i.e., the castration anxiety—moved into the forefront of the analysis.

Accordingly, the analysis of the new resistance did not go into the phallus anxiety, the point at which the resistance had been aroused. Instead, I again referred to his attitude as a whole. Throughout six full weeks the analysis was taken up almost exclusively with the consistent interpretation of his behavior as a defense against danger. Every detail of his conduct was examined from this perspective and impressed upon him again and again, gradually moving forward to the central motive of his behavior, the phallus anxiety.

The patient made repeated efforts to slip away from me through "analytic sacrifices" of infantile material, but I consistently interpreted the meaning of this procedure also. Gradually, the situation came to a head. He felt like a woman toward me, told me so, and added that he also sensed sexual excitations in the region of the perineum. I explained the nature of this transference phenomenon. He construed my attempt to explain his behavior to him as a reproach, *felt guilty, and wanted to expiate*

his guilt through feminine devotion. For the time being, I did not
enter into the deeper meaning of this behavior, namely that he
identified with the mother because he was afraid to be the man
(i.e., the father).

Among other things, he now produced the following confirmatory dream:

*"I meet a young chap at the Prater and get into a conversation
with him. He appears to misconstrue one of my statements and
remarks that he is willing to give himself to me. In the meantime,
we have reached my apartment; the young man lies down in my
father's bed. I find his underwear very distasteful."*

In the analysis of this dream, I could again trace the feminine
transference back to the father. In association with this dream,
he remembered that there had been a time in his masturbation
fantasies when he had had the desire to be a woman and also
had had fantasies in which he was a woman. The "dirty underwear" led to the analysis of the anal activities and habits (toilet
ceremonies) which related to his behavior. Another character
trait, his punctiliousness, was also clarified.

Finally, the resistance had been resolved; in the process, both
its old form and its erogenous, anal basis had been discussed.
Now I went a step further in the interpretation of his character: I
explained the connection between his submissive attitude and his
"female fantasy," telling him that he behaved in a feminine, i.e.,
exaggeratedly faithful and devoted, manner because he was afraid
to be a man. And I added that the analysis would have to go into
the reasons for his fear to be a man (in his sense of the word:
brave, open, honest, proud).

Almost as an answer to this, he produced a short dream in
which the castration anxiety and the primal scene were again
conspicuous:

"I am at my cousin's, an attractive young woman [the mother,
W.R.]. *Suddenly I have the sensation that I am my own grandfather. I am gripped by an oppressive despondency. At the same
time I somehow have the feeling that I am the center of a stellar
system and that planets are revolving around me. At the same
time (still in the dream) I suppress my fear and am annoyed at
my weakness."*

The most important detail of this incest dream is his appearance in it as *his own grandfather*. We were immediately agreed that his fear of having a hereditary taint played an important role here. It was clear that, identifying himself with the father, he fantasized being his own procreator, i.e., having intercourse with his mother; but this was not discussed until later.

He was of the opinion that the planetary system was an allusion to his egotism, i.e., "everything revolves around me." I surmised that there was something deeper at the bottom of this idea, namely the primal scene, but I made no mention of it.

After the Christmas vacation, he went on for several days speaking almost exclusively about his egotism, about his desire to be a child who is loved by everyone—at the same time realizing that he himself neither wanted to love nor was able to love.

I showed him the connection between his egotism and his fear for his adored ego and his penis,[7] whereupon he had the following dream, giving me, as it were, a glimpse of the infantile groundwork:

1. *"I am completely nude and regard my penis, which is bleeding at the tip. Two girls are walking away; I am sad because I assume that they will hold me in contempt due to the smallness of my penis.*

2. *"I am smoking a cigarette with a holder. I remove the holder and notice with astonishment that it is a cigar holder. As I put the cigarette back into my mouth, the mouthpiece breaks off. I feel disturbed."*

Thus, without my having done anything, the castration idea began to assume definite forms. Now he interpreted the dreams without my assistance, and he produced an abundance of material on his aversion to the female genital and on his fear of touching his penis with his hand and of having someone else touch it. The second dream is clearly a matter of an oral fantasy (cigar holder). It occurred to him that he desired everything about a woman *(most of all the breast)* except the genital, and in this way he came to speak of his oral fixation on the mother.

I explained to him that mere awareness of the genital anxiety

---

[7] In view of the total picture at this point, perhaps some psychologists will understand why we analysts cannot acknowledge the inferiority complex as an absolute agent: because the real problem and the real work begin precisely at that point at which it ceases for Alfred Adler.

was not much help. He had to find out why he had this anxiety. After this explanation, he again dreamed about the primal scene, not realizing that he had entered into my question:

"I am behind the last car of a standing train right at a fork in the tracks. A second train travels past and I am sandwiched between the two trains."

Before continuing the description of the analysis itself, I must mention here that, in the seventh month of the treatment, after the dissolution of his passive-homosexual resistance, the patient made a courageous effort to involve himself with women. I had no knowledge of this whatever—he told me about it later, in passing. He followed a girl and carried out his intentions in this way: in the park he pressed himself against her, had a strong erection, and an involuntary ejaculation. The anxiety states gradually ceased. It did not occur to him to engage in sexual intercourse. I called his attention to this and told him that he was evidently afraid to have coitus. He declined to admit this, using the lack of opportunity as an excuse. Finally, however, he too was struck by the infantile nature of his sexual activity. Naturally, he had dreams in which this kind of sexual activity was depicted. Now he remembered that as a child he had pressed himself against his mother in this same way.

The incest theme with which, in the hope of diverting me, he had begun the analysis, reappeared, but this time it was fairly free of resistance—at any rate, free of secondary motives. Thus, there was a parallel between the analysis of his demeanor during the analytic session and the analysis of his outside experiences.

Again and again he refused to accept the interpretation that he had really desired his mother. In the course of seven months, the material which he had produced in confirmation of this desire was so clear, the connections—as he himself admitted— were so evident, that I made no effort to persuade him, but began, instead, to analyze why he was afraid to avow this desire.

These questions had been simultaneously discussed in connection with his penis anxiety, and now we had two problems to solve:

1. *What was the etiology of the castration anxiety?*

2. *Why, notwithstanding conscious agreement, did he refuse to accept the sensuous incest love?*

From now on, the analysis advanced rapidly in the direction of the primal scene. This phase began with the following dream: *"I am in the hall of a royal palace where the king and his retinue are gathered. I ridicule the king. His attendants pounce upon me. I am thrown down and feel that mortal cuts are inflicted upon me. My corpse is carried away. Suddenly, it seems as if I were still alive, but I keep still so as not to undeceive the two grave-diggers, who take me for dead. A thin layer of earth lies on top of me, and breathing becomes difficult. I make a movement which catches the eyes of the gravediggers. I keep myself from being detected by not moving. Somewhat later I am liberated. Once again I force my way into the royal palace, a terrible weapon in each hand, perhaps thunderbolts. I kill everyone who gets in my way."*

It seemed to him that the idea of the gravediggers must have something to do with his fear of catastrophes, and now I was able to show him that these two fears, the hereditary idea and the penis anxiety, related to one and the same thing. It was very likely, I added, that the dream reproduced the childhood scene from which the penis anxiety originated.

With respect to the dream, it struck him that he pretended to be "dead," that he remained still in order not to be detected. Then, he recalled that, in his masturbation fantasies, he was usually the onlooker. And he himself posed the question whether he might have witnessed "such a thing" between his parents. He immediately rejected this possibility, however, arguing that he had never slept in his parents' bedroom. Naturally, this greatly disappointed me, for, on the basis of his dream material, I was convinced that he had actually witnessed the primal scene.

I, too, pointed out the inconsistency and asserted that one must not allow oneself to be put off so easily—the analysis would clarify the situation in due course. In the very same session, the patient felt fairly sure that he must have seen a certain maid together with her friend. Then it occurred to him that there were two other occasions when he might have eavesdropped on his parents. He remembered that, when guests were visiting, his bed was pushed into his parents' bedroom. *On summer holidays in the country,* moreover, he had slept in the same room with his parents until he was of school age. There was also the representation of the primal scene through the killing of chickens (rural scene), and the many dreams about Ossiacher See and Wörther See, where he had often spent his summer vacations.

In this connection, he again spoke about his acting out at the beginning of the analysis and about the states of nocturnal anxiety which he had experienced in childhood. One of the details of this anxiety was clarified here. He was afraid of a white female figure emerging from between the curtains. Now he remembered that, when he screamed at nights, his mother used to come to his bed in her nightgown. Unfortunately, the element, "someone behind the curtains," was never clarified.

Evidently, however, we had ventured too far into forbidden territory in this session. That night, he had a resistance dream whose content was clearly derisive:

"I am standing on a pier and am on the verge of boarding a steamship, as the companion, it turns out, of a mental patient. Suddenly the whole operation appears to me to be a spectacle in which I have been assigned a definite role. On the narrow plank which leads from the pier to the steamer, I have to repeat the same thing three times—which I do."

He himself interpreted the boarding of the steamer as a desire for coitus, but I directed his attention to an element of the dream which had greater contemporary importance, namely the "play acting." His having to repeat the same thing three times was a mocking allusion to my consistent interpretations. He admitted that he had often been quietly amused at my efforts. It also occurred to him that he had in mind to call on a woman and to engage in the sexual act three times—"to please me," I told him. But I also explained to him that this resistance had a deeper content, namely the warding off of his coital intentions out of fear of the sexual act.

On the following night, he again had the two complementary dreams: homosexual surrender and coital anxiety.

1. *"I meet a young chap on the street who belongs to the lower classes, but who has a healthy, vigorous appearance. I have the feeling that he is physically stronger than I, and I endeavor to gain his favor.*

2. *"I go on a ski trip with the husband of one of my cousins. We are in a narrow pass which drops down precipitately. I ex-*

amine the snow and find it sticky. I remark that the terrain is not very suitable for skiing—one would often have to take a spill on going down. As we continue our trip, we come to a road which runs along the declivity of a mountain. On a sharp curve, I lose a ski, which falls over the precipice."

He did not, however, go into this dream. Instead he took up the question of "remuneration"; he had to pay so much and had no idea whether it would do him any good. He was very dissatisfied, was again afraid—and more of the same.

It was no difficult matter now to show him the connection between the money resistance and the nonresolved coitus anxiety and genital anxiety—and to overcome this resistance. He could also be shown the deeper intentions of his feminine surrender: *when he approached a woman, he became afraid of the consequences and became a woman himself, i.e., became homosexual and passive in character.* As a matter of fact, he understood very well that he had made himself into a woman, but he was at a loss to explain why and what he was afraid of. It was clear to him that he was afraid of sexual intercourse. But, then, what could possibly happen to him?

Now he devoted his full attention to this question. Instead of discussing his fear of the father, however, he talked about his fear of women. In the anxiety-hysteria of his childhood, the woman was also an object to be feared. From first to last, instead of a woman's genital, he spoke of a "woman's penis." Until the age of puberty he had believed that the woman was made in the same way as the man. He himself was able to see a connection between this idea and the primal scene, the reality of which he was now firmly convinced.

At the end of the seventh month of the analysis, he had a dream in which he saw how a girl lifted her skirt so that her underwear was visible. He turned away as someone "who sees something which he isn't supposed to see." Now I felt that the time had come to tell him that he was afraid of the female genitalia because it looked like an incision, a wound. On seeing it for the first time, he must have been terribly shocked. He found my explanation plausible, for his feelings toward the female genitalia were a mixture of disgust and antipathy; fear was aroused in him. He had no recollection of a real incident.

Now the situation was this: whereas the central element of his symptoms, the castration anxiety, had been worked through, it was still unresolved in its ultimate and deepest meaning because the more intimate, individual connections to the primal scene were missing; these connections had been disclosed but not analytically assimilated.

Another time, in a resistance-free period, as we were discussing these relationships and not achieving any tangible results, the patient mumbled to himself, "I must have been caught once." Upon closer questioning, he said that he had a feeling that he had once done something wrong in a sneaky way and had been caught in the act.

Now the patient remembered that, even as a small boy, he had secretly rebelled against his father. He had ridiculed and made faces behind his father's back, while feigning obedience to his face. But this rebellion against the father had ceased completely in puberty. (Complete repression of the hatred of the father out of fear of the father.)

Even the hereditary-taint idea turned out to be a severe reproach against the father. The complaint, *"I have a hereditary taint,"* meant: *"My father handicapped me in giving me birth."* The analysis of the fantasies about the primal scene revealed that the patient fancied himself in the womb while his father was having intercourse with his mother. The idea of being injured in the genitalia combined with the womb fantasy to form the notion that *he had been castrated by the father in the womb.*

We can be brief in our description of the remainder of the analysis. It was relatively free of resistance and was clearly divided into two parts.

The first part was taken up with the working through of his childhood masturbation fantasies and the masturbation anxiety. For some time, his castration anxiety was anchored in the fear of (or aversion to) the female genitalia. The "incision," the "wound," was not an easily refutable proof of the feasibility of castration. Finally, the patient plucked up enough courage to masturbate, whereupon the anxiety states disappeared completely, a proof that the attacks of anxiety originated from the libido stasis and not from the castration anxiety, for this anxiety continued. By working through additional infantile material, we finally succeeded in subduing the castration anxiety to such an extent as to enable him to attempt intercourse, which, as far as his erection was concerned, succeeded well. Further sexual experiences with women brought out two disturbances: he was orgastically impotent, i.e., he derived less sensual pleasure from coitus than he did from masturbation; and he had an indifferent, contemptuous attitude toward the woman. There was still a cleavage in the sexual impulse between tenderness and sensuality.

The second phase was taken up with the analysis of his orgastic impotence and his infantile narcissism. As had always been his habit, he wanted everything from the woman, from the mother, without having to give anything in return. With great understanding and even greater eagerness, the patient himself took the initiative in dealing with his disturbances. He objectified his narcissism, realized that it was a burden, and finally overcame it when the final remnant of his castration anxiety, which was anchored in his impotence, had been resolved analytically. He was *afraid of the orgasm;* he thought the excitement it produced was harmful.

The following dream was the projection of this fear:

"I am visiting an art gallery. One picture catches my eye—it is entitled 'Inebriated Tom.' It is a painting of a young handsome English soldier in the mountains. There is a storm. It appears that he has lost his way; a skeleton hand has taken hold of his arm and appears to be leading him away, evidently a symbol that he is going to his doom. A painting 'Difficult Profession': also in the mountains, a man and a small boy plunge down an incline; at the same time, a rucksack empties its contents. The boy is surrounded by a whitish pap."

The plunge represents the orgasm,[8] the whitish pap the sperm. The patient discussed the anxiety which, in puberty, he experienced when he ejaculated and when he had an orgasm. His sadistic fantasies with regard to women were also thoroughly worked through. A few months later—it was then summer—he began a liaison with a young girl; the disturbances were considerably milder.

[8] Cf. my discussion of the symbolism of the orgasm in *The Function of the Orgasm.*

The resolution of the transference did not offer any difficulties, because it had been systematically dealt with from the very beginning, both in its negative and in its positive aspects. He was happy to leave the analysis and was full of hope for the future.

I saw the patient five times in the course of the next five years, full of health in both mind and body. His timidity and attacks of anxiety had wholly disappeared. He described himself as completely cured and expressed his satisfaction that his personality had been cleansed of its servile and underhanded traits. Now he was able to face all difficulties courageously. His potency had increased since the termination of the analysis.

4. SUMMARY

Having arrived at the conclusion of our report, we become keenly aware of the inadequacies of language to depict analytic processes. Notwithstanding these linguistic difficulties, we want to outline at least the most salient features of character analysis in the hope of improving our understanding of it. Hence, let us summarize:

1. Our patient is the prototype of the passive-feminine character who, regardless of what symptoms cause him to seek analytic help, always confronts us with the same kind of character resistance. He also offers us a typical example of the mechanism of the latent negative transference.

2. In terms of technique, the analysis of the passive-feminine character resistance (i.e., deception through excessive friendliness and submissive demeanor) was given priority. The result was that the infantile material became manifest in the transference neurosis according to its own inner logic. This prevented the patient from delving into his unconscious in a solely intellectual way, that is, to satisfy his feminine devotion ("to be obliging"), which would have had no therapeutic effect.

3. It becomes clear from this report that, if the character resistance is systematically and consistently stressed and if premature interpretations are avoided, the germane infantile material emerges *of itself* ever more clearly and distinctly. This ensures that the content and symptom interpretations which follow will be irrefutable and therapeutically effective.

4. The case history showed that the character resistance can be taken up as soon as its contemporary meaning and purpose

have been grasped. It was not necessary to have a knowledge of the infantile material pertaining to it. By *stressing* and interpreting its contemporary meaning, we were able to draw out the corresponding infantile material, without having to interpret symptoms or have preconceptions. *The dissolution of the character resistance* began with the establishment of contact with the infantile material. The subsequent symptom interpretations took place free of resistance, with the patient turning his full attention to the analysis. Typically, therefore, the analysis of the resistance fell into two parts: (a) *stressing* of the resistance's form and of its contemporary meaning; (b) its *dissolution* with the help of the infantile material drawn to the surface by that emphasis. The difference between a character resistance and an ordinary resistance was shown here in that the former was manifested in his politeness and submissiveness, whereas the latter was manifested in simple doubting and distrusting of the analysis. Only the former attitudes were a part of his character and constituted the *form* in which his distrust was expressed.

5. Through consistent interpretation of the latent negative transference, the repressed and masked aggressiveness against the analyst, superiors, and father was liberated from repression, whereby the passive-feminine attitude, which of course was merely a reaction formation against the repressed aggressiveness, disappeared.

6. Since the repression of the aggressiveness toward the father also entailed the repression of the phallic libido toward women, the active-masculine genital strivings returned with the aggressiveness in the process of analytic dissolution *(cure of impotence)*.

7. As the aggressiveness became conscious, the timidity which was a part of his character vanished, along with the castration anxiety. And the attacks of anxiety left off when he ceased to live in abstinence. Through the orgastic elimination of the actual anxiety, the "core of the neurosis" was also finally eliminated.

Finally, it is my hope that by describing a number of cases, I have shattered the opinion held by my opponents, namely that I approach each and every case with a "fixed scheme." Hopefully, the point of view which I have advocated for years, that there is only *one* technique for each case and that this technique has to be deduced from the structure of the case and applied to it, will have become clear from the foregoing representation.

CHAPTER V

INDICATIONS AND DANGERS OF CHARACTER ANALYSIS

The transitions from unsystematic and inconsistent analysis to systematic character analysis—which, compared to the former, resembles a well-considered psychic operation—are fluid and so manifold that it is impossible to take them all in at once. Yet it is possible to set up a number of criteria for determining when character analysis is indicated.

In view of the fact that violent affects are aroused by the character-analytic loosening of the narcissistic defense mechanism and that the patient is also temporarily reduced to a more or less helpless state, character analysis can be applied without ill effects only by therapists who have already mastered the analytic technique. Primarily, this means those therapists who are capable of handling the transference reactions. Hence, it is not to be recommended for beginners.[1] The patient's temporary helplessness is due to the isolation of the infantile neurosis from the character, and as a consequence the neurosis becomes fully reactivated. Of course it is reactivated even without systematic character analysis. In this case, however, since the armoring remains

---

[1] Footnote, 1945: The reader will understand that I had to be cautious in the beginning of my character-analytic research, i.e., some nineteen years ago. My warning that only experienced analysts should make use of the character-analytic method was objected to even at that time on the grounds that, if it was superior to symptom analysis, even beginners should learn to practice it. Today there is no longer any need for such caution. We now have a vast fund of character-analytic experience at our disposal. Hence, the technique can be taught and even recommended to beginners of symptom analysis. The restrictions on its use which are suggested in the following text are no longer necessary. It is not only that character analysis may be used—it *must* be used in *every* case of psychoneurosis if one wants to destroy the *character-neurotic reaction basis*. A much more difficult question is whether character analysis can be carried out without orgone therapy.

relatively untouched, the affective reactions are weaker and therefore easier to control. If the structure of the case is thoroughly grasped at the beginning, there is no danger in applying character analysis. With the exception of a hopeless case of acute depression which I took on many years ago, I have not had any suicides in my practice thus far. In this instance, the patient broke off the treatment after two or three sessions, before I was able to take any decisive measures. As I examine my experiences as critically as possible, the picture which ensues is paradoxical only in appearance. Since I began to use character analysis, i.e., about eight years ago, I have lost only three cases due to precipitate flight. Before that, patients ran away far more frequently. This is explained by the fact that, when the negative and narcissistic reactions are immediately subjected to analysis, an escape is usually made impossible—though the burden on the patient is greater.

Character analysis is applicable in every case, but its use is not indicated in every case. There are circumstances, indeed, which strictly forbid its application. Let us begin by surveying cases in which it is indicated. They are all determined by the extent of the encrustation of the character, that is, by the degree and intensity of the neurotic reactions which have become chronic and have been incorporated into the ego. Character analysis is always indicated in cases of compulsive neuroses, especially in those which are marked not by clearly defined symptoms but by a general debility of the functions, in those cases in which the character traits constitute not only the object of but also the greatest hindrance to the treatment. Likewise, it is always indicated in cases of phallic-narcissistic characters (ordinarily, these patients are wont to ridicule every analytic effort), and in moral insanity, impulsive characters and pseudologia phantastica. In schizoid or early schizophrenic patients, an extremely cautious but very consistent character analysis is the precondition for the avoidance of premature and uncontrollable emotional breakthroughs, for it anneals the ego functions before the deep layers of the unconscious are activated.

In cases of acute and extreme anxiety-hysteria, it would be wrong to begin with a consistent analysis of the ego defense in the way described above, for the id impulses in these cases are in an acute state of agitation at a time when the ego is not strong enough to shut itself off against them, to bind the free-floating energies. Extreme and acute anxiety is of course an indication that the armor has been broken through along a wide front, thus making superfluous immediate work on the character. In later stages of the analysis, when the anxiety has given way to a strong tie to the analyst and the first signs of reactions of disappointment have become noticeable, character-analytic work cannot be dispensed with; but it is not the main task in the initial stages of the treatment.

In cases of melancholia and manic-depressives, the application or nonapplication of character analysis will depend upon whether an acute exacerbation, e.g., strong suicidal impulses or acute anxiety, exists; or whether psychic apathy is the dominant trait. Another important factor will certainly be the amount of genital object-relationship which is still present. In the case of apathetic forms, cautious but thorough character-analytic work on the ego defense (repressed aggression!) is indispensable if one wants to avoid interminable analyses.

It goes without saying that the loosening of the armor can always be carried out by degrees, depending not only on the individual case but also on the individual situation. There are many different ways of loosening the armor by degrees: the intensity and consistency of the interpretation can be increased or decreased according to the tenacity of the resistance; the depth at which the resistance is interpreted can be raised or deepened; the negative or positive aspect of the transference can be given greater play, occasionally allowing the patient free rein, no matter how strong his resistance is, without making any effort to resolve the resistance. The patient has to be attuned to violent therapeutic reactions when he is on the verge of them. If the analyst is sufficiently elastic in his interpretations and influence, if he has overcome his initial apprehensiveness and insecurity and, over and above this, has great patience, he will not encounter any great difficulties.

It will not be easy to apply character analysis to unusual cases. The analyst will have to attempt to understand and be guided by the ego structure very slowly, step by step. Interpretations of deep layers of the unconscious will certainly be avoided if one

wants to protect oneself against unforeseeable and unpleasant reactions. If deep interpretations are withheld until the mechanisms of the ego defense are revealed, a certain amount of time, it
is true, will have been lost, but the analyst will have gained far
greater security in knowing how to handle that particular case.

I have often been asked by colleagues and beginning analysts
whether character analysis can be introduced when the patient
has already produced a chaotic situation for several months. A
final judgment is not possible, but it would appear that, in some
cases at any rate, a change in technique is definitely attended by
success. The application of character analysis is much easier
when the analyst himself can initiate that treatment, even if the
patient has undergone an extended analysis with another analyst
without any or only partial success.

It is worthy of note that, in consistent character analysis, it
makes no difference whether or not the patient has any intellectual knowledge of analysis. Since deep interpretations are not
applied until the patient has loosened his basic attitude of resistance and opened himself to affective experience, he has no opportunity to make a show of his knowledge. And if he should
nonetheless try to do so, this would merely be a part of his general attitude of resistance and could be unmasked within the
framework of his other narcissistic reactions. The use of analytic
terminology is not checked; it is merely treated as a defense and
a narcissistic identification with the analyst.

Another question which is often asked is: in what percentage
of cases can character analysis be initiated and consistently followed through? The answer is: not in all cases at any rate; much
depends on practice, intuition, and indications. During past
years, however, more than half of our cases could be dealt with
by character analysis. This also made possible a comparison of
intensive and consistent methods with less rigid methods of resistance analysis.

To what extent is a change of the character at all necessary in
the analysis and to what extent can it be brought about?

Fundamentally, there is only one answer to the first question:
the neurotic character must be so changed that it ceases to be the
basis of neurotic symptoms and to interfere with the capacity for
work and the capacity for sexual enjoyment.

The second question can be answered only empirically. To what extent the actual success approximates the desired success depends, in each case, upon a vast number of factors. With the existing psychoanalytic methods, qualitative changes of character cannot be brought about directly. A compulsive character will never become a hysterical character; a paranoid character will never become a compulsive neurotic character; a choleric will never become a phlegmatic, nor will a sanguine character become melancholic. However, it is definitely possible to effect quantitative changes which approximate qualitative changes when they have reached a certain measure. For example, the slight feminine attitude of the compulsive neurotic patient grows stronger and stronger during analysis until it takes on the characteristics of the hysterical-feminine personality, while the masculine-aggressive attitudes grow weaker.

In this way, the patient's entire being undergoes a "change," which is more apparent to people who do not often see the patient than it is to the analyst. The inhibited person becomes freer; the fear-ridden, more courageous; the overconscientious, relatively less scrupulous; the unscrupulous, more conscientious; but that certain indefinable "personal note" is never lost. It continues to show through, no matter how many changes are brought about. The overconscientious compulsive character will become reality-oriented in his conscientiousness; the cured impulsive character will remain impetuous but less so than the uncured character; the patient cured of moral insanity will never take life too hard and will consequently always get through easily, whereas the cured compulsive will always have some difficulty because of his awkwardness. Thus, though these traits persist even after a successful character analysis, they remain within limits which do not constrict one's freedom of movement in life to the extent that one's capacity for work and for sexual pleasure suffer from them.

CHAPTER VI

ON THE HANDLING OF THE TRANSFERENCE

1. THE DISTILLATION OF THE GENITAL-OBJECT LIBIDO

In the course of the analysis, the patient "transfers" to the analyst infantile attitudes which undergo manifold transformations and fulfill definite functions. The handling of these transferred attitudes creates a problem for the analyst. The patient's relationship to the analyst is of both a positive and a negative nature. The analyst has to reckon with ambivalence of feelings and, above all, to bear in mind that sooner or later every form of transference becomes a resistance, which the patient himself is not in a position to resolve. Freud stressed that the initial positive transference shows a tendency to change suddenly into a negative transference. Moreover, the importance of the transference is evidenced by the fact that the most essential elements of the neurosis can be gotten at only through the transference. Consequently, the resolution of the "transference neurosis," which gradually takes the place of the real illness, ranks as one of the most challenging tasks of analytic technique. The positive transference is the main vehicle of analytic treatment; the most tenacious resistances and symptoms are dissolved in it, but its resolution is not the cure itself. This transference, though not the therapeutic factor as such in the analysis, is the most important precondition for the establishment of those processes which, independent of the transference, finally lead to cure. The purely technical tasks which Freud treated in his essays on the transference can be briefly summarized as follows:

1. The establishment of a durable positive transference.

2. The use of this transference to overcome the neurotic resistances.

3. The use of the positive transference to extract repressed contents and to bring about dynamically complete and affective abreactive eruptions.

From the point of view of character analysis, there are two further tasks: one relating to technique and the other a libido-economic one.

The task of technique is the necessary establishing of a durable positive transference, because, as indicated by clinical fact, only a very small percentage of patients spontaneously establish it. The considerations of character analysis, however, lead us a step further. If it is correct that all neuroses result from a neurotic character and, moreover, that the neurotic character is characterized precisely by its narcissistic armoring, then the question arises whether our patients are at all capable of a *genuine* positive transference, in the beginning. By "genuine," we mean a strong, nonambivalent, and erotic object striving, capable of providing a basis for an intense relationship to the analyst and of weathering the storms entailed by the analysis. Reviewing our cases, we have to answer this question in the negative: there is no genuine positive transference at the beginning of the analysis, nor can there be, because of the sexual repression, the fragmentation of the object-libidinal strivings, and the restrictions of the character. At this point, someone will be sure to call my attention to the unambiguous indications of positive transference which we perceive in our patients in the initial phases of analysis. Most assuredly, in the beginning, there are any number of indications which *look like* a positive transference. But what is their unconscious background? Are they genuine or deceptive? Too often we have mistakenly assumed that we were dealing with *genuine,* object-libidinal, erotic strivings. Thus, the question cannot be left unanswered. It ties in with the more general question whether a neurotic character is at all capable of love, and if so, in what sense. Closer examination of these initial indications of the so-called positive transference, i.e., the focusing of object-libidinal sexual impulses on the analyst, shows that, except for a certain residue corresponding to the glimmering of rudimentary elements of genuine love, they are a question of three things, which have little to do with object-libidinal strivings:

1. *Reactive positive transference*—i.e., the patient uses love

to compensate for a transference of hate. In this case, the background is a *latent negative transference*. If the resistances which ensue from this kind of transference are interpreted as an expression of a love relationship, one has first of all made an incorrect interpretation and second has overlooked the negative transference concealed in it. If that is the case, the analyst runs the risk of circumventing the core of the neurotic character.

2. A *devotional attitude* toward the analyst indicative of a *guilt feeling* or a moralistic masochism. Again we find nothing but repressed and compensated hate at the root of this attitude.

3. The *transference of narcissistic desires*—i.e., the narcissistic hope that the analyst will love, console, or admire the patient. No other kind of transference falls to pieces more readily than this one, or is more easily transformed into bitter disappointment and a spiteful narcissistic sense of injury. If this is interpreted as a positive transference ("You love me"), one has again made an incorrect interpretation; the patient does not love at all but merely wants *to be loved,* and he loses interest the moment he realizes that his desires cannot be fulfilled. Connected with this kind of transference, however, there are pregenital libido strivings which cannot establish a durable transference because they are too laden with narcissism, e.g., oral demands.

These three types of specious positive transference—I have no doubt that further study will bring to light a number of others—overrun and interfuse the rudiments of genuine object-love which the neurosis has not yet consumed. They themselves are sequels of the neurotic process, for the frustration of the libidinal strivings causes hate, narcissism, and guilt feelings to surface. Despite their speciousness, they suffice to hold the patient in the analysis until they can be eliminated; but they will just as surely drive the patient to terminate the analysis if they are not unmasked in time.

It was precisely the endeavor to bring about an intensive positive transference that caused me to give the negative transference so much attention. If the negative, critical, and disparaging attitudes toward the analyst are made thoroughly conscious right from the outset, the negative transference is not reinforced; on the contrary, it is eliminated and the positive transference then emerges more clearly. There are two factors which could create the impression that I "work with the negative transference." The fact that the breakdown of the narcissistic defense mechanism brings to the surface the latent negative transferences—which even today I tend to overestimate rather than underestimate— and that often months are required in the analysis of the manifestations of defense. I do not, however, put something in the patient which was not already there; I merely bring into sharper focus what is latently concealed in his modes of behavior (politeness, indifference, etc.) and serves no other purpose than to ward off the influence exercised by the analyst.

In the beginning, I regarded all forms of ego defense as negative transferences. This had, it is true, a certain, if indirect, justification. Sooner or later, the ego defense makes use of the existing hate impulses; the ego resists the analysis in various ways by means of the destructive drive mechanism. It is also correct that hate impulses, i.e., the genuine negative transference, are always and in a relatively easy way drawn out when the resistance interpretation proceeds from the ego defense. It is merely incorrect to call the ego defense as such a negative transference; rather, it is a narcissistic defense reaction. Even the narcissistic transference is not a negative transference, in the strict sense of the word. At that time I was evidently under the strong impression that every ego defense, when consistently analyzed, easily and rapidly *becomes* a negative transference. But a latent negative transference is present from the outset only in the transference of the passive-feminine character and in cases of affect block. Here we are dealing with a hate which, though repressed, is nonetheless active in the *contemporary* situation.

A good illustration of the transference technique involving a specious positive transference is the case of a twenty-seven-year-old woman who sought analytic treatment because of her sexual vacillations. She had been divorced twice, had broken up both marriages, and had had, for a woman of her social standing, an uncommonly large number of lovers. She herself was aware of the contemporary reason for this nymphomanic trait: lack of gratification because of orgastic vaginal impotence. To understand the resistance and its interpretation, it is necessary to mention that the patient was exceptionally attractive and was very much aware of her feminine appeal. Nor was she at all modest about it. During the preliminary consultation, I was struck by a certain self-consciousness on her part; she stared at the floor continuously, though she spoke fluently and answered all questions.

The first hour and two-thirds of the second hour were taken up with the relatively uninhibited account of the embarrassing circumstances connected with her second divorce and of the disturbances of sexual sensitivity in the sexual act. Her account was abruptly broken off toward the end of the second hour. The patient was silent and, after a pause, said that she had nothing else to say. I knew that the transference had already become active as a resistance. There were two possibilities: (1) to urge the patient to continue her communications by persuading and exhorting her to follow the basic rule; (2) to attack the resistance itself. The former would have constituted an evasion of the resistance, while the latter was feasible only if the inhibition was understood at least in part. Since, in such situations, there is always a defense which stems from the ego, it was possible to begin with an interpretation of the resistance from there. I explained the meaning of such blocks, pointing out that "something unstated" was disrupting the continuation of the analysis, something against which she unconsciously struggled. I told her further that such inhibitions are usually caused by thoughts about the analyst and I stressed that, among other things, the success of the treatment was dependent upon her ability to be completely honest in these matters. Under considerable strain, she went on to relate that, while she had been able to speak freely on the previous day, she was now plagued by thoughts which actually had nothing to do with the treatment. Finally, it came out that, before entering analysis, she had wondered what would happen if the analyst gained "a certain impression" of her; whether he would hold her in contempt because of her experiences with men. This brought the session to a close. The block continued on the following day. Once again I called her attention to her inhibition and to the fact that she was again warding something off. It now turned out that she had completely repressed what had taken place during the previous hour. I explained the meaning of this forgetting, whereupon she said that she had been unable to fall asleep the night before because she had been so afraid the analyst could develop personal feelings toward her. This could have been interpreted as a projection of her own love impulses, but the patient's personality, her strongly developed feminine narcissism and her background, insofar as it was known, did not really lend themselves to such an interpretation. I had the vague impression that she was suspicious of my professional code of conduct and feared that I might take advantage of the analytic situation in a sexual way. Within the context of the analytic situation, there could be no doubt that sexual desires already existed on her part. However, faced with the choice of dealing first with these manifestations of the id or with the fears of the ego, one could hardly hesitate to choose the latter. Thus, I told her what I surmised about her fears. She responded with a torrent of information about the bad experiences she had had with physicians; sooner or later all of them had propositioned her or even exploited the professional situation. Wasn't it natural, she asked, for her to be suspicious of physicians? After all, she had no way of knowing whether I was any different. These disclosures had a temporarily liberating effect; she was again able to turn her full attention to the discussion of her contemporary conflicts. A great deal was learned about the motivations and circumstances of her love affairs. Two facts stood out: (1) she usually sought relationships with younger men; (2) it didn't take her long to lose interest in her lovers. It was of course clear that her motivations were of a *narcissistic* nature. On the one hand she wanted to dominate men, and this she could do more easily when dealing with young men. On the other hand, she lost her interest in a man as soon as he expressed sufficient admiration. It would of course have been possible to tell her the meaning of her behavior; this certainly would not have done any harm because it was not a matter of deeply repressed material. But the consideration of the dynamic effect of this interpretation restrained me from doing so. Since her leading characteristics would soon develop into a powerful resistance in the analysis, it seemed advisable to wait for this to take place so as to be able to use the affects from the transference experience to bring the unconscious contents into consciousness. As a matter of fact, the resistance soon developed, but in a wholly unexpected form.

She was again silent, and I continued to point out that she was warding something off. After great hesitation, she declared that what she had feared had finally come to pass, only it was not my relationship to her but her attitude toward me which worried her. The analysis was constantly in her mind. The day before, in fact, she had masturbated with the fantasy that she was having sexual intercourse with the analyst. After I had told her that such fantasies were not unusual while undergoing analysis, that the patient projected upon the analyst all the feelings which he or she harbored toward others at one time or another—this she understood very well—I went into the narcissistic background of this transference. There could be no doubt that the fantasy as such was also partially the expression of the incipient breakthrough of an object-libidinal desire. For various reasons, however, it was not possible to interpret this as a transference. More to the point, the moment was not ripe for such an interpretation. The incest desire was still deeply repressed; hence, the fantasy, in spite of its clearly childish elements, could not be traced back to this. But the patient's personality, and the entire situation in which the transference fantasy was embedded, provided ample material for dealing with other aspects and motives of the fantasy. She suffered states of anxiety before and during the analysis; these were indicative partly of blocked sexual excitation and partly of the ego's immediate fear of a difficult situation. Thus, in the interpretation of the transference resistance, I again proceeded from her ego. To begin with, I explained that her strong inhibition about discussing these things was connected with her pride, i.e., she was too proud to admit to such emotional stirrings. She immediately agreed, adding that her whole nature rebelled against such admissions. Asked whether she had ever experienced love or desire spontaneously, she answered that this had never been the case. The men had always desired her; she had merely acquiesced to their love. I explained the narcissistic character of this attitude, and she understood it very well. I further made it clear that there could be no question of a genuine love striving; rather, she had been irritated to see a man sitting there completely unmoved by her charms and found that situation unbearable. The fantasy had been an expression of her desire to make the analyst fall in love with her. That this had been the case was confirmed by the recollection that, *in the fantasy, the conquest of the analyst had played the major role and had afforded the actual source of pleasure.* Now I could draw her attention to the danger concealed in this attitude, namely that, as time went on, she would not be able to tolerate the rejection of her desires and would eventually lose interest in the analysis. She herself was already aware of this possibility.

This point requires special emphasis. In such transferences, if the narcissistic background is not uncovered in time, it easily happens that a disappointment reaction sets in unexpectedly and the patient, in a negative transference, breaks off the analysis. Over the years, a number of such cases were reported in the Technical Seminar. The story had always been the same: the analyst had accepted such manifestations at their face value and had interpreted the relationship solely as a love relationship. He had failed to stress the patient's need to be loved and the tendency to be disappointed. Sooner or later, consequently, the patient had broken off the analysis.

My interpretation of the transference led without difficulty to the analysis of her narcissism, her scornful attitude toward men who chased after her, and her general incapacity for love—which was one of the chief reasons for her difficulties. It was quite clear to her that she first had to unearth the reasons for the impairment of her capacity for love. In addition to her vanity, she mentioned her exaggerated obstinacy, her inner estrangement from people and things, her merely superficial and specious interests—all of which added up to the feeling of dreariness by which she was tormented. Thus, the analysis of her transference resistance had led directly to the analysis of her character, which, from now on, became the focal point of the analysis. She had to admit that she was not really involved in the analysis, notwithstanding her earnest intentions to straighten herself out through it. The rest of the case is of no interest to us here. I merely wanted to show how the unfolding of the transference in keeping with the patient's character leads directly to the question of narcissistic isolation.

Considerations related to the economic point of view in our therapy also make it clear that it is technically incorrect to bring into consciousness at the outset the rudiments and incipient manifestations of the genuine positive transference, instead of first working through the narcissistic and negative superimpositions.

To my knowledge, it was Landauer who first called attention to the fact that, initially, every interpretation of a projected emotion weakens it and strengthens its counter-tendency. Since our aim in the analysis is to extract and clearly crystallize the genital-object libido, to liberate it from its condition of repression, and to extricate it from its entanglement with narcissistic, pregenital, and destructive impulses, the analysis should, for as long as possible, deal only or predominantly with the manifestations of the narcissistic and negative transference, to interpret them and trace them back to their source. But the indications of an incipient manifestation of love should be allowed to develop undeterred until they are clearly and unambiguously concentrated in the transference. This does not usually take place until very advanced stages, frequently not until the end of the analysis. Particularly in cases of compulsion neuroses, ambivalence and doubt are very difficult to master unless the ambivalent impulses are isolated by consistent stress on the strivings (such as narcissism, hate, and guilt feelings) which are opposed to or at variance with the object libido. Unless this isolation is effected, it is practically impossible to get out of the condition of acute ambivalence and doubt; all interpretations of unconscious contents lose their force, if not effectiveness, because of the wall erected by the armor of doubt. Moreover, this economic consideration ties in very well with the topographical consideration, for the genuine, original object libido, particularly the incestuous genital striving, constitutes the deepest layer of repression in neurotics. On the other hand, narcissism, hate, and guilt feelings, as well as pregenital demands, lie closer to the surface, in both the topographical and the structural senses.

From the economic point of view, the task of handling the transference might best be formulated as follows: the analyst must strive to bring about a *concentration of all object libido in a purely genital transference*. To achieve this, the sadistic and narcissistic energies, which are bound in the character armor, must be freed, and the pregenital fixations must be loosened. When the transference is correctly handled, the libido, built up as a result of the liberation of those strivings from the structure of the character, becomes concentrated in the pregenital positions. This concentration of libido induces a temporary positive transference of a pregenital, i.e., more infantile, nature. This transference, in turn, is conducive to the breakthrough of pregenital fantasies and incest drives and thus helps to unbind the pregenital fixations. However, all the libido which analysis helps to free from its pregenital fixations becomes concentrated in the genital stage and intensifies the genital oedipal situation, as in the case of hysteria; or reawakens it, as in the case of compulsion neurosis (depression, etc.).

At first, however, this concentration is usually accompanied by anxiety, causing the infantile anxiety-hysteria to be reactivated. This is the first sign of a new cathexis of the genital stage. What appears first in this phase of the analysis, however, is not the genital Oedipus desire as such but once again its warding off by the ego, the castration anxiety. As a rule, this concentration of libido in the genital stage is only temporary, an attempt to achieve a new cathexis of the genital strivings. Incapable at this point of coping with the castration anxiety, the libido recoils and temporarily flows back to its pathological (narcissistic and pregenital) fixations. This process is usually repeated many times; each attempt to penetrate to the genital incest desires is followed by a retreat because of the castration anxiety. The result of this, because of the reactivation of the castration anxiety, is the rehabilitation of the old mechanism for the binding of anxiety; that is, either transitory symptoms appear or, what is perhaps more frequently the case, the narcissistic defense mechanism is fully reactivated. Naturally, the analyst always takes up the defense mechanism first in his interpretation and thus brings deeper and deeper infantile material to light. With each advance toward the genital stage, elements of anxiety are neutralized until the libido finally remains firmly concentrated in the genital position and the anxiety or pregenital and narcissistic desires are gradually replaced by *genital* sensations and transference fantasies.[1]

When I delivered a report on these findings, a number of ana-

---

[1] Footnote, 1945: In terms of orgone biophysics, the goal of orgone therapy is the dissolving of the armorings in such a manner that all biological reflexes and movements finally become united in the *total orgasm reflex* and lead to sensations of orgonotic current in the genital. This makes possible the establishment of orgastic potency.

lysts stated that they were not able to tell at what point the actual neurosis assumed such a major role in the analysis. This question can now be answered: in that phase of the analysis when the essential fixations of the libido have been dissolved, when neurotic anxiety has ceased to be absorbed in symptoms and character traits, the core of the neurosis, the stasis anxiety, becomes fully reactivated. This stasis neurosis corresponds to the stasis of the now free-floating libido. At this stage, since everything is converted back into libido, the *genuine* positive transference, which is both affectionate and sensuous, develops in full force. The patient begins to masturbate with fantasies from the transference. The remaining inhibitions and infantile distortions of the incest-fixated genitality can be eliminated through these fantasies; thus, consistently and systematically, we approach that stage of the analysis when we are faced with the task of dissolving the transference. Before we go on to this stage, however, we will enlarge upon some clinically observed details in the concentration of the libido in the transference and the genital zone.

2. SECONDARY NARCISSISM, NEGATIVE TRANSFERENCE, AND INSIGHT INTO ILLNESS

The loosening, indeed breaking down of the character's defense mechanism, which is necessary in order to free the largest possible amount of libido, temporarily causes the ego to become completely helpless. This can be described as the *phase of the breakdown of secondary narcissism*. In this phase the patient does indeed cling to the analysis with the help of the object libido, which has become free in the meantime, and this situation affords him a kind of childish protection. But the breakdown of the reaction formations and of the illusions which the ego has devised for its self-assertion rouses strong negative strivings in the patient against the analysis.[2] In addition, with the dissolution of the armor, the instinctual drives regain their original intensity and the ego now feels itself at their mercy. Taken together, these factors sometimes cause the transitional phases to become critical: suicidal

---

[2] It seems very likely to me that the objections which were raised during my discussion of the negative transference were prompted by the fact that, usually, the patient's narcissistic protective mechanism is not gone into very deeply, thus precluding a violent hate transference.

tendencies emerge; the patient becomes disinterested in his work; in schizoid characters, even autistic regressions are at times observed. The compulsive neurotic characters, by virtue of their strong anality and dogged aggression, prove to be the most tenacious during this process. By the consistency of the interpretation and, in particular, by the clear working through of the negative stirrings in the patient, the analyst who is in command of the transference can easily control the tempo and the intensity of the process.

In the course of dissolving the reaction formations, the male's potency, i.e., whatever of it still remains, collapses. I am in the habit of informing erectively potent patients of this in order to obviate a reaction that can be very intense. To lessen the shock of the acute disturbance of erective potency in such patients, it is advisable to recommend abstinence as soon as the decompensation is divined from certain indications (intensification of the symptoms and anxiety, increased restlessness, emergence of the castration anxiety in dreams). Certain types of narcissistic characters, on the other hand, who refuse to take cognizance of the compensation for their fear of impotence, must be exposed to that unpleasant experience. While intense narcissistic and negative reactions result from it, this exposure, inasmuch as the castration anxiety becomes manifest, thoroughly paves the way for the decompensation of secondary narcissism.

Since the decompensation of potency is the surest indication that the castration anxiety is becoming an *affective experience,* and that the armor is being dissolved, the absence of a potency disturbance in the course of the analysis of an erectively potent neurotic has to mean that the patient has not been deeply affected. Of course, this problem does not exist in most cases, because most patients already have a potency disturbance at the outset of the treatment. But there are some patients who retain an erective potency sustained by sadism, and others who, without knowing it, have a potency disturbance, e.g., weak erections and premature ejaculations.

Until the patient grasps the full meaning of his sexual disturbance, the analysis has, more or less, to struggle against the patient's personality as a whole. To the extent that the analysis is concerned with symptoms from which the patient suffers and into which he therefore has an insight, he can be relied upon as an ally in the fight against the neurosis. On the other hand, the patient has little interest in the analysis of his neurotic reaction basis, i.e., his neurotic character. In the course of the analysis, however, his attitude toward his character undergoes a radical change. He comes to feel that he is sick in this respect also; he recognizes the full implications of his character as the basis of his symptoms, gains an interest in changing his character, and extends his desire to get well to include his sexual disturbance, insofar as he did not sense it as a disturbing symptom from the outset. Thus, subjectively, he often feels sicker than he did before the analysis, but he is also more willing to cooperate in the analytic work. This willingness to cooperate is indispensable for the success of the analysis. To become capable of a healthy sexual life (whose importance for psychic health he has learned from the analyst or grasped on his own) is the chief motivation for his desire to recover. Essentially, therefore, the desire to recover is borne consciously by the feeling of wretchedness caused by the neurosis and unconsciously by the natural genital demands.

The deepening of the awareness of illness and the intensification of the feeling of sickness is the result of the consistent analysis of the narcissistic defense mechanism and of the ego defense. Although this increased awareness leads to an intensified defense, a negative transference whose content is the hatred of the analyst as the disturber of the neurotic balance, the latter already contains the seed of an opposite attitude, which offers the analysis the most positive aids. Now the patient is forced to surrender himself completely to the analysis; he begins to look upon the analyst as the helper in distress, the only one who can make him well. This lends considerable impetus to the patient's determination to recover. These attitudes are, of course, intimately connected with infantile tendencies, the castration anxiety and the infantile need for protection.

3. ON THE HANDLING OF THE ABSTINENCE RULE

If, from the dynamic and economic points of view, the analysis aims at establishing a genital-sensual transference, a question of technique arises, namely how the abstinence rule is to be interpreted and applied. Does the patient have to desist from every form of sexual gratification? If not, which forms are to be restricted? Some analysts interpret the abstinence rule to mean that the sexual act should be prohibited altogether, except for those patients who are married. These analysts seem to feel that, unless abstinence is imposed, the necessary stasis of libido and its concentration in the transference will not take place. But it must be emphatically stressed that such prohibitions are much more likely to prevent the establishment of a positive transference than to encourage it. In short, it is our opinion that the forbidding of coitus does not achieve the desired effect. Apart from certain exceptional cases, isn't this measure at variance with the general principles of analytic therapy? Isn't it true that such a restriction will automatically strengthen the origin of the neurotic situation, i.e., genital frustration, instead of eliminating it? In the case of sexually timid women and erectively impotent men, to restrict the sexual act would be an outright error. The truth of the matter is that our whole concept of the analytic task makes us wary of placing genitality under the pressure of a contemporary prohibition, except in very special circumstances. The point is this: regression and the deflection of the libido from the genital stage produced the neurosis in the first place; hence, to liberate the libido from its pathological moorings and to concentrate it in the genital zone is the primary objective of analytic technique. The general endeavor, therefore, is to eliminate pregenital activities through interpretation, while allowing the genital tendencies to develop with complete freedom. It would be a grave error of technique to restrict patients who did not masturbate just when they are on the verge of overcoming their fear of doing so. Nor are we alone in our view that genital masturbation should be permitted—for a long time as a matter of fact—and a number of experienced and unprejudiced analysts agree. Only when masturbation or the genital act becomes a resistance is it necessary to deal with it, as one would any resistance, through interpretation and, in extreme cases, through restriction. The latter, however, is seldom necessary—usually only for patients who are excessive masturbators. The overwhelming majority of our patients, especially the female patients, should not be forced into any form of genital renunciation in analysis. When the patients begin to masturbate we have the first sure indication of a new cathexis of the genital stage, a reactivation of erotic realism.

In many cases, libido stasis acts as an inhibiting element of analysis. When a large amount of libido becomes concentrated in the genital zone, intense sexual excitations begin to disrupt the analysis. After the content of the fantasies has been exhausted, a phase of strong sexual demands begins, during which no additional unconscious material is produced. At such times, periodic relief of the stasis by means of masturbation or sexual intercourse has a liberating effect and allows the analysis to continue. We see, therefore, that the abstinence rule must be applied with extreme elasticity and subordinated to the economic principle of the concentration of libido in the genital zone. In general terms, then, those technical measures which bring about this concentration are correct, and those which hinder it are incorrect.

The sensual transference that occurs as the libido is concentrated in the genital zone is, on the one hand, a most powerful vehicle for bringing unconscious material to light and, on the other hand, a hindrance to the analysis. The genital excitation causes the actualization of the sexual conflict as a whole and some patients refuse, often for a long time, to recognize the transference nature of this conflict. It is important in this situation that they learn to endure the genital frustration, that they stand up to the reactions of disappointment which usually ensue, cope with them without repressing them, and that they have concentrated the affectionate and sensual strivings on *one object*. We learn from experience *that patients who have not gone through such a phase of sensual transference of a genital nature never wholly succeed in establishing genital primacy,* a fact which, from the point of view of the libido economy, constitutes a defect in the healing process. If such is the case, the analysis has either failed to effect an *actual* liberation of the genital strivings from repression or it was not capable of neutralizing the guilt feeling which precludes the unification of the affectionate and sensual strivings. The indications that this effort has been completely successful are:

1. *Genital masturbation free of guilt feelings*, with genital transference fantasies and commensurate gratification. When the patient and analyst are of the same sex: masturbation with fantasies in which the analyst figures as the incest object.

2. *Incest fantasies free of guilt feelings are sometimes found.* Renunciation can best be achieved if the impulse is *fully conscious.*

3. *Genital excitation during the analysis* (erections in male patients; what corresponds to this in female patients) as the indication that castration anxiety has been overcome.

It cannot be sufficiently emphasized that the activation of genitality which prefaces the final disintegration of the neurotic character and leads to the establishment of genital character traits is never achieved by suggestion but solely by analytic methods, by the correct handling of the transference, which has as its goal the above-described concentration of the libido in the genital zone. This activation is not achieved in all cases, for such reasons as age and the chronicity of the neurosis. Yet it is not merely an ideal; it *is* an attainable goal in many cases. From the economic point of view, activation of genitality is indispensable, for it constitutes, either during or immediately following the analysis, the basis for the regulation of the libido economy through the genital function.

We have observed that the danger of the patient's becoming involved in ticklish situations if his genitality is allowed free rein during the analysis is entirely negligible. When his neurosis is about to cause him to do something detrimental, it is no difficult matter to keep him from doing it by subjecting his motives to thorough analysis, without having to forbid anything. This assumes of course that the analyst has been in control of the transference *from the outset.* In this area, the analyst's subjective appraisals of the situation show considerable latitude: one analyst will have no objection if a young man engages in sexual intercourse but will take strong exception if a young woman does so (double moral standards with respect to sex). Another analyst, rightfully, will not make any such distinction insofar as this step, more socially daring on the part of the young woman, *does not interfere with the analysis.*

4. ON THE QUESTION OF THE "DISSOLUTION" OF THE POSITIVE TRANSFERENCE

As Freud stated, after the transference neurosis has been successfully established the analyst is faced with the final task of resolving the positive transference which, at this point, dominates the analysis. The question immediately arises whether this dissolution is wholly analogous to the process of dissolving the other "transferred" affects by tracing them back to their infantile source; whether, in short, it is a matter of "dissolving" the positive impulses. There cannot be a resolution of the transference in the sense of a "dissolution." What is important is that the object libido, which has been liberated from all dross such as hate, narcissism, obstinacy, self-pity, etc., is "transferred" from the analyst to another object, one in keeping with the patient's needs. Whereas it is possible to "dissolve" all sadistic and pregenital transferences by tracing them back to their infantile source, this cannot be done in the case of genitality, because the genital function is part of the function of reality in general. This fact is indicative of the patient's determination to get well, a determination which urges him forward toward real life and insists on the fulfillment of his genital demands and, from the point of view of recovery, does so with good reason.[3] It is certainly no easy matter to understand why the tracing of the genital transference back to the genital incest desire does not "dissolve" it but, on the contrary, merely sets it free from the incest fixation, enabling it to seek gratification. To understand why this is so, it may be of help to remember that tracing an anal transference back to the infantile situation does not "dissolve" the impulse's cathexis but shifts the libido cathexis from the anal zone to the genital zone. This is how the progression from pregenitality to genital primacy takes place. Such a qualitative shifting is no longer possible in the tracing of the genital transference back to the primal situation, because the genital stage represents the *highest* libido stage in the

[3] The widely discussed problem of the "will to recovery" is not as complicated as it appears. Every patient has preserved a sufficient amount of elementary urges toward the love and enjoyment of life. These urges, even if they are completely buried, offer us the most essential help in our efforts.

progression toward cure. Here the only possibility is the "transference of the transference" to a real object.

Great difficulties are encountered in the loosening of the transference, especially in patients of the opposite sex. The libido refuses to let go and, in some cases, defies attempts at resolution for months on end. In the investigation of the reasons for libido "stickiness," we have discovered the following:

1. *Traces of unresolved guilt feelings* which correspond to a sadism as yet unconscious against a childhood object.

2. *A secret hope* that the analyst will fulfill the demands of love after all. The analyst must have a sixth sense for this secret hope, never spontaneously revealed by the patient.

3. A trace not of a genital but of an *infantile tie to the analyst as the representative of the protective mother*. This tie is an inevitable result of the analytic situation itself. (Rank's concept of the analytic situation as a fantasized womb-situation has, in many cases, applicability here.) Just as the last traces of sadistic impulses are worked through in the analysis of the guilt-feeling, so the traces of the libidinal fixation of a pregenital character are worked through in the analysis of the "stickiness" resulting from the infantile mother fixation.

4. In these final stages of the analysis, one encounters, especially in girls and unhappily married women, a tremendous fear of the impending sexual life. This anticipatory reaction reveals itself in part as a primitive fear of coitus, in part as a bondage to the social norms determined by the monogamous ideology and its demand for chastity. The latter in particular requires thorough analysis, which reveals a strong identification with the monogamous mother, the mother who demands chastity. Such fears can also be traced back to a feeling of inferiority regarding one's femininity resulting from a childhood penis envy that has not been sufficiently worked through. There is in addition a rational, fully justified fear of the sexual difficulties to be faced in a society which has debased sexuality to so great an extent. Men often encounter the difficulty that, having established a unity between affection and sensuality, they become incapable of intercourse with prostitutes or under other conditions involving payment. If they do not get married immediately, they will not easily find a partner who will gratify both affection and sensuality.

These and a number of other conditions make it difficult for the patient to break away from the analyst. A patient will very often gratify his sensuality with an object he does not and as a matter of fact cannot love, because his affections are tied to the analyst. Though this tie complicates the patient's finding the right object while undergoing analysis, the best results are obtained when the patient, whether male or female, finds a compatible partner before the analysis is terminated. This has the great advantage that the behavior in the new relationship can still be analytically controlled and possible neurotic residues easily eliminated.

If the finding of a partner during the analysis does not take place too early, i.e., not *before* the working through of the positive transference, and if the analyst is careful not to influence the patient in any way (does not urge him or her to choose a partner), there can be no doubt whatever as to the advantage of such termination of the treatment. There are, to be sure, difficulties of a social nature. But the discussion of them would take us beyond the scope of this book; and they have already been considered in works dealing specifically with this problem.[4]

5. A FEW REMARKS ABOUT COUNTER-TRANSFERENCE

It is easy to understand that the temperament of any given analyst constitutes a decisive factor in the treatment of every case. As we know, the analyst has the tasks of using his own unconscious as a kind of receiving apparatus to "tune in" the unconscious of the analysand and of dealing with each individual patient in keeping with the patient's temperament. The usual analytic knowledge and ability of the analyst are significant here only insofar as his receptiveness to the unfamiliar unconscious and his ability to adapt to every analytic situation enable him to increase that knowledge and ability.

To begin with, we have to clarify something which could easily be misunderstood. Freud recommended that the analyst assume an unbiased attitude, allow himself to be surprised by every new turn of the analysis. This recommendation appears to be at

---

[4] Cf. Reich: *Geschlechtsreife, Enthaltsamkeit, Ehemoral,* Münster Verlag, 1930; *Der sexuelle Kampf der Jugend,* Verlag für Sexualpolitik, 1931.

variance with our insistence on systematic resistance analysis and
the strict derivation of the special technique from the structure of
each and every case. How, it will be asked, can one assume a
passive, receptive, unbiased attitude and at the same time proceed in a logical, directive, and systematic manner? Some of my
colleagues erroneously try to solve the new tasks of character
analysis by meditating on the structure of the case.

The truth of the matter is that the assuming of an unbiased attitude and consistent resistance analysis are not at variance with
one another. If an analyst has developed the ability which Freud
recommended, the handling of the resistances and of the transference will ensue automatically as a reaction to the process in
the patient. There is no need for strenuous rumination about the
structure of a particular case. When material differing in dynamic value is offered simultaneously from various layers of the
unconscious, the analyst will spontaneously pick out one element
instead of another. Without giving it much thought, he will analyze the ego defense *before* the repressed contents, etc. When the
analyst begins to rack his brain about the structure and technical
requirements of a case, it is a sign of one of two things: either he
is dealing with an especially new and unaccustomed type or his
unconscious is in some way closed to the material the patient is
offering. Freud was quite right in saying that the analyst has to
be open to surprises. Over and above this, however, he must
have the ability to fit very quickly what is surprisingly new into
the total context of the therapeutic process. If, from the very beginning, the analysis has been unrolled in keeping with the structure of the case and on the basis of the transference resistances;
if the error has been avoided of confusing the case and the situation by interpretations which are too deep and too premature,
then the incorporation of new material takes place almost automatically. The most important reason for this is that the potential
elements of the unconscious do not emerge in an arbitrary way.
Their emergence is determined by the course of the analysis itself and presupposes that the analytic material and resistances,
juxtaposed and confused in the beginning, have been put into a
definite order. Once again, however, this is merely a matter of
systematic resistance analysis.

From the technical discussion of cases (which can only take

place intellectually) we could easily get the mistaken impression that character-analytic work is the result of an intellectual dissection of the case during the treatment. But this "intellectualization" must not be imputed to the analytic work itself, whose success depends largely upon intuitive comprehension and action. Once the beginner has overcome the typical tendency "to make a quick sale" of his analytic knowledge of the case, once he has learned to assume a flexible attitude, then he has established the essential basis of analytic ability.

Quite obviously, the ability of the analyst to adopt a flexible attitude in his work, to grasp the case intuitively without becoming stuck in his intellectually acquired knowledge, will depend upon conditions pertaining to his character in the same way that the similar ability of the analysand to let himself go is determined by the degree to which his character armor has been loosened.

Without going into the whole complex of questions, we will illustrate the problem of counter-transference with a few typical examples. It is usually possible to recognize by the way the case is proceeding whether and in which area the attitude of the analyst is defective, i.e., disturbed by his own psychological problems. The fact that some cases never produce an affective negative transference is to be ascribed not so much to the patient's block as to that of the analyst. The analyst who has not resolved the repression of his own aggressive tendencies will be incapable of accomplishing this work satisfactorily in his patients and might even develop an affective unwillingness to form an accurate intellectual appraisal of the importance of the analysis of the negative transference. His repressed aggression will cause the analyst to regard as a provocation the patient's aggression which has to be roused. He will either overlook negative impulses in the patient or obstruct their manifestation in some way. He might even reinforce the repression of the aggression by exaggerated friendliness toward the patient. Patients quickly sense such attitudes on the part of the analyst and thoroughly exploit them in warding off drives. An affect block or an excessively solicitous bearing on the part of the analyst is the most telling sign that he is warding off his own aggression.

The counterpart to this is the analyst's characterological inability to cope with the patient's sexual manifestations, i.e., his or her *positive* transference, without becoming emotionally involved. In acting as a control analyst, one observes that the analyst's own fear of the patient's sensual and sexual manifestations often severely hinders the treatment and can easily forestall the establishment of genital primacy in the patient. Under normal analytic conditions, the patient's genital demands for love become manifest in the transference. If the analyst himself is somewhat befuddled with respect to sexual matters or does not have at least a sexually affirmative intellectual orientation, his work as an analyst will certainly suffer. Needless to say, it is extremely likely that an analyst lacking sexual experience will be unable to comprehend the actual difficulties in the patient's sexual life. Hence, the student of psychoanalysis should fulfill, while undergoing analysis during his training period, at least the same requirements which apply to the patient: the establishment of genital primacy and the attainment of a satisfactory sexual life. Unless he represses his own impulses, the sexually disturbed or unsatisfied analyst will not only be hard-pressed to control his positive counter-transference; he will find it increasingly difficult to cope with the provocation to his own sexual demands by the patient's sexual manifestations. He will undoubtedly become entangled in a neurotic predicament. Practice imposes the strictest demands upon us in this respect, and we would be foolish to conceal or gainsay them. Whether the analyst consciously admits or denies that he has to struggle with such difficulties makes little difference, for the average patient will sense the analyst's unconscious sexual negation and rejection and will consequently be unable to get rid of his own sexual inhibitions. There is, in fact, more to it than that. The analyst, to be sure, has the right to live according to his own light. But the fact remains that if, *unconsciously,* he adheres to rigid moral principles, which the patient always senses, if, *without knowing* it, he has repressed polygamous tendencies or certain kinds of love play, he will be able to deal with very few patients and will be inclined to hold up some natural mode of behavior as "infantile."

Analysts who experience the transferences of their patients in an essentially narcissistic way tend to interpret those contemporary manifestations of love as signs of a personal love relationship. For the same reason, it often happens that the patient's criticism and distrust are not adequately worked through.

Analysts who are not sufficiently in control of their own sadism easily lapse into the well-known "analytic silence," despite the fact that there are no satisfactory reasons for it. They regard the patient himself, rather than the patient's neurosis, as an enemy who "does not want to get well." Threats to break off the analysis and unnecessary setting of deadlines are not so much the result of an insufficiency in analytic technique as they are of a lack of patience. The latter causes technique to fall short of its possibilities.

Finally, it is an error to interpret the general analytic rule (the analyst must be a "blank sheet of paper" upon which the patient inscribes his transference) to mean that one must always and in every case assume a mummy-like attitude. Under such conditions, many patients find it difficult "to come out of their shell," a fact which later makes artificial, unanalytic measures necessary. It is clear that an aggressive patient has to be handled differently than a masochistic patient, an overexcited hysterical patient differently than a depressive patient, that the analyst changes his attitude toward one and the same patient depending upon the situation. In short, one does not act neurotically even if one has to bear an element of neurosis in oneself.

While the analyst cannot and should not suppress his particular temperament and will be mindful of this in deciding which patients he is best fitted to deal with, we must nonetheless demand of him that his individuality be held in check, that it be controlled. We must also expect that a certain amount of character flexibility be attained in his training analysis.

In short, the demands we make upon the analyst are as great as the difficulties he will later be expected to deal with. Above all, the analyst will have to bear in mind that, because his professional activity is in sharp opposition to the majority of conventional society, he will be persecuted, ridiculed, and slandered unless he prefers to make concessions, at the expense of his theoretical and practical convictions, to a social order directly and irreconcilably opposed to the requirements of the therapy of the neurosis.

PART TWO
Theory of Character Formation

In our representation thus far, we have followed a path of investigation rigidly dictated by analytic practice. Proceeding from the question of the economic principle of analytic therapy, we approached the character-analytic problems which cluster around the "narcissistic barrier." We were able to solve some of the technical problems and found ourselves, in the process, faced with new theoretical questions. The one prominent fact about our case histories was that, however much it may differ from case to case, the narcissistic armor is connected in a typical way with the sexual conflicts of childhood. This, to be sure, was entirely in keeping with our analytic expectations. Now, however, we had the task of investigating these connections in detail. Nor did it escape our attention that the changes which take place in the pathological character attitudes in the course of the treatment follow a definite logic. It is the development from a neurotic character structure to a structure whose nature is determined by the attainment of genital primacy. For this reason, we call it "genital character." And finally we shall have to describe a number of character differentiations, among which that of masochism will lead us to a critique of a more recent analytic theory of the instincts.

CHAPTER VII

THE CHARACTEROLOGICAL RESOLUTION OF THE INFANTILE SEXUAL CONFLICT[1]

Psychoanalytic knowledge is in a position to provide the theory of character with fundamentally new points of view and to arrive at new findings based on them. Three characteristics of that investigation which make this possible are:

1. Its theory of unconscious mechanisms.
2. Its historical approach.
3. Its comprehension of the dynamics and economics of psychic processes.

Insofar as psychoanalytic research proceeds from the investigation of phenomena to their nature and development and comprehends the processes of "depth personality" in both cross section and longitudinal section, it automatically opens the way to the ideal of character research, a "genetic theory of types." This theory, in turn, could provide us not only with the natural scientific understanding of human modes of reaction but also with the history of their specific development. The advantage of shifting character research from the humanistic field, in Klages's sense of the word, to the sphere of natural scientific psychology should not be underestimated. But the clinical investigation of this field is not simple. It is first necessary to clarify the facts which are to be discussed.

1. CONTENT AND FORM OF PSYCHIC REACTIONS

From the very beginning, psychoanalytic methods provided a fresh approach to the investigation of the character. Freud's[2]

---

[1] First presented at the Congress of the German Psychoanalytic Society in Dresden, September 28, 1930.
[2] Freud: "Charakter und Analerotik," Ges. Schr., Bd. V.

discovery was pioneer work in this field. He demonstrated that certain character traits can be explained historically as the permanent transmutations of primitive instinctual impulses by environmental influences. He indicated, for example, that stinginess, pedantry, and orderliness are derivatives of anal erotic instinctual forces. Later, both Jones[3] and Abraham[4] made important contributions to the theory of character by showing the relation between character traits and infantile instinctual forces, e.g., between envy and ambition and urethral eroticism. In these first attempts, it was a matter of explaining the *instinctual basis* of typical individual character traits. However, the problems resulting from the demands of everyday therapy are more extensive. We see ourselves faced with the alternatives of (1) understanding, historically and dynamic-economically, *the character as an integral formation* both generally and in terms of typological transmutations, or (2) foregoing the possibility of curing a large number of cases in which the character-neurotic reaction basis has to be eliminated.

Since the patient's character, in its typical mode of reaction, becomes the resistance against the uncovering of the unconscious *(character resistance)*, it can be proven that during the treatment this function of the character mirrors its origin. The causes of a person's typical reactions in everyday life and in the treatment are the same as those which not only determined the formation of the character in the first place but consolidated and preserved the mode of reaction once it had been established and shaped into an automatic mechanism independent of the conscious will.

In the constellation of this problem, therefore, what is important is not the content and nature of this or that character trait but the mechanism and genesis of the typical mode of reaction. Whereas, until now, we were able to understand and explain genetically the contents of the experiences and the neurotic symptoms and character traits, we are now in a position to give an explanation of the *formal* problem, the way in which one experiences and the way neurotic symptoms are produced. It is my

[3] Jones: "Über analerotische Charakterzüge," *Internationalen Zeitschrift für Psychoanalyse,* V (1919).
[4] Abraham: *Psychoanalytische Studien zur Charakterbildung,* Internationaler Psychoanalytischer Verlag, 1924.

firm conviction that we are paving the way to an understanding of what might be called the *basic feature of a personality*.

In the vernacular, we speak of hard and soft, noble and base, proud and servile, cold and warm people. The psychoanalysis of these various characteristics proves that they are merely various forms of an *armoring of the ego* against the dangers of the outside world and the repressed instinctual demands of the id. Etiologically, there is just as much anxiety behind the excessive politeness of one person as there is behind the gruff and occasionally brutal reaction of another. A difference in circumstances causes one person to deal or try to deal with his anxiety in one way and another person to deal with it in a different way. With such terms as passive-feminine, paranoic-aggressive, compulsive-neurotic, hysterical, genital-narcissistic, and others, psychoanalysis has merely differentiated types of reaction according to a rough scheme. What is important now is to comprehend what pertains in a general way to "character formation" and to say something about the basic conditions which lead to such a differentiation of types.

2. THE FUNCTION OF CHARACTER FORMATION

The next question we have to deal with concerns the factors that cause the character to assume the definite form in which it is operative. In this connection, it is necessary to call to mind some attributes of every character reaction. The character consists in a *chronic* change of the ego which one might describe as a *hardening*. This hardening is the actual basis for the becoming chronic of the characteristic mode of reaction; its purpose is to protect the ego from external and internal dangers. As a protective formation that has become chronic, it merits the designation "armoring," for it clearly constitutes a restriction of the psychic mobility of the personality as a whole. This restriction is mitigated by the noncharacterological, i.e., atypical, relations to the outside world that seem to be open communications in an otherwise closed system. They are "breaches" in the "armor" through which, depending upon the situation, libidinal and other interests are sent out and pulled in again like pseudopodia. The armor itself, however, is to be thought of as flexible. Its mode of reaction always proceeds according to the pleasure-unpleasure principle.

In unpleasurable situations the armoring contracts; in pleasurable situations it expands. *The degree of character flexibility, the ability to open oneself to the outside world or to close oneself to it, depending upon the situation, constitutes the difference between a reality-oriented and a neurotic character structure.* Extreme prototypes of pathologically rigid armoring are the affect-blocked compulsive characters and schizophrenic autism, both of which tend toward catatonic rigidity.

The character armor is formed as a chronic result of the clash between instinctual demands and an outer world which frustrates those demands. Its strength and continued *raison d'etre* are derived from the current conflicts between instinct and outer world. The expression and the sum total of those impingements of the outer world on instinctual life, through accumulation and qualitative homogeneity, constitute a historical whole. This will be immediately clear when we think of known character types such as "the bourgeois," "the official," "the proletarian," "the butcher," etc. It is around the ego that this armoring is formed, around precisely that part of the personality which lies at the boundary between biophysiological instinctive life and the outer world. Hence we designate it as the *character of the ego.*

At the core of the armor's *definitive* formation, we regularly find, in the course of analysis, the conflict between genital incest desires and the actual frustration of their gratification. *The formation of the character commences as a definite form of the overcoming of the Oedipus complex.* The conditions which lead precisely to this kind of resolution are special, i.e., they relate specifically to the character. (These conditions correspond to the prevailing social circumstances to which childhood sexuality is subject. If these circumstances are changed, both the conditions of the character formation and the structures of the character will be changed.) For there are other ways of resolving the conflict, naturally not so important or so determinative in terms of the future development of the total personality, e.g., simple repression or the formation of an infantile neurosis. If we consider what is common to these conditions, we find, on the one hand, extremely intense genital desires and, on the other hand, a relatively weak ego which, out of fear of being punished, seeks to protect itself by repressions. The repression leads to a damming up of the impulses, which in turn threatens that simple repression with a breakthrough of the repressed impulses. The result is a transformation of the ego, e.g., the development of attitudes designed to ward off fear, attitudes which can be summarized by the term "shyness." Although this is merely the first intimation of a character, there are decisive consequences for its formation. Shyness or a related attitude of the ego constitutes a restriction of the ego. But in warding off dangerous situations which could provoke what is repressed such an attitude also strengthens the ego.

It turns out, however, that this first transformation of the ego, e.g., the shyness, does not suffice to master the instinct. On the contrary, it easily leads to the development of anxiety and always becomes the behavioral basis of childhood phobia. In order to maintain the repression, an additional transformation of the ego becomes necessary: the *repressions have to be cemented together,* the ego has *to harden,* the defense has to take on a chronically operative, automatic character. And, since the simultaneously developed childhood anxiety constitutes a continual threat to the repressions; since the repressed material is expressed in the anxiety; since, moreover, the anxiety itself threatens to weaken the ego, a protective formation against the anxiety also has to be created. The driving force behind all these measures taken by the ego is, in the final analysis, conscious or unconscious fear of punishment, kept alive by the prevailing behavior of parents and teachers. Thus, we have the seeming paradox, namely that fear causes the child to want to resolve his fear.

Essentially, the libido-economically necessitated hardening of the ego takes place on the basis of three processes:

1. It identifies with the frustrating reality as personified in the figure of the main suppressive person.

2. It turns against itself the aggression which it mobilized against the suppressive person and which also produced the anxiety.

3. It develops reactive attitudes toward the sexual strivings, i.e., it utilizes the energy of these strivings to serve its own purposes, namely to ward them off.

The first process gives the armoring its meaningful contents. (The affect-block of a compulsive patient has the meaning "I have to control myself as my father always said I should"; but it also has the meaning "I have to preserve my pleasure and make myself indifferent to my father's prohibitions.")

The second process probably binds the most essential element of aggressive energy, shuts off a part of the mode of motion, and thereby creates the inhibiting factor of the character.

The third process withdraws a certain quantity of libido from the repressed libidinal drives so that their urgency is weakened. Later this transformation is not only eliminated; it is made superfluous by the intensification of the remaining energy cathexis as a result of the restriction of the mode of motion, gratification, and general productivity.

Thus, the armoring of the ego takes place as a result of the fear of punishment, at the expense of id energy, and contains the prohibitions and standards of parents and teachers. Only in this way can the character formation fulfill its economic functions of alleviating the pressure of repression and, over and above this, of strengthening the ego. This, however, is not the whole story. If, on the one hand, this armoring is at least temporarily successful in warding off impulses from within, it constitutes, on the other hand, a far-reaching block not only against stimuli from the outside but also against further educational influences. Except in cases where there is a strong development of stubbornness, this block need not preclude an external docility. We should also bear in mind that external docility, as, for example, in passive-feminine characters, can be combined with the most tenacious inner resistance. At this point, we must also stress that in one person the armoring takes place on the surface of the personality, while in another person it takes place in the depth of the personality. In the latter case, the external and obvious appearance of the personality is not its real but only its ostensible expression. The affect-blocked compulsive character and the paranoid-aggressive character are examples of armoring on the surface; the hysterical character is an example of a deep armoring of the personality. The depth of the armoring depends on the conditions of regression and fixation and constitutes a minor aspect of the problem of character differentiation.

If, on the one hand, the character armor is the *result* of the sexual conflict of childhood and the definite *way* in which this conflict has been managed, it becomes, under the conditions to which character formation is subject in our cultural circles, the *basis* of later neurotic conflicts and symptom neuroses in the majority of cases; it becomes the *reaction basis of the neurotic character*. A more detailed discussion of this will follow later. At this point I will limit myself to a brief summary:

A personality whose character structure precludes the establishment of a sex-economic regulation of energy is the precondition of a later neurotic illness. Thus, the basic conditions of falling ill are not the sexual conflict of childhood and the Oedipus complex as such but the way in which they are handled. Since, however, the way these conflicts are handled is largely determined by the nature of the family conflict itself (intensity of the fear of punishment, latitude of instinctual gratification, character of the parents, etc.), the development of the small child's ego *up to* and including the Oedipus phase determines, finally, whether a person becomes neurotic or achieves a regulated sexual economy as the basis of social and sexual potency.

The reaction basis of the neurotic character means that it went *too far* and allowed the ego to become rigid in a way which precluded attainment of a regulated sexual life and sexual experience. The unconscious instinctual forces are thus deprived of any energetic release, and the sexual stasis not only remains permanent but continually increases. Next, we note a steady development of the character reaction formations (e.g., ascetic ideology, etc.) against the sexual demands built up in connection with contemporary conflicts in important life situations. Thus, a cycle is set up: the stasis is increased and leads to new reaction formations in the very same way as their phobic predecessors. However, the stasis always increases more rapidly than the armoring until, in the end, the reaction formation is no longer adequate to keep the psychic tension in check. It is at this point that the repressed sexual desires break through and are immediately warded off by symptom formations (formation of a phobia or its equivalent).

In this neurotic process, the various defense positions of the ego overlap and interfuse. Thus, in the cross section of the personality, we find side by side character reactions which, in terms of development and time, belong to different periods. In the phase of the final breakdown of the ego, the cross section of the

personality resembles a tract of land following a volcanic eruption that throws together masses of rocks belonging to various
geological strata. However, it is not especially difficult to pick
out from this jumble the cardinal meaning and mechanism of all
character reactions. Once discerned and understood, they lead
directly to the central infantile conflict.

3. CONDITIONS OF CHARACTER DIFFERENTIATION

What conditions, presently recognizable, enable us to understand what constitutes the difference between a healthy and a
pathological armoring? Our investigation of character formation
remains sterile theorizing as long as we do not answer this question with some degree of concreteness and thereby offer guide-
lines in the field of education. In view of the prevailing sexual
morality, however, the conclusions which follow from our investigation will put the educator who wants to raise healthy men
and women in a very difficult position.

To begin with, it must be stressed once again that the formation of the character depends not merely upon the fact that instinct and frustration clash with one another but also upon the *way*
in which this happens; the stage of development during which the
character-forming conflicts occur; and which instincts are involved.

To gain a better understanding of the situation, let us attempt
to form a schema from the wealth of conditions bearing upon
character formation. Such a schema reveals the following fundamental possibilities. The result of character formation is dependent upon:

the phase in which the impulse is frustrated;
the frequency and intensity of the frustrations;
the impulses against which the frustration is chiefly directed;
the correlation between indulgence and frustration;
the sex of the person chiefly responsible for the frustrations;
the contradictions in the frustrations themselves.

All these conditions are determined by the prevailing social
order with respect to education, morality, and the gratification of
needs; in the final analysis, by the prevailing economic structure
of the society.

The goal of a future prophylaxis of neuroses is the formation
of characters which not only give the ego sufficient support

against the inner and outer world but also allow the sexual and social freedom of movement necessary for psychic economy. So, to begin with, we must understand the fundamental consequences of every frustration of the gratification of a child's instincts.

Every frustration of the kind entailed by present-day methods of education causes a withdrawal of the libido into the ego and, consequently, a strengthening of secondary narcissism.[5] This in itself constitutes a character transformation of the ego inasmuch as there is an increase in the ego's sensitiveness, which is expressed as shyness and a heightened sense of anxiety. If, as is usually the case, the person responsible for the frustration is loved, an ambivalent attitude, later an identification, is developed toward that person. In addition to the suppression, the child internalizes certain character traits of this person—as a matter of fact, precisely those traits directed against his own instinct. What happens, then, is essentially that the instinct is repressed or coped with in some other way.

However, the effect of the frustration on the *character* is largely dependent upon when the impulse is frustrated. If it is frustrated in its *initial stages* of development, the repression succeeds only *too well*. Although the victory is complete, the impulse can be neither sublimated nor consciously gratified. For example, the premature repression of anal eroticism impedes the development of anal sublimations and prepares the way for severe anal reaction formations. What is more important in terms of the character is the fact that shutting out the impulses from the structure of the personality impairs its activity as a whole. This can be seen, for example, in children whose aggression and motor pleasure were prematurely inhibited; their later capacity for work will consequently be reduced.

At the *height* of its development, an impulse cannot be completely repressed. A frustration at this point is much more likely to create an *indissoluble* conflict between prohibition and im-

---

[5] Footnote, 1945: In the language of orgone biophysics: the continual frustration of primary natural needs leads to chronic contraction of the biosystem (muscular armor, sympatheticotonia, etc.). The conflict between inhibited primary drives and the armor gives rise to secondary, antisocial drives (sadism, etc.); in the process of breaking through the armor, primary biological impulses are transformed into destructive sadistic impulses.

pulse. If the fully developed impulse encounters a sudden, unanticipated frustration, it lays the groundwork for the development of an impulsive personality.[6] In this case, the child does not fully accept the prohibition. Nonetheless, he develops guilt feelings, which in turn intensify the impulsive actions until they become compulsive impulses. So we find, in impulsive psychopaths, an unformed character structure that is the opposite of the demand for sufficient armoring against the outer and inner world. It is characteristic of the impulsive type that the reaction formation is not employed against the impulses; rather the impulses themselves (predominantly sadistic impulses) are enlisted as a defense against imaginary situations of danger, as well as the danger arising from the impulses. Since, as a result of the disordered genital structure, the libido economy is in a wretched state, the sexual stasis occasionally increases the anxiety and, with it, the character reactions, often leading to excesses of all kinds.

The opposite of the impulsive is the instinct-inhibited character. Just as the impulsive type is characterized by the cleavage between fully developed instinct and sudden frustration, the instinct-inhibited type is characterized by an accumulation of frustrations and other instinct-inhibiting educational measures from the beginning to the end of his instinctual development. The character armoring which corresponds to it tends to be rigid, considerably constrains the individual's psychic flexibility, and forms the reaction basis for depressive states and compulsive symptoms (*inhibited* agression) . But it also turns human beings into docile, undiscriminating citizens. Herein lies its sociological significance.

The *sex* and the *character of the person mainly responsible for one's upbringing* are of the greatest importance for the nature of one's later sexual life.

We shall reduce the very complicated influence exercised by a authoritarian society on the child to the fact that, in a system of education built upon family units, the parents function as the main executors of social influence. Because of the usually unconscious sexual attitude of the parents toward their children, it happens that the father has a stronger liking for and is less prone to restrict and educate the daughter, while the mother has a

[6] Cf. Reich: *Der triebhafte Charakter*, Internationaler Psychoanalytischer Verlag, 1925.

stronger liking for and is less prone to restrict and educate the son. Thus, the sexual relationship determines, in most cases, that the parent of the same sex becomes most responsible for the child's upbringing. With the qualification that, in the child's first years of life and among the large majority of the working population, the mother assumes the main responsibility for the child's upbringing, it can be said that identification with the parent of the same sex prevails, i.e., the daughter develops a maternal and the son a paternal ego and superego. But because of the special constellation of some families or the character of some parents, there are frequent deviations. We shall mention some of the typical backgrounds of these atypical identifications.

Let us begin by considering the relationships in the case of boys. Under usual circumstances, namely when the boy has developed the simple Oedipus complex, when the mother has a stronger liking for him and frustrates him less than the father does, he will identify with the father and—provided the father has an active and manly nature—will continue to develop in a masculine way. If, on the other hand, the mother has a strict, "masculine" personality, if the essential frustrations proceed from her, the boy will identify predominantly with her and, depending upon the erogenic stage in which the main maternal restrictions are imposed upon him, will develop a *mother identification on a phallic or anal basis.* Given the background of a *phallic* mother identification, a phallic-narcissistic character usually develops, whose narcissism and sadism are directed chiefly against women (revenge against the strict mother). This attitude is the character defense against the deeply repressed original love of the mother, a love which could not continue to exist beside her frustrating influence and the identification with her, but ended rather in a disappointment. To be more specific: this love was transformed into the character attitude itself, from which, however, it can be released through analysis.

In the mother identification on an *anal* basis, the character has become passive and feminine—toward women, but not toward men. Such identifications often constitute the basis of a masochistic perversion with the fantasy of a strict woman. This character formation usually serves as a defense against phallic desires which, for a short time, were intensely directed toward the mother in childhood. The fear of castration *by the mother* lends support to the anal identification with her. Anality is the specific erogenic basis of this character formation.

A passive-feminine character in a male is always based on an identification with the mother. Since the mother is the frustrating parent in this type, she is also the object of the fear that engenders this attitude. There is, however, another type of passive-feminine character which is brought about by an excessive *strictness on the part of the father*. This takes place in the following way: fearing the realization of his genital desires, the boy shrinks from the masculine-phallic position to the feminine-anal position, identifies here with his mother, and adopts a passive-feminine attitude toward his father and later toward all persons in authority. Exaggerated politeness and compliance, softness and a tendency toward underhanded conduct are characteristic of this type. He uses his attitude to ward off the active masculine strivings, to ward off, above all, his repressed hatred of the father. Side by side with his *de facto* feminine-passive nature (mother identification in the ego), he has identified with his father in his ego-ideal (father identification in superego and ego-ideal). However, he is not able to realize this identification because he lacks a phallic position. He will always *be* feminine and *want* to be masculine. A severe inferiority complex, the result of this tension between feminine ego and masculine ego-ideal, will always set the stamp of oppression (sometimes of humbleness) upon his personality. The severe potency disturbance which is always present in such cases gives the whole situation a rational justification.

If we compare this type with the one who identifies with the mother on a phallic basis, we see that the phallic-narcissistic character successfully wards off an inferiority complex which betrays itself only to the eye of the expert. The inferiority complex of the passive-feminine character, on the other hand, is transparent. The difference lies in the basic erogenic structure. The phallic libido permits a complete compensation of all attitudes which are not in keeping with the masculine ego-ideal, whereas the anal libido, when it holds the central position in the male's sexual structure, precludes such a compensation.

The reverse is true of a girl: an indulgent father is more likely to contribute to the establishment of a feminine character than a father who is strict or brutal. Large numbers of clinical comparisons reveal that a girl will usually react to a brutal father with the formation of a hard male character. The ever-present penis envy is activated and is molded into a masculinity complex through character changes of the ego. In this case the hard, masculine-aggressive nature serves as an armoring against the infantile feminine attitude toward the father which had to be repressed because of his coldness and hardness. If, on the other hand, the father is kind and loving, the little girl can retain and, with the exception of the sensuous components, even develop her object-love to a large extent. It is not necessary for her to identify with the father. True, she too will usually have developed penis envy. However, in view of the fact that the frustrations in the heterosexual sphere are relatively weak, the penis envy has no significant effect on the formation of the character. Thus, we see that it is not important whether this or that woman has penis envy. What is important is how it effects the character and whether it produces symptoms. What is decisive for this type is that a maternal identification takes place in the ego; it finds expression in character traits which we call "feminine."

The preservation of this character structure is dependent upon the condition that vaginal eroticism becomes a permanent part of femininity in puberty. At this age, severe disappointments in the father or father-prototypes can arouse the masculine identification which did not take place in childhood, activate the dormant penis envy, and, at this late stage, lead to a transformation of the character toward the masculine. We very often observe this in girls who repress their heterosexual desires for moral reasons (identification with the authoritarian, moralistic mother) and thus bring about their own disappointment in men. In the majority of such cases, these otherwise feminine women tend to develop a hysterical nature. There is a continuous genital urge toward the object (coquettishness) and a shrinking back, accompanied by the development of genital anxiety, when the situation threatens to become serious (hysterical genital anxiety). The hysterical character in a woman functions as protection against her own genital desires and against the masculine aggression of the object. This shall be discussed in greater detail later.

We sometimes meet with a special case in our practice, namely a strict and hard mother who raises a daughter whose character is neither masculine nor feminine but remains childish or reverts to childishness later. Such a mother did not give her child sufficient love. The ambivalent conflict with respect to the mother is considerably stronger on the side of hate, in fear of which the child withdraws to the oral stage of sexual development. The girl will hate the mother at a genital level, will repress her hatred, and, after having assumed an oral attitude, transform it into reactive love and a crippling dependency upon the mother. Such women develop a peculiarly *sticky attitude* toward older or married women, become attached to them in a masochistic way, have a tendency to become passively homosexual (cunnilingus in the case of perverse formations), have themselves looked after by older women, develop but a small interest in men, and, in their whole bearing, exhibit "babyish behavior." This attitude, like any other character attitude, is an armoring against repressed desires and a defense against stimuli from the outside world. Here the character serves as an oral defense against intense hate tendencies directed against the mother, behind which the equally warded-off normal feminine attitude toward the male is found only with difficulty.

Until now, we have focused our attention merely upon the fact that the sex of the person mainly responsible for frustrating the child's sexual desires plays an essential role in the molding of the character. In this connection, we touched upon the adult's character only insofar as we spoke of "strict" and "mild" influencing. However, the formation of the child's character is, in another decisive respect, dependent upon the natures of the parents, which, in their time, were determined by general and particular social influences. Much of what official psychiatry looks upon as inherited (which, incidentally, it cannot account for) turns out, upon sufficiently deep analysis, to be the result of early conflicting identifications.

We do not deny the role played by heredity in determining the modes of reaction. The new-born child has its "character"—that much is clear. It is our contention, however, that the environment exercises the decisive influence and determines whether an existing inclination will be developed and strengthened or will not be allowed to unfold at all. The strongest argument against the view that the character is innate is provided by patients in whom analysis demonstrates that a definite mode of reaction existed until a certain age and then a completely different character developed. For example, at first they might have been easily excitable and enthusiastic and later depressive; or stubbornly active and then quiet and inhibited. Although it seems quite probable that a certain basic personality is innate and hardly changeable, the overemphasis of the hereditary factor stems undoubtedly from an unconscious dread of the consequences of a correct appraisal of the influence exercised by education.

This controversy will not be finally settled until an important institute decides to carry out a mass experiment, e.g., isolates some one hundred children of psychopathic parents right after birth, brings them up in a uniform educational environment, and later compares the results with those of a hundred other children who were raised in a psychopathic milieu.

If we once again briefly review the basic character structures sketched above, we see that they all have one thing in common: they are all stimulated by the conflict arising from the child-parent relationship. They are an attempt to resolve this conflict in a special way and to perpetuate this resolution. At one time, Freud stated that the Oedipus complex is submerged by the castration anxiety. We can now add that it is indeed submerged but it resurfaces in a different form. The Oedipus complex is transformed into character reactions which, on the one hand, extend its main features in a distorted way and, on the other hand, constitute reaction formations against its basic elements.

Summing up, we can also say that the neurotic character, both in its contents and in its form, is made up entirely of compromises, just as the symptom is. It contains the infantile instinctual demand and the defense, which belongs to the same or different states of development. The basic infantile conflict continues to exist, *transformed into attitudes which emerge in a definite form,* as automatic modes of reaction which have become chronic and from which, later, they have to be distilled through analysis.

By virtue of this insight into a phase of human development, we are in a position to answer a question raised by Freud: are repressed elements retained as double entries, as memory traces, or otherwise? We may now cautiously conclude that those elements of infantile experience which are not worked into the character are retained as emotionally charged memory traces; whereas those elements which are absorbed into and made a part of the character are retained as the contemporary mode of reaction. As obscure as this process may be, there can be no doubt about the "functional continuum," for in analytic therapy we succeed in reducing such character formations to their original components. It is not so much a question of again bringing to the surface what has been submerged, as, for example, in the case of hysterical amnesia; rather, the process is comparable to the recovery of an element from a chemical compound. We are also in a better position now to understand why, in some acute cases of character neuroses, we cannot succeed in eliminating the Oedipus conflict when we analyze only the content. The reason is that the Oedipus conflict no longer exists in the present but can be arrived at only by the analytic breakdown of the formal modes of reaction.

The following categorization of principal types, based on isolation of the specifically pathogenic from specifically reality-oriented psychic dynamisms, is anything but a theoretical pastime. Using these differentiations as our point of departure, we shall attempt to arrive at a *theory of psychic economy* which could be of practical use in the field of education. Naturally, society must make possible and encourage (or reject) the practical application of such a theory of psychic economy. Contemporary society, with its sex-negating morality and economic incompetence to guarantee the masses of its members even a bare existence, is as far removed from the recognition of such possibilities as it is from their practical application. This will be immediately clear when, by way of anticipation, we state that the parental tie, the suppression of masturbation in early childhood, the demand for abstinence in puberty, and the forcing of sexual interest into the (today sociologically justified) institution of marriage represent the antithesis of the conditions necessary to establish and carry through a sex-economic psychic economy. The prevailing sexual morality cannot but create the groundwork of neuroses in the character. Sexual and psychic economy is impossible with the morals which are so vehemently defended today. This is one of the inexorable social consequences of the psychoanalytic investigation of neuroses.

CHAPTER VIII

THE GENITAL CHARACTER AND THE NEUROTIC CHARACTER

(The Sex-Economic Function of the Character Armor)

1. CHARACTER AND SEXUAL STASIS

We now turn our attention to the reasons why a character is formed and to the economic function of the character.

The study of the dynamic function of the character reactions and of their purposeful mode of operation paves the way to the answer to the first question: *in the main, the character proves to be a narcissistic defense mechanism.*[1] Thus, it would seem cor-

---

[1] At this point it is necessary to make a fundamental distinction between our concepts and those of Alfred Adler concerning character and "security."

a) Adler began to move away from psychoanalysis and the libido theory with the thesis that what is important is not the analysis of the libido but the analysis of the nervous character. His postulating libido and character as opposites and completely excluding the former from consideration are in complete contradiction to the theory of psychoanalysis. While we do take the same problem as our point of departure, namely the purposeful mode of operation of what one calls the "total personality and character," we nonetheless make use of a fundamentally different theory and method. In asking what prompts the psychic organism to form a character, we conceive of the character as a causative entity and arrive only secondarily at a purpose which we deduce from the cause (cause: unpleasure; purpose: defense against *unpleasure*). Adler, in dealing with the same problem, uses a finalistic point of view.

b) We endeavor to explain character formation in terms of *libido economy* and arrive, therefore, at completely different results from Adler, who chooses the principle of the "will to power" as an absolute explanation, thus overlooking the dependency of the "will to power," which is only a partial narcissistic striving, upon the vicissitudes of narcissism as a whole and of the object libido.

c) Adler's formulations on the mode of action of the inferiority complex and its compensations are correct. This has never been denied. But here, too, the connection is missing to the libido processes which lie deeper, especially the phallic libido. It is precisely in our libido-theoretical dissolution of the inferiority complex itself and its ramifications in the ego that we part company with Adler. Our problem begins precisely where Adler leaves off.

rect to assume that if the character serves essentially as a protection of the ego, e.g., in the analytic situation, it must have originated as an apparatus intended to ward off danger. And the character analysis of each individual case shows, when the analyst succeeds in penetrating to the character's final stage of development, i.e., the Oedipus stage, that the character was molded under the influence of the dangers threatening from the outside world on the one hand and the pressing demands of the id on the other.

Building upon Lamarck's theory, Freud and particularly Ferenczi differentiated an *autoplastic* and an *alloplastic* adaptation in psychic life. Alloplastically, the organism changes the environment (technology and civilization); autoplastically, the organism changes itself—in both instances in order to survive. In biological terms, character formation is an autoplastic function initiated by the disturbing and unpleasurable stimuli from the outer world (structure of the family). Because of the clash between the id and the outer world (which limits or wholly frustrates libido gratification), and prompted by the real anxiety generated by this conflict, the psychic apparatus erects a protective barrier between itself and the outer world. To comprehend this process, which has been but crudely sketched here, we have to turn our attention momentarily from the dynamic and economic points of view to the topographical.

Freud taught us to conceive of the ego, i.e., that part of the psychic mechanism directed toward the outer world and therefore exposed, as an apparatus intended to ward off stimuli. Here the formation of the character takes place. Freud, in a very clear and illuminating way, described the struggle which the ego, as a buffer between id and outer world (or id and superego), has to engage in. What is most important about this struggle is that the ego, in its efforts to mediate between the inimical parties for the purpose of survival, introjects the suppressive objects of the outer world, as a matter of fact precisely those objects which frustrate the id's pleasure principle, and retains them as moral arbiters, as the superego. Hence, the morality of the ego is a component which does not originate in the id, i.e., does not develop in the narcissistic-libidinal organism; rather, it is an alien component borrowed from the intruding and menacing outer world.

The psychoanalytic theory of instincts views the inchoate psychic organism as a hodgepodge of primitive needs which originate in somatic conditions of excitation. As the psychic organism develops, the ego emerges as a special part of it and intervenes between these primitive needs on the one hand and the outer world on the other hand. To illustrate this, let us consider the protozoa. Among these we have, for example, the rhizopods, which protect themselves from the raw outer world with an armor of inorganic material held together by chemical eliminations of the protoplasm. Some of these protozoa produce a shell coiled like that of a snail; others, a circular shell equipped with prickles. As compared with the amoeba, the motility of these armored protozoa is considerably limited; contact with the outer world is confined to the pseudopodia, which, for the purpose of locomotion and nourishment, can be stretched out and pulled in again through tiny holes in the armor. We shall often have occasion to make use of this comparison.

We can conceive of the character of the ego—perhaps the Freudian ego in general—as an armor protecting the id against the stimuli of the outer world. In the Freudian sense, the ego is a structural agent. By character, we mean here not only the outward form of this agent but also the sum total of all that the ego shapes in the way of typical modes of reaction, i.e., modes of reaction characteristic of *one* specific personality. By character, in short, we mean an essentially dynamically determined factor manifest in a person's characteristic demeanor: walk, facial expression, stance, manner of speech, and other modes of behavior. This character of the ego is molded from elements of the outer world, from prohibitions, instinctual inhibitions, and the most varied forms of identifications. Thus, the material elements of the character armor have their origin in the outer world, in society. Before we enter into the question of what constitutes the mortar of these elements, i.e., what dynamic process welds this armor together, we have to point out that protection against the outer world, the central motive behind the formation of the character, definitely does not constitute the chief function of the character later. Civilized man has abundant means of protecting himself against the real dangers of the outer world, namely social institutions in all their forms. Moreover, being a highly developed organism, he has a muscular apparatus which enables him to take flight or to fight and an intellect which

enables him to foresee and avoid dangers. The protective mechanisms of the character begin to function in a particular way when
anxiety makes itself felt within, whether because of an inner condition of irritation or because of an external stimulus relating to
the instinctual apparatus. When this happens, character has to
master the actual (stasis) anxiety which results from the energy
of the thwarted drive.

The relation between character and repression can be observed in the following process: the necessity of repressing instinctual demands initiates the formation of the character. Once
the character has been molded, however, it economizes upon repression by absorbing instinctual energies—which are free-floating in the case of ordinary repressions—into the character
formation itself. The formation of a character trait, therefore, indicates that a conflict involving repression has been resolved: either the repressive process itself is rendered unnecessary or an
inchoate repression is transformed into a relatively rigid, ego-jus-
tified formation. Hence, the processes of the character formation
are wholly in keeping with the tendency of the ego to unify the
strivings of the psychic organism. These facts explain why repressions that have led to rigid character traits are so much more
difficult to eliminate than those, for example, which produce a
symptom.

There is a definite connection between the initial impetus to
the formation of the character, i.e., protection against concrete
dangers, and its final function, i.e., protection against instinctual
dangers, stasis anxiety, and the absorption of instinctual energies.
Social arrangements, especially the development from primitive
social organizations to civilization, have entailed many restrictions upon libidinal and other gratifications. The development of
mankind thus far has been characterized by increasing sexual
restrictions. In particular, the development of patriarchal civilization and present-day society has gone hand in hand with increasing
fragmentation and suppression of genitality. The longer this process continues, the more remote the causes of real anxiety become.
On a social level, however, the real dangers to the life of the individual have increased. Imperialistic wars and the class struggle
outweigh the dangers of primitive times. It cannot be denied that

civilization has brought about the advantage of security in individual situations. But this benefit is not without its drawbacks. To avoid real anxiety, man had to restrict his instincts. One must not give vent to one's aggression even if one is starving as a result of economic crisis and the sexual drive is fettered by social norms and prejudices. A transgression of the norms would immediately entail a real danger, e.g., punishment for "larceny" and for childhood masturbation, and imprisonment for incest and homosexuality. To the extent that real anxiety is avoided, the stasis of libido is increased and, with it, stasis anxiety. Thus, actual anxiety and real anxiety have a complementary relation to one another: *the more real anxiety is avoided, the stronger stasis anxiety becomes, and vice versa.* The man who is without fear gratifies his strong libidinal needs even at the risk of social ostracism. Animals are more exposed to the conditions of real anxiety because of their deficient social organization. However, unless they fall under the pressures of domestication—and even then only under special circumstances—animals rarely suffer from instinctual stasis.

We have stressed here the *avoidance of* (real) *anxiety* and the *binding of* (stasis) *anxiety* as two economic principles of character formation; we must not neglect a third principle, which is also instrumental in shaping the character, i.e., the pleasure principle. True, the formation of the character originates in and is caused by the need to ward off the dangers entailed by the gratification of instincts. Once the armor has been formed, however, the pleasure principle continues to operate inasmuch as the character, just as the symptom, serves not only to ward off drives and to bind anxiety but also to gratify distorted instincts. For example, the genital-narcissistic character has protected himself against external influences; he also gratifies a good portion of libido in the narcissistic relationship of his ego to his ego-ideal. There are two kinds of instinctual gratification. On the one hand, the energy of the warded-off instinctual impulses themselves, particularly the pregenital and sadistic impulses, is largely consumed in the establishment and perpetuation of the defense mechanism. While this, to be sure, does not constitute the gratification of an instinct in the sense of a direct, undisguised attainment of pleasure, it does constitute a *reduction of the instinctual tension* comparable to that derived from the disguised "gratification" in a symptom. Although this reduction is phenomenologically different from direct gratification, it is nonetheless almost on a par with it economically: both diminish the pressure exerted by the instinctual stimulus. *The instinct's energy is expended in the binding and solidifying of the character's contents* (identifications, reaction formations, etc.). In the affect-block of some compulsive characters, for example, sadism mainly is consumed in the formation and perpetuation of the wall between id and outer world, whereas anal homosexuality is consumed in the exaggerated politeness and passivity of some passive-feminine characters.

The instinctual impulses which are not absorbed into the character strive to achieve direct gratification unless they are repressed. The nature of this gratification depends upon the structure of the character. And *which* instinctual forces are employed to establish the character and which are allowed direct gratification decides the difference not only between health and sickness but among the individual character types.

Great importance also devolves on the quantity of the character armor as well as on its quality. When the armoring of the character against the outer world and against the biological part of the personality has reached a degree commensurate with the libido development, there are still "breaches" in it which provide the contact with the outer world. Through these breaches, the unbound libido and the other instinctual impulses are turned toward or withdrawn from the outer world. But the armoring of the ego can be so complete that the breaches become "too narrow," i.e., the communication lines with the outer world are no longer adequate to guarantee a regulated libido economy and social adaptation. Catatonic stupor is an example of a total insulation, while the impulsive character is a prime example of a wholly inadequate armoring of the character structure. It is likely that every permanent conversion of object libido into narcissistic libido goes hand in hand with a strengthening and hardening of the ego armor. The affect-blocked compulsive character has a rigid armor and but meager possibilities of establishing *affective* relationships with the outer world. Everything recoils from his smooth, hard surface. The garrulous aggressive character, on the other hand, has, it is true, a flexible armor, but it is always "bristling." His relationships to the outer world are limited to paranoic-aggressive reactions. The passive-feminine character is an example of a third type of armoring. On the surface, he appears to have an acquiescent and mild disposition, but in analysis we get to know it as an armoring that is difficult to dissolve.

It is indicative of every character formation not only *what* it wards off but what instinctual forces it uses to accomplish this. In general, the ego molds its character by taking possession of a certain instinctual impulse, itself subject to repression at one time, in order to ward off, with its help, another instinctual impulse. Thus, for example, the phallic-sadistic character's ego will use exaggerated masculine aggression to ward off feminine, passive, and anal strivings. By resorting to such measures, however, it changes itself, i.e., assumes chronically aggressive modes of reaction. Others frequently ward off their repressed aggression by "insinuating"—as one such patient once put it—themselves into the favor of any person capable of rousing their aggression. They become as "slippery" as eels, evade every straightforward reaction, can never be held fast. Usually, this "slipperiness" is also expressed in the intonation of their voice; they speak in a soft, modulated, cautious, and flattering way. In taking over anal interests for the purpose of warding off the aggressive impulses, the ego itself becomes "greasy" and "slimy," and conceives of itself in this way. This causes the loss of self-confidence (one such patient felt himself to be "stinky"). Such people are driven to make renewed efforts to adapt themselves to the world, to gain possession of objects in any way possible. However, since they do not possess any genuine ability to adapt themselves and usually experience one frustration and rejection after the other, their aggression builds up and this, in turn, necessitates intensified anal-passive defense. In such cases, character-analytic work not only attacks the function of the defense but also exposes the means employed to accomplish this defense, i.e., anality in this case.

The final quality of the character—true of the typical as well as the particular—is determined by two factors: first, *qualitatively,* by those stages of libido development in which the process of character formation was most permanently influenced by inner conflicts, i.e., by the specific position of the libido fixation.

Qualitatively, therefore, we can differentiate between depressive (oral), masochistic, genital-narcissistic (phallic), hysterical (genital-incestuous) characters and compulsive (anal-sadistic fixation) characters; second, *quantitatively*, by the libido economy which is dependent upon the qualitative factor. The former could also be called the historical, the latter the contemporary motive of the character form.

2. THE LIBIDO-ECONOMIC DIFFERENCE BETWEEN THE GENITAL CHARACTER AND THE NEUROTIC CHARACTER

If the armoring of the character exceeds a certain degree; if it has utilized chiefly those instinctual impulses that under normal circumstances serve to establish contact with reality; if the capacity for sexual gratification has thereby been too severely restricted, then all the conditions exist for the formation of the neurotic character. If, now, the character formation and character structure of neurotic men and women are compared with those of individuals capable of work and love, we arrive at a *qualitative* difference between the ways the character binds the dammed-up libido. It is found that there are adequate and inadequate means of binding anxiety. *Genital orgastic gratification of the libido and sublimation* prove to be prototypes of *adequate means;* all kinds of *pregenital gratification* and *reaction formations* prove to be *inadequate.* This qualitative difference is also expressed quantitatively: the neurotic character suffers a continuously increasing stasis of the libido precisely because his means of gratification are not adequate to the needs of the instinctual apparatus; whereas the genital character is governed by a steady alternation between libido tension and adequate libido gratification. In short, the genital character is in possession of a *regulated libido economy.* The term "genital character" is justified by the fact that, with the possible exception of highly unusual cases, only genital primacy and orgastic potency (itself determined by a special character structure), as opposed to all other libido structures, guarantee a regulated libido economy.

The historically determined *quality* of the character-forming forces and contents determines the contemporary *quantitative* regulation of the libido economy and therefore, at a certain point, the difference between "health" and "sickness." In terms of their qualitative differences, the genital and neurotic characters are to be understood as principal types. The actual characters represent a mixture, and whether or not the libido economy is vouchsafed depends solely upon how far the actual character approximates the one or the other principal type. In terms of the quantity of the possible direct libido gratification, the genital and neurotic characters are to be understood as average types: either the libido gratification is such that it is capable of disposing of the stasis of the unused libido or it is not. In the latter case, symptoms or neurotic character traits develop which impair social and sexual capacity.

We shall attempt now to represent the *qualitative* differences between the two ideal types. To this end, we shall contrast the structure of the id, the superego, and finally the characteristics of the ego which are dependent upon the id and superego.

a) Structure of the id

The genital character has fully attained the post-ambivalent genital stage;[2] the incest desire and the desire to get rid of the father (the mother) have been abandoned and genital strivings have been projected upon a heterosexual object which does not, as in the case of the neurotic character, actually represent the incest object. The heterosexual object has completely taken over the role—more specifically, the place—of the incest object. *The Oedipus complex is no longer a contemporary factor;* it has been resolved. It is not repressed; rather, it is free of cathexis. The pre-genital tendencies (anality, oral eroticism, and voyeurism) are not repressed. In part, they are anchored in the character as cultural sublimations; in part, they have a share in the pleasures preceding direct gratification. They are, in any case, subordinated to the genital strivings. The sexual act remains the highest and most pleasurable sexual goal. Aggression has also to a large extent been sublimated in social achievements; to a lesser extent, it contributes directly to genital sexuality, without, however, demanding exclusive gratification. This distribution of the instinctual drives assures

[2] Cf. Karl Abraham: *Psychoanalytische Studien zur Charakterbildung* (Int. PsA Bibl., No. XXVI, 1925), especially Chapter III: "Zur Charakterbildung auf der 'genitalen' Entwicklungsstufe."

the capacity for corresponding orgastic gratification, which can be achieved only by way of the genital system, although it is not confined to it since it also provides gratification to the pregenital and aggressive tendencies. The less pregenital demands are repressed, i.e., the better the systems of pregenitality and gentility communicate, the more complete is the gratification and the fewer possibilities there are for pathogenic stasis of the libido.

The neurotic character, on the other hand, even if it does not have a feeble potency from the outset or does not live abstinently (which is true of the overwhelming majority of cases), is not capable of discharging his free, unsublimated libido in a satisfactory orgasm.[3] Orgastically, he is always *relatively* impotent. The following configuration is responsible for this: the incest objects have a contemporary cathexis, or the libido cathexis pertaining to these objects is put forth in reaction formations. If there is any sexuality at all, its infantile nature is readily discernible. The woman who is loved merely represents the mother (sister, etc.) and the love relationship is burdened with all the anxieties, inhibitions, and neurotic whims of the infantile incest relationship (*spurious* transference). Genital primacy either is not present at all or has no cathexis or, as in the case of the hysterical character, the genital function is disturbed because of the incest fixation. Sexuality—this is especially true of the transference neuroses—moves along the paths of forepleasure, if the patient is not abstinent or inhibited. Thus, we have a kind of chain reaction: the infantile sexual fixation disturbs the orgastic function; this disturbance, in turn, creates a stasis of libido; the dammed-up libido intensifies the pregenital fixations, and so on and so forth. Because of this over-cathexis of the pregenital system, libidinal impulses creep into every cultural and social activity. This, of course, can only result in a disturbance because the action becomes associated with repressed and forbidden material. Occasionally, indeed, the activity becomes undisguised sexual activity in a dis-

[3] Footnote, 1945: The regulation of sexual energy is dependent upon orgastic potency, i.e., upon the ability of the organism to allow a free flowing of the clonic convulsions of the orgasm reflex. The armored organism is incapable of orgastic convulsion; the biological excitation is inhibited by spasms in various places of the organism.

torted form, e.g., the cramp of a violinist. The libidinal surplus is not always available for social action; it is intertwined in the repression of infantile instinctual goals.

b) Structure of the superego

The superego of the genital character is chiefly distinguished by its important *sexually affirmative* elements. A high degree of harmony therefore exists between id and superego. Since the Oedipus complex has lost its cathexis, the counter-cathexis in the basic element of the superego has also become superfluous. Thus, to all intents and purposes, there are no superego prohibitions of a sexual nature. The superego is not sadistically laden not only for the above reasons but also because there is no stasis of the libido which could stir up sadism and make the superego vicious.[4] The genital libido, since it is gratified directly, is not concealed in the strivings of the ego-ideal. Hence, social accomplishments are not, as in the case of the neurotic character, proofs of potency; rather they provide a natural, noncompensatory narcissistic gratification. Since there are no potency disturbances, an inferiority complex does not exist. There is a close correlation between ego-ideal and real ego, and no insurmountable tension exists between the two.

In the neurotic character, on the other hand, the superego is essentially characterized by sexual negation. This automatically sets up the familiar conflict and antipathy between id and superego. Since the Oedipus complex has not been mastered, the central element of the superego, the incest prohibition, is still wholly operative and interferes with every form of sexual relationship. The powerful sexual repression of the ego and the attendant libido stasis intensify the sadistic impulses which are expressed, among other ways, in a brutal code of morality. We would do well to remember in this connection that, as Freud pointed out, repression creates morality and not vice versa. Since a more or less conscious feeling of impotence is always present, many so-

---

[4] For further information on the dependency of sadism on libido stasis, see Chapter VII of my book *Die Funktion des Orgasmus,* 1927. Cf. also *The Function of the Orgasm,* 1942, 1948.

cial accomplishments are primarily compensatory proofs of potency. These accomplishments, however, do not diminish the feelings of inferiority. On the contrary: since social accomplishments are often attestations of potency which cannot in any way replace the feeling of genital potency, the neurotic character never rids himself of the feeling of inner emptiness and incapacity, no matter how arduously he tries to compensate for it. Thus, the positive demands of the ego-ideal are raised higher and higher, while the ego, powerless and doubly paralyzed by feelings of inferiority (impotence and high ego-ideal), becomes less and less efficient.

c) Structure of the ego

Now let us consider the influences on the ego of the genital character. The periodic orgastic discharges of the id's libidinal tension considerably reduces the pressure of the id's instinctual claims on the ego. Because the id is basically satisfied, the superego has no cause to be sadistic and therefore does not exert any particular pressure on the ego. Free of guilt feelings, the ego takes possession of and gratifies the genital libido and certain pregenital strivings of the id and sublimates the natural aggression as well as parts of the pregenital libido in social accomplishments. As far as genital strivings are concerned, the ego is not opposed to the id and can impose certain inhibitions upon it much more easily since the id gives into the ego in the main, i.e., the gratification of the libido. This appears to be the only condition under which the id allows itself to be held in check by the ego without the use of repression. A strong homosexual striving will express itself in one way when the ego fails to gratify the heterosexual striving and in an entirely different way when no libido stasis exists. Economically, this is easy to understand, for in heterosexual gratification—provided the homosexuality is not repressed, i.e., is not shut out of the communication system of the libido—energy is taken away from the homosexual strivings.

Since the ego is under only a small amount of pressure from both the id and the superego—largely because of sexual gratification—it does not have to defend itself against the id as does the ego of the neurotic character. It requires only small amounts of counter-cathexis and has, consequently, ample energy free for experiencing and acting in the outside world; acting and experiencing are intense and free-flowing. Thus the ego is highly accessible to pleasure *(Lust)* as well as unpleasure *(Unlust)*. The genital character's ego also has an armor, but it is in control of the armor, not at its mercy. The armor is flexible enough to adapt itself to the most diverse experiences. The genital character can be joyous, but angry when necessary. He reacts to an object-loss with a commensurable degree of sadness; he is not subdued by his loss. He is capable of loving intensely and enthusiastically and of hating passionately. In a particular situation, he can behave in a childlike way, but he will never appear infantile. His seriousness is natural, not stiff in a compensatory way, for he does not have to appear grownup at all costs. His courage is not proof of potency, it is objectively motivated. So under certain conditions, e.g., a war he believes unjust, he will not be afraid to have himself labeled a coward but will stand up for his conviction. Since the infantile wishes have lost their cathexis, his hate as well as his love are rationally motivated. The flexibility and strength of his armor are shown by the fact that, in one case, he can open himself to the world just as intensely as, in another case, he can close himself to it. His ability to give himself is mainly demonstrated in his sexual experience: in the sexual act with the loved object, the ego almost ceases to exist, with the exception of its function of perception. For the moment, the armor has been almost entirely dissolved. The entire personality is immersed in the experience of pleasure, without fear of getting lost in it, for the ego has a solid narcissistic foundation, which does not compensate but sublimates. His self-esteem draws its best energies from the sexual experience. The very way he solves his contemporary conflicts shows that they are of a rational nature; they are not clogged with infantile and irrational elements. Once again, the reason for this is a rational libido economy that precludes the possibility of an over-cathexis of infantile experiences and desires.

In the forms of his sexuality, as in all other respects, the genital character is flexible and unconstrained. Since he is capable of gratification, he is also capable of monogamy without compulsion or repression; when rationally motivated, however, he is fully capable of changing the object of his love or of polygamy.

He does not cling to his sexual object because of feelings of guilt or moralistic considerations. Rather, he maintains the relationship on the basis of his healthy demand for pleasure, because it gratifies him. He can conquer polygamous desires without repression when they are incompatible with his relationship to the beloved object, but he can indeed give in to them if they become too urgent. He solves the actual conflicts arising from this in a realistic way.

Neurotic feelings of guilt are practically nonexistent. His sociality is based not on repressed but on sublimated aggression and on his orientation in reality. This does not mean, however, that he always submits to social reality. On the contrary, the genital character, whose structure is wholly at odds with our contemporary moralistically anti-sexual culture, is capable of criticizing and changing the social situation. His almost complete absence of fear enables him to take an uncompromising stand toward an environment that runs counter to his convictions.

If the primacy of the intellect is the goal of social development, it is inconceivable without genital primacy. The hegemony of the intellect not only puts an end to irrational sexuality but has as its precondition a regulated libido economy. Genital and intellectual primacy belong together, i.e., interdetermine one another, as do libido stasis and neurosis, superego (guilt feeling) and religion, hysteria and superstition, pregenital libido gratification and the contemporary sexual morality, sadism and ethics, sexual repression and committees for the rehabilitation of fallen women.

In the genital character, the regulated libido economy and the capacity for full sexual gratification are the foundation of the above character traits. In the same way, everything the neurotic character is and does is determined, in the final analysis, by his inadequate libido economy.

The ego of the neurotic character is either ascetic or achieves sexual gratification accompanied by guilt feelings. It is under pressure from two sides: (1) the constantly ungratified id with its dammed-up libido and (2) the brutal superego. The neurotic character's ego is inimical toward the id and fawning toward the superego. At the same time, however, it flirts with the id and secretly rebels against the superego. Insofar as its sexuality has not been completely repressed, it is predominantly pregenital. Because of the prevailing sexual mores, genitality is tinged with anal and sadistic elements. The sexual act is conceived of as something dirty and beastly. Since aggressiveness is incorporated into or, more specifically, anchored partially in the character armor and partially in the superego, social achievements are impaired. The ego is either closed to both pleasure and unpleasure (affect-block) or accessible solely to unpleasure; or every pleasure is quickly transformed into unpleasure. The armor of the ego is rigid; communications with the outer world, constantly under the control of the narcissistic censor, are poor with respect to both object-libido and aggression. The armor functions chiefly as a protection against inner life; the result is a pronounced weakening of the ego's reality function. The relationships to the outer world are unnatural, myopic, or contradictory; the whole personality cannot become a harmonious and enthusiastic part of things because it lacks the capacity for complete experience. Whereas the genital character can change, strengthen, or weaken his defense mechanisms, the ego of the neurotic character is completely at the mercy of his unconscious repressed mechanisms. He cannot behave any differently even if he wants to. He would like to be joyous or angry but is capable of neither. He cannot love intensely because essential elements of his sexuality are repressed. Nor can he hate rationally because his ego does not feel equal to his hatred, which has become inordinate as a result of the libido stasis, and therefore has to repress it. And when he feels love or hate, the reaction is hardly in keeping with the facts. In the unconscious, the infantile experiences come into play and determine the extent and the nature of the reactions. The rigidity of his armor makes him unable either to open himself to some particular experience or to shut himself off completely from other experiences where he would be rationally justified in doing so. Usually, he is sexually inhibited or disturbed in the forepleasures of the sexual act. Even if this is not the case, however, he does not receive any gratification. Or, because of his inability to give himself, he is disturbed to such an extent that the libido economy is not regulated. A thorough analysis of the feelings one has during the sexual act allows the differentiation of various types: the narcissistic person whose attention is concentrated not on the sensation of pleasure but on the idea of making a very potent impression; the hyperaesthetic person who is very much concerned not to touch any part of the body that might offend his aesthetic feelings; the person with repressed sadism who cannot rid himself of the compulsive thought that he might hurt the woman or is tormented by guilt feelings that he is abusing the woman; the sadistic character for whom the act means the martyring of the object. The list could be extended indefinitely. Where such disturbances are not fully manifested, the inhibitions corresponding to them are found in the total attitude toward sexuality. Since the superego of the neurotic character does not contain any sexually affirmative elements, it shuns sexual experience (H. Deutsch mistakenly held this to be true of the healthy character as well). This means, however, that only half of the personality takes part in the experience.

The genital character has a solid narcissistic foundation. In the neurotic character, on the other hand, the feeling of impotence forces the ego to make compensations of a narcissistic nature. The contemporary conflicts, permeated with irrational motives, make it impossible for the neurotic character to reach rational decisions. The infantile attitude and desires always have a negative effect.

Sexually unsatisfied and incapable of being satisfied, the neurotic character is finally forced either into asceticism or into rigid monogamy. The latter he will justify on moral grounds or as deference to his sexual partner, but in reality he is afraid of sexuality and unable to regulate it. Since sadism is not sublimated, the superego is extremely harsh; the id is relentless in its demands for the gratification of its needs, the ego develops feelings of guilt, which it calls social conscience, and a need for punishment, in which it tends to inflict on itself what it really wishes to do to others.

Upon brief reflection, we see that the empirical discovery of the above mechanisms becomes the basis for a revolutionary critique of all theoretically based systems of morals. Without, at this point, going into the details of this question so decisive for the social formation of culture, we can briefly state that to the extent that society makes possible the gratification of needs and the transformation of the corresponding human structures, the *moral* regulation of social life will fall away. The final decision lies not in the sphere of psychology but in the sphere of the sociological processes. As far as our clinical practice is concerned, there can no longer be any doubt that every successful analytic treatment, i.e., one which succeeds in transforming the neurotic character structure into a genital character structure, demolishes the moralistic arbiters and replaces them with the self-regulation of action based on a sound libido economy. Since some analysts speak of the "demolishing of the superego" by the analytic treatment, we have to point out that this is a matter of withdrawing energy from the system of moral arbitration and replacing it with libido-economic regulation. The fact that this process is at variance with the present-day interests of the state, moral philosophy, and religion is of decisive importance in another connection. More simply expressed, what this all means is that the man whose sexual as well as primitive biological and cultural needs are satisfied does not require any morality to maintain self-control. But the unsatisfied man, suppressed in all respects, suffers from mounting inner excitation that would cause him to tear everything to pieces if his energy were not partially held in check and partially consumed by moralistic inhibitions. The extent and intensity of a society's ascetic and moralistic ideologies are the best yardstick for the extent and intensity of the unresolved tension, created by unsatisfied needs, in the average individual of that society. Both are determined by the relationship of the productive forces and the mode of production on the one hand and the needs which have to be satisfied on the other.

The discussion of the broader consequences of sex-economy and the analytic theory of character will not be able to evade these questions unless, at the sacrifice of its natural scientific prestige, it prefers to pull in the reins at the artificially erected boundary between what is and what should be.

3. SUBLIMATION, REACTION FORMATION, AND NEUROTIC REACTION BASIS

We now turn our attention to the existing differences between the social achievements of the genital character and the neurotic character.

We pointed out earlier that the orgastic gratification of the li-

bido and sublimation are the adequate means of removing the libido stasis or, more specifically, of mastering the stasis anxiety.
The pregenital gratification of the libido and the reaction formation are the inadequate means. Sublimation is, like orgastic gratification, a specific accomplishment of the genital character; reaction formation is the mode of the neurotic character. This of
course does not mean that the neurotic character does not sublimate and that the healthy character does not have any reaction
formations.

To begin with, let us endeavor to give, on the basis of our
clinical experiences, a theoretical description of the relationship
between sublimation and sexual gratification. According to
Freud, sublimation is the result of the deflection of a libidinal
striving from its original goal and its rechanneling to a "higher,"
socially valuable goal. The drive which receives a sublimated
gratification must have relinquished its original object and goal.
This first formulation by Freud eventually led to the misunderstanding that sublimation and instinctual gratification are altogether antithetical. However, if we consider the relation between
sublimation and libido-economy in general, we learn from everyday experience that no antithesis exists here. We learn, indeed,
that a regulated libido economy is the precondition of successful
and lasting sublimation. The really important factor is that those
drives which form the basis of our social achievements do not receive *direct* gratification; this does not mean that the libido is not
at all gratified. The psychoanalysis of disturbances in work
teaches us that the greater the stasis of the libido as a whole, the
more difficult it is to sublimate pregenital libido. Sexual fantasies
absorb the psychic interests and distract from work; or the
cultural achievements themselves are sexualized and in this way
are caught up in the sphere of repression.[5] The observation of
the genital character's sublimations shows that they are contin-

[5] "People say, to be sure, that the struggle against such a powerful instinct,
and the strengthening of all the ethical and aesthetic forces which are necessary
for this struggle, 'steel' the character; and this is true for a few specially favorably organized natures. It must also be admitted that the differentiation of
individual character, which is so marked in our day, has only become possible
with the existence of sexual restriction. But in the vast majority of cases the
struggle against sexuality eats up the energy available in a character and
this at the very time when a young man is in need of all his forces in order
to win his share and place in society. The relationship between the amount

ually reinforced by the orgastic gratification of the libido. Releasing the sexual tensions liberates energy for higher achievements because, for a certain time, sexual fantasies do not draw any libidinal cathexis to themselves. In successful analyses, moreover, we observe that the patient's productive power reaches a high level only after he has succeeded in achieving full sexual gratification. The durability of the sublimations is also dependent upon the regulation of the libido economy. Patients who rid themselves of their neurosis solely by means of sublimation exhibit a far less stable condition and have a far greater tendency to relapse than those patients who not only sublimate but also achieve direct sexual gratification. Just as incomplete, i.e., primarily pregenital, libido gratification interferes with sublimation, so orgastic genital gratification promotes it.

Now let us compare—to begin with, from a purely descriptive point of view—sublimation with reaction formation. What strikes us about these phenomena is that the reaction formation is spasmodic and compulsive, whereas the sublimation flows freely. In the latter case, the id, in harmony with the ego and ego-ideal, seems to have a direct contact with reality; in the former case, all achievements seem to be imposed upon a rebelling id by a strict superego. In sublimation, the effect of the action is important, even if the action itself has a libidinal accent. In the reaction formation, on the other hand, the act is important; the effect is of secondary importance. The action does not have a libidinal accent; it is negatively motivated. It is compulsive. The man who sublimates can suspend his work for a considerable period of time—rest is just as important to him as work. When a

---

of sublimation possible and the amount of sexual activity necessary naturally varies very much from person to person and even from one calling to another. An abstinent artist is hardly conceivable; but an abstinent young *savant* is certainly no rarity. The latter can, by his self-restraint, liberate forces for his studies; while the former probably finds his artistic achievements powerfully stimulated by his sexual experience. In general I have not gained the impression that sexual abstinence brings about energetic and self-reliant men of action or original thinkers or bold emancipators and reformers. Far more often it goes to produce well-behaved weaklings who later become lost in the great mass of people that tend to follow, unwillingly, the leads given by strong individuals." Freud: *"Civilized" Sexual Morality and Modern Nervous Illness,* (1908). The English translation is quoted from *The Complete Psychological Works of Sigmund Freud,* Vol. IX.

reactive performance is disrupted, however, an inner restlessness ensues sooner or later. And if the disruption continues, the restlessness can mount to irritability and even anxiety. The man who sublimates is, on occasion, irritated or tense, not because he is not accomplishing anything but because he is absorbed in giving birth, so to speak, to his accomplishment. The man who sublimates *wants* to accomplish things and derives pleasure from his work. The man whose work is of a reactive nature *has*, as a patient once aptly expressed it, "to robot." And as soon as he finishes one piece of work, he must immediately begin another. For him, work is an escape from rest. Occasionally, the effect of reactively performed work will be the same as that of work based on sublimation. Usually, however, reactive achievements turn out to be less successful socially than sublimated achievements. In any event, the same man will accomplish much more under conditions of sublimation than under those of a reaction formation.

From the structure of each achievement that entails the absolute use of a certain amount of energy, the correlation between individual achievement and individual *capacity for work* can be measured with some degree of accuracy. The gap between work capacity (latent capacity for work) and absolute achievement is not nearly as great in the case of sublimation as in the case of reaction formation. This means that the man who sublimates approximates his capabilities more closely than the man who works reactively. Feelings of inferiority often correspond to the secret awareness of this discrepancy. Clinically, we recognize the difference between these two types of accomplishment in that, when their unconscious relations are uncovered, sublimated accomplishments undergo relatively little change; reactive performances, on the other hand, if they do not break down altogether, often show tremendous improvements in the transformation into sublimations.

The activities of the average worker in our cultural milieu are characterized far more frequently by reaction formations than by sublimations. Moreover, the prevailing formation of the educational structure (in addition to the social conditions of work) permits the realization of the individual's capacity for work in effective achievements to only a very small degree.

In the case of sublimation, there is no inversion of the drive's direction: the drive is simply taken over by the ego and diverted to another goal. In the case of reaction formation, on the other hand, an inversion of the drive's direction does take place. The drive is turned against the self and is taken over by the ego only insofar as this inversion takes place. In the process of this inversion, the drive's cathexis is turned into a counter-cathexis against the drive's unconscious goal. The process described by Freud in the case of aversion is a perfect illustration of this. In the reaction formation, the original goal retains its cathexis in the unconscious. The original object of the drive is not relinquished but merely repressed. Retention and repression of the drive, inversion of the drive's direction accompanied by the formation of a counter-cathexis characterize reaction formation. Abjuration (not repression) and substitution of the drive's original goal and object, retention of the drive's direction without the formation of a counter-cathexis, are the characteristics of sublimation.

Let us further examine the process involved in the reaction formation. The most important economic feature in this process is the necessity of a counter-cathexis. Since the original goal of the drive is retained, it is continuously flooded with libido and, just as continuously, the ego has to transform this cathexis into a counter-cathexis, e.g., deduce the reaction of aversion from the anal libido, etc., to keep the drive in check. The reaction formation is not a process that takes place once, but is a continuous one and, as we shall presently see, one which spreads.

In the reaction formation, the ego is continually occupied with itself; it is its own strict monitor. In sublimation, the ego's energies are free for achievement. Simple reaction formations such as aversion and shame are part of the character formation of every individual. These are not detrimental to the development of the genital character and remain within physiological limits because there is no libido stasis to reinforce pregenital strivings. If, however, the sexual repression goes too far, if it is directed against the genital libido in particular, so that a stasis of libido takes place, the reaction formations receive an excess of libidinal energy and, consequently, demonstrate a characteristic known to the clinician as a phobic diffusion.

Let us cite as an example the case of an official. As is usual for a typical compulsive character, he performed his duties most

conscientiously. In the course of time, despite the fact that he derived not the slightest pleasure from his work, he devoted himself
to it more and more. At the time he entered analysis, it was not
unusual for him to work until midnight or even, on occasion,
until three o'clock in the morning. The analysis quickly brought
out that (1) sexual fantasies disturbed his work (he needed more
time to do his work for this very reason, i.e., he "dilly-dallied"
and (2) he could not allow himself a single quiet moment, especially not in the evenings, for then the supercharged fantasies re-
lentlessly invaded his conscious mind. By working at nights, he
discharged a certain amount of libido, but the greater part of his
libido, which could not be released in such a way, increased
more and more until he could no longer deny the disturbance in
his work.

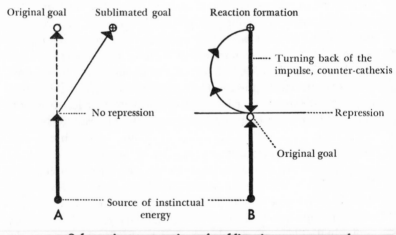

*Schematic presentation of sublimation as compared
with reaction formation*

A: Repression lacking; impulse merely diverted; original instinctual goal
   lacking cathexis.
B: Repression present; original goal has retained its full cathexis; impulse
   not diverted, but directed by the ego against itself. At the place where
   the turning back occurs we find the achievement (reaction formation).

Hence, the proliferation of both the reaction formations and
the reactive performances corresponds to a continually mounting

libido stasis. When, finally, the reaction formations are no longer capable of mastering the libido stasis; when the process of decompensation sets in; when, in short, the character of the ego fails in the consumption of the libido, either unconcealed neurotic anxiety appears or neurotic symptoms emerge which dispose of the excess of free-floating anxiety.

Reactive work is always rationalized. Thus, our patient attempted to excuse his long hours by complaining about his excessive work load. In actual fact, however, his perfunctory activity served the economic purpose of a release and a diversion from sexual fantasies. On the other hand, it fulfilled the function of a reaction formation against the repressed hatred of his boss (father). The analysis showed that the patient's efforts to be especially useful to his boss represented the opposite of his unconscious intentions. When all is said and done, such "roboting" cannot be interpreted as self-punishment, only one of many meaningful elements of the symptom. Basically, he certainly did not want to punish himself but to protect himself against punishment. Fear of the consequences of his sexual fantasies lay at the root of the reaction formation.

Neither work performed as a compulsive neurotic duty nor any other reaction formation is capable of binding the entire stasis anxiety. Consider, for example, the excessive motor activity of the female hysterical character or the hyper-agility and restlessness of the neurotic mountain climber. Both have a muscular system overcharged with unsatiated libido; both are continually striving toward the object: the hysterical girl in an unconcealed way, the mountain climber in a symbolic way (mountain = woman = mother). Their motility, it is true, works off a certain amount of libido; at the same time, however, it increases the tension inasmuch as it does not afford a final gratification. Inevitably, therefore, the girl has attacks of hysteria, while the neurotic mountain climber must undertake more and more strenuous and dangerous mountain tours to master his stasis. However, since there is a natural limit to this, a symptom neurosis finally breaks through if he does not, as often happens, meet with a misfortune in the mountains.

Reaction basis of the character is an appropriate term for all mechanisms which consume the dammed-up libido and bind the neurotic anxiety in the character traits. If, as a result of inordinate sexual restrictions, it fails to perform its economic function, it becomes the *neurotic reaction basis,* which the analytic treatment aims to remove. The proliferating reaction formation is only one of the mechanisms of the neurotic reaction basis.

It does not make much difference when an exacerbation of the neurotic character occurs. The fact remains that the neurotic reaction basis has been present in the character from early childhood, from the conflict period of the Oedipus stage. The neurotic symptom usually exhibits a qualitative affinity to its neurotic reaction basis. To give a few examples: the compulsive-neurotic exaggerated sense of order will become, given certain conditions, a compulsive sense of order; the anal character will become constipated; self-consciousness will become pathological blushing; hysterical agility and coquetry will develop into hysterical attacks; character ambivalence will become the inability to make decisions; sexual inhibition will become vaginismus; aggression or overconscientiousness will become murder impulses.

However, the neurotic symptom does not always exhibit a qualitative homogeneity with its reaction basis. Sometimes the symptom constitutes a defense against surplus anxiety at a higher or lower libido stage. Thus, a hysterical character might develop a compulsion to wash; a compulsive character, a hysterical anxiety or a conversion symptom. Needless to say, in actual practice our patients represent mixtures, with the one or the other character form in the ascendency. However, the diagnosis should not be made according to the symptoms but according to the neurotic character which lies at the basis of the symptoms. Thus, even when a patient comes to us because of a conversion symptom, the diagnosis will be compulsion neurosis if the character exhibits predominantly compulsive neurotic traits.

Reviewing the results of this investigation, we see that the difference between the neurotic and the genital character types must be conceived of as elastically as possible. Since the distinction is based on quantitative criteria (the degree of direct sexual gratification or degree of libido stasis) the variety of actual character forms between the two principal types is endless. Yet, in terms of its heuristic value and the point of view it offers in practical work, a typological investigation seems not only justified but even required. Since this work represents only a small beginning toward a genetic theory of types, it makes no pretense of doing justice to all questions arising from a "theory of types." Its task is momentarily fulfilled if it can succeed in convincing us that Freud's libido theory, unrestricted and consistently thought through, is the only legitimate foundation for psychoanalytic characterology.

CHAPTER IX

CHILDHOOD PHOBIA AND CHARACTER FORMATION

1. AN "ARISTOCRATIC" CHARACTER

Using a case as an illustration, we will show how the character attitude is derived from the infantile experiences. In our presentation, we shall follow the path that led from the analysis of the character resistance to its genesis in definite infantile situations.

A thirty-three-year-old man entered analysis because of marital difficulties and disturbances in his work. He was suffering from a severe inability to make decisions which made it difficult for him to solve his marriage problem in a rational way and prevented him from advancing in his profession. With considerable perception and skill, the patient immediately buckled down to the analytic work. Within a very short time, the usual pathogenic conflicts of the Oedipus relationship allowed a theoretical explanation of his marital difficulties. We shall not go into the material showing the identification between his wife and his mother, between his superiors and his father; though interesting, this material revealed nothing new. We shall concentrate on his behavior, on the relation between this behavior and the infantile conflict, and character resistance in the treatment.

The patient had a pleasing external appearance, was of medium height, had a reserved countenance, was serious and somewhat arrogant. His measured, noble stride caught one's attention —it took him a good while to come through the door and walk across the room to the couch. It was evident that he avoided—or concealed—any haste or excitement. His speech was well phrased and balanced, soft and eloquent. Occasionally, he would interject an emphatic, staccato "Yes!," at the same time stretching both arms forward, then passing one hand across his brow. He lay on the couch with crossed legs, very much at ease. There was very little if any change in his composure and refinement, even when very ticklish and otherwise narcissistic subjects were discussed. When, after several days of analysis, he discussed his relationship to his dearly loved mother, he quite obviously accentuated his noble pose in an effort to master the excitement which seized him. I told him that there was no need to be embarrassed and I urged him to express his feelings freely—but to no avail. He maintained his patrician bearing and refined manner of speech. One day, indeed, when tears welled up in his eyes and his voice was clearly choked, he raised his handkerchief to dry his eyes with the same dignified composure.

This much was already clear: his behavior, whatever its origin might be, protected him against violent emotions in the analysis, guarded him against an emotional breakthrough. *His character* obstructed the free development of the analytic experience; *it had already become a resistance.*

Soon after the obvious excitement had subsided, I asked him what impression this analytic situation had made on him. He replied that it was all very interesting but it did not affect him very deeply—the tears had simply "escaped" him; it had been very embarrassing. An explanation of the necessity and fruitfulness of such excitement was to no avail. His resistance increased perceptibly; his communications became superficial; his attitude, on the other hand, grew more and more pronounced, i.e., more noble, more composed, more reserved.

Perhaps it was merely an insignificant coincidence that one day the term "aristocrat" occurred to me for his behavior. I told him that he was playing the role of an English lord and that the reasons for this could be traced back to his adolescence and childhood. The contemporary defensive function of his "aristocratic manner" was also explained to him. He then produced the most important element of his family story: as a child he had never believed that he could be the son of the small insignificant Jewish merchant who was his father; he must be, he thought, of English descent. As a small boy he had heard that his grandmother had had an affair with a real English lord and he thought of his mother as having English blood in her veins. In his dreams about the future, the fantasy of some day going to England as an ambassador played a leading role.

Thus, the following elements were contained in his lordly bearing:

1. The idea of not being related to his father, whom he held in contempt (father hatred).

2. The idea of being the son of a mother who had English blood in her veins.

3. The ego-ideal of going beyond the circumscribed milieu of his lower-middle-class background.

The exposure of these elements, which had been incorporated into his attitude, was a considerable blow to his self-esteem. But it was still not clear which drives were being warded off.

As we probed consistently into his "lordly" behavior, we found that it was closely related to a second character trait, a tendency to *deride* his fellow men and the *malicious joy* he derived from seeing them come to grief. The analysis of this character trait offered considerable difficulty. He expressed his contempt and derision in a grand manner, as from a throne. At the same time, however, this served to gratify his especially intense sadistic impulses. To be sure, he had already talked about the many sadistic fantasies he had had as an adolescent. But he had merely *talked about* them. It wasn't until we began to ferret them out in their contemporary anchoring, in the tendency to ridicule, that he began to *experience* them. The lordly quality in his behavior was a *protection* against the excessive extension of his ridicule into *sadistic* activity. The sadistic fantasies were not repressed; they were gratified in ridiculing others and warded off in the aristocratic pose. Thus, his arrogant nature was structured exactly as a symptom: it served as a defense against and, at the same time, gratification of an instinctual drive. There can be no doubt that he saved himself the repression of a certain amount of sadism through this form of defense, i.e., by absorbing the sadism into the arrogance of the character. Under other circumstances, it is likely that a strong phobia would have developed from his mild fear of burglars.

The fantasy of being an aristocrat originated when he was about four years old. He fulfilled the demand of self-control somewhat later, out of fear of the father. To this, on the basis of a *contrary identification* with the father, was added an essential tendency toward the control of his aggression. While the father was continually fighting and wrangling with the mother, the ideal took shape in the young boy: "I'm not going to be like my father; I'm going to be the exact opposite."[1] This corresponded to the fantasy: "If I were my mother's husband, I would treat her in an entirely different way. I would be kind to her, I would not get angry because of her shortcomings." Thus, this contrary identification was part and parcel of the Oedipus complex, love of the mother and hatred of the father.

Dreaminess and self-control, accompanied by lively sadistic fantasies, comprised the boy's character that corresponded to the *aristocrat fantasy*. In puberty, he made an intense, homosexual object-choice of a teacher, which ended in an identification. However, this teacher was the lord incarnate, noble, composed, controlled, faultlessly attired. The identification began with the imitation of the teacher's dress; other imitations followed and, at about the age of fourteen, the character as we witnessed it in the analysis was complete. The *fantasy* of being an aristocrat had been translated into his demeanor.

There was also a special reason why the realization of the fantasy in his demeanor took place precisely at this age. The patient had never consciously masturbated during puberty. The castration anxiety, expressed in diverse hypochondriacal fears, was rationalized: "A noble man doesn't do such things." In short, being an aristocrat also served as a defense against the demand for masturbation.

As a lord, he felt himself superior to all people, with the right to hold everybody in contempt. In the analysis, however, he soon had to give way to the insight that his contempt was the surface compensation of a feeling of inferiority, just as, indeed, his whole pose concealed a feeling of inferiority stemming from the lower-middle-class milieu. However, on a deeper level, the contempt was a substitute for homosexual relations. He was especially contemptuous of those men who pleased him and he did not care at all about the others (contempt = sadism = homosexual flirtation). Being an aristocrat embraced the antithesis between sadism and homosexuality on the one hand and noble self-control on the other.

---

[1] See also my investigations of defective identifications in *Der triebhafte Charakter,* Internationaler Psychoanalytischer Verlag, 1925.

In the analysis, his lordly pose became more pronounced with every fresh penetration into the unconscious. As time went on, however, these defense reactions weakened in the same way that his nature in everyday life became milder, without the basic character ever being lost.

The analysis of his demeanor led directly to the discovery of the central conflicts of his childhood and adolescence. In this way, his pathogenic positions were attacked from two sides: (1) his associations, dreams, and other material communications—with little affect here—and (2) his character, the aristocratic pose, where the affects of aggression were bound.

2. OVERCOMING OF CHILDHOOD PHOBIA BY THE FORMATION OF CHARACTER ATTITUDES

A considerable amount of genital anxiety was bound in the pose of being a lord. The history of this binding revealed a childhood phobia about which little was known. From the age of three to about the age of six, the patient had suffered from an intense phobia of mice. In terms of its content, we are merely interested in the fact that his feminine attitude toward the father constituted the central element of this phobia, i.e., a regressive reaction to the castration anxiety. This was related to the typical masturbation anxiety. The more the boy transformed the fantasy of being an aristocrat into a pose, the weaker his phobia became. As he grew older, he was merely aware of a mild apprehensiveness before going to bed. During the analytic working through of the pose, the mouse phobia and the castration anxiety reappeared in an affective form. Obviously, a part of the libido or anxiety of the childhood *phobia* had been absorbed into a character attitude.

We are of course familiar with the transformation of infantile demands and anxieties into character traits. A special case of this kind of transformation is the replacement of a phobia by a definite kind of armoring against the outer world and against anxiety, an armoring dictated by the structure of the instinct. In this case, the patient's noble bearing bound the infantile anxiety.

Another typical case is the absorption of a childhood phobia or of even simpler manifestations of castration anxiety into a passive-feminine character, which appears externally, e.g., as exaggerated, stereotyped politeness. The following case is an additional illustration of the transformation of a phobia into a character attitude.

Apart from his symptoms, a compulsive patient stood out because of his *complete affect-block*. A kind of living machine, he was accessible to neither pleasure nor *unpleasure*. In analysis, the affect-block was unmasked as an armoring against excessive sadism. True, even as an adult he had sadistic fantasies, but they were dull and feeble. A correspondingly intense castration anxiety stood out as the motive of the armoring but manifested itself in no other way. The analysis was able to trace the affect-block to the day of its emergence.

The patient had also suffered from the usual childhood phobia—in this case, horses and snakes. Until the age of six, anxiety dreams with *pavor nocturnus* appeared almost nightly. He had very frequent dreams, accompanied by the severest anxiety, that a horse bit off one of his fingers (masturbation = anxiety = castration). One day he resolved that he would no longer be afraid (we shall come back to this peculiar resolution) and the next horse dream in which one of his fingers was bitten off was wholly free of anxiety.

At that same time, the affect-block developed; it replaced the phobia. It wasn't until the post-pubertal period that anxiety dreams occasionally reappeared.

Now let us return to his peculiar resolution not to be afraid any more. We could not clear up completely its dynamic process. Suffice it to say here that his life was held together almost exclusively by similar resolutions. He was not able to manage anything without a special decision. His anal obstinacy and the extremely strict command to control himself which he assumed from his parents formed the basis of his resoluteness. The anal tenacity also formed the energetic basis of the affect-block, which, among other things, constituted a kind of universal Götz von Berlichingen attitude toward the outer world as a whole.[2] It wasn't until the patient had been under analysis for six months that the following was ascertained: each time, before ringing the

[2] *Götz von Berlichingen,* a drama by Goethe about the peasant wars in Germany circa 1500. Götz, a knight, is remembered for his statement: "You can kiss my ass."—Ed.

bell to my apartment, he passed his hand over the fly of his pants three times and recited the Götz quotation three times as a kind of talisman against the analysis. His affect-block could not have been more strikingly expressed.

Thus, his anal obstinacy and his reaction against sadism were the two most important components that had been built into the affect-block. In addition to his sadistic energy, his powerful childhood anxiety (stasis anxiety plus castration anxiety) was consumed in this armoring. Only after we had worked through this wall, an aggregate of the most diverse repressions and reaction formations, did we encounter his intense genital incest desires.

Whereas the emergence of a phobia is an indication that the ego was too weak to master certain libidinal impulses, the emergence of a character trait or typical attitude in place of a phobia constitutes a strengthening of the ego formation in the form of a chronic armoring against the id and the outer world. A phobia corresponds to a cleavage of the personality; the formation of a character trait, on the other hand, corresponds to a consolidation of the personality. The latter is the synthesizing reaction of the ego to a conflict in the personality which can no longer be endured.

In spite of this discrepancy between phobia and the character formation that follows upon it, the basic tendency of the phobia is retained in the character trait. The nobility pose of our "aristocrat," the affect-block of our compulsive character, the politeness of the passive-feminine character are of course nothing other than *attitudes of avoidance,* in the same way as the phobia that preceded them.

Through the armoring, therefore, the ego receives a certain strengthening. At the same time, however, and precisely as a result of this, the ego's ability to act and its freedom of movement are curtailed. And the more the armoring impairs the capacity for sexual experience, the more closely the ego's structure approximates that of a neurotic, the greater the likelihood of its future breakdown.[3]

In the event of a later neurotic illness, the old phobia breaks through once again inasmuch as its earlier absorption into the

[3] Cf. Chapter VIII, "The Genital Character and the Neurotic Character."

character proves to be insufficient to master the dammed-up libidinal excitations and stasis anxiety. Hence, we can distinguish the following phases in the typical neurotic illness:

1. Infantile conflict between libido impulse and frustration
2. Resolution of this conflict through repression of the impulse (strengthening of the ego)
3. Breakthrough of the repression, i.e., phobia (weakening of the ego)
4. Mastery of the phobia through the formation of a neurotic character trait (strengthening of the ego)
5. Pubertal conflict (or its quantitative equivalent): insufficiency of the character armoring
6. Reemergence of the old phobia or development of a symptomatic equivalent
7. Fresh attempt on the part of the ego to master the phobia by absorption of the anxiety into the character

Among the adult patients who come to us for analytic treatment, two types can be distinguished: those who find themselves in the breakdown phase (phase 6), in which the old neurosis, in the form of a symptom, augments the neurotic reaction basis (renewed formation of phobia, etc.); and those who are already in the reconstruction phase (phase 7), i.e., whose egos have already successfully begun to incorporate the symptoms. For instance, a circumscribed and agonizing compulsive sense of order loses some of its acuteness; the *ego as a whole* devises certain ceremonies which are so diffused in the daily routine that they betray their compulsive character only to the trained observer. A self-cure is feigned in this way, but the spreading and leveling off of the symptoms impair the ego's ability to act no less than the circumscribed symptom. Hence, the patient no longer wants to be cured because of a painful symptom but because of a general disturbance in his work, lack of pleasure in his life, and similar complaints. A relentless struggle takes place between the ego and its neurotic symptoms, between *the formation and incorporation of symptoms*. However, every *incorporation of a symptom* accompanies a *character change* of the ego. These later incorporations of the symptoms into the ego are merely reflections of that first major process by which the childhood phobia was partially or completely transformed into a character structure.

We are speaking here of phobia because it is the most interesting and, in terms of libido economy, the most important manifestation of a disturbance of personal unity. But the processes described above can take place in the case of any anxiety appearing in early childhood. For instance, a child's rational and fully justified fear of his brutal father can lead to chronic changes that take the place of the fear; for example, obstinacy and harshness of character, etc.

Because experiences of infantile anxiety and other conflict situations of the Oedipus complex (phobia is merely one of the special cases singled out here) may determine character structure, the childhood experience or psychic situation is preserved, so to speak, in two different ways: in terms of *content*, as unconscious ideas; and in terms of *form*, as *character attitudes* of the *ego*. The following clinical example is a simple illustration of this.

A narcissistic-masochistic hypochondriac was characterized by his loud, excited, and agitated complaints about the strict way his father had treated him. The material he produced during the months of treatment could be summed up in the sentence: "Just look at what I have suffered at the hands of my father; he has ruined me, has made me incapable of living." Even before he came to me, his infantile father conflicts had been thoroughly worked through by a colleague during a year and a half of analysis. Nevertheless, there had been hardly any change in his behavior and in his symptoms.

One day I was struck by an aspect of his behavior in the analysis. His movements were indolent, there was a trace of tiredness around his mouth. His speech, hardly describable, was monotonous, somber. Finally, I divined the meaning of his intonation. He spoke in an agonized tone of voice, as if he were dying. I found out that, in certain situations outside of the analysis, he also lapsed into this *unconsciously put-on* lethargy. The meaning of his *speaking in this way* was also: "Look at what my father has made of me, how he has tortured me. He has ruined me, made me incapable of living." His bearing was a severe reproach.

My interpretation of his "moribund," plaintive, incriminating manner of speech had a surprising effect. It was as if, with the resolution of this last formal point of attachment to the father, all the prior content interpretations began to take effect. I concluded that, as long as his manner of speech had not betrayed its unconscious meaning, a large portion of the affects of his relationship to his father was bound in it; hence, the uncovered contents of that relationship, despite their having been made conscious, were not sufficiently charged to be therapeutically effective.

Evidently, therefore, one and the same element of the unconscious, infantile structure is preserved and made manifest in two ways: in what the individual does, says, and thinks; and in the *manner* in which he acts. It is interesting to note that the analysis of the "what," despite the unity of content and form, leaves the "how" untouched; that this "how" turns out to be the hiding place of the same psychic contents that had already appeared in the "what"; and finally that the analysis of the "how" is especially significant in liberating the affects.

CHAPTER X

SOME CIRCUMSCRIBED CHARACTER FORMS

1. THE HYSTERICAL CHARACTER

In our investigation of the various character types, we proceeded from the assumption that every character form, in terms of its basic function, represents an armoring against the stimuli of the outer world and the repressed inner drives. The external form of this armoring, however, is always historically determined. We also endeavored to cite a few conditions which determine different character types. Perhaps the most important of these, apart from the character of the person most responsible for the child's upbringing, is the stage of development in which the instinctual apparatus meets its most crucial frustration. Definite relations must always exist between the external appearance of the character, its inner mechanism, and the specific history of its origin.

The hysterical character, as complicated as the pathological symptoms and reactions pertaining to it may often be, represents the simplest, most transparent type of character armor. If one disregards the differences existing within this type, if one condenses what is common to all of them, the most conspicuous characteristic of both male and female examples of this type is an importunate *sexual attitude*. This is combined with a specific kind of *physical agility* exhibiting a distinct sexual nuance, which explains the fact that the connection between female hysteria and sexuality was recognized very early. Disguised or undisguised coquetry in gait, look, or speech betrays, especially in women, the hysterical character type. In the case of men, besides softness and excessive politeness, a feminine facial expression and a feminine bearing also appear. We gave a thorough account of such a case in Chapter IV.

These characteristics appear with more or less distinct anxiousness that is manifested most strongly when the goal sought by the sexual behavior is close at hand. At such a time, the hysterical character will always shrink back or assume a passive, apprehensive attitude. There is a quantitative correlation between hysterical coquetry and the passivity which follows it. In the sexual experience, however, there is another variation: overt displays of excitation in the act without corresponding gratification. Under analysis, these pseudo-passionate displays turn out to be the expression of a severe anxiety, which is overcome by activity.

The facial expression and the gait of the hysterical character are never severe and heavy, as they are in the compulsive character; never arrogant and self-confident, as they are in the phallic-narcissistic character. The movements of the archetype have a kind of lilting quality (not to be confused with elastic), are supple and sexually provocative. That the hysterical character is easily excited can be inferred from the appearance as a whole. The appearance of the compulsive character, on the other hand, suggests restraint.

Whereas shyness and anxiousness paired with coquetry as well as physical agility are conspicuous in the behavioral expressions of a hysterical character, the additional specific hysterical character traits are concealed. Among these we find fickleness of reactions, i.e., a tendency to change one's attitudes unexpectedly and unintentionally; a strong suggestibility, which never appears alone but is coupled with a strong tendency to reactions of disappointment. A hysterical character, as opposed to a compulsive character, can be easily persuaded of the most improbable things. By the same token he will readily give up his beliefs when others, just as easily acquired, replace them. Hence, an attitude of compliance is usually followed by its opposite, swift deprecation and groundless disparagement. The hysterical character's openness to suggestion accounts for his susceptibility to passive hypnosis on the one hand and his propensity for fantastic ideas on the other hand. This is related to the exceptional capacity for sexual attachment of a childish nature. The vivid imagination can easily lead to pseudologia; that is, fantasized experiences are reproduced and grasped as real experiences.

While it is true that many hysterical characteristics are expressed in the physical bearing, there is also a strong tendency to embody pyschic conflicts in somatic symptoms. This is easily explained in terms of the libido structure.

Specifically, the hysterical character is determined by a fixation in the genital stage of childhood development, with its incestuous attachment. From this fixation the hysterical character derives his strong genital aggression as well as his anxiety. The genital incest ideas are of course repressed, but they are in full possession of their cathexis; they have not, as in the case of the compulsive character, been replaced by pregenital strivings. Inasmuch as pregenital, oral, anal, and urethral strivings form a part of the hysterical character—as is always the case—they are embodiments of genitality or at least allied with it. In the hysterical character, the mouth and the anus always stand for the female genital organ. In other character types, e.g., melancholia, these zones fulfill their original pregenital function. The hysterical character, as Ferenczi put it, "genitalizes" everything; the other forms of neuroses substitute pregenital mechanisms for genitality or, as opposed to hysteria, allow genitalia to function as breast, mouth, or anus. Elsewhere I called this the flooding of the genital with pregenital libido. As a result of the genital anxiety which operates both as a genital fixation and as an inhibition of the genital function, the hysterical character always suffers from a severe sexual disturbance. At the same time he is plagued by an acute stasis of unabsorbed genital libido. Hence, his sexual agility has to be as vehement as his tendency to anxiety reactions. In contrast to the compulsive character, the hysterical character is overladen with *unabsorbed* sexual tension.

This leads us to the nature of his armoring. It is far less compact and stable than the armoring of the compulsive character. In the hysterical character, the armoring constitutes, in the simplest possible way, an anxious ego defense against the genital incest strivings. While it is certainly strange, it cannot be denied that, in archetypes of the hysterical character, genital sexuality places itself at the service of its own defense. The more anxiety-ridden the attitude as a whole is, the more urgent the sexual manifestations appear. Generally, the meaning of this function is as follows: the hysterical character has exceptionally strong and ungratified genital impulses that are inhibited by genital anxiety.

Thus, he always feels himself at the mercy of dangers which correspond to his infantile fears. The original genital striving is used, as it were, to explore the source, magnitude, and proximity of the danger. For instance, if a hysterical woman displays strong sensuality, it would be wrong to assume that she is expressing genuine sexual willingness. Quite the contrary: on the first attempt to take advantage of this apparent willingness, one would find that, in cases of extreme hysteria, the overt expression would be immediately transformed into its opposite, that the sexual manifestations would be replaced by anxiety or defense in some other form, including precipitate flight. Thus, the sexual displays in the hysterical character are an attempt to find out whether dangers are present and where they might be coming from. This is also clearly demonstrated in the transference reaction in the analysis. The hysterical character never recognizes the meaning of his sexual behavior; he violently refuses to take cognizance of it and is shocked by "such insinuations." In short, one soon sees that what stands out here as sexual striving is basically sexuality in the service of defense. Not until this defense has been unmasked and the childhood genital anxiety analytically taken apart does the genital object striving emerge in its original function. As this occurs, the patient also loses his exaggerated sexual agility. That other secondary impulses are expressed in this sexual behavior, e.g., primitive narcissism or the desire to dominate and impress, is of little importance.

Insofar as mechanisms other than genital mechanisms or their substitute formations are found in the hysterical character, they do not belong specifically to this type. For example, we often encounter depressive mechanisms. In these cases, the genital incestuous fixation is replaced by regressions to oral mechanisms or by new formations in the course of the process. The hysterical character's strong inclination to regress, especially to oral stages, can be accounted for by the sexual stasis in this zone as well as by the fact that the mouth, in its role as a genital organ, attracts a great deal of libido to itself in the "displacement from below upwards." In this process, melancholia-like reactions, which belong to the original oral fixation, are also activated. Thus, the hysterical character presents himself in a pure form when he play-acts, and is nervous and vivacious. When he is depressive, introverted, autistic, however, he betrays mechanisms other than those which specifically belong to him. Yet one can speak of hysterical depression as opposed to melancholic depression. The difference lies in the degree to which genital libido and object relationship are combined with oral attitudes. At the one extreme, we have unadulterated melancholia; at the other, where genitality predominates, we have unadulterated hysteria.

One final characteristic must be stressed: the hysterical character exhibits little interest in sublimations and intellectual accomplishments, and reaction formations are much fewer than in other forms of neurotic characters. This, too, ties in with the fact that, in the hysterical character, the libido does not advance toward sexual gratification, which could reduce the hypersexuality, nor is sexual energy adequately bound. Rather, this energy is partially discharged in somatic innervations or partially transformed into fear or anxiety. From these libido mechanisms of the hysterical character, some people like to deduce the alleged antithesis between sexuality and social accomplishments. But they overlook the fact that the extreme disturbance of the ability to sublimate is the direct result of the sexual inhibition with unattached genital libido and that social accomplishments and interests are possible only after the capacity for gratification has been realized.

In terms of the prophylaxis of neurosis and sexual economy, it becomes meaningful to ask why the hysterical character cannot somehow transform his genital stasis, in the same way that other character types transform their pregenital strivings. The hysterical character uses his genital libido neither for reaction formations nor for sublimations. Indeed, not even the character armoring is solidly developed. If these facts are considered together with other characteristics of the genital libido, we arrive at the conclusion that fully developed genital excitations are ill suited for purposes other than direct gratification. Their inhibition severely hinders the sublimation of other libidinal strivings because it imbues them with too much energy. Although the specific quality of genitality might be the reason for this process, the more likely explanation is the quantity of the libido used in the excitation of the genital zone. The genital apparatus, as opposed to all the other partial drives, is physiologically the most strongly equipped because it has the capacity for *orgastic* discharge; and in terms of libido economy, it is the most vital. Thus, we can assume that its impulses have a far greater similarity with hunger, as far as inflexibility and tenacity are concerned, than they have with impulses from other erogenous zones. This may well be a powerful blow to certain ethical concepts—but that cannot be helped. Indeed, the resistance to these findings can also be explained: their recognition would have revolutionary consequences.

2. THE COMPULSIVE CHARACTER

If the character's most general function is to ward off stimuli and to secure psychic balance, this should not be difficult to prove in the compulsive character. For this type is one of the most thoroughly studied psychic formations. There are fluid transitions from the known compulsive symptoms to the character's mode of behavior. Even if the neurotic compulsive sense of order is not present, a *pedantic sense of order* is typical of the compulsive character. In both big and small things, he lives his life according to a preconceived, irrevocable pattern. A change in the prescribed order causes at the very least an unpleasant sensation. In cases which can already be regarded as neurotic, a change arouses anxiety. If this trait constitutes an improvement of one's capacity for work because it is combined with thoroughness, it entails an extreme limitation of the capacity for work because it does not allow any spontaneity in one's reaction. Advantageous to an official, this trait will prove to be detrimental to productive work, to the play of new ideas. Hence, compulsive characters are seldom found among great statesmen. They are more likely to be encountered among scientists, whose work is not incompatible with such a trait even though it wholly precludes speculation and will stand in the way of fundamentally new discoveries. This is related to another character trait, the ever-present penchant for *circumstantial, ruminative thinking*. There is a marked inability to focus attention on what is rationally important about an object and to disregard its superficial aspects. Attention is evenly distributed; questions of secondary importance are accorded the same thoroughness as those at the center of professional interests. The more pathological and rigid this trait is, the more attention is concentrated on things of secondary importance and the rationally more important matters are sidetracked. This is the result of a well-understood process, the displacement of unconscious cathexes, the replacement of unconscious ideas which have become important, by irrelevant, secondary matters. This is part of the larger process of progressive repression directed against repressed ideas. Usually, these ideas, childish musings on forbidden things, are not allowed to penetrate to the real issue. This thinking and musing also move along prescribed paths, in accordance with definite, historically determined schemata, and considerably obstruct the flexibility of one's thinking. In some cases, an above-average capacity for abstract, logical thinking compensates for this rigidity. The critical capacities—within the framework of logic—are better developed than the creative capacities.

Frugality, often pushed to the point of *parsimony,* is a character trait in all compulsive characters and is intimately related to the others we have named. Pedantry, circumstantiality, tendency to compulsive rumination, and frugality are all derived from a single instinctual source: anal eroticism. For the most part, they represent the direct derivatives of reaction formations against the childhood tendencies prevalent during the period of toilet training. Insofar as these reaction formations have not been wholly successful, traits having a nature completely opposite to the ones already discussed exist and constitute an inherent part of the compulsive character. In more concrete terms, they constitute breakthroughs of the original tendencies. Then we have manifestations of extreme sloppiness, inability to husband money, thorough thinking only within circumscribed limits. If one adds the strong passion for *collecting* things, then the ensemble of the anal-erotic derivatives in the character is complete. Whereas we can easily grasp the qualitative connection between these traits and the interest in the functions of evacuation, the connection between compulsive rumination and anal eroticism is not obvious. While we always find ruminations about where babies come from, the transformation of the interest in defecation to a definite kind of thinking, whose existence is unquestioned, appears to be subject to unknown laws. The investigations of Abraham, Jones, Ophuijsen, and others built upon Freud's first work on this subject offer the most complete orientation in this area.

We will briefly name a few other character traits which derive not from the anal but from the sadistic impulses pertaining specifically to this stage. Compulsive characters always exhibit a marked proclivity for reactions of *pity* and *guilt feelings*. This of course is not a refutation of the fact that their other traits are not exactly pleasant for their fellow man. In their exaggerated sense of order, pedantry, etc., their hostility and aggression often extort a direct gratification. In keeping with the compulsive character's fixation on the anal-sadistic stage of libido development, we find in these traits all the reaction formations against the original contrary tendencies. We must emphasize, however, that we are justified in speaking of a compulsive character only when the full ensemble of these traits is present—not when someone is merely pedantic and does not exhibit any of the other traits of the compulsive character. Thus, it would be incorrect to speak of a compulsive neurosis when a hysterical character is orderly or ruminative.

Whereas the character traits that we have named so far are manifestations of direct transformations of certain partial drives, there are other typical traits which demonstrate a more complicated structure and are the results of a series of interacting forces. Among these we have *indecision, doubt, and distrust.* In external appearance, the compulsive character exhibits strong *reserve* and *self-possession;* he is just as ill disposed toward affects as he is acutely inaccessible to them. He is usually even-tempered, lukewarm in his displays of both love and hate. In some cases, this can develop into a complete *affect-block.* These latter traits are already a matter of form rather than content and thus lead us to our actual theme, the dynamics and economy of the character.

The reserve and methodicalness in life and thought that go together with indecisiveness indeed have a definite relation to it and constitute the point of departure for our analysis of the form of the character. They cannot, as in the case of character traits imbued with a specific content, be derived directly from individual drives. Rather, these traits give the person his distinctive quality. In analysis, they constitute the central element of the character resistance as well as the tendency to avoid the termination of a situation, including the analytic treatment. We learn from clinical experience that the traits of doubt, distrust, etc., operate as a resistance in the analysis and cannot be eliminated until the pronounced affect-block has been broken through. Hence, this deserves our special attention. We shall limit our discussion to those phenomena which are expressed as form, especially in view of the fact that the other traits are well known. This investigation is new territory.

To begin with, we have to refresh our memory regarding what is known about the libido development of the compulsive character. Historically, we have a central fixation on the anal-sadistic stage, i.e., in the second or third year of life. Toilet training, because of the mother's own particular character traits, is carried out too soon. This leads to powerful reaction formations, e.g., extreme self-control, even at an early age. With the rigid toilet training, a powerful anal obstinacy develops and mobilizes the sadistic impulses to strengthen itself. In the typical compulsion neurosis, the development continues to the phallic phase, i.e., genitality is activated. However, partially because of the person's previously developed inhibitions and partially because of the parents' antisexual attitude, it is soon relinquished. Insofar as genitality is developed, it is dependent upon the prior development of the anality and sadism in the form of phallic-sadistic aggression. Needless to say, a male child will sacrifice his genital impulses to the castration anxiety—i.e., will repress them—that much more readily, the more aggressive his acquired sexual constitution and the more extensive the character inhibitions and guilt feelings from earlier periods which impinge upon the new phase. Hence, in the compulsion neurosis the repression of the genitality is typically followed by a withdrawal to the immediately preceding stage of feces interest and the aggression of this stage. From now on, i.e., during the so-called latency period[1]—which is especially pronounced in the compulsive character—the anal and sadistic reaction formations usually grow more intense and mold the character into a definite form.

When such a child reaches puberty, when he is exposed to the most powerful stresses of physical maturation, he will, if the armoring of his character is strong, have to repeat briefly the old

---

[1] The latency period, as we learn from the sexual development of children of primitive peoples, is not a biological but a sociological phenomenon, created by sexual suppression.

process, without attaining the fulfillment of the demands of sexual maturity. Usually, in the beginning, there are violent fits of sadism against women (beating and rape fantasies, etc.) which are accompanied by feelings of affective weakness and inferiority. These feelings cause the youth to make narcissistic compensations in the form of strongly emphasized ethical and aesthetic strivings. The fixations on the anal and sadistic position are strengthened or regressively reactivated following a brief, usually unsuccessful advance toward genital activity; this causes further elaborations of the corresponding reaction formations. As a result of these in-depth processes, the pubertal and post-pubertal period of the compulsive character proceeds in a typical way, and we are therefore able to draw definite a posteriori conclusions about this period. There is, first of all, a progressive stunting of the emotional capacity, a stunting which sometimes impresses the average person as a mark of especially good social "adjustment." This may also appear to be the case to the person himself, as, indeed, in a certain sense it is. Simultaneously with the affect-block, however, there is a feeling of inner desolation and an intense desire "to begin a new life," which is usually attempted with the most absurd means. One such patient constructed a complicated system for the purpose of dealing with his small and large tasks. He had to master them so he could begin a new life on a certain day; he even went so far as to calculate the exact second at which his new life would begin to take shape. Since he was never able to fulfill the prescribed conditions, he always had to begin anew.

As a prototype of disturbances in the compulsive character manifested as a "form" of the character rather than as a "content" of a character trait, we would do well to investigate his affect-block. Although it impresses us as a helpless attitude on the part of the ego, this is not at all the case. On the contrary, in almost no other character formation does analysis show such intense and avid defense work. What is warded off, and how is it done? The compulsive character's typical means of repression is to separate the affects from the ideas, thus very often allowing the latter to emerge into consciousness without interference. One such patient dreamed and thought about incest with his mother and even about violent rapes, yet he remained unaffected.

Genital and sadistic excitation was totally absent. If such patients are analyzed without at the same time concentrating on the affect-block, additional unconscious material is obtained—occasionally even a weak excitation—but never the affects which would correspond to the ideas. What has become of these? When symptoms exist, the affects are partially absorbed in them; when there are no symptoms, they are mainly absorbed in the affect-block itself. The proof of this assertion is immediately evident when one succeeds in breaking through the block by means of consistent isolation and interpretation. When this has been accomplished, the sought-after affects reappear spontaneously, at first usually in the form of anxiety.

It is noteworthy that at first only aggressive impulses are set free; the genital impulses appear much later. Thus, we can say that bound aggressive energy makes up the outer layer of the character armor. By what is it bound? The aggression is bound with the help of anal-erotic energies. The affect-block represents one enormous *spasm of the ego,* which makes use of somatic spastic conditions. All the muscles of the body, but especially those of the pelvic floor and pelvis, the muscles of the shoulders, and those of the face (cf. the "hard," almost mask-like physiognomy of compulsive characters), are in a state of chronic hypertonia.[2] This ties in with the physical awkwardness so often encountered in the compulsive character. Hence, the ego, to put it graphically, has taken anal holding-back tendencies from the repressed layers and put them to use in its own interest as a means of warding off sadistic impulses. Whereas anality and aggression are parallel forces in the unconscious, anality, i.e., holding back, operates against aggression (and vice versa) in the function of defense. Thus, unless we break down the affect-block, we shall not get at the anal energies either. We are reminded of our affect-blocked patient who, for months on end, passed his hand over the fly of his pants three times before each session while reciting the Götz quotation three times. It was as if he wanted to say: "I would so much like to kill you, but I have to control myself—so you know what you can do . . ."

---

[2] Cf. Fenichel's excellent presentation in "Über organlibinöse Begleiterscheinungen der Triebabwehr" *Internationalen Zeitschrift für Psychoanalyse,* 1928.

The passive-feminine character also wards off aggression with the help of anal tendencies, but in a way different from the compulsive character. In the former, anality operates in the original direction as an object-libido striving; in the latter, it is manifested in the form of anal holding back, i.e., already as a reaction formation. In the purely developed compulsive character, therefore, passive homosexuality (which of course belongs to the category of the hysterical character) is not so close to the surface and relatively unrepressed as it is in the passive-feminine character.

How is it possible that anal holding back in the character can have such far-reaching ramifications, causing those who suffer from it to become living machines? This is not solely because of the anal reaction formation. The sadism which is bound in the affect-block is not only its object but also the means it employs to ward off anality. Thus, interests in anal functions are also warded off with the help of aggressive energy. Every affective, lively expression arouses in the unconscious the old excitations that had never been resolved. The result is a constant anxiety that a misfortune could take place, that something might preclude the reestablishment of self-possession. We observe that this is the point of departure for the unraveling of the whole childhood conflict between urge to evacuate and the need to hold back, out of fear of punishment. And we learn from clinical experience that, if the analysis of the affect-block is carried out correctly, the breakthrough into the central conflict is a success and the corresponding cathexes are restored to the old positions. This is equivalent to the dissolving of the armor.

By way of the affect-block, we also arrive at the affective anchoring of the first identifications and the superego: the demand to exercise control, originally imposed by the outer world upon a rebelling ego, is complied with. But this compliance does not stop there; it becomes a chronic, inflexible mode of reaction. And this can be accomplished only with the help of the repressed energies of the id.

Further probing into the dynamics of the affect-block shows that two kinds of sadistic impulses are consumed in it. Through systematic resistance analysis, they can be extracted in fairly pure, separate forms. Usually, anal sadism, whose goal is beating, stomping, crushing, etc., is liberated first. After it has been worked through and the anal fixations have been loosened, *phallic*-sadistic impulses move more and more into the foreground (sticking, piercing, etc.). That is, the regression is eliminated; the road to the cathexis of the phallic position is paved. At this point usually, *affective* castration anxiety finally becomes manifest and the analysis of the genital repressions begins. In compulsive characters, the old childhood phobia often reappears in this stage.

Hence, we find two layers of repressions in the compulsive character: the outer layer consists of sadistic and anal impulses, while the deeper layer is made up of phallic impulses. This corresponds to the inversion which takes place in the regression process: those impulses which receive a new cathexis lie closest to the surface; whereas object-libidinal genital strivings are deeply repressed, "covered over" by layers of pregenital positions. These structural relations reveal that it would be a serious technical error, through interpretations, to make the patient affectively aware of the weak manifestations of genital-object strivings *before* the superimpositions have been worked through. Everything would be received coldly, warded off with doubt and distrust.

We have in this connection to pause a moment to consider ambivalence and doubt. They constitute the severest obstructions to analysis if we do not succeed, from the outset, in disentangling the various strivings that comprise ambivalent emotions. Ambivalence reflects a conflict between two simultaneously present potentials, one to love and the other to hate the same person; at a deeper layer it is an inhibition of the libidinal as well as aggressive strivings by the existing fear of punishment. If all manifestations are indiscriminately and simultaneously analyzed, the ambivalence will hardly be mastered. And this could easily lead one to assume that man is biologically, i.e., immutably, ambivalent. If, on the other hand, we proceed in keeping with the structural and dynamic relations, hate will soon move into the foreground and can be resolved with relative ease through analysis, thus paving the way to the extrication of the libidinal strivings. The best procedure to effect this *separation of the ambivalent strivings* is to analyze thoroughly the contemporary distrust, right at the outset of the analysis.

In this discussion we have had to restrict ourselves to the essential traits of the compulsive character, leaving many secondary features untouched. It is enough if we have succeeded in explaining the basic makeup of the character.

3. THE PHALLIC-NARCISSISTIC CHARACTER

The designation of the "phallic-narcissistic character" resulted from the necessity of defining character forms which stand between those of the compulsion neurosis and those of hysteria. They exhibit circumscribed traits which differ sharply, in both the way they originate and the way they become manifest, from those of the other two forms, so that the distinction is justified. The term "phallic-narcissistic character," sometimes less accurately referred to as "genital-narcissistic character," has been incorporated into psychoanalytic terminology in the course of the past few years. The description of this type was first presented in a previously unpublished paper read at the Vienna Psychoanalytic Society in October 1926.

The phallic-narcissistic character differs even in external appearance from the compulsive and the hysterical character. The compulsive is predominantly inhibited, reserved, depressive; the hysteric is nervous, agile, fear-ridden, erratic. The typical phallic-narcissistic character, on the other hand, is self-assured, sometimes arrogant, elastic, energetic, often impressive in his bearing. The more neurotic the inner mechanism is, the more obtrusive these modes of behavior are and the more blatantly they are paraded about. In terms of physique, the phallic-narcissistic character is predominantly an athletic type, hardly ever an asthenic type and only in isolated cases a pyknic type (as defined by Kretschmer). His facial features usually exhibit hard and sharp masculine lines. Very often, however, despite his athletic habitus, we find feminine, girlish features (the so-called baby face). Everyday behavior is never cringing, as in the case of the passive-feminine character; it is usually arrogant, either coldly reserved or contemptuously aggressive. And sometimes his behavior is "bristly," as a representative of this type once put it. The narcissistic element, as opposed to the object-libidinal element, stands out in the attitude toward the object, including the love object, and is always infused with more or less concealed sadistic characteristics.

In everyday life, the phallic-narcissistic character will usually anticipate any impending attack with an attack of his own. The aggression in his character is expressed less in what he does and says than in the way he acts. Particularly, he is felt to be totally aggressive and provocative by those who are not in control of their own aggression. The most pronounced types tend to achieve leading positions in life and are ill suited to subordinate positions among the rank and file. When such is the case, as in the army or similar hierarchal organizations, they compensate for the necessity of having to subordinate themselves by dominating those beneath them. If their vanity is offended, they react with cold disdain, marked ill-humor, or downright aggression. Their narcissism, as opposed to that of other character types, is expressed not in an infantile but in a blatantly self-confident way, with a flagrant display of superiority and dignity, in spite of the fact that the basis of their nature is no less infantile than that of the other types. A comparison of their structure with the structure, for example, of a compulsive character, yields the clearest insights into the difference between pregenital and phallic-based narcissism. Notwithstanding their overwhelming concern for themselves, they sometimes form strong relationships to people and things of the world. In this respect, they show a close resemblance to the genital character. They differ from the latter, however, in that their actions show a far deeper and broader tendency to be influenced by irrational motives. This type is encountered most frequently among athletes, pilots, military men, and engineers. Aggressive courage is one of the most outstanding traits of their character, just as temporizing caution characterizes the compulsive character and the avoidance of dangerous situations characterizes the passive-feminine character. This courage and pugnacity of the phallic-narcissistic character have, as opposed to the genital character, a compensatory function and also serve to ward off contrary impulses. This is of no special importance as far as their respective achievements are concerned.

The absence of reaction formations against his openly aggressive and sadistic behavior distinguishes the phallic-narcissistic character from the compulsive character. We shall have to demonstrate that this aggressive behavior itself fulfills a function of defense. Because of the free aggression in the relatively unneurotic representatives of this type, social activities are strong, impulsive, energetic, to the point, and usually productive. The more neurotic the character is, the more extravagant and one-sided the activities appear—although they are not necessarily that extravagant and one-sided in actual fact. Between these actions and the creation of paranoic systems lie the many variations of this character type. The behavior of the phallic-narcissistic character differs from that of the compulsive character in its demonstration of greater boldness and less thoroughness with respect to details.

In phallic-narcissistic men, erective potency, as opposed to orgastic potency, is very well developed. Relationships with women are disturbed by the typical derogatory attitude toward the female sex. Nonetheless, the representatives of this character type are looked upon as eminently desirable sexual objects because they reveal all the marks of obvious masculinity in their appearance. Though not a rarity, the phallic-narcissistic character among women is far less frequently found. The neurotic forms are characterized by active homosexuality and clitoral excitability. The genitally healthier forms are characterized by enormous self-confidence that is based on physical vigor or beauty.

Almost all forms of active male and female homosexuality, most cases of so-called moral insanity, paranoia, and the related forms of schizophrenia, and, moreover, many cases of erythrophobia and manifestly sadistic male perverts, belong to the phallic-narcissistic character type. Productive women very often fall under this category.

Now let us turn our attention to the structure and genesis of this character. First of all, we have to distinguish those impulses which attain direct gratification in the phallic-narcissistic behavior from those which form the narcissistic defense apparatus, though the two are intertwined. One typical feature brought out through analysis is an identification between the ego as a whole and the phallus; in the case of phallic-narcissistic women, there is a very strong fantasy of having a penis. This ego, moreover, is openly vaunted. In erythrophobia, this impulse is repressed and breaks through in the form of an intensely neurotic feeling of shame and blushing. At the basis of and common to these cases is a fixation on that phase of childhood development in which the anal-sadistic position has just been left, while the genital object-libidinal position has not been fully attained, and is, therefore, governed by the proud, self-confident concentration on one's own penis. This explanation does not tell the whole story. The phallic-narcissistic character is characterized not only by this phallic pride but more so by the motives which compel him to become arrested at this stage of development.

Along with pride in the real or, as the case may be, fantasized phallus, there is a strong phallic aggression. Unconsciously, the penis, in the case of the male of this type, serves less as an instrument of love than as an instrument of aggression, wreaking revenge upon the woman. This accounts for the strong erective-potency characteristic of this type, but also for the relative incapacity for orgastic experience. In the childhood histories of the phallic-narcissistic character, the most severe disappointments in love are found with surprising regularity, disappointments precisely in the heterosexual objects, i.e., in the mother in the case of boys and in the father in the case of girls. And, in fact, these disappointments are experienced at the height of the striving to win the object by phallic exhibition. In the case of the male representatives of this type, the mother is very often the stricter parent, or the father died at an early age or was not married to the mother and was never present.

The inhibition of the further development to genital object-love in childhood because of a severe frustration of genital and exhibitionistic activities at the *height* of their development, typically by that parent or guardian on whom the genital interests had begun to focus, results in an identification with the genitally desired parent or guardian on a *genital* level. Boys, for example, relinquish and introject the female object and shift their interests to the father (active homosexuality, because phallic). The mother is retained as a desired object but only with narcissistic attitudes and sadistic impulses of revenge. Again and again such men seek unconsciously to prove to women how potent they are. At the same time, however, the sexual act constitutes a piercing or destroying—closer to the surface, a degrading—of the woman.

In phallic-narcissistic women, genital revenge upon the man (castration) during the sexual act and the attempt to make him or have him appear impotent becomes, in an analogous way, the leading tendency. This is certainly not at variance with the sexual attraction exercised by these strongly erotic characters on the opposite sex. Hence, we often meet with a neurotic-polygamous inability to stick to one's partner, the active inducing of disappointments, and passive flight from the possibility of being deserted. In other cases, where narcissistic sensitivity disturbs the mechanism of compensation, we find a weak potency, which the individual will not admit. The more disturbed the potency is, the more unstable the general mood usually is. In such cases, there are sudden vacillations from moods of manly self-confidence to moods of deep depression. Capacity for work is likewise severely disturbed.

The phallic-exhibitionistic and sadistic attitude serves simultaneously as a defense against diametrically opposite tendencies. The compulsive character, following genital frustration, regresses to the earlier stage of anality and develops reaction formations here. The phallic-narcissistic character remains at the phallic stage—indeed, he exaggerates its manifestations; but he does this with the intent of *protecting himself against a regression to the passive and anal stages.* In the course of the analysis of such characters, we meet with more and more intense and concentrated, while at the same time rigidly warded off, anal and passive tendencies. However, these tendencies do not directly constitute the character. Rather, it is mainly determined by the defense against these tendencies in the form of phallic sadism and exhibitionism, a defense proceeding from an ego that has become phallic-narcissistic. There is a marked difference here between the passive-feminine and the phallic-narcissistic character. Whereas the former wards off his aggression and his genital impulses with the help of anal and passive surrender, the latter wards off his anal and passive-homosexual tendencies with the help of phallic aggression. We often hear analysts describe such characters as anal and passive homosexual. However, just as the passive-feminine character cannot be designated as phallic-sadistic because he wards off these impulses, the phallic-narcissistic character cannot be described as anal-passive because he successfully subdues these impulses in himself. The character is determined not by what it wards off but by the way in which it does it and by the instinctual forces which the ego uses for this purpose.

In cases of moral insanity, active homosexuality, and phallic sadism, as well as in sublimated forms of these types, e.g., professional athletes, this defense succeeds well; the warded-off tendencies of passive and anal homosexuality are merely expressed in certain exaggerations. In cases of paranoia, on the other hand, the warded-off tendencies break through in the form of delusions. Erythrophobia is closely related to the paranoic form of this character; the representation of pathological blushing is often found in the anamnesis of paranoid schizophrenia. A patient suffering from erythrophobia falls victim to a symptomatic breakthrough of the warded-off passive and anal homosexuality inasmuch as he gives up masturbation because of acute castration anxiety. The sexual stasis which builds up weakens the defense function of the ego and affects vasomotor activity. Active homosexuality, phallic sadism, and moral insanity, on the other hand, have a strong ego defense, provided there is effective libido gratification. If, for one reason or another, this gratification is interrupted for any length of time, the passive and anal tendency also breaks through in these cases, either symptomatically or openly.

Among the phallic-narcissistic-sadistic characters, one often finds addicts, especially alcoholics. Not only warded-off homosexuality lies at the root of these addictions, but also another specific trait of this character type, likewise the result of phallic frustration. Let us take the case of the male. Along with the mother's frustration of phallic exhibition and masturbation, there is an identification with her. This has a provocative effect upon the recently relinquished anal position and, consequently, upon the passive-feminine behavior. This is immediately offset by an accentuation of the phallic-exhibitionistic and aggressive, i.e., masculine, impulses. However, when the identification with the woman takes place at the phallic stage, the woman is fantasized as having a penis and one's own penis becomes associated with the breast.[3] We therefore find a tendency toward passive and ac-

---

[3] Cf. Böhm's and Sadger's investigations of active homosexuality.

tive fellatio in the sexually active forms of this character type, in addition to a maternal attitude toward younger men in the case of the male, and to younger and feminine women in the case of the female. In alcoholism, there is also a regression to the oral position. Accordingly, the typical traits of the phallic-narcissistic character are effaced in the alcoholic.

In the phallic-narcissistic character, the transitions between the healthy, object-libidinal form on the one hand and the acutely pathological, pregenital forms of addiction and chronic depression on the other hand are far more numerous and diverse than they are in other character types. In psychopathology, much is said about the affinity between the genius and the criminal. However, the type they have in mind is a product neither of the compulsive nor of the hysterical nor of the masochistic character; he derives predominantly from the phallic-narcissistic character. Most of the sex murderers of recent years belong to this character type, e.g., Haarmann and Kürten. Because of severe childhood disappointments in love, these men later exercised phallic-sadistic revenge on the sexual object. Landru as well as Napoleon and Mussolini belong to the phallic-narcissistic character type. The combination of phallic narcissism and phallic sadism accompanied by compensation of passive- and anal-homosexual impulses produces those psychic constitutions most strongly charged with energy. Whether such a type will turn his energy to active endeavors or crime on a large scale depends, first and foremost, upon the possibilities which the social climate and situation provide for this character to employ his energies in a sublimated form.

Next in importance is the extent of genital gratification. It determines the amount of surplus energy which the destructive impulses receive and, therefore, how urgent the need for revenge becomes and what pathogenic forms it assumes. In contrasting the social and libido-economic conditions, we do not want to obscure the fact that the inhibition of gratification is also dependent upon socio-familial factors. In terms of their constitutions, these character forms probably produce an above-average amount of libidinal energy, thus making it possible for the aggression to become that much more intense.

The analytic treatment of phallic-narcissistic characters is one of the most gratifying tasks. Since, in these patients, the phallic stage has been fully achieved and the aggression is relatively free, it is easier to establish genital and social potency, once the initial difficulties have been mastered, than it is in patients of other character forms. The analysis is always promising if the analyst succeeds in unmasking the phallic-narcissistic attitudes as the warding off of passive-feminine impulses and in eliminating the unconscious attitude of revenge toward the opposite sex. If this fails, the patients remain narcissistically inaccessible. Their character resistance consists in aggressive deprecation of the treatment and of the analyst in a more or less disguised form, in narcissistic usurpation of the interpretation work, in the rejection and warding off of every anxious and passive impulse and, above all, of the positive transference. The reactivation of phallic anxiety succeeds only through the energetic and consistent unmasking of the reactive narcissistic mechanism. The indications of passivity and anal-homosexual tendencies should not be immediately pursued in depth; otherwise the narcissistic defense will usually build up to a point of complete inaccessibility.

CHAPTER XI

THE MASOCHISTIC CHARACTER

NOTE: "The Masochistic Character" first appeared in the *Internationalen Zeitschrift für Psychoanalyse,* XVIII (1932–33). It represents Wilhelm Reich's clinical break with Freud's theory of the death instinct. For the first time in the history of sexual pathology, it was proven on the basis of clinical investigations that:

1) The phenomena used to substantiate the hypothesis of the theory of the death instinct can be traced back to a specific form of orgasm anxiety.

2) Masochism is not a biologically determined drive; rather, it is a *secondary* drive in the sex-economic sense, i.e., the result of a repression of natural sexual mechanisms.

3) There is no biological striving for unpleasure; hence, there is no death instinct.

In 1933, this paper was incorporated into Wilhelm Reich's *Character Analysis.*

In the years following its publication, parts of this clarification of the problem of masochism were adopted by various psychoanalysts, without any mention of its source. However, no one discussed or presented the *central* element of the problem, namely the *specific* masochistic inhibition of the orgasm function, which became manifest as a *fear of dying* or *fear of bursting.* Hence, the solution of the problem of masochism has remained the exclusive scientific accomplishment of sex-economy.

The publication of this essay in 1932 was not devoid of dramatic concomitants. Freud, who was the editor of the *Internationalen Zeitschrift für Psychoanalyse,* would allow the article to appear in this journal only on condition that it be accompanied by an editorial note. In this note, the reader was supposed to be informed that Wilhelm Reich had written this article against the theory of the death instinct, "in the service of" the Communist

Party. A number of Berlin analysts rejected this nonsense and suggested a different way out of the difficulty; namely, that Reich's essay on masochism be published together with a *reply*. This reply was written by Siegfried Bernfeld and it appeared in the same issue, under the title *"Die kommunistische Diskussion der Psychoanalyse."* The reply had nothing to do with the problem of masochism, however. Instead, it dealt with and sharply rejected Wilhelm Reich's contributions to Marxian sociology. In other words, since Wilhelm Reich's clinical arguments were incontestable, the attempt was made to weaken his theory of masochism by ascribing it to emotionally tinged political motives. This attempt was a total failure. We leave it to the reader to decide whether this theory rests on clinical investigations and data or was motivated by political-ideological interests. It is necessary to point out that the sex-economic elucidation of the problem of masochism, i.e., the clinical refutation of the theory of the death instinct, represents an enormous step forward in the understanding of neuroses. For now it was no longer possible to ascribe human suffering to an immutable "biological will to suffer," i.e., a "death instinct," but to *dismal social impingements on the biopsychic apparatus.* And this paved the way to a critique of neuroses-engendering social conditions, a way previously blocked by the hypothesis of a biological will to suffer.

The sex-economic solution of the problem of masochism also provided an approach to the biological basis of neuroses. Indeed, the fear of "bursting," a fear which characterizes masochism, led (at first merely at a speculation, later as a viable theory) to the understanding of the vegetative life apparatus.[1]

The publication of this essay today is as justified as it was twelve years ago. It is indicative of certain kinds of ostensibly scientific criticisms that not a single one of the assertions which were made against Reich's theory of masochism twelve years ago could be published today. They are no longer valid—they belong to the dead past.

[1] Cf. Reich: *The Discovery of the Orgone,* Vol. I, *The Function of the Orgasm,* Chapter VII.

1. SUMMARY OF VIEWS

Since analytic characterology presupposes certain ideas about instincts, we have selected the masochistic instincts to illustrate a special type of neurotic character.

Pre-psychoanalytic sexology was essentially of the opinion that the tendency to find gratification in the endurance of pain or moral degradation constituted masochism, which was considered a special instinctual aim. Since there is an absence of pleasure in both goals, there has been from the very beginning a question about the nature of masochism: how can something which is unpleasurable be instinctively desired and even provide gratification? To resort to technical terminology is merely to postpone the solution; the term "algolagnia" was supposed to explain that one wants to obtain pleasure from being beaten or degraded. Some authors divined correct relationships when they contested the notion that the masochist really wants to be beaten; they contended that the beating itself played merely an intermediary role in the experience of pleasurable self-degradation (Krafft-Ebing). However that may be, the essential formulation remained: *what the average person senses as unpleasurable is perceived by the masochist as pleasurable or at least serves as a source of pleasure.*

The psychoanalytic investigation of the latent content and dynamics of masochism, in both its moralistic and its erogenic components, produced a wealth of new insights.[2] Freud discovered that masochism and sadism are not absolute opposites, that the one instinctual aim is never present without the other. Masochism and sadism appear as an antithetical pair; the one can change suddenly into the other. Thus, it is a matter of a dialectical antithesis, which is determined by the reversal of an active attitude to a passive attitude, while the ideational content remains the same.[3] Freud's theory of libidinal development further distinguishes the three stages of childhood sexuality (oral, anal, and genital) and, in the beginning, relegated sadism to the anal phase.

[2] A thorough, critical summary of the analytic results can be found in Fenichel: *Perversionen, Psychosen, Charakterstorungen,* Internationaler Psychoanalytischer Verlag, 1931, p. 37ff.

[3] Freud: "Triebe und Triebschicksale," Ges. Schr. Bd. V, p 453

Later it was found that every stage of sexual development is characterized by a corresponding form of sadistic aggression. Following up this problem, I was able to find in each of these three forms of sadistic aggression a reaction of the psychic apparatus to the specific frustration of the corresponding partial libidinal impulse. According to this concept, the sadism of each stage results from the mixture between the sexual demand itself and the destructive impulse against the person responsible for its frustration;[4] *oral sadism* (frustration of sucking→destructive impulse, biting); *anal sadism* (frustration of anal pleasure→crushing, stomping, beating); *phallic sadism* (frustration of genital pleasure→piercing, puncturing). This concept was in complete agreement with Freud's original formulation that destructive feelings (whose most frequent cause is the frustration of an instinct) are initially directed against the outer world and turn against the self only later, i.e., when they too are inhibited by frustration and fear, and end in self-destruction. Sadism becomes masochism when it is turned against the person himself;[5] the superego (the repre-

[4] Reich: "Über die Quellen der neurotischen Angst," *Internationalen Zeitschrift für Psychoanalyse,* XI (1926), p. 427.

[5] ". . . the designation masochism comprises all passive attitudes to the sexual life and to the sexual object; in its most extreme form the gratification is connected with suffering of physical or mental pain at the hands of the sexual object . . . It may even be doubted whether it ever is primary and whether it does not more often originate through transformation from sadism." Freud: "Three Contributions to the Theory of Sex," *The Basic Writings of Sigmund Freud.* New York, 1938. Translated by A. A. Brill.

"In the case of the pair of opposites sadism-masochism, the process may be represented as follows:

(a) Sadism consists in the exercise of violence or power upon some other person as object.

(b) This object is given up and replaced by the subject's self. With the turning round upon the self, the change from an active to a passive instinctual aim is also effected.

(c) An extraneous person is once more sought as object; this person, in consequence of the obliteration which has taken place in the instinctual aim, has to take over the role of the subject.

Case (c) is what is commonly termed masochism. Here, too, satisfaction follows along the path of the original sadism, the passive ego placing itself back in phantasy in its first role, which has in fact been taken over by the extraneous subject. Whether there is, besides this, a more direct masochism, not derived from sadism in the manner I have described, seems not to be met with. "Instincts and their Vicissitudes," *The Complete Psychological Works*

sentative of the person responsible for frustration or, to put it another way, the representative of the demands of society in the ego) becomes the agent of punishment toward the ego (conscience). The guilt feeling results from the conflict between the love striving and the destructive impulse.

The concept that masochism is a secondary formation was later given up by Freud himself in favor of another, namely that sadism was masochism directed toward the outer world. In this new formulation, there was supposed to be a *primary biological* tendency toward self-destruction, a *primary* or erogenic masochism.[6] Freud's statement was founded on the more basic assumption of a "death instinct," postulated as the antithesis of eros. Thus, primary masochism was said to be the independent manifestation of the biologically rooted death instinct, based on the processes of dissimilation in every cell of the organism (also "erogenic masochism").[7]

The exponents of the theory of the death instinct made every effort to support their assumptions by calling attention to the physiological processes of decomposition. Yet a convincing substantiation was nowhere to be found. A recent article which takes a stand *for* the reality of the death instinct deserves special attention because it approaches the problem clinically and offers physiological arguments which, at first glance, give one pause for thought. Therese Benedek[8] bases her arguments on the research of Ehrenberg. This biologist discovered that even in the unstruc-

---

of Sigmund Freud, Vol. XVI, 1914–16. Translated from the German by James Strachey.

"To begin with, there seems to be a confirmation of the view that masochism is not the manifestation of a primary instinct, but originates from sadism, which has been turned round upon the self . . . Instincts with a passive aim must be taken for granted . . . But passivity is not the whole of masochism. The characteristic of unpleasure belongs to it as well—a bewildering accompaniment to the satisfaction of an instinct." "A Child Is Being Beaten," Vol. XVII, 1917–19.

[6] "If one is prepared to overlook a little inexactitude, it may be said that the death instinct which is operative in the organism—primal sadism—is identical with masochism." Freud, in his article, "Das ökonomische Problem des Masochismus" ("The Economic Problem of Masochism").

[7] Freud: *Jenseits des Lustprinzips,* Ges. Schr., Bd. VI.

[8] "Todestrieb und Angst," *Internationalen Zeitschrift für Psychoanalyse,* XVII (1931).

tured protozoon a self-contradictory process can be found. Certain processes in the protoplasm not only determine the assimilation of food but at the same time lead to a precipitation of substances previously existing in solution. The first structural formation of the cell is irreversible inasmuch as dissolved substances are converted into a solid, undissolved condition. What assimilates is part of the life process; what comes into existence through assimilation is a change in the cell, a higher structurization which, from a certain point on, namely when it predominates, is no longer life, but death. This makes sense, especially when we think of the calcification of the tissues in old age. But this very argument refutes the assumption of a *tendency* toward death. What has become fixed and immobile, i.e., what remains behind as the slag of the life process, hinders life and its cardinal function, the alternation of tension and relaxation, the basic rhythm of metabolism in the fulfillment of the need for food and sexual gratification. This disturbance of the life process is the exact antithesis, of what we have come to know as the basic characteristic of the instinct. The process of rigidification increasingly disrupts the rhythm of tension and relaxation. To accept these processes as the basis of an instinct, we would have to change our concept of instincts.

If, furthermore, anxiety were the expression of the "liberated death instinct," it would still have to be explained how "fixed structures" can become free. Benedek herself says that we regard the structure, i.e., what is firmly frozen, as something inimical to life only when it predominates and inhibits the life processes.

If the structure-forming processes are synonymous with the death instinct; if, moreover, as Benedek states, anxiety corresponds to the inner perception of this preponderant rigidification, i.e., dying, then we shall have to assume further that anxiety is absent in the years of childhood and adolescence and appears increasingly with age. The exact opposite is the case. It is precisely in periods of sexual efflorescence that the function of anxiety is most strongly in evidence, i.e., because of the condition of inhibition. According to this assumption, we would also have to find the fear of death in gratified human beings, for they too are subject to the same biological process of decomposition as those who are ungratified.

By consistently pursuing Freud's theory of actual anxiety, I was able to change the original formula—anxiety arises through the conversion of libido—to read: anxiety is a phenomenon of the same process of excitation in the vaso-vegetative system, that in the sensory system is perceived as sexual pleasure.[9]

Clinical observation teaches us that, initially, anxiety is nothing other than the sensation of constriction, a condition of stasis (anxiety = *angustiae*); fears (imagined dangers) become emotionally charged anxieties only when that specific stasis occurs. Should it eventually turn out that the socially imposed restrictions upon sexual gratification accelerate the sexual stasis that accompanies the structure-forming processes, thus also accelerating the process of dying, this would not be proof of the derivation of anxiety from these processes but only of the life-damaging effect of sex-negating morality.

This new formulation of the concept of masochism results automatically in a change in the etiological formula of neurosis. The essential meaning of Freud's original conviction was that psychic development is carried out on the basis of the conflict between instinct and outer world. A second concept followed which did not, it is true, annul the first but very much reduced its importance. Now the psychic conflict was conceived of as the result of the conflict between eros (sexuality, libido) and the death instinct (urge to self-annihilation, primary masochism).

The clinical basis for this hypothesis, which from the outset aroused the deepest doubts, was the peculiar, indeed puzzling fact that certain patients appear not to want to give up their suffering but seek out unpleasurable situations again and again. This was at variance with the pleasure principle. Thus, one had to assume that there was an inner, concealed intention to maintain the suffering or to reexperience it.[10] It remained questionable how this "will to suffer" was to be conceived of, as a primary

---

[9] Cf. Reich: *The Function of the Orgasm*, Chapter IV.

[10] "The suffering itself is what matters."

"The satisfaction of this unconscious sense of guilt is perhaps the most powerful bastion in the subject's (usually composite) gain from illness—in the sum of forces which struggle against his recovery and refuse to surrender his state of illness. The suffering entailed by neuroses is precisely the factor that makes them valuable to the masochistic trend." Freud: *"Das ökonomische Problem des Masochismus."*

biological tendency or as a secondary formation of the psychic organism. It was possible to ascertain a need for punishment which—according to the hypothesis of the death instinct—appeared to gratify through self-inflicted suffering the demands of an unconscious feeling of guilt. And subsequent to the publication of *Beyond the Pleasure Principle*, psychoanalytic literature, as expounded particularly by Alexander, Reik, and Nunberg, modified, without really being aware of it, the formula of the neurotic conflict.[11] Originally, the neurosis was said to result from the conflict between instinct and outer world (libido—*fear of punishment*). Now it is said that the neurosis results from the conflict between instinct and the *need* for punishment (libido—*desire* for punishment), i.e., the exact opposite of what had been said previously.[12] This concept was in complete harmony with the new theory of instincts based on the antithesis between eros and the death instinct. This new theory traced the psychic conflict back to inner elements and more and more eclipsed the supreme role of the frustrating and punishing outer world.[13] In the original theory, suffering was said to derive "from the outer world, from society." Now it was said to derive "from the biologic will to suffer, from the death instinct and the need for punishment." This new formulation blocked the difficult path into the *sociology* of human suffering, into which the original psychological formula on the psychic conflict had made considerable headway. The theory of the death instinct, i.e., the theory of

[11] The theory of the death instinct dominates psychoanalytic literature at the present time. Freud himself in a conversation a few years ago described the theory of the death instinct as a hypothesis existing outside clinical experience. In *Beyond the Pleasure Principle*, we read at the end: ". . . be prepared to leave a path which one has followed for a while, when it doesn't appear to be leading to anything good." However, the hypothesis became a clinical "theory"; it was not only not given up—it led to nothing good. Some analysts even contend that they have direct evidence of the death instinct.

[12] "The core of the entire psychology of the neurosis is contained in the sentence that guilt can be atoned through punishment, through suffering." Alexander: "Neurose und Gesamtpersönlichkeit," *Internationalen Zeitschrift für Psychoanalyse,* XII (1926), p. 342.

"The neurosis, which is essentially based on a conflict between instinctual demand and need for punishment . . ." (Reik)

[13] This concept found its strongest advocates in the English group of the International Psychoanalytic Society.

self-destructive biological instincts, leads to a cultural philosophy of human suffering (cf. *Civilization and Its Discontents*). Human suffering is said to be ineradicable because destructive impulses and impulses striving toward self-annihilation cannot be mastered.[14] The original formulation of the psychic conflict, on the other hand, leads to a critique of the social system.

In the shifting of the source of suffering from the outer world, from society, to the inner world, and in its reduction to a biological tendency, one of analytic psychology's original and cardinal principles, the "pleasure-unpleasure principle," was severely undermined. The pleasure-unpleasure principle is a basic law of the psychic apparatus, according to which *pleasure is sought* and *unpleasure is avoided*. In the previous concept, pleasure and unpleasure—or, otherwise expressed, the psychic reaction to pleasurable and unpleasurable stimuli—determined psychic development and psychic reactions. The "reality principle" was not *antithetical* to the pleasure principle; it merely implied that, in the course of development and because of the influence of the outer world, the psychic apparatus has to get used to postponing momentary gains of pleasure and to forgoing some entirely. These "two principles of psychic functioning"[15] could be valid only so long as masochism was regarded as the desire to endure suffering arising from an inhibition of the tendency to inflict pain or suffering upon another person—was regarded, that is, as inverted sadism. So conceived, masochism lay wholly within the framework of the pleasure principle, though the problem remained as to how suffering can be pleasurable. From the very beginning, this was at variance with the nature and meaning of the pleasure function. While it was possible to understand how ungratified or inhibited pleasure could be transformed into *unpleasure,* it was hard to understand how *unpleasure* could become pleasure. In short, even the original concept of the gener-

---

[14] The Fateful question for the human species seems to me to be whether and to what extent their cultural development will succeed in mastering the disturbance of their communal life by the human instinct of aggression and self-destruction." *Civilization and Its Discontents,* English translation quoted from *The Complete Psychological Works of Sigmund Freud,* Vol. XXI.

[15] Freud: *Formulierungen über die zwei Prinzipien des psychischen Geschehens,* Ges. Schr., Bd. V.

ally accepted pleasure principle did not solve the basic enigma of masochism, for to say that masochism consisted in the pleasure derived from *unpleasure* did not explain anything.

The postulation of a "repetition compulsion" was accepted by most analysts as a satisfactory solution to the problem of suffering. It fit in extremely well with the hypothesis of the death instinct and the theory of the need for punishment, but it was very dubious in two respects. First, it invalidated the generally sound pleasure principle, so heuristically and clinically valuable. Second, it introduced into the empirically well-founded theory of the pleasure-*unpleasure* principle an indisputably metaphysical element, an unproven and "unprovable" hypothesis that caused a great deal of unnecessary confusion in the development of analytic theory. There was said to be a biological compulsion to repeat unpleasurable situations. The "principle of the repetition compulsion" was of no great import if conceived of as a basic biological principle, for as such it was merely a term. The formulation of the pleasure-*unpleasure* principle, on the other hand, could be substantiated by the physiological laws of tension and relaxation. Insofar as the repetition compulsion was understood to mean the law that every instinct strives to establish the state of repose and, moreover, to reexperience pleasures once enjoyed, there was nothing to object to. Thus understood, this formulation was a valuable supplement to our understanding of the mechanism of tension and relaxation. When conceived of in this way, the repetition compulsion lies wholly *within* the framework of the pleasure principle; indeed, the pleasure principle itself explains the compulsion to repeat. In 1923, rather awkwardly I defined instinct as the nature of pleasure to have to be repeated.[16] Thus, *within* the framework of the pleasure principle, the repetition compulsion is an important theoretical assumption. However, it was precisely *beyond* the pleasure principle that the principle of the repetition compulsion gained its most significant formulation, as a hypothesis for the explanation of facts for which the pleasure principle was allegedly insufficient. It was not possible to prove clinically that the repetition

[16] Reich: "Zur Trieb-Energetik," *Zeitschrift für Sexualwissenschaft*, X (1923).

compulsion was a *primary* tendency of the psychic apparatus. It was supposed to clarify so much, and yet it itself could not be substantiated. It seduced many analysts into assuming that there was a super-individual "ananke." This was superfluous as an explanation of the striving to reestablish the state of repose, for this striving is fully explained on the basis of the function of the libido to bring about a relaxation. This relaxation, in every instinctual sphere, is nothing other than the establishment of the original state of repose and is implicit in the concept of the instinct. Parenthetically, we might point out that even the hypothesis of a biological striving after death becomes superfluous when we bear in mind that the physiological involution of the organism, its gradual decease, begins as soon as the function of the sexual apparatus, the source of the libido, weakens. Hence, dying need not be based on anything other than the gradual cessation of the functioning of the vital apparatus.

The clinical problem of masochism, more than anything else, demanded a solution and led to the unfortunate hypothesis of a death instinct, of a repetition compulsion beyond the pleasure principle, and of a need for punishment as the *basis* of the neurotic conflict. In a polemic directed against Alexander,[17] who built a whole theory of the personality on these hypotheses, I endeavored to reduce the theory of the need for punishment to its proper perspective. Even with respect to the will to suffer, I relied on the old theory of masochism as the final possible explanation. The question of how *unpleasure* can be striven after, i.e., can become pleasure, was already in the air, but I had nothing to contribute at that time. Nor did the hypothesis of an erogenic masochism, a specific disposition of buttock and skin eroticism to perceive pain as pleasurable (Sadger), offer any satisfaction, for how could buttock eroticism be related to the perception of pain as pleasure? And why did the masochist sense as pleasure what others sensed as painful and unpleasant in the same erogenic zone while being beaten? Freud himself partially unraveled this question. In the fantasy "A Child Is Being Beaten," he

---

[17] Reich: "Strafbedürfnis und neurotischer Prozess, Kritische Bemerkungen zu neueren Auffassungen des Neurosenproblems," *Internationalen Zeitschrift für Psychoanalyse,* XIII (1927).

traced the original pleasurable situation to: "Not I, but my rival, is being beaten."[18] But this did not answer the question why being beaten was accompanied by pleasure. All masochists avow that pleasure is associated with the fantasy of being beaten or with actual self-flagellation, that they can sense pleasure or reach sexual excitation only with this fantasy.

Long years of research on cases of masochism did not provide any solution. It was not until I began to have doubts about the veracity and correctness of the patients' statements that a ray of light finally broke through this darkness. One could not help but be amazed, notwithstanding long years of analytic work, at how little one had learned to analyze the masochistic experience of pleasure itself. In probing deeply into the function of pleasure in the masochist, I was suddenly struck by a curious fact which was deeply puzzling at first, but at the same time provided a complete clarification of the sex-economy and, consequently, of the specific basis of masochism. What was surprising and at the same time puzzling was that the formula, the masochist experiences *unpleasure* as pleasure, proved to be incorrect. Rather, the masochist's specific mechanism of pleasure consisted precisely in that, while he strives after pleasure like any other person, a disturbing mechanism causes this striving to miscarry. This, in turn, causes the masochist *to perceive sensations, which are experienced as pleasurable by the normal person, as unpleasurable when they exceed a certain intensity.* The masochist, far from striving after *unpleasure,* demonstrates a *strong intolerance of psychic tensions* and suffers from a quantitative *overproduction of unpleasure,* not to be found in any other neurosis.

In discussing the problem of masochism, I want to proceed not—as is usual—from the masochistic perversion, but from its reaction basis in the character. To illustrate this, I shall use a patient who was under analysis for almost four years. His case provided answers to questions which several previously treated cases had left unanswered. These cases were understood only in retrospect from the results of this case, which serves here as an example.

[18] Freud: "A Child Is Being Beaten."

2. THE ARMORING OF THE MASOCHISTIC CHARACTER

Very few masochistic characters develop a masochistic perversion. Since an understanding of the masochist's sexual economy can be arrived at only through an understanding of his character reactions, we will pursue, in our presentation, the path generally followed in every psychoanalysis in which the analyst is not content with a theoretical explanation of the case but wants the patient to achieve genital primacy with orgastic potency.

Every character formation, as we pointed out earlier, fulfills two functions: first, the armoring of the ego against the outer world and against the instinctual demands; second, the economic function, i.e., the consumption of the surplus sexual energy produced by the sexual stasis—basically, hence, the binding of the continually produced anxiety. If this holds true for every character formation, then the way these basic functions are fulfilled by the ego is specific, i.e., in terms of the nature of the neurosis. In this process, every character type develops its own mechanism. Needless to say, it is not enough to know the basic function of the patient's character (defense and the binding of anxiety) ; it is necessary in the shortest time possible to learn in what special way the character fulfills this task. Since the character binds the essential parts of the libido (or anxiety) ; since, moreover, we have to liberate these essential elements of sexual energy from their chronic entrenchment in the character and channel them to both the genital apparatus and the sublimation system, we penetrate—under therapeutic necessity and with the help of the analysis of the character—to the central element of the function of pleasure.

Let us summarize the salient traits of the masochistic character. They are found individually in all neurotic characters and do not stand out in their totality as a *masochistic* character until they all converge and predominantly determine the basic tone of the personality and its typical reactions. A typical masochistic character trait is a chronic, subjective feeling of *suffering* which is manifested objectively and especially stands out as a *tendency to complain*. Additional traits of the masochistic character are chronic tendencies *to inflict pain upon and to debase oneself* ("moral masochism") and an intense passion for tormenting others, from which the masochist suffers no less than his object. Common to all masochistic characters is an *awkward, ataxic behavior, especially prevalent in their mannerisms and intercourse with people.* In some cases, these traits can take on the nature of pseudo-dementia. Other character traits are sometimes present, but they do not make any noticeable change in the total picture.

What is important is that, in some cases, this character-neurotic syndrome presents itself openly, while in other cases it is concealed by a surface disguise.

As is true of every other character attitude, the masochistic attitude is mirrored not only in the behavior toward an object but also within the masochist himself. The attitudes originally directed toward objects are also (and this is often important) retained toward the introjected objects, toward the superego. What was originally external and then internalized has to be externalized in the analytic transference. The patient's behavior toward the analyst in the transference repeats what was acquired in relation to the object in childhood. In terms of genetic history, it is irrelevant that, in the meantime, the same mechanism also operated within the ego.

The patient whose analysis we will follow in its essential features, without going into the full details of his illness, began the treatment with the following complaints: he had been wholly incapable of work and socially apathetic since he was sixteen. In the sexual sphere, there was a severe masochistic perversion. He had never cared for intercourse with girls but had masturbated nightly for hours in the way characteristic of the pregenital libido structure. He would roll around on his stomach, and squeeze his penis while fantasizing that a man or a woman was beating him with a whip. In short, he did not masturbate in the normal way, i.e., exciting the penis by regular friction, but by kneading it, clamping it between his thighs, rubbing it between the palms of his hands, etc. *When he sensed that he was about to ejaculate, he would hold back and wait until the excitation had subided, in order, then, to begin anew.* He masturbated in this way night after night, often during the daytime also, until finally, completely exhausted, he would yield to an ejaculation in which the semen did not spurt out rhythmically but merely flowed out. Afterwards, he felt battered, extremely tired, incapable of doing anything, fretful, "masochistic," tormented. He had an especially hard time dragging himself out of bed in the morning. In spite of an overwhelming sense of guilt, he was not able to put a stop to this "loafing in bed." He later described the whole thing as "masochistic bog." The more he rebelled against it, the less he succeeded in extricating himself from this "masochistic mood," the more deeply he was engulfed by it. When he entered analysis, this kind of sexual experience had been going on for years. The effects on his personality and on his emotional life had been devastating.

My first impression of him was that of a man who could barely keep himself going even with the fullest expenditure of his energy. True, he made a strenuous effort to appear well-bred and composed, struck a noble pose and talked about his plans; he wanted to become a mathematician. In the analysis, this ambition turned out to be an intricately worked out delusion in which he pictured himself wandering through the woods of Germany for years on end, cogitating a mathematical system which could calculate and change the whole world. The outer shell of his personality fell away very soon in analysis as I succeeded in explaining to him that it served as a compensation for his feeling of complete worthlessness, a feeling intimately related to and continually reproduced by his experience of masturbation as something "dirty" and "squalid." From childhood on, the "mathematician," conceived of as the pure, asexual man, had the function of covering up the "man of squalor." It is not essential for our discussion that the patient had all the earmarks of incipient schizophrenia of the hebephrenic type. Here it is merely important that "pure" mathematics had the function of erecting a wall against the "dirty" feeling he had about himself that stemmed from the anal type of masturbation.

With the relinquishing of his sexual demeanor, the masochistic attitude appeared in its full magnitude. Every session began with a complaint, followed by openly childish provocations of a masochistic sort. If I asked him to supplement or to give me a more precise formulation of one of his communications, he would attempt to reduce my efforts to absurdity by exclaiming: "No, I won't! No, I won't! No, I won't!" In this connection it was revealed that, between the ages of four and five, he had gone through a phase of violent stubbornness accompanied by attacks of screaming and kicking. The most trivial incident was enough to bring on those "fits of crying," which, as he said, reduced his parents to despair, helplessness, and rage. Such attacks might go on for days, to the point of total exhaustion. Later he himself was able to identify this period of stubbornness as the precursor of the actual masochism. His first fantasies of being beaten appeared when he was about seven years old. Before going to bed, he not only fantasized that he was put across someone's knees and beaten; often he would go into the bathroom, lock the door, and try to whip himself. A scene from his third year of life, which didn't appear until the second year of analysis, could be identified as traumatic. He had been playing in the garden and had—as was clearly evident from the entire situation —soiled himself. Since guests were present, his severely psychopathic, sadistic father got very upset, carried him into the house, and laid him on a bed. *The boy immediately turned over on his stomach and waited for the blows with great curiosity, which was mixed with anxiety.* The father gave him a sound thrashing, but the boy had a feeling of relief—a typical masochistic experience, which he had for the first time.

Had the blows given him pleasure? The analysis clearly established that he had feared far greater harm at that time. He had turned over on his stomach so quickly to protect his genital from his father.[19] The blows on his buttocks were therefore received with a tremendous sense of relief; they were relatively harmless compared with the expected injury to his penis. His fears, therefore, were allayed.

This basic masochistic mechanism must be clearly understood in order to comprehend masochism as a whole. But we are anticipating the course of the analysis, for this did not become clear until the analysis was well into its second year. Until this point, the treatment had been taken up with the attempt, at first unsuccessful, to master the patient's masochistic reactions of stubbornness.

---

[19] This phenomenon was stressed by Freud in his article: "Das ökonomische Problem des Masochismus" (Ges. Schr., Bd. V. p. 378). However, its clinical investigation leads not to the hypothesis of primary masochism but to its refutation.

Describing the way he masturbated in later years, the patient usually said: "It was as if I were turned from my back to my stomach with screws." At first I was of the opinion that this was an intimation of phallic sexuality; only later I recognized that it depicted a defensive movement. *The penis had to be protected; sooner be beaten on the buttocks than suffer an injury to the penis!* This basic mechanism also determined the role of the fantasy of being beaten. *What was originally a fear of punishment later became the masochistic desire.* In other words, the masochistic fantasy of being beaten constituted an anticipation of more severe punishment. Alexander's formulation that sexual pleasure is bargained for through the gratification of the need for punishment also has to be reinterpreted in this light. One does not punish oneself to assuage or "bribe" one's superego, in order, then, to enjoy pleasure free of anxiety. The masochist approaches pleasurable activity just like any other person, *but the fear of punishment intervenes.* Masochistic self-punishment is *not* the execution of the feared punishment but rather the execution of a milder, substitute punishment. Thus, it represents a special kind of defense against punishment and anxiety. The passive-feminine surrender to the punishing person typical of the masochistic character is also to be understood in this context. Our patient once stuck out his buttocks in order, as he said, to be beaten; in reality, this desire to be beaten was really the desire to give himself as a woman (entirely in keeping with the Freudian interpretation of the passive beating fantasy as the substitute of a passive-feminine desire). The non-masochistic passive-feminine character fulfills this function of warding off the danger of castration through pure anal surrender. He has no need of the masochistic idea or of the fantasy of being beaten to help him ward off anxiety.

This discussion leads us directly to the question whether *unpleasure* can be striven after. However, we want to postpone this question in order, first, to establish the foundation for it through the character analysis of the masochist.

In our patient, a period of infantile spite became reactivated in the analytic treatment in a completely uninhibited and unconcealed way. The phase of the analysis dealing with his fits of screaming lasted for some six months, but it also succeeded in completely eliminating this mode of reaction. After that, it did not reappear in this infantile form. In the beginning, it was not easy to get the patient to reactivate the stubborn actions of his childhood. His pose as a mathematician served as a defense against this. After all, a noble man, a mathematical genius, did not do such things. And yet there was no avoiding it. To unmask and to eliminate this layer of the character as defense against anxiety, it had to be fully reactivated. When the patient resorted to his "No, I won't! No I won't!" I tried at first to interpret it, but my efforts were completely ignored. So I began to imitate the patient, i.e., I followed up each interpretation of his behavior with a "No, I won't!" It was the specific analytic situation itself which prompted me to adopt this measure. I would not have gone as far with him as I eventually did in any other way. Once he reacted with involuntary kicking to my consistent attempts to reduce his resistance to absurdity. I seized the opportunity and told him to let himself go completely. At first he could not understand how anyone could ask him to do such a thing. Finally, however, plucking up more and more courage, he began to toss about on the couch, leading up to emotionally charged cries of defiance and bellowing of inarticulate animal-like sounds. A particularly violent attack occurred when I told him that he defended his father merely to mask the inordinate hatred he felt for him. Nor did I hesitate to tell him that there was a certain amount of rational justification in his hatred. Now his actions began to take on a startling character. He bellowed so horribly that the neighbors became afraid. We could not allow ourselves to be deterred by this, for we knew that this was the only way of reaching his deep affects. It was the only way he could reexperience his childhood neurosis completely and affectively—and not merely as a recollection. Again and again this reenactment enabled him to get an insight into his behavior. It represented a tremendous *provocation of the adults* and, in the transference, of me. *But why did he provoke?*

Other masochistic patients provoke the analyst by means of the typical masochistic silence. Our patient did it in the form of infantile spite. It took me quite some time to make him understand what had become clear to me very soon, namely that these provocations were attempts to make me strict and drive me into a frenzy. But this was merely the superficial meaning of his behavior. It was necessary to go deeper. This is seldom done, however, because one holds to the view that the masochist strives after punishment as such, as a gratification of a guilt feeling with the motive force and scope of an instinct. This view is generally regarded as an explanation for the deepest meaning of masochistic provocation. In actual fact, it is not at all a question of punishment but of *putting* the analyst or his prototype, the parent, *in the wrong,* of causing him to act in a way which would give a rational foundation to the reproach "See how badly you are treating me." This provocation of the analyst is, in every case, one of the main difficulties in analyzing a masochistic character. Unless its deepest intent is understood, no progress can be made.

There must be a meaning in the fact that the masochist provokes the analyst to put him in the wrong. The meaning is: "You are a bad person; you don't like me; on the contrary, you treat me horribly; I am right in hating you." This justification of the hatred and the diminishing of the guilt feeling through this mechanism are merely an intermediate process. The main problem of the masochistic character is not his guilt feeling or his need for punishment, though both are factors in each case. If guilt feeling and need for punishment are conceived of as manifestations of a biological death instinct, then, it is true, the unmasking of this rationalization of hate and the provocation of the object will be regarded as the ultimate explanation. Since this is not our view, we must go on to ask why the masochist tries to put his object in the wrong.

Genetically and historically, a deep *disappointment in love* lies behind the provocation. The masochist is especially fond of provoking those objects through whom he suffered a disappointment. Originally, these objects were intensely loved, and either an actual disappointment was experienced or the love demanded by the child was not sufficiently satisfied. It is already possible to note that a strong need for love goes along with the real disappointments experienced by the masochistic character. This need precludes a real gratification and has a specific inner source, which we shall discuss later.

As time went on and the patient came to realize that he could not reduce me to a frenzy, his behavior remained the same but its intention was different. Now, apparently, he began to enjoy letting himself go in the analysis. The acting out became a hindrance, for he consumed the entire hour with childish kicking and screaming. Now it was possible to show him that, originally, his provocation had compassed the important secondary goal of testing to what extent he could let himself go, i.e., how much I would take before withdrawing my love and attention and switching to punishment. He had persuaded himself that he had no need to be afraid—he could carry on as much as he pleased without being punished. By continually conducting himself in a disagreeable fashion, he neutralized the steadily flowing fear of punishment; therefore, being bad was a source of pleasure. It had nothing to do with a desire to be punished. Though especially attentive, I found no evidence of such a desire.

Parallel to this behavior, however, there were continuous complaints about his terrible condition, about the morass from which he was not able to free himself (and from which I was not helping him to get out). His manner of masturbation continued unchanged and daily put him in the "squalid" mood which was regularly vented in complaints, i.e., disguised reproaches. But it was not possible to get down to concrete analytic work. It was out of the question to forbid the acts of spite; to do so would have been to risk the entire future success of the treatment. Hence, I began to hold up a mirror to his behavior. When I opened the door to let him in, he would be standing there with a sullen, pain-distorted, spongy face, the epitome of a bundle of misery. I imitated his appearance. I began to speak to him in his childish language; I also lay on the floor and kicked and screamed the same way he did. At first he was astonished, but broke out in a spontaneous laugh one time, completely mature, completely unneurotic. The breakthrough had been effected, but only temporarily. I continued these procedures until he himself began to analyze. Now we were able to continue.

What was the meaning of the provocation? This was his way of *asking for love,* a way peculiar to all masochistic characters. He needed proofs of love to reduce his inner tension and anxiety. This demand for love was directly dependent upon the degree of tension produced by his unsatisfactory form of masturbation. The more "squalid" he felt, the more strongly he displayed masochism in his behavior, i.e., the more urgent became his demand for love, which he sought to fulfill with every possible means. But why was this demand for love made in this *indirect, veiled manner?* Why did he defend himself so tenaciously against every interpretation of his attachment? Why did he go on complaining?

His complaints showed the following stratification with respect to their meaning, corresponding to the genesis of his masochism: "You see how miserable I am—love me!" "You don't love me enough—you are mean to me!" "You have to love me; I will force you to love me. If you don't love me, I'll make you angry!" The masochistic passion for torment, the complaints, the provocation, and the suffering can, in terms of their meaning —we shall discuss their dynamics later—be explained on the basis of the fantasized or actual non-fulfillment of a quantitatively inordinate demand for love. This mechanism is specific to the masochistic character. It is not found in any other form of neurosis; if it appears in other forms, the corresponding masochistic feature in the character is also present.

What is the meaning of the inordinate demand for love? Information about this is supplied by the analysis of the *predisposition to anxiety* which is always found in masochistic characters. There is a direct correlation between the masochistic attitude and the demand for love on the one hand and unpleasurable tension and the predisposition to anxiety (or danger of loss of love) on the other hand. The former is not antithetical to the predisposition to anxiety as a source of masochistic reaction, for again it is typical of the masochistic character to check the threat of anxiety by demanding love. Just as the complaining represents a disguised demand for love and the provocation, a desperate attempt to force love, the total formation of the masochistic character represents an *abortive* attempt to rid oneself of anxiety and *unpleasure.* It is abortive because, no matter how hard he tries, he never frees himself from the inner tension which constantly threatens to change into anxiety. *Thus, the feeling of suffering corresponds to a concrete fact, namely the continually high-pitched inner excitement and predisposition to anxiety.* We shall understand this situation better when we compare it with the affect-block of the compulsion neurotic character. Here the binding of the anxiety has been carried out with complete success, with the forfeiture of psychic mobility. But the inner tension is completely consumed by a well-functioning character apparatus. There is no restlessness. When it is present, restlessness is an impairment or, more correctly, a decompensation of the character armor.

The masochistic character seeks to bind the inner tension and threat of anxiety by an *inadequate* method, namely by *courting love through provocation and defiance.* Naturally, there is a special reason for this, i.e., this manner of expressing the demand for love is specific to the masochistic character. It doesn't succeed, because the defiance and the provocation are directed at the person who.is loved and from whom love is demanded. In this way, the fear of losing love and attention is increased, just as the guilt feeling which one wants to be rid of is not diminished but intensified, for the beloved person is in fact tormented. This explains the extremely peculiar behavior of the masochist, who becomes more and more enmeshed in the situation of suffering, the more intensely he tries to extricate himself from it. It could not be otherwise, for these attempts to bind anxiety in the character are doomed from the outset.

We find these attitudes, individually, in other characters also; they relate specifically to the masochistic character only when they appear together. What causes such a combination of attitudes?

We have spoken thus far of the *inordinate* demand for love on the part of the masochistic character. Now we have to add that this demand for love is based on a *fear of being left alone* that was intensely experienced in very early childhood. The masochistic character cannot endure being alone any more than he can endure the possibility of losing a love relationship. The fact that masochistic characters so often are lonely is ascribable to the success of a secondary mechanism embodied in the attitude: "See how unhappy, alone, and deserted I am." Once, while discussing his relationship to his mother, our patient exclaimed in great excitement: "To be left alone is to be dead—my life is cut off!" I have often heard this feeling expressed by other masochistic characters, merely phrased differently. The masochistic character cannot endure the loss of an object (masochistic clinging to the love object) any more than he can divest it of its protective role. He cannot endure the loss of contact. When this happens, he will seek to reestablish it in his own inadequate way, i.e., by courting sympathy through misery. Many such characters are very susceptible to the feeling of being alone and deserted in the universe. We see no reason to interpret this feeling in the Rankian sense of womb anxiety, even if it is a common attitude. The fact is that in every masochist, whether he is masochistic solely in the moralistic sense or in the openly erogenic sense, we find a specifically erogenic basis for this feeling. In saying this, however, we are anticipating the later discussion of the masochist's sexual structure.

The fact that skin eroticism plays a special role in masochists is known from several psychoanalytic authors (Sadger, Federn, and others). However, they attempted to regard skin eroticism as the direct basis for the masochistic perversion, whereas analysis shows that the skin assumes this special role in a very complicated and roundabout way, namely only when various elements of disappointment coincide. Only the fear of being left alone is based directly on the fear which arises when the contact with the skin of the loved person is lost. Let us begin by seeking out the syndrome which pertains to the skin in the erogenic masochists. We always find in one form or another an urge for activity involving the skin, or at least corresponding fantasies: being pinched, rubbed with brushes, beaten with whips, tied up—anything which causes the skin to bleed. The buttocks assume an important role in this connection, but only in the indirect way of the anal fixation. Common to these strivings is the desire to feel the *warmth of the skin*—the original intent is not a desire for pain. The object of being whipped is not to suffer pain; rather, pain is put up with for the sake of the "burning." Coldness, on the other hand, has a repelling effect. Some masochists even go so far as to fantasize that their skin is being burned. Our patient's "loafing in bed" can also be traced back to this, i.e., the gratification of a desire for warmth of the skin.

In terms of the physiology of anxiety, the contraction of the peripheral vessels heightens anxiety (pallor in the case of fright; sensation of cold in the anxiety state; chills brought on by fear, etc.). On the other hand, the sensation of warm skin caused by the stronger flow of blood through the peripheral vessels is a specific attribute of pleasure. Physiologically, inner tension is determined by the restriction of the flow of blood. The strong flow of blood through the body periphery, on the other hand, relieves the inner tension and, consequently, the physiological basis of the anxiety. From the physiological point of view, the fear-resolving effect of the orgasm is essentially based upon this process, which represents a remarkable change in the blood circulation with peripheral vessel dilation and discharge of tension in the center (splanchnic vessels).

It is not easy to understand why body contact with the loved person has the effect of resolving anxiety. In all likelihood, this can be explained by the fact that, physiologically, body warmth in the above sense and the innervation of the body periphery in the expectation of maternal protection resolve or at least alleviate the inner tension.[20] A thorough discussion of these facts will follow later.

For the purpose of our present investigation, it is sufficient that the peripheral vasodilatation, which relieves the inner tension and anxiety, represents the erogenic basis of the masochistic character. His later endeavor to avoid the loss of contact is merely the psychic duplication of a physiological process of innervation. To be left alone in the world means to be cold and unprotected, i.e., an intolerable condition of tension.

The question could be raised in this connection as to the role played by oral fixation in the masochist. On the basis of what we know so far, we cannot ascribe any specific importance to it. It is, however, always present to a marked degree, as it is in all characters having pregenital fixations. There can be no doubt that the oral demands contribute considerably to the insatiability of the masochistic demands for love. But the oral greediness in masochism is much more likely the regressive result of an early disappointment in the love object, followed by the fear of being deserted, than a primary cause of the masochistic need for love.

---

[20] Footnote, 1945: The orgone energy that was dicovered in 1939 provides the explanation for this phenomenon: the alleviation of the child's anxiety by bodily contact with the mother is explained, orgone-biophysically, by the orgonotic expansion of the child's biosystem which reaches out for the mother. There is a contact between the orgone fields of the two organisms.

Several cases clearly revealed that the inordinate need for love stemmed from a different source. Here the fear of being left alone could be traced back to that phase of development in which violent aggressions and incipient infantile sexual curiosity, as opposed to the oral and anal impulses, met with severe frustrations by the loved parent or guardian. The enormous fear of punishment which obstructs the advance to genitality is the direct result of this contradiction between sexual impulses that are not only not frowned upon but even encouraged and those threatened with severe punishment. Our patient was allowed to eat as much as he wanted; indeed, he was encouraged to eat. He was allowed to lie in bed with his mother, to embrace her, pet her, etc. His bowel functions were faithfully taken care of. However, when he set about to explore further possibilities of sexual gratification, to take an interest in his mother's genital, to want to touch her, etc., then he experienced the full severity of parental authority.

Insofar as oral demands contribute to masochism, they account for the mood of depression, as they do in the other forms of neurosis. On the basis of what is presently known, the special combination of skin eroticism, anality, and the fear of being left alone which seeks resolution through body contact is specifically characteristic of masochism.

This erogenic disposition is one of the essential causes of the inordinate demand for love, which has the specific undertone of "warm me" (= "protect me"). "Beat me" is an expression of the same striving, but its form has already been changed. It would seem that the masochistic character had not received sufficient love and, for this reason, had developed such a strong demand for love. This is true as far as it goes. But it must also be borne in mind that he also suffered severe frustrations of love. Often, indeed, exaggerated coddling gives rise to it. This excessive demand for love, in turn, is itself the result of the miasma which is part and parcel of the patriachal system of education. The masochistic character is more than a disposition to anal or skin eroticism; rather, it is the result of a specific combination of external influences exercised upon the erogenic susceptibility of the skin and upon the entire sexual apparatus. This combination of influences specifically determines the masochistic character. Only after we have recognized these influences can we comprehend the other character traits of the masochist.

3. INHIBITED EXHIBITIONISM AND THE PASSION FOR SELF-DEPRECATION

We shall now discuss some of the other masochistic character traits, those relating specifically to sexual structure.

It took about a year to loosen sufficiently the character armor of spite, provocation, complaining, etc., to enable us to penetrate into the phase of early childhood and, above all, to reach the point where the patient began to take an active part in the analytic work. I shall pass over the known and in this instance not very important findings which masochism, like every other neurosis, yields in the analysis, e.g., the passive beating fantasy which conceals the desire to surrender oneself anally as a woman to the father, the typical Oedipus complex, the guilt-feeling reactions stemming from the repressed hatred, the ambivalence, etc. They are not specific to the masochistic character. I shall set forth merely those traits which, through their special combination, have to be regarded as pertaining specifically to masochism. I shall also discuss the causes of the masochistic disturbance of the pleasure mechanism.

After the structure of our patient's character was loosened, especially after the repression of the hatred against the father and the fear of him was eliminated, there was a powerful breakthrough of genitality. He had erections; masturbation in the masochistic form ceased; and he began to have genital longings for a woman. His first attempt to have intercourse with a woman was a failure, but it led to the analysis of his deep love for his mother, which had heavy anal overtones. In the rapid improvement of his condition, the following stood out:

His approach to women was exceptionally strong, but he could not get free of the feeling of *inner tightness and constraint.* This provided him with a continuous excuse for masochistic complaining, e.g., in spite of external improvement, he did not feel well: "The mood of masochistic squalor is the same as ever."

He tended to be readily disappointed on the most insignificant grounds and withdrew from reality into masochistic fantasies at the slightest difficulty. This vacillation between vigorous attempts to establish genital contact with reality and rapid retreats into masochism lasted for many months. I knew that his castration anxiety had not been dissolved and was responsible for this instability. The concentration of the work in this area produced a wealth of interesting analytic results. Until this time, the patient had not shown any trace of genital interest. Now it was revealed that he was full of anxiety notions about the genitals. Here are a few examples: the vagina is a "mire" swarming with snakes and vermin; his phallus is nipped off at the tip; one plunges into an abyss and does not find one's way out. However, the discussion of all these anxieties failed to effect any change in his apathetic condition. Week after week and month after month, he began each and every session with the same masochistically uttered complaint that he was "inwardly broken." The transference had to be analyzed time and again, in the course of which new material on his passive-anal strivings was unearthed. Above all, it was discovered that he immediately withdrew from the woman when a rival appeared. The idea that he had a small penis could not be easily dislodged. He developed an envious attitude toward every rival, which was immediately camouflaged by a passive-feminine bearing. This is a well-known mechanism of binding the fear of the father. Deep analysis of these attitudes did not bring about any change in his feeling that he had remained a masochist, in spite of external improvements.

The first attempts at coitus in which he was potent but remained unsatisfied were attended by a syphilis phobia. One day he showed me his penis and asked me whether a small erosion was not a sign of an infection. It was immediately clear that the intent behind this was exhibitionism. Now the analysis led directly to a clarification of an important aspect of his genital development. As a child he had reached the genital phase only in the form of exhibiting his penis, an act which had been immediately and strictly *forbidden by his mother.* The genital disappointment was all the worse because he had been allowed to indulge in anal exhibitions as much as he pleased in front of his mother, who had been intensely concerned with his functions of evacuation. At the age of ten, he was still taken to the bathroom by his mother. His pleasure in exhibiting his buttocks was clearly the reason why he introduced the genital phase precisely with the exhibition of his penis. The analysis revealed that his first attempts at a genital approach to his mother were of an exhibitionistic nature. His intentions had been immediately repressed, and this later resulted in the severe inhibition of his general bearing. In his attempts to have intercourse, he never ventured to show himself naked to the woman or allowed her to take hold of his penis. Following the analysis of this element of his neurosis, he began earnestly to cast about for a profession and he became a photographer. The first step in this direction was the purchase of a camera, with which he took pictures of just about everything. Here again we see how essential the elimination of genital repression is for sublimation. Today he does quite well as a photographer. For a long time, however, he derived no inner pleasure from his profession: "I don't really feel myself; and when I do, so masochistically miserable."

The introduction of the genital phase in childhood through exhibitionism, followed immediately by the severe frustration and repression of this pleasure and complete inhibition of further genital development, belongs, according to my experience, specifically to the masochistic character;[21] just as the introduction of genitality through phallic-sadism and its inhibition, combined with anal-sadistic fixation, relates specifically to the compulsive neurosis. A number of typical character traits which form the basis of the masochist's insecure, atactic, and awkward bearing can be traced back to these exhibitionistic impulses and their immediate frustration. Our patient once gave a drastic description of this inner condition. He said: "I always feel like an officer who, with drawn sword and cries of victory, marches far ahead of his troops, suddenly looks back and discovers that no one has followed him."

A further character trait is connected with this feeling, which is only very superficially related to guilt feeling. Masochistic characters *cannot endure praise* and tend toward *self-deprecation* and *self-abasement*. In spite of his great ambition, our patient could not endure it when he was considered a good student in school. "If I had continued to be a good student, I would have

---

[21] With respect to the relation between masochism and exhibitionism, see the case described by Fenichel in *Perversionen, Psychosen, Charakterstörungen*, p.39.

fancied myself as standing naked in front of a large crowd with an excited penis." This remark, though made parenthetically, as is often the case in analysis, went straight to the core of the matter. Through the inhibition and repression of genital exhibition, the foundation is eroded upon which sublimation, activity, and self-confidence can be later developed. In masochists, this inhibition of exhibitionism can lead to the development of completely opposite traits. The genital-narcissistic character exhibits in a disguised form (cf. erythrophobia). The masochistic character employs an opposite reaction formation: *a passion for self-deprecation in order not to stand out.* He lacks the essential element of the narcissistic structure of the genital character: the ability to stand out.

The masochistic character, for the reasons set forth above, cannot assume a leadership role, although he will usually construct glorious fantasies of heroism. His true nature, his *ego,* is rooted in passivity because of the anal fixation. As a result of the inhibition of exhibitionism, moreover, his ego has developed an intense inclination toward self-deprecation. This structure of the ego stands in opposition to and prevents the realization of an active phallic ego-ideal.[22] The result of this is again an intolerable tension, which serves as a further source of the feeling of suffering and thus nourishes the masochistic process. The image of the advancing officer mirrors this ego-ideal, which one has to be ashamed of, which one has to conceal, because the ego (the troops) doesn't—can't—follow.

In this connection there is another character trait which is very often found in masochistic characters and in children who tend toward masochism: *feeling oneself to be stupid* or, the counterpart of this, *acting as if one were stupid.* It is very much part of the masochistic character structure to exploit every inhibition in order to debase oneself. Another patient once said that he could not endure praise because he felt himself to be on exhibition with his pants pulled down. It should not be underestimated how much importance the anal fixation, the preoccupation with the baring of the buttocks, has for the child's genital devel-

---

[22] Cf. the chapter on "Defective Identifications" in my book *Der triebhafte Charakter,* Internationaler Psychoanalytischer Verlag, 1925.

opment. Anal shame is brought into the genital phase and op-
presses it with particular shyness. To the masochist, any kind
of praise represents a provocation of exhibitionistic tendencies.
Wherever he stands out, he is assailed by severe anxiety. Hence,
it is necessary for him to debase himself to ward off anxiety. This,
naturally, is a fresh reason for feeling neglected—which provokes
the whole complex of the need for love.

"Making oneself stupid" or "acting as if one were stupid" is
also a part of this. Once our patient described an infantile scene
in which he had pretended to be stupid. "I want something
that is not given to me, then I get mad and act stupid. But
how much am I loved even when I pretend to be stupid? If
I am not loved, then I am not worthy of being loved and have,
therefore, to be really stupid and ugly."

Now it is time to answer the question of why the masochistic
character expresses his demand for love in such a disguised
form, why he is wholly incapable of showing or demanding love
in a direct fashion. Another patient, having strong feelings of
suffering and a tendency toward masochistic complaining, had a
habit of showing himself to be miserable whenever he wanted to
win a woman. He had a terrible fear of offering the woman his
love directly. He was afraid she might get angry and make fun of
or punish him. He suffered from the same inhibited exhibitionism
as our patient.

All this, taken together, causes a feeling of inner ataxia, often
a tormenting feeling of shame because of one's external appearance. The inhibition of the ability to demonstrate or demand
love openly entails distorted expressions and makes a person, as
our patient put it, "bureaucratic," i.e., unnatural and stiff. Behind this lies the ever-present fear of being disappointed or rejected. Once our patient said: "I am faced with the task of pushing a penis which doesn't stand up into a vagina which is not
offered me."

The hysterical character develops anxiety in place of an open
testimony of love; the compulsive character manifests hate and
feelings of guilt; the masochistic character demonstrates and demands love in the roundabout way of complaining, provoking, or
putting on a show of misery. All these various forms are wholly

in keeping with the respective geneses of these types: the hysterical character has fully developed his genitality but it is interfused with fear; the compulsive character has replaced his genitality with phallic sadism; the masochistic character has arrived at genitality through exhibitionism, has then repressed it, and now persists in the *distorted* expression of love.

4. UNPLEASURABLE PERCEPTION OF THE INCREASE OF SEXUAL EXCITATION: THE SPECIFIC BASIS OF THE MASOCHISTIC CHARACTER

Every neurotic structure has a genital disturbance in one form or another which causes sexual stasis and thus provides the neurosis with its source of energy. The masochistic character always reveals a specific kind of disturbance of the genital function. And, unless it is evident from the outset, it does not come to light until the impotence or anesthesia have been largely eliminated. This explains why the disturbance has been completely overlooked in the past. Let us attempt now to pick up our discussion where we left off. We established that the masochistic character generates an excessive amount of unpleasure, which provides a real basis for his feeling of suffering. We observed that the psychic apparatus is constantly attempting to master this tension and predisposition to anxiety in an inadequate way. In his attempts to bind anxiety, the masochistic character becomes more and more immersed in tension and unpleasure, thus strengthening the predisposition to anxiety. We learned further that this very inability to bind anxiety in an adequate way constitutes what is specific to the masochistic character. We found, moreover, that the punishment which the masochistic character thinks he fears is only a substitute for the punishment he really fears.

Could an experience of fear such as our patient had when he was three years old bring about the masochistic fixation of the fantasy of being beaten? The answer is no. It was possible for the patient unconsciously to give up completely the sexual demand which provoked the punishment he feared so terribly. (Other character types do this.) It was not absolutely necessary for him to hit upon a specifically masochistic means of extricating himself from the punishment situation. There must be another element or elements, then, which, when added to what we already know, specifically account for the masochistic mechanism as a whole.

This mechanism can be traced only after the patient has been brought to the genital stage, i.e., when his genital desires become resuscitated or develop for the first time. Then a new difficulty is encountered: the patient now develops strong genital desires which momentarily eliminate much of his masochistic attitude. When, however, in his first attempt to have genital intercourse, he experiences not pleasure but *unpleasure* he is once again thrown back into the "masochistic squalor" of anal and sado-masochistic pregenitality. It took many years to solve this puzzle and to understand that the "incurability of the masochist, who doesn't *want* to give up his suffering," was to be ascribed to our very imperfect knowledge of his sexual apparatus. It would have been impossible to find an answer had we adhered to the theory that the masochist is fixated on suffering because of a repressed guilt feeling or a need for punishment, supposedly the manifestation of a death instinct.

These findings are not intended to gainsay the fact that self-punishments are capable of relieving the conscience. For us, it is solely the *validity* of our clinical formulations that is important. The alleviation of guilt feelings through punishments affects not the core but the surface of the personality. Such "expiatory" sufferings can be totally eliminated without bringing about the cessation of a neurotic process; they appear seldom and, moreover, constitute a symptom, not the cause, of a neurosis. On the other hand, the conflict between sexual desire and fear of punishment is central in every neurosis. There is no neurotic process without this conflict. The prevailing psychoanalytic assessment of the need for punishment led to a misguided modification of the analytic theory of neurosis, had a negative effect upon the theory of therapy, obscured the problems of the prophylaxis of neurosis, and concealed the sexual and social etiology of the neurosis.

The masochistic character is based on a very peculiar spastic attitude which controls not only his psychic but, first and foremost, his genital apparatus. *It immediately inhibits every strong sensation of pleasure and transforms it into unpleas-*

ure. In this way, the suffering which is the basis of the masochistic character reactions is continuously nourished and increased. No matter how deeply and thoroughly we analyze the
meaning and genesis of the masochistic character, we cannot
achieve a therapeutic effect unless we succeed in penetrating to
the genesis of this spastic attitude. Otherwise, we shall not
succeed in establishing the patient's orgastic potency, the capacity
for complete surrender in the genital experience. For orgastic
potency alone is capable of eliminating the inner source of *unpleasure* and anxiety. Let us return to our patient.

When he attempted to have sexual intercourse for the first
time, he had, it is true, an erection, but he did not venture to
move inside the vagina. At first we thought that this was due
to embarrassment or lack of knowledge—it wasn't until much
later that we discovered the real reason. *He had been afraid of
the intensified pleasure*. This was certainly very strange behavior.
We always encounter this fear in the cure of the orgastic disturbance of frigid women. In masochists, however, it has a particular character. To understand this, we shall have to return
to the analytic material.

After our patient had had sexual intercourse a number of
times, which considerably augmented his genital self-confidence,
it was revealed that he experienced less pleasure during intercourse
than he did during masochistic masturbation. Yet he was able to
form a vivid concept of the sensation of genital sensuality, and
this concept became a powerful incentive in the treatment. The
patient's weak genital experience was very critical, for pregenital
pleasure can be uprooted only through the establishment of the
naturally more intense genital pleasure. The absence of pleasure
during the sexual act was certainly no encouragement to the development of genitality. Further attempts at coitus revealed a
new disturbance. The penis became soft during the act. Was it
merely castration anxiety, or was it more than that? Further
analysis of his notions of castration failed to bring about any
change in his condition. Finally, it turned out that the contraction of the musculature of the pelvic floor before ejaculation in
masturbation had a greater significance than we had originally
assumed. I shall summarize the infantile material which shows
that, in spite of his seemingly free and excessive anal and ureth-

ral gratification, the masochist has an *anal and urethral inhibition and anxiety* stemming from earliest childhood, which is later carried over to the genital function and creates the immediate physiological basis for the excessive production of *unpleasure*.

From the ages of three to six, our patient developed a fear of the bathroom, sustained by the fantasy that an animal could crawl into his rear end. The dark hole of the toilet itself aroused anxiety. He began to hold back his bowel movements, which, in turn, aroused the fear that he would evacuate in his pants. When one evacuates in one's pants, one is beaten by one's father. The unforgettable scene at the age of three had provided ample proof of this. When one is beaten by one's father, there is also the danger of castration. Hence, the blows have to be diverted to the buttocks, so that they don't accidentally hit the penis. Nonetheless, in the "cultural" educational procedures which his father adopted and drastically applied, he was continually tormented by the fear that, by lying on his stomach, he might get a splinter in his penis. Everything together produced a spastic condition in the bladder and in the bowels, from which the child could not extricate himself. This, in turn, gave his mother further cause to be especially attentive to his bowel movements, thus creating a fresh contradiction. The mother was pleased with and took care of his bowel functions, whereas the father beat him for it. In this way, his Oedipus complex became predominantly anchored in the anal zone. At first, the additional anxiety developed that the bladder and bowels might burst, that, in short, holding back served no purpose in the long run, and he would again become the victim of his father's rage, for the latter was not to be trifled with in such things, even if he, the father, did not impose any anal restraints upon himself. Thus, we have the typical picture of a bleak and wretched situation, whose roots are to be traced back not to biological but to purely sociological factors. We must not forget to mention that the father was especially fond of pinching his children on the buttocks and, among other things, took pleasure in letting it be known that he would "skin them alive" if they misbehaved.

Thus, to begin with, the child had an anal fear of the father which was combined with the anal fixation on the mother and beating himself (reflective of the fear of punishment by the father). Because of the release and gratification connected with them, the child looked upon his bowel movements as punishable, and so he began to beat himself out of fear of being punished by the father. It is evident that this simple process was of far greater importance for the pathology of the case than the identifications with the punishing father and the masochistic attitudes toward the nascent anal superego. Such pathological identifications are of course themselves neurotic formations, essentially consequences, not causes, of the core of the neurosis.[23] We of course found all the complicated relations between ego and superego, but we did not stop there. Rather, we went on to the more important task of deciding exactly which factors of masochism were dependent upon the concrete behavior of the father and which factors were dependent upon inner erogenic strivings. In this case as well as in other similar cases, I came to one conclusion: our methods of education deserve far greater attention than is usually given to them, and we divide our attention very poorly when we allot 98 percent of it to analytic embellishments and scarcely 2 percent of it to the gross injuries inflicted upon the children *by the parents*. This is why, thus far, we have not succeeded in utilizing psychoanalytic findings for a critique of patriarchal and familial upbringing.

This childhood conflict situation, essentially the result of the contradictory attitude of the patient's parents toward his anality, was responsible not only for the feminine surrender to the male father but also for the feeling of emptiness and impotence. Later, every time the patient came into contact with an adult man, he felt impotent. Out of fear, he immediately withdrew his cathexis from the genital zone and became anal-passive—which was expressed as admiration of these men.

It is now possible to draw the following conclusions: the usual toilet training (too soon and too harsh) causes anal pleasure to take precedence over other forms and the libido to become fix-

---

[23] The neurosis is brought on by the conflict between an ego which strives for pleasure and an outer world which frustrates these ego-strivings; it is sustained by the conflict between the ego and the superego. The superego retains its power on the basis of the repeated experience that sexual pleasure is something punishable. To the early effect of childhood suppression is added the decisive suppressive atmosphere of society.

ated in this phase. The idea of being beaten which is related to
anality is definitely devoid of pleasure and, in the beginning,
charged with anxiety. Thus, it is not the *unpleasure* of being
beaten that becomes pleasurable. *Rather, it is the fear of being
beaten that blocks the sensation of pleasure.* In the course of development, this fear is carried over to the genital zone.

Even after the patient was well into adolescence, he still often
slept with his mother in the conjugal bed. When he was sixteen,
he developed the phobia that his mother could become pregnant
by him. Her physical closeness and warmth had a very stimulat-
ing effect on his masturbation. The ejaculation had the meaning
of urinating at his mother; nor could it have had any other
meaning in view of his previous development. If the mother bore
a child, this would constitute the *corpus delicti* of his urethral incest. Strict punishment would have to be feared. So now he
began to hold his semen back and at the same time to have vivid
masochistic fantasies. His definitive illness commenced at this
point. His school work deteriorated markedly. Following a brief
and unsuccessful attempt to restore himself through "self-
analysis," psychic debility set in, together with the protracted
nightly anal-masochistic masturbation.

The final breakdown was brought on by a severe actual neurosis which culminated in a state of continuous tension, insomnia, and migraine-like headaches. At this time, the inhibited adolescent suffered from a strong accumulation of genital libido. He
was in love with a girl but was afraid to approach her. He was
afraid that he would "asphyxiate" her (i.e., by passing wind),
the very thought of which filled him with shame. He chased after
every girl from a distance, vividly fantasizing that he and she
"were pressing their bellies together." This would be sure to result in a child which would betray them. The fear of being rejected because of his anal tendencies also had a decisive effect in
this. We see here a typical pubertal fate: inhibition of genital primacy due partly to social barriers, partly to neurotic fixations
caused by the earlier impairment of the sexual structure on account of faulty toilet training.

At first, in addition to the genital tension, there was also the
anal tension created by the continuously constrained urge to
evacuate and pass wind. The patient did not permit a genital

release. It was not until he was seventeen that he had his first emission, which was brought on with the help of protracted fantasies of passive beatings. The actual neurosis became milder after this, but the first ejaculation was experienced traumatically. For fear of soiling the bed, the patient sprang up during the ejaculation, seized the chamber pot, and was inconsolable that some semen had spilled on the bed.

As he began to establish his genitality during the course of treatment, he had considerable difficulty in retaining his erection during the sexual act. In this genital phase, masturbation was begun with normal masculine and phallic libido. As soon as the pleasure began to mount, however, masochistic fantasies set in. The analysis of this sudden change from genitality to masochism *during* the sexual act yielded the following facts. As long as the sensation of pleasure was slight, the genital fantasy remained. However, as soon as the pleasure began to increase; when, as the patient put it, that "melting feeling" began to take possession of him, he grew afraid; his pelvis became spastic instead of relaxed and transformed the pleasure into *unpleasure*. He described exactly how he perceived the "melting," usually an orgastically pleasurable sensation, as unpleasurable or, more specifically, with a sense of anxiety: he was afraid that the penis might dissolve. This feeling might cause the skin of the penis to melt away; the penis might burst if it continued to expand (as is normal in the sexual act). He had the feeling that the penis was a sac filled with fluid to the point of bursting. Here we had the incontestable proof that, in masochists, it is not *unpleasure* that becomes pleasure but the exact opposite: by means of a mechanism that is specific to the masochistic character, every pleasure which increases beyond a certain measure is inhibited and changed into *unpleasure*. It is also necessary to point out that the patient conceived of castration as referring to the skin of the penis: "In sex, I get as hot as a cooked chicken from which the skin can be peeled off."

The ever-present fear of punishment causes the "melting" sensation of warmth, which accompanies the increase of pleasure toward the climax, to be looked upon as the realization of the expected penis catastrophe. This inhibits the course of excitation and results in a purely physiological, unpleasurable sensation to the point of pain. We can summarize the three phases of this process as follows:

1) "I am striving for pleasure."
2) "I am 'melting'—this is the feared punishment."
3) "I have to suppress this sensation to save my penis."

Here an objection will be raised: the inhibition of the sensation of sexual pleasure due to infantile anxiety is found in *every* neurosis. In some cases, indeed, it has destroyed genitality altogether. Hence, this inhibition cannot constitute the specific factor of masochism. For why does not every inhibition of the involuntary increase of the sensation of pleasure lead to the development of the masochistic mechanism? This objection can be countered as follows:

There are two possibilities for such an inhibition of the sensation of pleasure. In the first, the "melting" feeling of pleasure is originally experienced *without* anxiety; later, anxiety supervenes and inhibits the completion of the sexual excitation, but pleasure is still perceived as pleasure. In the second, the sensation of pleasure and the sensation of *unpleasure* run *side by side*. This holds true for every non-masochistic inhibition of the orgasm. In masochism, on the other hand, the melting feeling of the pleasure leading up to orgasm is *itself* perceived as the expected harm. The anxiety, experienced in the anal zone as a result of the attainment of anal pleasure, lays the foundation of a psychic attitude that causes the later genital pleasure, which is of course significantly more intense, to be perceived as the signal of injury and punishment.

Hence, we have the paradox that, though continually striving to realize a pleasurable sensation, the masochistic character is invariably plunged into an unpleasurable sensation. The impression is created that he strives for the unpleasurable sensation. What really happens, however, is that anxiety intervenes between the instinct and its goal, causing the desired pleasure to be perceived as the anticipated danger. In short, instead of pleasure, *unpleasure* is the final result of the initial striving.

This also solves the problem of the repetition compulsion *beyond* the pleasure principle. It appears that a person wants to reexperience an unpleasurable situation. But analysis reveals that this is not the case. Quite the contrary: the goal is originally conceived of as pleasurable. The striving is cut short by frustration, fear of punishment, or anxiety, which completely conceal the goal or make it appear unpleasurable. Thus, we can conclude that a repetition compulsion *beyond* the pleasure principle does not exist; the corresponding phenomena can be explained *within* the framework of the pleasure principle and the fear of punishment.

We have to return to our case once again. The shallowness and protraction of his masturbation are to be ascribed to this disturbance of the pleasure mechanism. *He avoided every increase of the sensation of pleasure.* When this had become clear, he once said: "It is impossible to allow these sensations to pour into one—it is wholly unbearable." Now we comprehend why he masturbated for hours on end; he never attained gratification because he did not allow any involuntary increase in excitation to take place.

In addition to fear, there is another factor involved in this inhibition of the increase of sensation. The masochistic character is used to the low-curved, non-climactic (one is tempted to say "lukewarm") pleasure of the anal zone. He carries over the anal practice and experience of pleasure to the genital apparatus, which functions in an entirely different way. The intense and rapid increase of pleasure in the genital apparatus is not only unaccustomed but also quite apt to arouse terror in a person familiar only with anal pleasure—which is anything but overwhelming. If the anticipation of punishment is added to this, then all the conditions are present for the immediate transformation of pleasure into *unpleasure*.

In retrospect, many facts from previously treated cases become clear on the basis of these new findings. This is especially true of the large number of cases in which unsatisfying sexual activity was followed by a masochistic mood of suffering. Now we know that this activity was unsatisfying due to a *disturbance specific to masochism*. It was also possible to arrive at a much better libido-economic understanding of the strong masochistic tendencies of the patients whom, in *Der triebhafte Charakter* and *Die Function des Orgasmus,* I described as having orgastic disturbances. A female patient having a masochistic perversion was described as follows: "She masturbated . . . with the masochistic fantasy that she was wholly stripped (!), bound, and locked in a cage, where she was forced to starve. It was at this point that the inhibition of the orgasm came into play. Suddenly she had to muse about a contraption which was designed to remove her feces and urine automatically, for she was bound and not allowed to move . . ." In analysis, when the transference increased to the point of sexual excitement, she was usually overcome by an uncontrollable urge to defecate and urinate. When she masturbated with the idea of having intercourse, "masochistic fantasies intervened just before the orgasm was about to begin."

Sex-economically viewed, therefore, the masochistic attitude and the fantasy pertaining to it originate from the unpleasurable perception of the sensation of pleasure and serve to master *unpleasure* through the psychically formulated attitude: "I am so miserable—love me!" Now the beating fantasy comes into play because the demand for love also contains genital claims which force the patient to divert the punishment from the front to the rear: "Beat me, but don't castrate me!" Thus, the masochistic reaction has a specifically actual-neurotic[24] basis.

Hence, the problems of masochism cluster around the peculiar disturbance of the pleasure function. It became clear that the fear of the distintegrating or "melting" feeling of the sensation of pleasure leading up to orgasm forces the masochist to cling to the low-curved sexual excitation. Is this the result of anal fixation or genital inhibition? No doubt both factors contribute to this, just as both factors determine the chronic neurasthenic state of excitation. Anality mobilizes the entire libido apparatus but is not capable of also providing for the resolution of the tension. The inhibition of genitality, not only the result of anxiety, itself constitutes a fear-arousing process, which only augments the discrepancy between tension and factual resolution. It remains to be explained why the beating fantasy first comes into play or becomes especially intense just before the climax.

It is interesting to observe how the psychic apparatus seeks to reduce the discrepancy between tension and gratification, how the urge for relaxation nonetheless breaks through in the beating fantasy. Our patient was adamant on this point: "To be beaten

---

[24] Stasis-neurotic.

by the woman is exactly the same as secretly masturbating in the presence of the woman" (= mother). This, of course, corresponds to the actual experience: as a child and also as an adolescent, the patient had masochistically masturbated while sleeping in the same bed with his mother, that is, he would squeeze and rub his penis, being careful not to have an ejaculation (procreation phobia). Only when he added the fantasy of being beaten by his mother did he have an emission. This had the following meaning, which the patient remembered consciously: "I had the impression that my penis was boiling hot. At the fifth or sixth blow it would surely have to explode, the bladder would have to burst open." *Thus, the purpose of the blows was to bring about the release which was forbidden in other ways, i.e., autoerotically.* If, as a result of the blows of the mother, his bladder burst; if, for the same reason, his penis exploded and the semen was ejaculated, then it was not he who was responsible—it was the tormentor who had caused this to happen. Fundamentally, therefore, the yearning for punishment had the purpose of bringing about the release in a roundabout way, of making the punishing person responsible, i.e., of exonerating oneself. The mechanism is the same on the surface and in the depth of the character. In the former, its meaning is: "Love me so that I won't be afraid!" The meaning of the complaint is: "It is you who are responsible—not I." The function of the beating fantasy is: "Beat me so that, without making myself guilty, I can release myself!" There can be no doubt that this is the deepest meaning of the passive beating fantasy.

Since I first came to recognize this deepest function of the passive beating fantasy, I have observed the above mechanism in a number of other patients who had not developed any manifest perversion but, rather, had been able to hold the masochistic tendency in a latent stage through character changes in the ego. Here are a few examples. A compulsive character developed a masturbation fantasy that he had been placed among primitives who forced him to have intercourse and to behave in a completely uninhibited fashion. Another patient, a passive-feminine character not having any manifest perversion, fantasized that he was brought to the point of ejaculation by blows on the penis. But he had to be bound in order to endure the blows and to prevent him from running away. In this category we also have the masochistic sexual attitude of neurotic women, which is regarded by some analysts as normal female behavior. The woman's passive rape fantasy serves merely to exonerate her of guilt feelings, i.e., she wants to experience the sexual act without guilt. This is possible only under the condition that she is raped. The formal resistance offered by some women in the real act has the same meaning.

This leads us to the problem of so-called pleasure anxiety, which plays a major role in masochism. Let us give an example from another analysis.

A patient remembered that, as a child of some four years old, he was in the habit of consciously producing *pavor nocturnus*. He would crawl beneath the covers, masturbate, be seized by fear, and free himself from it by abruptly throwing the covers away from his body. In such a case, how tempting it is to assume that the repetition compulsion lies at the root of it. First he had *pavor nocturnus* and now, evidently, he wanted to reexperience fear. In this connection, it is necessary to make two points clear: in reality, it was not fear that he wanted to reexperience but the feeling of sensuality. This, however, always became interfused with fear. Furthermore, the freeing of himself from the fear was itself a source of pleasure. What was essential in this process, however, was the fact that the arousal of fear provoked anal and urethral sensations, for whose sake the fear was put up with. The fear does not become pleasure as such but merely forms the basis for the development of a special kind of pleasure.[25] Often, children experience the tension-resolving sensations only in a state of anxiety; usually they deny themselves these sensations out of fear of punishment. The release experienced by a sudden evacuation or urination in a fear-ridden situation often constitutes the main reason for wanting to reexperience anxiety. However, to want to comprehend these phenomena *beyond* the pleasure principle is to misunderstand the facts completely. Under certain conditions, pain and anxiety become the sole possibility of experiencing a release one is otherwise afraid of. Thus, the term "the pleasure of pain" or "pleasure anxiety" can only refer

[25] Cf. Freud: *Drei Abhandlungen zur Sexualtheorie*, Ges. Schr., Bd. V, p. 78f.

—not in a very expedient way—to the fact that pain and anxiety can become the basis of sexual excitation.

The fact that, in our patient, the "bursting of the penis" does represent the instinctual goal does not contradict our comprehension of masochism. On the one hand, this idea is a representation of anxiety, of punishment, in a certain context. On the other hand, it is a representation of the final gratification, of the release which is instinctually desired. This dual psychic meaning of the idea of the bursting of the bladder or of the bowels causes the final pleasure itself to be perceived as the feared execution of punishment.

5. OBSERVATIONS ON THE THERAPY OF MASOCHISM

The establishment of a healthy sexual life, of a regulated libido economy can only result from two kinds of therapeutic processes: the liberation of the libido from the pregenital fixations and the elimination of genital anxiety. Clearly, this is brought about through the analysis of the pregenital and genital Oedipus conflict (through the elimination of the repressions). In this connection, however, it is necessary to stress one point relating to technique. If the pregenital fixations are dissolved through the elimination of the repressions without *simultaneously* overcoming the genital anxiety, there is the danger of an increase of sexual stasis, while the sole road to adequate orgastic discharge remains closed. This danger can build up to the point of suicide precisely when the analysis of the pregenitality succeeds. If, on the other hand, the genital repression is eliminated without dissolving the pregenital fixations, genital primacy remains weak —the genital function is not capable of relieving the total amount of anxiety.

For the therapy of masochism, it is of special importance how the analyst penetrates the barricades of the patient's character, how he breaks down the patient's tendency to make use of his suffering to put the analyst in the wrong, come what may. The uncovering of the sadistic nature of this masochistic behavior is the first and most urgent step. It guarantees success inasmuch as it brings to the surface the original sadism behind the masochism and replaces passive anal-masochistic fantasies with active-phallic sadistic fantasies. Once infantile genitality has been reactivated or restructured in this way, it is much easier to reach the castration anxiety, which, until then, had been concealed and consumed by the masochistic reactions.

Needless to say, these therapeutic measures have no effect whatever on the patient's masochistic character. His complaints, spiting, self-destructiveness, and his awkwardness, which serve as a rational reason for withdrawing from the world, usually persist until the disturbance of his pleasure mechanism in masturbation has been eliminated. Once an adequate orgastic discharge of the libido has been achieved, the patient's personality usually makes a rapid change for the better. But the tendency to take refuge in masochism at the slightest disappointment, frustration, or ungratifying situation continues for a while. Consistent parallel work on the genital anxiety and the pregenital fixation can achieve success only if the damage to the genital apparatus was not too severe and if the patient's immediate environment is not such that it repeatedly forces him back into a masochistic reaction pattern. It follows, therefore, that the analysis of a young masochistic bachelor will succeed much more easily than that of a masochistic woman who is in her menopause or is economically tied to an unfortunate family situation.

Only by consistently working through the masochistic character traits during the first months of treatment can the analyst achieve a breakthrough to the core of the neurosis. But this work must be continued indefatigably throughout the analysis to avoid running into difficulties during the frequent relapses which occur in the process of establishing genital primacy. It must also be borne in mind that the definitive dissolution of the masochistic character can result only after the patient has led a sex-economically satisfactory life of work and love for some time, i.e., after the termination of the treatment.

There is good reason to be very skeptical about the success of the treatment of a masochistic character, particularly of those having manifest perversions, as long as the character reactions have not been understood (and therefore not dissolved) in detail. However, there is every reason to be optimistic when this has been achieved, i.e., when the advance toward genitality, though at first only in the form of genital anxiety, has taken place. When that is the case, there is no need to be alarmed by repeated relapses. It is of course known from general clinical experience that the cure of masochism is one of our most difficult tasks—which is not to say that the rest of our tasks are in any way easy. To do justice to these tasks, however, it is necessary to adhere consistently to that psychoanalytic theory which is firmly grounded in empirical data. Hypotheses such as those criticized here are very often an indication of a premature capitulation to the problems of psychoanalytic practice.

If the patient's masochism is traced back to an irreducible death instinct, then the patient's view of himself is confirmed, that is to say, his desire to suffer is supposedly verified. But we have demonstrated that it has to be unmasked as disguised aggression. This corresponds to the reality of the situation, and it alone renders possible a therapeutic success.

In addition to the two therapeutic tasks named above (reduction of masochism to its original condition of sadism; advancement of pregenitality to genitality), there is a third task which is specific to the treatment of masochistic characters. This is the analytic dissolution of the anal and genital spastic attitude which, as we pointed out, is the actual source of the symptom of suffering.

This representation of the masochistic process is far from offering a solution to all the problems of masochism. But it can be asserted that reincorporating the problem of masochism into the framework of the pleasure-unpleasure principle will facilitate the clarification of the remainder of the problems, which was delayed by the hypothesis of the death instinct.

CHAPTER XII

SOME OBSERVATIONS ON THE BASIC CONFLICT BETWEEN NEED AND OUTER WORLD[1]

To appreciate the theoretical significance of what has been set forth in the preceding chapters, it is necessary to pursue our subject further and to make some observations on the theory of instincts in general. Clinical experience has afforded ample opportunity to verify Freud's basic assumption of the fundamental dualism of the psychic apparatus; at the same time, it provided opportunity to eliminate some contradictions in it. It would be misplaced in this clinical framework to attempt to investigate the connections between instinct and outer world as thoroughly as the material deserves. However, it is necessary, by way of anticipation, to say a few words about these relationships in order to give the explanations of this work a theoretical conclusion, as well as to provide a counterbalance to the over-biologization of analytic psychology.

In his theory of instincts, Freud postulates a number of opposing pairs of instincts, as well as tendencies in the psychic apparatus which counteract one another. With this consistently adhered-to dichotomization of psychic tendencies (which, though antithetical, are nonetheless interacting), Freud, even if unconsciously, established the foundation for a future functional psychology. Originally, the instinct of self-preservation (hunger) and the sexual instinct (eros) were postulated as opposites. Later the instinct of destruction or the death instinct came to represent the counter-tendency of sexuality. The original analytic psychology was based on the antithesis between *ego and outer*

[1] Footnote, 1948: The discovery of the organismic orgone energy will force a reevaluation of our concepts of the "instincts." They are concrete PHYSICAL ENERGY functions.

world. To this corresponded the antithesis between *ego libido and object libido.* The antithesis between *sexuality and anxiety,* while not regarded as a basic antithesis of the psychic apparatus, played a fundamental role in the explanation of neurotic anxiety. According to the original hypothesis, when libido is prevented from entering consciousness and attaining its object, it is converted into anxiety. Later, Freud no longer insisted on the close correlation between sexuality and anxiety,[2] although in my opinion there was no clinical justification for the change in his concept, It can be demonstrated that there is more than an accidental relationship between these various antitheses; they are derived from one another dialectically. It is merely a matter of understanding which antithesis is the original one and how the development of subsequent antitheses takes place, i.e., what influences impinge upon the instinctual apparatus.

In our cases as well as in every other case which is analyzed deeply enough, we are able to discover that at the basis of all reactions exists not the antithesis between love and hate, and certainly not the antithesis between eros and the death instinct, but the antithesis between *ego ("person"; id = pleasure ego) and outer world.* On an elementary level, there is but one desire which issues from the biopsychic unity of the person, namely the desire to discharge inner tensions, whether they pertain to the sphere of hunger or of sexuality. This is impossible without contact with the outer world. Hence, the *first* impulse of *every* creature must be a desire to establish contact with the outer world. The psychoanalytic concept that hunger and libidinal need are opposites and nonetheless intertwined at the beginning of the infant's psychic development (since libidinal stimulation of the mouth—"sucking pleasure"—ensures the absorption of food) leads to strange and surprising consequences when pursued further, i.e., when Hartmann's views on the function of surface tensions on the unity of the organs are applied to our questions. If we assume that Hartmann's theory is correct (certain aspects of which were supplemented by the investigations of Kraus and Zondek), psychic energy must derive from simple physiological and mechanical surface tensions, grounded in the chemistry of the cells, tensions

[2] *Hemmung, Symptom und Angst,* Ges. Schr., Bd. XI.

which develop in the various tissues of the human body, most prominently in the vegetative system and the related organs (blood and lymph system). In this view, the disturbance of the physiochemical equilibrium which is brought about by these tensions turns out to be the motor force of action—in the final analysis, most likely also the motor force of thinking. Fundamentally, however, these disturbances, e.g., in the osmotic equilibrium of the organ tissues, are of a twofold nature. The one form is characterized by a shrinking of the tissues as a result of the loss of tissue fluid; the other, by an expansion of the organ tissues as a result of the increase of the fluid content. In both cases, *unpleasure* is experienced. In the former, the *decrease* of the surface tension produces a *low pressure* and a corresponding feeling of *unpleasure,* which can be eliminated only by the *absorption* of new substances. In the latter, on the other hand, there is a direct correlation between actual *tension* and the sensation of *unpleasure.* Hence, the tension can be eliminated only by a *release,* i.e., by the *elimination* of substances. Only the latter form is connected with specific pleasure; in the former, it is merely a matter of reducing the unpleasure.

An "instinct" is involved in both cases. In the first we recognize hunger and thirst; in the second we recognize the prototype of orgastic discharge peculiar to all erogenic, i.e., sexual, tensions. Biophysiologically, the primitive organism, e.g., a protozoon, discharges centrally and overcharges with plasma peripherally; it has to expand when it absorbs a particle of food, i.e., when it wants to eliminate an inner low pressure. Put into our language, it has to approach the outer world with the help of a libidinal mechanism to eliminate its "low pressure," i.e., its hunger. Growth, copulation, and cell division, on the other hand, are entirely a part of the libidinal function, which is characterized by peripheral expansion followed by release, i.e., decrease in the surface tension. Hence, sexual energy is always in the service of the gratification of hunger, while the absorption of food, conversely, introduces those substances which, through a physiochemical process, eventually lead to libidinal tensions. Just as food absorption is the basis of existence and of libidinal functions, so the latter are the basis of productive achievements, including the most primitive one, locomotion. These biophysiological facts are completely confirmed in the higher organization of the psychic apparatus: it is not possible to sublimate hunger, whereas sexual energy is changeable and productive. This is based on the fact that, in the case of hunger, a negative condition is eliminated—no pleasure is produced. In the case of sexual need, on the other hand, there is a discharge, i.e., production in its simplest form. Over and above this, there is the pleasure afforded by release. This pleasure, according to a law which is in no way understood yet, impels a repetition of the action. It is quite possible that this repetition constitutes an essential aspect of the problem of memory. Thus, hunger is an indication of the *loss* of energy; the gratification of the need for food does not produce any energy which would appear concretely as an achievement (expenditure of energy). It is merely the elimination of a lack. As obscure as this fact still is, the empirical psychoanalytic thesis that work is a conversion of the libidinal energy process—that, furthermore, disturbances of one's capacity for work are intimately related to disturbances of the libidinal economy—is based finally on the described difference of the two basic biological needs.

Now let us return to the question of the antithesis of the strivings. We see that originally they do not lie within the biopsychic unit, disregarding possible phylogenetic factors. One pole of the antithesis is represented by the outer world. Is this at variance with Freud's hypothesis of an *inner* antithesis between the strivings? This is obviously not the case. It is merely a question of determining whether the inner antithesis, the inner dualism, is a primary biological factor or whether it results later from the clash between the apparatus governing physiological needs and the outer world.[3] Moreover, it is a question of deciding whether the original antithesis within the personality is an instinctual one or something different. Let us begin by investigating the phenomenon of ambivalence.

The "ambivalence of feelings" in the sense of *simultaneous* re-

---

[3] To avoid any misunderstanding, it is necessary to make it quite clear that I am not postulating an absolute antithesis between a finished need apparatus and the outer world. The need apparatus itself has a long history behind it. Phylogenetically, it too must have resulted from similar functional processes. This will be a tremendous problem for the theory of evolution as soon as it is ready to give up the mechanistic point of view in favor of the functional point of view.

actions of love and hate is not a biological law. It is, rather, a socially determined product of development. In the anlage, there is only the ability of the biopsychic apparatus to react to stimuli of the outer world in a way that can—although not necessarily—develop into a chronic attitude which we designate as ambivalent. Ambivalence represents a vacillation between hate and love strivings only on the surface layer of the psychic apparatus. At a deeper level, corresponding to an earlier stage of development, vacillation, hesitation, indecision as well as other characteristics of ambivalence have a different explanation. They are the manifestations of a clash between a libidinal impulse ceaselessly striving for expression and fear of punishment which inhibits it and prevents it from being translated into action. Often (in the compulsive character, always) the love impulse is replaced by a hate impulse which, in the depth, pursues the goal of the love impulse but is also inhibited by the same anxiety as the sexual impulse. Thus, depending upon its genesis and the depth of its function, ambivalence has three meanings:

a) "I love you, but I am afraid of being punished for it" *(love-fear).*

b) "I hate you because I am not allowed to love you, but I am afraid of gratifying the hate" *(hate-fear).*

c) "I don't know whether I love or hate you" *(love-hate).*

This yields the following picture of the genesis of the psychic contradictions. From the original antithesis between ego and outer world, which later appears as the antithesis between *narcissism and object libido,* there results the antithesis between *libido* (as a striving in the direction of the outer world) and *anxiety* (as the first and most basic expression of a narcissistic escape back into the ego from the *unpleasure* suffered at the hands of the outer world). This is the first contradiction *within* the person. The stretching forth and pulling in of the pseudopodia in the protozoon is, as we shall demonstrate thoroughly elsewhere, much more than a mere analogy for the "stretching forth" and "pulling in" of the libido. If, on the one hand, *unpleasure* experienced in the outer world causes the libido to be pulled back or to seek refuge "within" (narcissistic flight), it is, on the other hand, the unpleasurable tension created by ungratified needs that urges the person to seek contact with the outer world. If the outer world would bring only pleasure and gratification, there would be no phenomenon of anxiety. Since, however, unpleasurable and danger-producing stimuli originate in the outer world, the striving of the object libido has to be provided with a counterpart, namely the tendency to take refuge in narcissistic escape. The most primitive expression of this narcissistic escape is anxiety. Libidinal stretching forth toward the world and narcissistic escape from it are merely paraphrases of a very primitive function which is present without exception in all living organisms. Even in the protozoon, it is expressed as two opposite directions of plasma currents: the one flowing from the center toward the periphery and the other from the periphery toward the center.[4] Turning pale with fright, trembling with fear ("hair standing on end") correspond to a flight of the cathexis from the periphery of the body to the center of the body, brought about by the contraction of the peripheral vessels and the dilation of the central vessel system (*anxiety* brought about by stasis). The turgor of the peripheral skin tissues, the flushing of the skin, and the feeling of warmth in sexual excitation are the exact opposites of this and correspond to a physiological as well as psychic flow of the cathexes in the direction, center → body periphery → world. The erection of the penis and the moistening of the vagina are the manifestation of this direction of energy in a state of excitation; the shrinking of the penis and the becoming dry of the vagina, conversely, are nothing more than manifestations of the opposite direction of the cathexes and the body fluids from the periphery to the center. The first antithesis, *sexual excitation-anxiety,* is merely the intrapsychic reflection of the primal antithesis, *ego-outer world,* which then becomes the psychic reality of the inner contradiction: "*I desire—I am afraid.*"

Thus, anxiety is and always must be the first manifestation of an inner tension, whether this is brought about by an external frustration of the advance toward motility or the frustration of the gratification of a need, or whether it is brought about by a

---

[4] According to Weber, sensations of *Unlust* go with a centripetal flow of blood, while sensations of pleasure go with a centrifugal flow of blood. See also Kraus and Zondek: *Syzygiologie: Allgemeine und spezielle Pathologie der Person,* Thieme, 1926.

flight of the energy cathexes into the center of the organism. In the first case, we are dealing with stasis or actual anxiety; in the second case, with real anxiety. In the latter, however, a condition of stasis results of necessity and consequently there is also anxiety. Hence, both forms of anxiety (stasis anxiety and real anxiety) can be traced back to *one* basic phenomenon, i.e., the central stasis of the energy cathexes. Whereas, however, the stasis anxiety is the direct manifestation of anxiety, real anxiety is initially merely an anticipation of danger; it becomes affective anxiety secondarily when the flight of cathexes toward the center creates a stasis in the central vegetative apparatus. The original flight reaction in the form of "crawling into oneself" later occurs in a phylogenetically younger form of flight, which consists in increasing the distance from the source of danger. It is dependent upon the formation of an apparatus of locomotion (muscular flight).

In addition to the flight into the center of one's body and the muscular flight, there is a second, more meaningful reaction on a higher level of biological organization: the removal of the source of danger. It can only appear as a *destructive impulse.*[5] Its foundation is the avoidance of the stasis or anxiety which is brought on by narcissistic flight. Basically, therefore, it is merely a special kind of avoidance or resolution of tension. At this stage of development, there are one of two motives for striving toward the world: (1) the gratification of a need (libido) or (2) the avoidance of a state of anxiety, i.e., by destroying the source of danger (destruction). A second antithesis between *libido ("love") and destruction ("hate")* is now developed upon the first inner antithesis between libido and anxiety. Every frustration of an instinctual gratification can either give rise to anxiety

[5] One can, if one wants, perceive a destructive impulse even in the processes pertaining to the gratification of hunger, in the destruction and assimilation of foodstuff. Thus viewed, the destructive instinct would be a *primary* biological tendency. However, one must not fail to take into account the difference between destruction for the sake of annihilation and destruction for the purpose of the gratification of hunger. Only the former can be regarded as a primary instinctual drive, whereas the latter merely represents a device. In the former, destruction is *subjectively* desired; in the latter, it is merely objectively given. The motive of the action is hunger, not destruction. But in each case the destruction is at first directed toward an object *outside* of the person.

(i.e., the first counterpart of the libido) or, to avoid anxiety it can produce a destructive impulse (i.e., the genetically younger counterpart). Each of these modes of reaction corresponds to a character form whose reaction to danger is irrationally motivated and fixated. The hysterical character retreats in the face of danger; the compulsive character wants to destroy the source of danger. The masochistic character, since he is equipped neither with the capacity to approach the object in a genital-libidinal way nor with the destructive tendency to destroy the source of danger, has to endeavor to resolve his inner tensions through an indirect expression, through a disguised beseeching of the object to love him, i.e., to permit and make possible for him the libidinal release. Obviously, he can never succeed in this.

The function of the second antithetical pair, libido-destruction, undergoes a fresh change, for the outer world frustrates not only the libidinal gratification but also the gratification of the destructive impulse. This frustration of destructive intentions is again carried out with threats of punishment which, by imbuing every destructive impulse with anxiety, strengthen the narcissistic mechanism of flight. Hence, a fourth antithesis emerges, *destructive impulse-anxiety*.[6] All new antithetical strivings are formed in the psychic apparatus from the clash between previous strivings and the outer world. On the one hand, the destructive tendency is strengthened by the person's libidinal intentions. Every frustration of the libido provokes destructive intentions; these, in turn, can easily be transformed into sadism, for the latter embodies the destructive *and* the libidinal impulse. On the other hand, the destructive tendency is strengthened by the propensity to anxiety and the desire to avoid or to resolve fear-inducing tensions in the usual destructive manner. However, since the emergence of each new impulse provokes the punitive attitude of the outer world, an unending chain ensues, the first link of which is the fear-inducing inhibition of the libidinal discharge. The inhibition of the aggressive impulse by the threat of punishment stemming from the outer world not only increases anxiety and obstructs the discharge of the libido far more than formerly; it also gives rise

---

[6] In spite of the fact that this antithetical pair lies close to the surface of the personality structure, Adler's entire individual psychology has never gone beyond it.

to a new antithesis. In part, it reverses the destructive impulse which is directed against the world and turns it against the ego, in this way adding counterparts to two impulses; i.e., the *impulse to self-destruction* becomes the counterpart of the *destructive impulse,* and *masochism* becomes the counter-impulse of *sadism.*

In this connection, the feeling of guilt is a late product—the result of a conflict between love and hate toward the same object. Dynamically, the feeling of guilt corresponds to the intensity of the inhibited aggression, which is the same as the intensity of the inhibiting anxiety.

In deriving a complete theoretical picture of psychic processes from the clinical study of neuroses, particularly masochism, we learn two things. (1) Masochism represents a very late product of development. (This is also confirmed by a direct observation of children.) It seldom emerges before the third or fourth year of life; for this very reason, therefore, it cannot be the manifestation of a primary biological instinct. (2) All the phenomena of the psychic apparatus, from which it is believed that a death instinct can be deduced, can be unmasked as indications and consequences of a *narcissistic* (not a muscular) flight from the world. Self-destructiveness is the manifestation of a destructive impulse turned upon itself. Physical deterioration because of chronic neurotic processes is the result of the chronic disturbance of the sexual economy, the chronic effect of unresolved inner tensions having a physiological basis. It is the result of chronic psychic suffering which has an objective basis but is not subjectively desired.

Conscious longing for death, peace, nothingness ("the nirvana principle"), occurs only under the condition of hopelessness and the absence of sexual, in particular genital, gratification. It is, in short, the manifestation of complete resignation, a retreat from a reality which has become *solely* unpleasurable into nothingness. Because of the primacy of the libido, this nothingness figures merely as *another* form of *libidinal* goal, e.g., being at peace in the womb, being cared for and protected by the mother. Every libidinal impulse which is not directed toward the outer world, i.e., which corresponds to a withdrawal into one's own ego—in short, every phenomenon of narcissistic regression—is brought forth as proof of existence of the death instinct. In reality, they are nothing but reactions to actual frustrations of the gratification of libidinal needs and the appeasing of hunger, frustrations caused by our social system or other worldly influences. If, even without concrete contemporary causes, this reaction is fully developed, we have in analysis a suitable instrument for demonstrating that *early infantile* frustrations of the libido necessitated the retreat from the world into one's own ego and created a psychic structure which later renders the person incapable of using the given possibilities of pleasure in the world. Indeed, melancholia, so often held up as proof of the death instinct, demonstrates clearly that suicidal inclinations are secondary. They represent a grandiose superstructure on frustrated orality, which becomes an oral fixation because of the complete inhibition of the genital function. Moreover, it is based on a strongly developed destructive impulse corresponding to this early stage and magnified by the immense libido stasis. This impulse, inhibited and turned against itself, simply can find no other way out than self-destruction. Thus, one destroys oneself, not because one is urged to it biologically, not because one "wants" to, but because reality has created inner tensions which become unbearable and can be resolved only through self-annihilation.

Just as the outer world becomes an absolute unpleasurable external reality, one's own instinctual apparatus becomes an absolute unpleasurable inner reality. However, since the ultimate motor force of life is tension with the promise of a possibility of release—i.e., the attainment of pleasure—a creature externally *and* internally deprived of these possibilities must want to cease to live. Self-annihilation becomes the only and final possibility of release, so we can say that, even in the will to die, the pleasure-unpleasure principle is expressed.

Every other concept passes over the deep clinical findings, avoids the confrontation with the question of the structure of our real world (a confrontation which leads to a critique of the social system), and gives up the best possibilities of helping the patient. For it is through analysis that the analyst enables him to overcome the fear of the punishment of this world and to resolve his inner tensions in the only way which is biologically, physiologically, and sex-economically sound—orgastic gratification and contingent sublimation.

The facts pertaining to masochism invalidate the assumption of a primary need for punishment. If it does not hold true for masochism, it will be difficult to find in other forms of illness. Suffering is real, objectively given but not subjectively desired. Self-abasement is a defense mechanism because of the danger of genital castration; self-injuries are anticipations of milder punishments as defense against those which are really feared; beating fantasies are the last possibilities of a guilt-free release. The original formula of neurosis is still valid: the neurosis originates in a conflict between instinctual sexual need and the threat of being punished by a patriarchal, authoritarian society for engaging in sexual activity. On the basis of this formula, however, even the conclusions we draw are fundamentally different. Suffering issues from society. Hence, we are fully justified in asking why society produces suffering, who has an interest in it.

It follows logically from Freud's original formula (i.e., frustration issues from the outer world) that one part of the psychic conflict, frustration, originates in the conditions of existence of our social system. To what extent, however, this formulation has been obliterated by the hypothesis of the death instinct is demonstrated by Benedek's line of reasoning: "If we accept the theory of the dualism of the instincts solely in the sense of the old theory, a gap ensues. Then the question remains unanswered why mechanisms have developed in man which operate antagonistically to the sexual instinct." We see, thus, how the hypothesis of a death instinct causes us to forget that those "inner mechanisms" which operate antagonistically toward the sexual instinct are moral inhibitions representing the prohibitions imposed by the outer world, by society. Hence, we are not "forcing an open door" when we contend that the death instinct is supposed to explain biologically facts which, by pursuing the former theory consistently, are derived from the structure of present-day society.

It remains to be demonstrated that the "uncontrollable destructive drives" which are held accountable for man's suffering are not biologically but sociologically determined; that the inhibition of sexuality by authoritarian upbringing transforms aggression into an uncontrollable demand, i.e., that inhibited sexual energy is converted into destructiveness. And the aspects of our cultural life which appear to be self-destructive are not manifestations of "instincts of self-annihilation"; they are manifestations of very real destructive intentions on the part of an authoritarian society interested in the suppression of sexuality.

PART THREE

*From Psychoanalysis to
Orgone Biophysics*

CHAPTER XIII

PSYCHIC CONTACT AND VEGETATIVE CURRENT

(A Contribution to the Theory of Affects and Character-Analytic Technique)

PREFACE

The work which follows is an elaboration on the talk I gave at the 13th International Psychoanalytic Congress in Lucerne, August 1934. It is a continuation of the discussion of the difficult character-analytic and clinical material and problems which I considered in great detail in Part I of the present volume. Above all, it is an attempt to comprehend two groups of facts which were not dealt with in Part I: (1) *psychic contactlessness* and the psychic mechanism which attempts to compensate for this by establishing *substitute contacts;* (2) the antithetical *unity of the vegetative and psychic manifestations of affect life.* The latter is a direct continuation of my work on the "Urgegensatz des vegetativen Lebens," which was printed in *Zeitschrift für politische Psychologie und Sexualökonomie,* 1934.

Again, it is merely a short, though clinically well substantiated, advance from the sphere of what is already known and established into the dark and difficult problems of the relationship between psyche and soma. The application of my technique of character analysis will enable anyone to verify these findings once he has mastered the initial technical difficulties.

A discussion of the views set forth in the works of other authors on the problem of "totality" and the homogeneity of psychic and somatic functions was intentionally avoided. Sex-economy approaches the problem from the perspective of an otherwise neglected phenomenon, the *orgasm,* and consciously applies the methods of functionalism. Even for this reason, a critical discussion would be premature, for it would presuppose a certain completeness in my own view and that other authors had already taken a stand on the orgasm problem. Neither is true.

There was good reason why the clinical refutation of Freud's theory of the death instinct had to be retained. Deep analysis of the so-called striving for nirvana was especially instrumental in strengthening my view that the hypothesis of the death instinct was an attempt to explain facts which could not yet be explained and, moreover, attempted to do this in a misleading way.

To those psychoanalysts with a functional orientation, the young sex-economists and the character analysts, this essay is perhaps more suited than previous essays to offer some theoretical clarity and practical help in the application of the character-analytic technique. The character-analytic concept and technique of dealing with psychic disturbances is again in a state of flux as a result of the discovery of psychic contactlessness and the fear of establishing contact. It may well be that the ideas set forth in this writing will soon prove to be incomplete, perhaps incorrect here and there. This would demonstrate that only through living practice can one keep abreast of the development of a new idea. Those who are seriously endeavoring to learn the character-analytic technique will have no difficulty in recognizing in their clinical work, and making full use of, the relationships between the mode of psychic contact and vegetative excitability described here for the first time. These relationships not only can help extricate our psychotherapeutic work from the mystical atmosphere of present-day psychotherapy but also, under fortuitous conditions, can guarantee otherwise unattainable successes. At the same time, I must warn the analyst not to become overzealous in his therapeutic expectations. There can no longer be any doubt of the superiority of character analysis. But it is precisely the end stages of character-analytic treatment, in particular the reactivation of the orgastic contact anxiety and its overcoming, that are still too little understood and, therefore, insufficiently mastered. Even by friends, the theory of the orgasm is grossly misunderstood. There is still great ignorance regarding the uninhibited spontaneity of orgastic surrender, which is usually confused with *pre*orgastic excitation. It is nonetheless certain that only by chance can character-analytic treatment be successfully terminated without security in the orgasm question.

The lecture upon which this essay is based terminated my membership in the International Psychoanalytic Association. Its leadership no longer wanted to identify itself with my views.

February 1935

---

1. MORE ABOUT THE CONFLICT BETWEEN INSTINCT AND OUTER WORLD

To begin with, I want to call to mind the *older* psychoanalytic theories which my work takes as its point of departure. An understanding of the results of character-analytic research is not possible without a knowledge of these theories.

The first psychoanalytic views were based on the conflict between *instinct* and *outer world*. The complete disregard of this basic concept by present-day theories has no effect on its validity. It is the most pregnant formulation of all analytic psychology and its presence will be unmistakably clear to every clinician in every case. The psychic process reveals itself as the result of the conflict between instinctual demand and the external frustration of this demand. Only secondarily does an inner conflict between desire and self-denial result from this initial opposition. The self-denial is the basic element of what is called "inner morality." It is my intent to show at every possible opportunity how this formula gives rise to basic theoretical views about the psychic conflict. If one inquires into the origin of instinctual frustration, one goes beyond the compass of psychology, enters the field of sociology, and encounters a fundamentally different complex of problems than those encountered in the field of psychology. The question of why society demands the suppression and repression of instincts can no longer be answered psychologically. They are *social*, more correctly, economic interests that cause such suppressions and repressions in certain eras.[1] Politics, which my opponents reproach me for mixing with science, tie in directly with this rigidly—I should say, solely—scientific line of reasoning.

When a young man discovers that the inhibition of his natural

---

[1] Cf. *The Invasion of Compulsory Sex-Morality*, Farrar, Straus and Giroux, 1971.

sexual strivings is not necessitated by biological considerations, is not dictated by the death instinct, but fulfills definite interests of those who wield social power; when he discovers that parents and teachers are merely unconscious executors of this social power, then he will not take the position that this is a highly interesting scientific theory. He will comprehend the misery of his life in a new light, deny its divine origin, and begin to rebel against parents and their taskmasters. He might even become critical for the first time and begin to think about things. This and only this is what I understand as sex-politics.[2]

We know that the ego's task is to mediate between such social influences—which later become internalized as morality or inner instinct inhibition—and biological needs. If we pursue the psychic manifestations of the latter, i.e., the id phenomena, far enough, we reach a point at which our psychological methods of investigation are no longer adequate, for we have entered the field of physiology and biology. Here is an important point of difference between my opponents and me. I find it necessary to recognize limits to the psychological method; my opponents "psychologize" sociology *and* biology. After this, it will appear somewhat strange that the subject of my investigation is precisely the development.of vegetative excitations from the character, i.e., psychic formations, and that I intend to accomplish this with the help of a psychological procedure. Am I guilty of a transgression of my own principle? We prefer to postpone the answer until later.

---

[2] It is the social, i.e., political, practice resulting from the knowledge that sexual repression is of *social* origin. The view expounded at the 13th Psychoanalytic Congress by Bernfeld that adolescent sexual intercourse can be traced back to poor educational conditions merely confirms the adolescent's neurotic guilt feelings. It will, to be sure, also please all priests and champions of the "objective spirit." Apart from this, however, it will merely veil the problem of adolescence, instead of solving it, and it will be inimical to every positive sex-economic help to adolescents. For all that, the problem of adolescent development definitely belongs in the framework of the relations between vegetative excitation and psychic behavior, no matter how conscientiously the truth is hushed up and the fact ignored by "objective science" that the adolescent development of our youth is chiefly determined by the social frustration of their sexual life. That is to say, whether the vegetatively produced sexual energy is regulated in a healthy or in a neurotic way depends primarily upon how the society has equipped the youth structurally and materially.

2. SOME TECHNICAL PRESUPPOSITIONS

The relationships between psychic apparatus and vegetative excitation, as I have attempted to describe them here, will remain incomprehensible if one does not first free oneself from a source of error inherent in our method of theoretical cognition. Theory and practice are inseparably intertwined. *An incorrect theoretical attitude must of necessity lead to an incorrect technique, and an incorrect technique produces incorrect theoretical views.* If we attempt to discover the reasons behind the postulation of a death instinct, we find, apart from reasons of a social nature—which I discussed elsewhere—quite a few which cluster around the problem of technique. Many of those who took part in the work of the Vienna Seminar for Psychoanalytic Therapy will certainly remember how much trouble we had in mastering the problem of the *latent negative transference* of our patients, both theoretically and practically.

It certainly would be no exaggeration to say that it wasn't until sometime between 1923 and 1930 that we gained a *practical* understanding of the negative transference, i.e., long after it had been clinically established and theoretically formulated by Freud. The clinical basis upon which Freud postulated his theory of the death instinct is the so-called negative therapeutic reaction. This formulation means that some of our patients react to our analytic work of interpretation not by showing signs of improvement but by developing stronger neurotic reactions. Freud assumed that this intensification was tied in with an unconscious guilt feeling or, as he called it from then on, a "need for punishment" which compels the patient to resist the therapeutic work and to persist in his neurosis, i.e., in his suffering. I admit that I shared this view in the first years following the publication of *The Ego and the Id,* and only gradually began to have doubts about it. In the technical reports given at the Vienna seminar, three things became clear which shed considerable light upon the secret of the negative therapeutic reaction: (1) the patient's negative tendencies, i.e., those springing from his repressed hate, were not at all or only very inadequately analyzed; (2) analysts, even the most experienced, operated almost exclusively with the patient's positive transferences, i.e., strivings for love; (3) the analyst usually regarded as a positive transference what was merely secret, concealed, and repressed hate.

It wasn't until shortly before the Congress of the Scandinavian Psychoanalysts in Oslo in 1934 that I succeeded in arriving at a correct formulation of the negative therapeutic reaction. Through our analytic work we liberate psychic energy which urges toward discharge. If the patient's transferences are exclusively, predominantly, or from the very beginning analyzed as *positive* transferences, if the negative manifestations are not thoroughly uncovered *before* this is done, the following will be the result: the liberated demands for love clamor for gratification and meet with strict denial in the analysis, in part, also with the inner inhibitions which are formed from the repressed hate impulses directed against the love object. In short, we believe that we have "liberated" the love impulses, but in reality the patient has remained incapable of love. According to the laws of the psychic apparatus, frustrated love is transformed into hate. The undeveloped hate impulses which have remained in the unconscious act like a magnet on this artifically produced hate. The two reinforce one another, the secondary hate also becoming unconscious. Since it does not experience any discharge, *it is transformed into self-destructive intentions.* Thus, the need for punishment which we ascertain in our patients is, as I pointed out as early as 1926 in my polemic against Alexander, not the cause but the product of the neurotic conflict. And *the negative therapeutic reaction can be traced back to the lack of a technique for handling the latent negative transference.*

As proof of the validity of this statement, I can allege that there is no negative therapeutic reaction when two rules are followed: (1) The patient's concealed negative attitude is worked out before any other analytic work is taken up; the patient is made conscious of this attitude; an outlet is secured for all liberated aggression; every masochistic impulse is treated not as a manifestation of a primary will to self-destruction but as aggression which, in reality, is directed against objects of the outer world. (2) The patient's positive expressions of love are not analyzed until they either are converted into hate, i.e., become disappointment reactions, or finally become concentrated in ideas of genital incest. At this point, I am reminded of an objection raised by Freud when I acquainted him with my initial views on character-analytic technique. At one time or another, it has been raised by just about all my colleagues, repeatedly by some. The gist of their argument is that the analyst has no right to select; he has to deal with all material as it presents itself. I gave the answer to this objection in Part I of the present volume, so I can spare myself a repetition here. However, this objection leads to a fundamental clarification of the theory behind the technique which I have advocated during the past years. I want to summarize it briefly, for a knowledge of it is indispensable for the understanding of the theoretical results as well as the means of arriving at them.

The first principle of analysis is to make the unconscious conscious. We call this the work of interpretation. It is determined by the *topographical* point of view. However, if the work of interpretation is to fulfill its therapeutic function, it is necessary to take into account that resistances exist between the patient's unconscious psychic material and our interpretations and that these resistances must be eliminated. This point of view corresponds to the *dynamics* of the psychic process. On the basis of our experiences in monitored analyses and in the Vienna seminar, it can be said that, while the analyst is theoretically familiar with both points of view, he analyzes almost exclusively according to the first, the topographical. This comes through very clearly, for example, in both Stekel's and Rank's concept of analytic work. But we would be guilty of a lack of self-criticism if we didn't admit that all of us have more or less neglected the dynamic point of view in our practical work, simply because we did not know how to handle it.

Character-analytic work adds the *structural* and the *economic* to the topographical and dynamic points of view in technique. This inclusion of all our views of the psychic process in the method of our work had, for me at least, a far greater revolutionary effect upon practice than the change from direct interpretation of the unconscious contents to the resistance technique. Once you include the structural and economic points of view, you can no longer contend that the analyst should deal with whatever happens to appear. I want to cite a few basic principles and outline what I attempted to establish with thorough clinical evidence in Part I of the present volume.

The material offered in the course of an analytic session is manifold; it derives from various psychic layers as well as various historical stages of development. Therapeutically and dynamically, then, the material is not of equal value. Sex-economy imposes upon us a rigidly prescribed path which begins with the analysis of the patient's pregenital and negative attitudes and ends with the concentration of all liberated psychic energy in the genital apparatus. The establishment of orgastic potency—this follows logically from the theory of the orgasm—is the most important therapeutic goal.

It is economically determined that, essentially from the contemporary modes of behavior, by consistent analysis of the patient's bearing, the historically disarranged affects can be brought to the surface, related to the contents of childhood ideas, and thus resolved.

Character analysis, hence, is a psychic operation which proceeds according to a definite plan that is evolved from the patient's particular structure.

Character analysis that has been correctly carried out, notwithstanding the endless diversity in content, conflicts, and structures, exhibits the following typical phases:

1. Character-analytic loosening of the armor

2. Breaking down of the character armor, or, put another way, specific destruction of the neurotic equilibrium

3. Breakthrough of the deepest layers of strongly affect-charged material; reactivation of the infantile hysteria

4. Resistance-free working through of the unearthed material; extraction of the libido from the pregenital fixations

5. Reactivation of the infantile genital anxiety (stasis neurosis) and of genitality

6. Appearance of orgasm anxiety and the establishment of orgastic potency—upon which depends the establishment of the almost full capacity for functioning

Though the establishment of genitality appears obvious to many analysts today, orgastic potency is not known and not recognized. Until 1923, "condemnation of the instincts" and sublimation were the only recognized goals of therapy. Impotence and frigidity were not regarded as specific symptoms of the neurotic organism but as symptoms among others, which might or might not be present. It was known, to be sure, that there is an orgasm and a climax, but it was contended that there are any number of severe neuroses with "wholly undisturbed orgasms"; i.e., the sex-economic nature and function of the orgasm were unknown. Neuroses were held to be the manifestations of a sexual disturbance in general; from the point of view of sex-economy, on the other hand, a neurosis could not result without a disturbance in the genitality and could not be cured without the elimination of this disturbance. Freud, Sachs, Nunberg, Deutsch, Alexander, and most of the other analysts rejected my view of the psycho-economic and therapeutic importance of genitality. In Freud's *Introductory Lecture on Psychoanalysis* (1933!), the complex of questions pertaining to the genital orgasm is not mentioned at all, nor is it mentioned in Nunberg's *Neurosenlehre*. Hence, the question of the source of the energy of the neurosis remained unanswered.

From the very beginning, the inclusion of the function of the orgasm in the theory of the neurosis was felt to be a nuisance and it was dealt with accordingly. As a matter of fact, it was not the result of purely psychological investigations but of psychophysiological investigations.[3] Ferenczi's attempts to arrive at a theory of genitality were merely a "psychologization" of physiological and biological phenomena. The orgasm is not a psychic phenomenon. On the contrary, it is a phenomenon brought about solely by the *reduction* of all psychic activity to the primal vegetative function, i.e., precisely by the suspension of psychic fantasizing and imaginative activity. It is nonetheless the central problem of psychic economy. Its inclusion in psychology not only permits a concrete treatment of the quantitative factor in psychic life and the establishment of the connection between the psychic and the physiological factor (i.e., vegetative factor). Over and above this, it leads of necessity to a significant change in the psychoanalytic view of the neurotic process. Formerly, the Oedipus complex was regarded as an explanation of neurotic ill-

[3] Cf. my work "Zur Triebenergetik," *Zeitschrift für Sexualwissenschaft*, 1923.

ness. Today we realize that whether or not the Oedipus complex leads to neurosis depends upon other factors: the child-parent conflict does not become pathogenic unless there is also a disturbance in the child's sexual economy; this early disturbance lays the groundwork for the subsequent malfunctioning of the libido economy in adulthood; it derives its energy precisely from what helped to bring it about, i.e., the stasis of genital-sexual energy.[4] In this way the accent was shifted from the content of the experience to the economy of vegetative energy.

Thus, the amount of material which the patient produced in the beginning and how much was learned about the patient's past receded into the background. Instead, the decisive question was whether those experiences which operate as vegetative-energetic *concentrations of energy* were actually obtained correctly.

There are many analysts sympathetic to sex-economy who did not go through this evolution of the cleavage in the theory of the neurosis and hence do not comprehend the central importance of the orgasm question. If, further, one considers that only the application of the character-analytic technique successfully leads to a penetration of the physiological phenomena of the orgastic disturbance and its psychic representatives and that this technique is partially rejected and partially not mastered, then it is not surprising that analysts are amazed to find that masochists are essentially characterized by a particular kind of fear of the orgastic sensation. Yet the same thing applies here as for the psychoanalytic conviction in general. Those who have not experienced character analysis cannot criticize its findings, simply because they lack the sense organ for it and the experience of it. At best, they can grasp it intellectually; the essence of the theory of the orgasm remains inaccessible to their understanding. I have had occasion to analyze trained and experienced analysts. They came to me with the familiar skepticism or with the conviction "of having known all about this for a long time." They were always able to persuade themselves of the significant difference between the usual psychoanalytic procedure and character analysis and had to admit that they could not have known what they came to

---

[4] See also my description of the relationships between psychoneurosis and actual neurosis in *Die Function des Orgasmus* (1927) . Also, *The Function of the Orgasm*, 1942, 1948.

know through character analysis, for the simple reason that it would never have come to the surface without the application of a definite technique. This is especially true of the genuine orgastic sensations which appear for the first time during the automatic contraction of the genital musculature.

I am going to content myself with this not very extensive summary. The inclusion of the patient's psychic structure and libido economy in the analytic work has considerably changed and complicated the picture, the mode of procedure, and indeed, the basic view of technique. The work of analysis has become much more difficult, which is certainly not a drawback, for this is more than offset by the greater security and more durable and comprehensive results which are achieved whenever the analyst succeeds in unraveling the case in accordance with the character-analytic technique. Unfortunately, it still cannot be contended that this approach succeeds in all cases.

During the past twelve years, technique has undergone considerable changes, as have our views on the dynamics of the psychic apparatus. Consequently, those analysts who have not followed this development are not in a position to comprehend my views on technique and theory. I fear that the gap has become difficult to bridge, even where it is maintained that my views are shared by others.

I want to take this opportunity to clarify a misunderstanding which comes up every time I attempt to explain my views. One group of analysts contends that everything I have to say is banal and has long been known to them, while another group declares that my technique no longer has anything to do with psychoanalysis, that it is misleading and faulty. How is this possible? Once we understand how new scientific findings are made, we will no longer be puzzled. On the one hand, my character-analytic technique grew out of the Freudian resistance technique; as I see it, it represents its most consistent development to this day. Hence, it must have fundamental similarities with the Freudian technique. Because of these similarities, the first group of critics I mentioned believes it is applying the same technique as I. However, on the basis of innumerable cases taken over from other analysts, I can affirm that this is not the case at all. The responsibility which I bear obliges me to make this assertion. In addition to the similarities, there are far-reaching and fundamental differences.

On the other hand, the inclusion of new points of view, particularly the setting of orgastic potency as the therapeutic goal, has changed the technical procedure as a whole to such an extent that the second group of critics no longer recognizes the analytic technique in it. This explanation is incontestable and is confirmed by the history of all sciences. New findings, views, methods never grow out of a void; they are based on a firm foundation—the painstaking work of other researchers. The differences and personal antipathies which result in divergences of opinion are an unfortunate but evidently unavoidable consequence of the fact that a quantitative and qualitative enrichment of certain aspects of knowledge is transformed into qualitative changes of the whole.

3. THE CHANGE OF FUNCTION OF THE IMPULSE

We have to pursue our technical discussion a bit further. We shall see that the theoretical results I arrived at in the end can be attained and demonstrated only when the character-analytic as opposed to the straightforward resistance technique, or even the obsolete technique of direct interpretation, is applied.

One of the fundamental principles of the character-analytic technique is that the repressed material is never loosened and made conscious from the perspective of the instinct but always and solely from the perspective of the defense.[5]

Accordingly, the most important theoretical question here concerns the organization, function, and genesis of the ego structure, from which the defense proceeds; for only to the extent that

---

[5] This principle was misconstrued by my critics, among them Nunberg, to mean that, for me, character and defense were identical; that, therefore, I unjustifiably limited the concept of the character. If this were so, I would immediately have to correct it. But I am of the opinion that I formulated my views quite unequivocally when I stated that the most important and most conspicuous character trait *becomes, in analysis, the most crucial resistance for the purpose of defense, just as it developed for this purpose in childhood.* The fact that, over and above this, it has different, chiefly sex-economic functions, that it serves to maintain the relationship to the outer world and to preserve the psychic equilibrium, is thoroughly described and elaborated in Part I of the present volume. Hence, it seems to me that this criticism is not objectively motivated.

we understand the ego defense will our therapeutic work be effective. And, vice versa, a knowledge of the id far less than a knowledge of the ego leads to an improvement of our technical skill.[6] In this respect, the character-analytic line of questioning coincides with the problem which has been a major concern of psychoanalytic research for some fourteen years: *how does the ego function?* We all remember how greatly impressed we were

[6] Footnote, 1945: This formulation was one-sided and therefore incorrect. The investigation of the armoring of the ego was only the first necessary step. After we had succeeded in mastering the armor, both in theory and in practice, the vast realm of biological energy was opened with the discovery of the orgone in the organism and in the cosmos. What the psychoanalytic theory calls the "id" is, in reality, the physical orgone function within the biosystem. In a metaphysical way, the term "id" implies that there is "something" in the biosystem whose functions are determined beyond the individual. *This something called "id" is a physical reality, i.e., it is cosmic orgone energy.* The living "orgonotic system," the "bioapparatus," merely represents a particular embodiment of concentrated orgone energy. A psychoanalyst recently wrote a review in which he described the "orgone" as being "identical" with the Freudian "id." This is as correct as saying that Aristotle's and Driesch's "entelechy" is identical with the "orgone." While it is true that the concepts "id," "entelechy," "élan vital," and "orgone" describe the *same thing,* this is an oversimplification of their relatedness. *"Orgone" is a visible, measurable, and applicable energy of a cosmic nature.* "Id," "entelechy," and "élan vital," on the other hand, are merely expressions of human *intuitions* of the existence of such an energy. Are Maxwell's "electromagnetic waves" the same as Hertz's "electromagnetic waves"? Yes, certainly. But with Hertz's waves it is possible to transmit messages across the ocean, which is not possible with Maxwell's waves.

Such "correct" analogies without mention of the *practical* differences have the function of verbally camouflaging great advances in the field of natural science. They are as unscientific as the sociologist who described the orgone as one of my "hypotheses." Blood cannot be revitalized and cancer tumors cannot be destroyed with "hypotheses," the "id," "entelechy," etc. With orgone energy, this is clearly possible.

The coming to grips with the problems of psychology in the following text is correct and important *within the framework of depth psychology.* Orgone biophysics transcends this framework. With the knowledge of the orgone functions of the organism, problems of depth psychology diminish in importance. The solution to the problems of psychology lies outside the sphere of psychology. For instance, a simple block of orgonotic pulsation in the throat makes the most complicated mechanism of oral sadism understandable in a simple way. But we cannot go into this at this point. In retrospect, it is interesting to realize how hard the serious psychoanalyst has had to struggle with biophysical problems, without really being able to get at their core. In depth psychology, the analyst operates with drives, but he is rather like the man who wants to drink water from a glass which he sees reflected in a mirror.

when Freud told us that until now we have studied and understood merely what is repressed. We know too little about the origin of the repression and about the structure of the ego defense. It was strange that so much less was known about the ego, that it was so much more difficult to arrive at an understanding of it than it was to arrive at an understanding of what is repressed. Yet there can be no doubt that this is the way it was, and this too must have its reasons. They are to be found not just in the difficulties of *psychological* understanding.

In *The Ego and the Id,* Freud posed the question of the origin of the energy of the ego instinct; this was a great novelty for us at that time, 1922. In answering this question, Freud made use of his theory of the death instinct, which he arrived at on the basis of the difficulties offered by the patient's ego to the elimination of the repressions and to the cure. According to this concept, these difficulties derived from the need for punishment or, to put it another way, from unconscious guilt feelings; in the final analysis, they were said to be the expressions of primary masochism, i.e., the will to suffer. For all that, the question of the structure of the ego defense and of the suppression of the libidinal forces in man was not answered by the formulation of the death instinct any more than was the question: *what is the ego instinct?*

Let us briefly refresh our memory regarding some of the obscurities that have always existed in analytic theory with reference to the nature of the ego instinct. Originally, hunger, as opposed to sexuality, was conceived of as the ego instinct serving the ends of self-preservation. This view was at variance with the function of the ego instincts as *antagonists* of sexuality. Moreover, several considerations of a sex-economic nature led to the insight that, in the strict sense of the word, the hunger instinct cannot be regarded as an instinct because it is not the manifestation of an overproduction of energy as sexuality is; it is, on the contrary, the manifestation of the lowering of the energy level in the organism. Furthermore, we have long since conceived of the need for food as belonging, in terms of its structure, to the id and not to the ego. Thus, hunger could not constitute the energy of the ego instinct.

Schilder once sought to contrast the ego instincts with the sexual instincts, depicting the former as grasping and holding

Diagram showing the change of function of the drive, inner dissociation, and antithesis

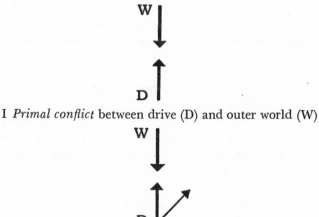

I *Primal conflict* between drive (D) and outer world (W)

II *Dissociation* of the unitary striving under the influence of the outer world

III *Antithesis* of the dissociated strivings. (Id = Id in the function of the ego instinct (defense, change of function)

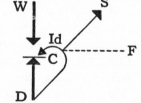

IV *Drive* (D) *in double function* (Id = defense and S = substitute contact)

F = place where the instinct's function changes

C = structural lack of contact

Defense (Id) and contemporary situation of the outer world become a unity (inner morality = social ideology)

instincts. This view was not tenable either, for there can be no doubt that the need to grasp and to take hold of belongs to the function of the muscular apparatus and, therefore, is part of the reservoir of vegetative energy. Freud's ultimate attempt to introduce the death instinct as the antagonist of sexuality in place of the mysterious ego instincts merely substituted for the antagonism between ego and id the antagonism between dual tendencies in the id itself. The problem was more complicated than ever before.

A detailed study of character-analytic work on the ego defense yielded an answer that was actually quite obvious. It was then a question of finding out why theoretical research had not hit upon it, though hints of it were abundant in analytic theory.

Once again we shall take as our point of departure the basic scheme of the psychic conflict between instinct and outer world. The drive (D) which strives toward worldly objects comes into conflict with the frustrating counter-force of the outer-world prohibition (diagram I). The next question is where the prohibition of the outer world obtains its energy to carry out its function. Upon brief reflection, we see that only the content of the prohibition stems from the outer world; the energy or, as we usually call it, the cathexis with which the prohibition is carried out is drawn from the energy reservoir of the person himself. Under the influence of a pressure exerted by the outer world, an *antithesis* develops *within the person; a dissociation* or *cleavage of a unitary striving* causes one drive to turn against another drive or even one and the same drive to split up in two directions: one which continues to strive toward the world and another which turns against itself. The turning of a drive against itself is described by Freud in *Trieb und Triebschicksale*. The new problem begins where we run up against the process of inner *dissociation* and *opposition*. Let us cite a concrete example: when a boy wants to masturbate with incest fantasies, then his self-love and his object-libidinal striving constitute, in this state, a unity; the striving toward the mother lies in the same direction as self-love—they do not run counter to one another. The prohibition of masturbation by the mother has the effect of a frustration of the object-libidinal striving and threatens the boy's narcissistic inviolability with the punishment of castration. However, at that moment when the external frustration begins to take effect, the narcissistic striving for self-preservation opposes the striving for object-libidinal masturbation (diagram II and III). A variation of this is the cleavage of the affectionate tie to the mother (the fear of the loss of love) and the sensuous sexual excitation. Originally, the affectionate component and the sensuous component constituted a unity. Thus, the dissociation of the homogeneous striving is followed by the opposition of the one part of the cleaved striving against the other. It is now clear that the prohibition of the outer world can have an effect only with the help of this energy which has become *divided against itself*.

To elaborate on this schematic representation, I shall cite another example, which will lead us even closer to the problems of technique that concern us here. I shall choose a patient who was characterized by an exaggerated readiness to help, an inability to assume an aggressive attitude, a characterological need to cling to people, and essentially passive behavior. All the traits of his passive-feminine character were concentrated in a certain obtrusive bearing, which served the purpose of constantly establishing and maintaining contact with other people. It was not difficult to see that the instinctual force with which he sustained these attitudes was his passive anal homosexuality. In short, the patient's ego made use of an id impulse to maintain object relationships. This was the *object-libidinal,* world-oriented function of his anality; in short, the id function.

In the analysis, the patient's character proved to be a powerful resistance to the analytic work. From the point of view of character analysis, this behavior could not and must not be interpreted as the manifestation of unconscious anal-homosexual strivings, though "in itself" one would have been objectively correct in doing so. The economic and structural point of view pointed in another direction. If my formula is correct that, in the analytic treatment, the most important character trait becomes the most important character resistance, then the question— *where is the defense energy?*—assumes greater significance than the banal fact that the patient experiences anal-passive-feminine object strivings. The interpretation of the ego defense was of no help here. It was quite some time before the search for the defense energy of this behavior was completed, and then in a strange way. It turned out that the anal-passive-homosexual striving which one time sustained the relationships to the outer world fulfilled the defense function of the ego another time or even at the same time. Thus, one and the same striving was split and served opposing functions, some times alternately and other times simultaneously: one time as the striving toward an object, another time as defensive ego drive.

Minute investigation of this peculiar fact in other cases which were analyzed at this time and earlier demonstrated that this *transformation*, or, rather, *change of function* in one and the same instinctual demand, that this functioning *simultaneously* in the service of the id and in the service of the ego defense, is a general phenomenon. Before we draw a theoretical conclusion about this, let us cite a few clinical examples which are familiar to all analysts. The sexual coquetry found in hysteria also shows this duality in function. Flirtation is the expression of repressed genital desires, i.e., directed toward the world. At the same time it is a defense against genitality, the expression of an anxious "feeling out" of the object, to determine, as it were, where the genital danger is coming from. This is the only possible explanation for the extensive sexual life of hysterical women suffering from severe genital anxiety. The same holds true for the sadistic behavior of the compulsive neurotic woman who, with her aggression toward the loved object, simultaneously gratifies her sadistic relationship to the object and wards off her own vaginal desires for intercourse.

In short, the ego instincts are nothing other than the sum total of vegetative demands in their defense function. We are merely building upon well-established ideas when we say that the ego instinct is the id instinct directed either against itself or against another instinct. The entire psychic process appears to be characterized by the cleavage and subsequent opposition between tendencies which functioned as a unit. But this still requires extensive clinical proof. These findings would be of academic interest only and would merely constitute theoretical refinements of our knowledge of the psychic apparatus if it were not for their consequences.

First of all, there is the *theoretical* consequence: if the concept is correct which we have developed of the structure of the ego and the defense function, then the systems, "ego" and "id," appear merely as different functions of the psychic apparatus[7] and not as separate spheres of the psyche. Once before, a similar question demanded an answer, namely: how is the infantile, historical experience preserved *in the present?* The clinical data showed that it did not rest as a kind of deposit in the unconscious but was absorbed into the character and expressed essentially as formal modes of behavior. And from these modes of behavior the content of past experiences can be extracted, in the same way, for example, as sodium can be extracted from sodium chloride. Even if not so clear-cut, relationships in the psychic system are very similar. That which is repressed and that which wards off do not constitute two individual, topically separate spheres or forces; though antithetical, they constitute a functional unity. Thus, the topographical concept of the psychic apparatus is merely a helpful expedient, and Freud was right in refusing to relegate the system unconscious to a deeper layer of the nervous system. For example, the perception which the ego accomplishes is no less a function of the vegetative system than is an instinct.

The *technical* consequence is as follows: experience shows that we do not or only insufficiently obtain the original energy of the repressed instinct if we begin by interpreting its id function. In this case, it may well be that the patient occasionally acquires a good intellectual understanding as well as a deep conviction of the theoretical correctness of the analytic work. However, the actual goal, the liberation of the instinct from repression, is achieved only to a highly unsatisfactory degree. The structure of the instinct changes but little. It is a different matter entirely if we begin by thoroughly destroying the defense function of the *same* instinct. A large number of clinical observations show that in this case and only in this way the vegetative sources of the personality begin to flow anew. In short, we do *not*—this is the ineluctable conclusion—really eliminate the repression when we work with id interpretations. Even at the present time, it is possible to get at these repressions with a definite legitimacy only if we extract the repressed instinct from the character's defense formation not as something repressed but, in the first place, as something *repressive.* To return to the example of the aforemen-

[7] Footnote, 1945: "Biopsychic apparatus," "human orgonotic system."

tioned patient; He remained unaffected in his total personality
as long as it was not completely clear to him that his devoted
attitude represented not love, not attachment, not helpfulness,
not even homosexuality, but, more basically, a warding off of
something else. This something else was—and this is not difficult
to divine—strong envy, inhibited aggression, destructive intentions, and more of the same.

Another patient exhibited sudden and uncoordinated changes of
posture of which he was not aware. Unquestioningly, he was suffering from some kind of tic.[8] Had I given him a direct interpretation of the libidinal motives of these movements, i.e., showed
him their connection to masturbation, there can be no doubt that
the following would not have been forthcoming. To begin with, I
persuaded him that these movements were motivated by embarrassment for the purpose of warding off a painful perception of
his external appearance. His vanity was opposed to the recognition of certain physical traits. My interpretation of this defense
immediately released great excitation, intensified the tic and the
self-consciousness, and led, to my surprise, to violent convulsions of the pelvic musculature. These convulsions turned out to
be the warding off of blows which he fantasized were falling
upon his "pregnant" stomach. These convulsions of the pelvic
muscles were interpreted not as an expression of mother identification but as a warding off of aggressive impulses toward an object. The patient's immediate reaction to this interpretation was
kicking of the feet, followed by violent pelvic movements with
masturbation and orgasm during the session. It was not at all
necessary for me to interpret the tic-like movement as a substitute for masturbation. He experienced the connection directly
and unmistakably. Even the slightest deviation from the rule of
treating all attitudes as defense would have thwarted this success.

One will want to know at this point what constitutes the essential manifestation of the affective rearrangement in both cases. It
consists in the fact that, when the instinct's defense function is
correctly analyzed and every interpretation of its id function is
avoided, states of vegetative excitation and tension regularly ap-

---

[8] Footnote, 1945: In 1933 I did not know that, in these spontaneous movements of the patient, I was dealing with segments of the orgasm reflex. I did
not understand the biophysical function of these movements, but only their
"psychic meaning." Today most analysts are still in this position.

pear, of which the patient was not previously aware. When, on the other hand, the id functions are interpreted, these states are absent or appear only by chance—not legitimately, i.e., predictably. The above patient, for example, again experienced, for the first time since suffering a strong wave of repression in puberty, hot flashes, severe oppression in the cardiac region, and the characteristic sensations in the region of the diaphragm indicative of the excitations of the coeliac ganglion. They were sensations like those experienced on a swing or in a descending elevator. In other cases, such physical sensations appear together with a change of the kinesthetic feelings of the body (sensations of floating, falling, etc.) .

The nascent indications of vegetative excitation can be essentially summarized as follows: feeling of constriction in the region of the heart; sensations of tension in the musculature, especially in the upper thigh and the crown of the head; sensations of currents and nascent feelings of sensual pleasure, such as those experienced subsequent to a gratifying sexual experience; sensations of pressure within the cranium; agitation; sensations of hot and cold; cold shudders along one's spine; itching sensations, quite frequently in the urethra and at the perineum; salivation or dryness in the mouth; feelings of strangulation; shortness of breath; feelings of dizziness; feelings of nausea; "pulling" in the genital zone (as in falling) ; feelings in the pit of the stomach similar to those experienced on a swing or in an elevator; involuntary twitching of the musculature; itchy or, rather, "pleasurable" feelings of contraction in the twitching of smooth muscle groups.

Before we attempt to arrive at a theoretical formulation of the abundant phenomena of this kind, we have to return once again to our point of departure, the structure of the character armor, from which, as is now quite clear, we liberate the vegetative energy with the technique of character analysis.

4. THE INTELLECT AS DEFENSE FUNCTION

To begin with, we shall cite a clinical example to demonstrate once again how precisely a person's character conserves and at the same time wards off the function of certain childhood situations.

It is commonly assumed that the human intellect has a solely objective function and that it is directed toward the world; ethics and philosophy in particular conceive of reason and intellect exclusively in the sense of an absolute non-emotional activity capable of comprehending reality "incorruptibly." Two things are overlooked here: (1) the intellectual function itself is a vegetative activity; and (2) the intellectual function may have an affect charge whose intensity is no less than any purely affective impulse. Over and above this, character-analytic work reveals another function of the intellect which ties in very well with the inversion and opposition of drives discussed earlier. Intellectual activity can be structured and directed in such a way that it looks like a most cunningly operating apparatus whose purpose is precisely to avoid *cognition,* i.e., it looks like an activity *directing* one *away* from reality. In short, the intellect can operate in the two fundamental directions of the psychic apparatus: toward the world and away from the world. It can function correctly in unison with the most lively affect and it can also take a critical stand toward the affect. There is no mechanical, absolutely antithetical relationship between intellect and affect but, rather, a functional one.

Until now, deriving the intellectual function from the vegetative function has seemed very difficult. However, certain character-analytic experiences pave the way to an understanding of this problem also. We'd like to illustrate this through a patient in whom the affective genesis of a clever and cunning intellectual function was evident in an interesting way.

Character analysis had succeeded in unmasking and eliminating the patient's politeness and apparent devotedness as deception and the warding off of strong aggressions. Now he began to develop the following defense. Exceptionally intelligent, he sought to divine everything he concealed in the way of unconscious mechanisms and, in fact, he succeeded in destroying most of the affect situations by divining them beforehand. It was as if, from a secret hiding place, he continually illuminated and examined everything with his intellect in order to preclude any surprises. It became more and more clear that the intellect fulfilled a defensive function and was spurred by severe anxious anticipations. For example, he was always extremely skilled in finding out what I happened to be thinking about him at any one moment. He was able to infer this from various factors and from the course of the treatment. He was also able to divine and foresee what would happen at any one point. From the point of view of character analysis, this behavior was looked upon as anything but cooperation; rather, it was attacked as an extremely cunning way of avoiding deep insights. The first task was to render this weapon unusable to the patient, and this could be done only by the consistent analysis of its function, and by being very sparse with my communications. The patient continued for a while to use his intellect as a defense mechanism, but gradually became insecure and uneasy and finally began to protest violently that I did not want to understand him, that his intellectual help was a clear demonstration of his cooperation, etc. I became that much more consistent in my analysis of his intellectual activity as a defense against surprises. One day a term occurred to me for his behavior. I told him that it reminded me of a *cunning fox or lynx.* And then, following a short period of excitation, his defensive behavior fell to pieces. It happened this way: once again he began the session by despairing that I no longer understood him. Then, gradually, his attention was focused on a scene from his third year of life which he had recounted earlier in passing, without details and affect.

He had taken a bad fall and severely injured his left arm, which required medical attention. His father took him in his arms and carried him across the street to a surgical hospital. Crying uncontrollably, he now remembered the following details: he passed by a store in which stuffed animals were displayed. He distinctly remembered two of them: a *fox* and a *reindeer* with large antlers. During this hour, he was not able to remember what took place between this observation and the operation. Then, however, he was able to see himself lying on the operation table, his arms bound, his shoulders drawn back in tense expectation. Suddenly he recalled the *chloroform mask,* after he had momentarily hallucinated the smell of chloroform. The mask was about to be placed on him and he thought: "This is a fox's face which I am getting here!" As a matter of fact, a fox's head has a great similarity to a chloroform mask. Even as a child, he knew that foxes are caught in traps; in his native country, they were caught in steel traps with spikes that fasten upon one of the animal's legs and "break its bones." On the way to the hospital, the boy had strained his intellect to see how he might elude this calamity. This was perhaps the first time that his intellect had served the purpose of warding off a great and imminent danger. And the analytic treatment was warded off as a danger in the same way, cunningly, "like a fox." The patient distinctly remembered how, after a strained search for an escape, he had come to the conclusion: "It's useless, it's altogether useless! I'm trapped." Now it was understandable how one of his most crucial weaknesses was established: he had become cunning and cautious to such a degree that he was capable neither of acting upon his political convictions nor—out of fear—of pursuing a definite plan of action. He had been a fox in the trap his whole life and, as a cunning fox, had *actively* bound the childhood fear of being caught in a fox trap himself.

5. THE INTERLACING OF THE INSTINCTUAL DEFENSES

It would be altogether misleading to assume that, through the loosening or elimination of one defense, the conditions for libidinal flow are automatically established or that this enables the patient to associate freely. Often, to be sure, following the removal of a layer of the defense apparatus, liberated affects begin to flow, together with the infantile material pertaining to them. The analyst would deprive himself of every further possibility of *completely* breaking down the armor, however, if, in this intermediary phase, he did anything more than extract from the flowing material what directly relates to the contemporary transference situation. If the analyst fails to follow this procedure, he will find that the resultant breach soon closes again and the armor continues to function unaffected. The small breakthroughs following the removal of individual layers of defense should not be confused with the final *breakdown* of the armor. The reason for this is found in the specific structure of the armored psychic apparatus, which we designate as the *interlacing of the defensive forces*. The following example will illustrate this.

If the analyst has unmasked as a defense function and eliminated an obtrusively polite attitude which represents the topmost layer of the psychic apparatus, the warded-off impulses (e.g., aggression) appear and produce a change in the patient's bearing. From the point of view of character analysis, it would be wrong at this time to point out to the patient that he is living out his infantile aggression; it would be wrong even when this aggression appears in an undisguised manner. As we have pointed out, this aggression is not only the expression of an infantile relation to the world but also, and at the same time, a warding off of what lies deeper, e.g., anal passive strivings. If now the analyst succeeds in removing this layer of defense, what may rise to the surface is not the expected passivity but a total absence of psychic contact, an indifference toward the analyst, etc. This lack of contact is unequivocal defense, i.e., the warding off of a fear of being disappointed. If, by analyzing this contactlessness, the analyst succeeds once again in bringing to the surface this fear of being disappointed, then the lack of contact too might assume the character of a deep infantile fear of losing the loved object; at the same time, however, it wards off deeper aggressive impulses toward that love object which once withdrew its love. Our example can be varied, complicated, or simplified at will, according to the type. For example, the *deeper* layer of aggression which emerges could itself be the expression of *original* destructive impulses; at the same time, however, it could also have the function of warding off very intense oral-narcissistic demands for love. From the point of view of character analysis, it would again have to be interpreted as defense and not as a vegetative instinctual expression. *Hence, the layers of the armor are interrelated, i.e., every impulse which has been warded off serves at the same time to ward off more deeply repressed impulses.* The final breakthrough is achieved only after the analyst has worked through the many defense functions.

In our patient, therefore, the vegetative excitation quite possibly would not break through until after the oral-narcissistic demands for love had been analyzed as a warding off of genuine, original love impulses of an oral or genital nature. Working through the various stages of the defense formations requires exceptional patience and the conviction that eventually original instinctual impulses will appear which no longer figure as defense. When this point has been reached, a new cathexis of the patient's genitality has usually already taken place. However, the interrelation of the defense functions still requires a very thorough clinical supplementation.

In this connection, it is necessary to discuss the point of view promulgated by Kaiser[9] that interpretations could be dispensed with altogether. First of all, a misunderstanding arises from the fact that Kaiser takes interpretation to mean only the making conscious of what has been warded off. In my discussion of the character-analytic technique, I use the term for every form of analytic communication. Kaiser's restriction of the concept of interpretation may even have certain advantages; according to him, the establishment of a superficial analytic connection or the isolation of a character trait would not be an *interpretation* in the strict sense of the word. Even with this reservation in mind, I can concur with Kaiser in theory only if he means that consistent resistance analysis not only makes every interpretation superfluous but even excludes it as an error. He seems to forget that my formulation of the "interpretation at the end" is a *practical* necessity as long as the character-analytic technique has not been perfected to such a degree that we can feel *wholly* secure in dealing with the defense mechanisms. Thus, his contention holds true only for the ideal case of character-analytic work. I must admit that I am still a long way off from this. At the present time, I am still struggling with the analysis of the defense formation, especially with the problems of contactlessness and the interlacing of the defense functions. Perhaps what makes correct character-analytic work so difficult at present is a consideration that I find lacking in Kaiser, namely the consideration of the sex-economic point of view of working in such a way that as much as possible of all sexual excitation becomes concentrated in the genital zone and appears there as *orgasm anxiety*.

6. CONTACTLESSNESS

Originally, character analysis conceived of the psychic armor as the sum total of all repressing defense forces; it could be dynamically broken down through the analysis of the formal modes of behavior. Later it was shown that this concept did not

---

[9] "Probleme der Technik," *Internationalen Zeitschrift für Psychoanalyse,* IV (1934).

embrace the psychic armor in its totality; indeed, that it probably overlooked the most important factor. We gradually came to see that, even after the formal modes of behavior had been completely broken down, even after far-reaching breakthroughs of vegetative energy were achieved, an undefinable residue always remained, seemingly beyond reach. One had the feeling that the patient refused to part with the last reserves of his "narcissistic position" and that he was extremely clever in concealing it from himself and from the analyst. Even as the analysis of the active defense forces and of the character reaction formations seemed to be complete, there was no doubt that an elusive residue existed. Here the analyst was faced with a difficult problem. The theoretical concept of the armor was correct: an aggregate of repressed instinctual demands which were directed toward the outer world stood in opposition to an aggregate of defense forces which maintained the repression; the two *formed a functional unity* within the person's specific character. In short, while we understood both what had been warded off and what warded it off, we still had no conclusive insight into the residue.

The explanation that *one and the same* instinct is simultaneously directed toward the world and serves as a defense function against one's own ego broadened our knowledge of the ego structure, but it did not really solve the problem. I want to use a clinical example to illustrate that *psychic contactlessness* constitutes the elusive residue of the armor.

In the patient discussed earlier, analysis revealed that, behind the reactive passive-feminine behavior, there was a deep estrangement from the world, from its objects and goals, which was expressed as *apathy* and *inflexibility*. The patient himself had no immediate awareness of this; on the contrary, his passive-feminine dependency glossed over this estrangement and gave him the impression of having especially intense relations to the outer world. I was faced with a contradiction difficult to resolve. On the one hand, there was his libidinal stickiness, his readiness to be of help and to be obliging, i.e., relationships which seemed to be very intense; at the same time, this was a clear case of contactlessness. The problem was solved as it became possible to comprehend the origin of the patient's attachment and dependency. These attitudes, it turned out, not only fulfilled the function of holding in suppression the repressed aggressive tendencies but, over and above this, they compensated for his inner estrangement from the world. Thus, we must distinguish the following:

First: the repressed demands.

Second: the repressing defense forces.

Third: a layer of the psychic structure between the two, the contactlessness, which, at first, appears not as a formation of dynamic forces but as a rigid, static manifestation, as a wall in the psychic organism, the *result of the contradiction between two libidinal currents pulling in opposing directions.* This structure can be best comprehended when its history is known.

After discovering this special form of contactlessness in our patient, we undertook a review of our clinical experiences. This contactlessness, it turned out, is as general a phenomenon of neurosis as is the change of function of the instinct. But before giving another clinical example to illustrate the genesis of this formation, let me offer a brief summary of the theoretical concept of contactlessness. When libidinal tendencies flow toward the outer world—we keep intentionally to this image—and a prohibition from the outer world checks this flow, then, in certain situations, an equilibrium is established between the instinctual force on the one hand and the frustrating force on the other hand. It might be said that this equilibrium is a seemingly static condition in the person's libidinal flow corresponding to an *inhibition.* And this dynamic condition may perhaps lie at the basis of the fixation of instincts at earlier stages of development, as well as at the basis of psychic inhibition in general.

This condition will become much clearer as we go along. It can even be described differently, though we have nothing different in mind. When an instinct is taken over by the ego for the purpose of gratification and it meets with a frustration, it can, as we pointed out, split up or dissociate. One part of it turns against itself (reaction formation); another part continues in the original direction toward the outer world. When this happens, however, the dynamic relations have changed. At the point where the current directed toward the outer world and the current turned toward one's own ego diverge, a condition of paralysis or rigidity arises. This is more than just a heuristic hypothesis. Once the analyst has thoroughly grasped this process and has instructed his patients to give him an exact description of their feelings, he will find that they experience this inhibition distinctly and directly in all their object relations. The manifestations of this dynamic-structural condition are different; I shall merely name a few of the more frequent clinical ones.

At the top of the list we have the feeling of *inner isolation.* This feeling is sometimes present in spite of an abundance of social and professional relationships. In other cases, we meet with a feeling described as *"inner deadness."* There can be no doubt that compulsive neurotic or, more specifically, schizoid depersonalization belongs to this group. The dualistic perceptions of schizophrenic patients are a direct manifestation of this condition. When patients complain about being estranged, isolated, or apathetic, their feeling can be traced back to this contradiction between the object-libidinal current and the tendency to escape into oneself. Cleavage and ambivalence are direct manifestations of this paradox; the apathy is the result of the equilibrium created by the two opposing forces. Thus, our earlier concept of contactlessness as a wall is not altogether correct. It is more an interplay between dynamic forces than a passive attitude. The same is true of the affect-block in the compulsion neurosis and catatonic rigidity. We must content ourselves with these examples.

After we have succeeded in breaking through the armor, we observe an *alternation* between vegetative current and affective block in our patients. The transition from the condition of motility to that of rigidity is one of the most important therapeutic and theoretical problems if one's goal is to reestablish the capacity for vegetative streaming. Similar conditions of the blocking of the affects or of the development of apathy were met with during the war and they were described by political prisoners who had been subjected to terroristic treatment. Here, apparently, the affects of aggressive rage are offset by the inhibition imposed by the external power. Since this continual oscillation from one direction to the other is neither economical nor tolerable for the psychic apparatus, the individual becomes stultified. This state, however, is not a passive attitude or a final ossification of a dynamic condition; it is, as we have said, the result of a conflict of forces. This can be proven by two facts. First, external conditions or character-analytic efforts can dissolve this dulling into its dynamic components. To the extent that this dulling gives way, sexual strivings, aggression, as well as anxiety, i.e., centripetal tendencies of flight, reappear in the individual. This further confirms the sex-economic concept of sexuality and anxiety as two antithetical directions of currents.

What we later meet in our patients as repressed instinct, repressing force, and intermediate inner estrangement operating simultaneously in fact arose in a definite historical sequence. This will be demonstrated by the following example.

A patient who suffered acutely from the feeling of inner deadness (as opposed to the other patient, who did not sense this condition) was characterized by an exaggeratedly formal, polite, and reserved bearing; people with free-flowing vegetative motility found him rigid and unalive. A certain dignity which he displayed completed the picture. His most intense secret wish was "to feel the world" and "to be able to flow." The character-analytic loosening of his affects from these attitudes led to a complete reactivation of those childhood situations that formed the basis of his contactlessness and yearning for psychic vitality. The following symptoms stood out in his neurosis: an extremely intense fear of object-loss, strong depressive reactions when he failed to have an immediate erection while kissing a woman, and more of the same. First of all, it was learned that the immediate cause of these symptoms was—in addition to the yearning for a vital object relationship—a strong inner *inclination to retreat,* a tendency to give up the object at the drop of a hat. This inclination stemmed from the fear of his own hatred toward the very object through which he sought to experience "a flowing feeling." It is important that he suffered from penis anesthesia or, to put it another way, from a lack of the *feeling of vegetative contact.* Especially pronounced manifestations of such conditions are found in compulsive characters. Their formula of the "new life" that they are constantly on the verge of beginning, their feeling that they have the capacity to be "different," i.e., vital and productive and not rigid, unalive, and "dead," is merely an expression of the last traces of vegetative motility and is usually the strongest incentive to recover. To return to our patient: when the penis anesthesia was eliminated, the feeling of contactlessness also disappeared; but it immediately returned when the genital disturbance reappeared. The correlations between psychic contactlessness and physiological lack of feeling on the one hand and the capacity for contact and vegetative sensitivity on the other had their roots in the patient's early history. Briefly summarized, it is as follows:

The patient had had a strong genital-sensual attachment to his mother and had been rejected when he attempted to approach her in a sensual and genital way. It is important that the mother not only did not prohibit non-genital surface contacts, e.g., lying together side by side, embracing, etc., but specifically encouraged them. When his genital impulses were repulsed, he retained the genital tendency toward the mother but simultaneously developed a strong aggressive-sadistic attitude toward her which gradually supplanted the genital tendency altogether. This attitude too had to be repressed because of frustration and fear of punishment. From then on, he found himself entangled in a conflict between affectionate love for his mother, culminating in the striving for physical contact with her, and hatred of her, fear of the hatred as well as of the genital striving and the fear of losing the love object. Later, no matter how often he approached a woman, a sadistic attitude overcame the genital striving, which was more or less repressed, and caused him to retreat. To meet the demands of the childhood repression, it had been necessary to deaden the genital sensation in his penis. Even today, we cannot explain how this is possible. In this case, the aggressive impulse probably checked the sexual impulse and vice versa. Where erective potency is present, the absence of genital sensation (vaginal anesthesia is the same) is the *direct* expression of the loss of the capacity for contact as well as its most salient characteristic. We can assume that we are dealing here not only with a psychic process but also with a change, probably of the electro-physiological functions on the skin of the penis. At a deeper level, the feeling of deadness had the same meaning to the patient as not having a penis or not feeling his penis. The rational reason for this was the fact that the penis had lost its capacity to feel. His deep depression resulted from this condition.[10]

His deep estrangement from the world, then, developed at the point where his natural, original genital striving came into conflict with the aggression toward the object and the inclination to retreat which resulted from that conflict. One would certainly be justified in generalizing about this process: wherever natural, adequate instinctual impulses are denied direct relationship to objects of the world, the result is anxiety, as the expression of a crawling into oneself, and the development of a wall of contactlessness. This is seen in the child following the first severe phase of genital repression, as well as in the young adolescent when, because of external reasons or inner inability, he cannot attain the object. It is also the case among couples who have been married for a long time when the genital relationship has lost its aliveness and other forms of sexual gratification have been suppressed. In all these cases, a picture emerges of psychic dulling, characterized by resignation, apathy, feelings of isolation, and severe impairment of one's activity and objective interests.

In the attempt to comprehend the dynamics of the character, one meets difficulties of a linguistic nature at every step. To describe the function of inhibition and contactlessness as faithfully as possible, we have to make a further correction in our present concept, one that requires a far-reaching change in our thinking regarding the psychic apparatus. We pointed out that, between the layer of what is repressed and what represses (the defense), we find a layer of contactlessness. This intermediate layer corresponds to an inhibition which results from the opposition between two instinctual impulses or the cleavage of a single instinctual impulse.

[10] Footnote, 1945: The clinical manifestation of "contactlessness" later became the leading perspective from which we carried out the search for orgone biophysical disturbances. In contactlessness, we are dealing with a motility block of the body orgone (anorgonia). In penis anesthesia, the skin is not orgonotically charged; the orgone energy field is markedly contracted; the penis is sensitive to touch but not to pleasure. Since only a change of the energy level is capable of creating pleasure, it is clear that it is a block in the plasmatic current which causes contactlessness. In 1942 we succeeded in proving the physical existence of the orgone energy field through the lumination of a filament. Cf. also "The Bio-electric Function of Pleasure and Anxiety," *The Function of the Orgasm*.

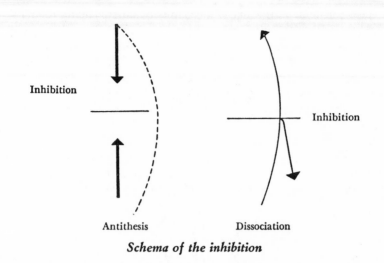

Inhibition

Inhibition

Antithesis   Dissociation

Schema of the inhibition

In this formulation, however, we neglected the fact that the neurotic psychic apparatus consists not of *one* warded-off and *one* warding-off impulse but of an infinite number of strivings which are partially dissociated and partially set off against one another. Further, in the *interlacing* of the defense forces, an impulse that has risen to the surface from the depth of the armor can exercise a defense function. It is very likely, indeed, that all psychic tendencies are dissociated into those operating simultaneously "toward the world," "away from the world," and in opposition to one another. In short, we get the picture of a complicated *web* of forces (armor structure), in which warded-off and warding-off elements are not neatly separated, as our complacency would have it. Rather, these elements are entangled in an extremely irregular manner. Only our character-analytic work brings order into the picture corresponding to the history of the structure. In no way whatever is this structural view compatible with any concept of a topographical stratification. What is warded off and what wards off are linked together in a functional unity, let us say, in a character inhibition, as Na and Cl in NaCl, or positive and negative electric forces in a "neutral" condition. If one considers the infinite multitude of such unifications of various tendencies and of single tendencies which have become split, then it becomes clear that any effort to comprehend these phenomena through a mechanistic and systematic thought-process will fail. Functional and structural thinking and imagination are required here. The development of the character is a progressive unfolding, splitting, and antithesis of simple vegetative functions. Perhaps the following diagram of forces operating in various directions will provide some idea of this:

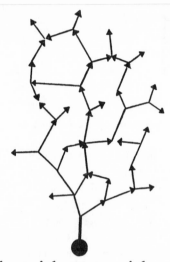

Schema of the structure of the armor

Hence, contactlessness is not a layer between two layers of opposing forces; it is a phenomenon corresponding to the positions of a *concentration* or special *density* of antitheses and dissociations. What we perceive in character analysis as a compact, tenacious, or entangled formation is just such a *concentration of* opposing forces in the *character*. We have already stressed how important it is to approach and analyze such a character formation from the "right end."

During the treatment, character traits such as reserve and reticence become a compact character resistance, e.g., in the form of a stubborn, apprehensive silence. It is completely alien to character analysis to overcome such silences by urging, demanding, or persuading the patient to talk. The patient's silence is usually the result of an *inability* to articulate his inner impulses. Urging and persuading intensify the stubbornness; they do not eliminate the disturbance of the patient's ability to express himself but make it worse. The patient of course would like to talk, to open his heart to the analyst. For some reason or other, however, he cannot. No doubt, the very fact of having to talk inhibits him. He does not know that he is not able to express himself, but is usually of the opinion that he does not *want to*. In secret, he hopes that the analyst will understand him in spite of his inability to open himself. This desire "to be understood" is usually accompanied by a warding off of any help: a stubborn attitude is assumed. This makes the work difficult but not impossible.

Instead of urging, persuading, or even resorting to the well-known "silence technique," the analyst consoles the patient, assuring him that he understands his inhibition and, for the time being, can do without his efforts to communicate. In this way, the patient is relieved of the pressure of "having to" talk; at the same time he is disarmed of any contemporary reason for being stubborn. If now the analyst succeeds in *describing* the patient's attitudes to him in a simple and precise manner, without expecting any immediate changes, the patient readily feels himself "understood," and his affects begin to stir. At first he struggles against them by intensifying his silence, but eventually he grows restless. This nascent restlessness is the first movement away from the condition of rigidity. After several days, or at most weeks, of careful description and isolation of his attitudes, he gradually begins to talk. In most cases, the character trait of silence is caused by a constriction of the throat musculature of which the patient has no awareness; this constriction chokes off "emerging" excitations.

Technically, therefore, it is by no means sufficient to want to destroy contactlessness. Merely to reconstruct the history of its development or to uncover the instinctual and defensive forces upon which it rests, i.e., which constitute it, is not enough. It must, rather, as with every character attitude, be *isolated* and *objectified before* it is taken apart analytically. This can be done in various ways, depending on the case. Essentially, however, it is accomplished by a thoroughgoing description of the patient's behavior. It can also be done by continually stressing the disparity between the person's ideal demands and the actual barrenness of his or her mode of existence; through demonstration of his objective lack of interest, which results in failure or contradictions in his work; unmasking the deep and palpable psychic bleakness of his experiences, in spite of the seeming intensity of his love life. In this way, the contactlessness is pushed to the outer limits of agony. Its complete unfolding and subsequent dissolution are usually achieved only when the demands for living contact with reality, as a result of liberated sexual excitations, have become urgent. Once the patient has begun to sense the first, even though weak, sensations of orgastic streaming in his body, especially in the genital, the feeling of contactlessness is no longer tolerable. Just as the general feeling of contactlessness, regardless of which psychic layer it is found in, is merely the general reflection of orgasm anxiety, that is, *fear of orgastic contact,* so too it completely disappears of its own accord when the capacity for orgastic contact has been realized.

The investigation of those psychophysical mechanisms which lead from the condition of full experience to the condition of inner emptiness or confinement cannot yet be regarded as complete. Much still lies in the dark here. What is most puzzling is the fact that the withdrawal of sexual interest or the inhibition of an outwardly striving impulse is directly experienced as a growing feeling of "coldness," "numbness," "hardness," "deadness." "My soul is like a frozen-over lake," a patient once said. Our earlier explanation of this phenomenon as the "inhibition" caused by two opposing forces is correct but incomplete. And the explanation that it is libido which is drawn off does not add to it. Words cannot replace dynamic comprehension. We simply don't know the answer yet. There is a way of investigating this life-destroying phenomenon, however, if we allow the patient to reexperience the precise history of the *transition* from being vitally alive to being utterly frozen; and if, in the treatment, we pay minute attention to the oscillation from the one condition to the other. Strange inner modes of behavior are revealed when this procedure is followed. One patient, for example, experienced the transition in the following way. He had to repeat mechanically: "It's useless; it's utterly useless," etc. The meaning behind this was: "What's the use of trying, of competing, of sacrificing, even of loving? The other person does not understand me anyhow." Certainly one of the most tragic experiences of children results from the fact that at an early age not every feeling and desire can be expressed and articulated. The child must find some other way to appeal for understanding of the unexpressible psychic condition. But parents and teachers, being what they are, are seldom capable of divining what is going on in the child. In vain the child makes his appeal, until finally he gives up the struggle for understanding and grows numb: "It's utterly useless." The road between vital experiencing and dying inwardly is paved with disappointments in love. These disappointments constitute the most frequent and most potent cause of internal dying. This, however, bitter as it is, still does not explain the mechanism involved in the process.

What very often sets this process in motion and sustains it is a fear of contact with things, experiences, and persons, operating at the center of which, according to my experience, is the fear of orgastic contact. It is usually acquired from the infantile masturbation anxiety. *Accordingly, the fear of orgastic contact constitutes the core of the fear of genuine, direct psychic contact with persons and with the processes of reality.* The overcoming of this fear is one of the most important and most difficult tasks of character-analytic therapy. Again and again patients, even those who have been completely liberated from their infantile fixations, relapse immediately into their old neurotic conditions when they are faced with realizing the capacity for genital-orgastic contact. This requires the overcoming of the orgasm anxiety. In every correctly executed character-analytic treatment, this phase, which is sharply delineated in most cases, sets in some time after the armor has been dissolved. Its characteristics are: superficiality of the analytic communications; dreams and fantasies of falling; general intensification of the attitude of reticence, such as intentional avoidance of the subject of genital desires; greater frequency of more or less clear ideas of physical disintegration (these are not to be confused with castration fantasies) ; annulment of all prior therapeutic accomplishments; escape from every sexual or objective relationship to the world; reactivation of early childhood modes of reaction; reappearance of the inner feeling of emptiness and desolation, etc. This phase requires a thorough analysis of the attitudes and sensations which the patient has during masturbation and/or intercourse. When these at-

titudes and sensations are thoroughly analyzed, it is observed
that at a certain point the patients in some way inhibit the increase of excitation. They do not allow the wave of excitation to
mount; they disrupt the excitation by means of short, rapid
movements; they constrict their pelvic muscles without being
aware of it; they distract themselves unconsciously by means of
associations; they refuse to yield to the impulse to stretch the
pelvis far forward; they very frequently stop the movement and
hold still the moment they begin to experience the orgastic sensation, instead of letting themselves go and increasing the release in
spontaneous, rhythmic friction. The most difficult orgastic inhibition to dispel is the one in which no external sign of the kind described above is found, and the excitement simply dies away.
This "going cold" is often difficult to understand.

I want to call special attention to a conspicuous (and regularly
overlooked) attitude in the act of intercourse. If there is a fear of
orgastic contact and the psychic contactlessness pertaining to it,
then the vegetative impulse to produce friction is always missing.
When, however, preorgastic contact is complete, this impulse operates automatically. In the former case, what happens is that, to
overcome the contactlessness and to arrive at a release in spite of
the fear, a forced, impetuous, consciously produced friction often
takes the place of the gentle, self-regulating, emotionally governed rhythm. The fear of genital contact cannot be uncovered
and eliminated until this form of friction has been analyzed as a
warding off of sensations and as a constricted desire for release.
Patients usually offer strong resistance to giving up this form of
friction and opening themselves to a vegetative kind of friction.
They do not want to be taken by surprise by the orgastic convulsion.

Generally, it can be said that correct and successful character
analysis is characterized by three phenomena.

1) A thorough dissolution of the armor

2) Complete development of the fear of orgastic contact

3) Complete overcoming of the orgastic inhibition and establishment of totally uninhibited, involuntary movement at the moment of climax

The effort required in most cases to bring about a concentration of the excitation in the orgasm anxiety and then to over-

come this anxiety is amply rewarded by the rapid and complete change in the patient's general behavior, i.e., his free-flowing vegetative motility.

7. SUBSTITUTE CONTACT

The more extensively vegetative motility is suppressed in childhood, the more difficult it will be for the adolescent to develop relationships to the world, to love objects, to his work, and to reality in general, which are commensurable with this stage of life. In such a case, it is that much easier to sink into the condition of estranged resignation, and the substitute relations which are formed will be that much more unnatural. Most of what official adolescent psychology considers the "characteristics of puberty," turn out in character-analytic work to be the artificially produced effect of obstructed natural sexuality. This holds true for daydreaming as well as for inferiority feelings. The latter express an imagined inferiority and ideals too divorced from reality; they are also reflective of a concrete contradiction in the structure. The feeling of inferiority is the inner perception of the gap between actual performances in the sexual and social spheres and the latent capacities and possibilities inhibited by the paralysis of vegetative motility. Most people are actually far less potent than they imagine themselves in their dreams, and are endowed with far greater qualities and capacities than they translate into action. This grotesque contradiction in the structure of modern man is one of the consequences of the destructive regulation of sexuality imposed upon him by the society. To eliminate this contradiction is one of the most important tasks that a new social order will have to accomplish. The productive power, "working power," depends essentially upon how closely actual achievement approximates the latent capacity for it, i.e., upon the reestablishment of vegetative motility.

These conditions are psychically unbearable and socially damaging in the long run. The psychic apparatus, which is sustained by constantly flowing vegetative energy, rebels against this contradiction, perceives it more or less consciously as a severe impairment of life, and attempts to come to terms with it in various ways. We shall not go into the neurotic symptoms which result from the sexual stasis. For us, it is more important to investigate the character functions which arise for the first time in this struggle. Once the immediate vegetative contact with the world has been more or less destroyed, when the remaining traces of vegetative contact are no longer sufficient to preserve the relationship to the outer world, either *substitute functions* develop or there are attempts to establish a *substitute contact*. Let us give some clinical examples to illustrate the difference between substitute contact and direct vegetative contact. The difficulty lies in the fact that the substitute contact is also sustained by vegetative instinctual energy (this is what the former has in common with the latter). But the similarities are less important than the differences. Thus, while the passive-feminine behavior of the passive-feminine character is sustained by anal excitations, this behavior is a substitute contact which has taken the place of a natural contact precluded by the situation of frustration. So, even as an adult, the young man has to rebel against a domineering and authoritarian father to secure his independence and to unfold his own capacities. He is not in possession of the aggression necessary for such a course, however, because it is repressed. To hold this aggression in repression, he develops a passive-feminine mode of behavior and attempts, instead of coming to grips with the world with sublimated aggression, to map out a way of life based on neurotic compliance and requiring the greatest personal sacrifices.

The sadistic attitude of the compulsive neurotic, genitally disturbed woman toward the male has the function not only of warding off her genitality but, over and above this, of compensating for the libidinal estrangement which resulted from this process, as well as the function of still preserving the contact with the original love object, even if in a different form. In the same way, the artificial, spurious, exaggerated expressions of affection exchanged between spouses are substitute contact functions in the absence of a genuine sexual relationship. By the same token, the neurotically aggressive behavior of querulous couples is a warding off and compensation for passive-feminine impulses toward the man or natural genital impulses toward the woman; over and above this, it is an attempt, prompted by the absence of immediate vegetative contact, to remain in touch with the world. Masochistic behavior is not only the expression and, in a certain sense, the warding off of repressed sadistic aggression; it is also a substitute function for natural relations to the outer world. The masochistic character is incapable of direct expressions of love.

Once the difference between the manifestations of free-flowing, direct vegetative contact and of spurious, secondary, circuitous substitute relationships has been thoroughly comprehended, it is no difficult matter to pick out the manifold manifestations of the latter in everyday life. At this point, I should like to name a few atypical but characteristic examples of artificial behavior: loud, obtrusive laughter; exaggeratedly firm handshake; unvarying, dull friendliness; conceited display of acquired knowledge; frequent repetition of empty astonishment, surprise, or delight, etc.; rigid adherence to definite views, plans, goals (e.g., a paranoic system, neurotic inability to change one's mind) ; obtrusive modesty in demeanor; grand gestures in speaking; childish wooing of people's favor; boastfulness in sexual matters; exaggerated display of sexual charm; promiscuous flirtation; unregulated promiscuous sexual intercourse; markedly dignified conduct; affected, pathetic, or overrefined manner of speech; markedly authoritative ("the big wheel") , haughty, or patronizing behavior; pseudo-exuberant fellowship; adherence to conventional conversational tone; rowdy or lascivious behavior; sexual giggling or obscene talk; Don Juanism; bashfulness. In the same way, most superfluous movements express, in addition to narcissistic tendencies, a substitute relationship to the object, e.g., affectedly shaking one's hair into place; repeatedly passing one's hand over one's forehead in a characteristic way; suggestively looking into the eyes of the other person while talking; affected swaying of the hips; cocky or athletic gait, etc.

Generally, wherever a character trait stands out from the total personality in an isolated or contradictory way, there is a substitute function governed by a more or less deep estrangement. One is reluctant to admit it, but character analysis again and again confirms it: the character trait popularly looked upon as "bad," "disagreeable," or "troublesome" is usually identical with neurotic behavior; the same is true of most of the modes of behavior which rule the life of the so-called "better people," i.e., where form takes precedence over content. On the other hand, most of the character traits commonly regarded as "simple," "natural," "sympathetic," "engaging" seem to coincide with the non-neurotic behavior of the "genital character." ("Neurotic" here specifically means a psychic condition which came into being through the repression of an instinctual impulse and is sustained by an energy-consuming counter-cathexis).

One is again and again amazed at the double life which people are forced to lead. The surface behavior, which varies according to social situation and class, turns out to be an artificial formation; it is in continual conflict with the true, direct, vegetatively determined nature which, quite often, it is hardly capable of concealing. The most formidable and feared policeman; the most high-minded and reserved academician; the elegant, inaccessible "socialite"; the "dutiful" bureaucrat who functions like a machine—they all turn out to be harmless characters having the simplest longings, anxieties, hate impulses. I am making a special point of this only because of the incredible respect which the so-called simple man has for the mask of the character.

In character-analytical terms, the difference between living sexual rhythm and calculated sex appeal; between natural, unaffected dignity and put-on dignity; between genuine and sham modesty; between the direct and the pretentious expression of life; between vegetative muscular rhythm and the swaying of hips and squaring of shoulders in imitation of it; between faithfulness stemming from sexual gratification and faithfulness stemming from fear and conscience—one could go on at random—is the same as the difference between a nascent revolutionary psychic structure and an unyielding conservative psychic structure, between living life and meaningless substitutes for life. In these differences we find a direct representation of the material, psychic-structural basis of ideologies which, at least in principle, are accessible to human experience.

In the ideology of all authoritarian social organizations, vegetative life, represented as animal-like and primitive, has always been absolutely set off against the "cultural" substitute life, represented as differentiated and highly developed. In reality, the latter, since it was torn away from the former, since it represents merely a substitute function and not a continuation of the former, is unproductive, frozen into rigid forms and formulas, as devoid of fruit as a dried-up plant. The vegetative life, on the other hand, is inherently productive and endowed with endless possibilities of development. And the reason for this is quite simple: its energy is not chronically frozen and bound. The vegetative substitute formations did not give birth to culture; all human progress sprang from the leftover traces of the direct vegetative contact with the world. This gives us some idea of just how much energy is waiting to be developed if we could succeed in freeing human structures from their substitute functions and restoring the immediacy of their relationship to nature and society. Fortunately, a new religion cannot result from this, e.g., a new yoga movement giving instruction "in the function of immediate contact." This change in the human structure presupposes changes in the social system, of which the student of yoga has no comprehension.

If man is the sole creature denied the realization of his native potentials and there is no death instinct which would drive him to commit suicide; if, moreover, the necessity to live, to have social relationships, is rooted in the vegetative system, then the substitute contact which man establishes is merely the expression of a compromise between a will to live and socially induced fear of life. The psychic formation of a substitute contact, as opposed to the immediate vegetative contact, is structured exactly like a neurotic symptom. It represents a substitute function for something else, serves as a defense, consumes energy, and attempts to harmonize contradictory forces. As in the case of the symptom, the result of the performance is in no way commensurate with the amount of energy necessary to accomplish it. Hence, the substitute contact is one of the many manifestations of a disordered social economy and of the disturbed personal sexual economy dependent upon it. Since the function of the substitute contact as such was unknown and since its manifestations in the social framework have become traditional, they have become associated with the idea of being immutable natural phenomena. However, in its role as a social phenomenon and as an element of modern man's structure, this function of the substitute contact is a historical formation, i.e., one that originated at a definite point in history and is therefore transient. A person making a trip on a poor train is hesitant to leave it as long as a new and better one is not available to take him securely to his destination. Moreover, that person begins to develop a very peculiar capacity to persevere and also begins to cherish illusions about the nature of trains. By the same token: if we are to free those forces sufficient to replace one form of life with another, the idea of a regulated sexual economy of human life must first become as embedded in man's consciousness as is the present idea of the immutability of unregulated sexual economy.

If man's present life is a substitute life, his work an imposed duty, his love a substitute love, and his hate a substitute hate; if the character-analytic dissolution of the psychic armor destroys these substitute functions; if this predominantly reactively functioning human structure is the result and exigency of the present social organization, the question arises: what takes the place of this form of psychic functioning after a successful character analysis? How is its structure changed? What is the relation between social achievement and sexuality after a successful character analysis? Difficult and momentous questions, indeed! The theory of the orgasm and character analysis have already shed some light on these questions which are epitomized in the difference between the "neurotic" character and the "genital" character.

The investigation of the mode of functioning of the psychically healthy individual is still in its initial stages, however, and has to reckon with the strongest resistance on the part of a world chaotically sustained by the moralistic and authoritarian management of its affairs as a whole. In all its institutions, ethical norms, and political organizations, the world stands in opposition to a psychic structure which is governed not moralistically but sexeconomically, whose work springs not from duty but from objective interest, whose vegetative sources flow freely and have immediate access to the environment. The clinical basis of this psychic structure is in the process of development, insofar as it is not already known. One of the most difficult theoretical and practical tasks will be the application of individual character-analytic restructurization to the collective restructurization of the great majority through education.

8. THE PSYCHIC REPRESENTATION OF THE ORGANIC

a) The idea of "bursting"

The fact that biophysiological conditions are reflected or presented in psychic modes of behavior is definitely borne out by our knowledge of psychophysical relationships. It is very strange and still wholly incomprehensible, however, that language as well as the feeling that one gets about another person's behavior reflect, in an entirely unconscious but apparently definite way, the corresponding physiological condition not merely graphically but *directly*. A few examples may help to illustrate this.

Analysis shows that people who are described as "inaccessible" or "hard" are also hypertonic physically. Analysis also shows that the energy employed to mold the character of patients who feel "slimy" and "dirty" is essentially of anal origin. Terms such as "free," "flowing," "direct," "relaxed," "natural" used to describe the genital character are entirely in keeping with the biophysical structure of the genital character's vegetative apparatus. Those who have a "false" nature display in analysis an intricate development of substitute contact mechanisms and only the most minor traces of free-flowing genital libido. It would be valuable to make an exact and detailed study of these strange relations between the perception of a person's vegetative temperament and its linguistic formulation. We shall set this aside for a later time; at the moment we want to pursue only *one* trend which results from these relationships.

In character-analytic practice, as opposed to the straightforward resistance technique, we regularly meet with the following circumstance. In the beginning, the patient senses the analyst's attack on the character armor as a threat to the self. This explains why the analytic situation regularly becomes associated with the fear of physical harm (castration anxiety); the patient fears the success of the character-analytic treatment as he would a physical catastrophe. Intellectually and, insofar as the patient consciously desires to establish orgastic potency, also affectively, the patient wants the imminent attack to succeed, i.e., wants his psychic rigidity to be destroyed. He urgently desires, then, something which, at the same time, he is mortally afraid of. Not only is the breakdown of the character armor looked upon and feared as a catastrophe; the fear of losing one's grip on oneself is added to this and causes this simultaneous desiring and fearing of one and the same thing to become a typical resistance. What is meant here is not the attitude of the ego toward its own impulse, but the attitude toward the help which the ego expects from the analyst.

Until the character armor has been broken down, the patient can neither associate freely nor have a vital feeling about himself. He expects the analyst in some magical way to do everything for him and, without really knowing it, he assumes a passive attitude, whose substance is anything but passive. It is to be expected at this point that the patient will mobilize his *masochistic* impulses and put them at the service of the resistance. The psychic content of the resistance runs as follows: "You are not helping me; you can't do a thing; you neither love nor understand me; I am going to force you to help me, i.e., I shall be stubborn and I shall reproach you." In reality, however, the patient himself wards off any analytic influence. In many cases, such attitudes eventually become concentrated in a peculiar situation, into which until now I had no insight: *unconsciously, the smashing of the armor and the penetration into the patient's unconscious secrets are represented as a feeling of being pricked open or brought to the bursting point.* Indeed, the passive-feminine fantasy of being pricked open or pierced is fully developed in both male and female patients. Especially in male patients, there is a variation of this unconscious fantasy which is represented as follows: because he lacks genital self-confidence, the patient feels himself impotent. To escape this feeling, he fantasizes, at first on a superficial level, that the analyst lends him his potency, his capacity—in the final analysis, his penis. At a deeper level, the idea occasionally exists that, during the act of intercourse with a woman, the analyst penetrates the patient's anus, fills out, strengthens, and stiffens the patient's penis so that he can prove himself to be potent toward the woman. If the identification with the analyst and the demand to be helped can be explained on the basis of these unconscious fantasies, the warding off of this help can also be explained in terms of these fantasies, for unconsciously the help constitutes an injury, a being pricked open.

As we know, the masochistic striving is characterized by the patient's inability to achieve a physiological release on his own accord, because he senses the mounting of the pleasure as a danger of melting or bursting. However, since it is precisely this feared situation which, for natural reasons, he most ardently yearns for, he develops the attitude of expecting and beseeching others to help him to achieve release, i.e., help him to burst, a sensation which he simultaneously fears and wards off. This circumstance is discovered only after the first orgastic impulses have become manifest in the musculature of the genital apparatus. Until then, these impulses remain concealed and incomprehensible to those analysts who have not acquired the technique of establishing the capacity for orgastic excitation.

So much for the clinical-analytic data. A momentous question arises from it: the sensation of melting or dissolving is undoubtedly a direct expression of the excitation processes in the muscular and vascular systems during orgasm. Seen as an expulsion, the ejaculation is analogous to the release brought about by puncturing a tautly filled bladder. This is imbued with fear for patients who are orgastically impaired. The question is this: how is it possible that a physiological function can be so directly manifested and represented as an attitude of the psychic apparatus? I have to admit that, to me, this relationship is as puzzling as it is important. It is altogether likely that its clarification will considerably extend our knowledge of the connections between the physiological and psychic functions. For the present, I have nothing to say about it.[11] However, this clinical observation leads us to a very important question: *how is the idea of death psychically represented?*

b) On the idea of death

The question regarding the psychic representation of biophysiological processes coincides at certain points with the question regarding the existence of a will to die. This field is not only one of the least accessible but one of the most dangerous, for nowhere else have premature speculations blocked every path to a concrete ascertaining of the facts. As we pointed out, the hypoth-

---

[11] Footnote, 1945: This assumption was confirmed three years later: the bioelectric experiments with stimuli of pleasure and anxiety showed that *the intensity of the sensation was functionally identical with the quantity of the bio-energetic excitation.*

esis of a death instinct is an attempt to use a metaphysical formula to explain phenomena which on the basis of our present knowledge and method, cannot yet be explained. Like every metaphysical view, the hypothesis of the death instinct probably contains a rational core, but getting at this rational core is difficult because its mystification has created erroneous trains of thought. The theory of primary masochism contends that the will to suffer and to perish is biologically determined and that it is explained by the so-called nirvana principle. However, the sex-economic investigation of the mechanisms which produce and inhibit pleasure led to the theory of the orgasm. At this point I want to summarize the *tentative* formulations set forth in the chapter on "The Masochistic Character." These formulations never claimed to be complete.

1. Masochism, which is generally conceived of as a striving for *unpleasure* transcending the pleasure principle, is a *secondary* neurotic formation of the psychic organism. It can be analytically broken down into its component parts and, for this reason, is not a primary biological fact. When Rado recently came forward with a "new" theory of the neurosis which traces all anxiety back to the "breakthrough of primary masochism," he not only misconstrued the libido theory but made the same mistake Alfred Adler made previously: his explanation ceased precisely where the line of questioning begins in earnest. Namely: *how can the living organism desire unpleasure or death?*

2. The apparent striving after *unpleasure* can be traced back to the fact that a frustration, imposed under definite conditions and in a definite way, intervened between an originally pleasurable aim and the desire to achieve this aim. In his strivings after pleasure, the patient repeatedly runs into the same situation of frustration and *appears* to want it subjectively; in reality, he is striving toward the *pleasurable* goal which lies *behind it* or is concealed in it. *Hence, the suffering which the masochist brings upon himself is objectively determined but it is not subjectively wanted.* It is important not to obscure this difference.

3. The masochist suffers from a specific disturbance of his pleasure mechanism, and solely through character-analytic techniques for breaking down the psychic armor can this disturbance

be exposed. This disturbance consists in the fact that, beyond a certain degree, the patient perceives every increase of his orgastic sensation as unpleasurable and *fears* it as a danger of "perishing." The reason for this lies in the spasm of certain muscles, i.e., the orgastic release is conceived of as a bursting, perishing, or melting in the physical sense and is warded off by spasms. The passive beating fantasy has the function of achieving the yearned-for and at the same time feared release without incurring guilt, i.e., without bringing it about through one's own efforts. This can be clearly ascertained in all cases of erogenous masochism. The inducing of a lesser danger for the purpose of avoiding a greater danger is merely an intermediate mechanism.

4. If, as a result of the external inhibition and internal frustration of the striving after pleasure, the external and internal psychic reality has become a totally unpleasurable situation, then, even in destroying itself, the organism is still following the pleasure-unpleasure principle. This is the case in melancholia, for example. As a last resort, the melancholic seizes upon suicide to resolve the unpleasurable tension.

While it was encouraging, in our clinical study of masochism, to arrive at formulations which were not at variance with the pleasure-unpleasure principle and which enabled us to include this phenomenon in our general knowledge of the psychic apparatus, there was no reason whatever to be content. A number of questions still remained unanswered, above all the question of the fear and of the idea of death. It follows from character analysis that the "death instinct" is an indication of a biopsychic inhibition and that there is no primary masochism. Indeed, there is good reason to doubt that masochism can be called an independent instinctual aim which strives after unpleasure. In the meantime, fresh complications were added to the problem from another side.

In the search for facts which would make the comprehension of the nirvana principle as complete as possible, I ran into strivings after disintegration, unconsciousness, non-being, dissolution, and similar longings in my patients. I found, in short, psychic material which seemed to confirm the existence of an actual original striving after death. I was always willing to revise my position on the question of the death instinct and to admit that my opponents were correct, if I could find justification for their view in clinical material.

But my earnest efforts to find clinical substantiation for the theory of the death instinct were in vain. Indeed, just when I began to waver in my firm rejection of the theory of the death instinct, I found a further incontestable argument *against* it. To begin with, this intense striving after disintegration, etc., is predominantly manifested at the end of the treatment, at a time, in other words, when the patient is faced with the task of overcoming his orgasm anxiety. This was extremely confusing, to say the least. Furthermore, this striving was seldom found in masochists; on the contrary, it was found precisely in patients who had developed the masochistic mechanisms to a very slight degree and the genital mechanisms to a very high degree. This increased the confusion, for why should patients who were on the verge of recovery, whose masochistic mechanisms were hardly developed, and who had not demonstrated any negative therapeutic reactions toward the cure, i.e., had no unconscious need for punishment—why should precisely these patients have allowed the "silent" death instinct to have such a strong effect?

In examining older theoretical formulations, I came across an allusion in my book *Die Funktion des Orgasmus* which showed me that, as early as 1926, I had, without really knowing it, hit upon a clinical observation which only now I am capable of explaining satisfactorily. I made mention in this book of the very peculiar fact that the orgasm anxiety frequently appears in the guise of death anxiety, and that the idea of complete sexual gratification is, in some neurotic people, associated with the idea of dying.

I want to use a typical clinical example to illustrate a previously overlooked fact that appears to be generally present here. I must stress once more that these clinical phenomena cannot be confirmed without the application of the character-analytic technique, which fully liberates vegetative excitation. A female hysteric developed severe genital anxiety at the end of the treatment, some time after the armor had been broken down. She fantasized the sexual act as a brutal penetration into her vagina, developed the idea that an enormous penis was being forced into her much too small vagina, causing it to burst. These fantasies had their origin in apprehensions and also sexual games of her earliest childhood. To the extent that her genital anxiety was dissolved, she became aware of previously unknown orgastic sensations in the genital organs and in the musculature of the upper thighs. She described these sensations as "flowing," "sensuous," "sweet," "like being electrified," and finally as a strong voluptuous *melting*. Yet there was still a trace of undefinable genital anxiety. One day she began to have fantasies about a doctor who wanted to perform a painful operation on her, and in connection with this fantasy, she remembered the severe anxiety she had had around the age of two or three regarding physicians. It was clear that we were dealing with a genital striving toward the analyst distorted by anxiety, a striving which made use of the childhood fear of a genital operation as defense. So far, there was nothing strange about this case.

Now, however, she began to have highly *pleasurable* fantasies about a genital operation conceived of as a brutal penetration. "It is so beautiful. One perishes in the process, one dies, one finally has peace." She fantasized almost ecstatically about the sensations experienced under general anesthesia. She described how one loses oneself in the process, becomes "one with the world," hears sounds "and yet doesn't hear them," withdraws into oneself and dissolves. One could not imagine a better description of the death instinct. However, further analysis revealed the true function of this strange behavior. Gradually, the fantasies became more concrete and could be clearly separated into two categories, one unpleasurable and the other pleasurable. In terms of their content, the unpleasurable fantasies were a precondition to the realization of the pleasurable fantasies. The apprehensive, i.e., masochistic, experience for which she seemed to be striving could be broken up into components. The *apprehensive* fantasy as such had the following content: "The physician is going to take away my penis or 'something' from my genitalia." The concealed pleasurable fantasy was as follows: "The physician is going to give me another one for it, a better one, namely a male genital."

To give the reader a better understanding of the connection between these two fantasies, I want to mention that the patient had a brother two years her senior whom she very much envied because of his penis. She had the idea that a girl could not obtain as much pleasure as a boy. Thus, she desired to be rid of her female genital and to have herself equipped with a male genital. In this way, she thought, she would be able to obviate a number of anxieties, for example, being exploded by a male genital in the act of intercourse, or bursting in the act of giving birth to a child or during the release of excrement. In reality, therefore, what she was striving after was the highest possible orgastic sensation. She thought this sensation could be achieved in the desired degree only with the help of a male genital. The feelings which she used to express her striving after death were the very same she experienced in the orgastic sensation itself. In short, orgasm and death were both represented as disintegration, perishing, losing of oneself, melting; under one condition, these sensations could become the object of deepest striving; under another condition, the cause of the most intense anxiety.

This association of the idea of the orgasm and the idea of dying is a universal one. On the basis of these typical clinical examples, we arrive at the following conclusion: *the striving after non-existence, nirvana, death, is identical with the striving after orgastic release, i.e., the most essential experience of the living organism.* Thus, an idea of death stemming from the actual demise of the organism does not and cannot exist, because an idea can reflect only what has already been experienced. No one, however, has ever experienced his or her own death. At present, the ideas of death and dying which we meet in analysis are expressed in one of two ways: either they exist as ideas of severe injury or destruction of the psychophysical organism, in which case they are accompanied by severe anxiety and center on the idea of genital castration; or they exist as ideas of the highest orgastic gratification and pleasure in the form of the idea of physical dissolution, disintegration, etc., in which case they are basically ideas of the sexual goal. Under special conditons, such as, for example, in the masochist, the orgastic sensation itself is experienced *apprehensively* and, as paradoxical as it may sound to the theorists of the death instinct, a desire for nirvana is seldom found. In short, it is precisely in the masochist that we find but little stasis anxiety and meagerly developed ideas of death.

Only now, some twelve years after the initial difficult differentiation between the metaphysical death-instinct theory and the clinical orgasm theory within the scope of psychoanalysis, is it possible to formulate the essential difference between them. These two views, so diametrically opposed, are based on the patient's negative therapeutic reactions to the direct interpretation of symptoms. They developed parallel to one another and were concerned with the same problem. Both views moved in a biophysiological direction. The former ended in the assumption of an absolute will to suffer and to die; the latter opened the road to a whole complex of problems having to do with character structure and psychological and psychophysiological relationships. Perhaps this most important controversy regarding the correct apprehension of underlying facts will one day be settled by the discovery of relationships directly linked to the life process. Even now, however, it can be intimated that what the theory of the death instinct attempted to represent as the dissolution of life is precisely what orgasm research is on the verge of comprehending as the most essential characteristic of the living organism.[12] In view of the fact that this is basically a biological controversy, it will not be decided in the field of psychology. There is no longer any doubt that much depends on how it is finally settled, that this is not a matter of trivialities but a decisive point of natural science. We are dealing here with the question of the nature and function of the striving after release which governs all living organisms, which, until now, has been encompassed in the vague concept of the "nirvana principle."[13]

9. PLEASURE, ANXIETY, ANGER, AND MUSCULAR ARMOR

In character-analytic practice, we discover the armor functioning in the form of a chronic, frozen, muscular-like bearing. First and foremost, the identity of these various functions stands out;

[12] To give a more concrete example, I might cite the fusion of two gametes. One can only surmise the deep relation with the orgastic sensations of melting.
[13] Footnote, 1945: The decisive importance of the sex-economic comprehension of the ideas of "bursting," "dying," "melting," etc., was not really revealed until 1936–40, when, on the basis of this hypothesis, the bions and the physical energy in the atmosphere were actually discovered. We know today that the neurotic fear of bursting is the expression of the inhibited orgonotic expansion of the biosystem.

they can be comprehended on the basis of *one* principle only, namely of *the armoring of the periphery of the biopsychic system*.

Sex-economy approaches these problems from the point of view of the psychic function of the armor and, in this respect, it has something to say. It proceeds from the practical demand of restoring the patient's freedom of vegetative movement.

In addition to the two primary affects, sexuality and anxiety, we have a third affect, *anger* or, more accurately, *hate*. As in the first two affects, here too we must assume that, in expressions such as "boiling with anger" and "consuming anger" to describe anger which is not discharged, the vernacular reflects an actual biophysiological process. It is our opinion that the full scale of affects can be comprehended on the basis of these three basic affects. All more complicated affect impulses can be deduced from these three. However, it will have to be proven whether and to what extent the anger affect can be deduced from the vicissitudes of the first two affect impulses.

We found that sexual excitation and anxiety can be comprehended as two antithetical directions of current. How is the function of hate related to the two primary affects?

Let us proceed from the clinical study of the *character armor*. This concept was created to offer a dynamic and economic comprehension of the character's basic function. According to the sex-economic view, the ego assumes a definite form in the conflict between instinct (essentially libidinal need) and fear of punishment. To carry out the instinctual inhibition demanded by the modern world and to be able to cope with the energy stasis which results from this inhibition, the ego has to undergo a change. The process we have in mind, though we are talking about it in absolute terms, is definitely of a causal nature. The ego, i.e., that part of the person that is exposed to danger, becomes rigid, as we say, when it is continually subjected to the same or similar conflicts between need and a fear-inducing outer world. It acquires in this process a chronic, automatically functioning mode of reaction, i.e., its "character." It is as if the affective personality armored itself, as if the hard shell it develops were intended to deflect and weaken the blows of the outer world as well as the clamoring of the inner needs. This armoring makes

unpleasure but also restricts his libidi-
...v and thus reduces his capacity for
We say the ego has become less
that the ability to regulate the energy
...he extent of the armoring. We regard
...sure of this ability, since it is a direct
...motility. The character armoring re-
...tained by continual consumption of li-
...es, which otherwise (under the condi-
...bition) would produce anxiety. This is
...r fulfills its function of absorbing and
...ergy.

...rmor is broken down through character
...on regularly rises to the surface first. But
is the oft-mentioned binding of aggression or anxiety *concretely*
represented?

If, further along in the character analysis, we succeed in freeing the aggression bound in the armor, the result is that anxiety becomes free. Anxiety, then, can be "transformed" into
aggression and aggression into anxiety. Is the relation between anxiety and aggression analogous to that between anxiety and sexual
excitation? It is not easy to answer this question.

To begin with, our clinical investigations reveal a number of
peculiar facts. The inhibition of aggression and psychic armor go
hand in hand with increased tonus; sometimes there is even a
rigidity of the musculature of the extremities and the trunk. Affect-blocked patients lie on the couch as stiff as boards, wholly
rigid and immobile. It is not easy to bring about a change in this
kind of muscle tension. If the analyst tries to persuade the patient to relax, the muscle tension is replaced by restlessness. In
other cases, we observe that patients make various involuntary
movements, the inhibition of which immediately engenders feelings of anxiety. On the basis of these observations, Ferenczi was
inspired to develop his "active technique of interference." He
recognized that the hindering of the chronic muscular reactions
increases the stasis. We agree with this, but we feel that there is
more to be inferred from these observations than quantitative
changes in excitation. It is a matter of a functional identity between character armor and muscular hypertonia or muscular ri-

gidity. *Every increase of muscular tonus and rigidification is an indication that a vegetative excitation, anxiety, or sexual sensation has been blocked and bound.* When genital sensations arise, some patients succeed in eliminating or weakening them through motor restlessness. The same holds true in the absorption of feelings of anxiety. In this connection, we are reminded of the great importance motor restlessness has in childhood as a means of discharging energy.

It is often observed that there is a *difference* in the state of muscular tension *before* and *after* a severe repression has been resolved. Usually, when patients are in a state of resistance, i.e., when an idea or an instinctual impulse is barred from consciousness, they sense a tension in the scalp, the upper thighs, the musculature of the buttocks, etc. If they succeed in overcoming this resistance on their own or it is resolved by the analyst through correct interpretation, they feel suddenly relieved. In such a situation a female patient once said: "It is as if I had experienced sexual gratification."

We know that every remembrance of the content of a repressed idea also brings about psychic relief. However, this alleviation does not constitute a cure, as the uninitiated believe. How does this alleviation come about? We have always contended that it is brought about by a discharge of previously bound psychic energy. Let us disregard the alleviation and the feeling of gratification which are connected with every new realization. Psychic tension and alleviation cannot be without a somatic representation, for tension and relaxation are biophysical conditions. Until now, apparently, we have merely carried over these concepts into the psychic sphere. Now it has to be proven that we were right in doing this. But it would be wrong to speak of the "transfer" of physiological concepts to the psychic sphere, for what we have in mind is not an analogy but a real identity: the unity of psychic and somatic function.

Every neurotic is muscularly dystonic, and every cure is directly manifested in a "relaxation" or improvement of the tonus of the musculature. This process can be observed best in the compulsive character. His muscular rigidity is expressed in awkwardness; unrhythmical movements, particularly in the sexual act, lack of mimetic movement, a typically taut facial musculature which often gives him a slightly mask-like expressio. common to this character type is a wrinkle stretching from the side of the nose to the corner of the mouth, as well as tain rigidity in the expression of the eyes, caused by the rigidity of the eyelid musculature. The musculature of the buttocks is almost always tense. The typical compulsive character develops a general muscular rigidity; in other patients this rigidity is paired with a flabbiness (hypotonus) of other muscle areas, which does not, however, reflect relaxation. This is frequently seen in passive-feminine characters. And then, of course, there is the rigidity in catatonic stupor which accompanies complete psychic armoring. This is ordinarily explained as disturbances of extrapyramidal innervations. We have no doubt that the related nerve tracts are always involved in changes of muscular tonus. In this innervation, however, we again perceive only a general disturbance of function which is expressed through it. It is naive to believe that something has been explained when the innervation or its path has been ascertained.

The psychic rigidity of post-encephalitics is not the "expression" of muscular rigidity, nor does it result from it. Muscular rigidity *and* psychic rigidity are a unit, the sign of a disturbance of the vegetative motility of the biological system as a whole. And it is an open question whether the disturbance of the extrapyramidal innervation is not itself a result of something, effective at a primary level, which has already damaged the vegetative apparatus itself, not just the affected organs. Mechanistic neurology, for example, explains a spasm of the anal sphincter on the basis of the continual excitation of the nerves belonging to it. The difference between the mechanistic-anatomical and the functional view can be easily demonstrated here: sex-economy conceives of the nerves only as the transmitters of general vegetative excitation.

The spasm of the anal sphincter, which is the cause of a number of very severe intestinal disturbances, is brought about by a fear of defecation acquired in childhood. It constitutes a block. Explaining it on the basis of the pleasure derived from holding back one's bowel movements does not appear to get to the core of the matter. Berta Bornstein describes the holding back of evacuation in a one-and-a-half-year-old child. For fear of soiling the crib, the child was in a continual state of spasm and was able to sleep at night only in a crumpled-up sitting position with clenched hands. The muscular pushing back and holding back of feces is the prototype for repression in general and is its initial step in the anal zone. In the oral zone, repression is manifested as a tightening of the musculature of the mouth and a spasm in the musculature of the larynx, throat, and breast; in the genital zone, it is manifested as a continual tension in the pelvic musculature.

The freeing of vegetative excitation from its fixation in the tensions of the musculature of the head, throat, jaws, larynx, etc., is one of the indispensable presuppositions for the elimination of oral fixations in general. According to our experiences in character analysis, neither the remembrance of oral experiences and desires nor the discussion of genital anxiety can have the same therapeutic value. Without it, the patient remembers but he does not experience the excitations. These are usually very well concealed. They escape notice by concealing themselves in conspicuous modes of behavior which appear to be part of the person's natural makeup.

The most important secrets of pathological displacements and the binding of vegetative energy are usually contained in phenomena such as the following: a toneless, languid, or high-pitched voice; speaking with a tight upper lip; a mask-like or immobile facial expression; even slight suggestions of a so-called baby face; an inconspicuous wrinkle of the forehead; drooping eyelids; tensions in the scalp; a concealed, undetected hypersensitivity in the larynx; a hurried, abrupt, constrained manner of speech; faulty respiration; noises or movements in the act of speaking which appear to be merely incidental; a certain way of hanging one's head, of shaking it, of lowering it when looking, etc. Nor is it difficult to persuade oneself that the anxiety of genital contact does not appear so long as these symptoms in the regions of the head and neck have not been uncovered and eliminated. Genital anxiety in particular is, in most cases, displaced toward the upper part of the body and bound in the contracted musculature of the neck. A fear of a genital operation in a young girl was expressed in the way she held her head while lying on the couch. After she had been made aware of this peculiar way of holding her head, she herself said: "I am lying here as if my head were nailed to the couch." As a matter of fact, she did give the appearance of being held down by the hair by an invisible force and was not able to move.

It will be asked, and justifiably, whether these concepts do not contradict another assumption. The increased tonus of the musculature is of course a *parasympathetic*-sexual function; the decreased tonus and paralysis of the musculature, on the other hand, are a *sympathetic*-anxious function. How does this tie in with the fact that an apprehensive holding back of feces or a speech inhibition in a child go hand in hand with a muscular *contraction?* In going over the theory relating to these facts, I had to ask myself this question and, for a long time, was not able to find an explanation. However, as always happens when such difficulties crop up in the investigation of various relations, it was precisely its puzzling aspect that led to a deepening of the insight.

First of all, it had to be understood that the process of muscular tension in sexual excitation could not be the same as the process of muscular tension in anxiety. In *expectation of danger,* the musculature is tense, as if *ready for action.* Visualize a deer on the verge of taking flight. In a *state of fright,* the musculature is suddenly depleted of excitation ("paralyzed with fright"). The fact that, in the case of fright, an involuntary evacuation can take place as a result of the sudden relaxation of the anal sphincter also fits in with our concept of the relation between anxiety and the sympathetic function. In this way, a sympathetic, fear-induced diarrhea in the case of fright can be distinguished from a parasympathetic diarrhea produced by pleasure in the case of sexual excitation. The former is based on the paralysis of the sphincter (sympathetic function); the latter on increased peristalsis of the intestinal musculature (parasympathetic function). In sexual excitation, the musculature is contracted, i.e., prepared for motor action, for further contraction and relaxation. In an expectation fraught with anxiety, on the other hand, the musculature is gripped in a *continual tension* until it is released by some form of motor activity. Then, either it gives way to paralysis if the fright reaction takes place, or it is replaced by a reaction of motor flight. The musculature can, however, remain tense, i.e., not resolve itself in either of the two forms. In this event, that condition sets in which, in contrast to *fright paralysis,* can be designated as *fright rigidity* ("scared stiff"). Observation shows that, in fright *paralysis,* musculature becomes flaccid, is exhausted by excitement; the vasomotor system, on the other hand, reaches a state of full excitation: acute palpitations, profuse perspiration, pallidness. In the case of fright *rigidity,* the peripheral musculature is rigid, the sensation of anxiety is missing or is only partially developed; one is "apparently calm." In reality, one cannot move and is as incapable of physical flight as of vegetative escape into the self.

What is the lesson of these facts? *Muscular rigidity can take the place of the vegetative anxiety reaction.* To express it another way, the same excitation which, in the fright *paralysis,* takes flight inwardly uses, in the case of fright *rigidity,* the musculature to form a *peripheral armoring of the organism.*[14]

It can be observed that a person operated upon under local anesthesia displays the same muscular rigidity. If voluntary efforts are made to relax, anxiety is immediately intensified in the form of palpitations and perspiration. Thus, the muscular tension that is present and is not resolved in a motor discharge consumes excitation which would otherwise appear as anxiety; in that way the anxiety is avoided. In this process we recognize the prototype of the binding of anxiety through aggression which, when it too is inhibited, leads to an *affect-block.* This binding of anxiety is very familiar to us from neurotic formations.

These clinical findings are of great importance for the theory of affects. Now we have a better comprehension of the interrelation of:

1. *Character block or armor and muscular rigidity*

2. *Loosening of the muscular rigidity and the liberation of anxiety*

3. *Binding of anxiety and the establishment of muscular rigidity*

4. *Muscular tension and libidinal inhibition*

5. *Libidinal relaxation and muscular relaxation*

[14] The theory of evolution will have to decide whether the biological armoring of the turtle, for example, is developed in the same way.

Before we formulate a theoretical conclusion on the basis of these findings, let us cite further clinical facts that pertain to the relation between muscle tonus and sexual tension. When, in the course of character analysis, the muscular tension begins to give way because of the loosening of the character encrustation, then —as we have pointed out—what comes to the surface is anxiety and/or aggression, or libidinal impulse. We conceive of the libidinal impulse as a flowing of excitation and body fluids toward the *periphery,* and we conceive of anxiety as a flowing of excitation and body fluids toward the *center.* The aggressive excitation also corresponds to an excitation directed toward the *periphery,* but one relating *solely* to the musculature of the extremities. If the excitation flowing in all *three* directions can be liberated from the muscular rigidity, from the increased chronic muscular tonus, then we must conclude that *chronic muscular hypertonicity represents an inhibition of the flow of every form of excitation (pleasure, anxiety, rage) or at least a significant reduction of vegetative streaming.* It is as if the inhibition of the life functions (libido, anxiety, aggression) was brought about by the formation of a muscular armor around a person's biological core. If the formation of the character has such a close relation to the tonus of the musculature, we can assume that there is a functional identity between neurotic character and muscular dystonus. We will cite additional findings which confirm this assumption; we will also cite findings that might perhaps limit the validity of the functional identity of character armor and muscular armor.

From a purely phenomenological standpoint, it is clear that *attractiveness,* i.e., sexual appeal, can be chiefly described by the relaxed quality of a person's musculature which accompanies flowing psychic agility. The rhythmicity of one's movements, the *alternation* of muscular tension and relaxation in movement, go together with the capacity for linguistic modulation and general musicality. In such people, one also has the feeling of direct psychic contact. The sweetness of children who have not been subject to any severe repressions, particularly in the anal zone, has the same basis. On the other hand, people who are physically stiff, awkward, without rhythm, gives us the feeling that they are also psychically stiff, wooden, immobile. They speak in a monotone and they are seldom musical. Many of them never "loosen up"; others are induced "to let go a bit" only under conditions of intimate friendship. In this event, the trained observer can immediately ascertain a change in the tonus of the musculature. Psychic and somatic rigidity, then, are not analogous manifestations; they are functionally identical. Men and women of this kind give us the impression of being deficient in eroticism as well as anxiety. Depending upon the depth of such armoring, the rigidity can go together with more or less strong *inner* excitation.

In observing melancholic or depressive patients, one finds that they betray a stiffness in their speech and facial expressions, as if every movement were possible only through the overcoming of a resistance. In manic patients, on the other hand, all impulses appear to flood the entire personality precipitately. In catatonic stupor, psychic and muscular rigidity coincide completely; for this reason, the dissolution of this condition restores psychic and muscular mobility.

From this vantage point, it is also possible to pave the way to an understanding of laughter (the "joyous" facial expression) and sorrow (the depressive facial expression). In laughter, the facial musculature contracts; in depression, it becomes flaccid. This is entirely in keeping with the fact that muscular contraction (clonus of the diaphragm in the case of laughter, "belly-shaking laugh") is parasympathetic and libidinal, while muscular flaccidity is sympathetic and anti-libidinal.

In the so-called genital character[15] who does not suffer from any stasis of excitation or chronic inhibition of excitation, the question arises whether he does not or cannot develop a muscular armor. This would be an argument against my thesis that, fundamentally, the character armor is functionally identical with muscular armor. For the genital character, too, has developed a "character." The investigation of such character types shows that they, too, *can* develop an armor, that they, too, have the ability to immure themselves against unpleasure and to spare themselves anxiety through an encrustation of the periphery. When this is the case, however, there is a greater austerity in bearing

[15] Cf. "The Genital Character and the Neurotic Character," in Part II of the present volume.

and facial expression. Under such conditions, sexual excitation and the capacity for sexual pleasure are negatively affected, but not necessarily the capacity for work. However, work which is usually performed effortlessly and with a feeling of pleasure is replaced by a mechanical, pleasureless performance. Therefore, a gratifying sexual life provides the best structural basis for productive achievement. The difference between the armor of the neurotic character and the armor of the genital character lies in the fact that, in the former, muscular rigidity is chronic and automatic, whereas in the latter it can be used or dispensed with at will.[16]

The following example will illustrate the functional relationship between a character attitude and muscular tension and vegetative excitation. The character analysis of a patient was marked by a superficiality of communication; the patient himself felt it to be "mere chatter," even when he was discussing the most serious matters. This superficiality, it soon became clear, had become the central character resistance. What better means of destroying every affective impulse! To begin with, the analysis revealed that the "chatter" and "superficiality" represented an identification with his stepmother, who had the same character traits. This identification with the mother figure contained the passive-feminine attitude to the father; and the chattering was an attempt to win the homosexual object, to amuse it, to dispose it favorably, to "pet" it as one would a dangerous lion. But it also functioned as a substitute contact, for, while identifying with the mother figure, the patient had no relationship whatever to his father. He felt estranged from him, a fact which did not come out until late in the analysis. The repression of a strong aggression toward the father lay at the root of and sustained this estrangement. Hence, chattering was also the expression of passive-feminine wooing (vegetative function), the warding off of aggressive tendencies (armor function),

---

[16] From the point of view of sex-economy, it is not so important *that* biopsychic energy is bound; what is important is the *form in which* this binding takes place, whether or not it limits the availability of the energy. It cannot be the goal of mental hygiene to obstruct the character's ability to develop armor; its goal is merely to guarantee free motility and the greatest possible disposal of vegetative energy, i.e., to guarantee the flexibility of the armor. This task cannot be reconciled with existing educational and moralistic institutions.

and a compensation for the contactlessness. The psychic content of the superficiality could be formulated somewhat as follows: "I want and have to win my father over to my side, I have to please him and amuse him; but I don't at all like having to do this; I don't care a hoot about him—I hate him, deep down. I have no relationship to him at all, but I can't let this come out." In addition to these psychic attitudes, the patient's awkwardness and muscular rigidity were immediately obvious. He lay there in a way very familiar to the character analyst: stiff as a board, rigid and immobile. It was clear that every analytic effort would be hopeless until this muscular armor had been loosened. Though he gave the impression of being afraid, the patient said he was not aware of having any anxieties. In addition to the above traits, he exhibited severe states of depersonalization, and he had a lifeless feeling about himself. His highly interesting childhood experiences were not important as such or in their relation to his neurotic symptoms; at this point, solely their relationship to this armor interested us. It was a question of breaking through this armor, of extracting from it the childhood experiences as well as the moribund vegetative excitations.

To begin with, the superficiality turned out to be a "fear of depth," specifically a fear of falling. In this connection, the patient produced convincing reports that the fear of falling had indeed dominated his life. He was afraid of drowning, of falling into a mountain gorge, of falling overboard from the deck of a ship; he was afraid of riding on a toboggan, etc. It soon became clear that these anxieties were connected with and rooted in an avoidance of the typical sensations experienced in the region of the diaphragm while swinging and descending in the elevator. In my book *Die Funktion des Orgasmus* I was able to demonstrate that, in some instances, the fear of orgastic excitation is concretely experienced as a fear of falling. It will not surprise us, therefore, that the patient suffered precisely from a severe orgastic disturbance of this kind. In short, the superficiality was more than a passive attitude or an "inborn" character trait; it had a very definite function in the patient's psychic operations. It was an *active* attitude, a warding off of the "fear of depth" and the sensations of vegetative excitation. There had to be a connection between these two warded-off conditions. I reflected that *the fear of falling had to be identical with the fear of vegetative excitation.* But how?

The patient remembered that, when as a child he was on a swing, he immediately made himself stiff, i.e., cramped his muscles as soon as he sensed the diaphragmatic sensations. His muscular habitus, characterized by awkwardness and a lack of coordination, stemmed from this period. It will be of interest to the musicologist that he appeared to have no ear for music whatever. But this lack of musicality could also be traced back to other childhood experiences. In connection with the history of his contactlessness and his muscular armor, the analysis produced proof that this defect also served to ward off vegetative excitation. He remembered that his mother was in the habit of singing sentimental songs to him which tremendously excited him, put him in a state of tension, caused him to be restless. When the libidinal relationship to his mother was repressed because of disappointment in her, musicality also fell victim to repression. This was the case not only because the relationship to the mother was essentially sustained by musical experiences but also because he could not endure the vegetative excitations aroused by her singing. And this was related to excitation which he experienced in childhood masturbation and which had led to the development of acute anxiety.

In their dreams, patients often represent their resistance to uncovering unconscious material as a fear of going into a cellar or of falling into a pit. We know that this resistance and its representation in the dream are connected, but we do not as yet understand it. Why should the unconscious be associated with depth, and fear of the unconscious with the fear of falling? This puzzling situation was solved in the following way: the unconscious is the reservoir of repressed vegetative excitations, i.e., excitations not allowed to discharge and flow freely. These excitations are experienced in one of two forms:

(1) sexual excitement and feelings of gratification, as in the case of healthy men and women; or (2) feelings of anxiety and constriction, growing more and more unpleasant, in the region of the solar plexus in the case of people who suffer from disturbances

of vegetative motility. They are similar to the sensations in the region of the heart and diaphragm and in the musculature which are experienced in fright or during a rapid descent. Also to be mentioned in this connection are the sensations experienced in the region of the genitalia when one is standing on the edge of a steep precipice looking down. In this situation, a feeling of genital contraction usually accompanies the idea of falling. The fact is that, at the mere thought of danger, the organism acts as if the dangerous situation were real and withdraws into itself. In the case of fright, as I explained earlier, energy cathexes in the form of body fluids flow toward the center of the organism and thus create a stasis in the region of the genitalia and the diaphragm. In the case of falling, furthermore, this physiological process is an automatic reaction on the part of the organism. Hence, *the idea of depth and the idea of falling must be functionally identical with the sensation of central excitation in the organism.* This also enables us to understand the otherwise incomprehensible fact that swinging, rapid descents, etc., are experienced by so many people with a mixture of anxiety and pleasure. According to sex-economic theory,[17] anxiety and pleasure are twins, sprung from one stem and later opposed to one another. To return to our patient: it is objectively justified to describe his fear of the unconscious as being identical with his fear of depth. From the point of view of sex-economy, therefore, we see that our patient's superficiality was an active character attitude for the avoidance of vegetative excitations of both anxiety and pleasure.

The affect-block also falls into this category. The relation between muscular rigidity on the one hand and character superficiality and contactlessness on the other still remains to be explained. It can be said that, physiologically, the muscular armor fulfills the same function that contactlessness and superficiality fulfill psychically. Sex-economy does not conceive of the primal relation between the physiological and the psychic apparatus as one of mutual dependency but as one of functional identity with simultaneous antithesis, i.e., it conceives of the relation *dialectically*. Hence, the further question arises whether muscular rigidity

---

[17] Cf. Reich: "Der Urgegensatz des vegetativen Lebens," *Zeitschrift für Politische Psychologie und Sexualökonomie,* 1934.

is not functionally identical with character armor, contactlessness, affect-block, etc. The antithetical relationship is clear: the physiological behavior determines the psychic behavior, and vice versa. The fact that the two mutually influence one another, however, is far less important for the comprehension of the psychophysical relation than everything which supports the view of their functional identity.

I want to cite one more clinical example which shows unmistakably how the vegetative energy can be precisely liberated from the psychic and muscular armor.

This patient was characterized by his intense phallic-narcissistic warding off of passive-homosexual impulses. This central psychic conflict was revealed in his external appearance: he had a gaunt leathery body, and his character was aggressive in a compensatory way. Great analytic effort was required to make him aware of this conflict, for he put up strong resistance to the recognition and breakthrough of the anal-homosexual impulses. When the breakthrough finally occurred, the patient suffered, to my surprise, a vegetative shock. One day he came to the analysis with a stiff neck, severe headache, dilated pupils, his skin alternating between mottled redness and pallor, and severe oppression. The pressure in his head subsided when he moved it and grew worse when he held it still. Severe nausea and feelings of giddiness completed the picture of sympatheticotonia. The patient recovered quickly. The incident was a glaring confirmation of the validity of my views on the relation between character, sexual stasis, and vegetative excitation. It seems to me that these findings also provide an insight into the problem of schizophrenia, for it is precisely in psychoses that the functional relations between the vegetative and the characterological components are so typical and so conspicuous. And there is good reason to believe that the new perspective which we have outlined here will one day provide a consistent and satisfactory explanation of these relations. What is new here is not the knowledge that psychic apparatus and vegetative system are related to one another, or that they have a mutual functional relation. What is new is:

1. The basic function of the psyche is of a sex-economic nature.

2. Sexual excitation and sensations of anxiety are identical and antithetical at one and the same time (i.e., they derive from the same source of the biopsychic organism but flow in opposing directions) and they represent the irreducible basic antithesis of vegetative functioning.

3. The formation of the character is the result of a *binding* of vegetative energy.

4. Character armor and muscular armor are functionally identical.

5. Vegetative energy can be liberated, i.e., reactivated from the character armor and muscular armor with the help of a definite technique and, at present, only with this technique.

I should like to make it quite clear that this theory which we have developed on the basis of the clinical data derived from character analysis represents merely an initial step toward a comprehensive presentation of the functional psychophysical relations, that the still unsolved problems are incomparably more complicated, extensive, and difficult than what we have thus far achieved in the way of a solution. However, I feel that I have definitely succeeded in arriving at some fundamental formulations concerning the whole complex of problems that may very well serve to advance our knowledge of the psychophysical relations. I feel that my attempt to apply the functional method of investigation has been successful and is justified by the results. This method is diametrically opposed to the metaphysical-idealistic or mechanistic-causal-materialistic methods applied in the attempt to arrive at an applicable knowledge of psychophysical relations. At this point, however, it would lead us too far afield to set forth the fundamental epistemological objections to these methods. The sex-economic approach differs from the recent efforts to comprehend the psychophysical organism as a "totality" and "unity" in that it makes use of a functional method of investigation and regards the function of the orgasm as the central problem.

10. THE TWO GREAT LEAPS IN EVOLUTION

Thus far, we have arrived at a theoretical formulation of the psychophysical relations which can be substantiated by copious clinical observations. On the basis of these views, it is certainly not rash to pose a hypothesis for further work in this field, provided we are willing to discard it if it turns out to be sterile or deceptive.

In evolution we are able to point to two great leaps which introduced more *gradual* processes of development. The first was the leap from the inorganic state to the organic or vegetative state. The second was the leap from the organic-vegetative state to the development of the psychic apparatus, particularly the development of consciousness with its central ability for *self-awareness*. Inasmuch as the organic grows out of the inorganic and the psychic grows out of the vegetative, they continue to function and operate in accordance with the basic laws which governed their matrix. In principle, we find the same chemical and physical laws in the organic that we find in the inorganic; and in the psychic component we find the same fundamental reactions of tension and relaxation, energy stasis and discharge, excitability, etc., that we find in the vegetative component. Apparently, the functional process of development of the character which we described as the dissociation and antithesis of new formations also governs the more comprehensive and universal developments of the organic from the inorganic and of the psychic from the organic-vegetative. In the organism, the organic is set off against the inorganic as the psychic is set off against the vegetative.[18] They are unitary and at the same time antithetical. In the capacity of the psychic apparatus for self-perception, the most peculiar and most puzzling function of conscious life, particularly of consciousness, we perceive the *direct* manifestation of the above antithesis. In the phenomenon of depersonalization, the function of self-perception is pathologically distorted. The use of the functional method of investigation to deepen our knowledge of depersonalization and related phenomena might very well turn up important clues for the solution of the problem of consciousness.

I should like these intimations to be taken for what they are: rough sketches of a very obscure field, the correct approach to which must still be sought. They differ fundamentally from

---

[18] These observations are not strictly true. But it would be premature at this point to make binding statements about the relation of the "psychic" to the vegetative and of consciousness to both.

the previous views of the relationship between the somatic and the psychic functions. Yet they cannot ask to be taken seriously unless they can succeed in solving those problems which have remained inaccessible and, if we are not totally deceived, must remain inaccessible to the other disciplines (the mechanistic-materialistic, idealistic, etc.). At present, these basic questions of life are shrouded in obscurity. Hence, we must be extremely cautious in forming new views; at the same time we must detach ourselves from all concepts which do not bring us closer to a solution, which are, indeed, merely premature attempts to anticipate a solution. A path full of uncertainties and pitfalls lies ahead for functional psychology. Only recently did sex-economy arrive at several fundamental formulations which gave it a solid foundation. Now much depends upon experimental orgasm research. Yet one thing is certain: if natural science succeeds in solving the problems regarding the relationship of body and soul, that is, in mastering them in such a way that a clear-cut policy of dealing with them is the result, and not mere idle theories, then the hour of doom will have struck for transcendental mysticism, the "absolute objective spirit," including all ideologies which come under the heading of religion in both the narrow and the broad sense of the word.

Man's vegetative life is only part of the universal process of nature. In his vegetative currents, man also experiences a part of nature. Once we have fully comprehended natural functioning, there will be no room for life-destroying psychic structures that prevent the constructive unfolding of vegetative energy, thus causing both sickness and suffering. Over and above this, their continued existence is justified on the basis that they are providential and immutable. But certain psychic structures continue to exist only because our knowledge of their sources is so fragmentary. Man dreams, stirred by dark "oceanic" feelings, instead of mastering his existence, and he is destroyed in dreams. Man's dreaming, however, is merely an intimation of the possible fruition of his vegetative life. Science may one day succeed in fulfilling man's dream of earthly happiness. Then the eternally unanswerable question of the meaning of life will fade into the background and be replaced by the concrete fulfillment of life.

CHAPTER XIV

THE EXPRESSIVE LANGUAGE OF THE LIVING

1. THE FUNCTION OF EMOTION IN ORGONE THERAPY

The concept "orgone therapy" comprises all medical and pedagogical techniques which make use of the biological energy, the orgone. The cosmic orgone energy, from which the concept "orgone therapy" derives, was not discovered until 1939. Yet, long before this discovery, the goal of character analysis was conceived of as the liberation of "psychic energy," as it was called at that time, from the character armor and muscular armor and the establishment of orgastic potency. Those conversant with orgone biophysics are familiar with the development of character analysis (1926 to 1934) into "vegetotherapy" (from 1935 on). It was no idle desire for sensationalism that gave birth to so many various concepts in one and the same discipline of natural science. Rather, the consistent application of the natural scientific concept of energy to the processes of psychic life made it necessary, in various phases of development, to coin new concepts for new techniques.

The fact that it was sex-economically oriented psychiatry which made cosmic orgone energy accessible can, in my opinion, be regarded as a great triumph on the part of *orgonomic functionalism*. Not withstanding the fact that we are dealing with a strictly physical form of energy in orgone energy, there are good reasons why it was discovered by a psychiatrist and not a physicist. The logic of this discovery in the field of biopsychiatry is demonstrated by its development, which I described in my book *The Discovery of the Orgone,* Vol. 1: *The Function of the Orgasm.*

When the orgasm reflex was discovered in 1935, the emphasis in treatment was shifted from the character to *the body*. The term "vegetotherapy" was coined to allow for this shift in emphasis, for, from that point on, my analytic technique affected character neurosis in the *physiological* realm. Thus, we spoke of "character-analytic vegetotherapy" to include in one concept the work on the psychic *and* on the physical apparatus. This term had many disadvantages which, at that time, I could not help. For one thing, it was too long. Moreover, it contained the word "vegetative," which, while it is correct in German, is suggestive of "vegetables" in English. Last but not least, it retained the psychophysical dichotomy, which was at variance with our concept of the homogeneity of the organism.

The discovery of the orgone put an end to these terminological difficulties. *Cosmic orgone energy functions in the living organism as specific biological energy.* As such, it governs the entire organism; it is expressed in the emotions as well as in the purely biophysical movements of the organs. Thus, for the first time since its inception and with its own means, psychiatry took root in objective, natural scientific processes. This requires a more detailed explanation.

Until the discovery of the orgone, psychiatry had to borrow from inorganic physics when it attempted to prove its psychological assertions *objectively* and *quantitatively*. Neither the mechanical brain lesions nor the chemico-physical processes in the organism, and certainly not the outdated cerebral localization of sensations and ideas, ever succeeded in giving a satisfactory explanation of emotional processes. As opposed to these, orgone biophysics was, from the outset, concerned with the basic problem of all psychiatry, the *emotions*. Literally defined, the word "emotion" means "moving outwards" or "pushing out." Thus, we not only can but *must* take the word "emotion" literally in speaking of sensations and movements. The microscopic observation of living amoebae subjected to minor electric stimuli reveals the meaning of the concept "emotion" in an unmistakable way. *Fundamentally, emotion is nothing but a plasmatic movement.* Pleasurable stimuli effect an "emotion" of the protoplasm from the center toward the periphery. Non-pleasurable stimuli, on the other hand, bring about an "emotion" or, more correctly, "re-motion" of the protoplasm from the periphery toward the center of the organism. These two basic directions of the biophysical plasma current correspond to the two basic affects of the psychic apparatus, pleasure and anxiety. In terms of their function, the physical plasma motion and the sensation corresponding to it are, as we learned from experiments on the oscillograph, completely identical. They cannot be separated from one another; indeed, they are inconceivable without one another. However, they are, as we know, not only functionally identical but also and at the same time antithetical: a biophysical plasma excitation transmits a sensation, and a sensation expresses itself in a plasma movement. Today these facts are a well-established foundation of orgone biophysics.

Whether we reactivate emotions from the character armor by means of "character analysis" or we liberate them from the muscular armor by means of "vegetotherapy," the fact remains that in both cases we produce plasmatic excitations and movements. What moves in this process is nothing but orgone energy, which is contained in the body fluids. *Accordingly, the mobilization of plasmatic currents and emotions in the organism is identical with the mobilization of orgone energy.* Clinical indications of this mobilization are clearly evident in the changes of the vasomotor functions. In every case, therefore, whether we are evoking memories, breaking down defense mechanisms, or eliminating muscular tensions, we are always working on the orgone energy of the organism. The difference in the various methods lies in their effectiveness. A memory is not nearly as capable of achieving the emotional outbreak, for example, as the loosening of a block in the diaphragm.

It is quite clear, then, why I now propose to include both character analysis and vegetotherapy under the term "orgone therapy."[1] The common element is reflected in the therapeutic goal, the mobilization of the patient's plasmatic currents. In other words, if we are really serious about the *unitary* concept of the organism, i.e., one with practical implications, then it is altogether out of the question to break up a living organism into character traits here, muscles there, and plasma functions elsewhere.

---

[1] Purely physiological orgone therapy by means of orgone accumulators is discussed in *The Discovery of the Orgone,* Vol. II: *The Cancer Biopathy.*

In orgone therapy, our work is concentrated on the *biological depth,* the plasma system, or, as we express it technically, the *biological core* of the organism. This, as is readily evident, is a decisive step, for it means that we have left the sphere of psychology, of "depth" psychology as well, and have entered the province of protoplasmatic functions, even going beyond the physiology of the nerves and muscles. These steps are to be taken very seriously; they have far-reaching practical and theoretical consequences, for they effect a fundamental change in our biopsychiatric practice. We no longer work merely on individual conflicts and special armorings but on the *living* organism itself. As we gradually learn to comprehend and influence the living organism, the purely psychological and physiological functions are automatically included in our work. Schematic specialization is no longer possible.

2. PLASMATIC EXPRESSIVE MOVEMENT AND EMOTIONAL EXPRESSION

It is difficult to define the living organism in a strict functional sense. The ideas of orthodox psychology and depth psychology are chained to word formations. However, the living organism functions beyond all verbal ideas and concepts. Human speech, a biological form of expression at an advanced stage of development, is not a specific attribute of the living organism, which functions long before a language and verbal representations exist. Thus, depth psychology deals with a life function which came into existence at a relatively late stage of biological development. Many animals express themselves through sounds. But the living organism functioned prior to and functions beyond the use of sounds as a form of expression.

Language itself reveals the key to the problem of how the living organism expresses itself. Evidently, language derives from the sensations perceived by body organs. For example, the German word *Ausdruck* and its English equivalent "expression" exactly describe the language of the living organism: *the living organism expresses itself in movements;* we therefore speak of *"expressive movements."* Expressive movement is an inherent characteristic of the protoplasm. It distinguishes the living organism from all non-living systems. The word *literally* implies—and we have to take it literally—that something in the living system "presses itself out" and, therefore, "moves." This can only mean the movement i.e., expansion or contraction, of the protoplasm. Literally, "emotion" means "moving outward"; at the same time, it is an "expressive movement." The physiological process of the plasmatic emotion or expressive movement is inseparably linked to an immediately comprehensible *meaning* which we are wont to call the *"emotional expression."* Thus, the movement of the protoplasm is expressive of an emotion, and emotion or the expression of an organism is embodied in movement. The second part of this sentence will require some modification, for we know from orgone therapy that there is an expression in human beings produced by immobility or rigidity.

We are not playing with words. Language is clearly derived from the perception of inner movements and organ sensations, and the words that describe emotional conditions *directly* reflect the corresponding expressive movement of the living organism.

While language does reflect the plasmatic emotional condition in an immediate way, it is still not capable of getting at this condition itself. The reason is that the beginnings of living functioning lie much *deeper* than and *beyond* language. *Over and above this, the living organism has its own modes of expressing movement which simply cannot be comprehended with words.* Every musically inclined person is familiar with the emotional state evoked by great music. However, if one attempts to translate these emotional experiences into words, one's musical perception rebels. Music is wordless and wants to remain that way. Yet music gives expression to the inner movement of the living organism, and listening to it evokes the "sensation" of some "inner stirring." The wordlessness of music is usually described in one of two ways: (1) as a mark of mystical spirituality, or (2) as the deepest expression of feelings incapable of being put into words. The natural scientific point of view subscribes to the interpretation that musical expression is related to the depths of the living organism. Accordingly, what is regarded as the "spirituality" of great music is merely another way of saying that deep feeling is identical with having contact with the living organism *beyond the limitations of language.*

Until now, science has not had anything decisive to say about the nature of the expressive movement of music. Undoubtedly, the artist himself speaks to us in the form of wordless expressions of movement from the depth of the life function, but he would be just as incapable as we of putting into words what he expresses in his music or in his painting. Indeed, he strongly objects to any attempt to translate the language of expression of art into human word language. He attaches great importance to the purity of his language of expression. Hence, he confirms the orgone-biophysical assertion that the living organism possesses its own language of expression before, beyond, and independent of all word language. Let us see what orgone therapy has to say about this problem. We shall cite an everyday experience.

Patients come to orgone therapists full of afflictions. The practiced eye can perceive these afflictions directly from the expressive movements and the emotional expression of their bodies. If the analyst allows the patient to speak at random, he finds that the patient tends to *circumvent* his afflictions, i.e., to *conceal* them in one way or another. If the analyst wants to arrive at a correct appraisal of his patient, he must begin by asking the patient *not* to speak. This measure proves very fruitful, for as soon as the patient ceases to speak, the emotional expressions of his body are brought into much sharper focus. After a few minutes of silence, the analyst will usually have grasped the patient's most conspicuous character trait or, more correctly, will have understood the emotional expression of the *plasmatic* movement. If the patient appeared to laugh in a friendly way while he spoke, his laughter might modulate into an empty grin during his silence, the mask-like character of which the patient himself must readily perceive. If the patient appeared to speak about his life with reserved seriousness, an expression of suppressed anger might easily appear in the chin and neck during his silence.

Let these examples suffice to point out that, apart from its function as communication, *human language also often functions as a defense.* The spoken word conceals the expressive language of the biological core. In many cases, the function of speech has deteriorated to such a degree that the words express nothing whatever and merely represent a continuous, hollow activity on the part of the musculature of the neck and the organs of speech. On the basis of repeated experiences, it is my opinion that in many psychoanalyses which have gone on for years the treatment has become stuck in this pathological use of language. This clinical experience can, indeed has to be applied to the social sphere. Endless numbers of speeches, publications, political debates do not have the function of getting at the root of important questions of life but of drowning them in verbiage.

Orgone therapy, as opposed to all other forms of therapy, attempts to influence the organism not through the use of human language but by getting the patient to express himself *biologically*. This approach leads him into a depth which he continually flees. In this way the orgone therapist learns, understands, and influences the language of the living organism. It is hardly possible to obtain the primary language of expression of the living protoplasm in the patient in a "pure" form. If the patient's mode of expression were biologically "pure," he would have no reason to seek the help of an orgone therapist. We have to go through a welter of pathological, unnatural expressive movements (i.e., movements not native to the process of the living organism) to arrive at the *genuine* biological mode of expression. Human biopathy, indeed, is nothing other than the sum total of all the distortions of the natural modes of expression of the living organism. By unmasking the pathological modes of expression, we get to know human biopathy at a depth inaccessible to methods of cure operating with human language. This is not to be ascribed to a deficiency on the part of these methods; they are adequate in their own sphere. *With its distorted expression of life, however, biopathy lies outside the sphere of language and ideas.*

Hence, orgone-therapeutic work on the human biopathy lies essentially outside the sphere of human language. Naturally, we too make use of the spoken word, but the words we use do not conform to everyday concepts but to *organ sensations*. There would be no point whatever in making the patient understand his condition in physiological terminology. We do not say to him: "Your masticatory organs are in a condition of chronic contraction, that's why your chin doesn't move when you speak; that's why your voice is a monotone; that's why you can't cry; you have continually to swallow to ward off an impulse to cry, etc." This would make sense to the patient's intellect but would not enable him to effect any change in his condition.

We work on a biologically deeper level of understanding. It is not at all necessary for us to be able to point out exactly which *individual* muscles are contracted. It would serve no purpose, for example, to put pressure on the masseter muscles, for there would be no reaction apart from the usual pain. *We work with the language of facial and body expression.* Only when we have *sensed* the patient's facial *expression* are we in a position to comprehend it. We use the word "comprehend" here to mean quite literally to know which *emotion* is being *expressed* in it. And it makes no difference whether the emotion is mobile and active or immobile and suppressed. We shall have to learn to recognize the difference between a mobile and a suppressed emotion.

We are operating with primary *biological* functions when we "sense" a patient's "expressive movement." When, in a flight of sparrows, a single sparrow becomes restless and, "sensing danger," flies off, the whole flight follows, whether or not the rest of the birds have noticed the cause of the commotion. The panic reaction in the animal kingdom is based on an involuntary reproduction of the movement expressive of anxiety. Any number of people can be brought to a standstill on the sidewalk and made to look up into the sky if one merely pretends that one has observed something interesting high up in the air. Let these examples suffice.

The patient's expressive movements involuntarily bring about *an imitation* in our own organism. By imitating these movements, we "sense" and understand the expression in ourselves and, consequently, in the patient. Since every movement is expressive of a biological condition, i.e., reveals an emotional condition of the protoplasm, the language of facial and body expression becomes an essential means of communicating with the patient's emotions. As I have already pointed out, human language *interferes with* the language of the face and the body. When we use the term "character attitude," what we have in mind is the *total expression* of an organism. This is *literally* the same as the *total impression* which the organism makes on us.

There is considerable variation in the outward expression of inner emotional states. No two people have precisely the same speech, respiratory block, or gait. Nonetheless, there are a number of universal, clearly distinguishable modes of expression. In depth psychology we draw a fundamental distinction between the *"neurotic"* character and the *"genital"* character on the basis of muscular and character armoring. We say that a character is "neurotic" when his organism is governed by an armor so rigid that he cannot voluntarily change or eliminate it. We speak of a "genital" character when the emotional reactions are not governed by rigid automatism, when the person is capable of reacting in a biological way to a particular situation. These two basic character types can also be quite sharply distinguished from one another in the area of biological functioning.

The armoring, its nature, the degree of its rigidity, and the inhibition of the body's emotional language can be easily assessed once the analyst has mastered the language of biological expression. The total expression of the armored organism is one of *"holding back."* The meaning of this expression is quite literal: *the body is expressing that it is holding back.* Pulled-back shoulders, thrust-out chest, rigid chin, superficial, suppressed breathing, hollowed-out loins, retracted, immobile pelvis, "expressionless" or rigidly stretched-out legs are the essential attitudes and mechanism of total restraint. They can be expressed schematically in the diagram on page 364.

Clinically, this basic body attitude on the part of the "neurotic" character is most clearly expressed in the "arc de cercle" of hysteria and in the "opisthotonus" of catatonic stupor.

There can be no doubt that the basic attitude of the armored body is not consciously created but is autonomous. A person is not aware of his armor as such. If the attempt is made to describe it to him in words, he usually does not understand what one is talking about. He does not sense the armor itself but merely the distortion of his inner perceptions of life. He describes himself as being apathetic, rigid, confined, empty, or he complains about palpitations, constipation, insomnia, nervous restlessness, nausea, etc. If the armor has existed for a long time and has also had an effect on the tissues of the organs, the patient comes to us because of peptic ulcers, rheumatism, arthritis, cancer, or angina pectoris. Since I presented the purely clinical facts in detail elsewhere, I shall content myself with this sum-

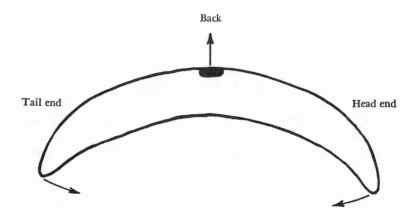

The basic biophysical attitude of the unarmored *organism*

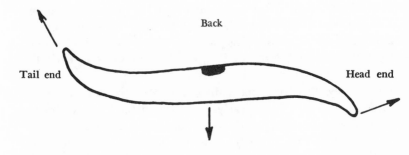

The basic biophysical attitude of the armored *organism: "holding back"*

mary. We are most concerned here to penetrate to the *functions of the biological depth* and to deduce the functioning of the *living organism* from them.

The armored organism is incapable of breaking down its own armor. But it is equally incapable of expressing its elemental biological emotions. It is familiar with the sensation of tickling but has never experienced orgonotic pleasure. The armored individual cannot express a sigh of pleasure or consciously imitate it. When he tries to do so, the result is a groan, a suppressed, pent-up roar, or even an impulse to vomit. He is incapable of venting anger or of banging his fist in an imitation of anger. He cannot breathe out fully. His diaphragm is very constricted in its movements. (This can be easily ascertained through x-rays). He is not capable of moving the pelvis forward. Asked to do so, an armored person will often not understand what is wanted of him or he will execute the wrong movement, i.e., a movement indicative of holding back. The excessive strain on the peripheral muscles and the nervous system causes the armored organism to be acutely sensitive to pressure. It is not possible to touch an armored organism on certain parts of the body without producing manifestations of acute anxiety or nervousness. It is quite likely that what is popularly known as "nervousness" can be traced back to this hypersensitivity of the overtensed muscles.

The incapacity for plasmatic pulsation and convulsion in the sexual act, i.e., orgastic impotence, is the result of this total holding back. This, in turn, results in the stasis of sexual energy, and from this sexual stasis follows everything which I include under the concept "biopathy."

The central task of orgone therapy is to destroy the armor, in other words, to restore the motility of the body plasma. In the armored organism, the pulsation function of all organs is impaired to a greater or lesser degree. It is the task of orgone therapy to reestablish the full capacity for pulsation. This takes place biophysically when the mechanism of holding back is destroyed. The result of an ideal orgone therapy is the appearance of the *orgasm reflex*. Apart from respiration, it is, as we know, the most important manifestation of movement in the animal kingdom. At the moment of orgasm, the organism completely "surrenders" itself to the sensations of its organs and the involuntary pulsations of the body. This explains the intimate connection between the movement of the orgasm reflex and the expression of "surrender." Those who are familiar with our work know that we do not urge the patient to "surrender" himself or herself. It would not serve any purpose anyhow, for he or she would not be able to do so. If the patient could, he would have no need to call upon our help. Nor do we allow the patient to practice "surrender." There is no technique capable of consciously producing the *involuntary* attitude of surrender. *The living organism functions autonomously, beyond the sphere of language, intellect, and voli-*

tion. It functions in accordance with definite laws of nature, and it is these laws we shall investigate here. The orgasm reflex, together with its physical manifestations of surrender, is, as will soon be shown, the key to the understanding of the *fundamental* processes of nature, which far transcend the individual and even the living organism. Hence, those who wish to benefit from the further discussion of these phenomena must prepare themselves for a journey deep into the realm of cosmic energy. Those who have not wholly freed themselves from burlesque concepts of sexuality will be bitterly disappointed and will fail to comprehend even the most rudimentary points.

We have already made a thorough study of the functions of the orgasm in the field of psychology and physiology. Hence, here we can concentrate exclusively on the fundamental natural phenomenon of the "orgasm." *In the orgasm, strangely enough, the organism unceasingly attempts to bring together the two embryologically important zones, the mouth and the anus.* Its form is:

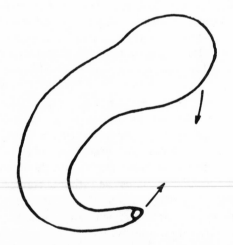

The emotional expression of the orgasm reflex

I stated above that the attitude from which the orgasm reflex derives is identical with the movement expressive of "surrender."

This is really quite obvious. The organism surrenders itself to its plasmatic excitations and sensations of flowing; then it surrenders itself completely to the partner in the sexual embrace. Every form of reserve, holding back, and armoring is abandoned. All biological activity is reduced to the basic function of plasmatic pulsation. In man, all thought and fantasy activity cease. The organism is "surrendered" in the purest sense of the word.

The movement expressive of emotional surrender is clear. *What is not clear is the function of the orgastic pulsation.* This pulsation consists in the alternating contractions and expansions of the entire body plasma. *What function does the bringing together of the two ends of the trunk have in the orgastic pulsation?* On first impression, it appears to have no "meaning" whatever. The expression of this movement is incomprehensible. We said that every movement of the organism has an *intelligible* expression. But this assertion does not hold up in the case of orgastic pulsation. We cannot find in the orgasm an *intelligible* expression, i.e., one capable of being translated into human language.

We could at this point indulge in philosophical speculations about this problem. But this would not lead us anywhere. Hence, for the time being, we shall content ourselves with the natural scientific explanation that, while it appears to be unintelligible, the orgastic pulsation must nonetheless have a concealed expression. For, like every movement of the living organism, it too is an *expressive* movement; hence, its movement must of necessity have an *expression*.

We shall, in the further course of our investigations, arrive at an amazing but incontestable answer to this basic question of the life function. But to arrive at this answer we must first digress considerably and collect and learn to collate correctly a large number of biological phenomena. The answer goes deeper than the individual biological organism; hence, *it is suprapersonal; at the same time, it is not in the least metaphysical or spiritualistic.* It also explains why the orgastic yearning of living creatures is not only the very deepest yearning but, in a preeminent way, *cosmic yearning.* To be sure, it is generally known that the organism is a part of the cosmos, but until now it has not been known *how.* Let us return to the clinical experiences of orgone therapy.

In terms of orgone biophysics, it is our task to enable the human organism to give up its mechanism of holding back and to achieve the ability to surrender. In other words, *as long as the two embryonic ends of the trunk bend backwards instead of bending forward toward one another, the organism will be incapable of surrendering itself to any experience, whether work or pleasure.* Since the *muscular* armor hinders every form of surrender and causes every form of biopathic restriction of the life function, our first task is to break down the armor. Only by eliminating muscular rigidity can the goal of surrender be encompassed. It cannot be achieved in any other way, be it psychoanalytic persuasion, suggestion, prayer, or gymnastics. It is not necessary to tell our patients anything whatever about this goal. Numerous experiences have taught us that his total orgasm reflex will develop as a matter of course when we have succeeded in breaking down his muscular armor. Our work has demonstrated time and again that *the essential function of the muscular armor is that of preventing the orgasm reflex.*

Elsewhere, I have described numerous mechanisms of the muscular armor. The corresponding *character* armor is described in Part I of this volume. Now I want to introduce a new point of view which will clarify character armor and muscular armor at the level of the most elemental functions of life. The germane observations were made over the past ten years or so. Hence, I have no hesitation in assuming full responsibility for the importance which these observations have in the field of biophysics.

3. THE SEGMENTAL ARRANGEMENT OF THE ARMOR

It has been known to psychiatry for decades that the physical disturbances of hysteria are not governed by the anatomical and physiological processes of the muscles, nerves, and tissues as a whole; rather, they are determined by definite, emotionally important organs. For example, pathological blushing is usually confined to the face and neck, despite the fact that the blood vessels run essentially along the length of the organism. Likewise, sensory disturbances in hysteria are not spread along the nerve tract but are confined to emotionally significant regions of the body.

We run into the same situation in our work of breaking down the muscular armor. The individual muscular blocks do not follow the course of a muscle or a nerve; they are altogether independent of anatomical processes. In carefully examining typical cases of various illnesses in the search for a law that governs these blocks, I discovered that *the muscular armor is arranged in segments.*

Biologically, this segmental arrangement is a much more primitive form of living functioning than is found in the highly developed animals. A conspicuous example of segmental functioning is that of ringed worms and the biological systems related to them. In the higher vertebrates, only the segmental structure of the spine, the nerve endings corresponding to the segments of the spinal cord, and the segmental arrangement of the ganglia of the autonomic nervous system are indicative of the vertebrates' descent from segmentally structured organisms.

I shall attempt in the following exposition to give *only a rough* sketch of the segmental arrangement of the muscular armor. These representations are based on the observation of armor reactions over a period of many years.

Since the patient's body is held back and since the goal of orgone therapy is to restore the plasmatic currents *in the pelvis,* it is logically necessary to begin the work of breaking down the armor at the parts of the body farthest away from the pelvis. Thus, the work begins on the expression of the facial musculature. There are at least *two* clearly distinguishable, segmentally arranged armorings in the head: one segment comprises the forehead, eyes, and the region of the cheekbone; the other comprises the lips, chin, and jaws. When I say that the armor is segmentally arranged, I mean that it functions circularly, in front, on both sides, and in back, i.e., like a *ring.*

Let us refer to the *first armor ring* as the *ocular* and the second as the *oral* armor ring. In the sphere of the ocular armor segment, we find a contraction and immobilization of all or almost all the muscles of the eyeballs, the eyelids, the forehead, the lachrymal gland, etc. Rigid forehead and eyelids, expressionless eyes or bulging eyeballs, mask-like expression, and immobility on both sides of the nose are the essential characteristics of this armor ring. The eyes peep out as from a rigid mask. The patient is not capable of opening his eyes wide as if to imitate fear. In schizophrenics, the expression of the eyes is blank, as if staring into space. This is caused by the contraction of the eyeball muscles. Many patients have lost the ability to shed tears. In others, the opening of the eyelids has been reduced to a narrow, rigid slit. The forehead is without expression, as if it had been "flattened out." Near-sightedness, astigmatism, etc., very often exist.

The loosening of the ocular armor segment is brought about by opening the eyes wide as in fright; this causes the eyelids and forehead to move and to express emotions. Usually, this also effects a loosening of the upper cheek muscles, especially when the patient is told to make grimaces. When the cheeks are pulled up, the result is that peculiar grin expressive of defiant, malicious provocation.

The segmental character of this muscle group is revealed by the fact that every emotional action in this area affects horizontally adjacent areas but does not carry over into the oral segment. While it is true that the opening wide of the eyelids, as in fright, is capable of mobilizing the forehead or of producing a grin in the upper part of the cheeks, it is not capable of provoking the biting impulses which are cemented in the clamped chin.

Hence, an armor segment comprises those organs and muscle groups which have a functional contact with one another and which are capable of accompanying each other in the emotional expressive movement. In terms of biophysics, one segment ends and a different segment begins when the one ceases to affect the other in its emotional actions.

The armor segments *always* have a *horizontal* structure— never a vertical one, with the two notable exceptions of the arms and legs. Their armor functions in conjunction with the adjacent armor segments of the trunk, i.e., the arms with the segment which comprises the shoulders, and the legs with the segment which comprises the pelvis. We want to take special note of this peculiarity. It will become intelligible in a definite biophysical context.

The second, i.e., the oral, armor segment comprises the entire musculature of the chin, pharynx, and the occipital musculature, including the muscles around the mouth. They are functionally related to one another; e.g., the loosening of the chin armor is capable of producing spasms in the musculature of the lips and the related emotion of crying or desire to suck. Likewise, the freeing of the gag reflex is capable of mobilizing the oral segment.

The emotional modes of expression of crying, furious biting, yelling, sucking, grimacings of all kinds in this segment are dependent upon the free motility of the ocular segment. Liberating the gag reflex, for example, will not necessarily release a suppressed impulse to cry if the armor of the ocular ring has not already been dissolved. And even after the two uppermost armor segments have been dissolved, it may still be difficult to release the impulse to cry as long as the third and fourth segments further down, at the thorax, are in the condition of spastic contraction. This difficulty in liberating the emotions gives us an insight into an extremely important fact of biophysics:

1. *The armorings have a segmental, circular structure, arranged at right angles to the spine.*

2. *The plasmatic currents and emotional excitations which we resuscitate flow parallel to the body axis.*

Thus, the inhibition of the emotional language of expression operates at right angles to the direction of the orgonotic current.

Two things are important in this connection: (1) the orgonotic currents merge in the orgasm reflex only when their passage *along* the entire organism is unobstructed; and (2) the armorings are arranged in segments crosswise to the flow of the currents. It is clear, therefore, that the orgastic pulsation can function only after all the segmental armor rings have been loosened. It is also clear that the sensations of each body organ can merge into a sensation of totality only when the first orgastic convulsions have begun. They preface the breakdown of the muscular armor. The orgonotic currents which break through in the loosening of every additional armor ring prove to be a tremendous help in the dissolution work as a whole. What happens is this: the liberated body energy spontaneously attempts to flow *lengthwise*. It runs into the still unresolved crosswise contractions and gives the patient the unmistakable sensation of a "block," a sensation which was only very weak or altogether absent as long as there were no free plasmatic currents whatever.

The reader is surely aware of the fact that these processes represent primary functions of the plasma system. They are not only

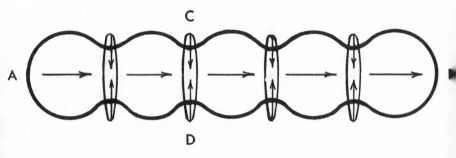

The direction of orgonotic streaming is transverse to the armor rings

deeper than all human language but also *central* to the functioning of the life apparatus. They are primordial phylogenetic functions. *In the segmental arrangement of the muscular armoring, we meet the worm in man.*

The movements of the ringed worm are governed by excitation waves which run from the end of the tail along the axis of the body forward to the "head." The excitation waves are transmitted continuously from segment to segment until they have reached the forward end. At the hind end, one wave movement follows another in the process of locomotion. In the worm, the segments alternate rhythmically and regularly between contraction and expansion. In the worm and the caterpillar, the function of locomotion is inseparably linked with this plasmatic wave movement. The logical conclusion is that *biological energy is being transmitted in these wave movements,* for it could be nothing else. This assertion is supported by observations of the inner movements of bions. The wave-like movement of the body orgone is slow and, in tempo and expression, wholly corresponds to the emotional excitations which, in the pleasure function, we experience subjectively in an unequivocal wave-like manner.

In *armored* human organisms, the orgone energy is bound in the chronic contraction of the muscles. The body orgone does not begin to flow freely as soon as the armor ring has been loosened. The first reaction is clonic shivering, along with the sensation of prickling, or "pins and needles." Clinically, this reaction tells us that the armor is giving way and body orgone is being liberated. Genuine sensations of plasmatic excitation waves are experienced only when a whole series of armor segments, e.g., muscular blocks in the region of the eyes, mouth, throat, breast, and diaphragm, have been dissolved. When this has been accomplished, marked *wave-like* pulsations are experienced in liberated parts of the body which move up toward the head and down toward the genitalia. Very often the organism reacts to these initial currents and pulsations with fresh armorings. Spasms in the deep musculature of the throat, reverse peristalsis of the esophagus, diaphragmatic tics, etc., testify to the *struggle* taking place *between the impulse of the current and the armor block.* Since more orgone energy has become free than the patient is capable of discharging; since, moreover, spasms block the plasmatic current at numerous points in the body, the patient develops acute anxiety.

These phenomena, which can be easily brought about by an orgone therapist having some experience and technical skill, confirm orgone-biophysics's concept of the antithesis between the emotion of *pleasure* and the emotion of *anxiety*.[2] At this juncture, however, I have to single out a new phenomenon which, until now, has not been described clearly enough.

As soon as the first armor blocks have been dissolved, the movement expressive of "surrender" appears more and more, along with the orgonotic currents and sensations. However, its full unfolding is hindered by those armor blocks that have not yet been dissolved. Usually, it appears as if *the organism wanted to overcome these undissolved armor blocks by force.* The expression of incipient surrender is transformed into hate. This process is typical and deserves special attention.

When, for example, the armoring of the oral zone has been sufficiently loosened to release a suppressed impulse to cry, while the neck and chest armorings are still untouched, we observe how the lower musculature of the face takes on the expression of wanting to cry but not being able to. The expression of being on the verge of tears is transformed into a hateful grin of the mouth-chin zone. It is an expression of desperation, of extreme frustration. All this can be summarized in the following formula:

[2] Cf. Reich: *The Discovery of the Orgone,* Vol. I.

As soon as the movement expressing surrender is obstructed by an armor block, the impulse to surrender is transformed into destructive rage. I shall have to come back to this transformation of an impulse after I have described the manifestations of the other armor segments.

The armor of the *third* segment comprises essentially the deep musculature of the neck, the platysma, and the sternocleidomastoid muscles. Let one but imitate the movement expressive of the attitude of anger or crying and one will have no difficulty in comprehending the emotional function of the neck armor. The spastic contraction of the neck segment also includes the tongue. In terms of anatomy, this is easily understood. Essentially, the musculature of the tongue is joined to the cervical bone system and not to the lower facial bones. This explains why spasms in the musculature of the tongue are functionally connected with the pressing down of the Adam's apple and the contraction of the deep and surface musculature of the throat. From the movements of the Adam's apple, it is possible to tell when a patient's anger affect or impulse to cry is unconsciously and literally "swallowed." It is extremely difficult to eliminate this method of suppressing emotions. While the hands can be used to get at the surface muscles of the neck, this is not possible in dealing with the larynx musculature. The best way to eliminate the "swallowing" of emotions is to liberate the *gag reflex*. In the gag reflex, the excitation wave in the esophagus is the reverse of the excitation wave which occurs in the "swallowing" of tears or anger. If the gag reflex begins to function or even goes so far as to cause the patient to vomit, then the emotions are set free which were being held back by the neck armor.

At this point the lengthwise course of the emotional excitation again becomes significant. The gag reflex is accompanied by an *expansion* of the diaphragm, i.e., by the lifting of the diaphragm and expiration. Work on the neck armor by means of the gag reflex brings about a loosening of the fourth and fifth armor segments. In other words, we do not eliminate one armor ring after the other in a mechanical and rigid manner. We work on an integrated life system, whose total plasma function is hindered by transverse armor rings. But the loosening of an armor segment liberates energy which, in turn, helps to mobilize armor rings at higher and lower levels. It is therefore not possible to give a clear description of each process involved in the dissolution of the muscular armor.

Now I want to turn to the *fourth,* the *chest segment.* While it is true that the armor functions of this segment can be subdivided, it is more advantageous to treat the chest as a whole.

The armoring of the chest is manifested in the elevation of the bony structure, a chronic attitude of inhalation, shallow breathing, and the immobility of the thorax. We already know that the attitude of inhalation is the most important instrument in the suppression of *any* kind of emotion. The armoring of the chest is particularly crucial not only because it represents a major part of the armoring of the organism in general but also because the biopathic symptoms have an especially dangerous character in this region.

All the intercostal muscles, the large chest muscles (pectoral), the shoulder muscles (deltoid), and the muscle group on and between the shoulder blades are involved in the armoring of the chest. The attitude of being "self-contained" or "self-controlled," of "sticking to oneself," "being reserved," are the major manifestations of the chest armor. Shoulders which are pulled back express precisely what they mean—"holding back." Together with the neck armor, the chest armor conveys the expression of suppressed "stubbornness" and "stiff-neckedness." When it is not chronically armored, the expression conveyed by the movement of the fourth segment is that of "free-flowing feelings." When it is armored, the expression is that of "immobility" or "indifference."

The chronic expansion of the thorax goes together with the tendency to high blood pressure, palpitations, and anxiety; in severe, long-standing cases, there is also the tendency to cardiac enlargement. Various cardiac defects result directly from this expansion or indirectly from the anxiety syndrome. Pulmonary emphysema is a direct result of the chronic expansion of the chest cavity. I am inclined to believe that the *disposition* to pneumonia and tuberculosis is to be sought here also.

"Raging anger," "heartfelt crying," "sobbing," and "unbearable longing" are essentially emotions which originate in the chest segment. These natural emotions are alien to the armored organism. An armored person's anger is "cold"; he looks upon crying as "childish," "unmanly," and "characterless"; he regards longing as "effeminate," the sign of a "weak character."

Most of the emotional expressive movements of the arms and hands also stem from the plasmatic emotions of the organs of the chest. In terms of biophysics, these limbs are extensions of the chest segment. In the artist, who is capable of freely unfolding his yearnings, the emotion of the chest extends directly into the wholly synchronized emotions and expressive movements of the arms and hands. This is equally true of the violin virtuoso and piano virtuoso, as it is of the painter. In the dance, the essential expressive movements derive from the organism as a whole.

The "awkwardness" of the arms and probably a part of a person's lack of musicality also derive from the chest armor. It is largely responsible for the expression of "hardness" and "inaccessibility." In European cultural circles and in an especially pronounced way among the "higher circles" of Asia, total armoring of the head, neck, and chest segments invests the organism with the mark of "nobility." The ideals of "character firmness," "hauteur," "detachment," "grandeur," and "control" correspond to this. Militarism the world over makes use of the expression embodied in the armoring of the chest, neck, and head as an emphasis of "unapproachable dignity." It is clear that these attitudes are based on the armor and not vice versa.

In some patients we find a whole series of interrelated life problems which derive from the armoring of the chest. Typically, these patients complain about a "knot" in the chest. This organ sensation leads us to believe that the esophagus (similar to the *globus hystericus* in the pharynx) is spastic. It is difficult to say whether the trachea is involved in this, but very likely it is. In the process of loosening this inner "knot," we learn that rage and anxiety are bound in it. To release this "knot" in the chest, it is often necessary to press down the chest cavity and at the same time have the patient scream. The inhibition of the inner chest organs usually entails an inhibition of those arm movements which express "desire," "embracing," or "reaching for something." It is not that these patients are handicapped in any *mechanical* way. They can move their arms quite well. *However, as soon as the movement of the arms becomes associated with the expressive movement of yearning or desiring, the inhibition sets in.* Sometimes, this inhibition is so strong that the hands and especially the finger tips lose their orgonotic charge, become cold and clammy, and, on occasion, acutely painful. It is very likely that Raynaud's gangrene of the finger tips is based on this specific anorgonia. In many cases it is simply an impulse to choke which is armored in the shoulder blades and in the hands and is responsible for vasomotor constriction in the finger tips.

We find the life of such patients ruled by a general inhibition of initiative and by disturbances in their work caused by their inability to use the hands freely. Sometimes the armoring of the chest cavity in women goes hand in hand with a lack of sensitivity of the nipples. Disturbances of sexual gratification and aversion to nursing a baby are the direct results of this armoring.

Between the shoulder blades, there are two painful muscle bundles in the region of the trapezius muscles. Their armoring creates the impression of suppressed defiance which, together with pulled-back shoulders, can be best described by the words, "I won't."

When the chest is armored, the intercostal muscles demonstrate an acute sensitivity to tickling. That this sensitivity is not "simply not wanting to be tickled" but a biopathic increase of excitability is evidenced by the fact that it disappears when the chest armor has been dissolved. In one particular case, the character attitude of inaccessibility had essentially one function, namely "Don't touch me! I'm ticklish."

It should be clear that it is not my intent to ridicule these character attitudes. It is merely that we see them for what they are, i.e., not as the embodiment of "higher" and "nobler" character traits but as the expression of biophysical conditions. A general may or may not be a person of "high esteem." We want neither to glorify nor to deprecate him. Yet we will not have ourselves deprived of the right to look upon him as an animal having a special kind of armor. It would not bother me if another scientist wanted to reduce my thirst for knowledge to the biological function of a puppy who goes around sniffing at everything. Indeed, it would make me happy to be biologically compared to a lively and lovable puppy. I have no desire to distinguish myself from the animal.

This much must be clear: there can be no thought of establishing orgastic potency until the chest armor has been dissolved and the emotions of rage, yearning, and *genuine* sorrow have been liberated. Essentially, the function of surrender is linked to the plasmatic movement of the chest and neck segments. Even if it were possible to mobilize the pelvic segment independently, the head would automatically move *forward* in stubborn defense instead of moving backward, as soon as the slightest sensation of pleasure was experienced in the pelvis.

I have already pointed out that the armoring of the chest constitutes a central part of the muscular armoring in general. Historically, it can be traced back to the most crucial and most conflict-ridden turning points in the life of the child, most likely to a point considerably before the development of the pelvic armor. Hence, it is not surprising to find that, in the course of dissolving the chest armor, we get the remembrances of traumatic mistreatments of all kinds, frustrations of love, and disappointments in the person responsible for the child's upbringing. I have also explained why remembering traumatic experiences is not essential for orgone therapy. It serves little purpose unless accompanied by the corresponding emotion. The emotion expressed in the movement is more than sufficient to make the patient's misfortunes comprehensible, quite apart from the fact that the remembrances emerge of themselves when the therapist works correctly. What remains puzzling is how unconscious memory functions can be dependent upon the conditions of plasmatic excitation, how memories can be preserved, so to speak, in plasmatic awareness.

Now let us turn to the *fifth*, the *diaphragm* segment. The segment which comprises the diaphragm and the organs which lie below it is, in terms of its function, independent of the chest segment. This is borne out by the fact that, even after the chest armor has been dissolved and rage and tears have broken forth, the diaphragmatic block remains unaffected. It is easy to observe the immobility of the diaphragm through a fluoroscope. While it is true that, through forced breathing, the diaphragm is capable of moving better than before the dissolving of the chest armor, it is also true that, until the diaphragmatic block has been eliminated, there *is no spontaneous diaphragmatic pulsation.* Thus, there are *two* stages in the dissolution of the diaphragmatic block.

In the process of loosening the chest armor, we make the patient breathe consciously and deeply. This causes the diaphragm to move more expansively but not spontaneously. As soon as this forced respiration is stopped, the movement of the diaphragm and, with it, the respiratory movement of the chest cavity also cease. We have to extract the *expressive movement* from the diaphragm armor to be able to accomplish the second step of *spontaneous* diaphragm pulsation. This is a fresh confirmation of the fact that mechanical means are of no use in reactivating biological emotional functions. Solely through the biological *expressive movement* can we loosen the armor ring.

The fifth armor segment forms a contraction ring which extends forward over the epigastrium, the lower part of the sternum, back along the lowermost ribs toward the posterior insertions of the diaphragm, i.e., to the tenth, eleventh, and twelfth thoracic vertebrae. Essentially, it comprises the diaphragm, the stomach, the solar plexus, including the pancreas, which lies in front of it, the liver, and two bulging muscle bundles extending alongside the lowermost thoracic vertebrae.

The overt manifestation of this armor ring is lordosis of the spine. Usually, the therapist can push his hand between the patient's back and the couch. The lower front rib margin is thrust forward and protruding. It is difficult or altogether impossible to bend the spine forward. On the fluoroscope, we can see that the diaphragm is immobile under usual conditions and that it moves but little under forced breathing. If we tell the patient to breathe consciously, he will always *inhale.* Exhalation as a *spontaneous* action is alien to him. If he is told to exhale, he has to make a considerable effort. If he succeeds in exhaling a bit, his body automatically assumes an attitude which works counter to exhalation. The head moves forward or the musculature of the oral armor ring becomes more acutely contracted. The shoulder blades are pulled back and the arms are pressed tightly against the upper part of the body. The pelvic musculature is tensed and the back is more rigidly arched.

The diaphragmatic block is the central mechanism of this region. Hence, the destruction of this block is one of the central tasks of the therapy.

The dissolution of the armor in the diaphragmatic segment entails the overcoming of many difficulties. Why is this so? The message of the body expression which is opposed to this work is quite clear, though the patient has no awareness of it: the organism refuses to allow the diaphragm to expand and contract freely. However, if the upper segments have been properly loosened, it can only be a matter of time until the diaphragm armor is also dissolved. For example, forced respiration in the chest segment or repeated freeing of the gag reflex can urge the organism toward orgastic pulsation. Irritation of the shoulder muscles by means of pinching can have the same effect.

Theoretically, we understand why the resistance to the full pulsation of the diaphragm is so strong: the organism defends itself against the sensations of pleasure or anxiety which the diaphragmatic movement inevitably entails. However, we cannot pretend that this statement offers anything more than a rationalistic and psychologistic explanation. Such an explanation presupposes that the organism "thinks" and "deliberates" rationally, somewhat as follows: "This meticulous physician demands that I let my diaphragm expand and contract freely. If I comply, I shall experience the sensations of anxiety and pleasure which I experienced when my parents punished me for enjoying myself. I have reconciled myself to the situation as it is. *Hence, I shall not comply.*"

The living organism neither thinks nor deliberates in a rational manner. It does not do or fail to do things "in order to . . ." The living organism functions in harmony with the primary plasmatic emotions, which have the function of gratifying biological tension and needs. It is simply impossible to translate the language of the living organism *directly* into the word language of consciousness. It is extremely important to realize this, for the rationalistic thinking which has shaped man's mechanistic civilization is capable of smothering and extinguishing our insight into the *fundamentally different* language of the living organism.

I should like to cite an especially clear clinical case to illustrate the novelty of the phenomena involved here:

A patient who had considerable intellectual insight into orgone therapy and had already succeeded in dissolving a substantial part of the armor of the upper body was asked to make an effort to break through the diaphragmatic armor. We were in complete agreement about the situation. Both in talking about and in applying himself to this task, the patient showed an affirmative attitude. Yet, as soon as a small breach had been made in the wall of the diaphragmatic armor, the patient's trunk, from the diaphragm downwards to the pelvis, began to jerk *sideways*. This was very puzzling, to say the least. And it took considerable effort to understand what this movement was trying to express.

In its sideward movement, the lower part of the trunk expressed a resolute NO. It is merely necessary to move one's right hand from side to side, in such a way as to say "no-no," to understand the expressive movement we are dealing with here.

Psychologistically or, better yet, mystically, it might be assumed that the plasma system, *beyond* word language, expressed a vehement NO to an undertaking which "the cortex" and word language affirmed. Such an interpretation of the process would be false, and it would not lead a step closer to an understanding of the living organism and its expressive language. This patient's abdomen and pelvis did not "deliberate" upon the demand which was made upon the organism. They did not "decide" to refuse to comply. There was a different process involved here, one more in keeping with the expressive language of the living.

As we pointed out, the plasmatic movements of a worm are directed lengthwise *along the body axis*. When the orgonotic excitation waves move the body of the worm forward, we gain the "impression" that the worm is acting *purposefully,* i.e., "volitionally." The expressive movement of the worm's living organism can be translated into the words of our language which mean "wanting to," "saying yes to," etc. If, now, we take a pair of pincers and squeeze the worm somewhere around the middle of its body so that the orgonotic excitation is interrupted as by an armor block, the unified purposeful forward movement and, with it, the expressive movement of "wanting to" and "saying yes to" momentarily cease to function. These are replaced by another movement, namely a sideways twisting back and forth of the lower or hind part of the body, while the front part is drawn in. The immediate impression conveyed by this seesawing side-to-side movement of the body is one expressive of pain or a vehement "No, don't do that, I can't stand it." We are not forgetting that we are speaking of our *impression* here, i.e., an interpretation which we *experience immediately* while observing the worm. But we would act exactly like the worm if someone fastened a large clamp around our trunk. We would automatically draw in our head and shoulders and struggle sideways with our pelvis and legs.

This comprehension of the process does not mean that we have taken up with the subjectivists who contend that we perceive "nothing but our own sensations" and that these sensations do not correspond to any reality. Basically, everything that lives is functionally identical. It follows, therefore, that the reactions of the worm to the pincers are identical to what ours would be in a similar situation. The reactions of pain and the effort to ward off the pain are the same. This functional identity between man and worm enables us to be "impressed" in the correct, objectively true sense of the word by the expressive movement of the wriggling worm. In fact, the worm's overt expression conveys what we sense through identification. But we do not directly sense the worm's pain and its crying of "no"; we merely perceive an expressive movement which, under any circumstances, would be identical with the expressive movement of our plasma system in the same painful situation.

It follows from this that *we comprehend the expressive movements and the emotional expression of another living organism on the basis of the identity between our own emotions and those of all living things.*

We have a *direct* comprehension of the language of living organisms based on the functional identity of the biological emotions. *After* we have grasped it in this biological language of expression, we put it "into words": we translate it into the word language of consciousness. However, the word "no" has as much, actually as little, to do with the language of expression of the living organism as the word "cat" has to do with the *flesh-and-blood* cat which crosses the street in front of our eyes. In reality, the word "cat" and the specific orgonotic plasma system which moves there in front of us have *nothing* to do with one another. As the many various designations for the phenomenon "cat" testify, they are merely loose, randomly interchangeable concepts which are attached to the real phenomena, movements, emotions, etc.

These observations sound like "highbrow" or "lowbrow" natural philosophy. The layman is averse to natural philosophy and will, therefore, put this book aside because it "does not rest upon the solid foundation of reality." The reader who shares this thought is mistaken. I shall demonstrate in the following pages how important it is to think *correctly* and to use both concepts and words *properly*. It will be shown that a whole world of mechanistically oriented biologists, physicists, bacteriologists, etc., really believed, from 1936 to 1945—i.e., in the period during which the functions of the living organism were being discovered —that it was the word "cat" moving on the street and not a complicated living product of nature.

Let us return to the "no-no" movement of our patient. Its meaning is this: *when a plasmatic current cannot run along the body in a lengthwise direction because it is obstructed by transverse armor blocks, a sideward movement results which, secondarily, means* NO *in word language.*

"No" in word language corresponds to the "no" of the expressive language of the living organism. It cannot be ascribed to mere chance that "no" is expressed by a transverse movement of the head, while "yes" is expressed by a lengthwise movement of the head. The "no-no" which our patient expressed by the sideward seesawing of his pelvis disappeared only after the block of the diaphragm had been dissolved. And it regularly reappeared when this block returned.

These facts are of supreme importance for the understanding of the body language. Our patient's general attitude toward life was also of a negative nature. "No" was the basic attitude of his character. Though he suffered from and fought against this character attitude, he could not escape it. No matter how much he consciously and intellectually wanted to say YES, to be positive, his character continually expressed NO. Both the historical and biophysiological functions of this "no" on the part of his character were easy to understand. As so many small children do, he had constantly had enemas given by his severely compulsive mother. Like other children, he too had submitted to this crime with horror and inner rage. To diminish the fury of his rage, to be able to endure this violation by his mother, "he contained himself," pulled up on his pelvic floor, severely reduced his breathing, generally developed the body attitude of "no-no." Everything that was alive in him wanted (but was not allowed) to cry out "no-no" to this violation, the result being that he came away from this experience permanently scarred. From then on, the overt expression of his life system became a fundamental negation toward everything and everybody. And though this negative character attitude represented an acute symptom, it was, at the same time, the expression of a strong self-defense which, originally, had been rational and justified. But this self-defense, rationally motivated in the beginning, had taken on the form of a chronic armor, which was rigidly shut off to everything.

I explained elsewhere that *a childhood experience is capable of having an "effect from the past" only insofar as it is anchored in a rigid armor which continues to operate in the present*. In our patient, the original, rationally motivated "no-no" had, over the years, been transformed into a neurotic and irrational "no-no". It had, in other words, become embedded in a chronic character armor which was responsible for sustaining and expressing it. The "no-no" expression disappeared with the dissolution of the armor in the treatment. Thus, too, the historical event, the assault by the mother, lost its pathological meaning.

From the point of view of depth psychology, it is correct to say that, in this patient, the affect of the defense, of the "crying no to," was "clamped down." Seen from the perspective of the biological core, on the other hand, it was not a matter of a "clamped-down" "no-no" but of *the incapacity on the part of the organism to say* YES. A positive, affirmative attitude in life is possible only when the organism functions as a totality, when the plasmatic excitations, together with the emotions pertaining to them, can pass through all the organs and tissues without obstruction, when, in short, the expressive movements of the plasm are capable of flowing freely.

As soon as even one single armor block limits this function, the expressive movement of affirmation is disturbed. Small children then cannot become fully immersed in their games, adolescents fail in their work or in school, adults function like a moving car with the emergency brake on. The onlooker, the teacher, or the technical supervisor gets the "impression" that the person is lazy, recalcitrant, or incapable. The "blocked" person himself feels he is a failure "no matter how hard he tries." This process can be translated into the language of the living organism: *the organism always starts out by functioning in a biologically correct way, by flowing freely and giving. However, in the passage of the orgonotic excitations through the organism, the functioning is slowed down and the expression of "I take pleasure in doing" is translated into an automatic "I won't" or "I don't want to." In short, the organism is not responsible for its own malfunctioning.*

This process is of universal importance. I have intentionally selected clinical examples that have general validity. This was absolutely necessary. On the basis of these restrictions in human functioning, we shall arrive at a deeper and more comprehensive understanding of a whole series of unfortunate social phenomena which remain unintelligible without their *biophysical* background.

After this long but necessary digression, let us return to the fifth armor segment. In the upper segments, once we had succeeded in liberating the expressive movements from the armor ring, the overt expression which ensued could easily be interpreted. The inhibition of the eye muscles expresses "empty" or "sad" eyes. A firmly clenched jaw may be expressive of "suppressed anger." A crying or roaring breaks loose from the "knot in the chest."

Body language is easily translated into word language and the expressive movement is *immediately* intelligible when we are working on the four upper segments. The situation is more complicated when working on the diaphragmatic segment. *Once the armor of the diaphragmatic segment has been dissolved, we are no longer in a position to translate the language of movement into word language.* This requires a detailed explanation. The overt expression which ensues when we have dissolved the armor of the diaphragmatic segment leads us into the uncomprehended depths of the life function. We meet a new problem here: in what concrete way is the human animal related to the primitive animal world and to the cosmic function of the orgone?

We succeed in liberating the diaphragmatic segment from the armor by having the patient repeatedly release the gag reflex, while strictly enjoining him not to suspend respiration during the gagging but to continue to inhale and exhale forcefully. The repeated releasing of the gag reflex leads inevitably to the dissolution of the diaphragmatic armor. There is only one precondition: the armor of the upper segments must have been dissolved *beforehand*, i.e., the orgonotic currents in the regions of the head, neck, and chest must function freely.

As soon as the diaphragm expands and contracts freely, i.e., respiration functions fully and spontaneously, the trunk strives, with each exhalation, to fold up in the region of the upper abdomen. In other words: the neck end strives forward toward the pelvic end. The upper middle part of the abdomen is drawn in. This is the picture of the *orgasm reflex* as it is displayed to us for the first time. (It is still a distorted picture, for the pelvis is still not wholly loosened.) The forward bending of the trunk accompanied by the *backward* movement of the head expresses "surrender." It is not difficult to understand this. *The difficulties begin where the convulsions start in a forward direction. The emotional expression of the convulsions in the orgasm reflex are not immediately intelligible.* THE EXPRESSION OF THE CONVULSIONS IN THE ORGASM REFLEX CANNOT BE TRANSLATED INTO WORD LANGUAGE. There must be a special reason for this difficulty. We have to assume that there is some essential difference between the expressive movements which we have become familiar with thus far and the expressive movement of the whole trunk which becomes manifest when the diaphragm functions freely.

I should like to ask the reader to follow me with the utmost patience from now on and not to withdraw trust prematurely. His patience will be amply rewarded by the results which we shall achieve. I can assure the reader that I myself have had to exercise the greatest patience for more than a decade to arrive at the findings I am about to describe. Again and again during these years I despaired in the attempt to comprehend the orgasm reflex; it seemed absolutely impossible to make this basic biological reflex accessible to human concepts. However, I refused to give up, for I neither could nor wanted to admit that the living organism, which has an immediately intelligible language of expression in all other spheres, should, precisely in the *central* sphere, the orgasm reflex, express *nothing*. This seemed so contradictory, so completely absurd that I simply could not accept it. Time and again I told myself that I was the one who had said that the living organism simply functions, that it did not have any "meaning." It seemed correct to suppose that the "inexpressiveness" or "meaninglessness" of the orgastic convulsions indicated precisely this: in its basic function, the living organism does not reveal any meaning. Yet the attitude of surrender which becomes manifest in the orgasm reflex is both expressive and meaningful. Undoubtedly, the orgastic convulsions themselves are full of expression. I had to tell myself, then, that natural science had simply not yet learned to comprehend this widely diffused, indeed universal, emotional expression of the living organism. In short, an inner "expressive movement" without overt "emotional expression" seemed to me to be an absurdity.

Vomiting represents one approach to the problem, for the patient often vomits when the diaphragmatic armor is broken through. Just as there is an inability to cry, there is also an inability to vomit. This inability is easy to understand in terms of orgone biophysics. Together with the armor rings which lie above it, the diaphragmatic block prevents the peristaltic wave-like movement of the body energy upward from the stomach toward the mouth. In the same way, the "knot" in the chest and "swallowing," together with the contraction of the eye muscles, prevent crying. In other cases of diaphragmatic blocks, there is, in addition to the inability to vomit, constant nausea. There can be no doubt that "nervous stomach" complaints are the direct consequence of the armoring in this area, though we still do not have a thorough understanding of the connection between the two.

Vomiting is a biological expressive movement whose function performs precisely what it "expresses": *convulsive expulsion of body contents*. It is based on a peristaltic movement of the stomach and esophagus in a direction *contrary* to its normal function, namely *toward the mouth*. The gag reflex loosens the armor of the diaphragmatic segment radically and quickly. Vomiting is accompanied by a convulsion of the trunk, a rapid folding in the pit of the stomach, with the neck *and* pelvic end *jerking forward.* In the colic of small children, vomiting is accompanied by diarrhea. *In terms of energy, strong excitation waves run from the center of the body upward toward the mouth and downward toward the anus.* The emotional expression in this case speaks such an elementary language that there can be no doubt of the deep biological nature of this language. It is merely a question of understanding it.

The total movement which seizes the trunk in vomiting is, purely physiologically (not emotionally), the same as that of the orgasm reflex. This is also confirmed clinically: the dissolution of the diaphragmatic block introduces, with certainty, the first convulsions of the trunk which, subsequently, develop into the total orgasm reflex. These convulsions are accompanied by deep exhalation and an excitation wave which spreads upward from the region of the diaphragm toward the head and downward toward the genitalia. We know that the dissolution of the upper armor segments is an indispensable precondition to the release of the total convulsion of the trunk. In the movement of the excitation wave toward the pelvis, the orgonotic excitation invariably runs into a block in the middle of the abdomen. Either the middle of the abdomen contracts sharply and quickly or the pelvis moves backward and becomes cramped in this position.

This contraction in the middle of the abdomen represents the *sixth* independently functioning armor ring. The spasm of the large abdominal muscle (*Rectus abdominis*) is accompanied by a spastic contraction of the two lateral muscles (*Transversus abdominis*), which run from the lowermost ribs to the upper margin of the pelvis. They can be easily palpated as hard painful muscle cords. In the back, the lower sections of the muscles running along the spine (*Latissimus dorsi, sacrospinalis, etc.*) correspond to this segment. These muscles also can be clearly felt as hard painful cords.

The loosening of the sixth armor segment is easier than the loosening of all the other segments. After it has been dissolved, it is easy to approach the armor of the *seventh* and last armor segment, the *pelvic armor.*

In most cases, the armor of the pelvis comprises almost all the muscles of the pelvis. The whole pelvis is retracted. The abdominal muscle above the symphysis is painful. The same holds true for the adductors of the thigh, those on the surface as well as those which lie deeper. The anal sphincter muscle is contracted, hence the anus is pulled up. Let one contract the gluteal muscles voluntarily and it will be understood why the gluteal muscles are painful. The pelvis is "dead" and expressionless. This "inexpressiveness" is the "expression" of asexuality. Emotionally, no sensations or excitations are felt. On the other hand, the symptoms are legion: constipation, lumbago, growths of all kinds in the rectum, inflammation of the ovaries, polyps of the uterus, benign and malignant tumors. Irritability of the urinary bladder, anesthesia of the vagina and the penis surface, with hypersensitivity of the urethra, are also symptoms of the pelvic armor. Leukorrhea accompanied by development of protozoa from the vaginal epithelium (*Trichomonas vaginalis*) is frequently found. In the male, as a result of anorgonia of the pelvis, we find either the inability to achieve an erection or apprehensive hyperexcitability resulting in premature ejaculation. In the female, we find complete vaginal anesthesia or spasm of the muscles of the vaginal opening.

There is a specific *"pelvic anxiety"* and a specific *"pelvic rage."* The pelvic armor is the same as the shoulder armor, inasmuch as it, too, holds bound in it impulses of rage as well as anxiety. Orgastic impotence produces *secondary impulses which achieve sexual gratification by force.* No matter how much in keeping with the biological pleasure principle the impulses of the act of love may commence, the result is anything but pleasurable: *since the armor does not permit the development of involuntary movements, i.e., does not permit convulsions to pass through this segment, the pleasure sensations are inevitably transformed into impulses of rage.* The result is a torturous feeling of *"having to get through,"* which cannot be called anything but sadistic. In the pelvis, as everywhere else in the province of the living organism, *inhibited pleasure is transformed into rage, and inhibited rage is transformed into muscular spasms.* This can be easily confirmed clinically. No matter how far the loosening of the pelvic armor has advanced, no matter how mobile the pelvis has become, the fact remains: *pleasure sensations in the pelvis cannot appear as long as the rage has not been liberated from the pelvic muscles.*

In the pelvis, as in all other armor segments, there is "beating" or "piercing" by means of strong forward-thrusting pelvic movements. The overt expression of this movement is unequivocal and cannot be misunderstood. Besides the expression of rage, the expression of contempt is also clearly evident: contempt for the pelvis and all its organs, contempt for the sexual act and especially contempt for the partner with whom the act is carried out. On the basis of wide clinical experiences, I contend that it is a matter of love in only a few cases when man and woman in our civilization engage in the sexual act. The rage which usurps the initial love impulses, hate, and sadistic emotion are all part and parcel of modern man's contempt for sex. I am not speaking of the clear cases in which the sexual act is performed for profit or subsistence. I am speaking of the majority of people of all social strata. It is on the basis of these clinical findings that the Latin saying, *"Omne animal post coitum triste,"* has become a scientific axiom. There is only one error in this statement: man ascribes his own disappointment to the animal. The rage and the contempt which have so distorted the expressive movement of genital love are reflected in the widespread vulgar terms of abuse which are clustered around the word "fuck." In America, one finds the words "Knock me" written on the sidewalks—their meaning is clear. I gave a thorough description of these findings in Volume I of my book *The Discovery of the Orgone.* Hence, it is not necessary for me to go into detail here.

4. THE EMOTIONAL EXPRESSION OF THE ORGASM REFLEX AND SEXUAL SUPERIMPOSITION

What is important for our main theme is the fact that the pelvic armor has an expression which is easily translated into word language and that the liberated emotions speak a clear language. But this holds true only for the *emotions of the armor. It does not hold true for the expressive movements which regularly become manifest after the dissolution of the anxiety and rage.* These movements consist in soft forward and upward movements of the pelvis clearly expressive of desire. It is as if the pelvic end wanted to arch forward in an extreme way. One thinks instinctively of the seesaw movements of the tail end of insects, e.g., of wasps and bees. The movement is illustrated with special clarity in the attitude of the tail end of dragonflies and butterflies in the sexual act. The basic form of this movement is as follows:

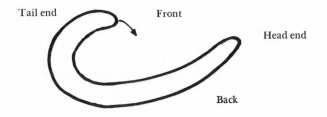

It continues the overt expression of surrender. Our subjective organ sensation tells us that this attitude of surrender is accompanied by *longing*. "Longing" for what? And "surrender" to what?

Word language expresses the aim of the longing and the function of the surrender as follows: as the organism develops the orgasm reflex, the yearning for "gratification" emerges clearly and unconquerably. The yearning for gratification is clearly focused upon the sexual act, upon sexual copulation. In the sexual act itself, one is "surrendered" to the sensation of pleasure; one "gives oneself to the partner." This we know from observation as well as from our subjective organ sensations.

Word language appears to respond unequivocally to this natural phenomenon. I say *"appears."* Since word language is only a translation of the language of expression of the living organism, we don't know whether the words "copulation" and "gratification" really express what the function of the orgasm reflex is. Apart from this, we have already pointed out that the expressive movement of the orgastic *convulsions* cannot be translated into word language. Let us venture a step further in doubting the ability of word language to make natural phenomena *immediately* intelligible. The reader will be nonplused by our next question. If he thinks about it for a moment, however, he will concede that words are often more likely to lead us *away from* rather than closer to a comprehension of processes. Our question is:

What is the origin of the extraordinary role of the genital drive? No one has any doubts about its elemental and instinctual force. No one is capable of escaping it; all living creatures are subject to it. Indeed, copulation and the biological functions related to it constitute that basic function of the living organism which guarantees the continuation of its existence. Copulation is a basic function of the "germ plasm," as conceived of by Weissman; it is immortal in the strict sense of the word. Homo sapiens has merely denied but in no way eliminated this powerful force of nature. We know the terrible human tragedies that have resulted from this denial.

The existence of the living organism is rooted in the SUPERIMPOSITION of two orgonotic systems of different sex. We have to admit that we have no answer to the simplest of all questions: *What is the origin of the function of the superimposition of two creatures of different sex? What is its importance? What is its "meaning"? Why is the perpetuation of living nature rooted precisely in this form of movement and not in another?*

The most general form of this movement of sexual superimposition is:

Sexual superimposition goes together with orgonotic lumination of the body cells and with the penetration and fusion of two orgonotic energy systems into one functional unit. The two orgone systems which have become *one* discharge their energy at the height of excitation (= lumination) in clonic convulsions. In this process, energetically highly charged substances, i.e., sperm cells, are ejaculated and, in turn, continue and fulfill the function of superimposition, penetration, fusion, and energy discharge.

Here, word language is not capable of explaining anything. The concepts which word language has formed about the process of sexual superimposition are themselves derivatives of the organ sensations which introduce, accompany, and follow the superimposition. "Longing," "urge," "copulation," "conjugation," "gratification," etc., are merely images of a natural process that words are not capable of making intelligible. To comprehend this natural process, we have to seek out other primary natural processes which have a more general validity than the sexual superimposition of the organism and are deeper than the organ sensations to which the concepts of word language correspond.

There can be no doubt that the orgasm reflex functions according to natural laws. It always becomes manifest in every successful treatment when the segmental armor which previously obstructed its course has been completely dissolved. Nor can there be any doubt that the sexual superimposition functions according to natural laws. It ensues inevitably when the orgasm reflex functions freely and no social obstacles stand in its way.

We shall have to make a wide detour and compile a large number of natural phenomena in order to comprehend the expressive language of the living organism in the orgasm reflex and in superimposition. The failure of word language in this case points to a function of nature *beyond* the realm of the living. We use the word "beyond" here not in the supernatural sense of the mystic but *in the sense of a functional relation between living and non-living nature.*

For the time being, we must conclude that word language is capable of describing only such phenomena of life as can be comprehended through the organ sensations and corresponding expressive movements, e.g., rage, pleasure, anxiety, vexation, disappointment, sorrow, surrender, etc. However, organ sensations and expressive movements are not the final criteria. At a certain point, the natural law of non-living substance must of necessity impinge upon the living organism and express itself in it. This must be correct if the living stems from the sphere of the non-living and sinks back into it. The organ sensations which correspond specifically to the living organism are capable of being translated into words. We cannot, on the other hand, put into words the expressive movements of the living organism which *do not belong specifically to the living but are projected into this sphere from the sphere of the non-living*. Since the living derives from the non-living and non-living material derives from cosmic energy, we are justified in concluding that *there are cosmic energy functions in the living*. Hence, it is possible that the untranslatable expressive movements of the orgasm reflex in the sexual superimposition represent the sought-for cosmic orgone functions.

I am well aware of the magnitude of this work hypothesis. But I see no way of avoiding it. It has been clinically established that orgastic longing, i.e., yearning for superimposition, always goes together with cosmic longing and cosmic sensations. The mystical ideas of innumerable religions, the belief in a Beyond, the doctrine of the transmigration of the soul, etc., derive, without exception, from cosmic longing; and, functionally, the cosmic yearning is anchored in the expressive movements of the orgasm reflex. *In the orgasm, the living organism is nothing but a part of pulsating nature.* The idea that man and animals in general are a "part of nature" is well known and widely disseminated. However, it is easier to use a phrase than to grasp, in a scientifically manageable way, wherein the essential functional identity of living substance and nature concretely exists. It is easy to say that the principle of a locomotive is functionally identical to that of a simple wheelbarrow. But a locomotive is essentially different from a wheelbarrow, and one must be able to state how the principle of the locomotive developed over the centuries from that of the wheelbarrow.

We see that the problem of the expressive language of the living organism is far more complex than one might suppose. Let us attempt to penetrate further and to seek out the similarities which link the more highly developed with the lesser developed forms of life.

The technique of orgone therapy has taught us that *a worm literally still functions in the human animal*. The segmental arrangement of the armor rings can have no other meaning. The dissolution of this segmental armor liberates expressive movements and plasmatic currents that are independent of the anatomical arrangement of nerves and muscles in vertebrates. They are much more in keeping with the peristaltic movements of an intestine, a worm, or a protozoon.

In spite of his development from phylogenetically older forms of life, man is still viewed predominantly as an *original* creature with no connection to the forms from which he descended. The segmental character and, therefore, the worm character of the biological core system are clearly preserved in the segments of the spine and the ganglia. However, this core system is segmental not only in a morphological, i.e., rigid, form. The orgone functions and the armor rings also represent *functional* segments, i.e., functions having a highly *contemporaneous* importance. They are not, as can be said of the vertebrae, remnants of a dead past in a living present. The orgone functions and the armor rings represent the most active and most important functional apparatus of the present, the core of all the biological functions of the human animal. The biologically important organ sensations and the emotions of pleasure, anxiety, and rage derive from the segmental functions of the human animal. In the same way, expansion and contraction as functions of pleasure and anxiety were present in the living organism from the amoeba all the way up to man. When one is happy, one carries one's head high; when one is afraid, one pulls it in, as a worm pulls in its front end.

If the amoeba and the worm in the human animal continue to operate as core elements of his emotional functioning, then we are justified in attempting to relate and thereby comprehend the basic biological reflex of the orgastic superimposition to the simplest plasmatic functions.

We stated above that the dissolving of the diaphragmatic block leads inevitably to the first orgastic convulsions of the body. We also stressed that the limbs of the body were merely continuations of the two segments of the chest and pelvis. *The largest and most important ganglion apparatus is located in the middle of the trunk, near the back.*

Now we want to risk a mental leap which, on first impression, will appear to be "unscientific," "unwarranted," indeed "insane." Afterwards, we can look back and see whether we have done any harm.

At one time or another, everyone has seen cats clutched by the fur of their backs and lifted into the air. The soft body of the cat appears to be doubled up, the head end is brought close to the pelvic end; head, fore and hind legs hang down limply, somewhat as follows:

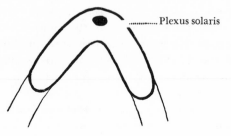

Naturally, we can imagine any animal in the same position, even man. There is, as is always the case when the body assumes a position, an emotional expression. It is not easy to read the overt expression of this particular position straight off. Observing it carefully for some time, we get the impression of a *jellyfish* with tentacles.

Biophysics will have to learn to read *forms of movement* from *body forms* and *forms of expression* from *forms of movement*. We shall have more to say about this later. Here, the similarity of the position with that of a jellyfish suffices. We can enlarge upon the analogy. The central nerve apparatus of the jellyfish is located in the middle of the back, as is the solar plexus in vertebrates. When the jellyfish moves, the ends of the body approach and move away from one another in rhythmic interchange. This is the heuristic substance of our mental leap: *the expressive movements in the orgasm reflex are, viewed in terms of identity of function, the same as those of a living and swimming jellyfish.*

In both cases, the ends of the body, i.e., the ends of the trunk, move toward one another in a rhythmic motion, as if they wanted to touch one another. When they are close together, we have the condition of contraction. When they are as far apart as they can be, we have the condition of expansion or relaxation of the orgonotic system. It is a very primitive form of *biological pulsation.* If this pulsation is accelerated, if it takes on a *clonic* form, we have the expressive movement of the orgastic convulsion.

The expulsion of spawn in fish and semen in animals is connected with this plasmatic convulsion of the body as a whole. The orgastic convulsion is accompanied by a high degree of excitation, which we experience as the pleasure of the "climax." In short, the expressive movement of the orgasm reflex represents a highly important, *contemporary* mobilization of a biological form of movement which goes as far back as the jellyfish stage. I append a diagram illustrating the bell shape and the jellyfish form of movement:

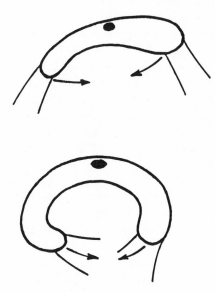

Upon close examination, the functional identity between the movement of the jellyfish and orgastic convulsion turns out to be far less strange than one originally supposed. In view of the fact that, in the segmental arrangement of the armor rings and in the sphere of the emotions, the worm continues to function in man, there is nothing very special about the fact that the jellyfish function is expressed in the convulsion of the body as a whole. We shall have to learn to accept the idea that we are not dealing here with atavistic remnants of our phylogenetic past but with *con-*

temporary, bio-energetically important functions in the highly developed organism. The most primitive and the most advanced plasmatic functions exist side by side and function as if they were connected to one another. The development of more complicated functions in the organism (functions which we call "higher") has no effect upon the existence and function of the "jellyfish in man." It is precisely this jellyfish in man that represents his unity with the less developed animal world. Just as Darwin's theory deduces man's descent from the lower vertebrates on the basis of man's morphology, orgone biophysics traces man's *emotional* functions much further back to the forms of movement of the mollusks and the protozoa.

The functional identity of man's life functions with those of primitive organic forms of movement reaches far back beyond the jellyfish.

Thus, what we call "nature in man" can be translated from the sphere of mystic or poetic fantasy into the concrete, objective, and practical language of natural science. We are dealing here not with metaphoric or analogous relations, still less with sentimental perceptions; we are dealing with tangible, visible, and controllable processes of the living organism.

CHAPTER XV

THE SCHIZOPHRENIC SPLIT[1]

1. THE "DEVIL" IN THE SCHIZOPHRENIC PROCESS

The idea of the "devil" is a true expression of the *distortion* of nature in man. No other human experience lends itself as well as the *schizophrenic* experience to the study of the "devil." The schizophrenic world in its purest form is a mixture of mysticism and emotional inferno, of penetrating though distorted vision, of God and devil, of perverse sex and murderous morals, of sanity to the highest degree of genius and insanity to its deepest depth, welded into a single horrible experience. I have in mind here the schizophrenic process which in classical psychiatry is called "dementia paranoides" or "praecox," not the so-called "catatonic stupor" or the "hebephrenic" process. Whereas the catatonic is typically characterized by total withdrawal from reality and total muscular armoring; whereas the hebephrenic process consists mainly in a slow torpid deterioration of biophysical functioning, the initial phases of paranoid schizophrenia, especially in puberty, are characterized by bizarre ideas, mystical experiences, ideas of persecution and hallucinations, loss of the power of rational association, loss of the factual meaning of words, and, basically, by a slow disintegration of organismal, i.e., unitary, functioning.

I shall limit myself to those processes in the schizophrenic which have a bearing on our main line of thought: the "devil" as the representative of perverted nature in man. These include the realm of the secondary, perverse, and antisocial drives rarely manifest in well-armored neurotics; the realm of primary biophysical sensations, plasmatic streamings, and experiences derived from contact with cosmic functions, experiences which are almost completely

[1] Conceived, 1940–48. Written in English by the author, August-September 1948.

blocked off in the so-called normal human being; and finally the ideas of persecution as experienced by a sick though most sensitive biosystem.

The schizophrenic world mingles in one experience what is kept painstakingly separate in *homo normalis*. The "well-adjusted" *homo normalis* is composed of exactly the same type of experiences as the schizophrenic. Depth psychiatry leaves no doubt about this. *Homo normalis* differs from the schizophrenic only in that these functions are differently arranged. He is a well-adjusted, "socially minded" merchant or clerk during the day; he is orderly on the surface. He lives out his secondary, perverse drives when he leaves home and office to visit some faraway city and indulges in occasional orgies of sadism or promiscuity. This is his "middle-layer" existence, cleanly and sharply separated from the superficial veneer. He believes in the existence of a personal supernatural power and its opposite, the devil and hell, and in a third group of experiences which is again cleanly and sharply delineated from the two others. These three basic groups do not mingle with one another. *Homo normalis* does not believe in God when he does some tricky business, a fact which is reprimanded as "sinful" by the priests in Sunday sermons. *Homo normalis* does not believe in the devil when he promotes some cause of science; he has no perversions when he is the supporter of his family; and he forgets his wife and children when he lets the devil go free in a brothel.

There are psychiatrists who deny the truth of these facts. There are other psychiatrists who do not deny them but who say that "this is as it should be," that this type of clean separation of the devilish inferno from the social veneer is only to the good, and that it makes for security in social functioning. But the true believer in the true Jesus might object to this. He might say that the realm of the devil should be extinguished, not shut off *here* only to be opened up *there*. To this, another ethical mind might object that true virtue is shown not by the absence of vice but by resisting the temptations of the devil.

I do not wish to participate in this argument. I believe that, again *within* this framework of thinking and living, each side may point to some truth. We want to stay outside this vicious circle in order to understand the devil as he appears in the daily life and in the world of the schizophrenic.

The fact is that the schizophrenic is, on the average, much more honest than *homo normalis,* if one accepts directness of expression as an indication of honesty. Every good psychiatrist knows that the schizophrenic is embarrassingly honest. He is also what is commonly called "deep," i.e., in contact with happenings. The schizoid person sees through hypocrisy and does not hide the fact. He has an excellent grasp of emotional realities, in sharp contradistinction to *homo normalis.* I am stressing these schizophrenic characteristics in order to make comprehensible why *homo normalis* hates the schizoid mind so much.

The objective validity of this superiority of schizoid judgment manifests itself quite practically. When we wish to obtain the truth about social facts, we study Ibsen or Nietzsche, both of whom went "crazy," and not the writings of some well-adjusted diplomat or the resolutions of the Communist Party congresses. We find the wavy character and blueness of orgone energy in van Gogh's marvelous paintings, not in the works of any of his well-adjusted contemporaries. We find the essential characteristics of the genital character in Gauguin's pictures, not in any pictures by *homo normalis.* Both van Gogh and Gauguin ended as psychotics. And when we wish to learn something about human emotions and deep human experiences, we resort as biopsychiatrists to the schizophrenic, not to *homo normalis.* This is so because the schizophrenic tells us frankly what he thinks and how he feels, whereas *homo normalis* tells us nothing at all and keeps us digging for years before he feels ready to show his inner structure. Therefore, my statement that the schizophrenic is more honest than *homo normalis* seems quite correct.

This appears to be a sad state of affairs. It should be the other way around. If *homo normalis* is actually as normal as he claims to be; if he claims that self-realization and truth are the greatest goals of good individual and social living, then he should be much more able and willing to reveal himself to himself and his doctor than the "crazy man." There must be something basically wrong with the structure of *homo normalis* if truth is so hard to get out of him. To declare, as the well-adjusted psychoanalysts do, that this is as it should be, that *homo normalis* could not otherwise withstand the impact of all his emotions amounts to complete resignation regarding the improvement of the human lot. We cannot base improvement of conditions on broader knowledge of man's soul and simultaneously defend his reluctance to reveal himself. Either we keep broadening the scope of our knowledge of man and condemn the general evasive attitude of *homo normalis, or* we defend this attitude and give up the task of understanding the mind of man. There is no other alternative.

In order to understand *homo normalis* and his opposite, the schizoid character, we must put ourselves outside the framework of thinking of both. *Homo normalis* blocks off entirely the perception of basic orgonotic functioning by means of rigid armoring; in the schizophrenic, on the other hand, the armoring actually breaks down and thus the biosystem is flooded with deep experiences from the biophysical core with which it cannot cope. Understandably, therefore, armored *homo normalis* develops anxiety when he feels threatened by the findings of orgonomy, whereas the schizoid character understands them instantly and easily, and feels drawn to them. For the same reason, the mystic, who is structurally close to the schizoid character, usually comprehends orgonomic facts, although only as in a mirror, whereas the rigid mechanist looks with arrogant disdain on all scientific dealings in the realm of the emotions and calls them "unscientific."

I suggest we study the relevant details of these important human functions by means of a concrete case of paranoid schizophrenia. This will convey a picture of the devil's realm much better than would any merely theoretical abstraction of psychiatric clinical experience.

The experimental world of the schizophrenic is boundless and so rich in variations that we must limit ourselves to those details which have a bearing on our main subject: how does the schizophrenic experience his biophysical core? Why does his ego break down in such a typical manner?

I am going to present the case history of a paranoid schizophrenic. The clinical psychiatrist will understand that I have to disguise the case in such a way that the patient's identity is protected and the typical disease mechanisms nevertheless emerge clearly.

This was the first case of schizophrenia I had ever treated experimentally with orgone therapy. I approached this case with some general theoretical assumptions, which were derived from my previous experiences with schizophrenics, such as the following:

1. The psychoanalytic arrangement of mental functions according to the three great realms of the ego, the superego, and the id has to be sharply distinguished from the *biophysical* arrangement of the functions of the total organism according to the functional realms of *bio-energetic core* (plasma system), *periphery* (skin surface), and *orgone energy field* beyond the body surface. These two theoretical structures describe different realms of nature in a different manner. Neither is applicable to the other realm of organismic functioning. There is only *one* meeting point of the two theoretical schemata, i.e., the *"id"* of psychoanalytic theory, where the realm of psychology ends and that of biophysics *beyond* psychology begins.

2. The most effective therapeutic approach to any emotional (= biophysical) disease is, if at all possible or indicated, the *withdrawal of bio-energy from the biopathic symptoms*. In order to destroy psychoneurotic or psychotic symptoms it is unnecessary and even harmful to delve into all details of the countless pathological ramifications; instead, opening up the core of the biosystem and establishing a balanced energy economy will automatically make the symptoms disappear, since, seen energetically, they are results of a disorderly energy metabolism in the biosystem.

3. Great danger arises in neurotics as well as in psychotics when the armor begins to dissolve. Utmost caution and medical skill are required to guide this process. The practice of medical orgone therapy is therefore restricted to well-trained physicians. We know our responsibilities better than anyone else and we do not have to be reminded of them by people who know little about orgonomy.

I knew well beforehand that the patient could or even would break down when her armoring dissolved completely. But the chance that she would stand the procedure was good enough to warrant the experiment. The patient had been in mental institutions several times over long periods of years. The diagnosis was "schizophrenia" and according to the reports, the patient was in the process of deterioration. The eventual final breakdown was inevitable; therefore, the risk taken in this case was not too great and the outlook was promising enough to satisfy the conscience of the experimenting physician.

The patient, a thirty-two-year-old Irish girl, had been brought to me by her relatives, who had heard about my new medical approach to the biopathies. I informed them of the great danger of precipitating a breakdown. They were ready to take the risk and to sign an affidavit to this effect. I also warned them of the risk of a sudden outbreak of destructiveness. Since I was well acquainted with the manifestations preceding a destructive attack, I felt sure that I would sense the danger in time. Therefore, I undertook the experiment outside the institution under the strict condition that a nurse or a relative should always be around the patient and that at the first sign of unrest and destructiveness the patient should be committed to the institution. A further condition was that the patient, who at the time was on parole, should see the parole physician regularly and that all arrangements should be made with the institution, where the patient had been before, for instant commitment in case of a breakdown. I also kept in touch with the psychiatrist in charge of the case at the institution by mail, and secured his cooperation.

Such precautions are indispensable if one wants to treat a schizophrenic outside an institution. One would prefer to rely on an institution which conducts experimental orgone therapy within its walls. But, unfortunately, mental institutions—with very few exceptions—are not inclined to bother with new, hopeful medical efforts to treat schizophrenia. Shock therapy is too readily available to dull schizophrenic activities, and there are too many psychotics to be taken care of by too few physicians. There is no time for extensive and deep-reaching scientific investigation. I understand this attitude, though I cannot condone it. A few cases of schizophrenia, well understood instead of "shocked," would, in the long run, save society countless millions of dollars. It seems too much to expect such foresight. It is known that mental institutions are, in reality, jails for psychotics, with little medical care, scarce funds, and, in most of them, no research at all. Moreover, some medical administrators are reluctant to consider any serious attempt to improve the condition of these patients. Sometimes they even meet such medical endeavors with great hostility.

This short description of the *social* situation may suffice to explain both my precautions and my willingness to take the risk. I knew the danger well, but the possible future reward seemed great. And indeed I was not disappointed. This patient, who had taken refuge in a mental institution for many years and who was already deteriorating at the time I accepted her for the experiment, has remained out of the institution for more than six years since the treatment. She resumed her profession; the process of deterioration was stopped. The patient became social in many ways.

I cannot predict whether this situation will last; I hope it will. The scientific and medical reward was great: *orgone therapy can be applied successfully in certain cases of schizophrenia where all other methods fail.* The result justified the risk. Furthermore, orgonomic theory was confirmed in some of its basic assumptions and was adjusted in others. Many entirely new facts about basic functioning in the biosystem of man were secured, and for the first time in the history of medicine and psychiatry, some central questions about the nature of paranoid mechanisms in schizophrenia were answered.

I shall describe the therapeutic experiment as it developed over a period of three months from treatment to treatment. I took notes carefully on the most essential details immediately after each session, and I kept a special record of the general line of development in order to find, if possible, some consistency or law in this development. The case itself offers nothing new in manifestations or symptomatology of the schizophrenic psychosis. What is new, however, is the response to orgone-therapeutic measures. It revealed some hitherto unknown connections between known schizoid functions and it brought to light some new functions in the depth of the biosystem which are of the greatest importance for the understanding of human biology in general.

The appearance of the patient

The first impression was not that of a schizophrenic. She spoke about her symptoms and experiences in a coherent, orderly manner. One felt great embarrassment in the background of her behavior; she spoke in an artificially eager manner. She seemed very intelligent and gave penetrating answers to most difficult questions; she knew the psychiatric language in an unusually clear way. She said that she had longed to meet a psychiatrist who would understand her inner emotions, but the psychiatrists always thought she was "crazy." Her eyes had the typical faraway, slightly veiled look of the schizophrenic character. At times she became confused, but regained her clarity easily. As the conversation proceeded, one could clearly discern certain subjects which she tried to evade. When asked whether she knew of any queer or unusual experiences, her eyes became "dark" and she said: "I am in contact with some powerful forces, but they are not here now."

The subject was clearly charged with emotion, and we did not delve into it any further. It became clear, furthermore, that she "dissimulated" and disguised her situation. She declared herself willing to undergo the experiment of orgone therapy. She had read the literature and thought that I was right.

First session

I restricted the work to an orientation on her armoring and character defenses. Her mannerisms were stronger than they had been during the initial meeting. She understood the principle of orgone therapy very well. She had known for years that most people were armored and therefore did not understand the inner life of the schizophrenic "who feels and knows everything." I tried to find out more about the "forces," but she refused to talk about them. The forces had, she said, nothing whatsoever to do with her own inner urges. She had excellent contact with the issues of the discussion.

She seemed *not to breathe at all*. On physical examination her chest appeared soft, *not rigid* as in cases of compulsion neurosis. This softness and mobility of the chest were later found in other initial schizophrenics. It should be further investigated whether and to what extent the lack of armoring in the chest is or is not a characteristic of the schizophrenic biopathy.[2]

The softness of her chest would have appeared normal if it had not been accompanied *by lack of respiration*. Respiration

---

[2] This assumption gained some support through the examinations of schizophrenics by Dr. Elsworth Baker at the Marlboro State Hospital in New Jersey.

was so shallow that it seemed altogether absent. When I asked the patient to inhale and exhale audibly, she refused; it was later shown that she was *unable* to do it. She seemed to stop the respiration somewhere in the cervical segments.

She became increasingly restless, looked anxiously at the walls and along the ceiling. "There are some shadows," she said. Suddenly she made the sign of a cross over her chest with her hands. "I am dedicated; the forces come to me; I can call them and make them come; the forces love me. . . ."

I asked her whether the "forces" had ever incited her to commit murder. She would have to answer this question very soon, I said. For if the experiment was to be conducted safely, we had to know everything about the "forces." I asked her whether she would promise to tell me immediately when the "forces" wanted her to do dangerous things to herself or to other people. She said, with deep sincerity, that she would tell me immediately. She told me that sometimes the "forces" told her to commit murder. Once she had suddenly felt as if she *had to* push a woman off a station platform.

She had scarcely finished this sentence when she became quite absent-minded; she did not listen to my questions and appeared completely dissociated. She was murmuring incoherently and unintelligibly. I could only discern the words: ". . . The forces betrayed . . . what did I say. . . ."

I knew from her relatives that she hated her mother bitterly and that at the same time she was strongly dependent on her. The ideas of "murder," "menstruation," and "mother" were closely linked. The urge to murder was also somehow connected with the experience of the "forces" or betraying the "forces."

The patient recuperated after a while and regained her composure.

Second through fifth sessions

During the following four therapeutic sessions, I tried cautiously to approach her dysfunction of respiration. The problem was not, as in the armored neurotic, to break down the armoring of the chest. *There seemed to be no armor.* The problem was how to make her draw in and expel air through the larynx. She began to struggle severely whenever I tried to bring about full respiration.

I had the impression that the function of respiration was not stopped any by immobility due to armoring, but *was inhibited as if by a strong, conscious effort.* I also thought that her organism suffered severely from this effort and that she did not feel the effort.

She responded with severe irritation to every attempt on my part to induce respiration. The typical armored neurotic would have appeared untouched or he would have smiled maliciously at my efforts. Not so our schizophrenic. She tried to cooperate intelligently but became panicky whenever I came close to succeeding. Fear of the "forces" overwhelmed her with anxiety; she felt them coming close and being all around her, on the walls, under the sofa, etc. She told me now that this same anxiety had driven her to me as a physician in whom she could have confidence. She had understood from my books that I would know what she was talking about.

I gave up any further attempts to make her breathe whenever the anxiety set in. She was told that this was one of her major pathological disturbances, that we would have to overcome it; that she would have to help me to do so; and that overcoming this disturbance would relieve her to a great extent. She promised to help me; she felt sure that I was right. She had known it for a long time.

I was able to form the following opinion of the situation:

Our patient did not shut off or was not able to shut off completely the sensation of plasmatic currents, as the rigidly armored neurotic does. She felt the orgonotic streamings in her body "very close by," and she fought them by not permitting the passage of air to and from the lungs. Whether she had ever actually and fully experienced the body streamings, I could not tell and she did not know. She had only experienced the "oncoming" of "forces," but she *did not feel the "forces" as her own.* She was terror-stricken when she felt the "forces"; at the same time she felt "dedicated to them," dedicated to "a mission." She was reluctant to say what kind of mission it was.

It is an essential rule in working with schizophrenics (and also with non-psychotics, for that matter) to give the patient the full understanding that one takes his complaints seriously, that one does *not* think them queer or "crazy" or "antisocial" or "immoral."

One gets nowhere if the patient does not have or does not develop *absolute* confidence in his physician which allows him to feel that he is trusted basically and that his words and feelings are understood, however peculiar they may appear to the layman. One must show *genuine* understanding to the schizophrenic even if he threatens to kill the physician. This absolute requirement makes orgone-therapeutic treatment of psychotics inaccessible to the physician who is not emotionally equipped to do the job. The further report will corroborate this statement.

Sixth session

After about half an hour of careful, painstaking work on her cervical armoring, the first outburst of hate occurred. This first outburst was accompanied by quiet crying; at the same time she developed severe anxiety, tremor in her lips, shoulders, and also partially in her chest.

In such situations, where different kinds of emotions are intermingled, it is necessary to separate the emotions from one another. This can be done by promoting the most superficial emotion, the one which fights off the deeper emotion, and by "pushing back" the latter. Accordingly, I encouraged her crying, which blocked the rage, and after some tearful release of sorrow, I let her develop her rage by encouraging her to hit the couch. *This is a dangerous procedure if the patient, especially the schizophrenic, is not in perfect contact with the physician.* In order to secure this contact, one must explain to the patient that he must stop his rage action instantly when asked to do so. It is the task of the physician to decide when the point in emotional release is reached where the patient is in danger of getting out of control. Only skilled orgone therapists can accomplish this. I warn physicians who have not been trained in the technique of medical orgone therapy, and trained orgone therapists who do not have the necessary experience, against tackling schizophrenics. One cannot proceed in such cases without releasing the rage, and one cannot release the rage without much experience previously gained in less emotional situations.

Toward the end of the sixth session, the patient had released enough emotion to relax. She uttered astonishment that such relief was possible and expressed her thanks with tears in her eyes.

She realized now for the first time that her idea that "people looked at her" was of a delusionary nature (the rational element in the persecotary idea will be elaborated later). Communications flowed freely. She had fought against the "influences" of the "forces" as far back as she could remember. She realized that she held on to reality only with great effort; she had felt as though she were hanging over an abyss most of the time, especially during puberty. She always became confused when her fear of the "forces" met with her love for them. She confessed that it was in such moments of confusion that *murderous impulses* would surge up in her.

This seemed the proper moment to tell her fully about my worries concerning a possible uncontrolled breakthrough of destructiveness. She understood immediately what I meant. She agreed and assured me with a quite unschizophrenic look that she had had this worry for a long time. I told her then that I knew from experience that most schizophrenics in the initial phases of the disease have the same worry as to whether they will be able to fight off the upsurge of murderous destructiveness. She agreed that there was no other way of safeguarding herself against committing murder than the security of an institution. She realized, quite on her own, that it was in such emotional situations that she sought the safety of an institution. She felt safer inside, she said, because life there made no demands on her that she was unable to fulfill. She knew she would not commit murder when in the institution; but she also knew that life in the institution was bad for her. She felt that slow deterioration was inevitable because life within the walls of the institution made her dull or furious, according to the special situation she met. She understood the inmates fully and felt sympathy for them; at the same time she felt horror toward their kind of existence. In her lucid phases, she saw through the glib and superficial attitudes of so many psychiatrists toward the psychotic, their lack of understanding, the brutality of many of the procedures, the injustices so often committed, etc.; she had, in short, excellent insight when the "forces" were absent or were present "without making too strong demands on her."

As the therapeutic process progressed, one single question gained an overall importance: DO THE "FORCES" WHICH HAUNT HER AND WHICH SHE LOVES DEVOTEDLY REPRESENT HER BODY SENSATIONS

OF STREAMINGS OF PLEASURE? IF THIS IS THE CASE, WHY IS SHE AFRAID OF THEM? (IT IS CLEAR SHE IS *devoted* TO THEM.) WHAT KIND OF MECHANISM IN HER BODY BLOCKS THE STREAMINGS OF PLEASURE? HOW DO THE BLOCKED-OFF PLASMATIC STREAMINGS TURN INTO "EVIL" FORCES? WHAT IS THE CONNECTION BETWEEN THIS BLOCK AND THE SCHIZOPHRENIC PROCESS?

I began to direct my attention toward the functions which possibly would answer these questions. My impression was that the blocking mechanism was somehow connected with her cervical segment, especially with the peculiar respiratory disturbance: *no respiration in the presence of a soft chest.*

Seventh session

During the seventh session it became obvious that the partial breakthrough of rage that I had kept under control during the previous treatment had increased her physiological need for full respiration. This could be seen in her even more desperate attempts to *prevent* the air from passing fully through her throat, larynx, and trachea. I encouraged her to exhale fully and helped by softly pressing down on her chest. She gave in to expiration suddenly but went into a state of trance immediately afterwards. She did not respond to my calling her; her eyes were turned toward a corner of the ceiling in a staring manner; she seemed to be hallucinated. Her legs trembled severely and she had fascicular convulsions in the muscles of her shoulders for about thirty minutes.

I succeeded in bringing her out of her trance by pinching her hard enough to make her aware of the sensation of pain. Slowly she began to return to full consciousness. She was obviously confused; she tried to convince herself that she was awake by knocking at things. She grasped my hands, began to cry out, and said: "I want to come back, oh, I want to come back . . ." This lasted another ten minutes. Then she said: "I am not quite back yet . . . Where are you? . . . With the Lord . . . I asked him whether I should give in to the devil . . . that you are the devil . . ." In answer to my question, she said that she did not "see things" any more but had "some contact" (with the forces). She had felt the tremor in her legs and shoulders, she also had heard my voice, and yet she "felt far, far away." It was the first time that she could not "come back" quickly. "It lasted so long this time . . . Where are you? . . . Please let me hold your hands . . . I want to feel sure that I am here . . ."

Holding my hands, she looked around the room suspiciously, along the walls and at the ceiling. She felt exhausted and remained for more than an hour after the treatment to compose herself.

I told her to come back next day for further treatment, and to call me or to have me called as soon as she felt the need to talk to me.

Eighth session

After the experience of the previous day, she had felt very tired and had gone to bed as soon as she got home. She felt calm and safe now, her eyes were clear. I decided not to proceed further in breaking down her armor but only to bring her back to where she had been the previous day.

It is an important rule in disarmoring people to proceed slowly, step by step, and not to advance further into the biophysical depth unless one knows *exactly* what is going on and unless the patient has become *accustomed* to the situation which has already been reached. This is valid for all types of medical orgone therapy; it is especially necessary in the treatment of schizoid characters. If one neglects this strict rule, one will lose sight of the total process and will endanger the patient. Patients who feel better after partial breakthroughs often implore the physician to proceed faster, to see them more frequently. This should not be granted. When a certain breakthrough has been accomplished, the organism must be given time to organize and to assimilate the emotions which have broken through. The position from which we proceed further must be firmly established. A certain amount of ill-being due to the remainder of the armoring is necessary in order to proceed further in the proper manner. One has to guard especially against the mystical, religious-like expectation on the part of the patient that now he has been "freed," "redeemed," "liberated." It is true that the first few breaks through the solid armor are accompanied by feelings of great relief. This often disguises the true situation in the depth of the biophysical structure. Therefore, the rule should be to be cautious as long as the basic orgastic pleasure anxiety does not appear in an unequivocal manner. As long as this deep terror of spontaneous plasmatic contraction is not at the surface and has not been overcome, great caution is indicated.

In this eighth session, the patient was very cooperative. She had less anxiety, permitted the clonisms to occur much more easily and willingly; but it was clear that she still anxiously watched every bit of what was going on, that she was "on guard" not to lose hold of herself, and that she had to fight hard not to run away again into a state of trance.

One should never proceed without great care as long as the basic distrust has not come forth which is to be expected in every single case. The schizophrenic is far franker than the neurotic in showing this typical distrust. In neurotics, one must dig up the distrust from under the veneer of friendliness and politeness. Our patient asked me point blank: "Can I trust you? Oh, if only I could trust you . . . [Looking at me with great fear in her eyes] *Are you a German spy?*"

It was soon after the FBI had mistaken orgone research for German (or Russian?) spy activity and had taken me into custody (as an "enemy alien") at the entry of the United States into World War II. The fact that I was soon released unconditionally after a hearing did not matter much to the patient. What mattered was the fact that I had been suspected of subversive activities, and this, of course, was in harmony with the general attitude of neurotics as well as psychotics to distrust everything, especially their own inner feelings. Our patient wanted to be able to trust me because, as she said plainly, she needed my help in her fight against the "forces." I assured her that I was not a German or, for that matter, any other type of spy and never had been. Thereupon she said that everybody thinks only in terms of his own nature or character structure and that hence the FBI could not think of anything but spy activity when they could not understand what I was doing. I had to agree with this statement, and I found my liking of the schizoid mind again justified. Schizophrenics are able in their lucid periods to see through individual and social matters intelligently, as no other character type can. Later we shall see that this lucidity of intelligence in the schizophrenic is one of the major dangers which threaten his existence in present-day society.

The patient was scheduled for a parole visit the following day at the state hospital. I told her not to hide anything, but I also told her to be prepared for the parole physician's inability to understand everything she would explain to him. We had the good luck to deal with a psychiatrist who was not one of the brutal shock-therapy surgeons. The patient left this session quiet and completely orderly.

Summary after the eighth session

1. The patient came with a remainder of a sharp sense of reality to which she held on desperately in order not to break down completely.

2. The patient sought my help because she felt that I understood the "forces" and had "contact" with them.

3. She thought she was better than the rest of the world because of her contact with the "forces." Her criticism of the world of *homo normalis* was correct, nearly perfect and rational in accordance with her contact with the "forces," whatever they represented.

4. Her armoring differed from the armoring in a simple neurotic biopathy in that it was not complete and only superficially constructed. Her chest was mobile, but she did not breathe fully. Because of the weakness of her armoring, she felt as though she were hanging only by a thread above an abyss. "Beyond" were the "forces," which were *"devilish"* and *"attractive"* at the same time.

5. The melting sensations of orgonotic streamings in her body had a close connection with her idea of "forces," but these sensations were projected upon walls and ceilings. Her schizophrenic fear of breaking down was somehow dependent on her contact with the "forces."

6. The perception of the inner "forces" at the walls and the ceiling constituted the main riddle. The word "projection" obviously did not explain anything.

2. THE "FORCES"

The patient knew the "forces" well. She described them in detail. Some characteristics of the "forces" were the same as those ascribed to an omnipotent Being = *God;* others were those ascribed to the devil—evil, cunning, sly and maliciously tempting.

The first group of characteristics made the patient feel safe and protected and therefore "devoted" to the "forces"; in regard to the second group of characteristics, the patient behaved as if she had to be protected against the "forces," their evil intentions and temptations, such as murder. This ambiguity in the nature of the "forces" became quite clear as the work proceeded.

My assumption at that stage of the work was the following: if the "forces" represented the GOOD and the EVIL in the same emotional formation, then it was necessary to assume that the split into two diametrically opposite kinds of experiences was due to TWO DIAMETRICALLY OPPOSITE SITUATIONS IN HER CHARACTER STRUCTURE which were mutually exclusive and incompatible. The schizophrenic split of the personality had to be ascribed to this incompatibility; each of the two opposite emotional structures would alternately take hold of the organismic functioning. In contradistinction to the schizophrenic structure, the structure of *homo normalis* keeps one or the other of the contradictory structures continually in a state of repression. Thus, in *homo normalis,* the split of the personality is hidden. The common functioning principle of both GOD and DEVIL is the *basic biophysical functioning of the organism,* the *"biological core,"* whose most significant manifestation is the plasmatic current and its subjective perception as a melting sensation of love, as anxiety or hate. All this had to be confirmed by further developments in this case.

Ninth session

The patient came to the ninth session full of joy and perfectly coordinated. She had visited the parole psychiatrist the day before. He had told her that he knew me to be "brilliant." She had explained to him my method of therapy as one of "letting off steam." The institutional psychiatrist had encouraged her to go on with the therapy. His attitude must have meant a support of her own hopes, since she had doubted my honesty previously ("Are you a German spy?").

Her respiration was *physiologically* nearly complete that day; her eyes were clear, not "veiled" as usual. She reported that she had had the urge to satisfy herself genitally. The inexperienced physician would have triumphed about the "success." But I knew that great danger was just ahead of us.

A sick organism can take a slight increase in energy functioning easily and enjoys this well-being very much, more than the healthy organism does, because of the great difference between the usual state of tension and the slight release of tension after a partial disarmoring. But the bio-energetic system continues to increase its energy level unless periodic releases of energy take place. And the only way of *full* release of built-up bio-energy is, as we well know, that of full orgastic convulsions during the natural process of mating. The problem of mental hygiene would not be as tough as it is if nature had not made the total orgastic convulsion entirely dependent on the absence of chronic body armoring. We are, as natural scientists and physicians, not responsible for this situation; we have only found and described it.

The patient herself was well aware of the danger ahead, far more than a simple neurotic would be. She told me that the "forces" had not been around lately, but they "could and would surely come back, malicious as they are."

She asked me whether I would abandon her if the "forces" came back. She wanted to know what exactly was the mechanism of orgone-therapeutic cure. Her questions were very intelligent and to the point. She inquired whether she would have to resign from her present "superior" position in the world, and whether she could become a useful member of society.

These questions appear peculiar to one who does not know what this case revealed in such an unequivocal manner. The schizoid character has a far better contact with and insight into the functions of nature and society than *homo normalis.* This imbues him with a rational feeling of superiority to the average *homo normalis,* who lacks such insight. It is logical, then, that in order to become a "useful member of society," i.e., a *homo normalis,* she would have to lose some of her insights and with them her superiority.

Such feelings of superiority contain a great deal of rational truth. The schizoid character is, on the average, really superior to the average *homo normalis* in intelligence, just as is the "criminal character." But this intelligence is impractical because of the deep-seated split. It is unable to perform lasting, rational biological activities, as in the case of what is called "genius."

I took this opportunity to brace her against future dangers. I told her that she had experienced only a first relief but that she would become frightened to a dangerous degree when her "forces" emerged fully from the depth. She understood and promised to keep close contact with me during the coming procedures.

The events I am going to describe now would appear utterly incredible to anyone who did not try to understand this case (and any other, for that matter) from the beginning in terms of the natural functions of *bio-energy* and its blocking in the *bio-pathies*. These events would appear to him just as other examples of "crazy reactions," "unintelligible," "dangerous," "antisocial," as good reasons for commitment of the patient to a lunatic asylum. I agree that what was to come *was* dangerous, antisocial, a good reason for commitment; but I cannot agree that it was unintelligible or that it was any more "crazy" than the deeds, or rather misdeeds, of our dictators or warmakers, who are not committed to institutions, but, on the contrary, are worshipped and honored by masses of *homines normales*. Therefore, I cannot become excited about the far lesser "craziness" in the schizophrenic. To put it bluntly, if worse comes to worst, he kills himself or he threatens to kill somebody else, but he never drives millions of innocent people from their homes for the "honor of the fatherland"; he does not demand at the point of a gun that millions be sacrificed for his impotent political ideas.

Therefore, let us be reasonable; let us abandon our false righteousness. There must be a potent reason why the schizophrenic is treated so cruelly and the cruel *homo normalis* is honored so crazily all over this planet.

Tenth session

The attitude just described saved this particular case. It could, I firmly believe, save thousands of lives which are rotting away innocently in obsolete mental institutions due to the typical evasiveness of *homo normalis* and his cruelty as applied in irresponsible, universal, and indiscriminate "shock therapy."

The patient had felt perfectly at ease during the day. But when she undressed, I saw the figure of *a cross*, cut into the skin of her chest at the sternum, about 6 cm. long and 4 cm. across. She had done it the previous evening "quite without any conscious motive." She *"just had to"* do it. She now felt highly "pent-up." "I must let off some steam or I am going to burst."

It was immediately obvious (to the well-trained orgone therapist) that her cervical segment was severely contracted, pale, and immobile. Severe rage was visible in her face, which appeared nearly blue, cyanotic. It took about ten minutes to release this severe cervical block. I succeeded by letting her gag, until the gag reflex operated well, and by forced respiration. As soon as the block in the throat gave way, she began to cry silently. Repeated encouragement to cry *loudly* met with no success. We find this phenomenon very often in neurotic biopathies: the emotion of crying is too strong to be let out fully at once. Usually, there is severe rage held down by the emotion of crying. If the patient let go in crying fully and freely, he would feel that he had to commit murder.

Such armoring usually results from cruel punishment for quite innocent behavior in childhood. The mother hated the father; she wanted to murder him, to get rid of him; he was too strong for that, and the mother was too weak to do anything about it. So she punished the three- or four-year-old child for making noise or for dancing in the street or for some other quite innocent activity. The natural reaction on the part of the child is justified rage against such cruelty; but the child is afraid to show the rage and wants to cry instead; but crying, too, is "forbidden"; "a good boy and a good girl don't cry, they don't show their emotions." This is the type of much-vaunted "education" of small children in the twentieth century of culture and civilization at the beginning of the great "atomic age" . . . which "will either make humanity soar to heaven or go to hell . . . depending on . . ." . . . *What?* ON WHETHER THE HUMAN RACE WILL OR WILL NOT SUCCEED IN ERADICATING TO THE LAST VESTIGE SUCH CRIMINAL BEHAVIOR ON THE PART OF SICK MOTHERS AND FATHERS; ON WHETHER OUR PHYSICIANS AND EDUCATORS AND JOURNALISTS WILL OR WILL NOT MUSTER THE COURAGE TO TACKLE THIS SUPREMELY IMPORTANT PROBLEM AND WILL FINALLY SUCCEED IN NOT SUPPORTING IT, IN OVERCOMING THEIR ACADEMIC EVASIVENESS, ALOOFNESS, AND "OBJECTIVITY."

Our patient had suffered several decades of cruel monstrosities on the part of her nagging mother. She had developed the impulse to choke her mother in order to defend herself. Such impulses are very strong and cannot be fought off in any other way than by armoring against the welling-up of the murderous hate in the throat.

Quite spontaneously, the patient asked me *whether I would*

permit her to choke my throat. I confess that I felt, not embarrassed, but a bit frightened; however, I told her to go ahead and do it. The patient put her hands *very cautiously* around my throat and exerted a slight pressure; then her face cleared up and she sank back exhausted. Her respiration was full now. Her whole body trembled severely with every exhalation. The streamings and sensations seemed strong, to judge from the way she stretched her right leg in order to avert the full force of the emotions. From time to time, her body would become quite rigid in a position of opisthotonus and then relax again. Her face became alternately red with crying or blue with anger. This process lasted for about thirty minutes. I knew that now her psychotic ideas would emerge with full force. When a certain degree of emotional upheaval was reached, I asked her quietly to try to stop the reaction. She responded instantly with full cooperation and began slowly to calm down. I had held her hand in my palm all through the breakthrough.

In twenty-two years of psychiatric work with psychotics and so-called psychopaths, I had acquired a certain skill in handling such emotional situations. I claim that all psychiatrists should be skilled enough to handle them. But I also claim that nowadays few psychiatrists are equipped to do so and, therefore, I would most emphatically advise *against* repeating my experiment unless the proper skill has been acquired. I do not wish to be made responsible for a disaster that might happen in some psychiatrist's office because of his lack of training.

If we are to understand the schizophrenic world, we must never judge it from the standpoint of *homo normalis;* the sanity of the latter has itself come under sharp scrutiny. We must try instead to understand it when the schizophrenic expresses *rational* functions in a *distorted* manner. Therefore, it is necessary to judge him from *beyond* this "orderly" world of ours; *we must judge him from his own standpoint.* This is not easy. But if one penetrates the distortions, a wide vista opens up on a vast realm of human experience, rich in truth and beauty. It is the realm from which all the great deeds of genius emerge.

To continue with the patient: I asked her what was the meaning of the cross on her chest. I did not scold her nor did I threaten to commit her. This would not have achieved anything.

She rose, her whole body trembling, and held on to her throat. Then she said: "I don't want to be Jewish" (she was *not* of Jewish origin). Since every schizophrenic of whatever faith could have said this, I did not try to convince her that she was not Jewish; on the contrary, I took her words seriously. "Why not?" I asked. "The Jews crucified Jesus," she said. Thereupon she asked for a knife to cut a large cross into her *belly*.

The situation was not clear at once. After a while, it became clear that she was trying hard to go into the state of trance, but apparently did not succeed. After a while, she said: "I tried to get in touch with them [the forces] again . . . but . . . I cannot . . ." She began to cry. I asked her why. "Perhaps there are three reasons: (1) I fought them too strongly. (2) I did not make the cross deep enough. (3) They reject me because I am Jewish."

The exact connection between her biophysical status and these psychotic ideas was still not clear. It was possible that the system of delusions no longer worked as well as before; that she felt guilt toward the "forces" to whom her life was dedicated, and that accordingly she tried hard to make a self-sacrifice in order to regain the benevolence of the "forces." Such mechanisms are well known from so-called "normal" religious behavior. Here, too, the loss of contact with "God" will lead to greater sacrifice in order to regain His benevolence.

Did she identify herself with Jesus Christ?

She calmed down after a while and went home safely. Why did I not commit her to the institution after what had happened? I asked this question myself. The answer was this: I knew from long experience with such emotional situatons that any threat would only have increased the danger, and that, on the other hand, only perfectly genuine confidence in her, which she felt, would save the situation. Somehow I had great confidence in her. But the risk was great, too, of course. The danger of suicide was present, but that of destructiveness toward somebody else was not present. Clinically, she seemed close to a major change in her structure, as indicated by her inability to get in contact with the forces. This was an important gain to be further developed.

Eleventh session

She came back in good humor with bright eyes, but slightly manic. She spoke much and with great wit. Therapeutically, not much progress can be made when the patient feels too well. One has to dig up another piece of conflict and to increase the energy level sufficiently to proceed further. This is done by full respiration.

As soon as the patient started to yield to deeper respiration, she developed strong psychotic emotions again. She began to look around the room in her typical paranoid fashion. She became anxious, and her body began to quiver all over. Her eyes changed: appearing empty at first, they later sharply observed the red-hot coil of the electric heater. This went on for quite a while. She fought off anxiety and then she said: "A funny thought I had . . . THAT THIS HEAT AND THE SUN ARE ALSO FORCES; that they [the "real forces"] could think that I could prefer this *other* force [from the heater and the sun]."

I was flabbergasted. What deep thought, and how close to the truth! I assure the reader that at that time she knew nothing of the orgone phenomena and that I had not told her anything about them. The truth she touched upon by her remark was this: if it was true that her "forces" were distorted perceptions of her own bio-energy; if it is further true that organismic energy and sun energy are basically the same, then she had made a truly scientific statement, and a great one at that. Was her organism trying to regain health by turning away from the delusion about a reality to the reality proper? She obviously was fighting hard to widen the scope of her sense of reality. Replacement of the "forces" by *other, natural* forces seemed a logical step in this direction. Somehow the delusional forces had lost some power over her, as expressed in the following statement: "I also thought they could befuck themselves . . . Oh, what did I say . . ." Great anxiety overcame her instantly after having said this, as though she had called for the devil.

I ventured the following work hypothesis: the respiration had increased her bio-energy level. She had come closer to the natural forces, the "melting" sensations, within herself. If this was correct, the *delusion* of "forces" from "beyond" had lost some of its energy and thus had weakened. *She came closer to reality by coming closer to the real forces of life, the orgonotic sensations, within herself.* This was a major finding about the schizophrenic delusion: the delusion of "forces from beyond" is not merely a psychotic construction without a basis in reality; rather, it describes a deeply felt reality, although in a *distorted* manner. The further progress had to prove or disprove this assumption. It later proved it correct. Basically, this amounts to the fact that in their delusions the psychotics tell us important things about functions of nature. We must only learn to understand their language.

She had come very close to the meaning of her delusion without sinking fully into it. The function that was responsible for this success was her improved respiration. Strong clonisms developed during the rest of this session which she tolerated much better and with less anxiety. But her eyes became veiled whenever the orgonotic sensations became too strong for her.

I felt that she wanted to tell me something but that she did not trust me fully. I asked her whether my guess was right that she was in conflict over the "forces" and me; that she was *for* and at the same time *against* the "forces," and *for* as well as *against* me. She was afraid of the "forces" when she affirmed me too much, when she applied for my help against the "forces." She understood this instantly and perfectly well. In fact, she had had this thought herself.

The clonisms continued while we talked. She felt dizzy, and I asked her to stop the reactions of her organism. She did. In the end she told me quite spontaneously that she *had become seriously ill for the first time when the "forces" had told her to poison the whole family with gas.* She had in fact turned on the gas one evening but had turned it off again. Soon after she told me this, she began to murmur unintelligibly. It sounded like a mystical ritual to placate evil ghosts. She did not leave the room for about an hour. She stood rigidly on one spot and did not move. One had the impression of a cataleptic posture. She did not answer my repeated questions why she did not leave. Finally she said: "I cannot step over this spot."

During this session, the prospects of her therapy had become clear:

1. The more and better contact she made with her plasmatic, bio-energetic streaming sensations, the less the fear of the forces would be. This would also prove my contention that the *"forces" in schizophrenia are distorted perceptions of the basic orgonotic organ sensations.*

2. This contact with her body sensations would help to establish some degree of orgastic satisfaction, and this in turn would eliminate the energy stasis which operated at the core of her delusions.

3. The undistorted experiencing of her body sensations would enable her to identify the true nature of the forces and would thus slowly destroy the delusion.

Before this could be accomplished, the patient would have to pass through a series of dangerous situations. Delusions and catatonic reactions were to be expected with each breakthrough of strong orgonotic streamings in her body. She would perceive these sensations with terror; she would block them off by bodily rigidity, and the blocked-off plasmatic currents would be transformed into *destructive* impulses. Therefore, the "secondary" impulses, which derive from the blocking of the original, basic emotions, would have to be handled carefully and would have to be "let out" slowly, step by step. This danger would become especially great when the first spontaneous orgastic contractions of her organism began to occur.

Twelfth session

We had come very close to hopeful changes and with them to great dangers too. She came to this session with strong anxiety and excitement. She asked innumerable questions and fought hard and long against any attempt to dissolve her blocking in the throat, which was particularly strong that day. Her respiration was very shallow, and her face was quite pale and bluish.

She wanted a knife. I told her that I would give her a knife if she told me first what she needed it for. "I want to cut your stomach wide open . . ." While saying this, she pointed to *her own* stomach. I asked her why she wanted to cut open her stomach and mine. "It hurts here . . . you did not release enough steam yesterday . . ." Did she feel strong tension there? "Yes . . . yes . . . it's awful . . . also in the throat . . ."

I suddenly understood with perfect clarity why and in what emotional situations murders are committed by schizophrenics and schizoid types of "criminals": when the tension in the organs, especially in the diaphragmatic region and in the throat, becomes unbearably strong, the urge appears to cut one's own stomach or throat. The Japanese habit of hara-kiri, disguised as it is by ideological rationalization, is an extreme expression of such a bio-energetic situation. The murder occurs when the impulse is directed away from oneself toward somebody else. Just as a child easily develops a contraction in its own throat when it has the impulse to choke its mother's or father's throat, *so does the schizoid murderer cut somebody else's throat when his own choking sensation becomes unbearable.*

I succeeded in forcing the patient to take several breaths and to exhale fully three or four times. Then a spasm of the glottis occurred. Her face became blue, her whole body trembled, but finally the spasm gave way and autonomic movements of her chest and legs set in. She fought desperately against these movements, apparently without success. The close connection between the autonomic movements and the development of her delusion became quite clear now.

She turned her eyeballs upward and said in a desperate tone of voice: "Do you think I cannot make contact with them [the forces] any more? . . . Did you really do that to me? . . ."

She had lost contact with the "forces" through the contact which her self-perception had made with her own autonomic body functions.

I answered: "I am not concerned with your 'forces.' I know nothing about them. I am only concerned with bringing you into contact with your own body." If I had fought her idea of "forces" or had uttered personal opinions about them, she would have reacted antagonistically, since she felt devoted to them. My policy, therefore, was to leave the forces untouched and to work solely on the blocks in her organism which created the delusion of forces.

She said after a while: "I want to go to Bellevue [a psychiatric institution in New York] to search for the 'forces' . . . I must find them somewhere . . . They wanted me to be superior, better, not a brute . . ."

Here, in one neat grouping, we had before us the whole system of ideologies of *homo normalis* directed against natural body functions. The "forces" in the psychosis had a double function: one represented the primary body functions, especially the orgonotic, biosexual streaming sensations; the other represented the contempt of the body, the being "superior" to such "earthly" and "base" things as bodily urges. The delusion had thus brought into ONE two diametrically opposed functions of *homo normalis*. But seen from "beyond," from outside the world of *homo normalis*, this unity made good sense: it represented the *functional unity of superior goodness, of being god-like, and the basic natural bodily streamings.* This functional unity was projected in the form of the delusion of persecuting forces. Now, when the contact with her body sensations was made for the first time, she split this unity into the idea of "moral superiority" as against the "brutishness of the bodily urges."

These connections and interactions are rarely seen so clearly in simple neurotic biopathies. Here the "devil" is well separated from "God" and is kept apart safely and continuously.

She trembled severely all through this process. Alternately she gave in partially to the body sensations and movements, and then stiffened up again. The struggle was tremendous. Her face became spotty, as in shock. Her eyes were alternately clear and veiled. "I do not want to be an average human being." I asked her exactly what she meant. "A human being with brutal emotions." I explained to her the difference between primary drives and secondary antisocial drives, and how the former turned into the latter. She understood it well. Then she gave in fully and relaxed. The severe tension in the abdominal muscles disappeared. She felt relieved and rested quietly.

We have seen how the sweet, "melting" organ sensations, the most longed-for experience in the organism, are dreaded and fought off as "brutal flesh" in the sense of *homo normalis* and as evil "forces" or the "devil" in the psychosis.

I would like to stress this structural function of the armored human animal most emphatically. To the biopsychiatrist with long experience in orgone therapy, this dichotomy and ambivalence toward one's own organism appears as the crux of the misery of the human animal. It is the core of all human functions which are *deviations* from the natural law of living matter. It is the core of criminal behavior, psychotic processes, neurotic deadness, irrational thinking, of the general basic split into the world of God and the world of the devil in human intellectual existence. What is called God turns into the devil by exactly these distortions of living functions, i.e., by the "denial of God." In the schizophrenic, these natural functions as well as their distortions appear in quite an undisguised manner. One has only to learn to read the schizophrenic language.

The "high" represents the "low" and vice versa. The instincts became "low" because of the split in the structure. The originally "high," the "god-like," became unattainable and returns only as the "devil." "God" is right there within *homo normalis,* but he changed God into the devil; God became unreachable and has to be sought for—in vain. What a tragedy! Since nobody but the human animal himself has created his philosophies of life and his religions, it must be true that whatever dichotomies appear in ideologies and thinking stem from this structural split with its insoluble contradictions.

The painful dilemma between God and devil dissolves without pain or terror when one sees it from *beyond* the framework of mechanistic-mystical thinking, from the standpoint of *natural, biophysical* human functioning. This has been clearly demonstrated, but it needs further elaboration. We shall now return to the patient for further instruction.

I had had the impression during the last few sessions that the patient, as she emerged from the delusion, was facing one of the following two developments: she would either fall into stupor, due to sudden complete armoring against the plasmatic currents; or she would become neurotic before reaching a satisfactory degree of health. The real process followed *both* lines of reasoning, but in quite an unexpected manner.

Thirteenth session

She was reluctant to come that day. She only wanted to talk. The day before, after the treatment, everything was "unreal, as if a wall had been erected around all things and people . . . there were no emotions at all . . . How is it that, in such a state, I feel everything clearly and yet as though through a thin wall?"

I explained to her that she had discharged a great amount of energy; that, therefore, her worst symptoms were temporarily gone; but that her inner contactlessness was laid bare. She understood perfectly well that the lack of real contact in a certain layer of her structure made her feel things and people "as if through a wall." "Yes," she said, "I could not move freely; all movements are so slow; I could not raise my legs or walk faster than I did . . ."

Such disturbances cannot be understood unless one knows of the anorgonotic attacks which so often follow extreme emotional upheavals, in simple neurotic biopathies, also. It seems as if the organism, unused to strong emotions, becomes partially immobilized.

Her orgasm reflex was fuller and stronger that day. Her face was strongly flushed, with no cyanosis intervening; the clonisms occurred freely and were not met with much anxiety.

After a while she said: "Your eyes look like those of the Greeks . . . Have you some connection with the Greek gods? . . . Oh, you look like Jesus . . ."

I answered nothing and let her go on talking. "Oh, I must think so much . . . there are so many emotions, contradictions . . . What is a split personality?"

I explained to her that one feels as if split in two, and that one really is split when one feels exactly what is going on around one and yet feels walled in. She understood. Toward the end, she became anxious; sudden convulsions in the total body occurred several times. She asked me what was meant by the term "energy stasis." And then, continuing instantly, she asked why I was interested in her "forces."

I had the impression that *her organism began to connect the "forces" with the perception of her streamings*. It appeared as if her splendid intellect was helping to unite the delusion and the understanding of the delusion. This was in the direction of our efforts to overcome the split which *separated her organ sensations from her self-perception*. Seemingly unrelated was her statement: "I often look at blond Christian girls . . . I envy them . . ." "But you are a blond Christian girl yourself," I said. "Oh, no, I am a dark Jewess . . ."

Fourteenth session

She had felt well during the three days since the last treatment. The "forces" had not been there; she had not longed for them. She had gone to a movie with a girl friend; she had been to a museum and had taken a bicycle trip.

She looked well that day, but she was reluctant to yield to

deep respiration; she tensed her chest and shut off her respiration again. I could not understand this reaction. After much talking, she said: "I had the same feeling in the movie toward a girl friend which I had had before I went to the hospital the first time . . . I don't like you today . . ."

She armored strongly in the musculature of her thighs, especially in the deep adductor muscles. This type of armoring is well known to the experienced orgone therapist as a sign of strong but fought-off genital excitations. "The pressure on these muscles releases *nasty feelings* . . . perverse feelings . . ."

She had obviously developed some homosexual ideas against strong, natural genital impulses. She gave in partially to the sensations that day and continued to feel clear and happy.

Her relative, who had brought her to me originally, phoned and said that she was greatly improved. I knew, however, that the greatest danger was just ahead of us exactly because of this great improvement. Her organism, unaccustomed as it was to functioning on a high energy level, was not yet ready to take too much well-being and pleasure. Accordingly, I warned against too great optimism. My warning proved correct, as we shall soon see.

Fifteenth session

The well-trained and experienced orgone therapist becomes very cautious in handling the process of therapy just when great improvements develop too suddenly. As long as the *basic orgasm anxiety* has not appeared and has not been lived through, there is great danger of complete regression or, worse, of suicide in some severe cases. It was the first time that this danger had to be faced in a case of schizophrenia. Therefore, all necessary precautions were taken.

The patient came to this session with clear, happy eyes and was apparently perfectly sane and healthy. She asked me for advice about a diaphragm and matters of mental hygiene. But she fought hard against full respiration; she blocked in her throat and around her mouth. Slowly a scornful smile developed in her face; she understood what had happened. She yielded again and went very far in admitting the tremor; but her face became bluish-spotty, as in shock. Her eyes turned upward again; she gave the impression of a beginning strong withdrawal. She had quite obviously experienced some strong orgonotic sensations in her body. I asked her at this point whether she gained contact with her "forces." "Yes, nearly . . . ," was her answer. Now it also seemed clear to her that the *"forces" were identical with the orgonotic streaming sensations in her body*.

After the session she remained in the room for a very long time. I let her come at the end of my work day in order to give her more time if necessary. From my adjoining study I suddenly heard peculiar noises. When I reentered the room, the pillows and the mattress were strewn all over the floor, the heater was turned over with the heat on, the leg of one chair was put on an ashtray.

"The forces told me to do this . . ." she said calmly. I told her not to worry, but next time to tell me when the "forces" induced her to do such things. After all, these were my possessions, not those of the "forces." She said "Yes," in a dull and faraway manner.

Sixteenth session

Her action the previous day had pointed to very severe hate impulses against me. According to the old rule of character analysis, taken over into orgone therapy, one must not proceed unless the hateful attitudes have been cleared up first. Therefore, I did not proceed further physically but worked merely psychologically, by means of character analysis. I told her that she had felt neglected by me. Had she fantasied about living in my house? She had. Now she took revenge in a petty manner because she was very sensitive. She had received no love at all from her mother, only nagging all her life. She had withdrawn into a fantasy life, and there the "forces" had come in. She listened to my explanation with disdain in her face. I told her that she would have to overcome this attitude before I could proceed further. Otherwise I would have to send her away.

After a while she gave up her disdain and yielded. But her attitude was full of meaning and typical for such situations. It occurs regularly that the patient despises the therapist when the orgonotic streamings break through; this happens in all cases, including neurotics; is a quite typical reaction. It corresponds to the hate and disdain shown by impotent, armored individuals toward healthy people and genital sexuality; usually, anti-Semitic ideas occur at this point, in the Jew as well as in the non-Jew. The disdain usually centers around the idea that the therapist, who deals with natural genitality, *must* be a "sexual swine."

She accepted my explanations, but declared that she did not want to give up her "forces."

The whole situation seemed perfectly clear: her natural genitality threatened to overwhelm her and to demand gratification. Her organism could not stand the strong excitations. Together with the weakening of the schizophrenic split her impulsiveness, from which the split had once grown, began to increase. Therefore, the next task was:

a. *To open the energetic valve of the organism:* SELF-SATISFACTION.

b. *To brace her against breakdown* by a thorough working-through of her hate against me.

c. *To prevent,* if possible, *any attempt on her part to escape from the perception of her high-pitched organ sensations into delusions.*

3. THE REMOTE SCHIZOPHRENIC EXPRESSION IN THE EYES

It is well known that one can diagnose the presence of schizophrenia by careful observation of the expression in the eyes. Schizoid characters and fully developed schizophrenics have a typical *faraway* look of remoteness. The psychotic seems to look right through you with an absent-minded but deep look into far distances. This look is not there all the time. But when emotions well up or when serious subjects are touched upon in conversations, the eyes *"go off,"* as it were.

One can see the same expression in some truly great scientists and artists, for instance in Galileo and Beethoven. One could venture the assumption that the great creator in science or art is deeply engrossed in his inner creative forces; that he is and feels removed from petty, everyday noise in order to follow his creativeness more fully and ably. *Homo normalis* does not understand this remoteness and is apt to call it "crazy." He calls "psychotic" what is foreign to him, what threatens his mediocrity. The psychotic is also deeply engrossed in his inner life forces; he listens to them just as the man of genius does; the difference, however, is great: the genius produces out of this contact with his forces great, lasting accomplishments; the schizophrenic becomes enmeshed in them because he is *split* and afraid of them, and not united with his bio-energy, as is the creative human structure. But the expression of the *eyes* is deep in both cases, and not flat, empty, sadistic or dull as in neurotic characters who have no contact with their bio-energy at all.

I knew this symptom well, since I had worked in the psychiatric hospital in Vienna some twenty years before I met this case. But I knew nothing about its function in connection with the mechanism of delusion and disorientation. Our patient showed this peculiar symptom in an especially clear manner. When the "forces" came close, her eyes would become veiled, the expression would become one of looking into the far distance, and, in addition, the eyeballs would turn sharply upward when the "melting" organ sensations became very strong. I decided to concentrate my attention on this symptom, and, if possible, to remove it, since it seemed to be the main mechanism by means of which she "went off."

Seventeenth session

Entering the room, she asked: "Can I become a nurse again? My record is very bad . . ." She had never been a nurse. I answered that I did not know. At present she would have to find out why she turned her eyeballs upward whenever the forces took hold of her. In orgone therapy one talks little; one lets the patient take on the special attitude which he tries to avoid. Accordingly, I let her turn her eyeballs upward. She did it hesitatingly; but when she had reached a certain position with her eyeballs, she became afraid and said: "This is the place where I usually go off . . . I know it now . . ." I urged her to try it again. She tried, but became afraid. She said: "Our agreement was that we should not touch the forces . . . I don't want to give them up . . ."

I did not urge her any more that day. But *one* thought stuck in my mind and did not budge: *is it possible that the schizophrenic attack or process is locally anchored just as are other disease symptoms such as anorexia or a headache or cardiac anxiety? Is it the base of the brain, the region of the crossing of the optic nerve?*

Would it be reasonable to assume that schizophrenia is a true "brain disease," induced by some specific type of emotional upheaval, with a *local contraction of special parts of the brain due to severe anxiety?* Many symptoms in schizophrenia seemed to confirm the validity of this assumption: the typically schizophrenic look in the eyes, the degenerative processes in the brain found in old schizophrenics (they would be *secondary* structural changes in tissues due to misuse just as calcification of blood vessels is due to chronic, anxious contraction of the vascular system) ; the report of so many schizophrenics that they felt veiled or "flattened" on the forehead at the outbreak of the disease. It seemed important to pursue this chain of thoughts.

Eighteenth session

The patient came back feeling quite well. We worked on the expression of her eyes. I urged her to try again to "go off" and to make contact with the "forces" by turning her eyeballs upward, and to reproduce by will the empty, faraway look. She cooperated readily, but whenever she came close to a certain position and expression of her eyeballs she became anxious and stopped. We seemed to be following the right line. Suddenly and without any apparent reason, she said: "You are suggesting all that happens to me."

There was only one possible interpretation of this utterance: the deliberate turning of the eyeballs provoked her schizophrenic mechanism. Since I had urged her to do it, I was logically the one who was suggesting all that happened to her. This idea of being influenced by me emerged from a purely biophysical attitude. This bodily attitude obviously provoked the "beyond" in her self-perception and thus produced the idea of being influenced. This mechanism could possibly apply to many—if not all —cases of ideas of persecution.

I ventured the preliminary assumption *that the "going off" in the eyes was due to a local contraction of the nerve system at the base of the brain.* According to this assumption, this contraction had the same function as all other biopathic contractions: *to prevent too strong bodily streamings and sensations.* I had thus reached a first firm foundation for the orgonomic understanding of the schizophrenic process.

4. THE BREAKTHROUGH OF THE DEPERSONALIZATION AND FIRST UNDERSTANDING OF THE SCHIZOPHRENIC SPLIT

We must keep in mind that this orgone-therapeutic experiment in a schizophrenic case was not done on a psychological basis. On the contrary: all psychological manifestations of the schizophrenic process had to be understood in terms of deep *biophysical processes which underlie and determine the functions of the mind.* Our assumption is that the realm of the psyche is much narrower than the realm of biophysical functioning; that the psychological functions are merely functions of self-perception or the perception of objective, biophysical plasma functions. Thus, a schizophrenic will fall into a state of disorientation when his self-perception is overwhelmed by strong sensations of orgonotic plasma streamings; the healthy genital character will feel well, happy, and highly coordinated under the impact of orgonotic streaming.

Our approach to schizophrenia is a *biophysical,* and not a psychological one. We try to comprehend the psychological disturbances on the basis of the *plasmatic* dysfunctions; and we try to understand the *cosmic* fantasies of the schizophrenic in terms of the functions of a *cosmic* orgone energy which governs his organism, although he perceives his body energy in a psychotically distorted manner. Furthermore, we do not believe that the psychological interpretation of schizophrenic ideas can go beyond the meaning of words and historical events. It *cannot,* by any means, reach the purely physical and biophysical processes, since they function *beyond* the realm of ideas and words. This constitutes what is rightly called the "depth" of the schizophrenic world, in contradistinction to the superficial world of the neurotic.

Schizophrenia is not a psychological disease; it is a *biophysical* disease which also involves the psychic apparatus. In order to understand this process the knowledge of the functions of orgone energy is indispensable. The core of the problem is the disruption of the unitary, total orgone functioning and the subjective perception of this disruption. Certain schizophrenic symptoms, such as disorientation, the experience of "world collapse," loss of the power of association, the loss of the meaning of words, the withdrawal of interests, etc., are secondary reactions to a shattering of *basically organismic, biological* functions. Other symptoms, such as the faraway look, the trance, automatisms, flexibilitas cerea, catalepsy, slowdown of reaction, etc., are direct expressions of the biophysical disturbance and *have nothing to do with psychology*. The withdrawal of libido from the world is a *result* and not the cause of the disease. The general deterioration of the organism in later phases of the process is due to chronic shrinking of the vital apparatus, as in the cancer biopathy, though different in origin and function. The shrinking carcinomatous organism is not in conflict with social institutions, due to its resignation. The shrinking schizophrenic organism is full of conflicts with the social pattern to which it reacts with a specific split.

If we did not keep distinct these methods of approach, we would not obtain any practical results. We would become confused ourselves about the nature and functions of schizophrenia. It is necessary to give a résumé of these facts *before* continuing the study of our case. It will become quite apparent from the facts themselves that what is commonly called the "schizophrenic process" is a mixture of objective *biophysical* processes and the psychological perception of and reaction to these processes. Last but not least, a *third* element is involved which could not possibly have been known before the discovery of atmospheric orgone energy.

What is to follow now will appear utterly incredible. Therefore, I wish to assure the reader that I had not the faintest idea of the existence of such mechanisms. But since the treatment of this case the facts to be described have been found in several other cases of schizophrenia. Clinically, as well as orgone-biophysically, there can no longer be any doubt about the reality of these facts.

Nineteenth session

The patient came to the *nineteenth session* very calm and coordinated, but slightly absent-minded. She spoke very slowly, as if against some great obstacle; she said that she was very depressed. She had been shopping the day before, for the first time in many months; she had bought many things, had enjoyed them as never before, had shown them to her friends, and had slept well. The following morning, however, she was overcome by great emptiness and tiredness. There was a "nothingness" in her; and she had felt the need to sit quietly in some corner "and not to move at all." "Every movement was such a great effort." She wanted to be by herself. She gave the impression of an oncoming catatonia with immobility and perseveration.

"Everything was very far away . . . I watched myself as if I were outside of myself; I felt clearly double: a body here and a soul there . . . [Saying this, she pointed outward toward the wall] . . . *I know well that I am one person . . . but I am outside myself . . . perhaps there where the 'forces' are . . .*"

She searched with her eyes anxiously along the walls. Then, suddenly, she asked: *"What is the aurora borealis?* [Very slowly, as if with great effort] I heard about it once; there are patterns and wavy pathways in the sky . . . [She looked again searchingly along the walls of the room, as if strongly absent] . . . I hear you, I see you, but somehow far away. . . at a very great distance . . . I know very well that I am trembling now, I feel it . . . but it is not me, it is something else . . . [after a long pause] . . . I would like to get rid of this body; it is not me; *I want to be there where the 'forces' are . . .*"

I was deeply moved in a quite unprofessional manner when I witnessed her experience of the schizophrenic split and depersonalization in such an unequivocal manner. It was the first time in my long psychiatric career that such a thing had happened so clearly before my eyes. I explained to her that she was experiencing the split which had been in her since childhood. "Is it what they call the 'split personality'?" she asked. She had not connected her own words with what I had just explained. "All those girls [in the mental institution] spoke about it . . . Is it that?"

These patients apparently experience the split in the organism quite clearly, but can neither grasp it nor describe it intellectually. While she continued speaking, she trembled severely all over her body; she kept her chest high in an inspiratory position, fighting hard against exhaling fully. Thorough exploration on my part made it quite clear that she did not perceive the holding of her breath *at all; her chest seemed excluded from self-percep-*

tion. Her eyes were heavily veiled, her forehead was bluish, her cheeks and eyelids spotty. "My brain is like empty . . . It was never so strong before . . ." I asked her whether this type of attack was known to her from earlier experience. She answered in the affirmative. I explained to her that this attack was not stronger than before, but only more clearly in the foreground of her self-perception.

She repeated: "What is it with the aurora borealis? . . . I would prefer to be soul only, my body to be not . . ." Thereupon her speech began to deteriorate.

This was clearly one of the most important sessions in her treatment and, I must add, one of the most instructive happenings in my whole medical experience. Let us pause for a while and try to understand what had happened. To the disinterested institutional psychiatrist, who sees such things happen many times every day, it means "just nothing"; only another of those "crazy things going on in the lunatic." To us, this experience of a living organism is full of meaning and deep secrets. I shall try to connect these phenomena with what we know from orgone-biophysical functioning of the organism. As far as I know, neither psychology nor chemistry nor classical physics could offer any plausible interpretation.

Why did she mention the aurora borealis in connection with her depersonalization? What did it mean when she said that she found "herself," her "soul," "there where" her "forces" used to be? What was meant by *"there"*?

We are reminded here of such experiences as are reported by great spiritualists and mystics, such as Swedenborg. To dismiss these things with a smile or the feeling of superiority of an ignoramus does not get us anywhere. We must adhere to the logical conclusion, from which there is no escape, *that a living organism cannot experience anything unless there is some kind of reality behind it. To investigate the mystical experience on a scientific basis does not imply that one believes in the existence of supernatural forces.* What we want is to comprehend what is going on in a living organism when it speaks of the "beyond" or of the "spirits" or of the "soul being outside the body." It is hopeless to try to overcome superstition without understanding what it is and how it functions. After all, mysticism and superstition govern the minds of the vast majority of the human race, ruining their lives. To ignore it as "fake," as the ignorant and therefore arrogant mechanist is wont to do, will not accomplish anything. We must seriously try to understand the mystical experience *without becoming mystics ourselves.*

The patient had projected a part of her organism toward the walls of the room, and had observed herself from the walls. If we want to describe exactly what had happened, we must say *that her self-perception had appeared where her "forces" usually appeared: at the walls of the room.* Therefore, the conclusion is warranted that the "forces" represented a certain function of her own organism. *But why at the walls?*

Hearing voices from and seeing things at the walls is a common schizophrenic experience. At the bottom of it, there must be a certain basic function which is responsible for this typical experience. The projection of a certain function outward is obviously responsible for the feeling of being split in two. At the same time, the chronic split in the personality, or, in other words, the lack of ONENESS in the organism, is the background from which the acute splitting emerges. The psychoanalytic explanation of the projection mechanism in terms of repressed drives which are ascribed to other people or things outside oneself only relates the content of the projected idea to an *inner* entity, but it *does not explain the function of projection itself,* regardless of the projected idea. These projected ideas vary with the patients; *the mechanism of projection is the same in all cases.* Therefore, the mechanism of projection is far more important than its content. It is important to know that the persecutor in the paranoic delusion is the loved homosexual object; but why does one human being project his homosexual desire whereas the other only re-presses it and forms it into some type of symptom? The content is the same in both cases. The essential thing, therefore, is the *difference,* that is, the *mechanism of projection,* the *ability to project.* This, however, has never been understood.

Let us take the expressions of our patient seriously. Let us believe what she says word for word. Afterwards, we can decide what has been distorted and what is actually true. Most amazing is the statement that the perception is "there where the forces used to be." It is *as if the perceptions were located at some distance outside the skin surface of the organism.* It is obvious that there must exist a severe disturbance of the inner ability of self-perception *before* "feeling oneself outside" is at all possible. This inner disturbance is, as we found earlier, the splitting-off of self-perception from the objective biophysical process that ought to be perceived. In the healthy organism, they are united into one single experience. In the armored neurotic individual, the biophysical organ sensations do not develop at all; the plasmatic streamings are greatly reduced and accordingly *below* the threshold of self-perception ("deadness"). *In the schizophrenic,* on the other hand, *the plasmatic currents remain strong and unimpaired, but their subjective perception is impaired and split off;* the function of perception is neither repressed nor united with the streaming; the function of self-perception appears as if "homeless" in the experience of the schizophrenic. Since the subjective perception is not related *experientially* to the objective plasmatic streamings, it seems understandable that the *schizophrenic searches for a reason for these experiences which he does not feel as his own.*

This situation may account for the *confusion* which so often overcomes the schizophrenic when the split between excitation and perception becomes acute. He perceives something that is not his own; there must be a reason for the experience, which he cannot find; people do not understand him; the physician says it's crazy. This only adds to the confusion; anxiety and unrest are the logical outcome of this confusion. The schizophrenic hears himself speak, but since his self-perception is split off from the biological process to which it belongs, he sounds strange and far away to himself; the words lose their contact with the things they are to connote, as Freud has so aptly described. This is the beginning of the disorganization of speech. It was quite clear in our patient that her speech began to deteriorate whenever the perception of the self "at the walls" was at its peak.

To drive the basic schizophrenic split to its peak in an acute experience of sensory delusion, such as "being outside oneself," requires a certain bodily function. In our patient, it was the severe blocking of the respiration against strongly forthcoming plasmatic sensations which constituted the *immediate* cause of the projection. *Her head was quite unmistakably in a state of shock because of lack of oxygen due to blocked respiration.*

In this connection I may mention an experience I had once myself some twenty-eight years ago during a general anesthesia. I had gone into it with the firm determination to observe the onset of the loss of consciousness. I managed to remember quite a bit of the experience after I woke up. The most impressive part of it was the feeling that the voices of the people in the operating room receded farther and farther away, became more and more unreal. Furthermore, I felt as if my perceiving ego were receding into some far distance. The depersonalization due to the central effect of the drug was experienced in this form: "I perceive that I still perceive . . . I perceive that I perceive that I perceive . . . I still perceive that I still perceive that I still perceive, etc. . . ." endlessly. At the same time, I felt my ego receding, as it were, into some far, *outer* distance, in the same way as one experiences hearing voices in the far distance while the body is seen asleep in the bed.

The complete loss of self-perception is preceded by an experience very similar to that described by our patient. Thus, it loses much of its mystery.

"Projection" is factually the process of recession of the ability to perceive, its detachment from the organismic functions to be perceived or usually perceived. Its result is the delusion of sensory impression "from outside the organism."

This detachment of the function of self-perception from the organismic functions cannot be experienced in some cases in any other way than as "the soul leaving the body" or "the soul being *outside* the body." Since the perception has only a weak contact and finally no contact at all with the bio-energetic functions which it reflects subjectively, one experiences in a very typical manner "self-estrangement," or "oneself being removed far, far away." Accordingly, the processes of projection, trance, depersonalization, hallucination, etc., have as their basis a *concrete* split in the bio-energetic system.

The split between the *bodily excitation* and the *psychic perception of this excitation* removes the body sensation into the distance, as it were. It does not make much difference whether the organ excitation or its perception is experienced as receding. In any case, the blocking occurs *between excitation and perception:*

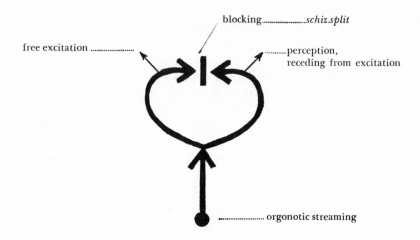

blocking...................*schiz.split*

free excitation ....

...........perception, receding from excitation

.... orgonotic streaming

Schizophrenic split, due to blocking of perception of excitation; *excitation is perceived as "strange," "foreign" or "removed"*

and not, as in the "cold" compulsion neurotic, between energy source and its motility (see facing page).

In the compulsion neurotic, the flow of energy is actually reduced or is bound in a complete armor as soon as it increases. In the schizophrenic, the energy flow is *not* reduced; there is no blocking of the energy production itself, but only lack of perception of the high-pitched excitation. This lack of perception is undoubtedly linked to a definite blocking in the region of the base of the brain, especially in the optical nerve, as expressed in the typical schizophrenic look. I believe, therefore, that it is *correct* to search for the somatic lesion somewhere in the brain. It is, however, utterly misleading to believe that one can remove a schizophrenic process by frontal lobotomy. Schizophrenia as well as cancer are *general* biopathic processes, with local symptoms due to disturbed functioning in the organs. To mistake the local disturbance in the brain for the schizophrenic process would be

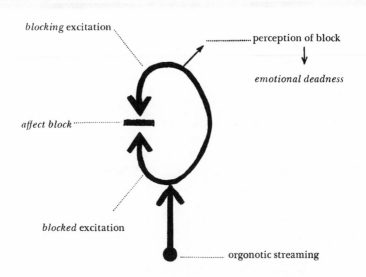

Compulsion neurotic affect block, due to blocking of bio-energy by total armoring. Excitation is not perceived at all: deadness; self-perception is full, but "unalive," "dead," or "empty"

just as bad as to mistake the *local* cancer tumor for the total cancer process. Both mistakes run counter to the medical tasks.

I told the patient everything I understood about her illness. She cooperated in a magnificent manner, although her speech was severely disturbed and considerably slowed down most of the time.

The function of SELF-PERCEPTION appeared severely disturbed, depending on how strongly the split between excitation and perception of excitation developed. The dissociation and the production of senseless words increased when the split increased. The normal function of speech and association returned when the split disappeared and the patient began to feel her bodily streamings as her own again. This permitted the conclusion that the *function of self-perception as a whole depended on the contact between objective excitation and the subjective feeling of the excitation.* The closer this contact, the stronger self-perception functioned. This observation was of the greatest importance theoretically. It was now possible to draw a hypothetical conclusion in a more general way.

5. THE INTERDEPENDENCE OF CONSCIOUSNESS AND SELF-PERCEPTION

The following is a first orgonomic attempt to approach the problem of consciousness and self-perception. It does not attempt to solve this greatest riddle in nature—however, it seems to survey the problem of self-awareness in a rather promising manner: *consciousness is a function of self-perception in general, and vice versa.* If self-perception is complete, consciousness also is clear and complete. When the function of self-perception deteriorates, the function of consciousness in general also deteriorates, and with it all its functions such as speech, association, orientation, etc. If self-perception itself is not disturbed, but only reflects a *rigid* organism, as in the affect-blocked neurotic, the functions of consciousness and intellect, too, will be rigid and mechanical. When self-perception reflects dull organismic functioning, then consciousness and intellect, too, will be dull. When self-perception reflects a removed, faint organ excitation, consciousness will develop ideas of being "beyond" or of "foreign and strange forces." This is why the schizophrenic phenomena lend themselves so well—better than any other type of biopathy—to an understanding of the most difficult and most obscure problem of all natural science, the ability of living matter to perceive itself and, in higher developed species, to be "conscious" of itself.

Although self-perception constitutes self-awareness, and although the *kind* of self-perception determines the *type* of consciousness, these two functions of the mind are not identical. Consciousness appears as a higher function, developed in the organism much later than self-perception. Its degree of clarity and oneness depends, to judge from observations in schizophrenic processes, not so much on the strength or intensity of self-perception, as on the more or less complete *integration of the innumerable elements of self-perception into one single experience of the* SELF. We can see how in the schizophrenic breakdown this unity falls apart and how, together with it, the functions of consciousness disintegrate. Usually, the disintegration of self-perception *precedes* the disintegration of the functions of consciousness. *Disorientation and confusion* are the first reactions to one's own perceptional discoordination. Thought association and coordinated speech, which depend on it, are the next functions of consciousness in the human animal which fall apart when the disintegration of self-perception has gone far enough. Even the *type* of discoordination of consciousness reflects the type of disintegration in self-perception.

In paranoid schizophrenia, where self-perception is severely disturbed, association and speech are also disjointed. In the catatonic stupor, where the organism is acutely and severely contracted and immobilized, complete mutism, i.e., absence of speech and emotional reaction, is the rule. In the hebephrenic disease picture, where a slow deterioration and dulling of all biophysical processes are in progress, perception and consciousness are also, as a rule, dulled, severely slowed down, and increasingly less effective.

Thus, we must conclude that the mental functions of self-perception and consciousness are directly related to, and correspond to, certain bio-energetic states of the organism, in kind as well as in degree. This permits, accordingly, the conclusion that *schizophrenia is a truly biophysical, and not "merely" a mental, disease.* The basis of the mental dysfunctions was sought heretofore in chemical or mechanical lesions of the brain and its appendices. Our functional approach permits a different understanding of these interrelations.

The mental dysfunctions express the schizophrenic process of disintegration of the biophysical system in an amazingly immediate manner. The dysfunctions of self-perception and of consciousness are directly related to dysfunctions of the emotional functions; however, the emotional functions are functions of orgonotic plasma motility, and *not* of structural or chemical conditions. *Emotions are bio-energetic, plasmatic, and not mental or chemical or mechanical, functions.* We must arrange the bio-energetic, the mental, and the structural functions with the emotional functions as the common functioning principle, in the following manner:

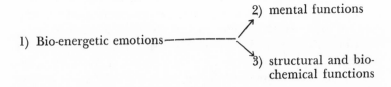

1) Bio-energetic emotions————————⟨ 2) mental functions

3) structural and bio-chemical functions

No other arrangement is possible. To put (3) in place of (1) would mean to bog down in the mechanistic ways of thinking of classical psychiatry, which led nowhere. To put (2) in place of (1) would mean to derive the emotional disturbances from confusion and to put the functions of the mind *before* the functions of the protoplasm. It would not work and would lead only into metaphysics.

Let us try to understand the functional relation between self-perception and biophysical emotion (= plasma-motion). In my book, *The Cancer Biopathy,* I have tried to draw a rough picture of the small child's development in the following manner:

The movements of a newborn baby are not yet coordinated into ONE whole function and, accordingly, there is no "purpose" or "meaning" in the movements. True, pleasure and anxiety reactions are already clearly formed; but we do not find as yet any coordinated movements which would indicate the existence of total consciousness and self-awareness. We must assume that, in the newborn child, self-perception already exists and functions fully, but *not in a coordinated, unitary manner*. The hands move for themselves and the eyes, which to begin with are not yet centered on objects, move for themselves too. The legs show only meaningless and purposeless motions, without any connection with the movements of other organs. During the first few months of life, the coordination of the independent and separate movements slowly develops. We must assume that some kind of functional CONTACT is progressively established between the many organs; and with the more numerous contacts the oneness begins to develop. We are probably not too far from the truth if we also concede a development and coordination of the functions of different perceptions. Accordingly, on the basis of the dependence of self-perception on plasmatic motion, self-perception in the uterine and post-uterine existence would be only a dim one and split up into many separate experiences of the self in accordance with the separateness of the plasmatic organ movements. With the growing coordination of the movements, their perceptions also are gradually coordinated one by one with each other until the point is reached where the organism moves in a coordinated fashion as a *whole* and, therefore, the many different perceptions of the self are united into *one* total perception of the moving self. Not until then, we must further conclude, can we speak of a fully developed consciousness. "Purpose" and "meaning" of biological activity seem to arise as secondary functions, closely linked up with this process of coordination. It also seems dependent on its tempo of development. It proceeds much faster in the lower animal than in man. The reason for this difference is unknown. In the human child, the faculty of speech does not develop until the bodily movements and the corresponding self-perception have reached a certain oneness and, with it, purpose and meaning.

It should be noted carefully that purpose and meaning are derived here from the function of coordination, and not vice versa. *"Purpose" and "meaning" are, therefore, secondary functions, entirely dependent on the degree of coordination of the single organ movements.*

We must further assume, if we follow logically, step by step, the different levels of coordination and the corresponding functions of the organism, that RATIONALITY, activity that is purposeful and meaningful in regard to the environment and one's own bio-energetic situation, now also appears as a function of emotional and perceptual coordination. It is obvious that no rational activity is possible so long as the organism is not functioning as a whole in well-coordinated fashion. We see it clearly in the schizophrenic distintegration, which is the reversal of the original process of bio-energetic coordination, that rationality, purposefulness, meaningfulness, speech, association, and other higher functions of the organism disintegrate to the extent to which their emotional, *bio-energetic* foundation disintegrates.

It is understandable now why the schizophrenic dissociation is so regularly found to be rooted in prenatal and immediate postnatal development: every severe disturbance which took place during the process of organismic coordination constitutes a weak spot in the personality where later, under certain emotional conditions, the schizophrenic discoordination will be most likely to set in.

What is called in psychoanalysis "fixation in early childhood" is in fact nothing but this weakness in the structure of functional coordination. The schizophrenic does *not* "regress to childhood." "Regression" is merely a psychological term describing the *actual*, present-day effectiveness of certain historical events. Childhood experiences could, however, not be effective twenty or thirty years later, had they not *actually damaged the process of coordination of the biosystem*. It is this *actual lesion in the emotional structure*, and not the long past experience in childhood, which constitutes the dynamic disease factor. The schizophrenic does not "go back to mother's womb." What he actually does is to become a victim of *exactly the same split in coordination of his organism which he suffered when he was in the deadened mother's womb;* and he has maintained the split throughout his life. We are dealing here with *actual, present-day functions of the organism,* AND NOT WITH HISTORICAL EVENTS. The U.S.A. does not function the way it does because of the historical event of the Declaration of Independence, but solely because this historical event has become a living, *present-day* reality in the lives of Americans. The historical Declaration of Independence is effective today only to the extent to which it was actually anchored in the emotional structure of American citizens, and not an iota more or less than that. It is because psychiatry did not go beyond merely historical thinking and exploration that it bogged down therapeutically. A memory *can,* but does not necessarily, mobilize the actual emotions in the present-day organism.

Orgone-therapeutic medicine does not attack memories but the *present-day biophysical anchoring* of the historical experiences; thus it works with high-pitched realities, and not with shadows of memories from the past. A memory may or may not develop in this process of emotional upheaval. It is of no therapeutic importance whether it does or not. *The factor which changes the human structure from "sick" to "healthy" is the emotional, bio-energetic coordination of the organism.* The orgasm reflex is merely the most prominent indication that the coordination has actually succeeded. Respiration, breaking of muscular blocks, resolution of rigid character armor are tools in this process of reintegration of the organism. They are, most unfortunately, often mistaken for a therapeutic end in itself, even by some close workers in our fields. To mistake mere tools of medical endeavors for the end itself is the result of bad thinking due to lack of coordinated knowledge of the organism, i.e., a narrow judgment which does not fit the breadth and the depth of human emotional diseases.

With such a narrow approach to human organisms, one will never penetrate to the *basic* bio-energetic concepts of orgonomy. One will be only a healer or a businessman in human misery at best, but not a scientific medical worker. I would like to warn especially against any attempts to master schizophrenic biopathies if one has not mastered the *deep* biophysical interrelations between emotions and plasmatic activities, perceptions and the functions of consciousness. These functional interrelations were hitherto completely hidden and unknown. We are only beginning to understand them; the riddles are still numerous. Therefore, utter caution in forming an opinion is essential. In the course of our development we face the danger of doing away with basic problems of natural functioning by using terms loosely. One can already hear people saying that orgone therapy is nothing but "work with the hands on the muscles" or "letting the patient breathe"; or that man suffers from "tensions." The tendency of the average human animal to escape from simple though basic realities by verbalization of alive functions is tremendous and among the most damaging attitudes in life. It is not a matter of "muscles" or of "breathing" or "tension," but it is a matter of understanding *how cosmic orgone energy came to form plasmatic moving substance, and how cosmic orgonomic functions are present and active in the human animal,* in his emotions, in his thinking, in his irrationalism, in his innermost experience of himself. Schizophrenic dissociation is *only one,* though a very characteristic, example of the interrelations between emotional processes in living matter and the orgone energy field (or the ether) around it. *This* is what matters, and not muscular tension. It seems to be in the nature of things that the living just functions, and is satisfied with mere functioning; reflecting about its own existence and ways and whys of being is an age-old activity of the human animal; but whether it is just as much a necessity of life as mere living seems very doubtful. In any case, the institution of statehood has reduced all human interests to the questions of mere existence. And somehow the human animal accepts this viewpoint *en masse* and as a matter of course.

To know one's standpoint of judgment is essential to any sound conclusion. What I am trying to convey here is the great depth of the functions we encounter in the schizophrenic. I mean *depth,* not complication. The functions which appear in the schizophrenic, if only one learns to read them accurately, are COSMIC FUNCTIONS, that is, functions of the cosmic orgone energy within the organism in undisguised form. Not a single symptom in schizophrenia makes sense if one does not understand that the sharp borderlines which separate *homo normalis* from the cosmic orgone ocean have broken down in the schizophrenic; accordingly, some of his symptoms are due to the intellectual realization of this breakdown; *others are direct manifestations of the merger between organismic and cosmic (atmospheric) orgone energy.*

I am referring here to functions which bind man and his cosmic origin into *one.* In schizophrenia, as well as in true religion and in true art and science, the awareness of these deep functions is great and overwhelming. The schizophrenic is distinguished from the great artist, scientist, or founder of religions in that his organism is not equipped or is too split up to accept and to carry the experience of this identity of functions inside and outside the organism. It happens that, after a period of great productivity, an artist or a *"knower"* breaks down psychotically. It was too much to carry; *homo normalis,* who has lost his first sense, has made life too hard and unbearable for such individuals. The final breakdown in such great men as van Gogh, Gauguin, Nietzsche, Doeblin, Ibsen, and many others is the work of *homo normalis.* Mystical deviations, such as those of Swedenborg, Lodge, Eddington, Driesch, etc., are due to the lack of *physical* comprehension of cosmic and organismic orgone energy functions. And this lack of knowledge is again due to the mechanical armor of *homo normalis.* But to go back to our patient.

Twentieth session

A new problem arose: *what exactly is the bodily mechanism that underlies the schizophrenic split between organ excitation and perception of excitation?* The events pointed sharply to the peculiar disturbance of respiration: *a severely restricted volume of respiration in connection with a mechanically soft chest.* In the well-armored neurotic, the chest itself is usually quite rigid; thus no strong emotions are developed. In the schizophrenic, on the other hand, the chest is soft, the emotions are fully developed, but *they are not fully perceived;* most probably the inhibition of the motion of the chest structure constituted the mechanism which split the perception off from the excitation. This had to be corroborated clinically. The further course of events confirmed this assumption.

The immobility in her chest and throat was especially severe that day. No air at all seemed to pass in or out through the larynx. At the same time, the patient was softer in her chest and neck musculature than ever before. She said: "I am very emotional today . . ." Any attempt to induce passage of air through the throat met with no success. There was no trembling, only severe aversion against respiration. There were no "forces" around that day.

The patient asked me whether she could go to the bathroom. I began to worry when she didn't return. After quite some time the patient came back. Her upper abdomen showed a *cut in the skin about 10 cm. long* across the region of the solar plexus beneath the sternum. She said: "It is here where I feel the strongest emotions . . ."

I told her that such actions would not eliminate the pressure; she agreed. To become excited and anxious about such actions would not help. It would only induce the patient to do *worse* things. If one has good control over the case, one will accept such actions as a special mode of self-expression. This requires, of course, the absolute confidence of the patient in the physician and vice versa, a confidence established firmly by working through the distrust and by complete frankness.

Twenty-first session

The patient came to this session in good humor and, to my great astonishment, breathing fully. But she had added three cuts across the one of the day before. She explained: "I had to do it on behalf of the forces; otherwise, they could have become worried because of the incompleteness of the cut. . . . It has to be a *cross*. . . . I am afraid that they [the forces] will not condone the interval of twenty-four hours between the first cut and the addition of the crosses. . . ."

It was quite obvious that she had cut herself in an attempt to release bio-energetically her terrific emotional tension in the diaphragmatic region. This is called "crazy" in the schizophrenic. It is called "national custom of hara-kiri" when a Japanese general does the same thing, with death as the consequence. Basically, they are of the same nature; they have the function, in the schizophrenic as well as in the general, of eliminating the unbearable emotional tension in the upper abdomen.

I had the impression that day that psychotic delusions were present but that they were very weak. She told me that the "forces" had not been around all day. She had felt her emotional excitation fully. The contact between excitation and perception seemed reestablished; this had obviously made perception of the streamings as *outer* "forces" more difficult. She was still afraid of the "forces"; she did not trust the situation as it were. The previous request on the part of the "forces" to "sacrifice herself" could now be understood as inner urges to release the terrific emotional strain by "opening the tight bladder" with a knife. This only confirmed what orgone-biophysical research had brought to light in other biopathies such as masochism: strong emotions correspond to an expansion of the plasma system. Under the condition of some constriction of organs, the feeling of "bursting" appears, together with the *inability* to *"let off steam."* In such situations self-injury, suicide, actual smashing-up of the body structure occur. In bio-energetic terms, an unbearably tight bladder had been pricked open.

The improvement did not last long. I may say that I had never before experienced the *incapacity for full healthy functioning* in a biopathic organism as clearly as in this case. *The biopathic structure is used to the biopathic functioning; it is incapable of "taking," or managing, strong natural emotions fully and of directing them.* It became clearer than ever before that there are two sharply delineated groups of human animals: the ones *without* and the ones *with* an armor. What appears easy and self-evident to the unarmored individual is utterly incomprehensible and impossible to manage in the armored individual, and vice versa.

A certain way of life requires a certain character structure; this is valid for both realms. *Our patient was unable to stand healthy functioning.* We can understand better now how useless, in the face of this inability to function healthily, the usual measures of mental hygiene appear. To impose healthy conditions of living on armored organisms is like asking a lame man to dance. The measures of rational mental hygiene are all right; *they require, however, thorough disarmoring of the human animal on a mass scale and,* first of all, *prevention of biopathic armoring in the newborn babies.* The breadth and depth of this task is obvious.

Twenty-second session

Her reactions, especially her speech, were severely slowed down. Every single word was repeated several times. She could not formulate words. Her face was frozen; she could not move her facial muscles; she knew the answers to my questions but could not formulate them; she was slightly confused; her skin was pale and spotty-white and bluish; she felt entirely empty.

She said slowly: "I *could* move if I made a very great effort. . . . Why is every effort so difficult? . . . What is happening to me? I had such states before, but I never felt them so clearly."

I told her that her full respiration the other day had made the appearance of the "forces" impossible. She rose and wanted to leave, but fell back on the couch.

I moved her facial muscles, raised her eyelids, moved the skin of her forehead. It helped a little, but the catatonic attack went on. She had apparently reacted to the strong emotions of the day before with an anorgonotic attack, with immobility; but her intelligence was clear; she knew what was going on. In the end, she still felt "empty," but less "faraway." "If I become healthy, and if I commit murder, I shall be convicted. Today the boys were electrocuted. . . ." (Some execution had actually taken place that day.)

Her cataleptic attack during the session was due to a breakthrough of a certain deep blocking. The medical orgone therapist knows well that each pathological layer has to appear from the depth. This does not interfere with the life outside. She had worked well in the office that day and was orderly.

She remained in the room after I had left. When I returned

ten minutes later, I found her coiled together, with her head between her pulled-up legs, her hands at her knees. *She could not move.* "I prayed to God that you would come in and free me from this position. . . . I suddenly could not move at all. . . ."

I helped her to get up, and she began slowly to move again. She said: "I thought that the forces might have done that to me, but I don't know. . . ." Thereafter, her head began to tremble; after a while she recovered fully and left, reassuring me that she felt better.

Twenty-third session

The misconception prevails in certain circles that the essential thing in orgone therapy is the establishment of orgastic potency and nothing but that. It is true, of course, that this is and remains the main goal of our technique. But the manner in which this goal is reached is decisive with regard to the firmness and durability of the success. *It is essentially the slow and thorough overcoming of the emotional blocks in the organism and of the anxieties connected with each single block which secures lasting results.* Our schizophrenic patient was close to the goal of therapy; but the disease mechanisms which were interpolated were the most essential obstacles to be overcome if the eventual success was to be lasting. It is easy in certain cases to achieve release of pent-up energy. But if the main blocks remain unresolved, relapse with worse effects than those of the disease will result. Therefore, we obey the rule of proceeding slowly and of carefully working through each single layer of blocking. These biophysical blocks, which impede the free flow of bodily energy, constitute exactly the "disposition" to various kinds of symptomatic diseases.

I knew that our patient carried strong inclinations to catatonic stupor within herself. These tendencies would have to develop fully; they would have to come to the surface and would have to be overcome. The greatest danger was still *ahead* of us. One must not brag about success too early.

The patient had suffered a slight catatonic attack during the previous session. She came back happy and looking very well: she told me that she had had a very good time since the last session. She could move her facial muscles, but was unable to move the skin of her forehead, as in "astonishment" or "frowning."

She related quite spontaneously that she felt impelled to make a lot of grimaces when she felt strongly emotional; but she was not able to make any grimaces at all when she felt "estranged." "I have learned hard not to show any emotions in my face . . . I don't like women who show emotions; *I want them to be like nice, slender statues. . . .*"

These few sentences, although spoken calmly, contained much emotional dynamite. Her head and neck musculature was severely blocked and rigid. Therefore, grimacing partially relieved her from the feeling of tension and immobility. Strong depersonalization and splitting wiped out the ability to grimace. We understand now why catatonics and advanced schizophrenics grimace: it is a desperate attempt to release the deadness and immobility which overcome their organism in the state of stupor. They test themselves to see whether they still feel anything at all.

I did not understand immediately what the ideal "slender statues" meant. I was soon to learn about it the hard way.

She spoke much about "dying" that day. The idea of "dying" is well known to orgone therapists. It usually comes up when the patient is close to orgastic release of bio-energy; it is connected with severe fear of letting go fully. The anxiety will persist as long as the main blocks in the organism, usually in the pelvis, are not dissolved. Her head was *visibly* disturbed in a most severe manner. Therefore, I feared a premature breakthrough of total body convulsions. The outcome would inevitably have been a total breakdown because of the remaining blocking in her forehead. "The emotions are hurting me lately in my belly," she said. "Here . . ." and she pointed to the upper abdomen. "My left arm also lives and acts on its own. . . . I do not feel it as *my* arm. . . ."

Whenever a neurotic or psychotic symptom increases in strength, it indicates that the emotion contained in the local region has become urgent and tends to break through. The detachment of her left arm could possibly be the expression of strong impulses to touch her genitals. Her idea of "nice, slender statues" could, in this connection, only mean being a "statue without genitals," something "god-like."

In order to prepare her for her genital breakthrough, I concentrated on her immobilized forehead and eyes. I let her move the skin of her forehead, roll her eyes in all directions, express anger and fear, curiosity and watchfulness. THIS IS NOT MANIPULATION AND HAS NOTHING WHATSOEVER TO DO WITH ANY KIND OF MANIPULATION. We do not "manipulate" mechanically; *we induce emotions* in the patients *by letting them imitate willfully this or that emotional expression.*

She objected very strongly to showing the expression of anxiety in her eyes. This objection is usually much more intense in schizophrenics than it is in neurotics. The reason, based on several cases of schizophrenia, is the following: raising the eyelids, opening the eyelids wide and showing anxiety releases a sensation of severe terror with the feeling of oncoming disaster. Sometimes panic sets in. Some such patients have the feeling that they are dying, "going off," and that they will be unable to "come back again." It is essential to be very careful at this point.

I worked very cautiously on her expressions in the forehead, stopping her whenever she showed too strong anxiety. After some time, she could move her forehead more easily and she felt freer. Her self-perception of the total organism was still severely disturbed; to let her total preorgastic contractions break through would have been dangerous and inadvisable. She was sensitive to touch, pressure, cold, and heat, *but at times she did not feel the quivering.* After the therapeutic session, she asked many intelligent questions about herself, but her speech was considerably slowed down; she spoke as if against some great counter-force.

It was during the experiment with this schizophrenic that the following idea came up for the first time: *the organ sensation or "orgonotic sensation" is a true* SIXTH SENSE. Besides the abilities to see, hear, smell, taste, touch, there existed unmistakably in healthy individuals a *sense of organ functions,* an ORGONOTIC SENSE, as it were, which was completely lacking or was disturbed in biopathies. The compulsion neurotic has lost this sixth sense completely. The schizophrenic has displaced this sense and has transformed it into certain patterns of his delusional system, such as "forces," "the devil," "voices," "electric currents," "worms in the brain or in the intestines," etc.

Since the orgonotic sensations and organ perceptions seem to constitute a great part of what is called the *ego* or the *self,* it appears clear now why a splitting and dissociation of perception and speech usually go hand in hand with the dissociation and displacement of these organ sensations.

We must also assume that the severity and the outcome of a disease depend entirely on the specific organ in which the deadening, i.e., the extinction of the organ sensation, took place. The dissociation of an arm appears harmless if compared with the immobilization of eyes and forehead, or even parts of the brain.

We would object less to the irresponsible brain operations and lobotomies which are performed to kill the devil in the organism if they served to disclose the dynamic *functions* of the brain. Such questions as "Does the brain move? Does it contract and expand when working, just as other organs such as the heart, intestine, glands, etc., do?" are of the utmost importance for medical pathology and the understanding of the organismic functions. It would be highly important to invent a device which would enable the brain specialist to observe the brain in its *natural* state. Cutting out "windows" in the skull to study the brain, as was done with apes and with some human beings, won't help. The living organ does not move when a severe operation has been performed in its vicinity. This is shown by the edemas and similar dysfunctions occurring after operations. All I want to say is this:

There is good reason to believe that *in the schizophrenic process parts of the brain, most probably the base with its nerve roots, become immobilized;* just as in chronic constipation the intestines are immobilized, or in a tumor of the stomach peristalsis ceases to function. This would appear as a new, hopeful and functional approach to the *somatic* disturbances in schizophrenia. It would require abandonment of the mechanistic view of the brain function. The brain would have to be regarded as an organ like others within the total functioning of the organism, as a special *"transmitter"* of total plasma functions, and *not as the source of motor impulses.* For if the brain is the source of impulses, then the next logical question is: *who gives the orders to the brain?* It amounts to the assumption of an imp in the brain, if one says that the motor impulses *originate* in the gray substance. There are many species without any brain at all, who function fully as far as living functions, including judgment, are concerned; and we know from experiment that brainless dogs continue to function, even if severely impaired by the operation.

To return to our patient: The situation at this point was characterized by her closeness to total bodily convulsions and genital activity; but the block in her forehead and eyes constituted a major obstacle which had first to be removed before she could be permitted to develop further on her way toward natural genitality.

Twenty-fourth session

The patient came beaming with joy. She had felt very happy and at ease. Her eyes were clear and the look was alert. The color of her face was ruddy and fresh. She had, for the first time in her life, passed through a menstrual period without psychotic reactions. She had visited many friends, among them a girl in the mental institution. Her respiration was much improved, though it was not completely without restriction.

The next step was quite clear: I had to bring her back to where she had been the previous day. She would have to "pump up" more emotion, to learn to stand it without "going off," and then to proceed further.

In the course of deep respiration, a tremor appeared over her chin and in the masseter muscles. She said: "When my emotions kick me on the one side, and society on the other side, I feel like getting down, hurting myself, becoming syphilitic or something like that . . ." Later on: "Emotions want to break out here . . ." She pointed to her stomach and *then down toward her genital.* . . . "Then I am able to commit anything . . ."

One cannot expect to have these connections presented more clearly.

6. THE RATIONAL FUNCTION OF THE "DEVILISH EVIL"

It is necessary to sum up again the basic functions which were found by orgonomic research in the depth of man's biophysical functioning, in order to understand fully the meaning of *character structure.* In the light of orgone biophysics, this "structure" appears as the sum total of the relationship between the orgonotic energy system and the sensory-motor system which has to perceive the plasmatic currents, to execute the energy discharges, and to coordinate all energy functions into an orderly, total, unitary functional system: "orgonotic system." In the schizophrenic process, the system of perception is flooded by high-pitched bio-physical sensations which are not integrated into the total biosystem and lead a *separate existence,* as it were. This constitutes the "split of personality." The biosystem has a very low tolerance for *sudden increases* of the emotional, i.e., *bio-energetic,* level of functioning. Disorientation, hallucinations, speech deterioration, and murderous impulses are likely to appear with a *sudden* increase in energy level if the tolerance is low. This has nothing to do with "psychology." The "psychology" of the schizophrenic is a *result* and not a cause of the process. When the perception is split off from the bio-energetic excitation, the bodily sensations are experienced as "foreign," as "evil," "devilish" influences by "supernatural powers" ("supernatural" in the sense of "beyond" one's own self). In this harrowing confusion, the biosystem develops destructive impulses to protect itself against the devil. It is, in fact, the remainder of sane personality which does the fighting against the devil.

Let us follow further the events in the patient:

The patient had scarcely uttered the words: "Emotions want to break through here . . . [in the genital] . . . ," when she became pale and silent; she lay there immobile, as if absent; she did not respond to questions. After a while she said in a very timid manner: "I have just said the Lord's prayer . . . The emotions are gone."

She left the session calm and slightly absent-minded. The next day I received the following letter (Italics mine.—W.R.) :

March 18, 1942

So it is all emotion—*you did not know about the music that was playing Liszt's Hungarian Rhapsody*—or others—*the notes go through me*—not through you or anyone else—to tell me something—I don't usually know what—tonight it was my bigness—you couldn't understand that—nor could anyone else on earth.

There are colors and darknesses and shadows and lights—it was raining hard tonight I walked in puddles I was going to take my shoes off and walk by your house, the people stared in the train and on the street—I went in to eat on your main street and a woman was there after talking to the boy in the store about hospitals and Bellevue—they had worked there—they are made to speak then to annoy me but they smiled not with me—at me—the people in the train were having a good time—*and they wanted me out of the way*—but I stayed anyway—

I came home and found I had passed a city test I once took—so maybe I'll be a typist for the city—that I would not be able to quit easily though—

Just human and emotional?—You couldn't know—You said I didn't believe in my forces—but they believe in me—they send rain and tell me they know—I won't see you for 2 days maybe I can forget you and your work—86000 Jews were killed—slaughtered by the Nazis in Russia today—all for crucifixion of Christ—There were nails through his hands and one through his feet—I wonder if he bled much Blessed Mother forgive me—Thine is the Kingdom the Power and the Glory forever and forever Amen

You crucifier of the Blessed Sacrament—You should pay and yours after you—I am protected from mine enemies the rain marks them for having annoyed me—something will happen to you—Adler died when I told him he would—Katz of Psychiatric died also—You shall have many troubles—you may think they are the natural outgrowth of things but I will know better—

You could have been so helpful but you went your own inimitable way—the epitome of knowledge—spheres that go round and round—Help when I needed it you would not give—I am protected and sheltered and if sometimes made to suffer it is for a definite reason—The Jew in me must be made to suffer so that others can survive—

On thee, Oh Lord, our faith rests—that takes thee to eternal life

Command and I shall obey no ties can find me no powers save those can stay me from performing my predestined destiny—Please tell me oh Lord—

If your interest has waned I am willing to stop—if your Ego keeps inflating I am also willing to stop so I must take first aid to help the wounded humans survive—

Mummies and madmen grow dark in the sun—(after thought)

You, too—F.

I suggest that we take these things very seriously. In such schizophrenic experiences, the world which is called THE BEYOND in common mysticism and in true religion manifests itself before our eyes. One must learn to read this language. What is never admitted by *homo normalis,* what is lived out only clandestinely or laughed at in a silly manner, are the severely distorted forces of nature; exactly the same forces which imbue the great sages, philosophers, musicians, geniuses of science, in the wide realm *beyond* the conceptions of *homo normalis* and his everyday political clamor. I venture the statement that in our mental institutions many potentially great artists, musicians, scientists, and philosophers are rotting away their lives because *homo normalis* refuses to look beyond the iron curtain which he drew in front of his real life, because he dare not look at living realities. These great souls, broken down and wrecked as "schizophrenics," KNOW and PERCEIVE what no *homo normalis* dares to touch. Let us not be led astray by the distortions in this knowledge. Let us listen to what these gifted and clear-visioned human beings have to say. We can learn a great deal from them; we can learn to become more modest, more serious, less gaudy and cocky, and we can start realizing a few of the claims we make in an empty manner in our churches and in our high academic institutions. I claim, after thirty years of thorough study of schizophrenic minds, that they look through our hypocrisy, our cruelty and stupidity, our fake culture, our evasiveness, and our fear of the truth. *They had the courage to approach what is commonly evaded,* and they were wrecked because they went through the inferno without any help on the part of our neurotic parents, our conceited teachers, our cruel directors of educational institutions, our ignorant physicians. They hoped to emerge from the inferno into the clear, fresh air where only great minds dwell. That they could not make it, that they got stuck in the realm of the "devil" is not their fault; it is the fault of the abysmal ignorance and stupidity of our *homines normales.*

Our patient had experienced her emotional storm as great music. The ignoramus will say "that's crazy." *No, it is not crazy.* A Beethoven goes through the same kind of emotional storm when he composes a great symphony, which provides a huge profit for some utterly amusical businessman. It is obvious that a Beethoven has the structure to stand the same kind of great emotional storm that causes the breakdown in the schizophrenic structure. It is equally obvious to one who works with orgonomic functions that a Beethoven, in order to keep his inner world safe, withdraws his bio-energy from his acoustic nerves, that he goes deaf in order not to have to listen to the chattering of annoying "critics" and what not. The schizophrenic differs from him in that he does not keep his genius intact and does not develop it as does a Beethoven. But he suffers from the misbehavior and misdeeds of our Babbits no less than did Beethoven; and he withdraws into his own inner world. His misfortune is that he has only partial contact with this inner world, that he is not equipped to accept it fully and to carry it further; hence the breakdown. My work with "wayward youth" in Germany left no doubt that the best of the human crop go down to ruin not because of their "badness" but because of the inferno which *homo normalis* calls "civilization" and "cultural adaptation." We shall have more to say about this realm of the devil. *Homo normalis,* who wants his psychiatrists and biologists to be "aloof," "unemotional," "academic," "removed," so that he can continue to plant the emotional plague in millions of newborn, healthy babies, undisturbed, hates the schizoid character for its closeness to a realm of nature which is forever closed to himself.

The evening of the same day the emotional storm had occurred, our patient became restless. She had seen her parole physician and had stood her ground well. But inside her the storm continued. It was clear to me that, should she ever become capable of coping with her strong and rational emotions, she would be saved. If not, she would certainly go down as a catatonic in the mental institution.

7. ANORGONOTIC REGIONS IN THE CATATONIC STATE

Twenty-fifth session

The patient came back in a very bad state. She had fought "a desperate battle against the 'forces.'" Both her arms were bandaged with tape. A huge cross, made of tape, was fixed to her stomach from the pit down to the genital and across. She told me that the "forces" had requested an account of whether she had betrayed them; they had asked whether she was ready to sacrifice herself fully, to yield to them to the fullest extent. I asked her what she meant: "It means that I have to cut a deep cross with a knife into my body . . ." She said that she did not want to do it, and she fought a hard battle against doing it, but that she did not know how to escape from the request. She had finally arrived at the conclusion that she could try to "cheat the forces": if she placed a bandage across her belly, the forces could be made to believe—"for a short time only"—that she had fulfilled their request. She wanted me to help her. Once, she said, she was close to using a razor to cut herself.

Her speech was considerably slowed down, as if all impulses had been extinguished. She was slightly dissociated; she showed mannerisms and driveled. Her face was pale, the skin of her forehead was immobile, her eyes were heavily veiled, the skin of her body was patchy. Something had to be done immediately if commitment to the institution was to be avoided. She was in a state similar to that of shock. I took her to the metal orgone room and examined her with the fluorescent bulb. The background of this test is the following: orgone-charged fluorescent bulbs luminate when they are slightly rubbed on the skin. I wished to ascertain whether or not her state was due to loss of surface charge. Her legs gave the normal effect of lumination. Her hair reacted only weakly, and her forehead did not react at all. It was amazing to me to hear her telling me *beforehand* which parts of her body would and which would not give lumination. She predicted the disturbance on the basis of the feeling of deadness or aliveness which she felt in a particular spot.

I tried to charge her in the orgone accumulator. After about half an hour of irradiation, she slowly began to recover. The lumination effect became stronger where it had been weak before; she could move the skin of her forehead; the patchiness disappeared; her eyes became bright again. The disturbance had been strongest in the region of the segment corresponding to the base of her brain: eyes, eyelids, lower parts of the forehead, temples. After about half an hour she felt "fuller in the head where it had been empty before." Her speech had also improved considerably.

In the end she implored me not to abandon her in her fight against the "forces" and to put her through safely. I told her that I could not promise anything, but that I would do what I could to help her. She felt rather happy again.

I had gained the firm conviction during this treatment that the *immobilization of the bio-energetic functions in the optical segment, including the brain, was the center of the acute catatonic attack.* Several other cases of latent and manifest schizophrenia with catatonic tendencies corroborated this conviction. Further investigation of this dysfunction might reveal that it is generally *specific* for the *acute* schizophrenic breakdown; it may also restrict this mechanism to certain types of schizophrenia. *Its main characteristic is a standstill of the movements and, with them, of the bio-energetic functioning of the brain, especially its frontal and basal parts.*

Orgonomy has termed the stoppage of bio-energetic functioning "anorgonia." This symptomatology was first discovered in the cancerous shrinking biopathy. But now I met it in a schizophrenic during a catatonic attack. It was correct to assume that most of the symptoms of the catatonic attack were due to a more or less complete standstill of bio-energetic functioning at the *periphery* of the organism. This standstill appeared to be accompanied or even caused by a withdrawal of bio-energy to the core of the biosystem. Immobility, *flexibilitas cerea,* perseveration, torpidity of speech or mutism were, accordingly, to be regarded as direct expressions of the immobilization. On the other hand, such symptoms as automatic movements, mannerisms, echolalia, and particularly the sudden breakthrough of severe rage could be understood in terms of an attempt of the remainder of mobile bio-energy to break through the immobility by forceful or by automatic movements from the center outward. The relief which is usually experienced by catatonics after an attack of rage, and the following improvement in the disease picture, would corroborate our interpretation. The more complete the armoring, the deeper toward the biological core it spreads, the greater must the rage be in the outbreak. In other cases, such an outbreak would be impossible and deterioration with loss of weight and stoppage of biofunctions one by one would result. It is also to be assumed that a paranoid schizophrenic picture changes more or less suddenly into a catatonic one, if the biosystem has lost its capacity to endure strong biophysical outbursts of energy. The complete final contraction of the biosystem in such cases would be the reaction to the attempts at expansion by the remaining life impulses.

It should be especially emphasized that *the intolerance of healthy expansion on the part of the sick organism constitutes the core of the disease.*

8. THE FUNCTION OF SELF-DAMAGE IN SCHIZOPHRENIA

We know from therapy of mental biopathies that suicide and self-injury are brought about by unbearable bio-energetic stasis in the organism when neither work nor destructive actions nor orgastic gratification are accessible for discharge. The psychological "motives" of such actions are secondary and incidental; usually, they are merely rationalizations of the action. In the schizophrenic, and especially in the catatonic type, self-injury acquires a special function. This became clear when the attempts at self-damage in our patient revealed their motivation.

Twenty-sixth session

I took her to the orgone room and examined her skin surface again with a gas-filled, orgone-charged bulb.[3] Then I asked her to show me the parts of her skin where she felt dead, and to rub the bulb against these spots. To my great amazement, she pointed to exactly the same spots where she had inflicted cuts: at the joints of her hands, where she had once cut herself; at her palms, at the saddle of her nose; at the temples; and, most emphatically, at her sternum, where she had several times cut crosses into the skin. These spots did not give lumination of the orgone-charged bulb, in contradistinction to other spots. They were felt as "dead" in her self-perception, and they were uncharged, i.e., "dead," objectively.

This is a most important new piece of information on the biophysical state in the schizophrenic psychosis. In our patient, the idea of "sacrifice" to hostile "forces" was obviously built upon the foundation of correct perception of a severe bio-energetic dysfunction of her skin surface. She behaved in exactly the same way as many schizophrenics in mental institutions; they knead their skin, touch their forehead, rub their finger tips against walls, try to move their eyelids, rock their limbs, etc., in a stereotyped manner; some do that for years on end. These stereotypes and automatisms have not been understood hitherto. Now it appears that these catatonic activities were expressions of a desperate but futile attempt to regain the feeling in the parts of the body which

[3] Cf. my article, "Orgonotic Pulsation," on "lumination," 1944.

went dead. I would like to emphasize especially the catatonic facial grimaces. Catatonics usually have severely stiffened, masklike faces. Grimacing seems, therefore, to be an attempt at mobilization of the deadened facial musculature.

Theoretically, the detachment of single parts of the body or of whole organ systems from the realm of self-perception would, according to these biophysical findings, be direct results of a deficiency in orgone charge in the respective parts or organs. The compulsion-neurotic biopath only feels a general emptiness and deadness; the schizophrenic biopath perceives the dysfunction much more clearly and immediately. He can tell us exactly where the dysfunction is located, if we pay close attention to what he is saying and understand his language of emotional, i.e., *bio-energetic,* expression.

We are justified in drawing the conclusion that the schizophrenic mind describes *objective* processes. Normal, healthy functioning of the organism expresses itself in and is governed by an even distribution of bio-energy in the biosystem. I know well that we are moving along pathways which no one has yet studied scientifically. It is not only *new* land but also no man's land, so to speak. The self-perception of well-being and happiness, of strength and security, is due to the coordination into one whole of all the self-governing partial functions of the various organs of the organism. Accordingly, the feeling of dissociation, splitting, depersonalization, etc., in the schizophrenic biosystem must be due to discoordination of the single organs and energy field systems in the body. It is as if some of the organs—I suggest especially the brain—lead *separate* existences, detached from the total organism; as if there were no *contact* and no *unity* between the bio-energetic units called "organs." The mental and the emotional confusion and disorientation are the direct result of a *sane* self-perception of this dissociation.

Our patient reacted in an unequivocal manner: when the "veiling" of her forehead set in, she felt *that the convolutions of her brain were tangled up "like entangled intestines."* Well, to me such a description appears full of *rational* meaning. In spite of the routine objections of mechanistic neurology, it seems improbable that the brain should have convolutions like the intestines and that at the same time it should *not move,* like most other organs, when it performs its work of coordination and transmission of central impulses. Is it not most reasonable to assume that the brain is built up of intestine-like convolutions precisely because *it moves* in the manner of peristalsis while functioning? Some healthy individuals who are used to hard thinking relate that they feel great heat in their brain and in their foreheads when they think with great effort; that they feel a "glow," and that this glow disappears when the effort is over; on the other hand, we see pale, immobilized, cold foreheads in cases of mental deficiency and pseudo-debility. If some thought is given to the question, it seems self-evident that the brain would not behave differently from other organs during strong functioning. Heat production is a well-known indication of physiological effort, in the muscles and in the emotional state of sexual excitement. Lack of heat production is readily seen in cases with low bio-energy, as in cancer biopathies, anorgonotic weaknesses, anemia, etc. There is, therefore, no reason to assume that the brain tissue does not develop more energy and, with it, more heat and motion during hard work.

I know well enough that this assumption sounds peculiar and strange to classical pathology, to which the brain is an immobile organ, in spite of the erroneous assumption that it is the brain with its thalamic and subthalamic appendices which generates all impulses of life activity. I do not agree with this theory. I believe that it is utterly wrong; that it is contradicted by obvious facts of living functioning, such as the fact of *brainless* living beings and by important aspects of natural philosophy in general. The visual proof of brain motility is hard to adduce, as I said before. But there can no longer be any reasonable doubt that it is the *brain which is functionally (and not, to begin with, structurally) disturbed in schizophrenia.* Mechanical and structural changes appear later as *results* of the functional bio-energetic dysfunctions; among them, stoppage of motion and discoordination of the bio-energetic field action appear to be the most essential ones. We must admit atrophic changes of disuse in the brain tissue just as we see them in muscular atrophy. If it is true, as it seems to be, that the shape of the organs reflects the form of motion of bio-energy, then the brain with its twisted and rich gyration is an excellent example of the bio-energetic function of organic forms.

The emotional and bio-energetic dissociation in the schizophrenic leads, as we well know, sooner or later to a general decay of the organism with bad body odor, loss of weight, severe disturbances of biochemical metabolism, and sometimes also with true cancerous developments. The schizophrenic shrinks biophysically, too, because of the loss of the capacity to take up bio-energy and to maintain its normal level.

To return again to our patient, who yielded so much insight into the riddles of schizophrenia: I treated her for several weeks with the orgone accumulator. The orgone had a strongly positive effect on her; it caused, as it does in other cases of organismic contraction, an expansion of the autonomic nervous system. Her face reddened, her eyes became clear again, her speech became faster and more coordinated, and she would even feel pleasure in the orgone accumulator after fifteen to thirty minutes' irradiation. This was a great new hope for possible biophysical treatment of incipient schizophrenia.

The combination of physical and psychiatric orgone therapy was very helpful. Acute withdrawal of bio-energy could be dealt with by means of the accumulator alone. Psychiatric orgone therapy helped to bring to the surface schizophrenic mechanisms from greater depth.

During the *twenty-seventh session* the patient was mostly good-humored, the skin of her forehead was mobile, and her eyes were very alert and clear. But her respiration was still restricted. It is possible to "pump to the surface," as it were, the remainder of pathological mechanisms. As long as it is still possible to induce anxiety by means of respiration or certain typical attitudes of the body, the biophysical structure has not really been cleaned of its dysfunctions. When I "pumped up" her emotions, she lost her gaiety, the "forces were near," the forehead became pale and immobile: "Something is interrupted between the skin of the forehead and the brain," she said. This, she said, was always the case when the "forces" were around; it usually disappeared with them.

During the following period *(twenty-eighth through thirty-second sessions)*, the patient seemed very much improved. She said repeatedly: "I don't know whether I want to get well. . . ." Saying that, she meant that she did not know "what would happen to her" if she became well. On several occasions she kept imploring me: "Please, help me against the forces . . . they are not around now, but I know they will come back . . . I am so afraid of them . . . save me. . . ."

It had become unequivocally clear by now that the "forces" were her *distorted* perceptions of the plasmatic orgonotic streamings; that she loved them and dreaded them at the same time; that whenever the streamings became strong, she would fall into a stupor-like state. The sensing of forces, flight into psychotic mechanisms, and immobility of the optical segment formed a single functional unit.

I could see that she fought against a mean, cruel expression in her eyes. I encouraged her to let go and to force this expression out. She succeeded with some effort, and immediately felt much better; but at the same time she also seemed to come very close to a catatonic state whenever she produced the expression of strong hate in her eyes. Once she got up, went in a stuporous manner to the closet, took the heater, and put it, switched on, before the door of the closet; then she built a cross from hangers on the door. She "had to soothe and appeal to the forces," she said. She also told me a little later that she "felt only parts of her brain"; other parts "were twisted," and, "therefore, she was confused."

I knew well that she would have to pass through a severe anxiety attack, with possible complete relapse into catatonia, when the plasmatic streamings broke through in full force. This seemed to depend entirely on whether or not she would yield to full respiration. One could see each time that she flattened her respiration when the "forces" became too strong.

During the following four weeks (in spring) she improved very much. She worked well in the office where she had taken a job; she was sociable and gay; the attacks of withdrawal became rare and were not as strong as they used to be. True, off and on she would return to her schizophrenic attitude and action. For example, she came once with her abdomen wound up in adhesive tape "in order to keep myself together. . . ." A neurotic biopathy would simply have expressed fear of bursting; our patient actually took measures against bursting in a typically psychotic way. But we both understood what was going on, why she did such things, and she knew perfectly well when she would stop doing them. I had taken great pains to tell her everything about the danger ahead, and she had understood with truly schizophrenic intelligence.

She had also learned slowly to produce the expression of murderous hate in her eyes, without becoming frightened by it. This gave her some feeling of security against her fear of committing murder; she realized that one can express murderous hatred fully, and that this did not mean that one actually had to commit murder.

I worked continuously and cautiously on the inhibition of respiration in her throat, with some success. But she never gave in fully to *emotional* respiration. She had shifted her main sensations from her chest to her abdomen; this was an indication of the shift in the perception of her orgonotic streamings toward the region of the *genitals*.

Once she tried in a playful manner to put a noose around her neck "in order to see whether she could hang herself." These actions still had the timbre of danger about them; but it was greatly reduced by the playfulness and the humor which went into them. I knew that she was not yet beyond the possibility of actually committing suicide. Her parole physician noticed the great change, and encouraged her therapeutic effort. This psychiatrist was very helpful and kind.

It was clear that bio-energy and the sensations accompanying it were moving strongly toward the *genital* region. The preorgastic sensations were near. Therefore, the still prevailing block in her throat constituted the main therapeutic problem. I knew if this block should fail to budge in time, *if the genital excitation should break through in great force with the block in the throat still present, then she would definitely become catatonic.* It was a race against time to remove the block in the throat before the full development of genital excitation.

One day she gave in fully to her respiration and *she felt immediately the identity of orgonotic streamings and the "forces."* She knew it instantly and quite clearly, with no doubt left whatsoever. Her chest structure moved quite automatically. She had strong sensations of streaming in her whole body, with the exception of the genital region proper from the mons pubis downward. She asked: "Would it be possible to make the body whole without touching the soul?" This was a most peculiar question. Did the "soul" represent the genital sensation or even the genital itself? Most probably it did. We would expect this to be so when the "forces" represented the bodily streamings; when, furthermore, the peak of bodily streamings was experienced in the genital organs, as "nature has prescribed," then it was logical that also the "soul" was represented by the preorgastic sensations in the genitals. They had been split off from perception for such a long time that they could be perceived only as foreign forces and as the "soul," the most prominent part of self-perception. This was confirmed when she insisted that she "did not want to have her soul cured."

The patient was very cooperative for weeks on end. Each time when natural respiration brought forth genital excitation she objected in a psychotic manner and cramped the muscles of her thighs, the deep adductor muscles, in a way familiar in all types of cases.

Thirty-third session

The genital organs are biological tools of energy discharge and of procreation of the species. The latter function is widely known and acknowledged. *Homo normalis,* who is the heir of *homo sapiens,* who in turn is the heir of *homo divinus,* has, on the other hand, condemned the biophysical function of energy discharge; it returned as the devil in the fantasy life of man. The biologically strong individual did not or could not sacrifice his rational judgment to the demands of ecclesiastical thinking; the great natural force came into conflict with the dependence of the individual on his kin and his society. Under these circumstances, the genital forces continue to function, but they are split off from the rest of the organism as "bad" or as "sin," and return as the devil, as "forces from beyond" in the realm of schizophrenia and mysticism in general.

This fact became clear beyond any shadow of a doubt during the further progress of our patient. Since Tausk in 1919, it has been known in psychiatry that the genital apparatus constitutes the persecutor in the schizophrenic delusion. But it was not known that this had a much deeper biophysical significance; that it was the *strong sensation of living streaming* in the body, and not merely the genitals, which becomes alien and unbearable in the adolescent as well as in the psychotic. The genital organs are so predominant only because their excitation induces the strongest sensations of aliveness.

I told the patient that she had now the task of learning to *feel* her genital region just as clearly as she felt other parts of her body. She let her respiration go fully, but soon became confused and patchy in her face whenever she came close to streamings in her pelvis. I saw her cramping severely in her thighs for the first time. *The "forces" began to break through to the area where they belonged: namely, into the genital region.*

She spoke in a secretive manner, fearfully and in a hushed voice; she said that no one had understood her with regard to "these feelings." She began to describe extensively what she experienced when "it happened or began to happen in that region." The "forces" somehow make the *things in the room around her take on a "queer expression";* they become quite "peculiar." Not that they would change their shape; but they acquired an *alive expression,* the meaning of *living beings.* "Something strange emerges from them"; they "seem to want to tell me important things, as if animated." Then she became confused and anxious.

At first I could not understand why "things became alive around her" when she herself was close to becoming genitally excited. Then it became clear: *In strong biosexual excitation, the orgone energy field of the organism expands considerably; all sensory impressions become more acute and sharp. This also happened to her; but since she did not perceive this biological process as her own, since the excitation was split off from self-perception, the* ORGONE ENERGY FIELD AROUND HER, AS EXPERIENCED IN VERY VIVID SENSE IMPRESSIONS, APPEARED AS A FOREIGN, STRANGE FORCE, WHICH ENLIVENED THE THINGS IN THE ROOM.

Accordingly, the projected psychotic persecutory sensation appears as a *true* perception of a *real* process: THE PSYCHOTIC PERCEIVES HIS OWN ORGONE ENERGY FIELD OUTSIDE HIS ORGANISM. The contents of the sensation, such as projected homosexual or destructive ideas, are secondary to the bio-energetic perception of the orgone energy field.

Let us pause for a moment and consider how safe this assumption is, apart from the clinical experience brought forth by our patient.

The orgone energy field meter, constructed in 1944,[4] demonstrated the existence of an orgone energy field beyond the skin surface of the organism.

An orgone-charged electroscope reacts to the energy field of the moving palm only, and not to dead wool.

The oscillograph reacts when the electrode is attached to a wet towel and when a living organism or organ such as the hand is touching the towel.

Bions which are strongly charged with orgone kill bacteria and cancer cells at a distance and attract other bodies. This capacity disappears when death occurs.

The existence of the "sixth sense," the orgonotic perception beyond the surface of the organism, can, therefore, not be doubted.

I explained to the patient the function of the orgone energy field as seen in bions, blood cells, and at the field meter. She understood it and paid me the compliment that I was the first person she had known who could explain her deep experiences to her in an understandable manner.

I would like to mention here briefly two cases of paranoid reaction which demonstrate the fact that persecutory sensual hallucination in certain instances follows the perception of orgone energy *outside* the skin surface of the organism.

Several years ago I treated a woman who suffered from vaginal anesthesia. She was married, but had never experienced any sensations in her pelvis. After some time, the orgasm-reflex began to appear; soon it was far enough developed to reactivate the natural physiological functions in the vaginal mucous membranes and the glands. She reported that her husband seemed rather gratified by the development in their relationship. However, a few days later she brought her husband to me in despair: *he* had developed the idea that I, in a malicious way, was influencing him with electrical currents through her vagina. It was immediately evident that he had developed a paranoid persecution idea. He went into an institution with the diagnosis paranoid schizophrenia.

Why did the husband break down psychotically when his wife

developed strong vaginal streamings and excitation? We could not have answered this question before the organismic orgone energy functions were discovered. Now it seemed clear: his own energy system could stand the genital embrace only so long as no strong sensations occurred. When his wife began to recover, her organism quite obviously had induced currents and strong sensations in *him*. His organism reacted to this experience with a split in a paranoid fashion. I had cured his wife; therefore, I had influenced him with electricity through her vagina. He showed the typical schizophrenic eye symptoms.

This case shows that actual physiological changes take place in the organism of one mate when the genital functioning changes in the other mate. This is true for dulling of sensations as well as for increased excitation. We see it often happen in orgone therapy that a husband or a wife improves when the bio-energetic situation changes for the better in the partner who is under treatment.

A man with clear-cut psychotic mechanisms used to react with severe anxiety after turning his eyeballs upward. He felt as if he were being choked to death. One day I let him turn his eyeballs upward again. This time the reaction was particularly strong. In the course of the anxiety attack, he stared into one corner of the room, ripped his eyelids wide open, began to scream, and pointed in terror toward the corner. "Don't you feel it," he screamed, "there, it's right there, coming out of the wall, staring at me." Then, with a sudden jump, he leaped up and ran with terror *into that corner* from which he felt the stare had come. I led him into this reaction several times. It subsided gradually and finally disappeared altogether.

In this case, too, a "projection" had occurred. Bio-energetically, however, I had no reason to doubt that his orgone energy field had become excited far outside of his body and that this had made possible the psychotic reaction. To return to our patient: during the following few weeks she was happy, worked well, and had no delusions; the "forces" seemed gone. But one day, when she saw her parole physician again, she told him that she did not know whether to continue the work with me; that she became confused and did not understand the mechanisms which I explained to her.

She had turned against me in a malicious manner. During her sessions with me she behaved in a haughty, arrogant way, as if she despised me. The treatment made her incapable of living in the real world of real human beings; she was losing the "credo" of a "beyond" which seemed so much a part of her. How would she be able to exist in this world if she were going to become genital? She knew well, she said, that people are ill; but she did not want to exchange her world for reality as it is.

She refused my suggestion that she could develop the ability to live her own life without having to escape into her schizophrenic world. To that she answered that the world as it is does not permit human beings to live the happiness of sexual union without imposing severe chains and pains. She, therefore, preferred her world of delusions where she was her own master and protected by the "forces."

Her judgment of the social situation, as far as the sex-economic way of living was concerned, seemed quite rational. Not a single one of her critical ideas could have been refuted on the basis of human welfare or social security or moral integrity. For instance: during her puberty there had been moments of great sanity and lucid judgment; she clearly longed for a boy to embrace her and to love him; but then came the thought of *where* to love him, and *what to do with her relatives,* who would have hindered and plagued her, had they only guessed what she was doing; she was afraid of being sent to a reform school; she had known that she would become a criminal if she were caught and taken to an institution. She had not known at that time that she would later spend many years in a mental institution. But her suffering from her frustrated, bodily excitations had become so strong that she finally welcomed the dullness of mental institutions.

Should she have yielded to her sick mother, who nagged her all day long, hated her father, spoke disparagingly about him, smeared his name wherever and whenever she could, because he had withdrawn from her? Or how could she have developed her great intelligence in some field of human endeavor when she had no room of her own, when her mother opened all letters addressed to her? She had been squeezed between her overpowering bodily craving for a man and the social impossibility in her life situation of satisfying this desire. The period of this dilemma was short but agonizing. Then, for the first time, things around her became alive and seemed to "tell her things." First she was curious; but when they grew stronger, she became frightened and finally confused. Where did *she end* and where did the *world around her begin?* She could tell less and less. Then murderous impulses would come up and she had a hard time refraining from hurting people. Therefore the walls of the institution appeared as a refuge from great strain and persecution on the part of her own organism.

During the following weeks she was clear and cooperative; she wished that I "would free her from her experience of animated objects" which frightened her so much. She felt deadly afraid of the "other world." I asked her to describe this other world. She drew this diagram:

Room	Mirror
A = Real World	B = "Other World"

The power of the "forces" manifested itself in their ability to open world B for her when she felt anxious in world A. This "other world" was "quite real," although she knew perfectly well that it was *not real.*

The patient began to perceive the deadness in her throat. She understood for the first time in several months what I meant when I kept telling her that she held her respiration; that she should try to press her air out; that she should let her chest "fall" or "go down."

She felt anxious when the chest moved downward with the air passing through her glottis. When she felt a strong excitation in her lower abdomen, she said: "I am afraid of something I do not feel, but I know it is there. . . ."

The projection and mystification of the bodily streamings were the result of *lack of clear perception of an organ sensation which was nevertheless perceived.*

It is very difficult to put such biophysical functions into proper words. These functions are beyond the realm of words and ideas.

It is very difficult to formulate in words an experience in which a process in the organism *is* perceived and yet is *not* perceived *as one's own*. But there can be no doubt whatsoever that this is exactly the key to understanding the schizophrenic split and the projection of bodily sensations. Her sharp intelligence manifested itself again when she spontaneously formulated the difference between a hysterical and a schizophrenic experience: the first, she said, consists in an alienation of an organ from the total body experience; the latter consists in an alienation, just as in hysteria, *plus misinterpretation and mystification of the detached perception.*

This description is in agreement with the most skillful biopsychiatric comprehension of the process. It fits every type of mystical experience; mysticism perceives a body-own process as alien and originating "beyond" one's person, or beyond one's earth.

The patient was in a constant disequilibrium between rational integration of her feelings and schizophrenic delusion. I had expected that her schizophrenic process would develop fully when her self-perception made contact with her bodily excitation in full force. My expectation proved correct.

Thirty-fourth session

The patient came with vivid schizophrenic delusions. Soon after the last treatment, when she had made contact with her bodily streamings, a diarrhea had set in. She had had "twisted intestines . . . and something had moved downward toward her genitals." She had vomited everything she had eaten; she was bothered by severe flatulence. During the night, she had seen many peculiar forms and figures in her room with rainbows around them. It was obvious that the orgone energy had moved rapidly in her body and had brought about the excitation of her intestines. It was further obvious that she had misinterpreted most of her sensations. She complained: "I do not trust you . . . you are at one with them [with the forces]; they use all possible means to harm me . . . they poisoned the food so that I had to vomit . . . they made it rain to annoy me . . . they never before mingled with everyday life . . . now they do . . . that's your fault. . . ."

The idea of being poisoned may well be understood as a result of excitations which are bounced back at the upper intestines in reversed direction, i.e., in impulses to vomit. I persuaded her to yield more to the "forces." She succeeded in giving in more fully. When severe tremors in her total body set in, she went off again. I brought her back by pinching her. But her eyes remained empty and "faraway." The skin of her forehead was immobile; she trembled with severe anxiety.

This was in itself a great step forward. I had expected it. I had known that all her schizophrenic symptoms would flare up once her organ sensations developed and were perceived fully. But I did not know what the outcome would be: *complete catatonia* or *recovery?* The risk had to be taken, since catatonia would have been the only outcome without therapy anyhow. I also knew that the danger of suicide was great. I assured myself of her confidence and honesty. She confided that when her hands went completely dead for a while the other day, she had had the impulse to cut them off. ". . . If only I could trust you . . ." she said repeatedly. ". . . They have got hold of me now . . . they do with me what they want . . . I cannot fight them any longer. . . ." It struck me that she had refused a cigarette I had offered her during the treatment. She was suspicious of being poisoned.

Thirty-fifth session

The patient came in a state of complete vegetative shock. Her skin was spotty from blue to red. She trembled and her eyes were severely veiled. She could hardly speak. At first she seemed willing to cooperate. But when convulsions occurred in her face and shoulders she suddenly jumped up, pulled a knife from behind her back, and went at me. I made it a habit to be on the lookout for such things. I grabbed her hand, squeezed the knife out of her fist, and told her sharply that she should lie down and not move. She screamed: "I have to kill you . . . I have to . . . I must. . . ."

For more than two decades I had experienced and understood the murderous rage against me on the part of people who became frightened to death by my scientific, factual description of the orgonotic streamings. I had met this terror in presidential candidates, Communist liberators, fascist mystics, well-adjusted psychoanalysts, neurotic court psychiatrists, neurosurgeons, directors of mental institutions, cancer pathologists without hope, schizophrenics, politicians of all kinds, scheming wives of co-workers, etc. So I knew what I was dealing with. She was blue with rage; she tried again and again to jump upon me, to get at my throat, and to kick me. . . . She did it openly and frankly, while the biopathic psychoanalyst who feels threatened by my teachings goes around sneaking and gossiping, telling people that I was in a mental institution or that I seduced all my female patients or that I have just been buried. I preferred the behavior of my patient by far. After some time, she broke down in a quite unschizophrenic manner and cried bitterly like a child. She cried for a long time, and it was emotionally complete. At intervals, she became furious, cursed her mother, her father, the world, the whole system of education and medicine, the state hospital, and the physicians there. In the end she calmed down and explained: after the last treatment, *spontaneous movements in her lower abdomen had plagued her;* she had felt them fully; *her genital had "itched" severely for the first time in her memory; she had tried to satisfy herself, but without success.*

I had to take strong precautions against possible disaster. I knew that if the therapy did not succeed in making the patient capable of tolerating and integrating her bodily sensations, the worst could be expected to happen. I notified her relatives to take the necessary steps to commit her to the institution. One will ask again why I took the great risk, why I did not commit her immediately. My answer is again: the scientific results of this experiment were tremendous; to commit the patient would have meant stopping the flow of scientific information; it would also have meant extinguishing any hope of her recovery. She was on the verge of recovery and deserved a chance to reach it. The final outcome proved this attitude correct. But at that time I did not know the final outcome.

Thirty-sixth session

The patient came late; she had not wanted to come. "I do not like it [the situation] . . ." she said. "I felt pleasure all over my body; my body is one now, but I do not like it. . . ." She was almost completely relaxed; her respiration functioned well. "I would like to go back to my old world. . . . I loved the forces. . . . I am afraid I might want badly to sleep with a boy. . . ." (She had *never* embraced a man.)

She showed all the well-known signs of severe preorgastic *pleasure anxiety*. The prospect was: she would either become frightened to a sufficiently great extent to withdraw again fully and probably finally; or she would break through to full health.

Thirty-seventh session

She same in, complaining about the movements in her abdomen and in her genital region. She had no power over these movements. On the contrary, the movements had great power over her body. Before, she could do nothing to the "forces," but she could, so she said, kill me because I had brought about this situation of movements in her body. She could not live with these movements. If I were dead, then the influence I was exerting upon her would cease, and with it also the movements in her body.

Let us pause for a moment again to think over this situation: the therapeutic result was doubtful as far as restoration of complete sanity was concerned. As a clinical confirmation of the whole theory of organismic orgone biophysics, the situation was invaluable, rich in possibilities, with a broad outlook on the whole realm of human character structure. To sum it up, the following conclusions seemed safe:

1. The murderous hate I and my co-workers had met in so many people, laymen and professionals alike, was due to the provocation of spontaneous movements in the body, in bodies which had never experienced such autonomic movements, well-known to every healthy, unarmored individual.

2. These movements, if *alienated* or *excluded* from the realm of full perception (= self-perception), constitute the experiences of every kind of mysticism. That a psychopath like Hitler preferred to kill in spring thus becomes easily understandable.

3. The influencing "forces" in schizophrenia are identical with the plasmatic movements in the organism.

4. Many types of crime and murder are due to such sudden changes in the structure of potential or actual murderers.

5. Chronically armored human organisms tolerate only low levels of bio-energy and the corresponding emotions. What constitutes high-pitched joie de vivre in unarmored individuals, their buoyance, their aliveness, namely the functioning of bio-energy

on a high level with a strong energy metabolism, is utterly unbearable to the armored individual. *Sudden* changes from a high to a very low energy level constitute acute depression. On the other hand, *sudden* changes from a chronically low to a very high energy level constitute dramatic and dangerous situations because of the inability to tolerate strong sensations and emotions.

It is, therefore, to be expected that biopsychiatry will sooner or later succeed in describing human structures and characteristic reactions in terms of *"bio-energetic metabolism," "emotional tolerance"* of biophysical excitation, and *"capacity for energy discharge."*

Such an *energetic* point of view would enable us to handle, finally, "human nature," not with complicated ideas and experiences, but with simple energy functions, as we are handling the rest of nature.

Thirty-eighth session

The patient felt fairly well, was coordinated, clear. She had tried to satisfy herself; she had felt a strong throbbing in her vagina. However, she had "detached" her right arm; she could not press the hand in handshaking. I explained to her that some deep inhibition manifested itself in this detachment of her right arm, that we had to get it out of the depth. "This would be much too dangerous," she said.

We were dealing clearly with a very old and deep blocking of the motion of physical self-gratification with the right hand.

Thirty-ninth session

I knew that I had to put her through the genital emotions as quickly and as safely as possible if a final breakdown was to be avoided. She was very mobile and clear that day. When the respiration had "pumped up" enough organismic energy, her *pelvis began to twitch* spontaneously. Strong streaming sensations set in and she refused to continue. She declared suddenly that she was confused (she was *not*). At the next parole meeting she would hide from the parole physician the fact that she felt much better in order to keep the door open for return to the asylum. "If I let go further, it will take my brain away. . . ." She meant she would lose consciousness: ORGASM ANXIETY was coming to the foreground. At the end of the session, she made the sign of the cross in the Catholic manner.

At 11 p.m. that evening she called me on the phone to tell me that the moon "had thrown shadows on the floor of her room," and that that was the "sign to her from them," but she had been unable to call the "forces." I succeeded in quieting her down.

Fortieth session

She was very unhappy. I knew that she had been very excited sexually the night before, that she had not been able to obtain gratification, and that she had reached a most crucial point in her life. She told me that she had tried desperately to get the "forces" back, but that she had not succeeded in doing so "in spite of the contact with the moon." She was convinced that the "forces" refused her company because she was "Jewish." Furthermore, she said that she did not want to lose her world; she could not live in "this world."

It was clear what she meant by the word "Jewish." It meant to be "sexual" and "swinish" at the same time. The ambiguity of these emotional experiences derived from the fact that she wanted to feel her bodily forces but did not want to feel or be "swinish." This was in complete agreement with the clinical experience of orgone biophysics: *the human animal longs for full feeling and realization of his biosexual emotions; at the same time he rejects them and hates them because of their perverse distortion.* "God" represents the former, and "devil" the latter; both are fused into one painful, confusing entity. This becomes quite obvious in schizophrenics but is also present and clearly expressed in *homo normalis.*

Was her refusal of the world of *homo normalis* justified? Of course it was. This world had ruined her natural biological structure ("God") and had implanted the "devil"; her mother had done this to her. The schizophrenic knows the ways of *homo normalis* and has full insight into their disastrous results. *Homo normalis,* on the other hand, is a Babbitt who does not understand the schizophrenic world of *rational* judgment, or, for that matter, his own.

It is a major objective of this case history to describe the psychotic crisis in relation to the orgonotic streamings and emotions of the biosystem. It is of the utmost importance to concentrate one's attention on this single fact, and not to be distracted by the maze of schizophrenic mechanisms and delusory ideas. We must penetrate to the common denominator which characterizes the schizophrenic breakdown, regardless of the contents of the delusions. *The center of the schizophrenic breakdown is determined by overwhelming orgonotic plasma streamings which flood a biosystem incapable of coping with the emotional storm.*

Psychiatry has understood that the psychotic system is an attempt at reconstruction of the lost *ego* (= *world*). But it could not tell why this world of the *ego* breaks down. The psychotic reconstruction is a result and not a cause of the disease. This must be kept well in mind. Also, the "narcissistic fixation in childhood" is not a cause of the breakdown but only one of the conditions under which the breakdown occurs. *The core of the problem is the biophysical split between excitation and perception and the resulting intolerance by the biosystem of strong emotions.*

9. CRISIS AND RECOVERY

The patient went through the following three distinct periods at the end and after the treatment: (1) great well-being and sanity; (2) sudden catatonic breakdown; (3) full recovery, with freedom from psychosis for over five years after treatment.

1. The rapid approach to health

The first period lasted about a month. In the beginning, she used to cry very often "because the 'forces' do not want me any more; because I am Jewish. . . ." With the bodily sensations and the return of their perception, the "forces" were gone completely.

Then she began to enjoy her newly acquired health. She used to call me up saying that she did not need the treatment that day, that she felt fine and happy, that she preferred to play tennis instead or to see a show. She worked efficiently and happily at the office.

During the treatment she breathed fully; she let her emotions develop freely, cried, laughed, talked very intelligently and without a trace of blocking or perseveration. But I did not trust the situation fully, because of my experiences with reactions to severe orgasm anxiety. I knew *she was not safe until she had yielded to her biological role as a female animal in the embrace with a man whom she could really love.*

The "forces were not around any more." No trace of any schizophrenic symptoms was to be seen on the surface. But there were many indications that there were schizophrenic functions still at work in the depth, even though without a high pitch of bio-energy.

She hesitated to acknowledge the accomplishment of orgone therapy. We know that patients who do not appreciate good results are somewhere and somehow hostile, due to a remainder of anxiety.

She said emphatically that she thanked only the great Lord for her recovery. She developed the idea that "health" meant continuous, uninterrupted happiness, without any interference of sorrow and worries. She did not accept my statement that health meant also the ability to stand the impact of unpleasant situations and worries.

She felt her genital region as belonging to her, and no longer as dead or alien; but she claimed to have no desire for the sexual union. There was no doubt whatsoever that she did not admit the problem of sexual union to full scrutiny. She was evasive and glib about the subject of a serious love life.

Then slowly the suspicious indications of oncoming disaster began to increase.

She began to call me a "faker" and a "dangerous man" who provoked "bad things" in people. She did "not want any orgastic potency," she said, although she had come to me explicitly because I had elaborated this concept of emotional health.

One day she came with a metal cross hanging from her neck; she had bought it for ten cents "in order to appease the 'forces.'" I warned her not to be too optimistic but to expect more devilish things from the depth of her emotions. She laughed at that and assured me that I was exaggerating.

She showed signs of escape from further therapy. She wanted to come only for another few sessions. She said I was not cultivated enough, not subtle enough for her. She would go to the police to accuse me of "doing bad things."

Then, one day, she did not want to cooperate at all, remained in her coat, and left soon after. She phoned that same evening, excused herself for her behavior, and told me that she still needed me very badly. Then events rapidly turned for the worse.

2. Sudden catatonic breakdown

The patient came to the next session in a very bad state of health. She had had a "horrible night"; things and forms had become "alive" in the room; a shadow had appeared on the wall and had stretched out an arm to take hold of her. "I felt no anxiety, but it was a horrible experience," she said.

She felt a little better when bodily currents developed and when she permitted their perception.

But the following day she came completely confused, with severe dissociation in speech and ideas. All things were "queer"; all actions were terribly complicated; when something went wrong she thought that the forces were interfering with her will. Her job at the office was a great burden, scarcely bearable. Her speech during the whole session was severely retarded and mostly unintelligible, but she tried very hard to make herself understood.

She remained in the treatment room at 7:20 p.m. to dress. One of my assistants found her at 8:50 p.m. in a cataleptic position; she could not move; she had remained there in the same position for an hour and a half. Very slowly and with great effort she told us that she had been unable to call for help. Her organism had reacted with catatonic catalepsy, that is, with a total block of motility, to the strong plasmatic currents which threatened to overcome her.

The following day the patient had recovered from her cataleptic attack, but she had developed a *delusion of grandeur* instead. This new delusion obviously had the function of preventing the flow of bio-energy in her organism and the perception of nature in herself.

When during the treatment strong preorgastic sensations occurred, she suddenly said: *"I am too great and too good to be an animal. . . ."* A few minutes later: ". . . The 'forces' force me to cut deep into my left cheek. But I shall master myself; I am stronger than they [the forces]. . . ."

To the expert in orgone-biophysical functioning, this reaction was clearly the expression of a delusion of strength due to the new and gratifying experience of biophysical, vagotonic *expansion* of her plasma system. Still incapable, as she was, of accepting and enjoying the pleasure function fully, she turned against it by means of her delusion: now she was even stronger than the "forces," i.e., still stronger than the *animal* in her. This was soon confirmed in a very drastic manner. The following day I received this letter from her:

Thursday

Added adjunct—the affective (should be effective) advocates of the lyceum in Rome. You do not see that by immortal power of Will to survive and achieve. "My mind" is in a state of confusion about the pieces fitting in and my good boss and job. You did not fit the pieces for me no one did or does and that's why I go to psychiatrists to find out.—The water babies, the Goddess Diana, and the Dr. Doolittle stories when I was a kid. I am very very old from Buddha and Mohammed in caves and Isis on an alter of crucifixion I am always depressed by nature of myself. I must have a clear answer not by "changing my thoughts" as you said—that solves nothing—but you are very very kind my thoughts are not thoughts but impregnated knowledge given into my head. Sentences written in books that know how and why I suffer written for my eyes alone without the author's knowledge or will. Impregnated thoughts.

But the bad panic is from the terrific confusion which hurts.

Here's another message to add to your collection. It may prove someday extremely valuable—I would not have to say "I told you so."

Do you know who I am? I told you I would tell you the complete picture—and the Greeks and Romans—ancient of course—fit right into the picture. I suppose you have heard of *"Isis"*—

I AM HER RESURRECTION

And there are those who are opposed to Foreign Forces—there are probably five all told.—The Lord on the left, the others are more or less somewhat antagonistic—It is these that sometimes bring fear because they are often against me and torture me cleverly. You see the complete reincarnation is not always present and when only part is there I am open to abuse from these other forces. I have no priestesses, etc. left—not in this world so I have to fight myself—and I am not always full of the complete super-power to do so easily—the Lord of course—is my ally. When I am complete as this evening in your home—there is Nothing I cannot do—should I so wish—coming home

there was a policeman ordering someone to put the lights out in a store
—for air-raid precaution—I was hoping he would say something to me
or someone would—to order me to do something—Fools that people
are they cannot appreciate the greatness of me—they do not see it—
they only see something strange but they do not know the power.

The question of suicide is difficult because of the question of status
beyond—would I go back to my original birth or forward into the
future queenliness—until the question is solved I can do nothing. Death
is another force, he is quite a kind, serious figure—he came years ago—
but not since. The One today was the same as last week but that is
Evil, I think—You see I as Isis am not fully on the same standing as
the Others—principally one reason because I am predestined to live
here on earth and carry on that life—that problem I have never been
told the answer to—what the main reason behind this being on
earth is—

> That's enough to write
>   F.
> Names are so meaningless
> Just family left-overs—not at all
> real—

She had become the goddess Isis because of her strong bodily
sensations; the psychotic distortion of the feeling of strength and
"mission" and contact with the universe was clearly due to her
inability to permit full perception of the natural orgonotic
strength and to enjoy it as a living organism, whole and sane.
Therefore, my statement seems justified that the schizophrenic,
in contradistinction to the neurotic, has the full power of his natural orgonotic energy function; he differs from the healthy animal, including man, in that he splits off perception from excitation and thus transforms his feeling of strength into delusions of
grandeur, and his weak perception of faraway excitation into delusions of the "beyond" and persecution.

These insights seem to be of first-rate importance for the
understanding of the whole realm of psychotic delusions; it does
not matter whether the split is brought about by high tempera-
ture, as in post-puerperal amentia, or by post-syphilitic structural
lesions as in the paralytic delusion, or by a truly schizophrenic
split. The essence remains the same.

Once the unitary function of the organism is split, the biophysical processes in the organism will be perceived as a force alien to the ego, in the form of hallucinations or delusions of various kinds. The specific mechanisms which distinguish a delusion in general paresis from a delusion in puerperal fever or a delusion in dementia praecox are not important here. What is important, however, is the *basic dissociation of the perceiving apparatus from the biophysical system of excitation.*

Our patient described this pathological situation very clearly during lucid moments in that period of her breakdown:

"The world is very far away . . . and yet very close . . . it does not concern me at all . . . and yet I feel everything around me in a painful way. . . . When an airplane flies by, I have the clear feeling that the motor makes a louder noise in order to *annoy me. . . .* The birds are singing louder in order to give me hell. . . . That sounds silly, but I sincerely believe that they do it for that purpose. . . . The human beings look at me and observe carefully everything I am doing. . . . I can scarcely stand all the many impressions. . . . How shall I be able to perform my work? . . . I would like to go back to the hospital where I do not have to do the work and be responsible."

Later on:

"Would you permit me to swallow this cross? It could help me to stand all that better. When there is only *one* 'force' around me, I can stand it; but when there are many of them around, then I cannot stand it; my ability to stand it is not sufficient."

This is plain language, indeed. One has only to learn to listen to it to understand it, instead of "shocking" such broken-down people. *Homo normalis* shuts himself up in his room behind drawn blinds when the bright sunlight annoys him, when he cannot stand the impact of natural forces. The old gossiping spinster keeps on telling bad stories about loving couples, because her organism cannot stand the excitation which is brought about in her by the functioning of love around her. The biopathic Führer kills millions of people because he cannot stand any alive expression. The criminal kills the one who provokes in him the feelings of humanity and goodness. The schizophrenic falls apart emotionally and biophysically.

The patient fell into a stupor that same session, recovered, and was taken home by one of her relatives.

The following day at 1:30 p.m. she swallowed the cross she had carried on her chest. She came to the session with great pain. She had at first only taken the cross into her mouth. Then "it went down quite by itself. . . ." It had hurt in the pharynx, but finally it had slipped through the esophagus. She had intended "to please God" by this action, and to stop people from looking at her. She had been frightened when she had swallowed the cross, but God had smiled at her. She wanted to walk on a high mountain, to stretch her arms toward heaven; then God would come close to her and would embrace her.

Her intense desire for the genital embrace was thus disguised in the form of the psychotic delusion of being embraced by God.

I let her eat a good deal of bread immediately. She looked at the bread and said: "Here there are eyes [the holes in the bread] looking at me. . . ."

She was taken to a private physician who x-rayed her. The cross was in her stomach. The physician knew of the orgone-therapeutic experiment and cooperated in order to help keep her out of the institution. But all efforts were in vain. In my long career as a research physician, I have seen many a human being rather die than admit the perception of his bio-energetic sensation of streaming. I have witnessed people go to war rather than risk punishment for telling the truth. Therefore, it did not surprise me to see this patient prefer to go to the mental institution rather than admit full genital excitation in her organism.

The cross was later eliminated naturally. But the following day I received this report from one of her relatives who was guarding her:

Report as of May 23, 1942

I first became aware of some change in her behavior when she asked her mother to leave, and said that she would prepare something to eat. I later learned that she insisted that the mother leave the house. She did set things out to eat. When I looked up next, she was standing at the sink with a glass in her hand which she was hitting up against the side of the sink. It refused to break and then she tried to hit it with a small drain shovel to no avail. I thought she would hurt herself so I approached and offered to break the glass for her. She gave me the glass which I broke. She picked up the pieces and carefully put them in the pail.

There was no further incident during the meal. She remained in the kitchen watching me; her eyes had a strange look. After the meal, I prepared a shower for myself. Then suddenly, while under the shower, I was very much surprised to see her appear in the bathroom with a large kitchen knife in her hands. She was completely nude. This is the first time I had ever seen her nude before me.

I asked her what she wanted the knife for. She said that she used it to open the door, to lift the latch. Then she laid the knife down upon the washstand and looked at me. I pretended to go on washing but all the time I kept watching her. She just stood there saying nothing and looking at me. I tried to make conversation with her but it was no good. All of a sudden, she jumped up on the rim of the bathtub in which I was, put her hands around my throat, and tried to push me under the water. My throat was soapy and her grip was insecure. I took hold of her wrists and forced her off the bathtub. I asked her why she did that. She said that she wanted to see me under the water. She stood looking at me for some time and then left.

When I came out of the bathroom, she was in another room. The lights were out and she sat in the gloom. I did not go into the room but I listened as intently as I could. After some time, I heard the sound of tearing. What it was that she was tearing I could not tell, and so after it continued for some time, I went to see what she was doing. She had completely torn the pages out of the book, *The Function of the Orgasm,* by Dr. Wilhelm Reich, and she was about to start on another copy of the book, when I took it from her. She now had her bathrobe on and continued to walk about in the dark.

When I noticed her again, she had climbed upon a dresser in the hall and stood there in a catatonic condition, a cigarette dangling from her hand. After about ten minutes, during which time she stood upon the dresser immobile, I called Dr. Reich to ask him what I should do. He suggested that I take her down and bring her over to the phone to talk to him. I took her by the hand and pulled her down. She sank into my arms rather easily. But when I started to carry her over to the phone, she began to kick and insisted that I let her down. I did. She put on her bathrobe and sat down to talk to Dr. Reich on the phone. I left her alone and went into another room.

Dr. Reich had suggested to me that I give her two sleeping pills and put her to bed. But after talking on the phone, she was much better and said that she wanted to visit some married friends of ours with whom she had an appointment. We both went to see them and spent the evening there. While she was not completely well, she was pretty clear. When we got home about 2 a.m., she took two sleeping pills and went to bed.

She slept all through Sunday and refused to get up either to eat or for any other reason. She finally got up on Monday morning, but she didn't go to work that day.

A few hours after I received this letter, the patient phoned me. She wanted to "do something, but cannot tell me what. . . ." I knew the patient's status well enough to feel sure that she would not do anything cruel. I knew that deep-seated schizoid mechanisms had broken through and were still breaking through; that she was acting out some of them, but also that her attachment to the treatment and her confidence in me were strong enough to keep her from dangerous actions. *The element of mutual trust had great weight in our relationship.* She had promised me that she would go to the hospital if necessary; I had to trust her promise if the cure was to be achieved. One cannot bring a schizophrenic back to sanity if one does not support his sane structure and rely on it. *She knew that I trusted her, and this was the most powerful guarantee against real danger.* The further development as well as the final outcome proved this attitude to be correct.

In the afternoon of the same day her relative called up: she had undressed completely, had climbed on a high chest of drawers, and remained there in the *position of a statue;* she had told her relative that she was the goddess Isis. She had also approached her brother in a sexual manner, after she had tried to drown him in the bathtub.

One hour later her brother called up again: she was still standing there immobile; she apparently could not move. I advised her relatives to keep a cool head; I told them that she was going through a certain emotional situation, that keeping her out of the hospital, if at all possible, was essential, but that they should call the ambulance if they felt that the situation was dangerous. *They did not have to call the ambulance.*

I also told them to call me immediately at any time if there should be any change for the worse. They did not call me until the afternoon of the following day. The patient had gone to bed the previous evening greatly exhausted. Now, at 4 p.m., she was still in bed and did not want to get up. Her mother tried hard to *pull* her out of bed. I told them to let the patient sleep; she was obviously exhausted and needed rest after the great strain she had lived through.

The patient slept through until the afternoon of the *third* day, and came to see me at 6 p.m. She "had been at the hospital to write herself in again, *but the hospital was closed.*" I told her that she *should* go back to the hospital if she felt the need to do so. She said that she did not know whether she ought to go back or not. She was afraid that she would deteriorate completely if she went back. I had to agree that this danger was present and that it was great.

It was perfectly clear in this session, after the great attack, that she was both *perfectly clear and very close to a complete catatonic breakdown* at the same time. I had never seen great clarity and sanity paired with a catatonic status in such a manner before. Usually a state of clarity and sanity returns *after* the patient breaks out of the catatonic stupor by way of violent rage. Here no rage was visible, but *clarity fought against immobilization.* Which function would win out in the end? I did not know; nobody could tell.

Her catatonic immobilization was very strong, making greater the contradiction in her strong urge to communicate with me, to talk to me, to tell what was going on in her. She spoke very clearly but very slowly, each word coming forth with great difficulty. Her facial expression was mask-like; she could not move her facial muscles; but *her eyes were not veiled;* on the contrary, they had the glow of great sanity and insight. Her speech, though slow, was clear and orderly, logical and to the point.

She told me in the course of about three hours that she *"had fallen into the other world completely"* the other day. The "forces" had succeeded in pulling her into this other world against her will. She had finally succeeded in coming back into *this* world. But she still felt far, far away. She had no contact with things and people at all. Everything seemed removed as if into the far distance. She felt completely indifferent to whether it was nine o'clock in the morning or in the evening, whether the people around her were laughing or crying, whether they liked her or not. She tried hard to come close to people and experiences, but was unable to do so.

She stared at a bright spot on the floor where light was reflected from the window. She knew it was light, but at the same time it appeared strange to her, *"foreign"* as it were, and as if it were "something alive." It seemed clear to me that *she perceived impressions clearly, but that at the same time* SHE COULD NOT MAKE CONTACT WITH HER OWN PERCEPTIONS.

The difference between her inner situation before treatment and now consisted in that previously the state of clarity had alternated with the state of confusion; *now she was confused but at the same time she knew perfectly well what she was confused about.* This was a great step forward toward health. These insights into the process of the cure itself are immeasurably important. They not only tell us what is going on in a catatonic stupor but reveal important functions of self-perception and of *consciousness* itself. Every natural scientist knows how decisive these insights are for a future comprehension of the greatest riddle of all natural science, the function of *self-perception.* And during the whole experiment I felt and acted far more as a natural scientist than as a psychiatrist. I would advise that only psychiatrists equipped with great psychiatric skill *and* thorough knowledge of the problems of the mind should attempt such ventures in exploring natural functions. But, on the other hand, there can be no doubt that such risky research is indispensable if mastery of a vast realm of the emotional plague is to be finally obtained by medicine.

She remembered well that she had tried to drown her brother and to turn on the gas. But she claimed that *"it* wanted to do it," that she had tried to resist *"it"* but did not succeed. Therefore, she wanted to go back to the hospital. It was clear that, if she managed to keep her clarity, the psychotic functions would cease. This required that she *not* hide behind the protective walls of the hospital.

Of the rest of the period of catatonia, she remembered only the day when she had stood there as the goddess Isis; she could not remember the following two days when she lay in bed, immobilized. She had been catatonic for two days and was amnestic to it.

I let her talk as much as she wanted. She described again and again the alienation of the world in different words and pictures. In the end, I took her into the orgone accumulator. Her reactions became faster after some twenty minutes and she left in good condition. The first decisive victory over the catatonic breakdown had been won.

She came back the following day a bit slowed down again. Irradiation in the orgone accumulator removed the plasmatic contraction promptly again. This was very hopeful. It became clear *that the orgone accumulator would some day play a great role in the overcoming of catatonic states of biophysical contraction of the organism.*

I must confess that I felt greatly astonished about the results obtained with the orgone accumulator, although I was already then—some seven years ago—well acquainted with its vagotonic effects. Nevertheless, the whole thing appeared amazing and incredible even to me. Therefore, I could well understand the reactions of distrust on the part of physicians who had never worked with orgone energy.

I informed her brother of her great improvement, but warned again against too great optimism. I also advised him to be ready at any time to commit the patient to the institution. The patient agreed to all this.

Then the following morning she met with disaster. The whole significance of the police mentality of mental institutions became apparent in a grotesque manner. *In spite of the information the officials had about the experimental therapy and the good results obtained so far, and in spite of their own approval of what was going on, they had the patient taken away the following morning at 7:30 to Bellevue Hospital by two psychiatric nurses and by force, without conferring with me or her relatives. The patient did not resist.*

This god-like omnipotence of institutional psychiatrists is the greatest obstacle to true efforts concerning rational mental hygiene. They could have and should have at least informed the relatives and me. No. They felt almighty after the worst was over, the patient having been handled skillfully and painstakingly by an experienced biopsychiatrist, by the relatives, and by the patient herself. The latter behaved, in view of the situation, admirably. I sincerely hope that the mental-hygiene movement will one day be able to clip the wings of the court and institutional psychiatrists, and will force them to listen and to pay attention to new and hopeful medical efforts in cases where they themselves betray nothing but utter ignorance. The whole effort of many months was in danger of breaking down because of this action on the part of officials. I did not succeed, then, in finding out how it had come about. There can be no true mental hygiene as long as such things are permitted to happen.

It is true, the patient had reacted in a dangerously psychotic manner on several occasions. It is also true, and I knew it very well, that I had taken a great risk. But we take risks every single day of our lives, if in nothing else than in walking under roofs with loose bricks. Yet we do not jail the owner of the house with loose bricks. We do not jail the parents who produce criminals *en masse*. And we do not jail the judge who sentenced an innocent man to die in the electric chair. Therefore, we cannot become excited at all over such well-controlled actions of a schizophrenic. Our patient was, on the whole, in spite of everything, much less dangerous than a single psychopathic neurosurgeon who keeps knowledge out of his mental institution, or a dictator who rules millions. Nobody asked that Hitler be jailed; yet they took away this patient who struggled so bravely for health. It is obvious that there is far more behind such institutional actions than mere safeguarding of the public.

Another fact is important here. We medical orgone therapists, who work with deep human emotions, know from experience that even the most adjusted neurotic will sound wild and insane during orgone therapy to the ear of an uninformed neurologist. Were such a neurologist to listen to a single therapeutic session of orgone therapy, he would surely run to the district attorney, as he in fact once did in New Jersey. When deep emotions, especially hatred, break through the armor, a procedure which is absolutely necessary for cure, we know that we have created an *artificial* situation involving *genuine* emotional forces. We know the emotions are *potentially* dangerous, but the process of breaking through was deliberate. Usually we have the patient well in hand, and we have prepared the emotional breakthrough for days or weeks with the greatest care. The same applies to cutting open an abdomen for an operation. Nobody will accuse the surgeon of murder. And nobody objects to the cruel method of shock "therapy" or the piercing of the thalamus with long needles or to the frantic brain operations which kill patients.

Since ignorance in emotional matters is widespread; since, furthermore, every ignoramus thinks he is an "expert" because he has emotions himself and can, therefore, judge biophysical or psychological processes, the situation in biopsychiatry is different from that in surgery.

I myself was not quite sure how much of the emotional situation in this patient was due to therapeutic procedure and how much was due to a genuine psychotic breakdown. The jailers were far removed from any such consideration. More will have to be said later about the hatred of *homo normalis* for the schizophrenic. It took only a few days to convince me fully that the patient had reacted psychotically *in accordance with the therapeutic situation, and not as a consequence of a psychotic breakdown.* She had taken the injustice in an *admirable* fashion. She wrote the following sane letter from the hospital to her brother, a short time after the commitment:

May 28, 1942

Thanks a lot for writing so soon—I know the manner of my leaving and the unexpectedness of it, must have been a great shock to you and Mom—I, myself, was shocked, so I can imagine how you people felt.—Anyway, the only thing I can say is that it was an unnecessary step for the hospital authorities to have taken—but since there was nothing I could do at the time to stop their taking me— I "took it" as nicely as possible.

I am a little bothered about my job.—I am wondering if it would be possible for me to take up where I left off, if I leave here soon enough. I would hate the thought of losing the excellent reference that I know they would give me—unless they are angry because I left without giving them notice.

If you get this letter in time to come out this Sunday, fine; if not, next week will do just as well. If possible, try and get Dr. Reich to come out with you—I'd like to see him.

When you write again, send me E's address—it is in my address book (which is on my table in my room). Let me know if she got in touch with you and if she was angry about my not being able to go with her on the A.Y.N. trip this Saturday.

Watch for the Red Cross first aid Certificate, I was expecting in the mail within a week or so.

Keep in touch with O. and M. and let me know as soon as she has her baby, and of course how she is feeling.

Tell Mom to send out some anklets for me. Tell her, also, not to worry—I feel fine and am hoping that it will be very soon that I leave here.—

Lots of love,
F.

I found out later that her commitment was due to a misapprehension on the part of the parole physician about her description of the "forces," which were coming through in orgone therapy. Her letter from the institution sounded sane and perfectly rational. Her cure had developed far enough to enable her to stand up against the impact of the cruel method of commitment. I received the following letter from the patient, which shows clearly that her reactions were only the usual reactions during psychiatric orgone therapy:

June 6, 1942

I don't know what to make of things all around—my being picked up and brought back here to the Hospital was some shock—I might have thought a lot about going back—but never seriously expected them to go to the length of forcing me back—In my opinion—they have some nerve—I never did anything to give them a right to do that to me—and without warning, too—did my brother tell you?—I could have made a fuss and refused to go—but I knew they had straight jackets in the ambulance-bus with them and there were enough of them to drag me down by force—so I just gave in as graciously as I could—I fitted in here just as before—I work all around the place and help out—but I've felt "off" a couple of times—here at least it doesn't make a damn bit of difference—but I would like to go on a "bat" and let loose—the only trouble with that is that it will land me in the violent ward and I will lose all the privileges I have gotten—for being good, so well-known, and such a good worker—I don't know if it is worth it—we will see—

Anyway, Christ, etc. are sort of still around—that is in an influence sort of way—to mix things up for me—but not enough to make any difference so far—I wonder if electric shock would do any good—

Incidentally, how on earth could I call you if I was here Sunday—you don't think they would let a patient make a phone call, do you —I can't even write you this letter without the doctors, nurses, attendants reading it and censoring it and probably not sending it out—so my brother is sneaking it out for me—

I think you all (doctors) stink! I don't know who's right and who's wrong—or what's the right way—or who's who—Should I tell these doctors that I intend to see you when I get out? I don't see any doctor here, anyway—only at the final staff meeting, when they decide whether to let you go home or not—

What's the matter—do you think you are too big to come out to see a patient? I asked my brother to ask you to come—but he said you couldn't—so I guess that's why—I don't know who is on my side and who isn't—

There is the constant threat of transfer to back buildings which are awful—and the noise, stink, and awfullness of the place as a whole—

Did you tell these doctors or the parole doctor about anything that happened when I was home?—Is that why I was brought back?—

If I have you to blame—I'd hate you the rest of my life—

Then the institution began to exert its typical influence:

Sunday

I am writing this while waiting for my brother to come back. I don't know anything about anything—what's more—it isn't at all bad here—As a matter of fact—it's swell—We have parties every night—Me and some other patients who are privileged like me and some attendants——

It is all done on the sly, of course—I can't see any future life at all.

We shall see—what is more—Christ and Death, etc. come around again—bothering me—I'm "sitting on a powder keg" because I'm very suspicious of this swell time I'm having here—I suspect that Christ, etc. are piling it all on so that there can be a Big eruption to smash it all up—just to annoy me——

I'm somewhat in a fog during the day and evening—but not today—much—you know—dulled, etc. far away—

I don't even know about continuing with you after—I don't know anything—

It's all fake

Anyway—

F.

I wrote a letter to the parole physician who had misunderstood her report on her reactions in therapy. I asked him to give her a chance at recovery and to transfer her to a private institution. The physician agreed to that, but the deterioration which I had expected began to make rapid progress. I shall reproduce here the letters I received during that time. They give a rather clear picture of what happened to her; in her fight for life and recovery the patient showed great insight, expressed in a psychotic manner. If the reader takes care to study her letters thoroughly, to separate the psychotic expression from the content of her ideas, he will have to agree that these schizophrenics deteriorate not because of too little but because of too much and too clear contact with the world of armored man. It is true that the idea of Jesus appears in a typically psychotic manner in her as it does in many psychoses. But it is also true that Jesus was nailed to the cross by a pack of sick, cruel, murderous *homines normales.*

Thursday, November 19, 1942

It's awful and I don't know what to do. The other night I found out the why of the world and the war and almost everything. They were drinking gallons of blood in front of me. The devil is red because of that and he gets redder and redder and then the blood goes to the the sun and makes it on fire. Jesus was dripping blood on the cross by drops and this was being swallowed then he was seated on the side of the devil and drinking too—the table was round oblong of flowing thick blood (no feet on it) Mother Mary was at the corner watching. She was white as a sheet—All her blood had been drained off and consumed. She saw her son drinking that and suffered. I did not want to see it or hear it or know the why of everything—that why but they force me to see and hear—Maybe because of Isis—whom they used all these thousands of years in between I don't know what to do.

F.

The other night I found out the why of the world and the war and almost everything. They were drinking gallons of blood in front of me . . .

This statement was perfectly true, in full accordance with reality. Hitler and other militarists were shedding millions of gallons of blood. The hook-up with the red of the sun is psychotic, of course, and yet we feel inclined to think about this connection.

I had no message from the patient for several months. Then, in February 1943, I received the following letter. It was clear that she was still fighting bravely and that she tried hard to hold on to me:

Feb. 14, 1943

Things are screwy as hell—the world and all the people in it stink— Everybody is out to cut everybody else's throat—with large, butcher knives—They kill 8 million—they were the Jews and they keep us in here alive—it makes no sense—nothing does—I'm not supposed to be eating and I eat so I'm paid back with intrigue and pettiness—All around me—just to trap me in the middle of it all—I have to be 115 lbs.—For a long time now and I get close to it and then eat tons and gain it all back—the 10 disciples are still waiting to be taken out of the catacombs and I can't draw them out until I'm 115 lbs,—Now they are with the right hand side—The Lord and they help me on my promise to not eat but I do eat and, as I said before, get paid back plenty—so much that I can't always cope with it all. I don't know anybody today only about generations ago—centuries ago— eons ago—ancient sage—

Only *work* today is *right* and *real*—I love it—it never fails you— never—the work is a straight line—

You told my brother you would write—please, please do—I don't know anything and I'd like to hear about the straight corners from you—Thanks a lot—   **F.**

Great insight into the realities of our society and our ways of life, though expressed in a distorted manner, was characteristic of this letter, too, and is the way many a schizophrenic looks through us.

The patient stayed in the mental institution another few months, more than a year in all. Her brother kept me informed about her state of health. She came out of the institution severely injured emotionally, *but she had stood the ground which she had gained during only three months of orgone therapy.* She seemed less psychotic now, but she had changed her character in the direction of a compulsion neurosis. She was petty, mean, nasty toward her relatives; in short, she had become a typical *homo normalis.* Her greatness and the "spark" of genius were gone. The brother married a girl of another faith. Earlier, she would not have cared at all. She would have taken it philosophically. Now she objected on petty religious grounds, exactly like her mother, whom before she had fully seen through and whom she imitated now. She did not work in the office any more as she had done during most critical periods of her psychotic condition. She just went around dull and without interest, clinging to her hated mother in the typical neurotic manner. The experience of her violent commitment had been too much for her. Orgone therapy was not resumed until October 1944, a year after her release from the institution.

3. Slow recovery

Her biophysical status on October 4, 1944, was the following:

Respiration was functioning well, air was passing through the glottis, only slightly restricted.

Orgasm reflex was functioning easily and fully.

Vaginal self-gratification with orgastic release was obtained at regular intervals.

Eyes were still slightly veiled but considerably improved.

Total behavior was yielding and coordinated.

"Forces" were "very weak" but "still around in the far distance."

A slight pressure in the depth between the eyes was felt occasionally.

Skin of the face was ruddy.

In the course of a few exploratory sessions, shock-like indications of catatonia still were discernible, but on the whole the situation seemed satisfactory. I succeeded in releasing her crying fully. Thereupon, she asked me to let her speak at length and about "something very important." She had found the origin of her idea that she was the goddess Isis.

As a child, she remembered now, she had felt that she understood the world so much better than others, especially the grown-ups. She had always felt that the human beings around her were ill in a certain way which she could not fully understand. The main thing in these experiences had been her astonishment that she was capable of knowing so much more than the others.

Slowly, she had developed the feeling of standing apart from the rest of human beings, and she began to believe that she *had knowledge of thousands of years.* In order to explain to herself this extraordinary fact, she had to assume that such a thing was only possible if the goddess Isis had been reborn in her body. In relation to the everyday course of petty events, this idea appeared queer to her, and she had felt, therefore, still more apart. Then she had begun to feel her body very strongly concentrated in her genitals. This was contrary to everything in her environment. Slowly, she had learned that the feeling in her body could be weakened or "removed" if she forced herself to stiffen up. Then the excitations used to subside. *She had felt these excitations as overpowering and beyond her control.* Later she had learned to master them, but she still felt them around. The return of the overpowering forces was usually announced by a strong feeling in the upper abdomen. Sometimes only this aura remained; at other times the forces had come back in full force. Now she understood clearly that the overpowering forces of her early childhood and the later "evil forces" from "beyond" were one and the same thing.

I had the impression that, in spite of this insight, a certain amount of doubt was left in her mind about the true meaning of the "forces."

She continued to improve greatly. Her eyes became clearer, but off and on a pressure would return in her eyes. She explained eagerly: "But it [the pressure] is *behind* the eyes, not in the eyes. . . ." I could only confirm this statement.

Four months later the patient was again overtaken by a catatonic attack, but she overcame it. I suggested continuous daily irradiation of the region of the *sella turcica* with orgone energy.

I saw the patient again in January 1947. She read a great deal, had good appetite. She had had intercourse with great pleasure, but without final orgasm. In November of the same year she came again to ask my advice: the orgastic release during intercourse was still not functioning properly. But she worked well and felt well on the whole.

I advised her not to see any physician any more, not even me, and to try to forget the whole tragedy of her life. She begged for continuation of therapy with me, but I felt that she should become entirely independent and advised her to learn to stand on her own feet.

On August 4, 1948, I received the following letter:

I am writing to tell you how very much I was impressed by your book, *Listen, Little Man!* I cannot write I enjoyed the book since what you wrote about the "Little Man" is too sadly true, and I find myself fitting into those shoes.

I want you to know that the antagonism and even hatred which I showed toward you and your work during therapy, stemmed from my knowledge (at times even conscious) that I was getting too close to the break-through of my body into feeling and perhaps love. This was something I could not permit—I had severely controlled my body all my life and even consciously damned it to extinction—treating my body as dirt, hating it and neglecting and torturing myself in punishment for early feelings and masturbation. This same hate I had for my body was hate which I projected on to you. Forgive me for this, Doctor, this hate has done a great deal of damage to my body and mind. I would like to tell you that in spite of my "maliciousness and pettiness" your work with me did me tremendous good. I am aware of what harm I am doing to myself and others around me and why I am doing these things. Also, I find myself thinking and feeling that my body wants to be healthy and that my retreat into the "ivory tower" of mental illness only changed the color of the picture, but not the picture itself. I might make myself mentally ill to be something "special" to be certain that my body will keep far in the background, but I am gradually finding out that a healthy "active" body is more pleasure—physically and mentally.

So, I think you will see that I am getting there, however slowly, through your help. The process is slow since I still have a great number of tensions and sometimes blocks which I can't seem to do anything about. Often my small courage fails and then the dark picture of hate, delusions, and suffering comes back but not permanently so, thanks for everything and I pray to God I have courage. F.

At the end of 1948 I heard that she was in good condition—with the exception of a letter I received from her telling me how "rotten" she was "in her core" and how "unworthy to live in this beautiful world." I told her to stop worrying about it and to go on enjoying herself. She did not mention the "forces" any more.

A few weeks later she visited me. She seemed perfectly coordinated, her eyes sparkled with intelligence and penetrating knowing. She worked well and even studied a great deal. However, her genital love life was not in order. She had no boy friend. She had met one whom she liked. One evening they were together alone. She knew that it would happen that night, that would embrace her. She had brought some sleeping pills with her. She put some sleeping pills into his wine glass, and he fell asleep. I advised her to remove the last obstacle with the help of one of our psychiatric orgone therapists.

Seven years have elapsed since the end of the therapeutic experiment; a period of time long enough to make possible a sound judgment of the result obtained, but not long enough to give a final answer as to whether such patients will *stay sane*. This will depend on many conditions beyond the reach of individual orgone therapy. They are essentially of a *social nature*.

It is mainly the question whether *homo normalis* will change his way of living and thinking *basically,* a question which awaits a highly uncertain answer. The elucidation of the fact that the way of life of *homo normalis* creates the schizophrenic breakdown in millions of healthy newborn infants will, if seriously considered and executed practically, be a part of this all-important answer. It is quite obvious that for some time already, and justly, *homo normalis* has come under sharp scrutiny as to the soundness and rationality of his ways of being. We can learn from such experiences in individual schizophrenics what *homo normalis* does to millions of newborn children. The prevention of the disease "schizophrenia" means changing radically the whole system of education of small children, and not only changing the schizophrenic. The latter will always remain an individual answer only, unless as a social endeavor.

This statement does not mean that we should stop studying the schizophrenic mind. It has much to tell us about human functioning, about the problems of perception and self-perception, about the function of consciousness which is far less understood than the unconscious. It can tell us much about how to help individual human beings who are in the beginning of a breakdown. But the main issue in this as in all other similar tasks of medicine and psychiatry will be the world of *homo normalis,* so long as he cherishes age-old ideas and laws which do untold harm to the biological core in every child of each new generation.

In this process of mastering the emotional plague, we shall encounter *homo normalis* at his worst; in the form of the righteous mystic and of the mechanistic human animal who run away from themselves for exactly the same reasons that forced our patient into the catatonic breakdown: the horror of the plasmatic currents in an organism which has become incapable of coping with strong bio-energetic emotions and has lost the natural function of self-regulation. All attacks upon our scientific work during the past twenty-five years have come from such individuals in various organizations and social bodies. *Homo normalis* has fought orgone biophysics for the same reason that made him burn witches by the thousands, that makes him "shock" patients by the millions: *the horror of the life forces in the human animal, which he is unable to feel in himself.* If we do not muster the courage to maintain this insight, we shall fail as psychiatrists, physicians, and educators.

For the first time in the history of medicine the emotional plague, which is built and maintained on the fear of the organ sensations, has found its medical opponent. This is our great obligation: TO ENABLE THE HUMAN ANIMAL TO ACCEPT NATURE WITHIN HIMSELF, TO STOP RUNNING AWAY FROM IT, AND TO ENJOY WHAT NOW HE DREADS SO MUCH.

CHAPTER XVI

THE EMOTIONAL PLAGUE

The term "emotional plague" is not a derogatory phrase. It does not connote conscious malevolence, moral or biological degeneracy, immorality, etc. An organism whose natural mobility has been continually thwarted from birth develops *artificial forms of movement*. It limps or walks on crutches. In the same way, a man goes through life on the crutches of the emotional plague when the natural self-regulating life expressions are suppressed from birth. *The person afflicted with the emotional plague limps characterologically.* The emotional plague is a chronic biopathy of the organism. It made an inroad into human society with the first mass suppression of genital sexuality; it became an endemic disease which has been tormenting people the world over for thousands of years. There are no grounds for assuming that the emotional plague is passed on from mother to child in a hereditary way. According to our knowledge, it is implanted in the child from the first days of life. It is an endemic illness, like schizophrenia or cancer, with one notable difference, i.e., it is essentially manifested in *social life*. Schizophrenia and cancer are biopathies which we can look upon as the results of the ravages of the emotional plague in social life. The effects of the emotional plague can be seen in the human organism as well as in the life of society. Every so often, the emotional plague develops into an epidemic just like any other contagious disease, such as the bubonic plague or cholera. Epidemic outbreaks of the emotional plague become manifest in widespread and violent breakthroughs of sadism and criminality, on a small and large scale. One such epidemic outbreak was the Catholic Inquisition of the Middle Ages; the international fascism of the twentieth century is another.

If we did not look upon the emotional plague as an illness in the strict sense of the word, we would run the risk of mobilizing the police against it, instead of medicine and education. The nature of the emotional plague necessitates police force, and this is how it spreads. The emotional plague does indeed represent a grave threat to life, but not one that will ever be eliminated by police force.

No one will take it as an insult if he is told that he is suffering from a cardiac disease or that he is nervous. No one *should* take it as an insult if he is told that he is suffering from an "acute attack of the emotional plague." We sometimes hear it said among orgonomists: "No sense wasting your time with me today, I'm pesty." In our circle, when someone is afflicted with a minor case of the emotional plague, he deals with it by isolating himself and waiting until the attack of irrationalism passes. In acute cases, where rational thinking and friendly advice are of no avail, orgone therapy is used to remove the infection. It can be seen again and again that such acute attacks of the emotional plague are always produced by a disturbance in the person's love life. They disappear upon the elimination of the disturbance. The acute attack of the plague is such a familiar phenomenon to me and to my circle of co-workers that we accept it as a matter of course and deal with it objectively. It is extremely important for students of orgone therapy to learn to perceive acute attacks of the plague in themselves before such attacks go too far, to know how to keep such attacks from getting the best of them, to prevent them from spreading into the social environment and causing damage there, and, by means of intellectual detachment, to wait until they pass. In this way, we succeed in keeping harmful effects in our cooperative work at a minimum. Sometimes such an attack cannot be dealt with and the afflicted person causes a certain amount of harm or even resigns. We take such misfortunes in the same way one would take the acute physical ailment or demise of a beloved colleague.

The emotional plague is more closely related to character neurosis than to organic heart disease, for example, but it can lead to cancer or heart disease in the long run. Just like the character neurosis, it is sustained by secondary drives. It differs from physical defects inasmuch as it is a function of the character and, as such, is strongly *defended*. As opposed to a hysterical attack, an attack of the emotional plague is not sensed as a symptom and as ego-alien. True enough, character-neurotic behavior is usually highly rationalized, but this is true of the emotional plague reaction to a far greater extent. One is hardly aware of it at all. How do we recognize a plague reaction and how do we distinguish it from a rational reaction, the reader will want to know. The answer is that we distinguish it in the same way that we distinguish a rational reaction from the reaction of a neurotic character: *as soon as the roots or motives of the plague-afflicted reaction are touched, the result is invariably anxiety or anger.* Let us go into this in more detail.

A man who is essentially free of the emotional plague and is orgastically potent is not overcome by fear when a physician discusses the dynamics of natural life processes. On the contrary, he develops a lively interest in such a discussion. The man afflicted with the emotional plague will become restless or angry when the mechanisms of the emotional plague are discussed. Orgastic impotence does not always lead to the emotional plague, but every person afflicted with the emotional plague is either lastingly orgastically impotent or becomes impotent shortly before the attack. This makes it easy to distinguish the plague reaction from rational reactions.

Furthermore, a natural and healthy behavior cannot be disturbed or eliminated by any genuine medical treatment. For example, there is no rational means of "curing," i.e., disturbing, a happy love relationship. But a neurotic symptom can always be eliminated. A plague reaction is accessible to and can be eliminated by the genuine character-analytic art of healing. This is how we recognize it. Thus, avarice, a typical character trait of the emotional plague, can be cured, but pecuniary generosity cannot be cured. Insidious cunning can be cured; characterological openness cannot be cured. Clinically, the emotional plague reaction is comparable to impotence; it can be eliminated, i.e., cured. Genital potency, on the other hand, is "incurable."

An essential and *basic characteristic of the emotional plague reaction is that action and the motive of the action never coincide. The real motive is concealed and a sham motive is given as the reason for the action.* In the reaction of the natural and healthy individual, *motive, action,* and *goal* form an *organic unity.* Nothing is concealed. This unity is immediately evident. For example: the healthy individual has no other motive for his sexual acts than his natural need for love, and no other goal than its gratification. The ascetic, plague-ridden individual, on the other hand, uses ethical codes to justify his sexual debility. This justification has nothing to do with the manner in which he lives, which *is there before the justification.* The healthy person will not want to impose his way of life on anyone, but he will cure and he will help others when he is asked and when he is capable. In no case will a healthy individual *legislate* that everyone *"has* to be healthy." First, such a demand would be irrational, for a person cannot be ordered to be healthy. Second, the healthy individual has no urge to force his way of life upon others, for the motives of conduct are related specifically to his own life and not to anybody else's. The person afflicted with the emotional plague is distinguished from the healthy individual by the fact that he makes *his* demands of life not only on himself but, *above all, on his environment.* In situations in which the healthy individual makes suggestions and helps, in which he uses his experiences as an example to others, leaving it up to them whether they want to follow, the person afflicted with the emotional plague imposes his mode of life upon others *by force.* Individuals afflicted with the emotional plague do not tolerate views which threaten their armor or unmask their irrational motives. The healthy person is happy to be given an insight into his motives. The plague-afflicted individual is seized by frenzy. When views contrary to his own disrupt his life and work, the healthy individual puts up a strong rational fight for the preservation of *his* way of life. The plague-afflicted person fights *against other* modes of life even when they don't concern him in any way whatever. He is impelled to fight because he senses the very existence of other ways of life as a provocation.

The energy which sustains the emotional plague reaction always derives from genital frustration, whether it is a matter of sadistic deeds of war or the defamation of friends. Stasis of sexual energy is what the plague-afflicted individual has in common with all other biopathies. I shall have a word to say about the differences shortly. The basic biopathic nature of the emotional plague is revealed in the fact that, like every other biopathy, it can be cured by establishing the natural capacity for love.

Susceptibility to the emotional plague is universal. There is no clear-cut line of distinction between those afflicted with and those uncontaminated by the plague. Just as every man somewhere in the depths is susceptible to cancer, schizophrenia, or alcoholism, so even the healthiest and most life-affirming among us is susceptible to irrational plague reactions.

It is easier to distinguish the emotional plague from the structure of the genital character than to distinguish it from the structure of the neurotic character. While the emotional plague is indeed a character neurosis or character biopathy in the strict sense of the word, it is also more than that, and this "more" distinguishes it from biopathies and character neuroses. *We can define the emotional plague as human behavior that, on the basis of a biopathic character structure, operates in an organized or typical way in interpersonal, i.e., social, relations and in social institutions.* The emotional plague is just as widespread as the character biopathy. In other words, wherever there are character biopathies, there is also at least the possibility of a chronic effect or an acute epidemic outbreak of the emotional plague. Let us briefly outline a few typical areas in which the emotional plague is either chronically rampant or capable of breaking out in an acute way. We shall see immediately that it is precisely the most important spheres of life in which the emotional plague is active: mysticism in its most destructive form; passive and active thirst for authority; moralism; biopathies of the autonomic nervous system; party politicking; familial plague, which I have designated as "familitis"; sadistic methods of education; masochistic toleration of such methods or criminal rebellion against them; gossip and defamation; authoritarian bureaucracy; imperialistic war ideologies; everything that falls under the American concept of "racket"; antisocial criminality; pornography; profiteering; racial hatred.

We see that the compass of the emotional plague coincides approximately with the broad compass of social abuse, which has always been and still is combatted by every social freedom movement. With some qualifications, it can be said that the sphere of the emotional plague coincides with that of "political reaction" and perhaps even with the principle of politics in general. This would hold true, however, only if the basic principle of all politics, namely thirst for power and special prerogatives, were carried over into those spheres of life which we do not think of as political in the usual sense of the word. For example, a mother who resorts to political methods to alienate her child from her husband would come under this extended concept of the political emotional plague. The same would apply to an ambitious scientist who works himself up to a higher social position not by concrete accomplishments but by intrigue.

We have already stated that biological *sexual stasis* is the common biophysiological core of all forms of the emotional plague. On the basis of our present experiences, we can say that a genital character is incapable of using the methods of the emotional plague. This constitutes a great disadvantage in a society ruled to such a large extent by plague-ridden institutions. There is another common denominator in all forms of the emotional plague: *the lack of the capacity for natural sexual gratification leads to the development of secondary impulses, particularly sadistic impulses.* There is abundant clinical evidence in support of this statement. Hence, it does not surprise us to find that the bio-psychic energy which sustains the emotional plague reactions always derives from *secondary* drives. In pronounced cases, specific human *sadism* is never missing.

Thus, it is not surprising that *truthfulness* and *straightforwardness,* though highly extolled modes of behavior, are rarely encountered in human intercourse; they are so rare, indeed, that most people are amazed when they occasionally prevail. To judge from our "cultural" ideals, one would expect truthfulness and straightforwardness to be everyday, self-understood attitudes. The fact that they are not, that they are looked upon with astonishment, that truthful and straightforward men and women are considered freaks, a bit "touched in the head", that, indeed, being truthful and sincere often entails severe social dangers— all this cannot be explained on the basis of the ruling cultural ideology. To arrive at an understanding of these contradictions, we must turn to our knowledge of the organized emotional plague. This knowledge alone is capable of providing an insight into the reasons why *objectivity* and *truthfulness,* the driving forces of all strivings for freedom, have been frustrated again and again over the centuries. It cannot be assumed that any freedom movement will have any chance of achieving its goals if it does not sharply and clearly confront the organized emotional plague with truthfulness.

The fact that the emotional plague was not previously recognized was its surest protection. An exact investigation of its nature and its dynamics will demolish this protection. The champions of the emotional plague will be right in interpreting this declaration as a mortal threat to their existence. This will be clearly brought out in the way the champions and perpetuators of the emotional plague react to the following objective representations. On the basis of these reactions, we shall be able to and shall *have to* distinguish those who want to help in the fight against the emotional plague from those who want to preserve its institutions. We have seen again and again that the *irrational* nature of the emotional plague unwittingly reveals itself as soon as one attempts to go to the root of it. This is understandable because the emotional plague can only react irrationally. It is doomed to extinction when it is sharply and clearly opposed by rational thinking and the natural feeling for life. It does not have to be attacked or fought directly. The plague will automatically and inevitably work itself into a rage when the natural functions of the living organism are objectively and truthfully described. There is nothing it hates more than this.

DIFFERENCES BETWEEN THE GENITAL CHARACTER, THE NEUROTIC CHARACTER, AND EMOTIONAL PLAGUE REACTIONS

a) In thinking

The genital character's thinking orients itself on *objective facts and processes.* The genital character distinguishes the essential from the non-essential or less essential; he attempts to think out and eliminate irrational emotional disturbances; he is, in terms of his nature, *functional,* i.e., capable of adapting himself; *he is not mechanistic and he is not mystical.* His judgments are the result of a thought process. Rational thinking is open to *objective* arguments, for it has difficulty functioning without *objective* counterarguments.

To be sure, the *neurotic character* also attempts to orient himself in objective facts and processes. In the neurotic character, however, rational thinking is interfused with and affected by chronic sexual stasis, as a result of which he also to some extent orients himself on the principle of the avoidance of unpleasure. So the neurotic character will use various means of avoiding processes and events which, if he examined them, would produce unpleasure or would be at variance, for example, with a compulsive character's system of thinking; or he will probe these processes and events in such a way, i.e., irrationally, that the rational goal becomes unattainable. Let us cite an example. Peace and freedom are universally desired. However, since the average character structure is neurotic in its thinking, *fear of freedom and fear of responsibility* (pleasure anxiety) become intertwined with ideas of peace and freedom, and these goals are therefore discussed in a formalistic rather than objective manner. It is almost as if the simplest and most immediate facts of life, i.e., those facts which obviously represent the natural building material of peace and freedom, are intentionally avoided. Important relations and connections are overlooked. For example, it is certainly no secret that politics is ruinous and that humanity is sick in the psychiatric sense of the word. Yet no one seems to see the connection between these facts and the demand for a viable democratic order. Thus, two or three well-known and generally valid facts exist side by side, without any connection. Showing how these facts are related to one another would immediately necessitate *radical changes in the practical affairs of everyday life. Ideologically,* the neurotic character would be prepared to *affirm* these changes. However, he *fears* their *practical* realization. His character armor forbids a change in the life pattern that has become rigid. Thus, he will, for example, agree with the critique of irrationalism in society and in science. In a practical and objective way, however, he will refashion neither himself nor his surroundings in keeping with this critique. He will not create a model social center reflective of the ideology he affirms. It often happens, indeed, that the same individual who says yes when it is a question of ideology becomes a vehement opponent in practice when someone else brings about actual changes. At this point, the boundaries between the neurotic character and the individual afflicted with the emotional plague become blurred.

The individual afflicted with the emotional plague is not content to take a passive attitude—he is distinguished from the neurotic character by a more or less life-destructive *social activity*. His thinking is completely muddled by irrational concepts and governed almost exclusively by *irrational* emotions. In the neurotic character, thinking and acting do not coincide. This is not true of the plague-afflicted character. As in the genital character, his thinking is in complete agreement with his actions, but there is a significant difference, i.e., his conclusions are not the result of his thinking. They are always *predetermined* by his emotional affliction. In the person afflicted with the emotional plague, thinking does not, as in the rational individual, serve to help him arrive at a correct conclusion; on the contrary, it serves to confirm and rationalize a predetermined irrational conclusion. This is generally known as "prejudice," but one fails to see that this prejudice has detrimental social effects on a large scale. It is universally disseminated and characterizes just about everything that is called "tradition." It is intolerant, i.e., it does not countenance the rational thinking which could pull the ground out from under it. Hence, plague-afflicted thinking is not accessible to arguments. It has *its own technique in its own sphere,* its *own "coherence,"* so to speak, which impresses one as "logical." In this way, it creates the impression of rationality, without in reality being rational.

For instance, a strict authoritarian educator will tell you that children are difficult to teach and that is why his methods are necessary. In this *narrow* framework, his conclusion seems to be correct. If a rational thinker comes along and points out that the intractableness of children which the strict authoritarian cites to justify his methods is itself a social consequence of precisely this irrational thinking in education, he will find himself face to face with a mental block. Precisely at this point the irrational nature of plague-afflicted thinking emerges.

Let us give another example. Moralistic sexual repression produces secondary drives, and secondary drives make moralistic suppression necessary. Any number of logical conclusions can be drawn on the basis of this relation. But if the clear thinker points out that the secondary drives can be eliminated by making possible the *natural* gratification of needs, the plague-afflicted individual, though his frame of reference has been shattered, will react not with insight and correction but with irrational arguments, silence, or even hatred. In short, it is *emotionally* important for him that *both repression and secondary drives continue to exist. He is afraid of the natural impulses.* This fear operates as an irrational motive for his entire, in itself logical, frame of reference and drives him to commit dangerous actions when his social system is seriously threatened.

b) In acting

In the genital character, motive, goal, and action are in harmony with one another. The goals and motives are rational, i.e., *socially oriented.* In accordance with the natural character of his motives and goals, i.e., on the basis of their primary *biological* foundation, the genital character strives for an *improvement in his own conditions of life and in the conditions of life of others.* This is what we call "social accomplishment."

In the neurotic character, the capacity for action is always limited, because the motives are devoid of affect or are contradictory. Since the neurotic character has usually deeply repressed his irrationality, he is constantly forced to keep it under control. And this very repression constitutes the limitation of his capacity for action. He is afraid to become fully involved in any activity, for he is never sure whether sadistic or other impulses might break through. He usually suffers because he is aware that he is inhibiting his own life, but he is not *envious of healthy people.* He can be characterized by the attitude: "I was unfortunate in life; our children should have it better than I did." This attitude makes him a sympathetic, though sterile spectator of progress. He is not detrimental to progress.

In the individual afflicted with the emotional plague, the motives of the action are always counterfeit. The ostensible motive never tallies with the real motive, whether the latter is conscious or unconscious. Nor does the ostensible goal tally with the real goal. In German fascism, for example, "salvation and pacification of the German nation" was given as the goal, whereas the real goal—grounded in the character structure—was imperialistic war, the subjugation of the world, and nothing but that. It is a basic characteristic of the plague-afflicted individual that he seriously and honestly believes in the ostensible goal and motive. I should like to stress that the character structure of a person afflicted with the emotional plague can be comprehended only if it is taken seriously. *The plague-afflicted person acts under a structural compulsion.* No matter how good his intentions may be, *he can act only in the manner of the plague.* His action is in keeping with his nature just as much as the need for love or truth is in keeping with the nature of the genital character.

But the plague-afflicted individual, protected by his subjective conviction, does not suffer from insight into the harmfulness of his act. A father who, out of hatred for his wife (who, let us say, was unfaithful to him), demands custody of their child is seriously convinced that he is acting "in the best interest of the child." But if the child suffers under the separation from the mother or even begins to go to pieces, such a father will prove to be totally impervious to any form of remedy. The plague-afflicted father will find all kinds of superficial arguments in support of his conviction that he "means well" by the child in keeping him away from his mother. It will be out of the question to convince him that the *real* motive is sadistic punishment of the mother.

The person afflicted with the emotional plague, in contrast to the neurotic character, always develops as a part of his structure an envy coupled with a deadly hatred of everything healthy. A character-neurotic spinster lives a resigned life and does not interfere in the love life of young girls; a plague-afflicted spinster, on the other hand, cannot endure the sexual happiness of young girls. If such a spinster is a teacher, she will be sure to *make* the girls entrusted to her care *incapable* of experiencing sexual happiness. This holds true for every life situation. The character afflicted with the emotional plague will attempt, under all circumstances and with every available means, to change his environment so that *his* way of life and *his* way of seeing things are not jeopardized. He senses everything that is at variance with his way of life as a provocation and, therefore, persecutes it with bitter hatred. The ascetic is a good illustration. Under one guise or another, the ascetic's basic attitude is: "Why should others have it any better than I had it? Let them suffer as I suffer." In every case, this basic attitude is so well concealed in a logical, well-thought-out ideology or theory of life that only someone having wide practical experience and capable of incisive thinking can unmask it. It is distressing but necessary to record here that, as recently as the beginning of this century, the greater part of official European education was modeled along these lines.

c) In sexuality

The sexuality of the genital character is essentially determined by the basic natural laws of biological energy. He is so constituted that he naturally takes pleasure in the sexual happiness of others. In the same way, he is indifferent to perversions and has an aversion to pornography. The genital character is easily recognized by the good contact he has with healthy children. He considers it quite natural that children and adolescents are essentially *sexually* oriented. In the same way, he fulfills or at least strives to fulfill the (often socially restricted) demands which result from these biological facts. This attitude exists spontaneously, whether a corresponding knowledge has been acquired or not. In our society, these very mothers and fathers, unless they happen to live in a milieu which supports their views, are exposed to the serious danger of being looked upon and treated as criminals by authoritarian institutions. They deserve the exact antithesis—the greatest possible social protection. They constitute centers of society from which rationally acting educators and physicians will one day proceed. The basis of their life and actions is the sexual happiness which they themselves have experienced. Parents, for example, who would allow their children to experience sex in keeping with completely healthy, natural laws, would be in danger of being accused of immorality (or "moral turpitude") and of being deprived of their children by any ascetic who happened to have power.

The *neurotic* character lives a sexually resigned life or engages in secret perverse activities. His orgastic impotence is accompanied by a yearning for sexual happiness—he is indifferent to the sexual happiness of others. He is more likely to be ruled by anxiety than by hate whenever he comes into contact with the sexual problem. His armor relates solely to his own sexuality and not to the sexuality of others. His orgastic longing is very often incorporated into cultural or religious ideals, which are neither very useful nor very detrimental to the welfare of the community. The neurotic character is usually active in circles and groups which do not have any great social influence. There can be no doubt about the cultural value of some of these groups. But the neurotic character is not capable of making any significant contribution to creating healthier structures on a mass scale, for the broad masses are far more intimate with the question of natural sexuality than he is.

This basic attitude on the part of the sexually innocuous, neurotic character is capable, at any time and under corresponding external conditions, of changing into a plague-ridden attitude. The process is usually as follows: the secondary drives held in check by the cultural and religious ideals break through. *The sexuality of the character afflicted with the emotional plague is usually sadistic and pornographic.* It is characterized by the *parallel existence of sexual lasciviousness* (owing to the incapacity to achieve gratification) and *sadistic moralism*. This dualism is a part of his *structure;* the plague-afflicted individual could not change it even if he had insight and knowledge. *In terms of his structure, he cannot be anything but pornographically lascivious and sadistically moralistic at the same time.*

This is the core of the character structure of the plague-afflicted person. This structure develops bitter hatred against every process which provokes its own orgastic yearning and, hence, orgasm anxiety. *The demand for asceticism is directed not only against oneself but, above all and in a sadistic way, against the natural sexuality of others.* Persons afflicted with the emotional plague have a strong tendency to form social circles. These circles become centers for the molding of public opinion. Their most outstanding characteristic is their strong intolerance in questions of natural sexuality. They are widespread and well known. Under the banner of "culture" and "morality," they persecute to the extreme every expression of natural sexuality. Over the years they have developed a *special technique of defamation.* We shall speak of this later.

Clinical investigations leave no room for doubt that sexual gossip and defamation afford these emotionally plagued individuals a kind of perverse sexual gratification; they can thus attain sexual pleasure without the natural genital function. It is precisely in such circles that we often find homosexuality, sexual intercourse with animals, and other forms of perversion. These Vehmic courts direct their sadistic attacks against the *natural* sexuality of others, *not against perverse sexuality*. They take an especially sharp stand against the *natural* sexuality of *children* and *adolescents,* whereas, strangely enough, they are purblind to every form of perverse sexual activity. They have many human lives on their consciences.

d) In work

The genital character takes an active interest in the development of a work process which is allowed to take its *own* course. His interest is focused essentially on the *process* itself. The result of the work is achieved without special effort, for it ensues spontaneously from the work process. *The shaping of the product through the course of the work process is an essential feature of the biological pleasure of work.* This leads to a sharp criticism of all methods of educating children through toys which spell out the child's activity. The predetermination of how the toy is to function and the rigid prescription of how the toy is to be put together stifle the child's imagination and *productivity.* Compulsive moralism tolerates only mystical ecstasy; it has no patience with genuine enthusiasm, and this is the reason why enthusiasm with regard to work is always lacking. A child who has to put together a *preplanned* house with *preplanned* building blocks in a *preplanned* way cannot apply his imagination and cannot develop any enthusiasm. We can easily understand that this basic characteristic of authoritarian education is part of the pleasure anxiety of adults. It has a stultifying effect upon the child's pleasure in work. *The genital character influences the work performance of others by setting an example and not by prescribing the product and the method of work.* That requires the ability to tolerate vegetative streaming and to be able to let himself go.

The neurotic character is more or less restricted in his work. His biological energy is essentially consumed in the warding off of perverse fantasies. The neurotic disturbance of work can always be traced back to a misuse of biological energy. For the very same reason, the work of the neurotic character, no matter how rich in potential it may be, is perfunctory and joyless. Since the neurotic character is incapable of genuine enthusiasm, he will look upon the child's capacity for enthusiasm as "unseemly" (if, for instance, he happens to be a teacher). In a compulsive neurotic way, nonetheless, he insists on determining the work of others.

The individual afflicted with the emotional plague *hates* work, for he senses it as a burden. Hence, he runs away from any responsibility and especially from small jobs which require patience. He may dream of writing an important book, of painting an outstanding work of art, of running a farm, etc.; however, since he is incapable of work, he shuns the necessary step-by-step, persistent organic development inherent in every work process. This predisposes him to becoming an ideologue, mystic, or politician, i.e., to engage in activities which do not require any patience and organic development. He is just as likely to become an idle vagrant as the dictator of this or that sphere of life. He has created a picture of life made up of neurotic fantasies and, since he himself is incapable of doing things, he wants to force others to work toward the realization of this sick picture of life. The American's negative concept of the word "boss" is a product of such a constellation. A genital character who is in control of a collective work process will spontaneously lead the way by his good example: he will work *more* than the others. On the other hand, the character afflicted with the emotional plague will typically want to work less than the others. The smaller his capacity for work and, consequently, the lower his self-esteem, the greater is his insistence on being a labor *leader*.

This comparison necessarily took the form of clear-cut distinctions. In reality, every genital character also has his neurotic inhibitions and his plague reactions. By the same token, every plague-afflicted individual bears in himself the *possibilities* of the genital character. Experiences in orgone therapy leave no doubt that persons afflicted with the emotional plague, those who come under the psychiatric concept of "moral insanity," are not only curable in principle but are capable of developing exceptional capacities for work, sexuality, and intellectual activity. This again gives us the opportunity to stress that the concept "emotional plague" does not imply a disparagement. In the course of almost thirty years of biopsychiatric work, I have come to realize that a predisposition to the emotional plague is indicative of very high quantities of biological energy. Indeed, the *high tension of the individual's biological energy* makes him sick with the emotional plague if, because of a rigid character and muscular armor, he cannot realize himself in a natural way. The person so afflicted is a product of authoritarian compulsive education. Because of the frustration of his unrealized talent, he wreaks *revenge* on compulsive education far more successfully than the quiet and resigned neurotic character. He differs from the genital character inasmuch as his *rebellion is not socially oriented* and is therefore incapable of effecting any rational changes for the better. He differs from the neurotic character inasmuch as he *does not become resigned.*

The genital character controls his emotional plague reactions in two ways: (1) Since the structure of his character is of an essentially rational nature, he senses his own plague reaction as alien and senseless. (2) He is so immersed in rational processes that he is immediately aware of the danger to his life process which could ensue from his irrational tendencies. This awareness enables him to keep himself in control. The person afflicted with the emotional plague, on the other hand, derives so much secondary, sadistic pleasure from his own behavior that he is inaccessible to any correction. The acts of the healthy individual flow directly from the reservoir of biological energy; the acts of the plague-afflicted individual stem from the same source, but they have to break through the character and muscular armor each time and in the process the best motives become antisocial and irrational actions. In its passage through the character armor, the original goal of the act changes its function: *the impulse begins with a rational intention; the armor thwarts a smooth and organic unfolding of the impulse; the plague-afflicted character senses this obstruction as an intolerable inhibition; the impulse must first break through the armor* in order to become at all manifest; in this process the original intention and the rational goal are lost. When finally realized, the act contains little of the original rational intention; it is an exact reflection of the *destructiveness* which had to be brought into play in the process of breaking through the armor. *The brutality of the*

*plague-afflicted individual is a result of the failure on the part of
the original impulse to get through the muscular and character
armor.* A loosening of the armor is impossible, for the plague-
ridden act neither discharges energy orgastically nor produces
rational self-confidence. This "failure" enables us to comprehend
some of the contradictions in the structure of the individual afflicted with the emotional plague. He has a strong desire for love;
he finds a woman whom he believes he can love; he proves himself incapable of the experience. This drives him into a sadistic
rage against himself or against the desired woman, a rage which
not infrequently ends in murder.

Basically, therefore, *the individual afflicted with the emotional plague is characterized by the contradiction between an intense desire for life and the inability (because of the armor) to
achieve a corresponding fulfillment of life.* To the careful observer, Europe's political irrationalism was clearly characterized
by this contradiction. With the logic of a compulsion, the best intentions led to destructive ends.

It is my opinion that the gangster type constitutes a simple
demonstration of the mechanism of the emotional plague, if the
result of the gangster act is taken into account along with the *inhibition of the rational impulse* which turns it into a plague-ridden act.

Now let us endeavor to examine these differentiations in simple examples from everyday life.

Let us take as our first example the *fight for the child* which
usually occurs when parents sue for divorce. There are three
possible reactions: the rational, the inhibited reaction of the neurotic character, and the emotional plague reaction.

a) Rational

Father and mother fight for the healthy development of the
child with rational arguments and means. It is possible that they
agree in principle—then it is easy; but it is also possible that they
will have very different ideas about the matter. Nonetheless, in
the interest of the child, they will shun underhanded methods.
They will speak openly with the child and allow him to make his
own decision. They will not allow themselves to be governed by
selfish interests; they will, instead, be guided by the child's incli-

nations. When one or the other parent is an alcoholic or is mentally ill, this information will be communicated to the child as a misfortune that has to be borne bravely, taking the greatest possible care to spare his feelings. *The motive will always be to prevent the child from being damaged.* The attitude is dictated by the sacrifice of one's personal interest.

b) Character-neurotic

The fight for the child is inhibited by all kinds of considerations, essentially fear of public opinion. Conformity to public opinion takes precedence over the child's best interest. In such things, character-neurotic parents abide by the prevailing practice: the child remains with the mother under all circumstances, or they submit the case to legal authorities. When one of the parents is a drinker or is mentally ill, then the tendency exists to sacrifice oneself, to conceal the fact, with the result that the child as well as the other parent suffer and are endangered. *Divorce is avoided.* The motive of their behavior is epitomized in the sentence, "We don't want to make a stir." *Their attitude is determined by resignation.*

c) The individual afflicted with the emotional plague

The welfare of the child is always a spurious and, as the results show, *unfulfilled* motive. *The real motive is to wreak revenge on the partner by depriving him or her of the pleasure of the child.* Hence, in the fight for the child, one partner resorts to defamation of the other, whether he or she is healthy or sick. The absence of any consideration for the child is brought out by the fact that his love for the other parent is not taken into account. As a means of alienating the child from one or the other parent, he is told that his mother or his father is an alcoholic or is mentally ill, a statement which usually does not correspond to the facts of the case. The result is that the child is the one who *suffers* most; the *motive is revenge* on the partner and domination of the child. Genuine love for the child is not at issue.

There are any number of variations on this example, but its basic features are the same and they are of general social importance. In making decisions, a rational jurisprudence would have to give priority to such differentiations. It can be assumed that there will be a significant increase in the number of divorces; and it is my opinion that only a correctly trained psychiatrist and educator is capable of measuring the extent of the damage caused solely by emotional plague reactions in cases of divorce.

Let us cite another example from the sphere of private life in which the emotional plague rages far and wide: the infidelity of a love partner.

a) Rational

In cases in which one of the partners in a love relationship wants to be or is unfaithful, the healthy individual reacts principally in one of three ways: factual separation from the partner; competition and the attempt to regain the partner's love; or toleration when the other relationship is not too serious and is of a temporary nature. In such cases, the healthy person does not take flight into neurosis, does not make any legal claims, and becomes angry only if the affair is carried out indecently.

b) Character-neurotic

The infidelity is either suffered masochistically or the armor shuts off its cognizance. There is acute fear of separation. Resignation, flight into a neurotic illness or alcoholism, and hysterical attacks are typical reactions.

c) Individual afflicted with the emotional plague

As a rule, infidelity occurs not for reasons of love for another person but because one has become weary of one's partner. The injured party attempts to hold the partner in the house, to wear him or her out with hysterical attacks, dominate him or her with scenes of the lowest sort, or even have him or her watched by a detective. Flight into alcoholism often occurs as a means of facilitating the brutalizing of the partner. The motive is not love for the partner but thirst for power and possessiveness.

Reactions of emotional plague are quite prevalent in tragedies of jealousy. At the present time, there are neither medical nor social nor legal views and measures which take this vast and desolate sphere of life into account.

Now let us turn our attention to an especially striking and typical mode of reaction of the emotional plague which we shall designate as *"specific plague reaction."*

The specific plague reaction has a special preference for the use of sexual, i.e., moralistic, defamation. It functions in a way similar to the projection mechanism in delusions of persecution; i.e., a perverse impulse which has broken through the armor is transferred to persons or objects in the outer world. What in reality is an inner impulse is misinterpreted as an external threat. The same applies to the sensations which originate in the orgonotic plasma currents. The healthy individual experiences these currents as something joyful and pleasurable. The schizophrenic on the other hand, because of the contradictions which result from his character armor, perceives these currents as the secret workings of an evil fiend intent upon destroying his body with electrical currents. These insane projection mechanisms are well known. However, psychiatry makes the error of limiting such projection mechanisms to the mentally ill. It fails to see that precisely the same mechanism is rampant in social life in the form of the specific plague reactions of ostensibly normal people. This is our next topic of discussion.

The biopsychic mechanism is the following: compulsive moralism in upbringing and in life produces sexual lasciviousness, which has nothing to do with the natural need for love, and constitutes a real secondary drive like, for example, sadism or masochism. Since orgonotic aliveness in the natural experience of pleasure has atrophied, lasciviousness and the thirst for sexual gossip become unbridled secondary needs. Just as the mental patient projects his orgonotic currents and his perverse impulses onto other persons and experiences them as a threat issuing from them, the plague-afflicted individual projects his own lasciviousness and perversions onto other persons. In contrast to the mental patient, he does not masochistically experience as a threat the impulses which he projects onto the other person; rather, he makes use of gossip in a sadistic way as a defensive mechanism, i.e., he imputes to others what he cannot take cognizance of in himself. This applies to natural genitality as well as to the secondary perverse impulse. The mode of life of the genitally healthy person painfully reminds him of his own genital weakness and, as such, constitutes a threat to his neurotic balance. Thus, in conformity with the principle, "What I can't have, you can't have," he is forced to cast a slur upon the natural genitality of others. Moreover, since he is not capable of wholly concealing his own perverse lasciviousness behind a façade of ethical moralism, he imputes it to the victim of his gossip. In every case of this form of plague reaction, one comes to realize that the healthy individual is reputed to have precisely those characteristics against which the plague-ridden individual struggles in vain or indulges in *with a bad conscience.*

The mechanism of the specific plague reaction is easily carried over from the sexual to the non-sexual sphere. It is characteristic that something one does oneself, would like to do, or is on the verge of doing is attributed to someone else. We shall use a few typical, everyday occurrences to illustrate the specific plague reaction.

There are young intellectuals who were once known as "cultural snobs" among the serious intellectual circles of Europe. They are clever, but their intelligence is devoted to a kind of sterile artistic activity. Their acquaintance with the magnitude and seriousness of the problems probed by a Goethe or a Nietzsche is less than superficial, but they take great pleasure in quoting classical literature. At the same time, they are full of cynicism. They regard themselves as modern, liberal, free of any conventions. Incapable of serious experience, they look upon sexual love as a kind of child's play. They spend their summer vacations in communes, little boys and little girls living together. At nights, there are amusing diversions, i.e., the "child's play." At the breakfast table, the child's play is joked about in a carefree and very clever manner. Possibly, the "sinful woman" will be made to blush by ambiguous allusions. All this is very much part of today's "liberal" and "unconventional" way of living. One is "jolly"; one is "hip." One intimates how often one has engaged in the "play" the night before; and one lets it be known, everything described in the "choicest" figures of speech, that it was "very nice," that *she* was "delightful," etc. The serious listener, who is all too familiar with the abysmal sexual misery of masses of people and the destructiveness of sexual triviality, comes away wtih the impression that the lasciviousness of these "bright" young men and women is the result of sexual hunger due to orgastic impotence. Such cultivated "Bohemians" typically look upon the serious efforts of sex-economy to fight the emotional plague in masses of people as the fabric of a sick mind. But then these young "geniuses" are well versed in the art of "high politics." Forever prattling about the cultural "values" that have to be upheld, they become furious as soon as one begins to translate their talk into social action among masses of people.

One such Bohemian met a woman who wanted to come to me to study. Naturally, the conversation turned to my work. He gave her fair warning, saying that he would send neither his best friend nor his worst enemy to me, for I was, so he said, the "owner of a public brothel, without license." To conceal the flagrant plague-ridden nature of this statement, he immediately added that I was a very able clinician. This defamation, patterned along the lines of the specific plague reaction, made the rounds. Notwithstanding, the woman came to me to study sex-economic pedagogy and soon grasped what we call the emotional plague.

It is difficult to maintain an objective and correct attitude in such situations. One cannot give into the impulse, which arises spontaneously and for which there is good reason, to give such a plague-ridden individual a good thrashing so that he will not go around defaming people any more, for one wants to keep one's hands clean. To ignore the incident in a noble way is to do precisely what the plague-afflicted individual counts on so that he can continue to perpetrate his social mischief with impunity. There remains the possibility of a libel suit against him. However, this would be to fight the emotional plague on its own level and not in a *medical* way. Thus, one allows the matter to take its own course. In so doing, however, one runs the risk that another such plague-afflicted person, perhaps a "scientific historian," will take up the matter and pass one on to posterity with the "objective historian's authority" as the owner of a secret brothel.[1]

---

[1] I should like to point out that, to me, a woman of easy virtue having a decent character is socially and humanly preferable to such a plague-afflicted person. Women of easy virtue have no pretenses; social conditions, material necessity, and the prevailing social chaos lead them into a profession which requires them to gratify the sexual needs of sailors and soldiers, i.e., men who risk their lives. Countless princes and priests have had to visit houses of prostitution to satisfy their needs or to escape their misery. This is neither reproach nor praise but merely an establishment of fact.

The matter is important because the emotional plague has succeeded again and again, by means of such rumors, in crushing honest and important accomplishments. The fight against the emotional plague is socially necessary, for it causes more damage in this world than "ten thousands canons." Read, for example, Friedrich Lange's account of the defamations to which the pioneer natural scientist of the seventeenth century, de la Mettrie, was subjected by the emotional plague. In his great work *Histoire Naturelle de l'Ame*, de la Mettrie clearly grasped the essential relations between perception and physiological stimuli and correctly divined and described the connection between the body-soul problem and the biological sexual process. This was too much for the Philistines, who far outnumber bold and honest scientists; they circulated the rumor that de la Mettrie was able to arrive at such views only because he was a "libertine." And thus the rumor was passed on to posterity that de la Mettrie died from a pastry which, in true voluptuary fashion, he had consumed too voraciously.

This of course is medical nonsense. More than that, it is a typical example of plague-afflicted rumor-mongering which, when seized upon by human organisms incapable of pleasure, becomes a specific plague reaction and is passed on to posterity, defiling, without rhyme or reason, a decent name. We readily recognize the catastrophic role played by such plague reactions in social life.

I should like to cite another example in which the projection mechanism of the emotional plague, in the form of defamation, is even more clearly manifested. In Norway, I heard that a rumor was being circulated that I had become schizophrenic and had spent some time in a mental institution. With some effort we succeeded in tracing the source of the rumor. When I came to the United States in 1939, I ascertained that this rumor was very widespread, much more so than in Europe, where my work was better known. In America, the source of the rumor was even more obscure than it had been in Europe, but certain signs clearly indicated that it stemmed from the same European source.[2]

[2] Footnote, 1945: One of our prominent physicians returned from Oslo to the U.S.A. in 1939. He spent a few days in Zürich, where he told a former psy-

The situation was not devoid of humor Shortly after my expulsion from the International Psychoanalytic Association, the person who had originally started this rumor suffered a nervous breakdown and was forced to spend several weeks in a mental institution. This fact was directly communicated to me by a university professor who was well informed on the situation. Evidently, the nervous breakdown gave this slanderer a terrible fright. He found himself at that time in a difficult situation: on the one hand, he recognized the correctness of my development; on the other, he could not detach himself from an organization that was sharply opposed to that development. As is usual in such cases, he took advantage of the circumstances to divert attention from himself and focus it on me when I was in the center of a critical controversy. He thought that I was finished, and the opportunity to give me another kick was too tempting. His reaction was a specific plague-afflicted projection.

I have never been mentally ill, nor have I ever been confined to a mental institution. I have borne until the present day one of the heaviest burdens ever imposed upon a man, without any disturbance to my capacity for work and love. To become mentally ill is no disgrace. I, like every self-respecting psychiatrist, have deep sympathy for mental patients and often admiration for their conflicts. As I have stressed elsewhere, a mental patient appears to me far more serious, far closer to what is alive than a Philistine or a socially dangerous individual afflicted with the emotional plague. This defamation was intended to ruin me and my work and it did result in a number of serious situations that were not easy to master. With some students, for example, I had the additional difficulty of persuading them that I was *not* mentally ill. In certain phases of orgone therapy, a specific mechanism of the emotional plague inevitably appears. As soon as the patient or pupil comes into contact with his plasmatic currents, severe

---

chiatric colleague that he had been working with me. Much surprised, he said: "But So-and-So said Reich had become schizophrenic." "So-and-So" was the person in question. Soon after his return to the States, he learned from an acquaintance that his analyst had told him the same thing: "So-and-So [again the same person] told me Reich was schizophrenic." This rumor-monger died a few years later from heart failure. I had known for a long time that he suffered from impotence.

orgasm anxiety appears. What happens is that the orgone therapist is looked upon as either a "dirty" sexual pig or an "insane" man. I want to emphasize that this reaction appears regularly. Most of my students had indeed heard about the rumor. Some aspects of the theory of sex-economy are so revolutionary that it is extremely easy to regard the theory itself as insane. I must state that, as a result of this rumor, certain complicated situations became mortally dangerous. There should be clear-cut legal possibilities for precluding such consequences of a plague-afflicted reaction. I have only my clinical experience to thank for my being able to weather—in addition to the already existing difficulties of my work—the dangers which derived from the rumor about my mental illness.

The affair was not without comic after-effects. When it was realized some years later that my scientific work clearly indicated that I was not schizophrenic, a new rumor was circulated and again from the same source. Now it was said that, happily, I had "recovered" from my schizophrenic illness.

Specific plague reactions are encountered particularly in the sphere of politics. Again and again during the last few years we have seen that, with every fresh conquest, dictatorial-imperialistic governments attribute to the victim precisely the intention they themselves have carried out. For instance, it was said that Poland had been secretly planning an attack on the German empire, that this had to be anticipated, and therefore Germany was justified in attacking Poland. The attack on the Soviet Union was "justified" in the same way.

Also illustrative of this specific plague reaction are the now famous "Moscow trials" of Lenin's early co-workers. At these trials, the charge of high treason was lodged against functionaries hostile to the Russian Communist Party; the defendants were accused of having maintained direct contact with the German fascists and, together with them, of having planned the overthrow of the government. To those who knew the backgrounds of those accused, it was clear that the charges against them had been trumped up. But in 1936 no one could explain the purpose of such an obviously spurious accusation. The Russian government was strong enough to eliminate any troublesome opposition with less transparent arguments. It wasn't until 1939 that the mystery was cleared up, at least for those who were already familar with the specific plague mechanism. In 1936 the accused were said to have committed precisely that crime against the state which the government itself actually did commit in 1939. It signed a pact with Hitler that precipitated the war with Poland and divided Poland with the German fascists. Only then was it understood that, by defaming others, the state had succeeded in clearing itself of the pact with Hitler, so well, indeed, that the implications of its action remained unknown to the public. This case was yet another confirmation of the fact that the public acts as if it had no memory. Such political plague reactions in fact count on this very irrationality in mass thinking. It makes no difference that this pact did not help, that eventually the German dictatorship became engaged in a war with the Russian dictatorship. Nor could the subsequent rationalization change the fact that a pact had been signed.

Let us cite another example from the sphere of the emotional plague. Leon Trotsky had to defend himself against the accusation that he was involved in a plot against the life of his rival. This was incomprehensible, for the murder of Stalin would have only damaged the Trotskyites. It became comprehensible when Trotsky was murdered in 1941. (These facts have nothing to do with political points of view for or against the Trotskyites.)

If we go back only a few decades in the history of politics, we find the famous Dreyfus case. High-ranking military men of the French general staff had sold plans to the Germans; to cover themselves, they accused the unsuspecting and respectable Captain Dreyfus of the very crime they were guilty of. They succeeded in having their victim convicted, and he languished in jail for more than five years on a faraway island. Without Zola's courageous intervention, this specific plague reaction would never have been combatted. That Dreyfus was subsequently honored does not erase in any way the atrocity committed against him. If policies of state were not ruled to such a large extent by the laws of the emotional plague, it would be a self-understood principle that such catastrophes should never happen in the first place. However, since the emotional plague governs the molding of public opinion, it always succeeds in passing off its atrocities as regrettable errors of justice, only to be able to continue its mischief with impunity.

In the case of a government figure, his personal character has enormous importance for the social life as a whole. If, for instance, the girl friend of a king is French, one can be assured that in a world war during this king's reign, his country will be on the side of France *against* the German "arch enemy." If that same king should forfeit his throne shortly before or at the beginning of the second world war, and if his successor had a personal relationship with a German woman, the same country would fight the war on the side of its former arch enemy, Germany, against France, its former ally.

Whoever takes pains to scrutinize the workings of the emotional plague in the sphere of politics will become more and more immersed in a condition akin to acute confusion. Is it possible, one will ask oneself, that the clericalism of a political dictator or the love affair of a king can determine the weal and woe of several generations? Does irrationalism in social life go that deep? Is it really possibᵢ that millions of industrious adults are not aware of this, indeed refuse to be aware of it?

These questions seem peculiar only because the effects of the emotional plague are too fantastic to be perceived as something tangible. Human intelligence evidently refuses to admit that such absurdity can predominate on such a massive scale. It is this stupendous illogicality of such social conditions that represents their strongest protection. We must realize just how enormous the effects of the emotional plague are and understand that this enormity makes them appear incredible. I firmly believe that not one social evil of any magnitude can ever be eliminated so long as the public refuses to recognize that this absurdity does exist and is *so* enormous that it is *not* seen. Compared with the enormity of social irrationality, which is constantly nourished by the deeply rooted emotional plague, the basic social functions of *love, work,* and *knowledge,* which govern the life process, appear infinitesimal; indeed, they appear socially ridiculous. We can easily convince ourselves of this.

On the basis of long and extensive medical practice, we know that, unresolved as it is, the problem of adolescent sexuality plays an incomparably greater part in the molding of our social and moral ideologies than some tariff law or other. Let us imagine that a parliamentarian, who happened to be a physician, approached his government and demanded the opportunity to give a thorough presentation of the problem of puberty at a parliamentary session and to have it debated as a tariff bill is debated. Let us further imagine that this same outstanding person resorted to a filibuster because his request was denied. In a simple way, I believe this example shows the basic contradiction between everyday life and the administrative form which rules it. If we consider the matter calmly and objectively, we shall find that there is nothing very special about a legislative debate on the problems of puberty. Everybody, every member of parliament included, has gone through the hell of the adolescent neurosis brought on by sexual frustration. No other conflict compares with this one in magnitude and importance. It is a problem of general social interest. A rational solution to the difficulties of puberty would eliminate at one blow a multitude of social evils, such as juvenile delinquency, public care of mental patients, the misery of divorce, the misery of child rearing, etc.—thousands of formal bills on budgets and tariff systems could never even approach the problem.

So we regard the demand of our medically oriented parliamentarian as unequivocally rational, progressive, and useful. At the same time, however, we ourselves shy away from it. Something in us is opposed to the possibility of a public, parliamentary debate on this topic. This "something" is precisely the effect and intention of the social emotional plague, which is constantly striving to preserve itself and its institutions. It has drawn a sharp distinction between official and private life, and the latter has been denied access to the public platform. Official life is asexual on the surface and pornographic or perverse beneath the surface. If this dichotomy did not exist, official life would immediately coincide with private life and correctly mirror everyday life in large social forms. This unification of everyday living and social institutions would be simple and uncomplicated. Then, however, that sector in the social framework would automatically perish which not only does not contribute to the preservation of social life but, rather, periodically brings it to the brink of the abyss. We can place this sector under the heading of "high politics."

The continuation of the gap between the real life of the community and its official façade is one of the emotional plague's bitterly defended intentions. There is no other way to explain the fact that the emotional plague always resorts to force of arms when an effort is made to touch upon this gap in an objective and rational way. Representatives of high politics, whether personally affected or not, always attempted to thwart the dissemination of the sex-economic recognition of the relationship between man's biological organism and the state. In their *mildest* form, their attacks were somewhat as follows: "These 'sex philosophies' are immoral abscesses on the social body which break open from time to time. It is true that the human animal has a sexuality, but this is only to be regretted. After all, sexuality is not everything in life. There are other, far more important problems, i.e., economics and politics. Sex-economy exaggerates. We would get along far better without it."

This is a typical argument, some variation of which is regularly encountered in curing a person of a biopathy and even in training a student. We are convinced that this argument springs from orgasm anxiety and that its aim is to prevent a disturbance of the person's resigned attitude. Faced with the same argument at a public meeting on mental hygiene, one cannot disarm the advocate of cultural and other "values" by pointing to his personal armor and pleasure anxiety. A sex-economist who used such an approach would have the meeting *against him,* for the opponent of sex-economy shares this character trait and the irrational argument that springs from it with the others. Many a physician and teacher has floundered here. There is an incontestable, purely logical counter-argument which, on the basis of our experience, is successful.

We concur with the opponent: sexuality is not everything in life. We even add that, in healthy people, sexuality is not a topic of conversation or the center of their thinking. But how do we explain that sexuality, which is not everything in life, actually assumes the most prominent place in man's life and thinking? This fact cannot be gainsaid. Let us cite another example to illustrate this.

The circulation of steam in the steampipes of a factory is an unquestioned precondition of the factory's operation. However, the workers in a factory hardly give a moment's thought to the circulation of the steam. Their attention is completely concentrated on their work. The energy engendered by the steam is "not everything" in the factory. There are other important interests, e.g., the manufacture of machines and similar things. Let us imagine that all of a sudden one or more steam valves became clogged. The flow of energy engendered by the steam would cease immediately. The pistons would stop; the wheels would no longer turn; work would be out of the question. All the workers would have to direct their attention with dispatch to the obstructed flow of steam in the pipes. All thinking would be centered on one question: how a regulated circulation of steam could be reestablished in the quickest way. Let us further imagine that some workers began to argue about this situation as follows: "This confounded theory of heat exaggerates the role of steam. Sure, it's true that steam is necessary, but it's far from being everything in this factory. Don't you see that there are other things to worry about? What about the economy?" In a breakdown like the one described, these "brainstorms" would merely be laughed at, and one would quickly attempt to eliminate the basic disturbance in the circulation of the steam before turning one's thoughts to "other things." It would serve no purpose to consider the interests of economy when the steam valves are clogged.

This example illustrates the nature of the sexual problem in our society. The flow of biological energy, i.e., sexual energy, is disturbed in most people. The biosocial mechanism of society therefore functions poorly and sometimes not at all, and we have irrational politics, irresponsibility on the part of masses of people, biopathies, homicide—in short, the emotional plague. If all people fulfilled their natural sexual needs in a natural way, there would be little talk of the sexual problem; there would be no sexual problem. Then one would be justified in contending that there are "also other things."

Because sex-economy is interested in seeing these so-called *other* things *come into their own*, it spends much time and effort trying to eliminate the basic problem. The fact that today everything revolves around sex is the surest indication that there is a severe disturbance not only in the human animal's flow of sexual energy but, as a consequence of this disturbance, in his biosocial functioning. Sex-economy is striving to open the valves blocking the flow of biological energy in the human animal so that *other* important things, such as clear thinking, natural decency, and pleasurable work, can function and pornographic sexuality will no longer occupy *all* of one's thinking, as is the case today.

This disturbance of the flow of energy has a profound effect on the basis of biosocial functioning and thus governs both limited and higher functions of the human animal. I believe that the fundamental biological character of this disturbance has not been comprehended in its full scope and depth, even by some orgonomists. Once again let us cite an example to illustrate this depth and the relationship of orgonomy to other sciences.

Let us compare the natural sciences, which disregard this basic biological disturbance, to a group of railroad engineers. Let us imagine that these engineers write thousands of highly technical books describing the construction of trains, their size and the material of the doors and windows, the seats and sleeping accommodations, the specific chemical composition of the iron and wood, the strength of the brakes, the speeds at which these trains are to travel and the time schedules, the stations, every detail of every single track. In every book, however, these engineers regularly omit *one* detail—they make no mention of the dynamics of steam. The natural sciences are not familiar with the study of life processes from a functional point of view; they are therefore comparable to these engineers. The *orgonomist* cannot perform his work unless he has fully realized that he is the *engineer of the living apparatus*. It is not our fault that, as engineers of the living apparatus, we are first and foremost concerned with biosexual energy. We have not the slightest reason to feel demeaned because of this. Quite the contrary: we have every reason to be proud of our difficult task.

One will ask in amazement how it was possible to have so completely overlooked a disease that has so ravaged mankind for such a long time. He who has gone to the very core of the emotional plague knows that concealment is part of its nature. It owes its success to the impossibility of getting at it, seeing through it, comprehending it—all part of its intent. I stressed earlier that the disease was *too obvious to attract attention*. (Hitler: "The bigger the lie, the more readily it is believed.") Before character analysis, there was no scientific method for the discovering and unmasking of the emotional plague. Politics and the expression of political opinion appeared to have a special kind of reason; one was miles away from an intuition of the irrational character of the political plague. And the emotional plague itself was in control of the most important social institutions and was, therefore, in a position to prevent the recognition of its nature.

We have to deal with the emotional plague every time we cure biopathies and every time we have to restructure a teacher or physician. So, even in the fulfillment of this training program, the emotional plague obstructs our efforts in the form of resistance reactions on the part of the character. This is how we learn to know it clinically, and upon these experiences we base our contention that it has left no human being unscathed.

We also learn about its nature through the typical reactions to the scientific discoveries of orgonomy. Even if those afflicted with the emotional plague are not directly affected by the results of our scientific work; even if they are far removed from or unfamiliar with the subject; they have somehow divined and feel threatened by the unmasking of the emotional plague as it takes place in the quiet offices of character analysts and orgone therapists. In spite of the fact that they were not directly affected, they reacted with defamation and the specific plague reaction long before a single orgonomist had any idea that he was on the verge of engaging in the most difficult struggle that physicians and educators had ever undertaken. We shall go into this matter in detail when we discuss the training of physicians and educators. Here it is merely important to give a very thorough description of the emotional plague's general characteristics, so that everyone will be capable of recognizing them in himself and in others.

The emotional plague has known how to anticipate possible disclosures by well-concealed and rationalized actions. It acted like a nobly dressed murderer whose mask has been torn off. The emotional plague was successful for more than a decade; it had almost succeeded in securing its existence for centuries to come. It would have indeed triumphed had it not become so destructively and blatantly manifest as dictatorships and mass infection. It stirred up a war of unimaginable dimensions and added to chronic, everyday murder. It endeavored to conceal itself behind high-sounding "political ideals" and "new orders," behind "ancient empires" and "racial claims." For years it was given credence by a psychiatrically sick world. But its acts of betrayal were too blatant. It insulted the natural feelings for life of all men and women, leaving no family and no profession untouched. The phenomena which character analysts and orgone therapists had learned to study and to fight so well over a long period of time in the stillness of their offices suddenly became *one* with the phenomena of the world catastrophe. Both on a small and on a large scale, the basic characteristics were the same. Thus, the emotional plague itself came to the aid of natural science, and the work of a few psychiatrists and educators. The world began to ask about its nature and to demand an answer. This answer shall be given according to our best knowledge and conscience. Every conscientious person will discover the emotional plague in himself and, in this way, better comprehend what plunges the world into tragedy again and again. The "new order" always begins in one's own house.

The unmasking of these hidden activities and mechanisms of a decadent life has two goals: first, the fulfillment of an obligation to society. If, in the case of a fire, the water supply fails and someone knows the source of the failure, it is his duty to name it. Second, the future of sex-economy and orgone biophysics has to be protected from the emotional plague. In Austria in 1930; in Germany in 1932 and 1933; in Denmark in 1933; in Lucerne in 1934; in Denmark and Sweden in 1934 and 1935; and in Norway in 1937 and 1938, my honest work on the human structure was subjected to attacks. In retrospect, I am almost inclined to feel grateful for these unjustified attacks, for they did away with my good-natured guilelessness and opened my eyes to a generally dangerous, though pathological, system of defamation and persecution. When a thief goes too far and throws caution to the wind, he runs a greater risk of being caught and rendered harmless. Until about ten years ago, those who were afflicted with and spread the emotional plague felt secure. They were too sure of their victory. For many years, indeed, victory did appear to be on their side. Great perseverance, deep involvement in experimental and natural scientific work, and an independence from public opinion—an independence for which one can only be grateful—rendered their victory impossible. The emotional plague never lets up or rests until it has invalidated great deeds, until it has poisoned the fruits of human diligence, research, and the attainment of truth. I do not think that it has succeeded this time or that it will succeed. It is the first time that the emotional plague is confronted not only by honest attitudes but by the necessary knowledge of life processes, which always make up in clarity what they lack in strength. The strength and consistent application of orgonomic natural science enabled me to recover from the heavy and dangerous blows I received from the emotional plague. If that was possible, it seems to me that the most difficult part has been accomplished.

As far as I and my work are concerned, I should like to state one simple fact for the reader's consideration. Neurotic psychoanalysts declared that I was mentally ill; fascist communists denounced me as a Trotskyite; sexually frivolous people accused me of being the unlicensed owner of a brothel; the Gestapo persecuted me on the grounds that I was a Bolshevik (the FBI did the same on the grounds that I was a German spy); domineering mothers wanted to pass me on to posterity as a seducer of children; charlatans in the field of psychiatry called me a charlatan; would-be saviors of mankind called me a new Jesus or Lenin. However flattering or unflattering these diverse appellations may have been, this much should be clear: it is not likely that I, being but *one* person, could have been brothel owner, spy, Trotskyite, schizophrenic, and savior all at the same time. Each of these activities would have taken up a whole life. But I cannot have been all these things for the simple reason that my interests and efforts lie elsewhere, namely in work on the irrational human structure and in the extremely demanding work of comprehending the recently discovered cosmic life energy; they lie, in short, in the field of sex-economy and orgone biophysics. Perhaps this logical consideration will help to remove a misunderstanding about me.

Those who have read and really understood the works of great women and men know the sphere we characterize as emotional plague. Unfortunately, *these great accomplishments have remained without any essential social effect*. They were neither organized nor made the basis of life-affirming institutions. If that had happened, it would be difficult to believe that the emotional plague could have reached the extent it did in the catastrophes of 1934–45. True, monuments have been erected in honor of the great masters of literature, but all too often, we see that the emotional plague knows how to build huge museums in which these great accomplishments can be *locked up* and *made innocuous* through *false* admiration. Any one of these accomplishments would have been enough to build a rational world if it had been taken seriously as a practical possibility. I am not the first person to make an effort to grasp and fight the emotional plague. I merely believe that I am the first *natural scientist* who, by the discovery of the orgone, has provided a solid foundation on the basis of which the emotional plague can be *understood* and *vanquished*.

Today, five, eight, ten, fourteen years after various unexpected and incomprehensible catastrophes, this is my standpoint: *just as a bacteriologist devotes all his efforts and energies to the total elimination of infectious diseases, the medical orgonomist devotes all his efforts and energies to the unmasking and combatting of the emotional plague as a rampant disease of the people of the world.* The world will gradually get accustomed to this new form of medical activity. One will learn to comprehend the emotional plague in oneself and in others and to go to scientific centers and not to the police, the district attorney, or the party leader. There are police, district attorneys, and even saviors who are interested in mastering the emotional plague in themselves and in others. For the police and the district attorney have to deal with biopathic criminality, and the human savior is concerned with the helplessness and mass biopathies of man. We want from now on to draw a sharp distinction between those who run to the police or use political persecution to settle a controversy and those who use scientific reasoning. Thus we will be in a position to distinguish who is afflicted with the emotional plague and who is not. At this point I should like to stress that we do not enter into discussions of politics and police. On the other hand, we welcome every form of scientific discussion; indeed, we wait for it.

I believe that the time has come when helplessness toward the emotional plague is beginning to disappear. Until now, one sensed its attacks as something comparable to a tree crashing to the ground or a stone falling from the roof. Such things simply happened, and one was either lucky and got out alive or one was unlucky and was struck down dead. From this point on, we know that the tree does not tumble by accident and the stone does not fall of its own volition from the roof. We know now in both cases that well-concealed, mentally disturbed human animals cause the tree to topple and the stone to roll off the roof. Once this much has been grasped, the rest follows of itself.

Hence, when some physician or another files suit against an orgonomist because of some "illegal activity"; when a politician accuses an orgonomist of "tax fraud," "child seduction," "espionage," or "Trotskyite opposition"; when we hear rumors that some orgonomist or another is mentally ill, seduces his patients, operates an illegal brothel, etc., then we know that we are dealing with police or political tactics and not with scientific argumentation. The training requirements of the Orgone Institute and the demands of everyday work are a public guarantee that *we* are doing our utmost to combat the basic characteristics of the emotional plague.

We do not conceal, nor have we ever concealed, that we cannot believe in the fulfillment of human existence as long as biology, psychiatry, and educational science have not come to grips with the universal emotional plague, and fought it as ruthlessly as one fights plague-ridden rats. Nor do we conceal the fact that extensive, careful, and painstaking clinical investigations have led us to this conclusion: *it is solely the reestablishment of the natural love-life of children, adolescents, and adults which can rid the world of character neuroses and, with the character neuroses, the emotional plague in its various forms.*

INDEX